Exam 70-667: Pro: Configuring Microsoft SharePoint 2010

OBJECTIVE

INSTALLING AND CONFIGURING A SHAREPOINT ENVIRONMENT	
Deploy new installations and upgrades.	Chapter 2, Lesson 2
	Chapter 9, Lessons 1 and 2
Configure SharePoint farms.	Chapter 1, Lessons 2 and 3
	Chapter 2, Lesson 2
	Chapter 3, Lessons 1, 2 and 3
	Chapter 8, Lesson 2
	Chapter 9, Lessons 1 and 2
	Chapter 11, Lesson 1
Configure service applications.	Chapter 5, Lessons 1 and 2
	Chapter 6, Lessons 1 and 2
	Chapter 8, Lessons 1, 2, 3, 4, 5, and 6
	Chapter 9, Lessons 1 and 2
Configure indexing and search.	Chapter 7, Lessons 1, 2 and 3
MANAGING A SHAREPOINT ENVIRONMENT	
Manage operational settings.	Chapter 4, Lesson 1
	Chapter 12, Lessons 1, 2, and 3
Manage accounts and user roles.	Chapter 1, Lessons 2 and 3
	Chapter 2, Lessons 1 and 2
	Chapter 4, Lessons 1 and 2
	Chapter 9, Lesson 2
Manage authentication providers.	Chapter 3, Lesson 2
DEPLOYING AND MANAGING APPLICATIONS	
Manage Web Applications.	Chapter 1, Lesson 3
	Chapter 2, Lesson 2
	Chapter 3, Lesson 1, 2 and 3
	Chapter 4, Lessons 1 and 2
Manage site collections.	Chapter 1, Lesson 3
	Chapter 2, Lesson 2
	Chapter 4, Lessons 1 and 2
	Chapter 5, Lessons 1 and 2
	Chapter 9, Lessons 1 and 2
	Chapter 10, Lessons 1, 2 and 3
	Chapter 12, Lesson 4
Deploy and manage SharePoint solutions.	Chapter 10, Lessons 2 and 3
MAINTAINING A SHAREPOINT ENVIRONMENT	
Back up and restore a SharePoint environment.	Chapter 11, Lesson 2
Monitor and analyze a SharePoint environment.	Chapter 12, Lessons 1, 2 and 3
Optimize the performance of a SharePoint environment.	Chapter 9, Lesson 2
	Chapter 12, Lesson 4

Exam Objectives   The exam objectives listed here are current as of this book's publication date. Exam objectives are subject to change at any time without prior notice and at Microsoft's sole discretion. Please visit the Microsoft Learning Web site for the most current listing of exam objectives: *http://www.microsoft.com/learning/en/us/Exam .aspx?ID=70-667#tab2.*

DATE DUE

MC ning
Kit
Con t
Sha

Dan Ho
Alistair

GAYLORD

PRINTED IN U.S.A.

PUBLISHED BY
Microsoft Press
A Division of Microsoft Corporation
One Microsoft Way
Redmond, Washington 98052-6399

Library of Congress Control Number: 2011934666
ISBN: 978-0-7356-3885-3

Printed and bound in the United States of America.

First Printing

Microsoft Press books are available through booksellers and distributors worldwide. If you need support related to this book, email Microsoft Press Book Support at mspinput@microsoft.com. Please tell us what you think of this book at http://www.microsoft.com/learning/booksurvey.

Microsoft and the trademarks listed at http://www.microsoft.com/about/legal/en/us/IntellectualProperty/Trademarks/EN-US.aspx are trademarks of the Microsoft group of companies. All other marks are property of their respective owners.

The example companies, organizations, products, domain names, email addresses, logos, people, places, and events depicted herein are fictitious. No association with any real company, organization, product, domain name, email address, logo, person, place, or event is intended or should be inferred.

This book expresses the author's views and opinions. The information contained in this book is provided without any express, statutory, or implied warranties. Neither the authors, Microsoft Corporation, nor its resellers, or distributors will be held liable for any damages caused or alleged to be caused either directly or indirectly by this book.

Acquisitions Editor: Jeff Koch
Developmental Editor: Karen Szall
Project Editor: Karen Szall
Editorial Production: Christian Holdener, S4Carlisle Publishing Services
Technical Reviewer: Bob Hogan; Technical Review services provided by Content Master, a member of CM Group, Ltd.
Copyeditor: Becka McKay
Indexer: Maureen Johnson
Cover: Twist Creative • Seattle

Contents at a Glance

Contents

What do you think of this book? We want to hear from you!

Microsoft is interested in hearing your feedback so we can continually improve our
books and learning resources for you. To participate in a brief online survey, please visit:

www.microsoft.com/learning/booksurvey/

Chapter 6   Configuring User Profiles and Social Networking   341

Chapter 8 Implementing Enterprise Service Applications 453

Chapter 10 Administering SharePoint Customization   571

Chapter 11 Implementing Business Continuity   625

Chapter 12 Monitoring and Optimizing SharePoint Performance   675

What do you think of this book? We want to hear from you!

Microsoft is interested in hearing your feedback so we can continually improve our books and learning resources for you. To participate in a brief online survey, please visit:

www.microsoft.com/learning/booksurvey/

Introduction

This training kit is designed for information technology (IT) professionals who support or plan to support SharePoint Server 2010 and who also plan to take the Microsoft Certified Technology Specialist (MCTS) exam 70-667, *TS: Microsoft SharePoint 2010, Configuring.*

The material covered in this training kit and on exam 70-667 relates to SharePoint products and technologies, which enable business collaboration in an enterprise and on the web. It is assumed that before you begin using this training kit, you have a solid, foundation-level understanding of Microsoft Windows client and server operating systems and common Internet technologies. The MCTS exam and this book assume that you have at least one year of experience configuring SharePoint and related technologies, including Internet Information Services (IIS), Windows Server 2008, Active Directory, DNS, SQL Server, and networking infrastructure services.

The topics in this training kit cover what you need to know for the exam, as described on the Skills Measured tab for the exam, which is available at *http://www.microsoft.com/ learning/en/us/exam.aspx?ID=70-667&locale=en-us#tab2.*

By using this training kit, you will learn how to do the following:

- Deploy SharePoint Server 2010 farms.
- Create a logical architecture of web applications, content databases, site collections, and sites.
- Manage security of SharePoint content by configuring authentication and access controls.
- Configure SharePoint services including search, user profiles, and the managed metadata service.
- Optimize, monitor, and troubleshoot performance of SharePoint servers and services.
- Ensure that data is protected and highly available.
- Deploy and manage customized SharePoint functionality and solutions.

Refer to the Objective map in the front of this book to see where in the book each exam objective is covered.

System Requirements

Practice exercises are a valuable component of this training kit. They allow you to experience important skills directly, reinforce material discussed in lessons, and even introduce new concepts.

Each lesson and practice describes the requirements for exercises. Many lessons require only two computers, one configured as a domain controller for a sample domain named contoso.com and the second configured as a SharePoint server running Microsoft SQL Server 2008 R2 and SharePoint Server 2010. However, some lessons require additional computers acting as a second server in the SharePoint farm.

The companion media includes the "Lab Environment Build Guide" document, which contains detailed setup instructions for the computers used throughout this training kit. Lessons that require additional computers provide guidance regarding the configuration of those computers.

Hardware Requirements

You can perform exercises on physical computers. Each computer must meet the minimum requirements for RAM, free hard disk space, and processor cores shown here:

- **Domain Controller**   1.5 GB RAM, 40 GB free disk space, and at least 1 processor core.
- **SharePoint server**   6 GB RAM, 128 GB free disk space, and at least 2 processor cores.
- **Additional SharePoint server**   4 GB RAM, 128 GB free disk space, and at least 2 processor cores.

To minimize the time and expense of configuring the computers required for this training kit, it's recommended that you perform the practices in this training kit on virtual machines. The training kit assumes you will use virtualization software that supports snapshots, so that you can roll back to a previous state after performing an exercise.

You can create virtual machines by using Hyper-V—a feature of Windows Server 2008 and Windows Server 2008 R2—or other virtualization software, such as VMware Workstation. The Lab Environment Build Guide details the configuration of the virtual machines required for this training kit. Refer to the documentation of your selected virtualization platform for hardware and software requirements, for instructions regarding host setup and configuration.

If you choose to use virtualization software, you can run more than one virtual machine on a host computer. The host computer must have sufficient RAM for each virtual machine that you will run simultaneously on the host, plus sufficient RAM to meet the RAM requirements of the host operating system.

If you plan to run all virtual machines on a single host, the host must have at least 12 GB of RAM. For example, one of the most complex configurations you will need is one domain controller using 512 MB of RAM, and two SharePoint servers using 6 GB and 4 GB of RAM. On a host computer with 12 GB of RAM, this would leave just over 1 GB for the host.

The host computer must have sufficient disk space for each virtual machine plus snapshots. We recommend that you have at least 512 GB of free disk space if you want to run all virtual machines on a single host computer. Note that you never use more than three virtual machines together at the same time.

If you encounter performance bottlenecks while running multiple virtual machines on a single physical host, consider running virtual machines on more than one physical host.

Ensure that all machines—virtual or physical—that you use for exercises can network with each other. It is highly recommended that the environment be totally disconnected from your production environment. Refer to the documentation of your virtualization platform for network configuration procedures.

We recommend that you preserve each of the virtual machines you create until you have completed the training kit. After each chapter, create a snapshot of the virtual machines used in that chapter so that you can reuse them, as required in later exercises.

Finally, you must have a physical computer with a CD-ROM drive with which to read the companion media. (If you have the eBook, you can retrieve the companion media from the book's web page.) You must also have Internet connectivity so that you can download the evaluation versions of software, as specified in the "Lab Environment Build Guide."

Software Requirements

The following software is required to complete the practice exercises:

- Windows Server 2008 R2
- SQL Server 2008 R2 (64-bit)
- SharePoint Server 2010 (Enterprise Client Access License features)
- SharePoint Designer 2010
- Office Professional Plus 2010
- Silverlight

You can download evaluation versions of the products from the TechNet Evaluation Center at *http://technet.microsoft.com/en-us/evalcenter*. If you use evaluation versions of the software, pay attention to the expiration date of the product. The evaluation version of Windows Server 2008 R2, for example, can be used for up to 60 days.

If you have a TechNet or MSDN subscription, you can download the products from the subscriber downloads center. These versions do not expire. If you are not a TechNet or MSDN subscriber, it is recommended that you subscribe so that you can access benefits such as product downloads.

To configure the computers and to access files on the companion media, the following software is required:

- If you are not using virtualization software, you need software that allows you to handle .iso files. This software needs to perform either of the following functions:
  - Burn .iso files to CDs or DVDs. (This solution also requires CD/DVD recording hardware.)
  - Mount .iso files as virtual CD or DVD drives on your computer.
- A web browser such as Internet Explorer version 8 or later.
- An application that can display PDF files, such as Adobe Acrobat Reader, which can be downloaded at *http://www.adobe.com/reader*.

> **IMPORTANT**   **LAB ENVIRONMENT BUILD GUIDE**
>
> Be sure to read the "Lab Environment Build Guide" on the companion media for detailed instructions regarding the setup of computers for this training kit.

Using the Companion CD

A companion CD is included with this training kit. The companion CD contains the following:

- **Practice tests**   You can reinforce your understanding of the topics covered in this training kit by using electronic practice tests that you customize to meet your needs. You can run a practice test that is generated from the pool of Lesson Review questions in this book. Alternatively, you can practice for the 70-667 certification exam by using tests created from a pool of more than 200 practice exam questions, which give you many practice exams to ensure that you are prepared.
- **Practice files**   Some practices in this training kit refer to files in the Practice Files folder on the companion media. When you prepare for practices by following the instructions in the Lab Environment Build Guide, these files are copied to the C:\70667TK folder on the disk drive of the SharePoint server, so that during the practices you can access the files without the companion media.
- **An eBook**   An electronic version of this book is included for when you do not want to carry the printed book with you.
- **Practice answers**   At the end of each lesson, one or more hands-on practice exercises challenge you to apply the concepts and skills discussed in the lesson to real-world scenarios. Each exercise presents high-level instructions, similar to what you might receive from a manager, colleague, or end user in an enterprise environment. We recommend that you try to complete the exercise by recalling and reviewing what

you've learned in the lesson. If you cannot complete a step or exercise, you can use the practice answers on the companion CD, which include detailed, step-by-step instructions for each exercise.

> **NOTE   COMPANION CONTENT FOR DIGITAL BOOK READERS**
>
> If you bought a digital-only edition of this book, you can enjoy select content from the print edition's companion CD. Visit *http://go.microsoft.com/FWLink/?Linkid=223198* to get your downloadable content.

How to Install the Practice Tests

To install the practice test software from the companion CD to your hard disk, perform the following steps:

1. Insert the companion CD into your CD drive and accept the license agreement. A CD menu appears.

> **NOTE   IF THE CD MENU DOES NOT APPEAR**
>
> If the CD menu or the license agreement does not appear, AutoRun might be disabled on your computer. Refer to the Readme.txt file on the CD for alternate installation instructions.

2. Click Practice Tests and follow the instructions on the screen.

How to Use the Practice Tests

To start the practice test software, follow these steps:

1. Click Start, All Programs, and then select Microsoft Press Training Kit Exam Prep.

    A window appears that shows all the Microsoft Press training kit exam prep suites installed on your computer.

2. Double-click the lesson review or practice test you want to use.

> **NOTE   LESSON REVIEWS VS. PRACTICE TESTS**
>
> Select the (70-667) *TS: Microsoft SharePoint 2010, Configuring* lesson review to use the questions from the "Lesson Review" sections of this book. Select the (70-667) *TS: Microsoft SharePoint 2010, Configuring* practice test to use a pool of 200 questions similar to those that appear on the 70-667 certification exam.

Lesson Review Options

When you start a lesson review, the Custom Mode dialog box appears so that you can configure your test. You can click OK to accept the defaults, or you can customize the number of questions you want, how the practice test software works, which exam objectives you want the questions to relate to, and whether you want your lesson review to be timed. If you are retaking a test, you can select whether you want to see all the questions again or only the questions you missed or did not answer.

After you click OK, your lesson review starts.

- To take the test, answer the questions and use the Next and Previous buttons to move from question to question.

- After you answer an individual question, if you want to see which answers are correct—along with an explanation of each correct answer—click Explanation.

- If you prefer to wait until the end of the test to see how you did, answer all the questions and then click Score Test. You will see a summary of the exam objectives you chose and the percentage of questions you got right overall and per objective. You can print a copy of your test, review your answers, or retake the test.

Practice Test Options

When you start a practice test, you choose whether to take the test in Certification Mode, Study Mode, or Custom Mode:

- **Certification Mode** Closely resembles the experience of taking a certification exam. The test has a set number of questions. It is timed, and you cannot pause and restart the timer.

- **Study Mode** Creates an untimed test during which you can review the correct answers and the explanations after you answer each question.

- **Custom Mode** Gives you full control over the test options so that you can customize them as you like.

In all modes, the user interface when you are taking the test is basically the same but with different options enabled or disabled depending on the mode. The main options are discussed in the previous section, "Lesson Review Options."

When you review your answer to an individual practice test question, a "References" section is provided that lists where in the training kit you can find the information that relates to that question and provides links to other sources of information. After you click Test Results to score your entire practice test, you can click the Learning Plan tab to see a list of references for every objective.

How to Uninstall the Practice Tests

To uninstall the practice test software for a training kit, use the Program And Features option in Windows Control Panel.

Acknowledgments

Although the authors' names appear on the cover of this book, we are but one part of the incredible team that has brought this—the first training kit for SharePoint administration published by Microsoft Press—to fruition. Our technical reviewer is Bob Hogan, and the copy editor is Becka McKay. Both of them went well beyond the call of duty, and their attention to detail and to accuracy added tremendous value to this work. Christian Holdener is our project manager. He coordinated the many reviews and, more important, kept the production schedule moving despite the challenges we threw at him. Most important is the astounding Karen Szall, our editor *extraordinaire*, with whom I've worked on many Microsoft Press titles. She has earned herself a place in editorial heaven with this one. We the authors are deeply grateful for the efforts of this talented group of colleagues. Dan also extends a big *mahalo* to Wyatt, Keith, Maddie, Jack, and the team at AvePoint for their support and soul-nourishment over the course of this project.

Support & Feedback

The following sections provide information on errata, book support, feedback, and contact information.

Errata

We've made every effort to ensure the accuracy of this book and its companion content. Any errors that have been reported since this book was published are listed on our Microsoft Press site at oreilly.com:

http://go.microsoft.com/FWLink/?Linkid=223199

If you find an error that is not already listed, you can report it to us through the same page.

If you need additional support, email Microsoft Press Book Support at *mspinput@microsoft.com*.

Please note that product support for Microsoft software is not offered through the addresses above.

We Want to Hear from You

At Microsoft Press, your satisfaction is our top priority, and your feedback our most valuable asset. Please tell us what you think of this book at:

http://www.microsoft.com/learning/booksurvey

The survey is short, and we read every one of your comments and ideas. Thanks in advance for your input!

Stay in Touch

Let us keep the conversation going! We are on Twitter: *http://twitter.com/MicrosoftPress.*

Preparing for the Exam

Microsoft certification exams are a great way to build your resume and let the world know about your level of expertise. Certification exams validate your on-the-job experience and product knowledge. While there is no substitution for on-the-job experience, preparation through study and hands-on practice can help you prepare for the exam. We recommend that you round out your exam preparation plan by using a combination of available study materials and courses. For example, you might use the Training Kit and another study guide for your "at home" preparation, and take a Microsoft Official Curriculum course for the classroom experience. Choose the combination that you think works best for you.

Microsoft
CERTIFIED
Technology
Specialist

CHAPTER 1

Creating a SharePoint 2010 Intranet

Microsoft SharePoint Server 2010 offers a broad range of functionality that addresses a vast number of business collaboration scenarios. In this Training Kit, you will learn to configure and support SharePoint Server 2010, but of course you must begin at the beginning, and in this chapter you will learn what it takes to get SharePoint up and running—from preparing your infrastructure, to configuring related technologies and products, to deploying SharePoint servers and farms using both out-of-the-box installation wizards and scripts, and finally to creating a simple web application to serve as a corporate intranet.

> **IMPORTANT**
>
> ### Have you read page xxxi?
>
> It contains valuable information regarding the skills you need to pass the exam.

Exam objectives in this chapter:

- Deploy new installations and upgrades.
- Configure SharePoint farms.
- Manage accounts and user roles.
- Manage web applications.
- Manage site collections.

Lessons in this chapter:

Before You Begin

To complete the lessons in this chapter, you must build your lab environment according to the instructions found in the Introduction to this Training Kit.

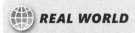

REAL WORLD

Dan Holme

Nothing could be easier than installing SharePoint Server 2010, right? Not so fast. SharePoint 2010 relies on a deep, rich stack of technologies, including 64-bit versions of Windows Server, SQL Server, Internet Information Services (IIS), the .NET Framework, and Windows PowerShell. There's also a lengthy list of software and configuration prerequisites. So although it's possible to log on as a domain administrator, pop the SharePoint Server 2010 DVD into a server, and have a stand-alone installation of SharePoint up and running in less than an hour, that doesn't mean it's a production-ready farm that meets all of the technical, security, and business requirements of your SharePoint governance plan. Even something as seemingly straightforward as SharePoint installation requires careful preparation, consideration for least privilege and other security best practices, and preferably a small investment in scripting and automation to ensure a smooth and consistent installation in both test and production environments.

Lesson 1: Prepare for SharePoint 2010

Microsoft SharePoint Server 2010 is a platform that relies on a wide range of other Microsoft technologies. Before you can install SharePoint 2010, you must prepare your hardware and software environment to support the dependencies and interactions with SharePoint products and technologies.

After this lesson, you will be able to:

- Identify the roles and topologies of SharePoint farms.
- Describe the infrastructure requirements for installing SharePoint 2010.
- Describe the client browser and application requirements for installing SharePoint 2010.
- Describe the interaction between SharePoint services, Active Directory, and Microsoft SQL Server.
- Create the user accounts required to install SharePoint.
- Assign permissions and rights required to install SharePoint.
- Describe the software and configuration prerequisites for installing SharePoint 2010.
- Install the software prerequisites for SharePoint.

Estimated lesson time: 60 minutes

Prepare the Server Infrastructure

Before you can install SharePoint Server 2010, you must prepare one or more servers to host the SharePoint farm. The following sections outline the considerations and requirements for your SharePoint server infrastructure.

SharePoint Components and Topologies

A SharePoint implementation consists of numerous components, including web applications, services, and databases. Web applications are websites with which users interact, such as your corporate intranet. Services include the crawler that indexes content for search. All SharePoint content and most SharePoint configurations are stored in databases hosted by one or more instances of SQL Server.

These components can be hosted by one or more servers in a SharePoint farm. The consolidation or distribution of components determines the farm's topology. A single-server farm runs both SQL Server and SharePoint—and all SharePoint components—on one server. A single-server farm is often appropriate for training and development environments, and may be used for sites with low utilization patterns, such as a small, remote office.

SQL Server performance is critical to the overall performance of a SharePoint farm. For that reason, most organizations choose to run SQL Server on a server or cluster that is separate from the servers running the SharePoint farm. A farm with a dedicated server running all SharePoint components, separate from the SQL Server server or cluster, can support higher levels of utilization.

However, a SharePoint farm with only one server running SharePoint offers no redundancy for SharePoint itself. If the server fails, SharePoint sites are not available. For this reason, it is a best practice to have at least two servers running SharePoint in a farm, and to run components on both servers that are important to the operations of your organization, based on the service-level agreements (SLAs) specified by your SharePoint governance plan. For example, most organizations would want search services to be available in the event of the failure of a single server. To achieve this service objective, you must ensure that a search query component is installed on both servers in the SharePoint farm. Similarly, if it is important that the intranet web application is available even if a server fails, you must ensure that the web application is accessible on both servers in the farm.

By distributing and load balancing web applications, and by installing services on multiple servers, you also gain performance efficiencies. Load balancing distributes requests for content from web applications across servers. SharePoint automatically distributes requests to services across the servers that run those services.

> **BEST PRACTICES** **SCALING OUT THE FARM**
>
> You might imagine that the best practice to scale out a farm is simply to add more servers and to continue adding all services to each server. In fact, in larger and more complex environments performance is optimized by dedicating servers to specific tasks. For example, indexing content from numerous content sources is a performance-intensive task. It is therefore common for organizations to configure a SharePoint server with only the search index component, allowing the server to focus its resources on this task.
>
> As you scale out your farm, you should first ensure that services and web applications are redundant to a level that meets the SLAs of your governance plan. You must also ensure that performance is optimized. By balancing availability and performance, you can determine the correct topology for your SharePoint implementation.

Topology Terminology

In previous versions of SharePoint, much documentation referred to *web front-end* (WFE) servers, which hosted only user-facing web applications, and *application servers*, which hosted services such as indexing. In SharePoint 2010, although you can still create a topology in which user-facing web applications and SharePoint services run on separate servers, the range of available topologies is much greater. It will therefore be more common to mix services and web applications on the same server, with the goal of optimizing availability and performance. However, old habits are hard to break, and the SharePoint community, SharePoint resources and documentation, and even this Training Kit are likely to continue referring to WFE and application servers.

Hardware and Software Requirements

SharePoint Server 2010 is a powerful platform that can scale to meet the most demanding enterprise scenarios. As such, the hardware requirements for SharePoint begin with a minimum hardware base with at least four processor cores running 2.5 GHz and 8 GB of RAM.

SharePoint 2010 is a 64-bit platform, and therefore you must use 64-bit versions of the operating system on each SharePoint server and for SQL Server. Windows Server 2008 with Service Pack 2 (SP2) (64-bit) or Windows Server 2008 R2 (which is only 64-bit) is required.

SQL Server is the required database platform. SharePoint 2010 requires one of the following:

- SQL Server 2005 with Service Pack 3 (SP3) with Cumulative Update 3 (64-bit)
- SQL Server 2008 SP1 with Cumulative Update 2 or Cumulative Update 5 or later (64-bit)
- SQL Server 2008 R2 (which is only 64-bit)

> **MORE INFO** **MINIMUM HARDWARE AND SOFTWARE REQUIREMENTS**
>
> You can find the minimum hardware and software requirements for SharePoint Server 2010 in a Microsoft TechNet article at *http://technet.microsoft.com/en-us/library/cc262485.aspx*.

It is highly recommended that you use the latest versions of the operating system and SQL Server to take advantage of the maximum number of features. For example, you need SQL Server 2008 R2 to take advantage of failover, PowerPivot, and Access Services reporting features.

EXAM TIP

While it is recommended that you use the latest versions of the operating system and SQL Server in a production environment, the exam may test your awareness of minimum supported versions as well.

If you are investing in infrastructure for Microsoft Office SharePoint Server 2007, invest in 64-bit servers, operating systems, and software now to reduce the number of steps required to migrate to SharePoint Server 2010. Migration from 32-bit to 64-bit platforms is detailed in Chapter 9, "Deploying and Upgrading to SharePoint 2010."

Microsoft allows you to install SharePoint on a client operating system to support development. The following are supported, with at least 4 GB of RAM:

- Windows Vista with Service Pack 1 (SP1) or later (64-bit)
- Windows 7 (64-bit)

Such platforms should not be used for production purposes.

> **MORE INFO** **PREPARING A DEVELOPMENT ENVIRONMENT**
>
> You can learn more about installing SharePoint on a Windows client in a Microsoft TechNet article at *http://go.microsoft.com/fwlink/?LinkID=164557*.

You can also access SharePoint through a hosted service such as one of the following offerings from Microsoft and its partners:

- Microsoft Online (*http://www.microsoft.com/online*) offers Office 365, a per-user subscription to SharePoint as well as to Microsoft Exchange and Microsoft Office LiveMeeting. Microsoft Online also offers dedicated SharePoint hosting to large customers.

- Microsoft will offer customers the ability to serve their public-facing web sites on hosted instances of SharePoint Server 2010. Details are not available at the time of publication.

- Microsoft's consumer and small business services, such as Windows Live, provide some SharePoint functionality. For example, Windows Live SkyDrive allows users to edit Word, Excel, PowerPoint, and OneNote documents in the browser, which is functionality provided by Office Web Apps.

You can mix and match internally hosted farms with externally hosted services to meet varied business requirements.

SharePoint Licensing

SharePoint licensing is complex because of the number of products that are involved. It is important that you consult with your licensing representative to ensure compliance for your SharePoint implementation.

The most typical implementation involves purchasing licenses for Windows Server 2008 or Windows Server 2008 R2 for each SharePoint server and a quantity of per-user client access licenses (CALs) for each SharePoint user. SQL Server is typically installed with a per-processor license, which does not require CALs for users.

If you are using SharePoint Foundation 2010, no additional license is required. If you are using SharePoint Server 2010, however, you need a server product license for each SharePoint server and CALs for each user. SharePoint Standard CAL provides access to the basic level of SharePoint Server 2010 functionality including My Sites and search. With the Enterprise CAL, which is an add-on to the Standard CAL, you can deploy features such as Excel Services and Office Web Applications.

> **MORE INFO** **SHAREPOINT EDITIONS**
>
> You can learn more about and compare the features of SharePoint Foundation, Standard, and Enterprise at *http://sharepoint.microsoft.com/en-us/buy/Pages/Editions-Comparison.aspx*.

If you provide content to users or devices that cannot be counted—for example, if you expose SharePoint content to the Internet for public access—you must use the SharePoint server-only license model, in which you purchase licenses to SharePoint Server for Internet Sites, Standard or Enterprise. If these servers provide content to both public and internal users, the licensing becomes more complex.

To minimize the cost of an enterprise SharePoint implementation, you should consider implementing multiple SharePoint farms, each with a level of functionality that supports the business requirements of users in different scenarios. For example, you might build a SharePoint farm in your enterprise datacenter on which you host your enterprise search, user My Sites, and Excel Services for business insights. This farm would support Enterprise features of SharePoint, and would be licensed accordingly.

If you also have a remote office where users require support for collaboration around documents and lists, you might build a farm running SharePoint Foundation in that remote site, instead of hosting the users' collaboration sites at the enterprise datacenter, across the wide area network (WAN) link. Users in the remote office would continue to use the enterprise SharePoint farm for search and My Site functionality, but their day-to-day collaboration would take place on the local SharePoint Foundation farm, which would provide optimal performance and availability without increasing the cost of SharePoint licensing.

Browser and Application Requirements

SharePoint 2010 generates most of its content using web-standard eXtensible Hypertext Markup Language (XHTML) that renders well across most browsers. Microsoft categorizes browsers into two categories—Level 1 and Level 2—to help customers align browser choice with the desired level of functionality.

Level 1 browsers support ActiveX and all SharePoint functionality on user and administrative pages, as shown in Table 1-1.

TABLE 1-1 Level 1 Browser Requirements

OPERATING SYSTEM	BROWSER
■ Windows XP	■ Internet Explorer 7 (32-bit)
■ Windows Vista	■ Internet Explorer 8 (32-bit)
■ Windows Server 2003	■ Mozilla Firefox 3.5*
■ Windows Server 2008	
■ Windows 7	■ Internet Explorer 8 (32-bit)
■ Windows Server 2008 R2	■ Mozilla Firefox 3.5

__Note__: Features provided by ActiveX controls, such as list Datasheet view and the control that displays user presence information, do not work in Mozilla Firefox 3.5, which does not support ActiveX.

Level 2 browsers support basic read, write, and administrative activities, as shown in Table 1-2.

TABLE 1-2 Level 2 Browser Requirements

OPERATING SYSTEM	BROWSER
■ Apple Mac OS X Snow Leopard	■ Apple Safari 4.*x* ■ Mozilla Firefox 3.5
■ Windows XP ■ Windows Vista ■ Windows Server 2003 ■ Windows Server 2008	■ Internet Explorer 7 (64-bit) ■ Internet Explorer 8 (64-bit)
■ Windows 7 ■ Windows Server 2008 R2	■ Internet Explorer 8 (64-bit)
■ UNIX/Linux 8.1	■ Mozilla Firefox 3.5

Other standards-based browsers work with SharePoint with the same limitations as Level 2 browsers. However, Microsoft has not done extensive testing on browsers other than those listed, and does not support use of other browsers. If you want to use a browser other than one listed in the preceding tables, you should perform testing to ensure that the browser delivers an acceptable user experience.

For published sites, page designers can apply Web Content Management features to control markup and styling so that published sites are compatible with additional browsers, including Microsoft Internet Explorer 6. However, it is the page designer's responsibility to create pages that target the browsers that are designated for support. Page designers and content authors must use a standards-based browser, such as Internet Explorer 8 or Firefox 3.5 to author content.

SharePoint compatible applications can provide a rich, client-side interaction with SharePoint. Microsoft Office 2003 and later are compatible with SharePoint.

> **MORE INFO   PLANNING BROWSER SUPPORT**
>
> The following article provides additional details regarding browser support for SharePoint 2010: "Plan Browser Support" at *http://technet.microsoft.com/en-us/library/cc263526.aspx.*

Prepare User Accounts for SharePoint Administration and Services

SharePoint has close relationships with, and dependencies on, SQL Server and Active Directory.

Active Directory provides identity and authentication services. In other words, it stores user accounts (user names and passwords) and validates account logons. These services support users logging on to SharePoint sites. They also support the accounts used by SharePoint and SQL services themselves.

SQL Server stores almost all of the configuration and content of a SharePoint farm. SQL Server services, like all Windows services, run using an identity and log on with credentials consisting of a user name and password.

SharePoint services also run with Active Directory credentials. The credentials are used by SharePoint to access data in SQL Server. These accounts must have SQL logins so that SQL can authorize the access. These SQL logins are created automatically by SharePoint during setup and the creation of web applications.

To support the administration and services of SQL and SharePoint, you must create identities in Active Directory, and you must ensure that appropriate permissions have been granted. It is important that you adhere to the security practice of *least privilege*, in which an account is given only the permissions required to perform its tasks. The following accounts enable a least-privilege implementation of SharePoint in a typical environment:

- SQL Server administrator account: SQL_Admin
- SQL Server service account: SQL_Service
- SharePoint setup user and administrator account: SP_Admin
- SharePoint farm account: SP_Farm
- Web and service application pool account(s): SP_WebApps and SP_ServiceApps
- Search indexer (crawler) account: SP_Crawl
- User profile synchronization account: SP_UserSync

The following sections provide detail about each of these accounts. Because these accounts are privileged, they should be dedicated for the indicated purpose, and should not be used for any other purpose in the enterprise.

SQL Server Administrator Account: SQL_Admin

To install SQL Server, an identity must be a member of the local Administrators group on the server that will host SQL Server. It is recommended that you use a unique account to install SQL Server instead of using your own account. This allows for future growth and change in the enterprise—when you get promoted or leave the organization, your account is not tied to the ownership of SQL Server or its databases. For example, you can create an account named SQL_Admin and add it to the local Administrators group of the server. Log on as SQL_Admin and install SQL Server. The SQL_Admin account will thus become the first administrator of the SQL Server instance, and the owner of several components and databases of SQL Server.

During or after the installation, you can specify additional administrators of SQL Server. At that time, add your account as an additional SQL Server administrator. You thus gain administrative privileges to SQL Server without registering your account as the owner of the SQL Server instance.

SQL Server Service Account: SQL_Service

SQL Server services use identities, or accounts. Like most Windows services, you can configure SQL Server services to use special identities such as System, Network Service, or Local Service, but it is a highly recommended best practice to use a domain user account. If SQL Server is running on a different server than SharePoint, you are required to use a domain account. The SQL Server service account is used as the identity for the MSSQLSERVER and SQLSERVERAGENT services. For example, create an account named SQL_Service. During installation of SQL Server, configure two services, MSSQLSERVER and SQLSERVERAGENT, to log on as SQL_Service.

SharePoint Administrator and Setup User Account: SP_Admin

The setup user account—for example, SP_Admin—is used by a human being to install and configure SharePoint.

During setup and configuration, SharePoint creates SQL databases and logins, and modifies the server itself (for example, by creating local groups). SharePoint setup and configuration use the credentials of SP_Admin to perform such tasks, so SP_Admin must be a domain user account that has been assigned the *securityadmin* and *dbcreator* roles on the SQL server. The account must also be a member of the local Administrators group of any server that will run SharePoint.

SP_Admin is the only account for which a SQL login must be manually created, and to which SQL roles must be assigned. During installation of SharePoint, the credentials of SP_Admin are used by the setup routines to automatically create SQL logins for—and to assign roles to—other accounts, such as SP_Farm.

SharePoint Farm Service Account: SP_Farm

During installation and configuration, the setup user, SP_Admin, assigns an account to the SharePoint farm. This account—for example, SP_Farm—is used by the Central Administration site's application pool and as the identity for the Timer service. It must be a domain user account.

The permissions required by SP_Farm are assigned automatically during farm setup by the SharePoint Products Configuration Wizard. Specifically, the account is given a SQL Server login that is assigned the *dbcreator* and *securityadmin* fixed server roles. The account is also associated with the *dbo* login or assigned the *db_owner* fixed database role for all SharePoint databases in the farm. When additional servers are added to a farm, SP_Farm is automatically given the permissions it requires on those servers.

Both the SP_Admin and SP_Farm accounts are highly privileged. SP_Admin is used by a human being to install SharePoint, configure the farm, and add servers to or remove servers from the farm. On a day-to-day basis, SP_Farm acts as the service account for the farm, supporting Central Administration, timer jobs, and other components.

Web and Service Application Pool Accounts: SP_WebApps and SP_ServiceApps

Each web application runs in an application pool. The application pool identity is a domain user account that is functionally equivalent to a service account, with permissions to access the content database for the web application on the SQL Server. Service applications and services, such as Search or the Office Web Applications, also use domain user identities for application pool and service accounts.

When you assign an account to a web application, service, or service application, SharePoint 2010 automatically grants the account the permissions it needs. For example, when you assign an account as the default crawl account, which is used to index SharePoint content for search, SharePoint automatically grants the account permission to read all content in all sites.

You can use one or more accounts for web applications, service applications, and services based on your requirements for manageability and security. By using unique accounts for each application and service, you can create a least-privileged environment in which each application or service account has only the permissions required for that component. Additionally, you can more easily audit and troubleshoot because logs will clearly identify the account—and therefore the service—in question.

By using a single account for all applications and services, you eliminate the need to manage multiple accounts. However, the account will have the cumulative permissions required for all applications and services, which means that any one application or service process will run with more permissions than it needs. And it will become more difficult to audit and troubleshoot certain scenarios, because logs will identify a single account and you cannot directly associate that account with a specific service or application.

In many products, it is difficult to manage service accounts because of password synchronization. When a service account's password is changed in Active Directory, you must manually update the logon information for the service on each system on which the service is installed.

SharePoint 2010 introduces *managed accounts*, a feature that reduces the management overhead for service accounts. A managed account is a domain user account that is registered with SharePoint and assigned to one or more web applications, service applications, or services. When you change the password of a managed account, SharePoint automatically updates the logon information of the associated components. Additionally, SharePoint can automatically manage password changes so that changes are made just prior to the expiration of the password based on domain password policy.

As a result, managing service accounts for SharePoint 2010 is significantly easier than in previous versions of SharePoint, or in other products. By reducing the management burden of service accounts, SharePoint 2010 makes it possible for you to use one account per service or application. You will learn more about managed accounts in Chapter 9.

In this Training Kit, a single account, SP_ServiceApps, will be used for most service applications, and another account, SP_WebApps, will be used as the application pool identity for user-facing web applications. In a production environment, you should define accounts based on your requirements for security and manageability, with the understanding that defining unique accounts for each service and web application is a best practice.

Search Indexer (Crawler) Account: SP_Crawl

The search crawler account is used to index content. It is automatically given permissions to read all SharePoint content. It should be a unique account that cannot access content at any higher level. You must manually give it permission to read any other content source that you configure it to index, such as shared folders on servers.

User Profile Synchronization Account: SP_UserSync

SharePoint user profile synchronization uses an account to synchronize profile attributes between Active Directory and SharePoint. This account will be detailed in Chapter 6, "Configuring User Profiles and Social Networking."

Install SharePoint Prerequisites

You must apply a long list of software and configuration prerequisites before you install SharePoint. The following are required:

- Microsoft SQL Server
- The Web Server (IIS) server role
- The Application Server server role
- Hotfix for Microsoft Windows (KB976394 for Windows Server 2008, KB976462 for Windows Server 2008 R2)
- Windows Identity Foundation (KB974405)
- Microsoft Sync Framework Runtime v1.0 (x64)
- Microsoft Chart Controls for Microsoft .NET Framework 3.5
- Microsoft Filter Pack 2.0
- Microsoft SQL Server 2008 Analysis Services ADOMD.NET
- Microsoft Server Speech Platform Runtime (x64)
- Windows PowerShell 2.0 (for Windows Server 2008)
- Microsoft Server Speech Recognition Language (Optional component supports phonetic search)
- Microsoft SQL Server 2008 R2 Reporting Services (SSRS) Add-in for SharePoint Technologies (Optional component supports reporting services integration and Access Web services reporting)

The following sections will equip you to install these prerequisites. Details and links to all prerequisites can be found in the article "Hardware and software requirements (SharePoint Server 2010)" at *http://technet.microsoft.com/en-us/library/cc262485.aspx*.

Install SQL Server

You must install one of the versions of SQL Server discussed earlier in this lesson before you can install other SharePoint prerequisites. The Lab Environment Build Guide on the companion media provides instructions for preparing the lab environment for the practices in this Training Kit. The instructions include procedures for installing SQL Server. To install SQL Server in a production environment, you must follow the guidance in the SQL Server documentation. See *Microsoft SQL Server 2008 Administrator's Pocket Consultant, Second Edition* by William R. Stanek for more information.

Microsoft SharePoint 2010 Products Preparation Tool

Microsoft SharePoint 2010 Products Preparation Tool (Preparation Tool), also known as the *prerequisite installer*, can download and install all of the prerequisites for you automatically.

To run the Preparation Tool, log on as the setup user account—for example, SP_Admin. The setup user account is described earlier in this lesson. Then, launch the tool from the Install Software Prerequisites link on the SharePoint Server 2010 Start page (default.hta), shown in Figure 1-1, or launch the tool directly by starting PrerequisiteInstaller.exe from the root of the installation media.

The Preparation Tool scans for each prerequisite. If a prerequisite is not found, the tool downloads, installs, and configures the prerequisite.

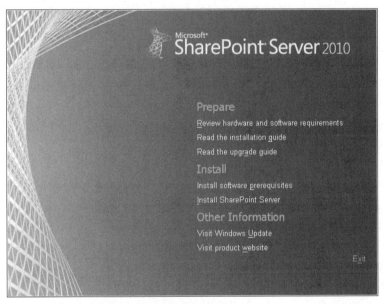

FIGURE 1-1 SharePoint Server 2010 Start page

In the event of an error—for example, if downloading a prerequisite fails—the tool stops and produces an error message that indicates which prerequisite failed. You can find the details of the failure in the error log, which is located in the %TEMP% folder, or by clicking the Review The Log File link in the wizard. The tool displays a link to the log. After you have remedied the problem, rerun the tool. Repeat the process until all prerequisites have been installed and configured successfully.

Two prerequisites are optional: Microsoft Server Speech Recognition Language and Microsoft SQL Server 2008 R2 Reporting Services (SSRS) Add-in for SharePoint Technologies. If the Preparation Tool cannot find or install these prerequisites, it generates an error, but you can continue to the next step in installing SharePoint Server 2010.

Offline and Scripted Installation of Prerequisites

Many organizations do not allow servers to have direct access to the Internet. The Preparation Tool can be directed to install prerequisites from a specific location, such as a shared folder, rather than downloading prerequisites from the Microsoft Download Center.

First, you must use a system that does have Internet connectivity to download all prerequisites to a shared folder. You can find links to prerequisites by using one of the following two options:

- Links to prerequisites are listed at *http://technet.microsoft.com/en-us/library/cc262485.aspx*.

- Run the Preparation Tool and examine the log for error messages that are generated when the tool attempts to download each prerequisite. The URL to each prerequisite is listed.

PrerequisiteInstaller.exe supports parameters that specify the location of each prerequisite. The syntax of each parameter is */PrerequisiteName:PathToInstallationFile*. The path can be a local or Universal Naming Convention (UNC) path to which the setup user (SP_Admin) account used to run the Preparation Tool has Read permission.

For example, the parameter used to indicate the location of the Microsoft Filter Pack 2.0 installation file is the following:

```
/FilterPack:\\ServerName\SharedFolder\Path\FilterPack64bit.exe
```

You can type **PrerequisiteInstaller.exe /?** to display the full list of parameters.

You can use PrerequisiteInstaller.exe and its parameters to script the installation of SharePoint prerequisites by using one of two methods:

- Start Command Prompt, and then type a command line with **PrerequisiteInstaller.exe** and all of the parameters on a single command line.

- Start Notepad and enter all parameters on a single line. Save the file as PrerequisiteInstallerArguments.txt in the same folder as PrerequisiteInstaller.exe. Then, run PrerequisiteInstaller.exe. It automatically looks for the arguments file, called PrerequisiteInstallerArguments.txt, in the working directory.

You will create and use a PrerequisiteInstallerArguments.txt file in the Practice for this lesson.

The */unattended* parameter causes the Preparation Tool to run in silent, unattended mode. No prompts or messages are displayed. Use this mode only when you are confident that prerequisite installation will be successful.

Additional Prerequisites

You must install and configure several prerequisites manually. The first two are updates that should be evaluated in the context of your enterprise. Use the following Knowledge Base articles to determine whether the update is appropriate in your environment.

- The ADO.NET Data Service Update is used by services like REST Web services: "An update is available that provides additional features and improvements for ADO.NET Data Services in the .NET Framework 3.5 SP1 on a computer that is running Windows 7 or Windows Server 2008 R2" at *http://support.microsoft.com/kb/976127.*

- Update KB979917 for ASP.NET is required if you use claims-based authentication. "Two issues occur when you deploy an ASP.NET 2.0-based application on a server that is running IIS 7.0 or IIS 7.5 in Integrated mode" at *http://support.microsoft.com/kb/979917.*

You must also consider whether you need to disable loopback checking. Windows Server 2008 (and Windows Server 2008 R2) blocks access to a website if the request for the website originates from the IP address of the server itself.

Loopback checking prevents you from using a browser on a SharePoint server to browse to a site on the same server farm. In a production environment, it is not recommended that you log on to a SharePoint server and use a browser on the server. However, this usage scenario may be more common in a development, testing, or training environment.

Loopback checking also prevents SharePoint services—most notably the search crawler that indexes SharePoint content—from accessing sites on the same server farm. The crawler, which runs on a SharePoint server, will request content to index, and the request will be denied. The crawl process will generate Access Denied events, and no content will be indexed.

The problem is solved by removing or controlling loopback checking. Details can be found in the Microsoft Knowledge Base article "You receive error 401.1 when you browse a Web site that uses Integrated Authentication and is hosted on IIS 5.1 or a later version" at *http://support.microsoft.com/kb/896861.*

The article discusses two options. Method 1 involves specifying all sites hosted on the server so that the server allows requests to those sites to originate from the same server. Method 2 entails disabling loopback checking altogether for all sites. Method 2 reduces the security of the server more than Method 1. Therefore, Method 2 is recommended only for development and test environments. Method 1 requires closely managing the servers on a SharePoint farm. Each time a new web application is added to the farm, its fully qualified host name must be added to the list of sites for which loopback checking is skipped.

PRACTICE   Prepare to Install SharePoint 2010

Practices are designed to guide you through important procedures. The instructions in this Training Kit are high-level instructions that will challenge you to think carefully and to apply the procedures that are covered in this lesson and elsewhere in the Training Kit. If you need assistance, consult the detailed, step-by-step instructions in the Practice Answers on the companion media.

In this practice, you will prepare a server for installation of SharePoint Server 2010.

Prepare for the Practice

Before you perform this practice, you must ensure that your lab environment has been built according to the instructions found in the Introduction to this Training Kit.

1. Apply the snapshot SQL INSTALLED to CONTOSO-DC.

2. Apply the snapshot SQL INSTALLED to SP2010-WFE1.

3. Start CONTOSO-DC.

   Wait for the virtual machine to complete startup, at which time the Press Ctrl+Alt+Del prompt appears.

4. Start SP2010-WFE1.

EXERCISE 1   Create Active Directory Accounts

In this exercise, you will create accounts for SharePoint administration, services, and access to SQL Server.

1. Log on to SP2010-WFE1 as **CONTOSO\Administrator** with the password **Pa$$w0rd**.

2. Start Active Directory Users And Computers.

3. In the Service Accounts OU, create the following user accounts. For each account, set the password to **Pa$$w0rd**, clear the User Must Change Password At Next Logon check box, and select the Password Never Expires check box.

   After creating each user, set its *Description* to the same value as the *Full Name* shown in the following table. Then set the email address of the account to *UserLogonName*@contoso.com—for example, SP_Admin@contoso.com.

FULL NAME	USER LOGON NAME
SharePoint Administrator and Setup User	SP_Admin
SharePoint Farm Service	SP_Farm
SharePoint Service Applications	SP_ServiceApps
SharePoint Web Applications	SP_WebApps
SharePoint Search Crawler	SP_Crawl
SharePoint User Profile Synchronization	SP_UserSync

4. Close Active Directory Users And Computers.

EXERCISE 2   Create a SQL Server Login for the SharePoint Administrator

In this exercise, you will create a login and assign roles on SQL Server for the new SharePoint Administrator account.

1. Start SQL Server Management Studio and connect to SP2010-WFE1.

2. Create a login for CONTOSO\SP_Admin.

3. Assign the login the *dbcreator* and *securityadmin* server roles.

4. Close SQL Server Management Studio.

EXERCISE 3 Delegate Administration of the SharePoint Server

In this exercise, you will add the SharePoint Administrator account to the local Administrators group of the SharePoint server. You will also add the user to the DnsAdmins group in the domain, so that the SharePoint Administrator can create DNS records for web applications in the SharePoint farm.

1. Add CONTOSO\SP_Admin to the DnsAdmins group of the Contoso domain.

2. Add CONTOSO\SP_Admin to the local Administrators group of SP2010-WFE1.

3. Log off of SP2010-WFE1.

EXERCISE 4 Copy the SharePoint Installation Files to the Server

1. Log on to SP2010-WFE1 as **CONTOSO\SP_Admin** with the password **Pa$$w0rd**.

2. Copy the contents of the SharePoint Server 2010 installation media to a new folder, C:\Software\SharePoint Server 2010.

3. Share the folder with the share name SP2010. Configure share permissions to grant the Everyone group Read permission.

EXERCISE 5 Attempt to Install SharePoint Prerequisites

1. Run C:\Software\SharePoint Server 2010\default.hta.

2. Click Install SharePoint prerequisites.

    The Preparation Tool reports There Was An Error During Installation.

3. Review the information provided by the Preparation Tool.

4. Review the log file. Locate the portion of the log file that documents the attempt to download the hotfix for Microsoft Windows (KB976462). Identify the URL from which the Preparation Tool attempted to download the hotfix.

    The URL is *http://go.microsoft.com/fwlink/?LinkID=166369*.

    This is the URL from which you can manually download the prerequisite.

5. Close the log file and all open windows.

EXERCISE 6 Download SharePoint Prerequisites

In this exercise, you will obtain the SharePoint prerequisites and save them in a shared folder.

1. Create the folder C:\Software\SharePoint Prerequisites.

2. Share the folder with the share name SP2010Prereqs. Configure share permissions to grant the Everyone group Read permission.

3. On a system with Internet connectivity, browse to ***http://technet.microsoft.com/ en-us/library/cc262485.aspx*** and then download the prerequisites for SharePoint Server 2010.

4. Copy the files to the C:\Software\SharePoint Prerequisites folder.

EXERCISE 7   Create a Script for Offline Installation of Prerequisites

In this exercise, you will create a PrerequisiteInstaller.Arguments.txt file that contains parameters with paths to the installation files for SharePoint prerequisites.

1. Run C:\Software\SharePoint Server 2010\PrerequisiteInstaller.exe /?.

   The About window opens. Do not close the window.

2. Start Notepad.

3. Using the list of install parameters in the About window as a reference, create a script for the prerequisite installer that contains parameters for each prerequisite with the path to the installation file for that prerequisite.

   For example, the parameter for the installation of the Microsoft Chart Controls for Microsoft .NET Framework 3.5 is */ChartControl:\\SP2010-WFE1.contoso.com\ SP2010Prereqs\MSChart.exe*.

   Because you are installing SharePoint on a server running Windows Server 2008 R2, you will not need parameters for Windows Server 2008 SP2, the Microsoft .NET Framework 3.5 SP1, Windows PowerShell 2.0, or KB976394.

   All parameters must be on one command line, although you can use Word Wrap in Notepad to facilitate your view of the command line.

4. Save the file as C:\Software\SharePoint Server 2010\PrerequisiteInstaller.Arguments.txt.

5. Close Notepad and the About window.

EXERCISE 8   Perform an Offline, Scripted Installation of SharePoint Prerequisites

In this exercise, you will run PrerequisiteInstaller.exe with the PrerequisiteInstaller.Arguments.txt script to perform an offline installation of SharePoint Prerequisites.

1. Run C:\Software\SharePoint Server 2010\PrerequisiteInstaller.exe.

2. Step through the Preparation Tool to prepare the server.

3. Validate that the Preparation Tool reports Installation Complete.

   If the system restarts automatically, log on as CONTOSO\SP_Admin with the password Pa$$w0rd. The Preparation Tool might open automatically after logon. If not, run PrerequisiteInstaller.exe again. Repeat this process until the Installation Complete page appears.

   If errors occur, examine the log file generated by the Preparation Tool. Verify that the PrerequisiteInstaller.Arguments.txt file contains no errors.

4. Restart SP2010-WFE1.

   Prerequisite installation might continue when you log on. If so, follow the instructions provided by the Preparation Tool. If an error is reported, run the Preparation Tool one more time to determine whether the Preparation Tool can resolve the issue. Restart the system after all prerequisites have been installed successfully.

> **ON THE COMPANION MEDIA** **VERIFYING THE FILE IS CORRECT**
>
> To ensure that the file is correct, copy the PrequisiteInstaller.Arguments.txt file from the companion media (in the Practice Files\01_01 folder) to the C:\Software\SharePoint Server 2010 folder. Then verify that the correct prerequisite installation files exist in the paths specified by each of the parameters in the PrequisiteInstaller.Arguments.txt file.

Lesson Summary

- SharePoint servers can host user-facing Web sites, services, service and administrative applications, or a combination thereof.
- SharePoint Server 2010 requires 64-bit versions of Windows Server 2008 or Windows Server 2008 R2, along with a database running a 64-bit version of SQL Server 2005 SP3, SQL Server 2008, or SQL Server 2008 R2. Each fundamental prerequisite requires appropriate service packs and updates.
- Several user accounts are required for a least-privilege installation of SharePoint 2010. Most importantly an account for setup and administration (for example, SP_Admin) and an account for farm services and Central Administration (for example, SP_Farm). You must configure the permissions for SP_Admin. During configuration of SharePoint 2010, SharePoint automatically assigns permissions to other accounts.
- You can install and configure software prerequisites by using the SharePoint 2010 Products Preparation Tool, also known as the Prerequisite Installer. The Preparation Tool can be automated using parameters of PrerequisiteInstaller.exe, which can be provided on the command line used to launch the Prerequisite Installer or in a PrerequisiteInstaller.Arguments.txt file.

Lesson Review

You can use the following questions to test your knowledge of the information in Lesson 1, "Prepare for SharePoint 2010." The questions are also available on the companion CD in a practice test if you prefer to review them in electronic form.

> **NOTE** **ANSWERS**
>
> Answers to these questions and explanations of why each answer choice is right or wrong are located in the "Answers" section at the end of the book.

1. You are planning to upgrade your Microsoft Office SharePoint Server 2007 installation to SharePoint Server 2010. Your current SharePoint farm stores its data on a 32-bit version of SQL Server 2000. What is the minimum version of SQL Server to which you must upgrade your database server?

   A. SQL Server 2005 (64-bit)

   B. SQL Server 2005 SP3 (64-bit)

   C. SQL Server 2008 (64-bit)

   D. SQL Server 2008 R2

2. Which of the following SQL Server roles must be assigned to the setup user account? (Choose all that apply.)

   A. sysadmin

   B. serveradmin

   C. dbcreator

   D. securityadmin

3. Which of the following methods can be used to prepare a server with the configuration and software prerequisites for SharePoint 2010? (Choose all that apply.)

   A. Run setup.exe from the SharePoint 2010 installation media.

   B. Click Install SharePoint Prerequisites on the SharePoint 2010 Start Page on a server that is disconnected from the Internet.

   C. Create a PrerequisiteInstaller.Arguments.txt file, and then run PrerequisiteInstaller.exe.

   D. Run PrerequsiteInstaller.exe with parameters.

Lesson 2: Install and Configure SharePoint 2010

You can use several methods to install and configure a SharePoint 2010 farm. In this lesson, you learn how to install SharePoint by using the wizard-driven setup and configuration tools, which make it easy to create a simple farm. In Chapter 9, you learn about ways to upgrade an existing farm to SharePoint 2010.

After this lesson, you will be able to:

- Describe the process for installing and configuring SharePoint 2010.
- Identify the configuration parameters required to install SharePoint.
- Install SharePoint to create a single-server farm.
- Configure SharePoint on a single-server farm.
- Perform post-installation configuration.

Estimated lesson time: 60 minutes

Prepare for Installation and Configuration

Installing SharePoint is a multiphase process. The following four high-level steps are used to install and configure SharePoint:

- Install the prerequisites.
- Install the SharePoint binaries.
- Configure the SharePoint server.
- Configure services and applications on the farm.

You can perform each phase using user interface tools or commands or scripts. In the previous lesson, you learned to install SharePoint prerequisites. In the following sections, you will learn how to perform the remaining three phases.

Before you begin installation and configuration, you must collect information that is required during the installation. Use the following items as a preinstallation checklist:

- You must know the user name and password for each of the accounts discussed in the previous lesson.
- You must know the SQL Server server name and instance name.
- You will be prompted for a configuration database name. Determine a naming strategy for SharePoint databases.

    A typical name for the farm configuration database is *SharePoint_Config*. However, if your SQL Server database will service multiple farms, your naming convention should provide a way to easily determine the configuration database for a specific farm.

- You will be prompted for a port on which to host Central Administration. You must determine this port based on your network infrastructure. The port must be allowed through firewalls that sit between the Central Administration application and the clients from which administrators will access the application.

- You will be prompted for a farm passphrase. You must determine this.

  You use the farm passphrase when making certain changes to the farm, such as when adding a new server to the farm. With the farm passphrase, an administrator can perform farm-level changes without needing to know the password for the SharePoint farm account (SP_Farm). The farm passphrase should be long, complex, unique, and should not be the same as the password used by any of the SharePoint administrative or service accounts. Be sure to document the password and store it in a physically secure location.

- You must know the product key or trial key. You must enter the product key during setup, but you can change it later in Central Administration.

Install the SharePoint Binaries

After you have installed the SharePoint prerequisites and gathered the information that you will be required to provide during installation, you can proceed to install the SharePoint binaries. Run Setup.exe on the SharePoint Server 2010 installation media. A wizard guides you through installation, during which program files are installed, components are registered, security settings are applied, and services are configured but not enabled.

To install SharePoint binaries, perform the following steps:

1. Log on as the setup user account—for example, *SP_Admin*.

2. Start the SharePoint Server 2010 Start Page (default.hta).

3. Click Install SharePoint Server.

   As an alternative to steps 2 and 3, run Setup.exe.

   Installation requires administrative credentials, so the User Account Control dialog box opens.

4. Click Yes.

5. On the Enter Your Product Key page, enter your product key or a trial key.

   You can change the key after installation from the System Settings page of Central Administration.

6. On the Read The Microsoft Software License Terms page, select the I Accept The Terms Of The Agreement check box.

7. On the Choose The Installation You Want page, shown in Figure 1-2, click Server Farm.

> **IMPORTANT USE THE CORRECT INSTALLATION TYPE**
>
> It is recommended that you use the Server Farm installation.

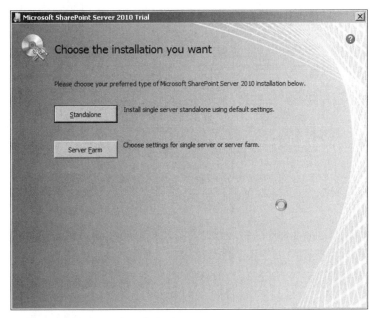

FIGURE 1-2 Selecting an installation type

The Standalone installation fully installs and configures SharePoint Server 2010 with all defaults, including the installation of SQL Server 2008 Express as the database server on the same server. The result is a stand-alone, single-server farm with all roles on one server. Standalone installation is not supported on a server that is a domain controller because SQL Server Express cannot be installed on a domain controller.

It is not possible to add servers to a farm that was installed with the Standalone installation. Therefore, it is recommended that you use Standalone only for the most simple testing or development environments.

In all other scenarios, you should use the Server Farm installation option. A farm can be one server, but with a Server Farm installation, you have the option to later add servers to the farm and move roles to other servers in the farm. Before you can perform a Server Farm installation you must have already installed SQL Server on the same server or on another server.

If you select a Server Farm installation, you can specify the location of the SharePoint binaries and the SharePoint Root (formerly known as the 12 Hive and now known as the 14 Hive) on the File Location tab.

8. On the Server Type tab, shown in Figure 1-3, select Complete.

The Stand-alone option presented on this page of the installation wizard creates a single-server farm with all components and roles. It is not possible to add another server to a farm that was installed with the Stand-alone option. This option is identical to the Standalone installation option discussed in an earlier step.

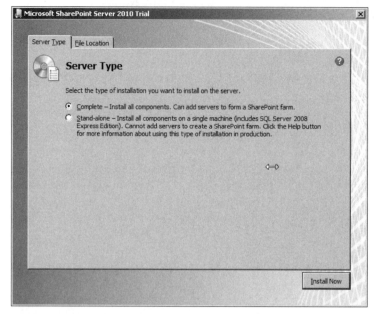

FIGURE 1-3 Selecting a server type

Installation proceeds.

At the end of the installation phase, the setup wizard offers you the chance to proceed to the configuration phase.

   9. On the Run Configuration Wizard page, clear the Run The SharePoint Products Configuration Wizard Now check box.

   10. Click Close.

The result is a SharePoint Server that is ready to add to a farm. However, the server is not yet functioning as an active server in your farm.

Script the Installation of SharePoint Binaries

You can script the installation of SharePoint binaries by specifying installation parameters in an Extensible Markup Language (XML) file named Config.xml by default.

Microsoft provides sample Config.xml files in the SharePoint distribution in the Files folder. You can simply modify these files to match your environment. Table 1-2 lists sample Config. xml files that are available in the Files folder in the SharePoint distribution.

TABLE 1-2 Available Sample Config.xml Files

CONFIGURATION FILE	DESCRIPTION
Setup\Config.xml	Stand-alone server installation using Microsoft SQL Server 2005 Express Edition
SetupFarm\Config.xml	Server farm installation

CONFIGURATION FILE	DESCRIPTION
SetupFarmSilent\Config.xml	Server farm installation in silent mode
SetupFarmUpgrade\Config.xml	In-place upgrade of an existing farm
SetupSilent\Config.xml	Stand-alone server installation using SQL Server 2005 Express Edition in silent mode
SetupSingleUpgrade\Config.xml	In-place upgrade of an existing single-server installation

The following Config.xml file installs a SharePoint server using the Server Farm installation option and the Complete server type:

```
<Configuration>
    <Package Id="sts">
        <Setting Id="LAUNCHEDFROMSETUPSTS" Value="Yes"/>
    </Package>
    <Package Id="spswfe">
        <Setting Id="SETUPCALLED" Value="1"/>
    </Package>
    <Logging Type="verbose" Path="%temp%" Template="SharePoint Server Setup(*).log"/>
    <PIDKEY Value="AAAAA-BBBBB-CCCCC-DDDDD-EEEEE-FFFFF" />
    <Display Level="none" CompletionNotice="no" />
    <Setting Id="SERVERROLE" Value="APPLICATION"/>
    <Setting Id="USINGUIINSTALLMODE" Value="0"/>
    <Setting Id="SETUP_REBOOT" Value="Never" />
    <Setting Id="SETUPTYPE" Value="CLEAN_INSTALL"/>
</Configuration>
```

Compare the file to the Config.xml file in the SetupFarm folder. You will see that in most cases, you only need to modify the Config.xml file to remove the comment tags (<!-- and -->) and enter a valid product ID.

After you have modified the Config.xml file, run SharePoint setup with the */config* parameter pointing to the appropriate configuration file. For example:

```
"C:\Software\SharePoint Server 2010\setup.exe" /config "C:\Software\SharePoint
Server 2010\Files\SetupFarmSilent\config.xml"
```

The *Display Level* element of the configuration file controls the type of user interface that is presented during installation. If the *Display Level* value is *none*, no user interface is presented—installation is silent. You can monitor the progress of the SharePoint installation using any of these methods:

- Click Start, type **%temp%,** and then press Enter. Open the log named SharePoint Server Setup*.log.

- Start Task Manager and then monitor processes including setup.exe, msiexec.exe, mscorsvw.exe, and psconfigui.exe.

MORE INFO **CONFIG.XML**

The following article provides additional details regarding Config.xml: "Config.xml reference (SharePoint Server 2010)" at *http://technet.microsoft.com/en-us/library/cc261668.aspx*.

Configure the SharePoint Server

After installing the SharePoint binaries, you can configure the server and, in the process, create a SharePoint farm or add the server to an existing farm.

Configuration with the user interface is wizard-driven. As long as you know the configuration information presented earlier in this lesson, configuration is very straightforward.

1. Log on as the setup user account—for example, SP_Admin.

2. Start SharePoint 2010 Products Configuration Wizard, which you can find in the Microsoft SharePoint 2010 Products program group on the Start menu.

   The SharePoint Products Configuration Wizard opens.

3. On the Welcome To SharePoint Products page, click Next.

   The SharePoint Products Configuration Wizard warning opens. It reminds you that IIS and SharePoint services will be restarted during configuration.

4. Click Yes.

5. On the Connect To A Server Farm page, click Create A New Server Farm, and then click Next.

   The Specify Configuration Database Settings page opens, shown in Figure 1-4.

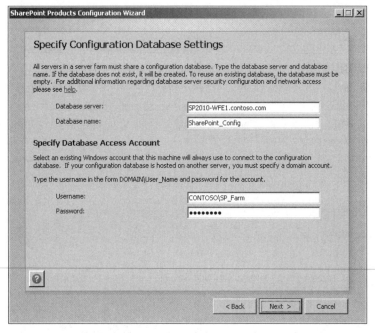

FIGURE 1-4 Specifying the SQL Server and SharePoint farm credentials

6. In the Database Server box, type the name of the database server or use the syntax *SERVER\instance* if you are connecting to a specific instance of SQL Server.

7. In the Database Name box, type the name for the SharePoint farm configuration database.

8. Enter the user name and password of the farm account—for example, **SP_Farm**.

   The SharePoint Products Configuration Wizard will create the configuration database on the specified SQL Server and assign database and server roles to the farm account.

9. Click Next.

10. On the Specify Farm Security Settings page, in the Passphrase and Confirm Passphrase boxes, type the farm passphrase and then click Next.

11. On the Configure SharePoint Central Administration Web Application page, enter the port number on which Central Administration will be hosted.

12. On the same page, select an authentication provider: NTLM or Negotiate (Kerberos). NTLM is the default authentication provider. It allows Central Administration to use Active Directory as the authentication provider. You will learn more about authentication providers in Chapter 3, "Managing Web Applications."

13. Click Next.

14. On the Completing The SharePoint Products Configuration Wizard page, review the configuration, and then click Next.

   Configuration takes several minutes. When it is complete, the Configuration Successful page opens.

15. Click Finish.

   SharePoint 2010 Central Administration opens.

Script the Configuration of SharePoint

You can automate the Microsoft SharePoint 2010 Products Configuration Wizard using a Windows PowerShell script. Windows PowerShell is discussed in Chapter 2, "Administering and Automating SharePoint," so it is beyond the scope of this section to explain Windows PowerShell. The cmdlets (pronounced *command-lets*) listed in this section are for reference purposes. However, in the Practice for this module, you have the option of using a preexisting Windows PowerShell script to automate the configuration of the farm.

> **MORE INFO** **DEPLOYING SHAREPOINT USING WINDOWS POWERSHELL**
>
> The following article provides an overview of the use of Windows PowerShell to install and configure SharePoint: "Quick start: Deploy single server in an isolated Hyper-V environment (SharePoint Server 2010)" at *http://technet.microsoft.com/en-us/library/ee805951.aspx*. A more complete technical reference, along with a downloadable Windows PowerShell module that greatly facilitates installation and configuration tasks, can be found in the following article: "Install SharePoint Server 2010 by using Windows PowerShell" at *http://technet.microsoft.com/en-us/library/cc262839.aspx*.

Configure the Farm

After you have installed Microsoft SharePoint 2010 on your first server in the farm, and after you have run the SharePoint Products Configuration Wizard, you still must configure services, accounts, and settings on the farm itself.

SharePoint 2010 introduces wizards in Central Administration. These wizards make it easier to perform common tasks. The Farm Configuration Wizard, for example, creates services, proxies, proxy groups, and accounts, and configures those components with default settings.

The wizard makes it easy to get a farm up and running using out-of-the-box defaults. It is particularly well suited to configuring a SharePoint farm for testing, training, or development when there are no requirements for farm or service customization.

To run the Farm Configuration Wizard, perform the following steps:

1. Start SharePoint 2010 Central Administration. If you clicked Finish in step 15 of the previous lesson then skip to step 4.

2. In the Central Administration Quick Launch, click Configuration Wizards.

3. In the Farm Configuration section, click Launch The Farm Configuration Wizard.

   If the Help Make SharePoint Better page opens, click Yes, I Am Willing To Participate (Recommended), and then click OK.

4. On the Configure Your SharePoint Farm page, click Start The Wizard.

5. In the Service Account section, click Create New Managed Account.

6. In the User Name box, type the name of the SharePoint service applications account—for example, **CONTOSO\SP_ServiceApps**.

7. In the Password box, type the password for the account—for example, **Pa$$w0rd**.

8. Observe the list of service applications that will be created by the Farm Configuration Wizard.

9. Click Next.

   Farm service applications are created and started. This takes several minutes. Optionally, you can open SQL Server Management Studio to follow the progress of the service application database creation.

   When the configuration is complete, the Create Site Collection page opens.

10. On the Create Site Collection page, click Skip.

11. On the Initial Farm Configuration Wizard page, click Finish.

In most production environments, however, business requirements lead to farm topology designs and configuration that are not the same as SharePoint's out-of-the-box defaults. Therefore, it is generally recommended to configure the farm manually in a production environment.

At a minimum, you should be aware of the service applications that most often require configuration that differs from the default settings. For example, the User Profile Synchronization service application, which synchronizes profile information between Active

Directory and SharePoint and hosts user My Sites, typically requires enterprise-specific configuration. Therefore, you can use the Farm Configuration Wizard to deploy those service applications that do not require specific configuration, and then manually deploy and configure service applications such as the User Profile Synchronization service.

Through the lessons in this Training Kit, you will learn how to configure services, service applications, proxies, application proxy groups, managed accounts, and other farm components. In the Practice for this chapter, you will use the Farm Configuration Wizard to deploy all service applications except User Profile Synchronization. Later, in Chapter 6, you will create and configure the User Profile Synchronization service application.

Understand Service Applications

The Farm Configuration Wizard creates selected service applications using default settings, and configures those service applications to run using the selected managed account. Service applications are a very important concept to understand in SharePoint 2010. Although they perform a role similar to Shared Service Providers (SSPs) in SharePoint 2007, there are significant differences between service applications and SSPs.

A *service application* provides specific functionality, such as search, that may be required by a web application. In the end, web applications connect to and consume the service provided by a service application.

The following are examples of service applications:

- The Search Service Application, which supports crawling, indexing, and querying
- The Business Connectivity Service, which enables SharePoint to connect to external data sources
- The Managed Metadata Service, which provides taxonomy and managed content types
- The User Profile Service, which maintains properties of users to support personalized content and social tagging.

A service application's *application connection*, also called *proxy*, creates the connection point for the web application. If a web application needs search functionality, for example, the web application must be connected to the Search Service Application's application connection. The application connection controls the interaction between the web application and the service application. For example, the application connection can have permissions applied so that a web application can access only a subset of functionality of the service application.

Typically, a web application requires more than one service application, and several web applications require the same service applications. To make it easier for you to manage the connections between web applications and service applications, *application connection groups*, also called *proxy groups*, create a logical grouping of service application connections (proxies). A web application connects to an application connection group and thereby connects to all of the connections that are members of that connection group.

The Farm Configuration Wizard sets up all service applications and creates a single application connection group, named *default*, that is available and can be used by any web app in the farm. By default, all new web apps are connected to the *default* connection group. So, by default, all web apps in the farm are connected to all service applications in the farm.

This default provides maximum functionality and ease of setup. However, one of the most important features of SharePoint 2010's service application model is that you are not limited to this "all apps connect to all services" topology. (Topology is discussed later in this section.)

Service applications are part of SharePoint Foundation 2010. This means that the architecture is part of the platform, in contrast to SharePoint 2007 in which SSPs were introduced by Microsoft Office SharePoint Server 2007 and not by Windows SharePoint Services v3.

In SharePoint 2010, most new services are built on the Windows Communications Framework (WCF), which means they have optimization built into their protocol, using binary streams instead of XML to transfer data.

Service apps are administered in Central Administration like all web applications. In Microsoft Office SharePoint Server 2007, the SSP had a separate administrative application. Service apps can be remotely managed and monitored. Service apps can be administered by using Windows PowerShell.

A service application provides a single set of functionality. A web application can, through application connection groups, connect to one or more service applications based on the needs of the web app. This is in contrast to the SSP in SharePoint 2007, which contained a bundle of services and a web application that was connected to the SSP and incurred the overhead of all services in the SSP.

A service app can also be published so that it can be consumed by applications on another farm.

As you learned earlier in this section, by default all web apps use the *default* connection group, which connects them to all service applications, providing maximum functionality and ease of setup. But it is useful to manage the connections more granularly, creating custom connection groups to ensure that web apps connect only to the services that they require.

You will learn more about many of the individual service applications throughout this Training Kit. Chapter 5 will detail the concepts of service application management and topology that have been introduced here.

Managed Accounts

In Windows operating systems and other Microsoft technologies, *service accounts* are user accounts used by a service to log on to a system. When you configure a service, you associate an identity—a user name and password—with the service. When the service starts, it authenticates using that account just as a user authenticates when logging onto a system. The service account must have sufficient permissions for the service to perform its tasks.

Traditionally, service accounts have been difficult for enterprises to manage because when you change the password of the service account in Active Directory, you must then reconfigure the service with the new password; otherwise, it will be denied logon. Because of this challenge, enterprises have typically sacrificed security best practices and have configured service accounts with passwords that never expire.

To address this management and security challenge, SharePoint 2010 introduces the concept of managed accounts. *Managed accounts* are service accounts with which SharePoint services run. Unlike traditional service accounts, however, SharePoint is able to perform password resets on the accounts in Active Directory, and it can update the service with a new password. All of this can be done automatically, without administrative intervention.

A managed account starts like any service account: a domain user account is created in Active Directory. You then register the account as a managed account using SharePoint 2010 Central Administration. At that time, you enter both the user name and password of the account.

When you configure a service application, application pool, or any other component that requires an identity, you can specify which managed account should be used. In this way, SharePoint is able to maintain a database of associations between managed accounts and services.

Additionally, and in contrast to SharePoint 2007, when you assign an identity to a service application, SharePoint 2010 configures any permissions or rights required for the identity.

When it comes time to change the password of a managed account, you do so with SharePoint Central Administration, rather than with Active Directory Users And Computers. SharePoint is able to change the password of the account in the domain, and it can reconfigure the services associated with that identity to allow the use of a new password.

You can also configure SharePoint to change passwords automatically based on the domain password expiration and complexity policies. In this way, the managed account passwords are known only to the farm, and cannot be used by an administrator—accidentally or intentionally—to cause damage to the farm.

The managed account credentials are encrypted. The encryption process begins with the farm passphrase that is specified during SharePoint configuration. The farm passphrase is stored in a secure key of the Registry. The farm passphrase encrypts a private key that is stored in the SharePoint configuration database. Private keys are used to encrypt account credentials.

Chapter 9 details the administration of managed accounts.

Perform Post-Installation Configuration

After you have deployed service applications by using the Farm Configuration Wizard, Central Administration, or Windows PowerShell, you must continue to configure farm-level settings that provide functionality that is important for even the simplest test or development farm.

Farm Administrators

The Farm Administrators group represents the accounts that can use the Central Administration application to perform administrative tasks. By default, the setup user account (for example, SP_Admin), the farm account (SP_Farm), and the local Administrators group are members of the Farm Administrators group. In a secure, least-privileged configuration, a SharePoint administrator will rarely be logged on as one of those accounts. Therefore, immediately after creating your farm, you should add appropriate user accounts to the Farm Administrators group.

For example, after you install and configure SharePoint while logged on as the setup user account (SP_Admin), you should add your administrative user account—the Active Directory account that is assigned to you as an individual—to the Farm Administrators group. From that point forward, you should not log on as the setup user and administrator (SP_Admin) account, except to install additional products on the server or to perform major, farm-level operations such as installing a service pack.

To manage the Farm Administrators group, perform the following steps:

1. In the Central Administration quick launch, click Security.

2. In the Users section, click Manage The Farm Administrators Group.

Members of the Farm Administrators group have permissions to and responsibility for all servers in the server farm. Members can perform all administrative tasks in Central Administration for the server or server farm. Members of this group can also use Windows PowerShell to create and manage configuration database objects and can perform command-line operations such as Stsadm.exe. They can assign administrators to manage service applications, which are instances of shared services.

The Farm Administrators group does not have permissions to access individual sites or their content, by default. However, members can take ownership of a site collection by assigning themselves as site collection owners in Central Administration. For example, if a site collection administrator leaves the organization and a new administrator must be added, a member of the Farm Administrators group can take ownership of the site collection to make the change.

Outgoing E-mail Settings

SharePoint sends numerous notifications via email. Users can create alerts to monitor changes to lists, libraries, items, and documents. Administrative alerts notify you of sites that have been unused for a long period of time, or that are close to filling their storage quota. For these messages to be sent successfully, SharePoint must be pointed to an SMTP server. If outgoing email settings have not been configured, users will not see the Alert Me button on the Ribbon.

To configure outgoing email settings, perform the following steps:

1. In the Central Administration Quick Launch, click System Settings.

2. In the E-Mail And Text Messages (SMS) section, click Configure Outgoing E-Mail Settings.

Your SharePoint governance plan should specify how SharePoint-related email will be managed in your enterprise. Determine which user or users will receive SharePoint-related alerts.

As a best practice, create unique email addresses for each service account, and assign a unique email address to the SharePoint farm as the *from* address. Unique accounts make it easier to identify the source and reason for an email notification. Then, create a single inbox that is associated with all of those email addresses. In other words, although notifications are sent to unique addresses, they all end up in the same inbox. Give your SharePoint administration team permission to the inbox, so that all administrators can monitor incoming alerts and messages. The result is a group inbox that represents the SharePoint service in your enterprise, but the unique email addresses can be used to create processing rules within that inbox.

If your SharePoint implementation involves teams that are dedicated to specific purposes, you can create one inbox per team, and direct specific addresses to the appropriate inboxes. For example, if you have a team dedicated to managing search, that team can have permission to an inbox that is associated with the email address for the SharePoint Search Service Application managed account.

Additional Settings

The settings that have been described in this section are those settings that require configuration even on the simplest farm, and that deserve attention immediately after completing installation and configuration of the server and farm. Of course, you must configure numerous settings to align SharePoint with your design and governance plan. Throughout this Training Kit, you will learn about these settings in the context of specific functionality and services.

PRACTICE **Install and Configure SharePoint 2010**

Practices are designed to guide you through important procedures. The instructions in this Training Kit are high-level instructions that will challenge you to think carefully and to apply the procedures that are covered in this lesson and elsewhere in the Training Kit. If you need assistance, consult the detailed, step-by-step instructions in the Practice Answers on the companion media.

In this practice, you will install and configure a single-server farm running SharePoint Server 2010.

In this practice, certain exercises provide alternate procedures. For example, you will notice that the practice has Exercise 1A and Exercise 1B. The first procedure, Exercise 1A, applies the SharePoint user interface—the Central Administration Web application. The second procedure, Exercise 1B, applies command-line automation and scripting. You can choose to perform one procedure or the other. Alternately, you can take a snapshot of your virtual machines before beginning the practice, then perform the first procedure, then revert to the snapshot—effectively undoing your changes—and then perform the second procedure.

Prepare for the Practice

Before you perform this practice, you must ensure that your lab environment has been built according to the instructions found in the Introduction to this Training Kit. You must also have completed the Practice for Lesson 1 of this chapter.

1. Start CONTOSO-DC.

   Wait for the virtual machine to complete startup, at which time the Press Ctrl+Alt+Del prompt appears.

2. Start SP2010-WFE1.

EXERCISE 1A Install SharePoint Server

In this exercise, you will install SharePoint Server 2010 by using the SharePoint Server installation wizard.

1. Log on to SP2010-WFE1 as **CONTOSO\SP_Admin** with the password **Pa$$w0rd**.

2. Install the SharePoint binaries. Use the following specifications and guidance:

   - Choose a Server Farm (Complete) installation.

   - When installation is complete, clear the Run The SharePoint Products Configuration Wizard Now check box.

EXERCISE 1B Script the Installation of SharePoint Server

In this exercise, you will perform a scripted installation SharePoint Server 2010 by creating a custom Config.xml file.

1. Log on to SP2010-WFE1 as **CONTOSO\SP_Admin** with the password **Pa$$w0rd**.

2. Modify the properties of C:\Software\SharePoint Server 2010\Files\SetupFarmSilent\ config.xml:

   - Ensure that the file is not read-only.

   - Grant your user account Full Control permission.

3. Edit Config.xml. Use the following specifications and guidance:

   - Replace the placeholder for the product ID with the product ID you received when you downloaded or otherwise obtained the SharePoint 2010 installation media.

   - Remove the comment tags before and after the *PIDKEY* element.

   - Replace the *Display* element with the following:

```
<Display AcceptEULA="yes"
         Level="basic"
         CompletionNotice="yes" />
```

   In a production environment, you would leave the *Display* element with its default values (Level="none" and CompletionNotice="no") for a completely unattended installation.

   In this exercise, you change the values of the *Display* element so that installation can be monitored.

4. Start Command Prompt using the Run As Administrator option.

5. From the C:\Software\SharePoint Server 2010 folder, start SharePoint setup with a parameter that directs setup to the configuration file you just modified.

   Installation takes approximately 7 to 10 minutes. A progress bar is displayed.

6. When installation is complete, clear the Run The SharePoint Products Configuration Wizard Now check box.

EXERCISE 2A   Run the SharePoint Products Configuration Wizard

In this exercise, you will configure a single-server SharePoint farm by using the SharePoint Products Configuration Wizard.

1. Start the SharePoint 2010 Products Configuration Wizard.

2. Configure a single-server SharePoint farm. Use the following specifications and guidance:

   ■ Database server: SP2010-WFE1.contoso.com

   ■ SharePoint farm account username: CONTOSO\SP_Farm

   ■ SharePoint farm account password: Pa$$w0rd

   ■ Farm passphrase: My Farm Pa$$phrase

   ■ Central Administration port: 9999

   When configuration is complete, Internet Explorer opens and loads the Help Make SharePoint Better page. This is the Customer Experience Improvement survey page of the SharePoint 2010 Central Administration website.

3. Click No, I Don't Wish To Participate.

   The virtual machine does not have Internet connectivity.

4. Close Internet Explorer.

   You configure SharePoint in the next exercise.

EXERCISE 2B   Perform a Scripted Configuration of SharePoint Server

In this exercise, you will execute a Windows PowerShell script that configures a single-server SharePoint farm.

1. Mount the companion media to the CD/DVD drive of SP2010-WFE1.

   > *ON THE COMPANION MEDIA*   Use the Mount an ISO Image or Mount a DVD
   > procedure in the Lab Environment Build Guide on the companion media.

2. Start Windows PowerShell using the Run As Administrator option, Navigate to *<cdrom>*:\Practice Files\01_02, type the following command, and then press Enter.

   ```
   .\ConfigureSharePoint.ps1
   ```

3. Use the following specifications and guidance:
   - Credentials user name: CONTOSO\SP_Farm
   - Credentials password: Pa$$w0rd
   - Farm passphrase: My Farm Pa$$phrase

   After a few moments, configuration status will be displayed. Configuration proceeds for 7 to 10 minutes.

   Because the local farm does not yet exist, and will be created by the configuration script, the following warning is expected during the configuration of SharePoint:

   ```
   The Local Farm Is Not Accessible. Cmdlets With Featuredependencyid Are Not
   Registered.
   ```

   You can monitor the progress of the SharePoint installation by performing these steps:
   a. Start Task Manager, click the Processes tab, and click Show Processes From All Users.
   b. Monitor processes including powershell.exe, sqlservr.exe, and owstimer.exe.

4. At the Press Enter To Exit prompt, press Enter, and then close Windows PowerShell.

   You will configure SharePoint in a later practice.

EXERCISE 3 Create the SHAREPOINT INSTALLED AND CONFIGURED Snapshot

The SHAREPOINT INSTALLED AND CONFIGURED snapshot captures SP2010-WFE1 after SharePoint binaries have been installed and the SharePoint Products Configuration Wizard has been run. Perform this procedure for each of the following virtual machines: SP2010-WFE1, CONTOSO-DC.

1. Shut down the virtual machine.
2. Unmount any ISO image currently mounted to the CD/DVD drive.

   Use the Unmount an ISO Image procedure in the Lab Environment Build Guide on the companion media.

3. Create a snapshot named SHAREPOINT INSTALLED AND CONFIGURED.

   Use the Create a Snapshot procedure in the Lab Environment Build Guide on the companion media.

EXERCISE 4 Run the Farm Configuration Wizard

In this exercise, you will deploy services and service applications by using the Farm Configuration Wizard.

1. Log on to SP2010-WFE1 as **CONTOSO\SP_Admin** with the password **Pa$$w0rd**.
2. Start SharePoint 2010 Central Administration. Use the Farm Configuration Wizard to configure the farm with the following guidance and specifications:
   - Create a new managed account based on the SharePoint Service Applications account you created in Lesson 1. The user name is CONTOSO\SP_ServiceApps and the password is Pa$$w0rd.

- Observe the list of service applications that will be created by the Farm Configuration Wizard.
- Clear the User Profile Service Application check box.

Farm service applications are created and started. This takes several minutes. Optionally, you can open SQL Server Management Studio and refresh the view of the Databases node to monitor the creation of service application databases.

When the configuration is complete, the Create Site Collection page opens.

3. On the Create Site Collection page, click Skip. (You will create an intranet in Lesson 3.)

4. On the Initial Farm Configuration Wizard page, click Finish.

EXERCISE 5   Create the FARM CONFIGURATION WIZARD DEFAULTS Snapshot

The FARM CONFIGURATION WIZARD DEFAULTS snapshot captures SP2010-WFE1 after the SharePoint farm has been configured. Perform this procedure for each of the following virtual machines: SP2010-WFE1 CONTOSO-DC.

1. Shut down the virtual machine.

2. Unmount any ISO image currently mounted to the CD/DVD drive.

   Use the Unmount an ISO Image procedure in the Lab Environment Build Guide on the companion media.

3. Create a snapshot named FARM CONFIGURATION WIZARD DEFAULTS.

   Use the Create a Snapshot procedure in the Lab Environment Build Guide on the companion media.

Lesson Summary

- Installation and configuration of a SharePoint farm consists of several phases. First, you install prerequisites. Then, you install SharePoint binaries. Next, you configure the server. Finally, you configure the farm.

- You install SharePoint binaries by using Setup.exe from the SharePoint installation media. You can automate the installation by running Setup.exe with the */config* parameter pointing to a Config.xml file.

- You configure the SharePoint server by using the SharePoint Products Configuration Wizard, or by using Windows PowerShell.

- Service applications and managed accounts can be deployed and configured by using the Farm Configuration Wizard, by manually deploying and configuring them in Central Administration, or by using Windows PowerShell.

Lesson Review

You can use the following questions to test your knowledge of the information in Lesson 2, "Install and Configure SharePoint 2010." The questions are also available on the companion media in a practice test if you prefer to review them in electronic form.

1. Which of the following is required to automate the installation of SharePoint binaries?

    A. PrerequisiteInstaller.Arguments.txt

    B. Config.xml

    C. Unattend.xml

    D. Windows PowerShell

2. After installing the SharePoint binaries, which of the following can be used to configure the server? (Choose all that apply.)

    A. SharePoint Products Configuration Wizard

    B. Setup.exe

    C. Windows PowerShell

    D. Central Administration

3. Which of the following are configured by the Farm Configuration Wizard? (Choose all that apply.)

    A. Farm Administrators group membership

    B. Managed account

    C. Service applications

    D. Connections to back-end data sources

    E. Outgoing email server

4. Which of the following are members of the Farm Administrators group by default? (Choose all that apply.)

    A. The Administrators group of the SharePoint server

    B. Domain Admins

    C. Users who are assigned the *dbowner* role on the SQL server

    D. The farm account, such as SP_Farm

    E. The setup user account, such as SP_Admin

Lesson 3: Create a SharePoint Intranet

Now that the SharePoint farm is installed and configured, you can turn your attention to the creation of web applications, site collections, and sites. These are the primary components of the SharePoint logical structure. In this lesson, you will learn how to create the architecture for a very simple SharePoint intranet. In subsequent chapters, you will learn the concepts, procedures, and best practices related to configuring and administering each of these components.

After this lesson, you will be able to:

- Identify components of a logical architecture.
- Describe the high-level transactions that deliver a Web page to a browser.
- Create a web application.
- Create a site collection.
- Create a list or library.

Estimated lesson time: 60 minutes

SharePoint Logical Structure

Figure 1-5 represents the logical structure of SharePoint.

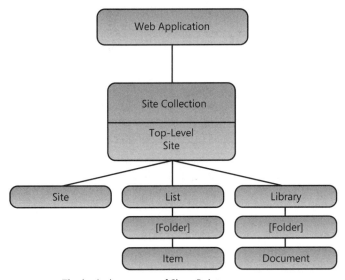

FIGURE 1-5 The logical structure of SharePoint

The diagram shows the hierarchy of objects related to content within a farm, including the following:

- A *web application* is the highest-level component of the logical structure within a farm. A farm can have one or more web applications.

- Within a web application are one or more *site collections*. Site collections have a URL that is a *managed path*.

- A site collection contains one or more *sites*. When you create a site collection, you also create the top-level site in that site collection. Below that top-level site can be one or more additional sites, often referred to as *subsites* or *subwebs*.

- Within a site are pages, lists, and libraries.

- Lists and libraries can contain folders.

- Within lists and libraries—possibly organized into folders—are items and documents, respectively.

An important element of the diagram in Figure 1-5 is that when you create a site collection, you also create a top-level site. They are two separate components, but they always go hand-in-hand. You can't have a site collection without a top-level site, and you can't have a top-level site without also having a site collection.

Request a Page from a SharePoint Site

The top-level logical component within a farm is the web application. A web application in SharePoint corresponds to a site and Internet Information Services (IIS).

To understand the configuration parameters you must provide when you create a web application, it is helpful to understand how a client—a web browser, for example—connects to a site. The following steps explain, at a high and somewhat simplistic level, the process that is used:

1. A user enters a URI (Universal Resource Identifier), also called a URL (Uniform Resource Locator) into the address bar of a browser, or clicks a hyperlink to a URI. The URI is the *request*. For example, the user might request *http://intranet.contoso.com/default.aspx*.

   The URI includes a protocol, such as *http:* and an address, typically specified as a domain name system (DNS) name, such as *intranet.contoso.com*. Often, the URI also includes a path or page that specifies a resource within the target site, such as */default.aspx*.

2. The browser must send the request to the server hosting the website. Therefore, the DNS name of the server must be resolved to its IP address. The DNS client on the user's computer sends a query to its DNS server requesting a lookup of the web server's DNS name, such as *intranet.contoso.com*.

3. The DNS server resolves the query and returns the IP address of the server—for example, 10.0.0.11.

4. The client can now send the request to the web server using the server's IP address. The request is sent to a specific port on the server based on the protocol or a port specified in the URI. For web requests, port 80 is used unless otherwise specified.

5. IIS, running on the server, receives the request and must retrieve the requested content from the correct site. The server knows which site should get the request based on the site's *bindings*. A site can be bound to a specific IP address or port. Typically, however, a web server hosts multiple sites and it is not efficient or sometimes even possible to assign a unique IP address or port to each site. Therefore, it is typical to see a web server hosting multiple sites all bound to the same IP address and port—port 80.

   How then can the server know which site should handle the inbound request? While the inbound request targets a specific IP address and port, the http request packet itself contains the DNS name of the website in a field called the *host header*. Sites on the server can be bound to the host headers that correspond to the DNS name of the site. Therefore, while requests for different sites may be coming into the same IP address and port, IIS is able to examine the host headers in each request packet, and forward requests to the corresponding sites.

6. If a site happens to be a SharePoint site, SharePoint takes the request, examines the URI, and retrieves the content from the appropriate content database on the SQL Server.

7. At each point in the process, security controls can be applied to ensure that users can get only to the content they need.

Create a Web Application

A web application is a logical unit that contains one or more site collections. A web application is associated with an IIS Web site, but can have up to five IIS Web sites with which it is associated.

Each web application's IIS Web site runs in the context of an application pool. An *application pool* is the process hosted by IIS. You can think of an application pool like a service—it runs in the context of a user account that gives the process the permissions it needs to host the web application. Microsoft supports up to 10 application pools per web server; however the limit is dependent largely upon the amount of RAM allocated to front-end servers and the workload that the farm is serving: the user base and its usage characteristics. Before you create a web application, you must determine whether you want to assign the web app to an existing application pool or to a new application pool. The factors you should consider are described in Chapter 3.

SharePoint uses managed accounts as identities for application pools. If you will be creating a new application pool for the new web application, you must decide whether to use an existing managed account or whether you will register a new managed account for the application pool. The factors you should consider are described in Chapter 9. If you choose to register a new managed account for a new application pool, you should do so before creating the web application. The following procedure registers a new managed account using the SP_WebApplications account you learned about in Lesson 1.

REGISTER A MANAGED ACCOUNT USING CENTRAL ADMINISTRATION

The following procedure creates a managed account.

1. In the Central Administration quick launch, click Security.

2. In the General Security section, click Configure Managed Accounts.

    The Managed Accounts page opens.

3. Click Register Managed Account.

4. In the User Name box, type the name of the Active Directory account, with the syntax *DOMAIN\username*—for example, **CONTOSO\SP_WebApps**.

5. In the Password box, type the account's password.

6. Click OK.

CREATE A WEB APPLICATION USING CENTRAL ADMINISTRATION

The following procedure creates a web application that uses classic-mode authentication, with NTLM as the authentication provider. The web application will use your Active Directory domain for authentication. The procedure assigns the web application to a new application pool that runs using an existing managed account.

1. In the Central Administration Quick Launch, click Application Management.

2. In the Web Applications section, click Manage Web Applications.

3. On the Web Applications tab of the Ribbon, click New.

    The Create New Web Application page opens.

4. In the Authentication section, select the authentication method, such as Classic Mode Authentication.

    For more information, see Chapter 3.

5. In the IIS Web Site section, in the Port box, type **80**.

    The default port number for HTTP access is 80, and the default port number for HTTPS access is 443. If you want users to access the web application without typing in a port number, they should use the appropriate default port number.

6. In the Host Header box, type the unique DNS name for the web application—for example, **intranet.contoso.com**.

    This field is used so that a server can host more than one web application on the same port. If the server is hosting only one web application on the specified port, this field can be left blank.

7. In the Name box, type a descriptive name for the web application—for example, **Intranet – intranet.contoso.com**.

    SharePoint populates the Name box automatically, based on the port and host header. You should always use a meaningful, descriptive name for the website. Use the naming standards of your organization to determine the name.

8. In the Application Pool section, ensure that Create New Application Pool is selected.

9. In the Application Pool Name box, type **SharePoint Web Applications**.

   You should use a meaningful, descriptive name for each application pool that you create. Use the naming standards of your organization to determine the name.

10. Under Select A Security Account For This Application Pool, in the Configurable list, select the managed account that will be used as the identity for the application pool, such as CONTOSO\SP_WebApps.

11. In the Database Name and Authentication section, in the Database Name box, type a name for the database—for example, **SharePoint_Content_Intranet**.

   You should always use a meaningful name for your content databases. Use the naming standards of your organization to determine the name.

12. Click OK.

   The web application and content database will be created. When this process is complete, the Application Created page opens.

13. Click OK.

   The new web application is displayed on the Web Applications Management page.

Be sure that you have created a host record in DNS for the web application, otherwise you will be unable to access the web application after creating it.

You will learn more about the characteristics and management of web applications in Chapter 3, "Managing Web Applications."

MORE INFO   CREATING A WEB APPLICATION

The following article provides additional details regarding the creation of web applications: "Create a Web Application (SharePoint Server 2010)" at *http://go.microsoft.com/ fwlink/?LinkID=192703*.

When you create a web application by using Central Administration, you also create a content database on a SQL server. The content database, as its name implies, will contain the content of the web application. However, no content will be generated in the content database until you create a site collection.

Create a Site Collection

A site collection is a group of SharePoint websites that share common ownership and administrators, as well as common settings, such as quotas, locks, site use confirmation and deletion, and self-service site creation.

When you create a site collection, you also create a top-level site in the site collection. The top-level site can be configured to use a template, also called a *site definition*. You must assign a site collection administrator when you create a site collection. When you create a site collection by using Central Administration, you can also assign a second site collection administrator.

CREATE A SITE COLLECTION USING CENTRAL ADMINISTRATION

The following procedure creates a site collection and top-level site based on the Team Site site definition:

1. In the Central Administration Quick Launch, click Application Management.

2. In the Site Collections section, click Create Site Collections.

   The Create Site Collection page opens.

3. In the Web Application section, ensure that you are focused on the web application in which you want to create a site collection.

   If necessary, click the Web Application picker, shown in Figure 1-6, and then click Change Web Application. Click the correct web application.

FIGURE 1-6 The Web Application picker control

4. In the Title box, type a title for the site collection, such as **Contoso Intranet**.

5. In the Template Selection section, select the site definition you want to apply to the top-level site of the new site collection—for example, Team Site on the Collaboration tab.

6. In the Primary Site Collection Administrator section, in the User Name box, type the user name of the site collection administrator—for example, **CONTOSO\SP_Admin**.

7. Click OK.

   The site collection is created, and the Top-Level Site Collection page opens.

8. Click OK.

   When you create a site collection, you also create a top-level site within that site collection. The top-level site is typically created using a site definition—for example, Team Site or Publishing Site—but it is also possible to create a blank top-level site that can then be customized later.

You will learn more about the characteristics and management of site collections in Chapter 4, "Administering and Securing SharePoint Content."

> **MORE INFO**   **CREATING A SITE COLLECTION**
> The following article provides additional details regarding the creation of site collections: "Create a site collection (SharePoint Server 2010)" at *http://technet.microsoft.com/en-us/ library/cc263094.aspx*.

Create a List or Library

Lists and libraries are the most important user-facing container for content. A list is a SharePoint object containing related items, and an item is a collection of columns. In database terminology, a list is like a table, with each item like a record (or row) in the table and each column like a field. The actual storage of a list in the SharePoint content database is much more complex than that, but from a conceptual standpoint, the metaphor works. A library is a specialized form of a list, designed specifically to contain documents of any type.

Users collaborate around items and documents in lists and libraries. Out of the box, SharePoint Server 2010 can create document libraries, picture libraries, wiki page libraries, contact lists, calendars, task lists, and more. You can also create custom lists and libraries out of the box, and you can develop SharePoint solutions that deploy custom lists and libraries with properties and behaviors specific to your SharePoint sites.

CREATE A LIST OR LIBRARY
The following procedure creates a list for a company calendar on the Contoso intranet:

1. Click Site Actions, and then click More Options.

2. Select the type of list or library you want to create, such as Calendar.

   Use the Browse From panel to filter the list of available options.

3. In the Name box, type the name of the list or library as it will appear in the URL for the list or library. For example, type **CompanyCalendar**.

   When you create a list or library and configure its Name, the value is used to create the URL of the list or library. Use best practices for URL naming: keep the name short, with no spaces, and use mixed case for readability.

4. Click Create.

After you create a list or library, you should examine the settings that were applied, and modify any settings that do not meet the business requirements for the list or library.

MODIFY LIST OR LIBRARY SETTINGS

The following procedure configures the title of the new calendar to be different than the URL you created in the previous procedure:

1. On the list Ribbon, click List Settings.

   The List Settings page opens.

2. Click Title, Description And Navigation.

3. In the Name box, type the name of the list or library as it will appear in the user interface. For example, type **Company Calendar**.

   When you change the *Name* of a list or library on the Title, Description and Navigation page, it does not change the URL.

4. In the Navigation section, select whether to display the list or library in the Quick Launch.

5. Click Save.

You will learn more about the characteristics and management of lists and libraries throughout this Training Kit, and particularly in Chapter 4.

PRACTICE   Create a SharePoint Intranet

Practices are designed to guide you through important procedures. The instructions in this Training Kit are high-level instructions that will challenge you to think carefully and to apply the procedures that are covered in this lesson and elsewhere in the Training Kit. If you need assistance, consult the detailed, step-by-step instructions in the Practice Answers on the companion media.

In this practice, you will create a simple SharePoint intranet, consisting of a home page and a site collection for the Information Technology (IT) organization. Along the way, you will experience and remediate two common troubleshooting scenarios.

Prepare for the Practice

Before you perform this practice, you must ensure that your lab environment has been built according to the instructions found in the Introduction to this Training Kit. You must also have completed the Practices for Lessons 1 and 2 of this chapter.

1. Apply the FARM CONFIGURATION WIZARD DEFAULTS snapshot to CONTOSO-DC.

2. Apply the FARM CONFIGURATION WIZARD DEFAULTS snapshot to SP2010-WFE1.

3. Start CONTOSO-DC. Wait for startup to complete, at which time the Press Ctrl+Alt+Delete prompt appears.

4. Start SP2010-WFE1.

EXERCISE 1   Register a Managed Account

In this exercise, you will register a managed account that will be used as an application pool identity in the next exercise.

1. Log on to SP2010-WFE1 as **CONTOSO\SP_Admin** with the password **Pa$$w0rd**.

2. In Central Administration, register a managed account using the CONTOSO\ SP_WebApps user account. The password of the account is Pa$$w0rd.

EXERCISE 2   Create a New Web Application

In this exercise, you will create a new web application for the Contoso Intranet. Create a new web application using the following specifications and guidance:

- Name: Contoso Intranet

- Authentication: Classic Mode Authentication

- Port: 80

- Host Header: intranet.contoso.com

- Create a new application pool named SharePoint Web Applications. Configure the application pool to use the CONTOSO\SP_WebApps managed account.

- Database Name: SharePoint_Content_Intranet

EXERCISE 3   Create a New Site Collection

In this exercise, you will create a new site collection for the Contoso Intranet. The new site collection will use the Publishing site definition. Create a new site collection in the intranet web application using the following specifications and guidance:

- Title: Contoso Intranet

- URL: *http://intranet.contoso.com*

- Template: Team Site

- Primary site collection administrator: CONTOSO\SP_Admin

EXERCISE 4   Attempt to Open the New Site

In this exercise, you will attempt to open the Contoso Intranet website.

- In Internet Explorer, in the address bar, type **http://intranet.contoso.com** and then press Enter.

  An Internet Explorer Cannot Display The Webpage error page is displayed.

Question: What is the cause of this error?

EXERCISE 5   Add a DNS Host Record for the New Web Application

In this exercise, you will remediate the name resolution problem you identified in the previous exercise. You will add a DNS host record that resolves *intranet.contoso.com* to the IP address *10.0.0.21*.

1. Start DNS Manager.

2. Create a host record for intranet.contoso.com, which resolves to the IP address 10.0.0.21.

EXERCISE 6   Attempt to Open the New Site

In this exercise, you will attempt to open the Contoso intranet website.

- In Internet Explorer, in the address bar, type **http://intranet.contoso.com** and then press Enter.

    An Internet Explorer Cannot Display The Webpage error is displayed. If this error does not appear on your system, continue to the next exercise.

  Question: What is the cause of this error?

EXERCISE 7   Flush the DNS Client Cache

In this exercise, you will remediate the name resolution problem you identified in the previous exercise. You will flush the DNS client cache.

1. Start Command Prompt, and then flush the DNS client's cache.

2. In Internet Explorer, in the address bar, type **http://intranet.contoso.com** and then press Enter.

    The website begins to load. Because this is the first time that the site has been requested from the server, it must be compiled. This takes several seconds.

    When the Windows Security dialog box opens, continue to the next exercise.

EXERCISE 8   Attempt to Open the New Site

In this exercise, you will attempt to open the Contoso intranet website.

1. In Internet Explorer, navigate to *http://intranet.contoso.com*.

    The Windows Security dialog box opens, prompting you to enter credentials to access the website.

2. Enter the user name **CONTOSO\SP_Admin** and the password **Pa$$w0rd**.

    The Windows Security dialog box opens again. It appears that credentials are not being accepted. Repeat this step. Then click Cancel to close the Windows Security dialog box.

  Question: What is the cause of this problem?

EXERCISE 9   Disable Loopback Checking

In this exercise, you will disable loopback checking for the SharePoint server.

- Add the following entry to the Registry:

    - Key: HKEY_LOCAL_MACHINE\SYSTEM\CurrentControlSet\Control\Lsa

    - Value: DisableLoopbackCheck

- Type: REG_DWORD
- Data: 1

EXERCISE 10   **Open the New Site**

In this exercise, you will open the Contoso intranet website.

- In Internet Explorer, in the address bar, type **http://intranet.contoso.com** and then press Enter.

    The website begins to load. Because this is the first time that the site has been requested from the server, it must be compiled. This takes several seconds.

EXERCISE 11   **Create and Configure a Company Calendar**

In this exercise, you will add a company calendar to the Contoso intranet website.

1. Create a new calendar on the Contoso intranet with the following specifications and guidance:

    - URL: *http://intranet.contoso.com/CompanyCalendar*. Note that there is no space in the name of the list, CompanyCalendar.

    - List type: Calendar.

    - List title: Company Calendar. Note the list title includes a space.

EXERCISE 12   **Create the CHAPTER 01 snapshot**

The CHAPTER 01 snapshot captures the state of the environment at the end of Chapter 01. Perform this procedure for each of the following virtual machines: SP2010-WFE1, CONTOSO-DC.

1. Shut down the virtual machine.

2. Unmount any ISO image currently mounted to the CD/DVD drive.

    Use the "Unmount an ISO Image" procedure in the Lab Environment Build Guide on the companion media.

3. Create a snapshot named CHAPTER 01.

    Use the "Create a Snapshot" procedure in the Lab Environment Build Guide on the companion media.

Lesson Summary

- A SharePoint farm's logical structure contains one or more web applications, each of which contains one or more site collections. When you create a site collection, you also create a top-level site in the site collection. A site collection can contain other sites, lists, and libraries. Lists and libraries contain items and documents, respectively, which can be grouped into folders.

- A SharePoint Web application consists of an IIS website bound to an IP address, port, or host header. The web application runs in an application pool, the credentials of which are those of a managed account. When you create a web application, you create a content database associated with that web application.

- A site collection is a content and administrative container. Until you create a site collection, a web application has no content.

- When you create websites, lists, and libraries, you should follow best practices related to URLs: no spaces, mixed case, and short.

Lesson Review

You can use the following questions to test your knowledge of the information in Lesson 3, "Create a SharePoint Intranet." The questions are also available on the companion media in a practice test if you prefer to review them in electronic form.

> **NOTE ANSWERS**
>
> Answers to these questions and explanations of why each answer choice is right or wrong are located in the "Answers" section at the end of the book.

1. Which of the following is required when you are creating a web application on a server that hosts other web applications on the same IP address and port?

   A. A unique authentication provider

   B. A unique host header

   C. A unique application pool

   D. A unique application pool identity

2. Which of the following are created when you create a new web application by using Central Administration? (Choose all that apply.)

   A. An IIS Web site

   B. A DNS host record

   C. A content database

   D. A home page

3. Which of the following are configured when you create a new site collection? (Choose all that apply.)

   A. A top-level website

   B. An IIS website

   C. A content database

   D. A home page

   E. Lists and libraries

Chapter Review

To further practice and reinforce the skills you learned in this chapter, you can perform the following tasks:

- Review the chapter summary.
- Review the list of key terms introduced in this chapter.
- Complete the case scenarios. These scenarios set up real-world situations involving the topics of this chapter and ask you to create a solution.
- Complete the suggested practices.
- Take a practice test.

Chapter Summary

- SharePoint depends upon a variety of other Microsoft technologies and platforms. To create a SharePoint farm, you must install and configure a variety of prerequisites, including the operating system, SQL Server, service packs and updates, server roles and features, and user accounts in Active Directory.
- SharePoint installation and configuration is a multi-phase process that includes prerequisite installation, installation of SharePoint binaries, configuration of the server, and configuration of the farm. Each of these phases can be scripted to automate the process.
- SharePoint's logical structure consists of web applications, site collections, sites, lists, libraries, folders, items, and documents.

Key Terms

The following terms were introduced in this chapter. Do you know what they mean?

- Least privilege
- Managed account
- SharePoint 2010 Preparation Tool (Prerequisite Installer)
- Service application
- Application connection (Proxy)
- Application connection group (Proxy group or connection group)
- Site definition

Case Scenario: Deploying SharePoint Servers and Farms

In the following case scenario, you will apply what you've learned about preparing to install SharePoint Server 2010. You can find answers to these questions in the "Answers" section at the end of this book.

You are planning the deployment of SharePoint at Contoso, Ltd. The company needs the following:

- A training environment in which five administrators can learn how to configure SharePoint farms
- A development environment for the SharePoint developer
- A test environment that reflects the configuration of the production farm
- A production environment

1. What type of installation will allow students in the training environment to configure SharePoint without impacting each other's servers or the production SharePoint and SQL environments?

2. You want to minimize the cost and complexity of the development environment by allowing developers to work on their laptops, which have 4 GB of RAM. What approach will you use to provide a development environment?

3. How can you ensure consistency in the installation and configuration of servers in the test and production farms?

Take a Practice Test

The practice tests on this book's companion media offer many options. For example, you can test yourself on just the lesson review content, or you can test yourself on all the 70-667 certification exam objectives. You can set up the test so that it closely simulates the experience of taking a certification exam, or you can set it up in study mode so that you can look at the correct answers and explanations after you answer each question.

> *MORE INFO* **PRACTICE TESTS**
>
> For details about all the practice test options available, see the "How to Use the Practice Tests" section in this book's Introduction.

CHAPTER 2

Administering and Automating SharePoint

I n Chapter 1, "Creating a SharePoint Intranet," you used Central Administration to perform common administrative tasks related to the installation and configuration of Microsoft SharePoint Server 2010.

In this chapter, you learn more about what it means to be an administrator of a SharePoint farm and what it takes to administer SharePoint using both Central Administration and command-line options.

Among the most powerful tools at your disposal as a SharePoint administrator is Windows PowerShell. SharePoint 2010 offers rich support for Windows PowerShell as the primary command-line interface for administering and automating SharePoint, and in this chapter you learn the fundamentals of Windows PowerShell for SharePoint.

Exam objectives in this chapter:
- Manage accounts and user roles.
- Deploy new installations and upgrades.
- Configure SharePoint farms.
- Manage Web Applications.
- Manage site collections.

Lessons in this chapter:

Before You Begin

To complete the lessons in this chapter, you must have performed the practices in Chapter 1.

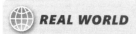
REAL WORLD

Dan Holme

This chapter will illuminate what are, for many SharePoint administrators, among the most confusing and difficult-to-grasp concepts and skills. SharePoint 2010 (which, technically, is SharePoint version 4) is almost unrecognizable when compared to early versions; however, the legacy of those early versions comes back to haunt you, with terminology that is used by the underlying engine—the object model and command-line parameters—quite different than the terminology used in the user interface and documentation. Lesson 1 will clarify the administrative roles and the options you have for administering SharePoint—specifically, Central Administration, Stsadm.exe, and Windows PowerShell. Lesson 2 will introduce what is undoubtedly the most important administrative change in SharePoint 2010—the introduction of Windows PowerShell as the preferred command-line and automation interface. SharePoint has traditionally suffered from a dearth of tools that could examine, monitor, and operate across multiple websites, site collections, and web applications. Windows PowerShell steps in to fill those gaps, and to enable administrators to be far more productive than would be possible with Central Administration and Stsadm.exe alone.

Lesson 1: SharePoint Administrative Roles and Interfaces

Thus far, you have installed and configured SharePoint using a highly privileged account, SP_Admin, which is a member of the SharePoint Farm Administrators group as well as the local Administrators group on a SharePoint server. And you have performed most configurations by using the Central Administration Web application. In this lesson, you will refine your administrative model, delegating administrative roles to specific users; you will learn to use Stsadm.exe, one of SharePoint's two primary command-line administrative interfaces; and you will explore Central Administration itself.

> **After this lesson, you will be able to:**
> - Describe and manage SharePoint administrative roles.
> - Describe the options for administering SharePoint farms.
> - Administer SharePoint from the command prompt with Stsadm.exe.
> - Configure and manage the Central Administration Web application.
>
> **Estimated lesson time: 45 minutes**

Administrative Roles

In previous versions of SharePoint, it was difficult to delegate administrative control over specific collections of settings or services. SharePoint 2010 offers a more granular set of administrative roles, including the following:

- Farm Administrators
- Windows Administrators
- Service Application Administrators
- Service Application Feature Administrators
- Site Collection Owners
- Site Collection Administrators
- Site Groups

Each of these roles is detailed in the sections that follow.

Farm Administrators

As you learned in Chapter 1, the Farm Administrators group represents the accounts that can use the Central Administration application to perform administrative tasks. By default, the setup user account (such as SP_Admin), the farm account (SP_Farm), and the local Administrators group are members of the Farm Administrators group. Chapter 1 reminded you that, after installing SharePoint, you should add appropriate user accounts to the Farm Administrators group. For example, you should add your administrative user account to the Farm Administrators group, after which you should log on with that account, rather than as SP_Admin. You should continue to use SP_Admin, however, when performing major product- or farm-level changes, such as installing products, language packs, and service packs, and when adding or removing servers in the farm.

MANAGE THE MEMBERSHIP OF FARM ADMINISTRATORS

1. In the Central Administration Quick Launch, click Security.

2. In the Users section, click Manage The Farm Administrators Group.

Members of the Farm Administrators group have permissions to and responsibility for all servers in the server farm. Members can perform all administrative tasks in Central Administration for the server or server farm. Members of this group can also use Windows PowerShell to create and manage configuration database objects and can perform command-line operations, such as Stsadm.exe. They can assign administrators to manage service applications, which are instances of shared services.

The Farm Administrators group does not have permission to access individual sites or their content, by default. However, members can take ownership of a site collection by assigning themselves as a site collection administrator in Central Administration. For example, if a site collection administrator leaves the organization and a new administrator must be added, a member of the Farm Administrators group can take ownership of the site collection to make the change.

Windows Administrators

Members of the Administrators group on a SharePoint server that runs Central Administration are members of the Farm Administrators group by default. Therefore, members of the Administrators group on the local server can perform all farm administrator tasks. In addition, local administrators can install new products or applications, deploy Web Parts and new features to the global assembly cache, create new web applications and new Internet Information Services (IIS) Web sites, and start services.

Like farm administrators, members of the Administrators group on the local server have no access to site content, by default, but can take ownership of a site collection and thereby give themselves access to content.

> **BEST PRACTICE MANAGE THE ADMINISTRATORS GROUP**
>
> Ensure that the membership of the Administrators group of a SharePoint server is minimized, to reduce the risk of accidental or malicious viewing of or damage to content. It is also important to keep the membership of the Administrators group consistent across all SharePoint servers in a farm.

Service Application Administrators

In Chapter 1, you learned that service applications are the logical management instance of SharePoint services such as search. Many service applications have configurations that must be managed. Farm administrators always have rights to manage all service applications. Those rights cannot be removed. SharePoint 2007 did not make it easy to delegate the administration and configuration of an individual service, but in SharePoint 2010 you can delegate the administration of service applications.

Service application administrators are delegated by members of the Farm Administrators group. The administrators of a service application can configure settings for a specific service application in a farm. However, these administrators cannot create service applications, access any other service applications in the farm, or perform any farm-level operations, including topology changes. For example, the service application administrator for a Search service application in a farm can configure settings for that Search service application only.

DELEGATE ADMINISTRATION OF A SERVICE APPLICATION

1. In the Central Administration Quick Launch, click Application Management, and then, in the Service Applications section, click Manage Service Applications.

2. Click the row of a service application.

   Do not click the *name* of a service application. Most service application names are links to the service application's management application.

3. In the Ribbon, click Administrators.

When you assign a service application administrator, and the user is not already a member of the Farm Administrators group, the user is added to the Delegated Administrators group in Central Administration. This gives the user the ability to access the Central Administration website.

Service Application Feature Administrators

Some service applications have features that can be further delegated. For example, the User Profile service application supports the Audiences feature. Audiences define a collection of users based on criteria, and content can be targeted to an audience to personalize the users' experience with SharePoint.

A feature administrator is associated with a specific feature or features of a service application. These administrators can manage a subset of service application settings but not the entire service application. In later chapters, you will learn about SharePoint service applications and, in the context of those discussions, you will learn about the features and delegation of feature administration.

When you assign a service application administrator, and the user is not already a member of the Farm Administrators group, the user is added to the Delegated Administrators group in Central Administration. This gives the user the ability to access the Central Administration website.

Site Collection Owners

Each site collection can have two *owners*: the primary owner and the secondary owner. When you create a site collection by using Central Administration, you assign the Primary Site Collection Administrator and the Secondary Site Collection Administrator. Although the user interface of Central Administration suggests that these are site collection administrators, they are actually owners and site collection administrators. You cannot create a site collection without a primary owner (a primary site collection administrator), and you can use Central Administration to change the primary owner, or to add, change, or remove the secondary owner.

ASSIGN SITE COLLECTION OWNERS
1. In the Central Administration Quick Launch, click Application Management.
2. In the Site Collections section, click Change Site Collection Administrators.

Only Farm Administrators can modify site collection owners by using Central Administration.

When you assign a service application feature administrator, and the user is not already a member of the Farm Administrators group, the user is added to the Delegated Administrators group in Central Administration. This gives the user the ability to access the Central Administration website.

Site Collection Administrators

A site collection can have one or more site collection administrators. Site collection administrators have full control of all websites in a site collection. They have access to all content in all sites in that site collection, even if they do not have explicit permissions to that content. Site collection administrators can configure all settings of the site collection.

ASSIGN SITE COLLECTION ADMINISTRATORS
1. At the top-level site of a site collection, click Site Actions, and then click Site Settings.
2. In the Users And Permissions section, click Site Collection Administrators.
3. Add or remove users from the semicolon-delimited list of site collection administrators.

Any site collection administrator can change the list of site collection administrators. There can be one or more site collection administrators. The primary and secondary owners of the site collection are automatically site collection administrators, and there is no way to segregate owners (which have both site collection administration and contact roles) from site collection administrators. If a site collection has only one or two site collection administrators, those same users are the primary and secondary owners of the site collection as well.

Site Collection Administrators Clarified

SharePoint's terminology and user interface lead to a lot of confusion about site collection administrators, so it is helpful to remember that primary and secondary site collection owners are attributes of a site collection: the *Owner* and *SecondaryContact* properties of the *SPSite* object. Those properties are exposed in the *OwnerLoginName* and

SecondaryOwnerLoginName properties of the *SPSiteAdministration* object of the farm configuration. There are only two owners.

The site collection administrators designation exists only within the site collection itself. When a user is added as a site collection administrator, the user's identity is flagged with the *bit2* column in the user information list of the site collection. Theoretically, every user in a site collection could be a site collection administrator—you are not limited to two.

From a functional perspective, the two owners are site collection administrators, but the owners are also contacts. They receive email notifications for events, such as the pending automatic deletion of inactive sites and requests for site access.

When you change owners by using Central Administration, the list of site collection administrators will be updated automatically. However, if you change site collection administrators from the site settings of the top-level site, changes are not always reflected in the owners' properties. For example:

- Adding a second site collection administrator to the site does not make the user the secondary owner.

- Removing the primary owner from the list of site collection administrators is only possible if the secondary owner is assigned, at which point the secondary owner becomes the primary owner.

- Using the site to change the order of two site collection administrators that are already owners does not swap the primary and secondary owner properties.

- Removing the secondary owner from the list of site collection administrators removes that user as the secondary owner as well, but does not add the next site collection administrator as an owner.

- If you add a user as a third (or later) site collection administrator, and then promote the user to an owner by using Central Administration, and then remove the user as an owner, the user is automatically removed from the list of site collection administrators, which may not be what you wanted—you might still want that user to have full control of the site collection.

- A user assigned as a site collection administrator can promote himself or herself to owner by removing the current owners from the list of site collection administrators. This may or may not reflect an acceptable capability within your governance plan, and if it does not you must monitor and audit for such changes.

As you can see, the user interface labels that refer to site collection administrators when they should distinguish between administrators and owners, and the behavior of the user interface controls can be confusing and problematic.

Therefore, best practice is to use Central Administration to manage the primary and secondary owners according to your governance plan, remembering that the owners receive email notifications and are automatically site collection administrators, and then to assign full control ownership of a site collection by managing the list of site collection administrators in the top-level site.

Alternately, access the SharePoint object model by using a tool such as Windows PowerShell. In the object model, owners are clearly called owners … or contacts. I guess it's confusing no matter how you go about it!

 Quick Check

1. What are the differences between the site collection administrators as defined in Central Administration and the site collection administrators as defined in the site collection itself?

2. Do both sets of site collection administrators have the same permissions to a site collection?

Quick Check Answers

1. There can be only two site collection administrators as defined in Central Administration, and these two users receive email notifications including quota and site use confirmation messages. More than two site collection administrators can be defined in the site collection itself, and these users do not receive those email notifications.

2. Both sets of site collection administrators have Full Control permission to the site collection.

Site Groups and Permissions

Each site has groups that are assigned permissions to the site. The default site Owners group, for example, has Full Control permission to the site. By default, site permissions are inherited by each child site, list, library, folder, item, and document. Therefore, the Owners group of a top-level website in a site collection has full control of content—as do site collection administrators.

The Owners group—or any group with Full Control permission to a site—can perform administrative tasks for the site and for any list or library in that site. Unlike site collection administrators, the Owners group's Full Control permission to content can be blocked by disabling inheritance. Furthermore, although the Owners group can change certain site-level settings, it cannot change all settings, including those that apply to the site collection as a whole.

In Chapter 4, you will learn more about administering site groups and permissions.

> *NOTE* **TERMINOLOGY HEADACHES CONTINUED**
>
> SharePoint terminology obviously takes another turn for the worse here: the Owners group of a site is not the same as the site collection owners, which themselves are called site collection administrators in the Central Administration user interface, even though site collection owners receive email notifications that the site collection administrators do not. Confused? So is everyone else. Spend time understanding the roles and the scope of those roles so that regardless of the term that is used by a colleague or document, you can interpret which role is really being referred to.

SharePoint Administrative Tools

SharePoint has introduced new administration interfaces with each successive version of the product. In SharePoint 2007, Microsoft redesigned Central Administration and introduced Stsadm (Stsadm.exe), which exposed 182 commands. As you learn in the next topic, Stsadm has been deprecated but is still supported in SharePoint 2010.

In SharePoint 2010, Microsoft has again redesigned Central Administration, providing a task-based organization and a Ribbon-centric interface for many administrative pages. At the command line, SharePoint 2010 aligns with other Microsoft technologies around the use of Windows PowerShell as the primary command-line interface for administration. SharePoint 2010 provides more than 600 Windows PowerShell cmdlets to support administration of a SharePoint farm. Windows PowerShell provides a superset of capabilities found in Central Administration. Windows PowerShell 2.0 is required to install SharePoint and is installed by the Microsoft SharePoint Products Preparation Tool (PrerequisiteInstaller).

Stsadm

Stsadm.exe is a command-line administrative tool located in the C:\Program Files\ Common Files\Microsoft Shared\web server extensions\14\BIN folder. Stsadm is deprecated but is included to support compatibility with previous product versions. However, for a small number of Stsadm operations, no Windows PowerShell equivalent exists.

Some Stsadm operations are no longer supported because of feature or architectural changes in SharePoint 2010. For example, commands used to create, enumerate, and manage Shared Service Providers (SSPs) are not supported because SSPs have been replaced by service applications.

To use Stsadm, you must open a Command Prompt on a SharePoint server with the Run As Administrator option, and then navigate to the folder that contains Stsadm.exe: C:\Program Files\Common Files\Microsoft Shared\web server extensions\14\BIN. You can avoid having to navigate to this deeply nested folder by adding the path to the folder to the *Path* environment variable. For example, type the following command:

```
set path=%path%;C:\Program Files\Common Files\Microsoft Shared\web server extensions
\14\BIN
```

Alternately, use SharePoint 2010 Management Shell or Windows PowerShell with the SharePoint snap-in loaded. Each of these adds the path to the \BIN folder in their *Path* variable.

Stsadm exposes functionality through *operations*. Each operation is invoked with this syntax:

```
stsadm -o <OperationName> [-parameter <Value> ...]
```

Where:

- *<OperationName>* is the name of an Stsadm operation.
- *<Value>* is the value for a parameter used by the operation.

To discover the operations that are supported, type the following command:

```
stsadm -?
```

To read documentation about a specific operation and the parameters it supports, type the following command:

```
stsadm -help <OperationName>
```

Windows PowerShell

Windows PowerShell is the current administrative framework for administering and automating Microsoft technology platforms from a command line. SharePoint 2010 provides a snap-in for managing SharePoint with Windows PowerShell that exposes more than 600 cmdlets. Lesson 2 of this chapter introduces you to administering SharePoint with Windows PowerShell.

SharePoint 2010 Management Shell

In addition, when you install SharePoint 2010, you install the SharePoint 2010 Management Shell. This is the preferred interface for performing task-based commands and for running scripts. The SharePoint 2010 Management Shell supports both Stsadm and Windows PowerShell. Therefore, it is not a separate administrative tool; rather, it is an interface within which the two primary command-line interfaces can be used.

SharePoint 2010 Management Shell already includes in its *Path* variable the folder that contains Stsadm.exe: C:\Program Files\Common Files\Microsoft Shared\web server extensions\14\BIN. So you can run Stsadm operations without having to navigate to that folder. However, remember that you must open SharePoint 2010 Management Shell with the Run As Administrator option; otherwise, Stsadm operations will fail.

SharePoint 2010 Management Shell also includes a Windows PowerShell profile that loads the SharePoint snap-in and configures several settings that optimize Windows PowerShell performance for SharePoint administration. You will learn more about SharePoint 2010 Management Shell in Lesson 2.

Central Administration

Central Administration is the web application that you have used thus far in this Training Kit to configure SharePoint 2010. Like any web application, access to the application can be restricted. Your ability to access the application is based on the security permissions for Central Administration: Your administrative user account must be a member of Farm Administrators to successfully open Central Administration. In Chapter 1, you learned that after installing SharePoint 2010 in the context of the Setup User and Administration account (such as SP_Admin), you should add your own administrative identity to the Farm Administrators group.

Users who have been delegated administrative roles for service application or service application features can also open Central Administration, but the interface is *security trimmed*. The user interface presents only the navigation links and commands to which the user has permission. All other navigation links and options are hidden.

The Security Context of Central Administration

Once you have been granted access to Central Administration, the tasks you perform are not executed in the context of your account's identity. Every change you request in Central Administration is implemented using the application pool identity for the Central Administration Web application and the timer service—for example, SP_Farm.

If something is not working, be sure that the SP_Farm identity has the permissions it requires. For example, some tasks performed in Central Administration require the account to have the following attributes:

- Local Administrators group membership on each SharePoint server. Typically, SP_Farm should not be a member of the Administrators group, and SharePoint 2010 will generate a notification message in Central Administration if it detects that SP_Farm is a member of Administrators. However, the account must be a member of Administrators to successfully provision the User Profile Synchronization service application.

- Microsoft SQL Server permissions. During configuration of SharePoint, the SP_Farm account is assigned the permissions it requires on the SQL Server and on each database. However, if permissions are later removed directly on SQL Server, SharePoint functionality may be negatively impacted or administrative tasks may fail.

Change the Port of Central Administration

When you run the SharePoint Products Configuration Wizard (Psconfigui.exe), you specify the port to which the Central Administration website is bound. You cannot change the port on which Central Administration is hosted from Central Administration itself. You can, however, change the port using either Stsadm or Windows PowerShell.

CHANGE THE PORT OF CENTRAL ADMINISTRATION USING STSADM

You can use the *setadminport* operation of Stsadm to modify the port to which Central Administration is bound.

```
stsadm -o setadminport -port <PortNumber>
```

Where:

- *<PortNumber>* is an available port.

CHANGE THE PORT OF CENTRAL ADMINISTRATION USING WINDOWS POWERSHELL

You can use the *Set-SPCentralAdministration* cmdlet *-Port* parameter to modify the port to which Central Administration is bound.

```
Set-SPCentralAdministration -Port <PortNumber>
```

Where:

- *<PortNumber>* is an available port, greater than 1023 and less than 32767.

You will learn more about Windows PowerShell in the next lesson.

> **MORE INFO**   **CHANGING THE CENTRAL ADMINISTRATION PORT**
>
> You can learn more about how to change the port of Central Administration in the TechNet articles "Change the Central Administration Web site port number (SharePoint Server 2010)" at *http://go.microsoft.com/fwlink/?LinkID=192720* and "Setadminport: Stsadm Operation (Office SharePoint Server)" at *http://go.microsoft.com/fwlink/?LinkID=192721*.

PRACTICE   Configure SharePoint Administration

Practices are designed to guide you through important procedures. The instructions in the Training Kit are high-level instructions that will challenge you to think carefully and to apply the procedures that are covered in this lesson and elsewhere in the Training Kit. If you need assistance, consult the detailed, step-by-step instructions in the Practice Answers on the companion media.

In this practice, you will delegate administration of Central Administration, of service applications and features, of site collections, and of sites. You will also configure the port for Central Administration by using Stsadm.

Prepare for the Practice

Before you perform this practice, you must ensure that your lab environment has been built according to the instructions found in the Introduction to this Training Kit.

1. Apply the snapshot CHAPTER 01 to CONTOSO-DC.

2. Apply the snapshot CHAPTER 01 to SP2010-WFE1.

3. Start CONTOSO-DC.

   Wait for the virtual machine to complete startup, at which time the Press Ctrl+Alt+Delete prompt appears.

4. Start SP2010-WFE1.

EXERCISE 1   Add a User to the Farm Administrators Group

In this exercise, you add a user account to the Farm Administrators group.

1. Log on to SP2010-WFE1 as **CONTOSO\SP_Admin** with the password **Pa$$w0rd**.
2. Add Pat Coleman to the Farm Administrators group. Pat Coleman's username is PatC.

EXERCISE 2   Sign in as a Different User

In this exercise, you sign in with the account that you just added to the Farm Administrators group.

- Sign in to Central Administration as **CONTOSO\PatC** with the password **Pa$$w0rd**.

EXERCISE 3   Assign a Site Collection Owner

In this exercise, you add a site collection owner of the Contoso intranet.

- In the Central Administration add Pat Coleman as the Secondary Site Collection Administrator for the intranet site collection.

EXERCISE 4   Assign a Site Collection Administrator

In this exercise, you add a site collection administrator of the Contoso intranet.

1. Open a new tab in Internet Explorer, and then browse to ***http://intranet.contoso.com***.
2. Add April Meyer as a site collection administrator. April's username is AprilM.

EXERCISE 5   Assign a Site Owner

In this exercise, you add a site owner of the Contoso intranet website.

- Add Kevin Cook to the Contoso Intranet Owners group. Kevin's username is KevinC.

EXERCISE 6   Assign a Service Application Administrator

In this exercise, you delegate administration of the Managed Metadata Service service application.

- In the Central Administration, delegate administration of the Managed Metadata Service to April Meyer. Give her Full Control permission.

EXERCISE 7   Change the Port of Central Administration

In this exercise, you change the port of Central Administration.

1. Open a Command Prompt using the Run As Administrator option.
2. Type the following command and then press Enter:

```
stsadm -o setadminport -port 9998
```

An error message is displayed.

3. Determine the cause of the error and enter the command correctly so that it executes successfully.

4. In Internet Explorer, browse to ***http://sp2010-wfe1:9998***.

   Central Administration opens. Because the web application must be recompiled and cached, it takes a few moments for this to occur.

5. Open a Command Prompt, change the port for Central Administration back to port 9999.

6. In Internet Explorer, browse to ***http://sp2010-wfe1:9999***.

   Central Administration opens. Because the web application must be recompiled and cached, it takes a few moments for this to occur.

Lesson Summary

- SharePoint administrative roles include SharePoint's Farm Administrators group, the Administrators group on the SharePoint server, service application and feature administrators, the primary and secondary owners of site collections, site collection administrators, and site groups with administrative permissions.

- Farm Administrators can modify the primary and secondary owners of a site collection by using Central Administration. Primary and secondary owners are automatically site collection administrators. They also receive email notifications regarding site use, site deletion, quotas, and site access requests.

- Site collection administrators can change the list of site collection administrators from the site settings of the top-level site in the site collection. Certain changes to this list can result in changes to the primary and secondary owner of the site collection.

- SharePoint 2010 provides Central Administration, Stsadm, and Windows PowerShell interfaces for administration. SharePoint 2010 Management Shell supports both Stsadm.exe and SharePoint cmdlets for Windows PowerShell.

- Stsadm.exe is supported in SharePoint 2010, but Windows PowerShell is the preferred command-line and automation interface.

- Access to Central Administration is granted to members of the Farm Administrators group and to service application and feature administrators.

- Actions performed in Central Administration are executed within the security context of the Central Administration application pool identity, such as SP_Farm.

Lesson Review

You can use the following questions to test your knowledge of the information in Lesson 1, "SharePoint Administrative Roles and Interfaces." The questions are also available on the companion CD in a practice test if you prefer to review them in electronic form.

1. You want to assign five users the ability to enable or disable features for the departmental site collection of the Sales department. Which of the following can you use?

    A. Change Site Collection Administrators in Central Administration

    B. Site Collection Administrators in the department's top-level site Site Settings

    C. Sales Owners

    D. Sales Designers

2. You want to ensure that Lola Jacobsen receives email notifications when her department's site collection reaches its quota. Which of the following must you do? (Choose all that apply. Each correct answer is a part of the complete solution.)

    A. Add Lola as the third member of the Site Collection Administrators group by using the Site Settings page of the site.

    B. Assign Lola as the Primary Site Collection Administrator by using Central Administration.

    C. Configure a quota template named Sales Quota with a storage limit.

    D. Configure a quota template named Sales Quota with a warning level.

    E. Apply the quota template named Sales Quota to the Sales site collection.

    F. Select Individual Quota on the Site Quotas And Locks page.

    G. Configure the outgoing email settings of the farm.

    H. Configure the incoming email settings of the farm.

3. You receive an Access Denied error when you attempt to use Stsadm.exe to assign the primary owner of a site collection. The site collection currently has only one owner. Which of the following must you do to correct the problem?

    A. You cannot configure the primary owner of a site collection by using Stsadm.

    B. Start Stsadm using the Run As Administrator option.

    C. Add the path to Stsadm to the *Path* environment variable.

    D. Remove the current primary site collection administrator.

Lesson 2: Automate SharePoint Operations with Windows PowerShell

In this lesson, you are introduced to Windows PowerShell, which is the recommended tool for administering and automating SharePoint 2010 from the command line. Windows PowerShell certainly deserves its *Power* moniker. As you will discover, it enables you to perform tasks that would require multiple clicks in Central Administration with a single command line and, better yet, it allows you to perform repetitive tasks with ease.

> ### After this lesson, you will be able to:
> - Identify the role of Windows PowerShell for administering SharePoint.
> - Describe the SharePoint 2010 Management Shell.
> - Examine the SharePoint logical structure.
> - Use Windows PowerShell features to discover cmdlets and get help about the cmdlets.
> - Distinguish between user interface and object model terminology for SharePoint logical structural components.
> - Describe objects, members, properties, and methods in Windows PowerShell.
> - Describe how to select, sort, and format output in Windows PowerShell.
> - Describe how to filter objects.
> - Create a SharePoint intranet by using Windows PowerShell.
> - Explain the concepts of iteration and variables.
> - Automate SharePoint operations with Windows PowerShell.
> - Delegate permissions to use Windows PowerShell
> - Run Windows PowerShell scripts.
>
> ### Estimated lesson time: 90 minutes

EXAM TIP

This section introduces you to Windows PowerShell so that you can become familiar with this important administrative tool. You are not expected to create Windows PowerShell scripts on the 70-667 exam; however, you should be able to recognize cmdlets used for SharePoint administrative tasks such as those described in this training kit. If you want to learn more about creating automation scripts for Windows PowerShell, refer to *Windows PowerShell 2.0 Administrator's Pocket Consultant* by William R. Stanek (Microsoft Press, 2009).

Introducing Windows PowerShell

Windows PowerShell is a task-based command-line shell and scripting language designed especially for system administration. Built on the Microsoft .NET Framework, Windows PowerShell helps IT professionals control and automate the administration of several Microsoft technologies, including the Windows operating system, SharePoint 2010, Active Directory Domain Services, and Microsoft Exchange Server.

With Windows PowerShell commands, called *cmdlets*, you can perform management tasks from the command line. With Windows PowerShell *providers,* you can access data stores, such as the registry and certificate store, as easily as you access the file system. In addition, Windows PowerShell has a rich expression parser and a fully developed scripting language.

Windows PowerShell includes the following features:

- Cmdlets for performing common system administration tasks.

- A task-based scripting language.

- Support for existing scripts and command-line tools. For example, you can perform most Cmd.exe commands with Windows PowerShell.

- Consistent design. Because cmdlets and system data stores use common syntax and naming conventions, data can be shared easily and the output from one cmdlet can be used as the input to another cmdlet without reformatting or manipulation.

- Providers that expose system resources such as the registry, certificate store, and directory service for simplified navigation by using the same techniques that users employ to navigate the file system.

- Powerful object manipulation capabilities. You can manipulate objects directly or send them to other tools or databases.

- Extensible interface. Independent software vendors and enterprise developers can build custom tools and utilities to administer their software.

Stsadm and Windows PowerShell have significant overlap in support for operations that are common to both SharePoint 2007 and SharePoint 2010. However, Windows PowerShell provides unique capabilities related to the management of all new features, including support for the following tasks:

- Installation and configuration of SharePoint 2010

- Management of service applications

- Granular control of backup and restore

One of the most important new features of Windows PowerShell 2.0 is *remoting*, with which you can execute Windows PowerShell commands on remote systems. Remoting is a Windows PowerShell feature, rather than a feature specific to SharePoint, so it is beyond the scope of this training kit. The following TechNet article addresses remoting with Windows PowerShell: "Running Remote Commands" at *http://go.microsoft.com/fwlink/?LinkID=192745*. Also see the following blog entry: "SharePoint 2010 with Windows PowerShell Remoting Step by Step" at *http://blogs.msdn.com/b/opal/archive/2010/03/07/sharepoint-2010-with-windows-powershell-remoting-step-by-step.aspx*.

SharePoint 2010 Management Shell

You can manage SharePoint with Windows PowerShell in two ways: the Windows PowerShell console and SharePoint 2010 Management Shell. In Lesson 1, you learned that the SharePoint 2010 Management Shell is the preferred tool with which to administer SharePoint from the command line because it supports the use of both Windows PowerShell and Stsadm.exe.

OPEN SHAREPOINT 2010 MANAGEMENT SHELL

To open the SharePoint 2010 Management Shell, perform the following procedure:

- Click Start, All Programs, Microsoft SharePoint 2010 Products, and then click SharePoint 2010 Management Shell.

To use Stsadm and some Windows PowerShell cmdlets, you must be running SharePoint 2010 Management Shell with administrative privileges. These cmdlets along with Stsadm fail unless you use the Run As Administrator option when opening SharePoint 2010 Management Shell.

OPEN SHAREPOINT 2010 MANAGEMENT SHELL WITH ADMINISTRATIVE PRIVILEGES

To start the shell with administrative privileges, perform the following procedure:

1. Click Start, All Programs, Microsoft SharePoint 2010 Products, hold the Shift key and right-click SharePoint 2010 Management Shell, and then click Run As Administrator.

   The User Account Control dialog box opens.

2. Click Yes.

cmdlets

In traditional shells such as Command Prompt (Cmd.exe), you issue commands such as *dir* or *copy* that access utilities built into the shell, or you call executable programs such as Attrib.exe or Xcopy.exe, many of which accept parameters from the command line and return feedback in the form of output, errors, and error codes.

In Windows PowerShell, you issue directives by using cmdlets. A cmdlet is a single-feature command that manipulates an object. SharePoint Server 2010 ships with more than 500 cmdlets for Windows PowerShell, so it is not recommended that you try to memorize them all. Instead, you should know how to discover—and get help—about a cmdlet when you need it. Over time, you will memorize the cmdlets that you use regularly.

Luckily, Windows PowerShell is a modern command-line and automation interface, and it benefits from lessons learned from past command-line environments, such as Command Prompt. One of the most immediately useful sets of features are those that help you discover cmdlets and learn syntax easily.

The *Get-Command* cmdlet lists cmdlets. Simply type the following command to list all cmdlets available within the Windows PowerShell session:

```
Get-Command
```

Cmdlets are not case-sensitive. Therefore, the following cmdlets are equivalent:

- Get-Command
- get-command
- GET-COMMAND

Cmdlets always follow the *Verb-Noun* format, also called the *Action-Object* format. The *Noun* is always singular. For example, the cmdlet to list all services running on a computer is *Get-Service*. To list all processes running on a computer, type the following command:

```
Get-Service
```

A limited number of verbs can be listed with the *Get-Verb* cmdlet. Nouns follow naming standards managed by the Windows PowerShell team. For example, all SharePoint nouns begin with *SP*.

LIST ALL SHAREPOINT CMDLETS

To list all SharePoint cmdlets, type the following command:

```
Get-Command -noun SP* | more
```

Windows PowerShell supports much of the same syntax as Command Prompt, which eases the transition to Windows PowerShell. As in Command Prompt, adding | *more* to a command pages the output of the command.

The command shown at the beginning of this section is a shortcut based on the fact that all SharePoint nouns begin with *SP*. A more technically accurate approach is to list all of the commands in the SharePoint snap-in for Windows PowerShell. Windows PowerShell is an extensible framework, and its commands can be extended by adding snap-ins. SharePoint 2010 installs the SharePoint snap-in for Windows PowerShell. To list the commands in the snap-in, type the following command:

```
Get-Command -pssnapin Microsoft.SharePoint.PowerShell
```

Get-Help

Once you have found a cmdlet that appears to support a task you want to perform, you can expose the documentation for the cmdlet using the *Get-Help* cmdlet. The simplest form of help is provided by typing the *Get-Help* cmdlet followed by the cmdlet name you want help with. For example:

```
Get-Help Get-Service
```

Without a parameter, the *Get-Help* cmdlet shows a synopsis, a more detailed description, and the syntax of the cmdlet. The following optional parameters of *Get-Help* produce various types and levels of detail:

- **-examples**   Shows usage examples of the cmdlet.
- **-detailed**   Shows detailed information about the cmdlet and each of its parameters. Also shows examples.
- **-full**   Shows all documentation of the cmdlet.

For example, to get help, including examples, about the *New-SPContentDatabase* cmdlet, type the following:

```
Get-Help New-SPContentDatabase -detailed
```

The Windows PowerShell *Get-Help* cmdlet is the best place to start looking for information about cmdlets, especially when you are just getting started with Windows PowerShell. Windows PowerShell cmdlets are well documented with a standard documentation format, and the *Get-Help* cmdlet, with the *-examples*, *-detailed*, and *-full* parameters, exposes that documentation.

> **MORE INFO**   **EXPLORE SHAREPOINT CMDLETS**
>
> The following article, and its related articles, provide additional details regarding the fundamentals of Windows PowerShell cmdlets: "Windows PowerShell Basics" at *http://technet.microsoft.com/en-us/library/dd347730.aspx*.

Objects

Unlike Command Prompt, in which commands return text that then must be parsed and processed as text, Windows PowerShell returns *objects*—representations of the component itself.

An object is a programming construct. From a technical perspective, a .NET object is an instance of a .NET class that consists of data and the operations associated with that data. Think of an object as a virtual representation of a resource of some kind. For example, when you use the *Get-Service* cmdlet in Windows PowerShell, the cmdlet returns one or more objects representing services. Objects can have *properties*—also called *attributes*—that represent data maintained by the resource. An object representing a service, for example, has properties for the service name and its startup state. When you get a property, you are retrieving the data of the resource. When you set a property, you are writing that data to the resource.

Objects also have *methods*, which are actions that you can perform on the object. The service object has *start* and *stop* methods, for example. When you perform a method on the object that represents the resource, you perform the action on the resource itself.

For example, the *Get-Service* cmdlet returns objects representing services on a computer. Type the following to retrieve all services on a computer:

```
Get-Service
```

To limit the services returned, use a parameter of the *Get-Service* cmdlet. For example, the *-Name* parameter limits services returned based on their name. The following command retrieves all services on a computer with names that begin with *SP*, many of which are SharePoint-related services:

```
Get-Service -Name SP*
```

The *-Name* parameter is the default parameter for the *Get-Service* cmdlet, so it can be omitted:

```
Get-Service SP*
```

Windows PowerShell cmdlets do not pass commands or parameters to other utilities or programs as in Cmd.exe. Instead, Windows PowerShell cmdlets operate on .NET objects directly. The *Get-Service* cmdlet returns a *collection* of objects, one object for each service on the computer. The cmdlet presents the results of the cmdlet as a table showing several properties of each service: status, name, and display name, as shown in Figure 2-1.

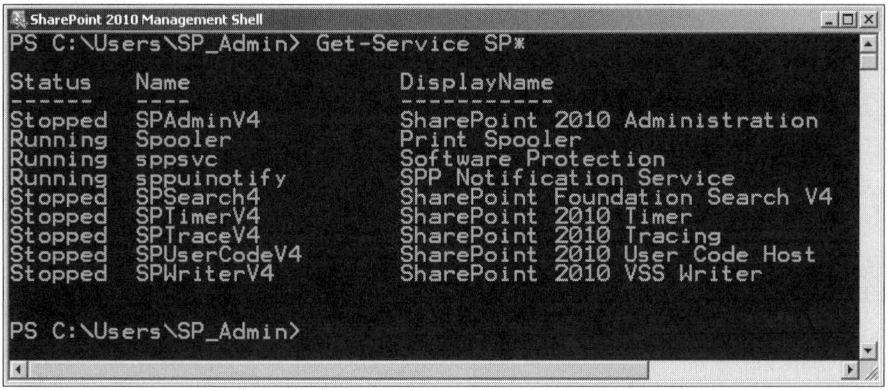

FIGURE 2-1 The *Get-Service* cmdlet

Pipeline

In the examples thus far, you have not yet done anything with the objects other than showing properties. However, objects returned by a cmdlet can be stored in variables for later use or piped to a subsequent cmdlet as input for the cmdlet. Windows PowerShell features a *pipeline*—a channel through which the output of a cmdlet can be passed to the following cmdlet. The pipeline is represented by the pipe character (|).

For example, type the following to stop all processes named iexplore on a computer:

```
Get-Service SPTimerV4 | Stop-Service
```

The *Get-Service* cmdlet gets an object representing the SharePoint Timer service, *SPTimerV4*, and passes the object down the pipeline to the *Stop-Service* cmdlet, which stops the service.

As you learn later in this lesson, one of the most important differences between Windows PowerShell and Command Prompt is that cmdlets return *objects*, not text. In Command Prompt, commands return text, and the text can be piped to another command. In Windows PowerShell, cmdlets return objects, which can be manipulated in much more powerful ways further down the pipeline. For example, the *Get-Service* cmdlet returns an object representing the SPTimerV4 service. The next command in the pipeline stops the service, but it could just as easily be a cmdlet that changes a property of the service or returns specific information about the service.

In addition, when a cmdlet returns more than one object—known as a *collection* of objects—and passes the collection down the pipeline, a subsequent cmdlet can operate on each of the objects it receives. For example, to stop all services with *SharePoint* in their display name, type the following command:

```
Get-Service -DisplayName *SharePoint* | Stop-Service
```

The *Get-Service* cmdlet returns approximately 10 service objects and pipes the collection to the *Stop-Service* cmdlet. The *Stop-Service* cmdlet iterates through the collection of objects and stops each one.

Extend the Pipeline to More Than One Line

A Windows PowerShell task may involve multiple cmdlets, parameters, and expressions. More complicated tasks may create a long pipeline with structures including functions, iterative loops, and conditional statements. Often, the pipeline is extended to more than one line to improve readability. There are several ways to enter one line of a pipeline, and then to continue the pipeline on a subsequent line:

- **The tick mark (`)**   When a tick mark is the last character of a line, it serves as a line break and line continuation marker. Windows PowerShell assumes that the subsequent line is a continuation of the current line. The following two-line command uses a tick mark to break the line for readability:

```
Get-Service -DisplayName *SharePoint* | `
Stop-Service
```

- **The pipe symbol (|)**   When the pipe symbol is the last character of a line, it too serves to indicate that the command is not complete, so Windows PowerShell continues the command with the subsequent line, as in the following example:

```
Get-Service -DisplayName *SharePoint* |
Stop-Service
```

- **A left curly brace ({)**   Curly braces enclose a structure such as an expression or a procedure. A left curly brace suggests that a structure follows. You will see examples of this later in this lesson.

When you type a line in the Windows PowerShell console and the line ends with one of these characters, the console returns a double right chevron prompt, shown in Figure 2-2.

This prompt is a visual indication that the command is being continued. To indicate that the command is complete, you must enter a blank line at the prompt, as shown in Figure 2-2. When Windows PowerShell receives the blank line, it executes the multi-line command.

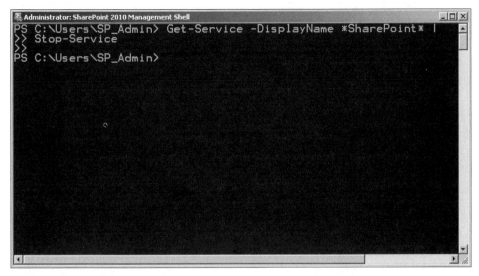

FIGURE 2-2 A multi-line command

> **MORE INFO**   **THE WINDOWS POWERSHELL PIPELINE**
>
> The following article provides additional details regarding the Windows PowerShell Pipeline: "Understanding the Windows PowerShell Pipeline" at *http://go.microsoft.com/ fwlink/?LinkID=192732*.

Aliases

Windows PowerShell allows a cmdlet to have *aliases*, which are alternate names for the cmdlet. For example, *gsv* is an alias for *Get-Service*. The *Get-Alias* cmdlet lists aliases. Without a parameter, *Get-Alias* lists all aliases in the current Windows PowerShell session. To list aliases for a specific cmdlet, type the following command:

```
Get-Alias -definition <cmdlet>
```

where *<cmdlet>* is the cmdlet for which you want to list aliases.

If you see a cmdlet that does not follow the *Verb-Noun* syntax, the cmdlet is using an alias. Sometimes it can be difficult to interpret what a command is doing when an alias is used. To list the cmdlet associated with a specific alias, type the following command:

```
Get-Alias <Alias>
```

where *<Alias>* is the alias you want to define.

Windows PowerShell aliases enable you to use common Command Prompt (Cmd.exe) and UNIX commands. For example, *dir* and *ls* list the objects in a directory—they are aliases for the *Get-ChildItem* cmdlet. You can clear the Windows PowerShell console screen with the *Clear-Host* cmdlet, or you can use the alias *cls*.

> **MORE INFO** **USING FAMILIAR COMMAND NAMES**
>
> The following article provides additional details regarding Windows PowerShell aliases: "Using Familiar Command Names" at *http://go.microsoft.com/fwlink/?LinkID=192733*.

Tab Expansion

Windows PowerShell supports *tab expansion*, also called *tab completion*, so that you can type a few letters and then press Tab to complete your typing. This applies not only to paths, which is possible in Command Prompt as well, but also to cmdlets and their parameters.

To experience tab completion, perform the following steps in SharePoint 2010 Management Shell, which creates a new content database for a web application:

1. Type **New-SPCont** and then press Tab.

    Windows PowerShell completes the name of the cmdlet, *New-SPContentDatabase*.

    The first parameter of the *New-SPContentDatabase* cmdlet is the name of the database you want to create.

2. Press Spacebar, type **TestContentDB** and then press Spacebar.

    The next parameter is the name of the database server on which to create the content database.

3. Type **-Da** and then press Tab.

    Windows PowerShell completes the name of the parameter, *-DatabaseServer*.

4. Press Spacebar, type **SP2010-WFE1** and then press Spacebar.

    The other required parameter is the name of the web application with which the content database is associated.

5. Type **-W** and then press Tab.

    Windows PowerShell completes the name of the parameter, *-WebApplication*.

6. Press Spacebar and then type "**http://intranet.contoso.com**".

7. Press Ctrl+C to cancel the command without executing it.

Examine and Document the SharePoint Logical Structure Using Windows PowerShell

Now that you have an understanding of Windows PowerShell fundamentals, let's use Windows PowerShell to explore the SharePoint logical structure, and to document aspects of a SharePoint implementation. At the end of this discussion, you should be able to produce a report of blogs in your SharePoint farm, sorted by the date on which they were last updated. To achieve this task, you will need to learn how to do the following tasks:

- Use *Get-SP** cmdlets to return objects representing components of the SharePoint logical structure.
- Use the pipeline to create a collection of objects representing websites in the farm.
- Use the *Select-Object* cmdlet to work with specific properties.
- Use the *Where-Object* cmdlet to filter specific objects.
- Use cmdlets such as *Format-** and *Export-** to produce reports.

Examine the SharePoint Logical Structure with *Get-SP**

A SharePoint farm's logical structure consists of the farm, web applications, site collections, sites, documents and lists that can optionally be divided into folders, and lists and items. In this chapter, you will use cmdlets with the *Get* verb to retrieve objects from the first few layers of the SharePoint object model. The logical structure and the related *Get-SP** cmdlets are shown in Figure 2-3.

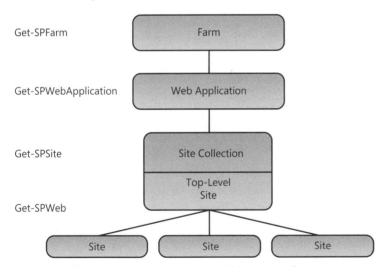

FIGURE 2-3 The SharePoint logical structure and *Get-SP** cmdlets

To retrieve an object that references the farm, type the following command:

```
Get-SPFarm
```

The output of the command is the name of the farm, which is the SharePoint configuration database name by default.

To retrieve a collection representing the web applications in the farm, type the following command:

```
Get-SPWebApplication
```

The *Get-SPWebApplication* cmdlet excludes Central Administration by default as a measure of protection against scripts that are designed to perform actions against every web application in a farm. To include the Central Administration Web application, add the parameter *-IncludeCentralAdminsitration*, as in the following example:

```
Get-SPWebApplication -IncludeCentralAdministration
```

To retrieve a collection of site collections in the farm, type the following command:

```
Get-SPSite
```

To prevent runaway memory and processing, the *Get-SPSite* cmdlet limits the number of site collections it returns to 20 by default. Add the *-Limit* parameter to increase this limit or add *-Limit All* to return all site collections. The *Get-SPSite* cmdlet always excludes the Central Administration site collection unless the Central Administration Web application is specified as the *-Identity* parameter or piped to the cmdlet.

The *Get-SPWeb* cmdlet, unlike *Get-SPSite* or *Get-SPWebApplication*, does not retrieve a collection of website objects. In fact, without a parameter that specifies a scope, the *Get-SPWeb* cmdlet returns an error.

Get-SPWeb followed by a URL returns an object that references a single website, as in the following example:

```
Get-SPWeb http://intranet.contoso.com/sites/Sales/Blogs
```

Get-SPWeb followed by the *-Site* parameter retrieves a collection of websites in the specified site collection. For example, the following command retrieves the websites in the intranet site collection:

```
Get-SPWeb -Site http://intranet.contoso.com
```

The *Get-SPWeb* cmdlet limits the number of objects it returns to 200 by default. As with the *Get-SPSite* cmdlet, you can use the *-Limit* parameter to increase this limit, or you can use *-Limit All* to return all websites in a site collection.

User Interface Terminology vs. Object Model Terminology

As you've no doubt noticed in this discussion, terminology used to describe the logical hierarchy of SharePoint is different in Windows PowerShell from terminology in the user interface. That's because the SharePoint object model, which drives terminology used by developers and by the .NET Framework, has a legacy that dates back to the beginning of SharePoint time.

The terminology is particularly tricky around the word *site*. Notice the different ways in which the word *site* is used both in describing the components of SharePoint as shown in the user interface and in the object model.

USER INTERFACE AND DOCUMENTATION	OBJECT MODEL
Farm	SPFarm
Web application	SPWebApplication
Site collection	SPSite
Site, Web site, Web, subweb, subsite	SPWeb

It gets even trickier when users say something like, "I can't access my site." Is that a site collection (SPSite), Web site (SPWeb), or are they really saying that they're typing *http://intranet.contoso.com* and getting an error, in which case it may even be the web application (SPWebApplication) or DNS that needs to be examined?

It's recommended that when you discuss SharePoint—particularly when you are gathering information for troubleshooting—that you avoid the word *site* by itself. Clarify: *web application*, *site collection*, or *website*.

 Quick Check

- In the context of Windows PowerShell, what SharePoint object is an SPSsite?

Quick Check Answer

- A site collection.

Use the Pipeline to Enumerate a Specific Part of the Logical Structure

As you learned in the previous section, the *Get-SPWeb* cmdlet uses a *-Site* parameter to specify the site collection in which websites should be returned. For example, the following command retrieves all websites in the intranet site collection:

```
Get-SPWeb -Site "http://intranet.contoso.com" -Limit All
```

The *Get-SPSite* cmdlet, also discussed earlier, retrieves all site collections in the farm. If you use an *-Identity* parameter, it retrieves only matching site collections. The *-Identity* parameter is the default parameter, so the parameter name can be omitted. For example, the following command retrieves only one site collection:

```
Get-SPSite "http://intranet.contoso.com"
```

You can use the site collection returned by *Get-SPSite* instead of the *-Site* parameter of *Get-SPWeb*, as long as you pipe the site collection retrieved by *Get-SPSite* to *Get-SPWeb*. For example, the following command also retrieves all websites in the intranet site collection:

```
Get-SPSite "http://intranet.contoso.com"| Get-SPWeb -Limit All
```

You can use the pipeline to pass an object representing a specific part of the logical structure of your SharePoint farm to a cmdlet that *enumerates*, or lists, the objects contained within the passed object. For example, to list all site collections in the intranet web application, type the following command:

```
Get-SPWebApplication "http://intranet.contoso.com" | Get-SPSite -Limit -All
```

The object representing the intranet web application, retrieved by *Get-SPWebApplication*, is piped to *Get-SPSite*, which uses the object as its *Identity* parameter.

If we combine the previous two commands using the pipeline, we create the following command:

```
Get-SPWebApplication "http://intranet.contoso.com" | Get-SPSite -Limit All |
Get-SPWeb -Limit All
```

This command enumerates all websites in the intranet web application. First, the *Get-SPWebApplication* cmdlet retrieves an object representing the intranet web application. That object is piped to *Get-SPSite*, which retrieves all site collections in the intranet web application. Those objects are piped to *Get-SPWeb*, which enumerates all websites in the site collections.

To list all websites in the farm, including Central Administration, type the following command:

```
Get-SPWebApplication -IncludeCentralAdministration | Get-SPSite -Limit -All |
Get-SPWeb -Limit All
```

Discover Object Members (Methods and Properties) Using *Get-Member*

Now that you can list all websites in the farm, we need to get more specific about which sites we want to work with. Remember, a goal of this discussion is to identify blog sites in the farm, and to document when those sites were last updated. To do that, we need more detailed information about each site.

As you learned in the previous lesson, Windows PowerShell cmdlets operate on and return one or more *objects*—representations of the specified components. For example, the following command returns an object that references the Sales Blog website on the Contoso intranet:

```
Get-SPWeb "http://intranet.contoso.com/sites/Sales/Blogs"
```

Objects have *members*—most important, their *methods* and *properties*. Methods are actions—things you can do with or to the object. Properties are attributes. A special kind of property is a *collection*, which can contain zero, one, or more items.

To discover what methods and properties are exposed by a particular object, pipe the object to the *Get-Member* cmdlet. The *Get-Member* cmdlet exposes the members of an object. *Get-Member* takes an object as input. The following commands list the members of an object:

```
object | Get-Member -MemberType Methods
object | Get-Member -MemberType Properties
```

For example, to see the methods and properties of the Sales Blog website, type the following command:

```
Get-SPWeb "http://intranet.contoso.com/sites/Sales/Blogs" | Get-Member
```

The cmdlet returns all members, including methods, properties, events, and alias properties. In the scope of this discussion, you are interested only in the properties of the website. You can narrow down the output of the *Get-Member* command by adding *-MemberType Properties* for properties and *–MemberType Methods* for methods. The following commands list the methods and properties, respectively, of an object:

```
object | Get-Member –MemberType Methods
object | Get-Member –MemberType Properties
```

Among the dozens of properties exposed by an *SPWeb* object are *Url* (the website address), *WebTemplate* (the name of the template used to create the website), and *LastItemModifiedDate* (the date on which the last change to the site's content was made).

> **MORE INFO** *GET-MEMBER*
>
> The following article provides additional details regarding the *Get-Member* cmdlet: "Viewing Object Structure (Get-Member)" at *http://technet.microsoft.com/en-us/library/ dd315243.aspx*.

Write-Output

If you type the following command:

```
Get-SPWeb "http://intranet.contoso.com/sites/Sales/Blogs"
```

The URL of the Web site is returned. As you know, Windows PowerShell works with objects, but when a command completes—at the end of the pipeline—an implicit *Write-Output* cmdlet displays the default properties of the objects at the end of the pipeline. In the example shown, the default property is *Url*, and the default display format is a table.

Display Properties with *Select-Object* (Alias: *Select*)

You can change which properties are displayed at the end of the pipeline by using the *Select-Object* cmdlet, which has the alias *Select*. To display all properties of pipeline objects, add *Select ** to the end of the pipeline. For example, the following command displays all properties of the Sales Blogs website:

```
Get-SPWeb "http://intranet.contoso.com/sites/Sales/Blogs" | Select *
```

You can specify the properties that are displayed by adding property names to the *Select* cmdlet. For example, the following command displays the URL and template of the sales website:

```
Get-SPWeb "http://intranet.contoso.com/sites/Sales/Blogs"|
Select URL,WebTemplate,LastItemModifiedDate
```

If you type the following command:

```
Get-SPWebApplication | Get-SPSite -limit all | Get-SPWeb -limit all
```

all websites in the farm are displayed, except Central Administration. To display the URL and template of all websites in the farm, add the *Select* cmdlet to the pipeline. Type the following command:

```
Get-SPWebApplication | Get-SPSite -limit all | Get-SPWeb -limit all |
Select-Object URL,WebTemplate
```

 REAL WORLD *Get-SPWebApplication* **Isn't Really Necessary**

Dan Holme

In the preceding command, the *Get-SPWebApplication* cmdlet, which returns all Web applications in the farm, except Central Administration, is not really necessary. The *Get-SPSite* cmdlet returns all site collections in the farm, except Central Administration, and websites are contained in site collections. So the same result would be obtained with the following command:

```
Get-SPSite -limit all | Get-SPWeb -limit all | Select-Object
URL,WebTemplate
```

However, the *Get-SPWebApplication* cmdlet will be shown throughout this lesson for two reasons. First, it emphasizes the SharePoint logical structure and the related *Get-SP** commands. Second, *Get-SPWebApplication* is necessary if you want to include Central Administration. Add the *-IncludeCentralAdministration* parameter to *Get-SPWebApplication*, and then the resulting list of websites will include Central Administration.

MORE INFO *SELECT-OBJECT*

The following article provides additional details regarding the *Select-Object* cmdlet: "Selecting Parts of Objects (Select-Object)" at *http://go.microsoft.com/ fwlink/?LinkID=192739.*

Sort the Pipeline with *Sort-Object* (Alias: *Sort*)

As you work with larger collections of objects, you will often want to sort the results. To sort objects, you can use the *Sort-Object* cmdlet, which has the alias *Sort*. For example, the following command displays the URL and template of the all websites in the farm, sorted by template name:

```
Get-SPWebApplication | Get-SPSite -limit all | Get-SPWeb -limit all |
Select-Object URL,WebTemplate | Sort WebTemplate
```

You can add the *-Descending* parameter to the *Sort* cmdlet to sort in descending order. The default is ascending order, and there is no *-Ascending* parameter.

> **MORE INFO   SORT-OBJECT**
>
> The following article provides additional details regarding the *Sort-Object* cmdlet: "Sorting Objects" at *http://go.microsoft.com/fwlink/?LinkID=192740*.

Display Results with *Format-Table* and *Format-List* (Aliases: *ft* and *fl*)

The format of the output of cmdlets depends somewhat on how many properties of how many objects are returned. Some of the commands shown in previous sections return properties as lists, and others return properties as tables.

You can specify a particular display format using the *Format-List* (alias *fl*) and *Format-Table* (alias *ft*) cmdlets. For example, the following command displays the URL and template of the all websites in the farm, sorted by template name and formatted as a list:

```
Get-SPWebApplication | Get-SPSite -limit all | Get-SPWeb -limit all |
Select-Object URL,WebTemplate | Sort WebTemplate | Format-List
```

> **NOTE   FORMAT-LIST ADDS AN IMPLICIT SELECT ***
>
> Using *Format-List* (or *fl*) at the end of the pipeline adds an implicit *Select ***. All properties are returned. If you want to limit properties returned, add the properties to the *Select* cmdlet.

> **MORE INFO   FORMAT COMMANDS**
>
> The following article provides additional details regarding the *Format-** cmdlets: "Using Format Commands to Change Output View" at *http://go.microsoft.com/fwlink/?LinkID=192741*.

Manage Output Formats

Windows PowerShell can save, export, and convert objects to a wide variety of formats. Some of the most useful include the following:

- Comma-separated value (CSV) files
- Extensible Markup Language (XML) files
- The GridView

To save output to a CSV file, add | *Export-CSV <filename>* to the end of the pipeline.

You can add | *ConvertTo-XML* to the end of the pipeline to convert output to an XML object. An XML object is not immediately viewable because it is an object, not the text output of an XML file. Therefore, you must save the pipeline, and thereby save the XML file. Follow this template:

```
( command | ConvertTo-XML ).Save("filename")
```

For example, the following command creates an XML file consisting of the URL and template of all the websites in the farm, sorted by template name:

```
(Get-SPWebApplication | Get-SPSite -limit all | Get-SPWeb -limit all |
Select-Object URL,WebTemplate | Sort WebTemplate |
ConvertTo-XML).Save("C:\Users\SP_Admin\Desktop\SharePointWebsiteTemplates.xml")
```

Windows PowerShell 2.0 includes an Integrated Scripting Environment (ISE), which provides a datagrid view application. You must make sure that the Windows PowerShell ISE feature is installed. If it is not, add the ISE feature by using Server Manager's Add Features Wizard.

The following example outputs to the datagrid view application:

```
Get-SPWebApplication | Get-SPSite -limit all | Get-SPWeb -limit all |
Select-Object URL,WebTemplate | Sort WebTemplate |
Out-GridView -Title "Web Site Templates Report"
```

The resulting datagrid is shown in Figure 2-4.

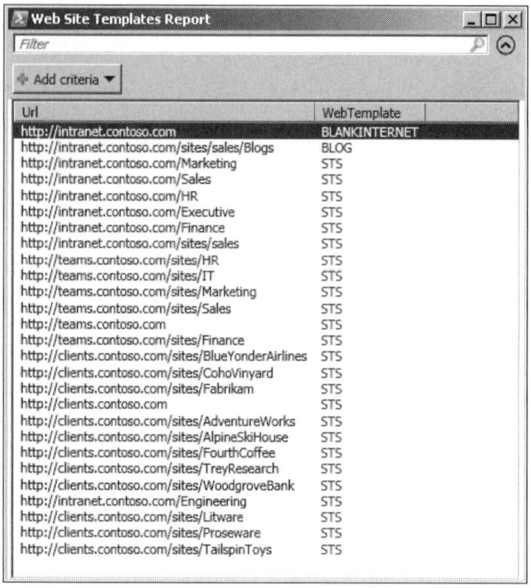

FIGURE 2-4 Datagrid view

> **MORE INFO   OUT-* CMDLETS**
>
> The following article provides additional details regarding the *Out-** cmdlets:
> "Redirecting Data with Out-* Cmdlets" at *http://go.microsoft.com/fwlink/?LinkID=192742*.

Filter the Pipeline with *Where-Object* (Aliases: *Where, ?*)

Sometimes you need to work with a subset of objects. In the previous topic, for example, the *Get-SPWeb* cmdlet returned all websites. You sorted the results by the template used for the website, but what if you wanted to return only websites that were based on the Blog site definition?

The *Where-Object* cmdlet filters objects in the pipeline. Subsequent cmdlets in the pipeline operate on only the objects that made it through the filter. For example, the following command retrieves all websites in the farm that are based on the Blog site definition by using the *WebTemplate* property of the *SPWeb* object:

```
Get-SPWebApplication | Get-SPSite -Limit All | Get-SPWeb -Limit All |
Where-Object { $_.WebTemplate -eq "BLOG"}
```

The filter—the criterion against which websites are being evaluated—is an *expression* surrounded by curly braces. The expression states that an object's *WebTemplate* property must be equal to "BLOG." If a website fails to meet this criterion, it is removed from the pipeline.

Notice the use of the special variable, *$_*. The special variable *$_* represents the current object in the pipeline. A collection of all websites in the farm is piped to *Where-Object* from *Get-SPWeb*. *Where-Object*'s job is to filter the pipeline, allowing only websites that use the blog template through the filter. You can imagine that *Where-Object* loops through each website in the collection and tests the website against the criterion. The special variable *$_* represents the current website at each iteration of *Where-Object*.

> **MORE INFO** **FILTERING WITH *WHERE-OBJECT***
>
> The following article provides additional details regarding the *Where-Object* cmdlet: "*Removing Objects from the Pipeline (Where-Object)*" at *http://go.microsoft.com/ fwlink/?LinkID=192743*.

Server-Side Filtering Using *-Filter*

When you perform filtering using the *Where-Object* cmdlet, Windows PowerShell retrieves all objects from the server and then filters the objects locally on the client computer. In the example shown previously, all objects are retrieved by the *Get-SPWeb* cmdlet, and then the Windows PowerShell client must filter the objects. You can reduce the burden on the server by using server-side filtering whenever possible. A limited number of cmdlets support a *-Filter* parameter, which uses server-side filtering.

The *SPWeb* object can be filtered server-side for the *Title* and *Template* properties. The *SPSite* and *SPSiteAdministration* objects can be filtered server-side for *Owner*, *SecondaryContact*, and *LockState*.

Because you have the option in this example of using server-side filtering, it is recommended you do so. For example, the following command retrieves the websites that are based on the Blog site definition by using server-side filtering of the *SPWeb* object:

```
Get-SPWebApplication | Get-SPSite -Limit All | Get-SPWeb -Limit All -Filter {$_.Template
-eq "BLOG#0"}
```

You might have noticed that the expression in the server-side filter looks for a *Template* property equal to "BLOG#0." This is different from the filter we used on the client, which looked for a *WebTemplate* property equal to "BLOG". "BLOG" is the *Title* property of the template; "BLOG#0" is the *Name* of the template.

Operators

In the filter expressions shown earlier, you might have noticed the *-eq* comparison operator, which means *equals*. The following operators are commonly used in expressions:

- **-lt** Less than
- **-le** Less than or equal to
- **-gt** Greater than
- **-ge** Greater than or equal to
- **-eq** Equal to
- **-ne** Not equal to
- **-like** Like; uses wildcards for pattern matching
- **-and** Logical and
- **-or** Logical or

Build an Effective Pipeline

As objects are passed through the pipeline of a Windows PowerShell command or script, there is a common approach and order to working with those objects:

- **Get** Use the Get verb to retrieve objects.
- **Filter** Use the Where cmdlet to filter objects so that the only objects remaining in the pipeline are those with which you want to work. In the few cases where server-side filtering is available, add a *-Filter* parameter to the *Get* commands.
- **Manipulate** Do something to the objects by using cmdlets appropriate for the type of objects in the pipeline.
- **Select** Use the Select cmdlet to select the properties of objects that you want to output.
- **Sort** Use the Sort cmdlet to sort the results, before output.
- **Output** Use the *Format-**, *Export-**, and *Out-** cmdlets to produce output in the desired format. If you want to convert the pipeline object(s) to a specific format, you can use the *Convert-** cmdlets to do so, and then use the Save method of the pipeline to save an object to a file. An example is shown earlier in which pipeline output is converted to an XML object, and then saved to an XML file.

Although the preceding list shows pipeline activities in a typical and effective sequence, many Windows PowerShell commands will not include all activities listed.

Examine the following example:

```
Get-SPWebApplication | Get-SPSite -Limit ALL | Get-SPWeb -Limit ALL |
Where-Object { $_.WebTemplate -eq "BLOG"} |
Select URL,Title,WebTemplate,LastItemModifiedDate | Sort LastItemModifiedDate |
Export-CSV desktop\BlogActivityReport.csv
```

This command does the following:

- Gets objects, specifically all websites in the farm

  ```
  Get-SPWebApplication | Get-SPSite -Limit ALL | Get-SPWeb -Limit ALL
  ```

- Filters the pipeline so that only websites that use the Blog template remain

  ```
  Where-Object { $_.WebTemplate -eq "BLOG"}
  ```

- Selects properties of the websites

  ```
  Select URL,Title,WebTemplate,LastItemModifiedDate
  ```

- Sorts the results by the date at which the last item in the Web site was modified

  ```
  Sort LastItemModifiedDate
  ```

- Exports the results to a .csv file

  ```
  Export-CSV desktop\BlogActivityReport.csv
  ```

Create a SharePoint Intranet Using Windows PowerShell

You can use Windows PowerShell to create logical components of SharePoint, just as you did by using Central Administration in Chapter 1.

Create a Web Application Using *New-SPWebApplication*

The following example shows the use of the *New-SPWebApplication* cmdlet to create a new web application:

```
New-SPWebApplication -Name <Name> -Port <Port> -HostHeader <HostHeader> -URL <URL>
-ApplicationPool <ApplicationPool> -ApplicationPoolAccount <ApplicationPoolAccount>
-DatabaseName <DatabaseName>
```

Where:

- *<Name>* is the name of the new web application.
- *<Port>* is the port on which the web application will be created in IIS.
- *<HostHeader>* is the host header, in the format *server.domain.com*.

  Note that the *Get-Help* documentation for the cmdlet states that the format for *<HostHeader>* is *http://server.domain.com*. The documentation is incorrect.

- *<URL>* is the public (load-balanced) URL for the web application.
- *<ApplicationPool>* is the name of the application pool.

- *<ApplicationPoolAccount>* is the managed account that the application pool will use. This parameter is required if you are specifying an *<ApplicationPool>* that does not already exist. Use the *Get-SPManagedAccount* cmdlet as shown in the following example. If the *<ApplicationPool>* already exists, do not include this parameter.

- *<DatabaseName>* is the name for the first content database for the web application.

For example, the following command creates the Intranet Web application with configuration similar to the intranet that was created by using Central Administration in Chapter 1.

```
New-SPWebApplication -Name "Contoso Intranet" -Port 80
-HostHeader "intranet.contoso.com" -URL "http://intranet.contoso.com:80"
-ApplicationPool "SharePoint Web Applications"
-ApplicationPoolAccount (Get-SPManagedAccount "CONTOSO\SP_WebApps")
-DatabaseName "SharePoint_Content_Intranet"
```

The command creates a new application pool. If the application pool already exists, you would not include the *-ApplicationPoolAccount* parameter and value.

Delete a Web Application

To delete a web application, use the *Remove-SPWebApplication* cmdlet. For example, the following command deletes the intranet web application, including the IIS Web site and the content databases:

```
Remove-SPWebApplication http://intranet.contoso.com
-DeleteIISSite -RemoveContentDatabase -Confirm:$false
```

The verb that is used to delete a web application is *Remove*, not *Delete*. In fact, *Delete* is not a valid Windows PowerShell verb. For each object that you can create in this lesson using a *Create-SP** cmdlet, there is an equivalent *Remove-SP** cmdlet.

Note the use of the *-Confirm:$false* parameter. The *-Confirm* parameter is common to all Windows PowerShell commands that have potentially detrimental effects. The default is to confirm an action (*-Confirm:$true*); the cmdlet will prompt for confirmation. Specifying *-Confirm:$false* suppresses such prompts.

You can also use the *-WhatIf* parameter to simulate a command and report its effects. The *-WhatIf* parameter is particularly helpful when you are performing a command on a variable or collection of objects so that you know exactly what is being done to which objects.

Create a Site Collection Using *New-SPSite*

The following example shows the use of the *New-SPSite* cmdlet to create a new site collection.

```
New-SPSite -Url "<URL for the new site collection>"
-ContentDatabase <Content Database Name> -Name "<Name for Top-Level Site>"
-OwnerAlias "<domain\user>" -Template <Template>
```

Where:

- *<URL>* is the URL of the site collection you want to create.

- *<Content Database Name>* is the name of the content database within which the site collection should be created. This parameter is optional.

- *<Name>* is the name of the top-level website. The name will appear in the title and heading of the top-level website.

- The *-OwnerAlias* parameter's *<domain\user>* value defines the primary site collection administrator. The *-SecondaryOwnerAlias* parameter is used to define the secondary site collection administrator.

- *<Template>* specifies the site definition for the top-level site—for example, BLANKINTERNET#0, the Publishing Site, or STS#0, the Team Site.

For example, the following command creates a site collection at the root of the intranet web application and creates a top-level site with the Publishing site definition.

```
New-SPSite -Url "http://intranet.contoso.com" -Name "Contoso Intranet" -OwnerAlias
"CONTOSO\SP_Admin" -Template "BLANKINTERNET#0"
```

List Available Site Definitions

How do you know which value of *<Template>* to use? Type the following command for a list of available site definitions:

```
Get-SPWebTemplate
```

The *Name* column contains the value that you use when configuring a new site collection's top-level site or when creating a new website.

Create a Website

The following example shows the use of the *New-SPWeb* cmdlet to create a new website:

```
New-SPWeb <Identity> -Name <Name> -Template "STS#0"
```

Where:

- *<Identity>* is the URL of the new website.

- *<Name>* is the name of the website.

- *<Template>* specifies the site definition for the website, for example, BLANKINTERNET#0, the Publishing Site, BLOG#0, the Blog Site, or STS#0, the Team Site.

For example, the following command creates a child website for a company blog on the intranet website:

```
New-SPWeb "http://intranet.contoso.com/Blogs" -Name "Contoso Blogs" -Template "BLOG#0"
```

Variables

As you begin to find and create Windows PowerShell commands and scripts for real-world scenarios, you must understand the concept of *variables*. Variables are memory locations that store a value or object and are represented in Windows PowerShell by a name that starts with a dollar sign ($).

To assign a variable—that is, to create and define a variable—simply use the following syntax:

```
$variable = value
```

For example, the following script stops the SharePoint Timer service:

```
$service = "SPTimerV4"
Get-Service $service | Stop-Service
```

The result is the same as the one-liner shown earlier. However, by separating the name of the service from the line that performs the action of finding and stopping the service, you can more easily modify the script. Or you could use the *Read-Host* cmdlet to prompt a user for the name of a process, instead of hard-wiring the name of the process into the script.

To assign a string value to a variable, enclose the value in single or double quotation marks, as shown earlier. Variables can also store one or more objects. Examine the following script:

```
$websites = Get-SPSite http://intranet.contoso.com -Limit ALL | Get-SPWeb -Limit ALL
$websites | Select name, URL, WebTemplate
```

In this example, the variable *$websites* is set to the collection of processes named *iexplore*. The variable is then used in the following command, which reports the name, URL, and template of each website in *$websites*.

Windows PowerShell has built-in variables, including the following:

- **$true**   Boolean true
- **$false**   Boolean false
- **$error**   Contains the error object of the last error

Windows PowerShell also has automatic variables, including the $_ variable you encountered earlier in this lesson.

MORE INFO   VARIABLES

The following article provides additional details regarding variables: "Using Variables to Store Objects" at *http://go.microsoft.com/fwlink/?LinkID=192734*.

Iterate with *ForEach-Object* (Aliases: *%, ForEach*)

One of the strengths of Windows PowerShell is the ease with which you can perform an operation on multiple objects. Many cmdlets automatically *iterate*, or loop, through objects in the pipeline. Look at the following example:

```
Get-SPWebApplication | Get-SPSite -Limit ALL | Get-SPWeb -Limit ALL
```

This command returns all websites in the farm except for Central Administration. The *Get-SPWeb* cmdlet receives a collection of *SPSite* (site collection) objects from the *Get-SPSite* cmdlet. It iterates through each site collection, returning a collection of websites in that site collection.

However, some cmdlets cannot operate on multiple objects. For example, the *Enable-SPFeature* cmdlet turns on a SharePoint feature for the scope, such as a website, site collection, or farm. The scope is specified by the cmdlet's *-Url* parameter. For example, to enable the content rating feature for the Contoso intranet site collection, type the following command:

```
Enable-SPFeature "Ratings" -Url "http://intranet.contoso.com"
```

This cmdlet cannot operate on more than one object. Therefore, if you wanted to turn on the content ratings feature for all site collections in the farm, you could not use the following command:

```
Get-SPWebApplication | Get-SPSite –Limit ALL | Enable-SPFeature "Ratings"
```

The command would fail because the pipeline objects—the site collections returned by *Get-SPSite*—are neither expected nor understood.

This is why the *For-Each* cmdlet is one of the most important cmdlets for working on multiple objects. *ForEach-Object* has a commonly used alias, *ForEach*, and another, super-abbreviated alias, *%*.

The *ForEach-Object* cmdlet iterates through each object in the pipeline, performing one or more actions that are contained in a *script block*. The script block is enclosed in curly braces.

For example, the following command enables the Ratings feature for all site collections in the farm:

```
Get-SPWebApplication | Get-SPSite –Limit ALL |
ForEach-Object { Enable-SPFeature "Ratings" -Url $_.url }
```

Notice the use of the *$_* special variable. Again, this represents the current object in the pipeline. The *ForEach-Object* cmdlet is iterating through all objects in the pipeline, passing each object, one at a time, to the *Enable-SPFeature* cmdlet. The *Enable-SPFeature* cmdlet accepts a URL as a scope, and the *-Url* parameter's value is set to the *URL* attribute of the current site collection.

You might notice a similarity to the *Where-Object* cmdlet that was discussed earlier. *Where-Object* applies a filter to all objects in the pipeline, and the examples you examined used similar syntax, with curly braces surrounding an expression that used the *$_* special variable.

MORE INFO **ITERATION WITH *FOREACH-OBJECT***

The following article provides additional details regarding iteration with *ForEach-Object*: "Repeating a Task for Multiple Objects (ForEach-Object)" at *http://go.microsoft.com/fwlink/?LinkID=192744*.

Create Multiple Websites with a Windows PowerShell Script

Examine the following script, which creates intranet sites for HR, Marketing, and Finance:

```
$departments = ("HR", "Marketing", "Finance")
ForEach($dept in $departments)
{
New-SPWeb -Url http://intranet.contoso.com/$dept –Name "$dept" -Template "STS#0"
}
```

This topic examines this script line by line.

```
$departments = ("HR", "Marketing", "Finance")
```

This line creates an *array*—a collection of multiple items. In this case, the items are string values. The array items are separated by commas. The parentheses around the items are optional, but they make it easier to read. The array is assigned to the variable, *$departments*. You have learned that variables always start with a dollar sign ($), and the name of the variable can be anything except for a reserved word (such as *true*).

```
ForEach($dept in $departments)
```

This line starts the iteration. *ForEach* executes the script block for each value in the array variable *$departments*. The current object in the array during each iteration is assigned to the variable *$dept*. During each iteration, *$dept* contains the current string value—the current department.

The script block is enclosed in curly braces.

```
{
```

The left brace begins the script block.

```
New-SPWeb -Url http://intranet.contoso.com/$dept –Name "$dept" "-Template "STS#0"
```

The *$dept* variable is used to create a unique URL for each department's website—the variable is the last element of the URL. The *$dept* variable is also used to create a unique name for each website.

```
}
```

The right brace ends the script block.

A blank line is at the end of the script. If you are entering the script directly in the Windows PowerShell console, you must enter a blank line to begin the execution of the script.

Iterate with the *For-Each* Statement

A confession: I slipped in a new element without telling you. In the previous topic's script, we used *ForEach*, but this is *not* the *ForEach* alias of the *ForEach-Object* cmdlet you learned about earlier in this lesson. This is the *ForEach statement*.

The distinction is small but important. The *ForEach-Object* cmdlet, or its alias *ForEach*, typically operates in the middle of a pipeline, iterating through a collection of objects in the pipeline, and executing a script block for each object. The *ForEach* statement typically operates at the beginning of the pipeline, creating a collection of objects and then iterating through the collection, executing the script block for each object. So although *ForEach-Object* is piped the objects with which it works, the *ForEach* statement has its own objects—in this case, an array of string values of department names.

As a new Windows PowerShell user, you can take solace in the fact that the practical effect of the two is very similar. But the subtle differences between the statement and the cmdlet will arise as you learn more about Windows PowerShell, so it's worth knowing that *ForEach* can be either a statement or a cmdlet.

Windows PowerShell Scripts

Windows PowerShell scripts can be entered directly in the console, as you learned in the previous topic. More traditionally, scripts are saved as text files with a .ps1 extension.

Read and Create Scripts

As you discover Windows PowerShell scripts that others have written, you'll find that many are not written in ways that make them easy to read or interpret. Some people make a sport out of making scripts more obtuse than they need to be, and of creating *one-liners*—a complex script in which each command line is separated by a semicolon (;).

In Windows PowerShell, the semicolon is used to combine separate commands into a single line. The following one-liner would generate websites for two more departments on the Contoso intranet:

```
$departments = ("Manufacturing", "Purchasing") ; ForEach($dept in $departments)
{ New-SPWeb -Url http://intranet.contoso.com/$dept -Name "$dept" -Template "STS#0" }
```

As you can see, combining lines makes a script difficult to read. It is a best practice to keep commands on separate lines.

Some people overuse aliases, making it difficult for others to make sense of the script. This is particularly true for single- and double-character aliases such as % (*ForEach-Object*), and ? (*Where-Object*). Aliases reduce the time it takes to type a single command directly into the console, but they reduce readability. If you're only going to execute a command one time, use an alias, but if you are documenting a command or creating a script, use the full cmdlet name or a readable alias so that when you return to the script in the future, you can easily interpret the script's functionality. Don't forget that you can always use tab completion to make it easier to type cmdlet and parameter names into the console.

Run Windows PowerShell Scripts

By default, Windows PowerShell scripts are not allowed to run. This is done to prevent malicious scripts from damaging your environment. Although that's the default, the chances are good that you will want to change the setting.

The Windows PowerShell *ExecutionPolicy* property determines which scripts are allowed to run. *ExecutionPolicy* can be set to one of the following values:

- **Restricted**   No scripts can run. *Restricted* is the default execution policy for Windows PowerShell.
- **AllSigned**   Only signed scripts can be run. Scripts, including scripts that you write, must be signed by a trusted publisher.
- **RemoteSigned**   Scripts that are downloaded from the Internet must be signed by a trusted publisher. Other scripts can run without a signature. Installing SharePoint 2010 changes the default execution policy to *RemoteSigned*.
- **Unrestricted**   All scripts can run. However, if you run an unsigned script that was downloaded from the Internet, you are prompted for confirmation before it runs.
- **Bypass**   All scripts can run, and there are no blocks, warnings, or prompts.
- **Undefined**   The execution policy in the current scope is removed. This value will not remove an execution policy that is set in a Group Policy scope.

To determine the current *ExecutionPolicy*, type the following command:

```
Get-ExecutionPolicy
```

To allow locally created scripts to run, type the following command:

```
Set-ExecutionPolicy -RemoteSigned
```

As you enable the execution of scripts, reduce the level of trust by removing the requirement for signatures, and disable warnings and blocks, security risks increase, of course.

When you begin to run Windows PowerShell scripts, you are likely to encounter several common challenges. The first challenges relate to the fact that Windows PowerShell will not execute a script by name only—it must know the path of the script.

You can put a script in a folder that is included in the *Path* variable. Type **$env:path** to examine the current *Path*. If a script is in the *Path*, you can launch the script by name. Alternately, put the script in the current folder and type **.\scriptname**, or type the full path and filename of the script.

If a specified path or filename of a script includes a space, you must surround the path with quotes and precede it with the *Call* statement or its alias, *&*, as shown in the following example:

```
& "C:\Scripts\My Folder\Script.ps1"
```

To execute a script from the Command Prompt, the Run command, or a scheduled task, use the following template:

```
powershell.exe -noexit &'path\script.ps1'
```

The *-noexit* parameter causes the Windows PowerShell console to remain open after the script executes, so that you can observe the results of the script. The *-noexit* parameter must immediately follow the *Powershell.exe* command. If you want the script to execute silently, and you do not need to see its output, simply exclude the parameter.

You can use Task Scheduler to schedule a Windows PowerShell script. The command of the scheduled task is *Powershell.exe*. The argument is *-command 'path\script.ps1'*. Of course, the scripts run only if the execution policy allows. You will schedule a Windows PowerShell backup script in Chapter 11, "Implementing Business Continuity."

Local, Global, and Remote Commands

The two categories of SharePoint cmdlets are local and global. Local cmdlets affect something on a single SharePoint server. For example, to start a service on a server, use the *Start-SPServiceInstance* cmdlet. To connect a new SharePoint server to a farm, use the *Connect-SPConfigurationDatabase* cmdlet. To perform a command on multiple servers in a farm—for example, to start a service on multiple servers—you need to iterate through the servers in the farm.

Global cmdlets affect the farm as a whole, generally by making changes to a SQL Server database. For example, when you set the property of a web application using the *Set-SPWebApplication* cmdlet, the property is written to the content database and thus affects all servers hosting that web application. You do not need to configure each server individually. Similarly, when you create a new site collection with *New-SPSite*, the site collection is available to all SharePoint servers.

The SharePoint Management Shell Windows PowerShell Profile

SharePoint 2010 Management Shell loads a Windows PowerShell profile located in the SharePoint root, by default: C:\Program Files\Common Files\Microsoft Shared\Web Server Extensions\14\CONFIG\POWERSHELL\Registration\SharePoint.ps1. A Windows PowerShell profile is a script that configures the initial user environment for Windows PowerShell. In the case of SharePoint 2010 Management Shell, the profile does three important things:

- **Loads the SharePoint snap-ins**   The SharePoint 2010 Management Shell profile loads the SharePoint snap-ins.

  If you run Windows PowerShell instead of SharePoint 2010 Management Shell, you cannot actually perform any SharePoint tasks because the snap-ins are not loaded by the default profile. To load the SharePoint snap-in, you must run the following command:

  ```
  Add-PSSnapin Microsoft.SharePoint.PowerShell
  ```

> **NOTE**   **REFLECTION IS NO LONGER NECESSARY IN SHAREPOINT 2010**
>
> Another way to add SharePoint functionality to Windows PowerShell is to use a process called *reflection*, through which you load the SharePoint .dll files directly. This was required in SharePoint 2007 but is not recommended in SharePoint 2010 now that the SharePoint snap-in is available.

- **Adds the Stsadm (*SharePoint Root*/BIN folder) to the path**   The SharePoint snap-in adds the path to the Stsadm.exe command to the *Path* environment variable. This allows you to use Stsadm to perform tasks, in addition to Windows PowerShell.

- **Sets the *PSThread* option to *ReuseThread***   This is a setting that improves the utilization of memory in Windows PowerShell and reduces the likelihood of memory leaks. In Windows PowerShell, each line—each command—is started in its own thread, or process. When *ThreadOptions* are set to *ReuseThread,* each command is run in the same thread. If you use Windows PowerShell, you must run the following command:

  ```
  $Host.Runspace.ThreadOptions="ReuseThread"
  ```

> **MORE INFO**   **PSTHREAD OPTION**
>
> The following article provides additional details regarding *PSThread*: "PSThreadOptions Enumeration" at *http://go.microsoft.com/fwlink/?LinkId=183145*.

Delegate Permissions to Use Windows PowerShell

To use Windows PowerShell to administer SharePoint 2010, an administrator must be assigned the *SharePoint_Shell_Access* role on any databases against which Windows PowerShell will be used. For example, to perform tasks that read or manipulate data in the configuration database, an administrator must have the *SharePoint_Shell_Access* role for the configuration database. Likewise, to work with a specific site collection, the administrator must have the *SharePoint_Shell_Access* or *db_owner* role for the appropriate content database.

Additionally, the administrator's account must be a member of the WSS_ADMIN_WPG local group on all servers in the farm.

To assign these two roles, and thereby to delegate permission to use Windows PowerShell, you can and should use the *Add-SPAdmin* cmdlet. The process is straightforward.

DELEGATE PERMISSIONS WITH ADD-SPSHELLADMIN

1. Open SharePoint 2010 Management Console.

2. Use the *Add-SPShellAdmin* cmdlet to grant a user the ability to use Windows PowerShell against that content database. Use the following example:

```
Add-SPShellAdmin -username <DOMAIN\user>
-database (Get-SPContentDatabase <Content Database Name>)
```

So, with just one command, you can give a user *the SharePoint_Shell_Access* role on the database and add the user to the WSS_ADMIN_WPG local group on each server in the farm. If the user is currently logged on, the user will of course have to log off and log back on for the new local group membership to take effect.

Of course, your account must have permissions to delegate Windows PowerShell access. To successfully run *Add-SPShellAdmin*, your account must have the *securityadmin* server role for the SQL Server instance and the *db_owner* role for the database, and you must be in the Administrators group of each server in the farm. In other words, you must be a high-level administrator to delegate to another user the ability to use Windows PowerShell. Practically speaking, you'll likely be an administrator of the SQL Server and of each server in the farm, though technically speaking you don't need *quite* that much power.

When you delegate Windows PowerShell access to a content database, you also delegate access to the configuration database. This is required, and it's not possible to delegate access only to a content database and not to the configuration database.

If you use Windows PowerShell to create a content database, your account is automatically given the *db_owner* role for the database.

You must also be a site collection owner, as defined in Central Administration, to use Windows PowerShell against a site collection in the content database.

To assign a site collection owner by using Windows PowerShell, follow this example:

```
Set-SPSiteAdministration <SiteCollectionURL> -OwnerAlias <DOMAIN\user>
-SecondaryOwnerAlias <DOMAIN\user>
```

Where:

- *<SiteCollectionURL>* is the URL of the site collection.
- The *-OwnerAlias* parameter's *<DOMAIN\User>* is the primary site collection administrator.
- The *-SecondaryOwnerAlias* parameter's *<DOMAIN\User>* is the secondary site collection administrator.

Quick Check

- If you are a member of the Farm Administrators group, can you use Windows PowerShell to administer SharePoint?

Quick Check Answer

- No. You must be delegated permission to use Windows PowerShell. You can delegate permission by using the *Add-SPShellAdmin* cmdlet.

PRACTICE **Administer SharePoint Using Windows PowerShell**

Practices are designed to guide you through important procedures. The instructions in the Training Kit are high-level instructions that will challenge you to think carefully and to apply the procedures that are covered in this lesson, and elsewhere in the Training Kit. If you need assistance, consult the detailed, step-by-step instructions in the Practice Answers on the companion media.

In this practice, you will explore Windows PowerShell functionality. You will then build a SharePoint intranet web application, site collection, and site. Finally, you will run reports that document your SharePoint implementation.

Prepare for the Practice

Before you perform this practice, you must ensure that your lab environment has been built according to the instructions found in the Introduction to this Training Kit. You must also have performed the practice in Lesson 1 of this chapter.

EXERCISE 1 Use Familiar Commands in Windows PowerShell

In this exercise, you start SharePoint 2010 Management Shell and use commands with which you are already familiar.

1. Log on to SP2010-WFE1 as **CONTOSO\SP_Admin**.
2. Start SharePoint 2010 Management Shell using the Run As Administrator option.
3. Type **dir** and then press Enter.

4. Use the *Get-Alias* cmdlet to answer the following question: For which cmdlet is *dir* an alias?

5. Type **ipconfig /all** and then press Enter.

6. Type **cls** and then press Enter.

7. Type **stsadm -help**.

EXERCISE 2 Delegate Permissions to Use Windows PowerShell to Administer SharePoint

In this exercise, you discover that you do not have permission to use Windows PowerShell to administer an existing content database. You then grant the SP_Admin account permissions to use Windows PowerShell to administer that database.

1. Create a report of all websites in the Farm, including Central Administration.

   An error appears.

   Question: What does the error suggest is the cause of the problem? How can you address this problem?

2. Remediate the problem that you encountered in the previous step.

   Tip: To solve the problem, you will need to assign appropriate permissions to the CONTOSO\SP_Admin account. To assign those permissions, you will need to run a Windows PowerShell cmdlet using a more privileged account, specifically CONTOSO\ Administrator with the password *Pa$$w0rd*.

3. Close all instances of SharePoint 2010 Management Shell.

4. Start SharePoint 2010 Management Shell with the SP_Admin using the Run As Administrator option.

5. Create a report of all websites in the Farm, including Central Administration.

EXERCISE 3 Identify and Explore a Windows PowerShell Cmdlet

In this exercise, you identify the command needed to create a new web application, and you explore its built-in documentation.

1. List the SharePoint cmdlets for Windows PowerShell.

2. List the cmdlets that perform tasks related to web applications.

   Question: What noun represents SharePoint Web applications?

   Question: Which cmdlet creates a SharePoint Web application?

3. Display the summary help documentation for the *New-SPWebApplication* cmdlet.

4. Display usage examples for the cmdlet.

   Tip: You can press Up Arrow to select the previously entered command, and then type the additional parameter.

5. Display detailed help for the cmdlet.

   Question: What parameter is required only if the application pool does not already exist?

EXERCISE 4   Create a Web Application Using Windows PowerShell

In this exercise, you create a web application, site collection, and top-level site by using Windows PowerShell.

1. Create a web application called *teams.contoso.com*. Use the following specifications and guidance:

   - Name: Contoso Teams
   - Port: 80
   - Host header: *http://teams.contoso.com*
   - URL: *http://teams.contoso.com:80*
   - Application pool: SharePoint Web Applications
   - Content database name: SharePoint_Content_Teams

2. List the available SharePoint website templates.

   Question: What is the name of the team site template?

3. Create a site collection at the root of the teams.contoso.com web application. Use the following specifications and guidance:

   - URL: *http://teams.contoso.com*
   - Content database for the site collection: SharePoint_Content_Teams
   - Name: Contoso Teams
   - Primary site collection administrator: CONTOSO\SP_Admin
   - Template: the Team Site template

4. Create a team site for the Finance department in the *teams.contoso.com* web application. Use the following specifications and guidance:

   - URL: *http://teams.contoso.com/Finance*
   - Name: Finance
   - Template: the Team Site template

5. Create a team site for the Marketing department in the *teams.contoso.com* web application. Use tab completion to type the cmdlet and parameter names more efficiently. Use the following specifications and guidance:

   - URL: *http://teams.contoso.com/Marketing*
   - Name: Marketing
   - Template: STS#0

6. Create a new blog site under the Marketing site in the teams.contoso.com web application. Use the following specifications and guidance:

   - URL: *http://teams.contoso.com/Marketing/Blogs*
   - Name: Marketing Blogs
   - Template: the Blog template

EXERCISE 5 Generate Reports About Your SharePoint Farm

In this exercise, you generate reports about the websites in your SharePoint farm.

1. List all websites in the *teams.contoso.com* web application. Create a command that returns all websites in the web application even if the web application contains many site collections and websites.

2. Assign the Marketing Blogs website to a variable named *$website*.

3. Enumerate the members of an *SPWeb* object by using the *$website* variable and the *Get-Member* cmdlet.

4. Enumerate only the properties of an *SPWeb* object by using the *$website* variable and the *Get-Member* cmdlet.

5. List all of the properties and their values of the Marketing Blogs site by using the *$website* variable and the *Select-Object* cmdlet.

   Question: Which property exposes the fact that the website is a blog?

6. Create a report of all websites in the farm, including Central Administration. In the report, show the URL, template, and the last date that the site was updated.

EXERCISE 6 Create Websites by Using a Windows PowerShell Script

In this exercise, you create and execute a Windows PowerShell script to provision websites in the Contoso intranet.

1. Create the following script:

```
$departments = ("HR","IT","Sales")
ForEach ($dept in $departments)
{
New-SPWeb "http://teams.contoso.com/$dept" -Name "$dept" -Template "STS#0"
}
```

2. Save the script to your desktop with the following name: **CreateSites.ps1**.

3. Run the script by using SharePoint 2010 Management Shell.

   The sites are created.

4. Produce a report of all websites in the teams.contoso.com web application.

5. Produce a report of all websites in the farm, including Central Administration.

   Type the following command, and then press Enter:

```
Get-SPWebApplication -IncludeCentralAdministration | Get-SPSite -Limit ALL |
Get-SPWeb -Limit ALL
```

EXERCISE 7 Create the CHAPTER 02 Snapshot

The CHAPTER 02 snapshot captures the state of the environment at the end of Chapter 02. Perform this procedure for each of the following virtual machines: SP2010-WFE1, CONTOSO-DC.

1. Shut down the virtual machine.

2. Unmount any ISO image currently mounted to the CD/DVD drive. Use the procedure "Unmount an ISO Image" in the Lab Environment Build Guide on the companion media.

3. Create a snapshot named CHAPTER 02. Use the procedure "Create a Snapshot" in the Lab Environment Build Guide on the companion media.

Lesson Summary

- Windows PowerShell is the preferred command-line administration and automation interface for SharePoint 2010.

- SharePoint 2010 Management Shell loads the Microsoft SharePoint PowerShell cmdlets automatically, is optimized for administering SharePoint, and supports Stsadm.

- Windows PowerShell cmdlets follow strict standards, including their *Verb-Noun* syntax with singular nouns, and their help documentation.

- The *Get-Command, Get-Help,* and *Get-Member* cmdlets enable you to discover commands, syntax, and parameters and to explore the structure of objects.

- Windows PowerShell works with .NET objects. A cmdlet returns objects and sends them down the pipeline to subsequent cmdlets or into variables for later use.

- The SharePoint object model, and therefore also Windows PowerShell cmdlets, use terminology that can be quite different than the terminology used in the user interface.

- Constructs such as variables and iterative loops enable you to build powerful scripts, which can be executed by Windows PowerShell as long as the execution policy permits scripts to run.

- You must be delegated permission to use Windows PowerShell to administer SharePoint.

Lesson Review

You can use the following questions to test your knowledge of the information in Lesson 2, "Automate SharePoint Operations with Windows PowerShell." The questions are also available on the companion CD in a practice test if you prefer to review them in electronic form.

> *NOTE* **ANSWERS**
>
> Answers to these questions and explanations of why each answer choice is right or wrong are located in the "Answers" section at the end of the book.

1. Which of the following can the *Get-SPWebApplication* cmdlet do? (Choose all that apply.)

   A. Create a website.

   B. Return an object representing a single web application.

   C. Return a collection of objects representing all web applications in the farm.

   D. Create an Excel Services service application.

2. You want to delete a site collection. Which of the following can you use?

   A. *Delete-SPSite*

   B. *Remove-SPWebApplication*

   C. *Remove-SPWeb*

   D. *Remove-SPSite*

3. You want a report of all site collections in the farm, including Central Administration. Which of the following will you need? (Choose all that apply. Each answer is part of the complete solution.)

   A. The *Get-SPWebApplication* cmdlet

   B. The *-IncludeCentralAdministration* parameter

   C. The *Get-SPSite* cmdlet

   D. The *-Limit ALL* parameter

Chapter Review

To further practice and reinforce the skills you learned in this chapter, you can perform the following tasks:

- Review the chapter summary.
- Review the list of key terms introduced in this chapter.
- Complete the case scenarios. These scenarios set up real-world situations involving the topics of this chapter and ask you to create a solution.
- Complete the suggested practices.
- Take a practice test.

Chapter Summary

- SharePoint administration can be managed and delegated to assign only the permissions and roles that are required to perform specific administrative tasks.
- SharePoint can be administered by using Central Administration, Stsadm, or Windows PowerShell.
- By using Windows PowerShell—the preferred command-line administration and automation interface for SharePoint 2010—you can perform most administrative tasks from the command line, interactively, or by executing scripts.
- Windows PowerShell is extraordinarily powerful, because it exposes and works directly upon .NET objects representing SharePoint resources. And yet, Windows PowerShell provides numerous features that makes it easy to discover, explore, and learn the cmdlets you need to perform both simple and complex tasks.

Key Terms

The following terms were introduced in this chapter. Do you know what they mean?

- cmdlet
- remoting
- pipeline
- alias
- object
- members, properties, and methods
- variable
- iterate
- first term

Case Scenario: Reporting Properties of the SharePoint Farm

In the following case scenario, you will apply what you've learned about the subjects of this chapter. You can find answers to these questions in the "Answers" section at the end of this book.

Your compliance officer has requested a weekly report of websites in the farm, and of updated activity on the sites. Additionally, she would like to know which sites are blogs, to ensure that she is able to monitor content posted on the blogs for material that is inconsistent with Contoso's Information Technology Acceptable Use Policy. She wants the reports in a format that she can sort and analyze by using Microsoft Excel. You want to generate the reports automatically, so that the reports are always available for her without requiring effort on your part.

1. What Windows PowerShell cmdlets can you use to create a list of websites in the farm along with their template and the last date on which content was modified?

2. What Windows PowerShell cmdlet can you use to save the report in a format that can be opened and analyzed by using Microsoft Excel?

3. What Windows feature can you use to automatically run the report once a week?

4. What credentials and permissions are necessary for this solution?

Suggested Practices

To help you successfully master the exam objectives presented in this chapter, complete the following tasks.

Practice 1: Explore the Security-Trimmed Administrative Interfaces

In the practice of Lesson 1, you delegated administration of service applications, site collections, and sites. SharePoint's user interface is *security-trimmed*—it removes links to tasks that you do not have permissions to perform. Log on as each of the users that were delegated permissions in the practice of Lesson 1, and browse the administrative interfaces of Central Administration and the Site Settings page of the Contoso intranet, *http://intranet.contoso.com*. Pay attention to the tasks that are—and are not—available to each of the users.

Practice 2: Administer User Roles Using Windows PowerShell

In Lesson 2, you learned how to use Windows PowerShell, and you discovered features and cmdlets that make it easy to learn how to perform new tasks. Use those features and cmdlets, including *Get-Command*, *Get-Help*, and *Get-Member*, to determine how you can delegate administration by using Windows PowerShell. How can you add or remove a user from the Farm Administrators group? How can you add or remove a site collection owner—the primary and secondary site collection administrator as defined in Central Administration? How can you add a site collection administrator to a site collection? In addition to the information provided in this chapter, search Microsoft TechNet and the Internet for more information.

Take a Practice Test

The practice tests on this book's companion media offer many options. For example, you can test yourself on just the lesson review content, or you can test yourself on all the 70-667 certification exam objectives. You can set up the test so that it closely simulates the experience of taking a certification exam, or you can set it up in study mode so that you can look at the correct answers and explanations after you answer each question.

> **MORE INFO** **PRACTICE TESTS**
>
> For details about all the practice test options available, see the "How to Use the Practice Tests" section in this book's Introduction.

CHAPTER 3

Managing Web Applications

Web applications are the top component of the logical hierarchy of SharePoint content within a farm. All user access to SharePoint content is performed within the context of a web application. Although content itself is contained within site collections and stored in content databases, web applications and their associated IIS Web sites manage important functions, including authentication and SSL encryption. Web applications also scope configuration, including important settings that enforce consistent security across all site collections in the web application. In this chapter, you will learn the procedures and settings related to web applications, and you will master important concepts including Claims Based Authentication, access mappings, and zones. In Lesson 1, you will explore, in detail, the numerous settings that you can configure when you create a web application. Lesson 2 is dedicated to managing authentication. In Lesson 3, you will learn how to configure access to web applications in more complex scenarios, in which users access web applications via more than one URL.

Exam objectives in this chapter:
- Configure SharePoint farms.
- Manage web applications.
- Manage authentication providers.

Lessons in this chapter:

Before You Begin

To complete the lessons in this chapter, you must have done the following:

- Performed the practices in Chapter 1.

REAL WORLD

Dan Holme

A web application is a SharePoint component that is closely related to and dependent on—but separate from—an IIS Web site. Thrown in the mix are access mappings and zones, each of which relate to the URLs with which a web application is accessed. The tangled relationship between these components is not seamless to manage. Vague terminology and documentation make it easy for even a seasoned SharePoint veteran to make configuration mistakes that prevent access to a website. I've worked hard in this chapter to clarify concepts and procedures that are quite confusing for many SharePoint administrators, and I've centered the discussion of these concepts and procedures around the real-world scenarios you will face as you manage SharePoint web applications in your enterprise.

Lesson 1: Configure Web Applications

Web applications are at the top of the logical hierarchy of a SharePoint farm. A SharePoint farm will typically have at least two web applications: Central Administration and a web application that contains content accessed by users, such as *http://intranet.contoso.com*.

A web application is composed of a collection of settings stored in the farm's configuration database, one or more content databases, one or more site collections containing content, and one to five zones—each supported by Internet Information Services (IIS) Web sites running with a single application pool. All of these are accessible using URLs called *access mappings* that enable a request to reach the correct SharePoint web application and enable content to be rendered properly to a user.

A diagram of the components related to a SharePoint web application is shown in Figure 3-1.

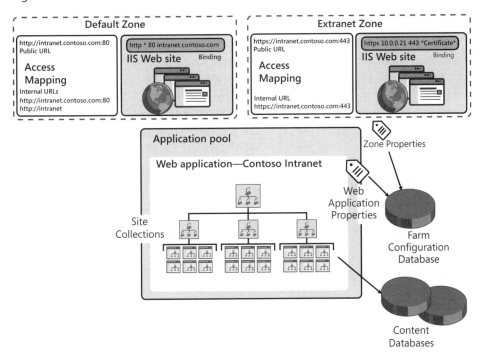

FIGURE 3-1 SharePoint web application components

In this lesson, you will learn to create a web application and to configure many web application settings. In Lesson 2, you will learn to configure authentication. And, in Lesson 3, you will learn to manage access mappings and zones.

Understand Web Applications and IIS Web Sites

When you create a web application, you create a site in Internet Information Services (IIS). An IIS Web site has *bindings*, which can include a unique IP address, a host header, or a port. Bindings enable IIS to determine which site is being requested by an inbound HTTP request.

When a user requests a page with a unique resource indicator (URI), such as *http://intranet.contoso.com/SitePages/Home.aspx*, the client creates an HTTP request packet. The client determines the IP address by querying DNS to resolve the host name—in this example, *intranet.contoso.com*. The client adds the host name to the host header field of the packet. The client then sends the packet to the server's IP address over the default HTTP port (80) unless otherwise specified. If the request is an HTTPS request, the destination port is 443 unless otherwise specified. IIS receives and parses the request and identifies that the request is for the *Contoso Intranet* IIS Web site, which is bound to port 80 with the host header *intranet.contoso.com*.

After IIS has determined the Web site from which content is being requested, it begins a series of processes that return the requested content to the client. IIS first looks into the web application's physical path, also called the *root directory*. When you create a SharePoint web application, you specify the physical path. For example, the intranet web application is stored at C:\inetpub\wwwroot\wss\VirtualDirectories\clients.contoso.com80. In traditional ASP.NET websites, actual content is stored in the root directory. However, as you learned in previous chapters, SharePoint stores content in content databases on a SQL server. IIS has no idea how to locate and access this content. However, the configuration file, Web.config, in the root directory of the IIS Web site defines the site as a SharePoint application and instructs IIS to pass the request to SharePoint.

SharePoint then parses the URI to determine which site collection and thereby which content database is being requested. SharePoint can then access the content from SQL and return the content to IIS, which then delivers the content to the user.

The request is handled by IIS and SharePoint within the context of the application pool of the IIS Web site. The application pool is an isolated memory space that is routed to one or more worker processes (w3wp.exe) that handle requests sent to a server for the sites associated with the application pool. The application pool identity is a domain user account that is registered as a managed account in SharePoint.

When you create a web application, SharePoint creates a content database and assigns the application pool identity the permissions it requires to access content. SharePoint also creates the physical path, the Web.config file, the IIS Web site, and several virtual directories.

As you will learn later in this lesson, SharePoint does not manage the configuration of a security certificate. Although SharePoint specifies that a web application uses SSL, you must install a certificate and bind the certificate to the site in IIS Manager on each server in the farm. Additionally, SharePoint does not give you the option of binding a web application to a specific IP address. If you want to bind a web application to one or more specific IP addresses, you must do so manually in IIS Manager on each server in the farm.

> **TIP   MANAGE WEB APPLICATIONS BY USING CENTRAL ADMINISTRATION OR WINDOWS POWERSHELL**
>
> Do not create or change settings directly on sites by using IIS Manager, except when assigning an IP address binding to a site or binding a certificate to a site that uses SSL. When you manage configuration with SharePoint, the settings are stored in the configuration database, and are applied to each new server that you add to the farm. If you change settings in IIS Manager, you must make the same changes on each server in the farm.

Design Considerations: One or More Web Applications

More web applications are necessary if your governance requirements must be implemented using configuration that is scoped to web applications. For example, if your governance plan requires isolation of internal and external content from cross-site scripting attacks, you can divide content into separate web applications, each of which will have a distinct IIS Web site with a unique domain name, such as *http://intranet.contoso.com* and *http://clients.contoso.com*. Doing so will also physically isolate content in separate content databases that can optionally be hosted on separate SQL servers with distinct SQL authentication configuration.

Later in this chapter, you will explore the numerous settings that are scoped to a web application. Although the importance of each setting will vary between enterprises, among the most important settings scoped to a web application are the following:

- **Service application connections**   Each web application is connected to the services it requires, such as Search. Not all scenarios require all services. For example, a small team site might not require the PerformancePoint Service Application. For performance and governance reasons, you should connect web applications only to the service applications they require.

- **Recycle Bin settings**   You can configure whether deleted items are moved to SharePoint's two-stage Recycle Bins, how long items are retained before being permanently deleted, and what storage limits will be.

- **Self-service site collection creation**   You can allow users to create site collections, which reduces administrative overhead.
- **Blocked file types**   You can configure the file types that are allowed to be uploaded within a web application.

If every scenario that you will support with SharePoint can be implemented with a single set of configuration—for example, if every scenario requires the same services, the same Recycle Bin settings, and the same settings for self-service site collection creation and blocked file types—you need only one web application. However, it is likely that some scenarios will require different sets of configuration. For example, all scenarios might require the same Recycle Bin settings as dictated by your governance plan, but you might want to block audio and video file types on the intranet web application while allowing them within a team site. To support two different collections of settings that are scoped to web applications, you must create two web applications.

In this chapter, and throughout this Training Kit, you will learn about settings that apply to a web application, to a site collection, to a content database, to zones (which you will learn about in Lesson 3), or to other components of the SharePoint logical structure. Pay attention to the scope of settings, because you must consider them when you translate your information management requirements into a SharePoint logical architecture for your enterprise.

Design Considerations: One or More Application Pools and Identities

Because the application pool is a process (w3wp.exe) and an isolated memory space, two web applications running in two separate application pools are isolated from each other. If one web application contains poorly written code that causes the site to crash or consume too many resources, the other application pool and web application will continue to function. And if security is compromised in one application pool, other application pools are not exposed.

You might think that you should create a new application pool for each new web application. In fact, the default settings on the Create New Web Application page encourage you to do just that. However, application pools are a limited resource—each running application pool requires a memory footprint and places performance overhead on the server. Microsoft supports up to 10 application pools per web server; however, the limit depends largely upon the amount of RAM allocated to front-end servers and the workload that the farm is serving: the user base and its usage characteristics. It is therefore recommended that you create web applications in a shared application pool unless there is a significant requirement for process isolation.

Each application pool has an identity—a domain user account that is used by the application pool process. When you create a new application pool, you can use an identity that is shared with other application pools, or you can assign an identity unique to the application pool. The decision of whether to use a shared or unique application pool identity depends on the level of security your governance plan requires. The two primary considerations are access and auditing.

If an application pool identity is breached, it is possible that other application pools running with the same identity might also be exposed. Therefore, if the content accessed by web applications in two application pools shares similar security profiles, you might choose to use a single identity for both application pools. If the security profiles are different, you might choose to use a separate identity for each. For example, Central Administration should run in a separate application pool because the identity used by Central Administration is the SharePoint farm service account—for example, SP_Farm—which is highly privileged. That level of privilege is not appropriate for user-facing web applications. The application pool that is used for user-facing web applications should be a different identity.

If you use unique identities for each application pool, it can be easier to review event log or audit entries and, by examining the identity reported in an event, to distinguish the specific application pool that generated an event.

As you learned in Chapter 1, "Creating a SharePoint 2010 Intranet," SharePoint 2010's managed accounts feature makes it much easier to manage password changes for accounts used by services and application pools. Therefore, it is suggested that when you create a new application pool, you consider using a unique identity; however, this is not required. In the Practice for this lesson, you will create an extranet web application for Contoso, Ltd. Because the extranet website is exposed to the Internet, you will create the web application in a separate application pool. Because the security profile of the extranet application is similar to other user-facing web applications, but is quite different than Central Administration, you will assign the new application pool the same identity as other user-facing application pools: CONTOSO\SP_WebApps. In Chapter 9, "Deploying and Upgrading to SharePoint 2010," you will learn how to configure managed accounts and how to assign and change application pool identities.

By default, service applications such as Search and Managed Metadata share a single application pool. Although this application pool is separate from the application pool shared by user-facing applications, it is recommended that all service applications share an application pool unless, again, there is a significant driver for process isolation.

Configure a New Web Application

In Chapter 1, you learned to create a web application by using Central Administration. In Chapter 2, you learned to use the *New-SPWebApplication* cmdlet to create a web application. In Chapter 9, you will learn to use the *New-SPManagedAccount* cmdlet to create a managed account, which you can then use as the application pool identity for the *–ApplicationPoolAccount* parameter of the *New-SPWebApplication* cmdlet.

You have learned that a web application is a combination of an IIS Web site and a content database. The configuration for each is stored in the configuration database of the farm. In this section, you will explore the most important settings that can be configured when you create a web application using the Create New Web Application page in Central Administration, shown in Figure 3-2.

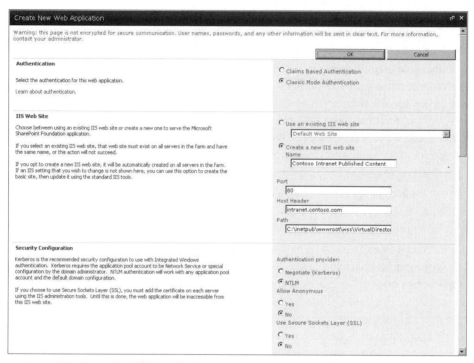

FIGURE 3-2 The Create New Web Application page

Authentication

The first setting that appears on the Create New Web Application page is Authentication. SharePoint Server 2010 offers two types of authentication:

- **Classic Mode Authentication**   Classic Mode Authentication is the same type of authentication that was used in Microsoft Office SharePoint Server 2007. Classic Mode Authentication relies on Active Directory to authenticate users.

- **Claims Based Authentication**   Claims Based Authentication is a new feature in SharePoint 2010. With Claims Based Authentication you can use Windows authentication (Active Directory); Forms Based Authentication (FBA) against an authentication provider such as Active Directory Lightweight Directory Services (AD LDS), a SQL database of users, or an ASP.NET membership provider; or Security Assertion Markup Language (SAML) tokens generated by trusted authorities such as Windows Live ID or Active Directory Federated Services 2.0 (ADFS 2.0).

If you are new to SharePoint, you should select Claims Based Authentication only if you need to implement Forms Based Authentication or SAML token-based authentication, or if the web application will use code that uses claims. Otherwise, you should select Classic Mode Authentication. Some SharePoint features, including audiences, become more difficult to implement in a web application that uses Claims Based Authentication.

You will learn about each provider and method in Lesson 2. When you understand the various authentication providers, and the nuances of configuring and managing authentication, you can make a more informed decision about whether to select Classic Mode Authentication or Claims Based Authentication when you require only Windows authentication. As you will learn in Lesson 2, you can change the authentication mode from Classic Mode Authentication to Claims Based Authentication by using Windows PowerShell.

IIS Web Site

As you've learned, when you create a SharePoint web application, you also create a corresponding site in IIS. In the Name box, type a name for the web application. This name will appear in Central Administration as the name of the web application and in IIS as the site name. Follow your organization's naming standards, which should be designed to ensure that an administrator can easily identify the purpose of a SharePoint web application or IIS Web site.

Next, in the Port box, configure the port number to which the site will be bound. By default, the Create New Web Application page specifies a random port number, but the port is usually 80 for HTTP or 443 for HTTPS.

When more than one web application is bound to a single IP address and port, a host header is required to allow IIS to route an inbound request to the correct site. Earlier in this lesson you learned that a client embeds the host name portion of the URL in the host header field of the HTTP request packet.

In the Host Header box, type the host header for the web application, which should be the fully qualified domain name (FQDN) of the web application.

Finally, you can configure the root directory by changing the default value in the Path box. The content stored in the root directory of a SharePoint site is minimal, because most content is stored in the content database(s) of the web application. Therefore, you have little reason to change the root directory, unless your governance policies require you to do so. If you do change the path, ensure that the drive letter exists on every SharePoint server in the farm. Also, verify that NTFS permissions allow the root directory to be created successfully on each server in the farm.

The settings discussed in this section are required when you create a new IIS Web site. However, you can also select the Use An Existing IIS Web Site option, and the web application will read the site configuration from IIS on the server running Central Administration. This option is rarely used. Its primary purpose is to fix a broken web application by re-creating the web application and connecting it to the previously created IIS Web site.

Note the following guidelines related to the creation of the IIS Web site for a SharePoint web application:

- It is not recommended to use flat host names without a domain name component as the host header. In other words, do not configure a host header of *http://intranet*. Instead, use *http://intranet.contoso.com*.

- When you create a new SharePoint web application, you cannot specify a unique IP address for the new IIS Web site within SharePoint. After creating the IIS Web site, you must use IIS Manager to modify the bindings of the IIS Web site so that the site is bound to an IP address. You must repeat this process on each server in the farm. This configuration is not recorded by SharePoint, and therefore it is not backed up by SharePoint. If you restore a web application by using SharePoint, you must manually reconfigure the IP address binding. Bindings are backed up when you back up IIS configuration.

- Enter the host header correctly entered when you create a web application. The host header is recorded in the configuration database and cannot be changed after the web application is created. You can change host header bindings directly in IIS, but you must remember to do so each time you add a new server to the farm, and to update existing servers if you restart the Microsoft SharePoint Foundation Web Application service. If you need to change the host header of the web application, it is recommended that you delete and re-create the web application.

- Only one host header can be defined during the creation of a web application creation. If users will access the web application with more than one host name, such as *http://intranet.contoso.com* and *http://portal.contoso.com*, you must extend the web application to create additional zones. You will learn more about zones in Lesson 3.

Security Configuration

The options that appear in the Security Configuration section depend on whether you selected Claims Based Authentication or Classic Mode Authentication in the Authentication section at the top of the Create New Web Application page. The settings that appear if you selected Classic Mode Authentication are shown in Figure 3-3.

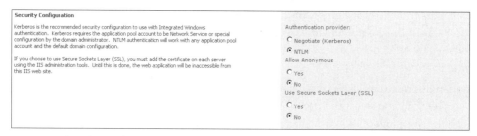

FIGURE 3-3 Security Configuration settings

If you selected Classic Mode Authentication, you must designate the authentication provider for the web application. You can select NTLM or Negotiate (Kerberos) as the authentication provider. Classic Mode Authentication essentially uses IIS to authenticate users with built-in Windows authentication providers, including NTLM, Kerberos, and Basic authentication. However, you cannot select Basic authentication when you create a web application—you must configure Basic authentication after the web application has been created. You will learn more about Windows authentication providers later in this lesson.

If you selected Claims Based Authentication, the authentication provider is configured in the Claims Authentication Types section of the Create New Web Application page.

For both authentication types, you must specify whether anonymous authentication is allowed and whether SSL is enabled in the Security Configuration section. By default, anonymous access and SSL are disabled. Later in this lesson, you will learn about the additional steps required to implement anonymous access and SSL.

Claims Authentication Types and Sign In Page URL

The Claims Authentication Types and Sign In Page URL sections are visible only if you selected Claims Based Authentication. One or more authentication providers, and a sign-in page are required for Claims Based Authentication. You will learn more about these settings later in this chapter.

After you have configured security and authentication settings, you must configure additional settings for a web application, shown in Figure 3-4.

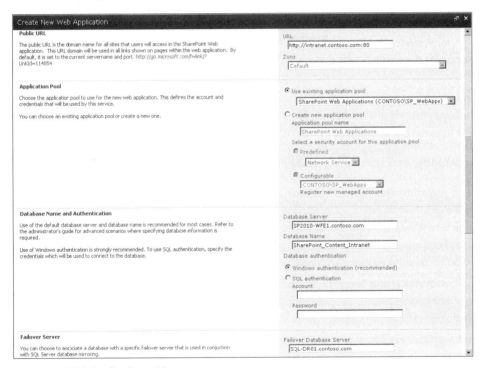

FIGURE 3-4 Web Application settings

Public URL

The Public URL represents the user-accessible URL of the web application. In the URL box, type the protocol, the fully qualified domain name (FQDN) of the web application, and the port that will be used in URIs of requests to the site, such as *http://intranet.contoso.com:80*.

You will notice that the Public URL is associated with the zone named Default, and you cannot change the zone when creating a new web application. A zone is a path through which content in a web application is actually accessed. When SharePoint receives a URI—for example, *http://intranet.contoso.com/SitePages/Home.aspx*—SharePoint examines the protocol, FQDN, and port of the URI and uses those three elements to identify both the SharePoint web application that is being requested and the zone through which the request is received—in this example, the default zone of the Contoso Intranet Web application.

> **NOTE SHAREPOINT 2007**
>
> In SharePoint 2007, this setting was called the *Load Balanced URL*.

Application Pool

Use the controls in the Application Pool section to specify whether the web application will be hosted within an existing application pool, running in the context of the identity that has been already assigned to the application pool, or within a new application pool running in the context of a managed account that you select in the Configurable list. Earlier in this lesson, you learned that it is a best practice to use a shared application pool for web applications unless there is a significant driver for process isolation, because application pools incur memory and performance overhead and are therefore a limited resource of IIS.

Database Name and Authentication

The Database Server box is prepopulated with the name of the server that hosts the farm's configuration database. If you want to host the web application's content database on another server, replace the value using the *<SERVERNAME\instance>* format, where *SERVERNAME* is the FQDN of the database server and *instance* is the Microsoft SQL Server instance you want to use, if more than one instance is running on the server.

The Database Name box is prepopulated with a sample name that includes a globally unique identifier (GUID). Most database administrators (DBAs) prefer to follow a naming standard that uniquely identifies the database with a descriptive name that does not include a GUID. Replace the default name with a name that follows your naming standards. A guideline is to use a name that follows this example: *SharePoint_Content_Intranet*, where the first two elements of the name identify the database as a SharePoint content database, and the remaining elements of the name correlate to the web application and site collections contained in the database.

In the Database Authentication section, select the method used to connect to the content database. The default and recommended method is Windows authentication, which uses the credentials of the application pool identity to connect to SQL Server. Windows authentication automatically encrypts the password.

If you have configured the SQL Server for mixed mode authentication, you can select SQL authentication. You must specify the credentials that the web application will use to connect to the database. Type the user name in the Account box and the password in the Password box. The user account with which you are logged on to Central Administration must have permission to create and secure databases on the server.

Failover Server

SharePoint 2010 supports failover to a second instance of the database. If you have configured database mirroring in SQL Server, SharePoint can failover to another server in the event that the current database server becomes unresponsive. In the Failover Database Server box, type the name of a specific failover database server for the content database. This setting does not configure SQL database mirroring—it only instructs SharePoint to failover to an already-configured backup instance of the database. You will learn about failover in Chapter 11, "Implementing Business Continuity."

Search Server

The Search Server setting is automatically configured, and cannot be changed, if SharePoint Server 2010 is installed. On a SharePoint Foundation 2010 farm, you associate a search server running SharePoint Foundation 2010 Search service with the content database for the new web application.

Service Application Connections

A web application connects to service applications for shared services such as search. Service application connections are grouped into application connection groups, also called *proxy groups*. In the Service Application Connections section, select either an existing application connection group, or select Custom from the drop-down list and then select the specific service applications you want the web application to use. You will learn more about service application management in Chapter 5.

Customer Experience Improvement Program

Click Yes or No to opt in or out, respectively, of the Customer Experience Improvement Program. If you choose Yes, certain information will be sent to Microsoft that will help Microsoft understand performance and usage patterns of SharePoint implementations in the real world.

Delete a Web Application

You can delete a web application by using Central Administration. As with other changes that involve components of both SharePoint and IIS, you should not use IIS Manager to delete an IIS Web site that services a SharePoint web application. Exercise care when deleting a web application. Before doing so, verify that you have a backup of the web application and of the farm's configuration.

DELETE A WEB APPLICATION USING CENTRAL ADMINISTRATION

1. In the Central Administration Quick Launch, click Application Management.
2. In the Web Applications section, click Manage Web Applications.
3. Click the Web application you want to delete.
4. On the ribbon, click Delete.

   The Delete Web Application page opens.
5. If you want to delete the content databases, click Yes in the Delete Content Databases section.
6. If you want to delete the IIS Web sites associated with the web application, click Yes in the Delete IIS Web Sites section.

> **NOTE UNDERSTAND YOUR OPTIONS**
>
> It is possible to delete the definition of the web application in the farm configuration database while leaving both the content databases and the IIS Web sites in place. Although rarely used, this option can be helpful if the configuration of a web application has been corrupted.

7. Click Delete.

DELETE A WEB APPLICATION USING WINDOWS POWERSHELL

The following example shows the use of the *Remove-SPWebApplication* cmdlet to delete a site:

```
Remove-SPWebApplication <URL> -DeleteIISSite -RemoveContentDatabase -Confirm:$false
```

Where:

- *<URL>* is the URL to the web application that you want to delete.
- The *-DeleteIISSite* switch parameter, if present, instructs SharePoint to delete the IIS Web site associated with the web application.
- The *-RemoveContentDatabase* switch parameter, if present, instructs SharePoint to delete the content databases associated with the web application.
- The *-Confirm:$false* parameter suppresses confirmation prompts.

Secure Communication with a Web Application Using SSL

Transport Layer Security (TLS) and its predecessor, Secure Sockets Layer (SSL), are cryptographic protocols used to encrypt the contents of communications over a network, at the application layer. In the case of SharePoint, the communication is between a client and an IIS Web site, or communications between SharePoint web applications and service applications.

SSL is particularly important if sensitive information will be transmitted to or from a website—without SSL, the information is transmitted in clear text and could be intercepted by a packet sniffer. SSL becomes more important when transmission of information is over untrusted networks, such as the Internet.

Secure communication is made possible with certificates and keys. When a client initiates contact with a secured website, the website provides the client a certificate. Through the series of ensuing processes, the two endpoints agree on a secret—a key—that is used to encrypt and decrypt communications.

The client can also use the server's certificate to verify the identity of the server, by validating the digital signature of the certificate against a trusted certificate authority. In this way, SSL can be used to authenticate a server prior to sending sensitive information to the server. For example, if Internet Explorer cannot verify that a server's certificate is valid, it warns the user and the user can then decide whether to accept the inherent risks and to continue communicating with the server.

To secure communications with a SharePoint web application, you must perform the following steps:

1. Configure the SharePoint web application to use SSL.
2. Create a certificate.
3. Bind the certificate to the IIS Web site of the SharePoint web application.

When you enable SSL for the SharePoint web application, you change the web application scheme to SSL in the configuration database, and you enable SharePoint to recognize the HTTPS protocol in the URL. But SharePoint Server 2010 does not itself provide SSL services and does not store the certificate used to authenticate the web application. These roles are performed by IIS.

Configure a SharePoint Web Application to Use SSL

When you create a new web application, you can enable SSL by clicking Yes for the Use Secure Sockets Layer (SSL) setting of the Create New Web Application page. The procedure to create a web application was introduced in Chapter 1, and the settings for a new web application were detailed earlier in this lesson.

To change an existing HTTP web application to use HTTPS, you must modify access mappings and zones. These procedures will be detailed in Lesson 3.

After the SharePoint web application has been configured to use SSL, you must manage certificates and bindings on each web server in the farm.

Create a Certificate

SSL relies on a certificate provided by the web server to the client. If you want the client to be able to verify the server's identity, you must create a certificate request and send that request to a known certificate authority (CA), such as VeriSign or GeoTrust, or obtain a certificate from an online CA in your domain—for example, from Active Directory Certificate Services.

In a test environment, you can create a self-signed certificate on the web server. The certificate can be used to test SSL configuration and communication with an IIS Web site, but clients will be unable to verify the identity of the server.

CREATE A SELF-SIGNED CERTIFICATE

1. In IIS Manager, in the console tree, click the node representing the server, for example SP2010-WFE1.

> **TIP** **SELECT THE SERVER**
>
> **Be sure that you select the server node in the IIS console tree, not an IIS Web site. Certificates are stored in the Windows Server certificate store, not in IIS itself.**

2. In the IIS section, double-click Server Certificates.

3. In the Actions panel, click Create Self-Signed Certificate.

    The Create Self-Signed Certificate dialog box opens.

4. In the Name box, type a friendly name for the certificate, such as **Test Certificate**.

5. Click OK.

Bind an SSL Certificate to an IIS Web Site

After you have added a certificate to IIS, you can bind the certificate to an IIS site.

CREATE AN SSL BINDING FOR AN IIS WEB SITE

1. In IIS Manager, in the console tree, click the node representing the IIS Web site for which you want to create an SSL binding.

2. In the Actions panel, click Bindings.

    The Site Bindings dialog box opens.

3. Click Add.

    The Add Site Binding dialog box opens.

4. In the Type list, select HTTPS.

5. Optionally, in the IP Address list, select a specific IP address. Otherwise, accept the default value, All Unassigned.

    If you are hosting more than one SSL-enabled web application on a server, you might want to bind each to a specific IP address to avoid using a wildcard SSL certificate. IP address bindings also make it easier to configure network load balancing for high availability and performance.

    Wildcard SSL certificates allow you to secure multiple subdomains under a single parent domain. For example, you could obtain a wildcard SSL Certificate for *.contoso.com*. Wildcard certificates do not allow clients to verify the identity of a specific web application, and can make it more difficult to trace network traffic.

6. Optionally, in the Port box, type a port number or accept the default value, 443.

The default port for the HTTPS protocol is 443.

7. In the SSL Certificate list, select the certificate—for example, Test Certificate.

The resulting configuration is shown in Figure 3-5.

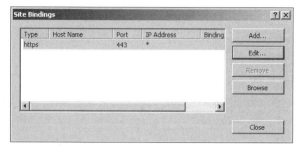

FIGURE 3-5 An SSL binding for an IIS Web site

8. Click OK and then click Close.

After you have added a new binding for SSL, you can remove any other bindings that are no longer needed.

MORE INFO **CONFIGURING SSL**

The following article provides additional details regarding the configuration of SSL: "How to Set Up SSL on IIS 7" at *http://go.microsoft.com/fwlink/?LinkId=187887*.

IMPORTANT **RESTORE IIS CONFIGURATION WHEN YOU RESTORE SHAREPOINT**

SSL certificates, SSL bindings, and IP address bindings are not stored in the farm configuration database. If you must restore a web application or web server, you will need to reconfigure IIS Web sites or restore IIS configuration.

 Quick Check

- When you configure SSL for a SharePoint web application, what must you do on each server in the SharePoint farm?

Quick Check Answer

- Bind the SSL certificate to the IIS Web site

Configure Web Applications

After creating a web application, you can specify additional configuration for the web application. In Lesson 2, you will learn to configure authentication. In Lesson 3, you will learn to configure authentication zones and alternate access mappings. You must also create one or more site collections and, if needed, additional content databases. You will learn about site collections and content databases in Chapter 4, "Administering and Securing SharePoint Content."

> **IMPORTANT NEXT, CREATE A SITE COLLECTION**
>
> Until you create a site collection, a new web application contains no content. Users navigating to the web application will be presented with an error page when a site has no content.

On the Web Applications Management page of Central Administration, you can select a web application and then configure settings for the web application by clicking buttons on the ribbon, shown in Figure 3-6. The remainder of this lesson will cover a variety of web application settings, and will point you to other locations in this Training Kit that provide additional detail.

FIGURE 3-6 The Web Applications Management page and ribbon

Master Page Setting For Application _Layouts Pages

Administrative pages for SharePoint sites are common across all sites in the farm. For example, a site's Site Settings page, Settings.aspx, is the same ASPX page used by all sites in the farm. This is possible because each SharePoint site is created with a virtual directory called _layouts that points to a common location. Of course, the content that is displayed by the page might be different for each site, based on the site's features and configuration, but the page itself is common. Because administrative pages are located in the _layouts virtual directory, administrative pages are often called _layouts pages.

Like other ASPX pages, an administrative page refers to a master page, which determines the look and feel and functionality of all pages that refer to it.

CONFIGURE APPLICATION _LAYOUTS MASTER PAGES

1. On the Web Applications Management page of Central Administration, select the web application that you want to configure.

2. On the ribbon, click the General Settings drop-down arrow, and then click General Settings.

   The Web Application General Settings page opens.

3. In the Master Page Setting For Application _Layouts Pages section, for the Application _Layouts Pages Reference Site Master Pages setting, click Yes or No.

4. Click OK.

If the Application _Layouts Pages Reference Site Master Pages setting is disabled (set to No) the administrative pages will use the application.master page in the SharePoint Root directory as their master page. This master page presents the default look and feel of SharePoint Server 2010.

If you have customized the master pages of a site to incorporate custom functionality or branding, you probably want those changes to be visible both on standard content pages and administrative pages. It would not be acceptable for administrative pages to lose the customizations you have made to the site. Therefore, by default, this setting is enabled (set to Yes). This instructs SharePoint to use the site's master pages—rather than the standard, shared application.master page—when you access an administrative page in a site.

However, this presents a risk that if a site's master pages become corrupt or inaccessible, an administrative page will not be able to load, and you could be locked out of the ability to manage a site. Therefore, even if this setting is enabled, if SharePoint cannot render a vital page, such as the Settings.aspx page, because of problems with the site's master pages, the page will be rendered with the default SharePoint master pages, so that the page can be returned to the user successfully.

Recycle Bin Configuration

SharePoint sites support a two-stage Recycle Bin by default. When a user deletes content, the content is moved to the first-stage Recycle Bin, from which the user can restore the content or empty the Recycle Bin. When the Recycle Bin is emptied, content is moved to the second-stage Recycle Bin. Once the content is in the second-stage Recycle Bin, only a site collection administrator can restore it. When the second-stage Recycle Bin is emptied by a site collection administrator, or after another configurable time frame, the content is permanently deleted from the content database. By default, the Recycle Bin is enabled for a new web application, and default configuration is applied.

You should modify Recycle Bin settings in accordance with your specifications.

CONFIGURE RECYCLE BIN SETTINGS FOR A WEB APPLICATION

1. On the Web Applications Management page of Central Administration, select the web application that you want to configure.

2. On the ribbon, click the General Settings drop-down arrow, and then click General Settings.

   The Web Application General Settings page opens.

3. In the Recycle Bin section, in the Recycle Bin Status section, click On to enable the Recycle Bin or click Off to disable the Recycle Bin.

   If you disable the Recycle Bin, all content will be expunged from both first and second stages on Recycle Bins of all sites and site collections in the web application.

4. If you enable the Recycle Bin, you can configure the Delete Items In The Recycle Bin setting and the Second Stage Recycle Bin setting, as discussed later in this section.

5. Click OK.

If the Recycle Bin is enabled, as it is by default, you can configure the time-based expiration of content. Content in a Recycle Bin will be permanently deleted after the number of days that you specify. This time limit does not apply to the first- or second-stage Recycle Bins individually, nor is the time reset when an item is moved to the second-stage Recycle Bin. Instead, the time limit is measured from the time at which the content was deleted.

You can disable the second-stage Recycle Bin by clicking Off in the Second Stage Recycle Bin Setting group. By default, the second-stage Recycle Bin is on, and SharePoint limits the second-stage Recycle Bin size to 50 percent of the storage limit quota for the site collection. However, by default, new site collections have no quota applied, which effectively means that the second-stage Recycle Bin size is also unlimited.

As you can see, you should carefully plan and configure Recycle Bin settings.

General Settings

The Web Application General Settings page exposes many common web application settings, including the Recycle Bin and Master Page Setting For Application _Layouts Pages configuration discussed earlier.

MODIFY WEB APPLICATION GENERAL SETTINGS

1. On the Web Applications Management page of Central Administration, select the web application that you want to configure.

2. On the ribbon, click the General Settings drop-down arrow, and then click General Settings.

   The Web Application General Settings page opens.

3. Modify the settings, as described below, and then click OK.

The following additional settings can be configured on the Web Application General Settings page.

- **Default Time Zone** By default, each web application uses the time zone of the host operating system, and each site uses the time zone of the parent web application. It is recommended that you manually configure the time zone to prevent potential inconsistencies, particularly across servers of a multi-server farm.

- **Default Quota Template** When you create a site collection, you can configure the quota for the site collection, which establishes storage limits and warning levels at which administrators can be notified by email that the size of a site collection is approaching its storage limit. This setting, at the web application level, determines the default quota template for new site collections. You must have previously created a quota template before you can configure the Default Quota Template for a web application. See Chapter 4 for more information about quotas.

- **Person Name Actions And Presence Settings**   This setting determines whether online status of users will be displayed within the web application. Online status can be queried from Microsoft Office Communicator Server (OCS), and can be displayed next to a user's name wherever the user's display name appears. Additionally, if you right-click a user name, additional commands will appear that allow you to communicate directly with the user. By default, this setting is enabled for a new web application.

- **Alerts**   Alerts are email notifications regarding changes to content in a list, library, folder, page, item, or document. By default, users are allowed to create alerts—up to 500 alerts across all sites in the web application. It is recommended that you do not configure the limit too high, or choose Unlimited, because it opens the possibility that a user might create sufficient alerts to degrade the performance of SharePoint or Exchange Server.
- **RSS Settings**   Really Simple Syndication (RSS) feeds allow users and applications to monitor content in lists and libraries. For example, a user can subscribe to alerts in a list or library using an RSS reader such as Internet Explorer or Microsoft Outlook 2010. By default, RSS feeds are enabled for a web application, and the RSS feed of each list and library is enabled. You can disable RSS at the web application level.

  If RSS is enabled for the web application, you can enable, disable, and customize the RSS feed of a specific list or library. Open the Settings page for the list or library, and then click RSS Settings. The Modify RSS Settings page opens, with which you can configure RSS settings.
- **Blog API Settings**   The MetaWeblog API is a standard API used by many blog applications to accept blog posts published directly from blogging applications, including Microsoft Office Word 2010. By default, the blog API is enabled. You can also configure whether the web application's authentication will be used to authenticate the user, or whether the API should accept the user's user name and password.
- **Browser File Handling**   By default, SharePoint protects users by preventing certain types of files, such as HTML files, from being executed locally when a user clicks the file on the SharePoint site. SharePoint adds headers to these sensitive file types that cause

the browser to prompt the user to download the file, rather than allowing the browser to open the file immediately. This default setting, called Strict, should not be changed unless you have specific reasons to do so and you are in a controlled environment. The Strict setting also prevents attacks such as cross-site scripting from compromising the integrity of your server farm by forcing code in such files to be executed on the client browser, instead of on the SharePoint server.

- **Web Page Security Validation** When enabled, as it is by default, this setting prevents a client session from being used indefinitely. By default, 30 minutes after authentication of a request for a page, the client's security validation expires. Therefore, after 30 minutes of inactivity, the user must refresh the page or otherwise reestablish the connection, at which point authentication will be performed.

  The setting does not produce a visible effect for web applications that use Classic Mode authentication, which uses Windows authentication mechanisms. Internet Explorer will transparently re-authenticate the user, as long as the web application's URL is in Internet Explorer's Trusted Sites or Local Intranet security zone. If the web application uses other authentication providers, a sign-in page will be presented and the effect of re-authentication will be more noticeable.

- **Send User Name And Password In E-mail** SharePoint 2010 can be installed in Active Directory account creation mode. This mode is included for Internet Service Providers and is being deprecated. The mode is not enabled by default, is being deprecated from SharePoint, and is included primarily to support upgrades of legacy environments for SharePoint hosting services. It is not recommended that you configure an organizational SharePoint farm in Active Directory account creation mode. SharePoint also ignores this setting when it is not installed in Active Directory account creation mode. Therefore, you can ignore this setting.

- **Maximum Upload Size** By default, a user cannot upload a single file, group of files, or other piece of content greater than 50 MB in size. You can modify this limit, but you must be cognizant of timeouts when transferring large files using HTTP, which is the transfer mechanism used by SharePoint, particularly over slow or high-latency networks such as the Internet or a WAN link.

NOTE **2 GB MAXIMUM FILE SIZE**

There is a fixed limit of 2 GB for any file stored in SharePoint. It is not possible to store files larger than 2 GB in a SQL record. Some third-party solutions might address scenarios that require SharePoint-based interaction with files larger than 2 GB.

IMPORTANT **MAXIMUM UPLOAD SIZE AFFECTS UPLOAD MULTIPLE FILES**

The Maximum Upload Size setting limits the aggregate size of a single upload action, which includes uploads using the Upload Multiple Files command. For example, by default, you cannot upload 10 files of 10 MB each with the Upload Multiple Files command because the total size of 100 MB exceeds the default limit of 50 MB.

- **Customer Experience Improvement Program**   See the description of this setting in the "Configure a New Web Application" section.

Workflow Settings

From the General Settings menu, you can configure workflow settings for a web application. The Workflow Settings page exposes the following configuration:

- **Enable User-Defined Workflows**   By default, this option is set to Yes and workflows are enabled for a new web application. Users can create declarative workflows—workflows that are based on building blocks that are available by default, such as SharePoint Designer workflow activities, or code that has been deployed to the server by an administrator. Users cannot add new compiled code workflows to the server. Users must have at least the Design permission level for a site to create a workflow in that site.

- **Alert Internal Users Who Do Not Have Access**   Enabled—set to Yes—by default, this option will send an email notification to a user who has been assigned a task in a workflow. The email will include a hyperlink that will generate an access request for the site, at which point an administrator can grant the user the permissions necessary to perform the workflow task. If this option is disabled—set to No—a user who does not have access to the target item of the workflow task will not be notified of the task.

- **Allow External Users To Participate In Workflow**   When this option is enabled, SharePoint will email a copy of a document to a user who has been assigned a workflow task related to the document. For security reasons, and to reduce the proliferation of independent copies of documents, this option is disabled by default.

Outgoing Email Settings

Outgoing email settings are required for alerts to function. You learned in Chapter 1 that after creating a SharePoint farm you should configure the outgoing email settings for the farm. By default, a web application will use those farm-level outgoing email settings. However, you can override the outgoing email settings for a specific web application. You must define the SMTP Relay Server, From Address, and Reply To Address.

CONFIGURE OUTGOING E-MAIL SETTINGS FOR A WEB APPLICATION

1. On the Web Applications Management page of Central Administration, select the web application that you want to configure.

2. On the ribbon, click the General Settings drop-down arrow, and then click Outgoing E-mail. The Web Application Outgoing E-Mail Settings page opens.

3. In the Outbound SMTP Server box, type the FQDN of an SMTP-compliant server to which SharePoint can connect to using TCP port 25.

> **IMPORTANT**   The SMTP server must be accessible over TCP port 25, and must permit relay from servers based on IP address. SharePoint products do not support SMTP authentication mechanisms.

4. In the From Address box, type the email address that will be used as the sender's address of outgoing email messages.

5. In the Reply-To Address box, type the email address to which replies should be sent.

6. In the Character Set list, select the character set for email messages. The default is 65001 (Unicode UTF-8), which is the character set most commonly used for email, and supports characters in all languages supported by Unicode.

7. Click OK.

> **IMPORTANT** SharePoint allows you to configure only one SMTP server address. If you want to ensure availability in the event of a failure of an SMTP server, you must configure redundancy outside of SharePoint's configuration.

Text Message Service Settings

If users do not have smart phones with which to monitor SharePoint email alerts, you can send alerts via text message, which allows alerts to be sent to almost any cellular telephone.

You must first subscribe to a third-party SMS service provider. The SMS provider relays alerts, based on the email address of the user in the alert, to the user's mobile phone.

> **MORE INFO** **SMS PROVIDERS**
> You can find an up-to-date list of SharePoint 2010 compatible SMS providers at *http://messaging.office.microsoft.com/HostingProviders.aspx?src=O14&lc=1033*.

Your costs will vary based on factors including your geographic location, volume of SMS alerts, and fees imposed by your cellular telephone provider.

> **IMPORTANT** **THROTTLING MOBILE ALERTS**
> There is no way to throttle alerts sent by SharePoint. If users create many alerts, and those alerts are sent via SMS, your costs might skyrocket. Consider throttling capabilities of your SMS provider as a way to limit out-of-control costs of mobile alerts.

CONFIGURE SMS-BASED ALERTS

1. On the Web Applications Management page of Central Administration, select the web application that you want to configure.

2. On the ribbon, click the General Settings drop-down arrow, and then click Mobile Account.

   The Web Application Text Message (SMS) Service Settings page opens.

3. In The URL Of Text Message (SMS) Service box, type the URL provided by your SMS provider.

4. In the User Name box, type the user name provided by your SMS provider.

5. In the Password box, type the password provided by your SMS provider.

6. Click Test Service to test the configuration of the service.

7. Click OK.

Self-Service Site Creation

By default, you must be a member of the Farm Administrators group to create a site collection in a web application. However, in certain scenarios—a team or project collaboration web application, for example—you might want users to be able to create site collections without administrator intervention. To support these scenarios you can enable self-service site collection creation, which is disabled by default, by using one of two interfaces in Central Administration.

ENABLE SELF-SERVICE SITE CREATION FROM THE WEB APPLICATIONS MANAGEMENT PAGE

1. Select the web application for which you want to enable self-service site creation.

2. In the Web Applications ribbon, click Self-Service Site Creation.

   The Self-Service Site Collection Management page opens.

3. In the Enable Self-Service Site Creation section, click On.

   Optionally, select the Require Secondary Contact check box. If this check box is selected, a user will be required to provide a secondary contact when the user creates a site collection. The secondary contact becomes the secondary site collection administrator. A primary site collection administrator is always required.

4. Click OK.

ENABLE SELF-SERVICE SITE CREATION FROM THE APPLICATION MANAGEMENT PAGE

1. In the Central Administration Quick Launch, click Application Management.

2. In the Site Collections section, click Configure Self-Service Site Creation.

   The Self-Service Site Collection Management page opens.

3. Click the Web Application picker, and then click Change Web Application.

   The Select Web Application page opens.

4. Click the name of the web application for which you want to enable self-service site creation.

5. In the Enable Self-Service Site Creation section, click On.

6. Optionally, select the Require Secondary Contact check box.

7. Click OK.

In Chapter 4, you will learn how to create a site collection when self-service site creation is enabled for the web application.

Blocked File Types

SharePoint Server 2010 allows you to prevent certain types of files from being uploaded to a web application, based on file extension.

CONFIGURE BLOCKED FILE TYPES

1. On the Web Applications Management page of Central Administration, select the web application that you want to configure.

2. On the ribbon, click Blocked File Types to open the Blocked File Types page.

   You can open the Blocked File Types page with an alternate method. In the Central Administration Quick Launch, click Security. Then, in the General Security section, click Define Blocked File Types. The Blocked File Types page opens. Click the Web Application picker, and then click Change Web Application. The Select Web Application page opens. Click the name of the web application for which you want to define blocked file types.

3. Add or remove extensions, each on a separate line of the list, and then click OK.

The extension-based protection provided by the Blocked File Types list is rudimentary. Users can change the extension of a file and then upload it for storage. For example, you can rename a blocked .exe file with a .txt extension, and then upload the file to a document library. SharePoint looks only at the extension. However, you cannot upload a file and then change the extension.

Other Settings in the Web Applications Ribbon

The Web Applications ribbon also exposes a number of additional settings that are scoped to a web application. The following settings are discussed in Chapter 10, "Administering SharePoint Customization":

- **SharePoint Designer governance** From the General Settings menu, you can manage what users are able to do with SharePoint Designer within the web application.

- **Manage Features** Features are bundles of functionality that can be enabled or disabled for scopes of the SharePoint logical architecture, including web applications, site collections, and sites.

- **Web Part Security** You can define the availability, behavior, and security of web parts in the web application.

Chapter 4 details the following settings:

- **User Permissions** You can configure the granular permissions available to be used in permission levels defined for sites in the web application.

- **User Policy** You can define access policies at the web application that override any permissions, or lack thereof, for content within the web application. For example, the SharePoint search crawling account is assigned a Full Read permission policy for each new web application. This enables the search crawling account to index all SharePoint content, without the need to explicitly assign permissions to content in the web application. User policy is actually scoped to zones, not to web applications. You will learn more about zones in Lesson 5.

- **Permissions Policy** Permission policies are collections of permissions that can be assigned to a user or group as a user policy, as described earlier. SharePoint 2007 had a fixed number of permission policies: Full Control, Full Read, Deny Write, and Deny All. In SharePoint 2010, you can define custom permission policies.

The remaining settings are discussed later in this Training Kit:

- **Resource Throttling** SharePoint 2010 introduces resource throttling, which is designed to protect a server and the users of a server from the negative impact of large queries and other performance-degrading activities. Resource throttling allows you to control resource utilization and optimize server performance. Resource Throttling settings are exposed by the General Settings menu. You will learn about resource throttling in Chapter 12, "Monitoring and Optimizing SharePoint Performance."

- **Managed Paths** Managed paths specify the URLs in a web application at which site collections can be created. While managed paths are a property of a web application, they are conceptually more related to site collections, and are therefore detailed in Chapter 4.

- **Service Connections**   You can specify the application connection group with which a web application is associated, or you can specify individual service applications to which a web application connects. Service applications, application connection groups, and web application associations are discussed in Chapter 5.

- **Authentication Providers**   Lesson 2 of this chapter details the configuration of web application authentication. Authentication providers are scoped to the zone, not to the entire web application. You will learn more about zones in Lesson 3 of this chapter.

- **Anonymous Policy**   Anonymous access restrictions are described in Lesson 2.

PRACTICE   Configure Web Applications

Practices are designed to guide you through important procedures. The instructions in the Training Kit are high-level instructions that will challenge you to think carefully and to apply the procedures that are covered in this lesson and elsewhere in the Training Kit. If you need assistance, consult the detailed, step-by-step instructions in the Practice Answers on the companion media.

In this practice, you will create a web application to support collaboration with Contoso partners. The web application will be accessible from the Internet, so you want to ensure that communication between clients and the web application is secure. Therefore, you will configure the web application to use SSL. Finally, you will make configuration changes to support both the business and governance requirements of the partner collaboration website.

Prepare for the Practice

Before you perform this practice, you must ensure that your lab environment has been built according to the instructions found in the Introduction to this Training Kit.

1. Apply the snapshot CHAPTER01 to CONTOSO-DC.
2. Apply the snapshot CHAPTER01 to SP2010-WFE1.
3. Start CONTOSO-DC.

    Wait for the virtual machine to complete startup, at which time the Press Ctrl+Alt+Del prompt appears.

4. Start SP2010-WFE1.

EXERCISE 1   Add DNS Host Records for New Web Applications

In this exercise, you add DNS host records for web applications you will create in subsequent exercises.

1. Log on to SP2010-WFE1 as **CONTOSO\SP_Admin** with the password **Pa$$w0rd**.
2. Start Command Prompt.
3. Use Dnscmd.exe to create a new host (A) records on the DNS server (*contoso-dc .contoso.com*) for *partners.contoso.com* that resolve to the IP address *10.0.0.21*.

4. Use Dnscmd.exe to create a new host (A) records on the DNS server (*contoso-dc .contoso.com)* for *extranet.contoso.com* that resolve to the IP address, *10.0.0.21*. Then close Command Prompt.

EXERCISE 2   Create a Web Application Using Central Administration

In this exercise, you create a web application for collaboration with partners of Contoso.

1. Use Central Administration to create a web application collaboration with partners. Use the following specifications and guidance:

   - Authentication: Classic Mode Authentication
   - Name: Contoso Partner Portal
   - Port: 443
   - Host header: partners.contoso.com
   - Authentication provider: NTLM
   - Anonymous authentication: No
   - Secure Sockets Layer (SSL): Yes
   - URL: *https://partnerss.contoso.com:443*
   - Application pool: SharePoint Extranet Applications
   - Application identity: CONTOSO\SP_WebApps
   - Content database name: SharePoint_Content_Partners

EXERCISE 3   Create a Site Collection Using Central Administration

In this exercise, you use Central Administration to create a site collection at the root of the new web application.

1. Use Central Administration to create a site collection. Use the following specifications and guidance:

   - Web application: *https://partners.contoso.com*
   - Title: Contoso Partner Portal
   - Description: Sites for collaboration with partners
   - URL: *https://partners.contoso.com/*
   - Template: Team Site
   - Primary site collection administrator: CONTOSO\SP_Admin

2. Open a new tab in Internet Explorer and browse to ***https://partners.contoso.com***.

   An Internet Explorer Cannot Display The Webpage error page opens. The site cannot be accessed using HTTPS because SSL has not been configured for the IIS Web site associated with the application.

EXERCISE 4   Create a Self-Signed Certificate

In this exercise, you create a self-signed certificate that, in the next exercise, you will bind to the site to enable SSL.

- In IIS Manager, create a self-signed certificate named **Test Certificate** in the certificate store of SP2010-WFE1.

EXERCISE 5   Create an SSL Binding for an IIS Web Site

In this exercise, you bind the certificate you created in the previous exercise to the Contoso Partner Portal IIS Web site.

1. Bind the certificate named *Test Certificate* to the Contoso Partner Portal IIS Web site by modifying the site's existing incomplete binding.

2. In Internet Explorer, browse to ***https://partners.contoso.com***.

   An error page opens: *There is a problem with this website's security certificate.*

   Question: Why does this error appear?

3. Click Continue To This Website (Not Recommended).

   The site is loaded, compiled, and cached for first-time access, and then authentication proceeds. The Windows Security dialog box opens.

   Question: Why does this dialog box appear?

4. Authenticate as **CONTOSO\SP_Admin** with the password **Pa$$w0rd**.

   The site is loaded, compiled, and cached for first-time access, and then the site opens.

   If an error appears, refresh the page. It is possible that the client timed out while the site was being loaded by IIS.

EXERCISE 6   Configure Web Application Settings

In this exercise, you enable self-service site creation, configure the Recycle Bin to retain items for 60 days, and prevent users from uploading MP3 files.

1. Switch to the Internet Explorer tab that displays Central Administration. Navigate to the Web Applications Management page, and then make the following changes to the configuration of the Contoso Partner Portal Web Application:

   - Enable Self-Service Site Creation. Require that users add a secondary site collection administrator.

   - Configure the Recycle Bin to retain items for 60 days.

   - Block the upload of MP3 files. For additional manageability and elegance, add the MP3 file extension to the list of blocked file types in alphabetical order.

2. Use Notepad to create a file named **TEST.MP3**.

   Ensure that the file extension is MP3, and that a TXT extension is not added.

3. Attempt to upload the MP3 file to the Contoso Partner Portal's Shared Documents document library.

   An error message appears. It indicates that the file has been blocked by an administrator.

Lesson Summary

- When you create a SharePoint web application, you create an IIS site including a folder, a Web.config file, bindings, and a virtual directory. You should manage all configuration by using Central Administration or Windows PowerShell, except for binding a security certificate to a site, which must be performed in IIS Manager on each server in the farm.

- It is recommended that you create all web applications within a single application pool, unless you have a significant requirement for process-level isolation. If you create more than one application pool, your requirements for auditing and access are likely to drive you to create a unique managed account as the identity for each application pool.

- You can encrypt communication between clients and a SharePoint web application by configuring the web application to use the HTTPS protocol, which relies on SSL. You must also add the certificate to the server, and add an SSL binding to the IIS Web site.

- Numerous settings are scoped to a web application, including self-service site collection creation, service application connections, and Recycle Bin settings. If your requirements call for more than one collection of these settings, you will need more than one web application to support those requirements.

Lesson Review

You can use the following questions to test your knowledge of the information in Lesson 1, "Configure Web Applications." The questions are also available on the companion media in a practice test if you prefer to review them in electronic form.

> **NOTE ANSWERS**
>
> Answers to these questions and explanations of why each answer choice is right or wrong are located in the "Answers" section at the end of the book.

1. You want to enable SSL encryption for a new SharePoint web application. The server farm currently has no IIS Web sites that use SSL. What do you need to do? (Choose all that apply. Each correct answer is a part of the complete solution.)

   A. Add a binding to the IIS site.

   B. Configure the new SharePoint web application to use SSL.

   C. Add a certificate to the SharePoint configuration database.

   D. Add a certificate to the server.

2. You want to distribute email alerts to different SMTP servers based on the site from which the alert originates. Where can you do this?

   A. Site Collection Administration settings on the Site Settings page of each site.

   B. The Configure Outgoing E-Mail Server command on the General Settings page of Central Administration.

   C. The SMTP Relay settings of the SMTP server.

   D. The Outgoing E-Mail Server setting on the Web Application General Settings page.

3. Your information security and compliance requirements state that if a user accidentally deletes an item, the user must be able retrieve the item for 75 days. How can you configure SharePoint to support this requirement?

   A. Configure Recycle Bin Settings for the web application.

   B. Configure permissions so that the user cannot delete items.

   C. Configure information management policy.

   D. Configure a User Policy for the web application.

Lesson 2: Configure Authentication

SharePoint Server 2010 is a distributed application that is logically divided into three tiers: the front-end web server tier, the application server tier, and the back-end database tier. SharePoint can also interact with external systems—for example, by presenting data stored in an external database in a list. Each tier or system is a trusted subsystem, and authentication is required by default. *Authentication* is the process of verifying the identity of a user making a request to an application. The application must be assured that the user is authentic before the system performs *authorization*, which is the process of verifying that the user has permission to make the request, and *personalization*, which determines how the application interacts with the user.

SharePoint 2010 supports numerous methods by which users can be authenticated, including Windows authentication methods such as NTLM or Kerberos, forms-based authentication with methods that use LDAP directories or SQL databases as sources of user credentials and groups, and claims authentication using Security Assertion Markup Language (SAML) tokens. In this lesson, you will master the concepts and procedures related to authentication in SharePoint.

> **After this lesson, you will be able to:**
> - Describe classic-mode authentication and identify the authentication provider and methods it supports.
> - Configure classic-mode authentication.
> - Describe integrated Windows authentication.
> - Configure Kerberos authentication.
> - Describe additional Windows authentication methods.
> - Describe claims-based authentication and identify the authentication providers and methods it supports.
> - Configure claims-based authentication using Windows authentication methods.
> - Configure forms-based authentication.
> - Configure SAML token authentication.
> - Convert an upgraded or other web application using Classic Mode Authentication to Claims Based Authentication.
>
> **Estimated lesson time: 120 minutes**

Configure Anonymous Access

Let's start our exploration of authentication by detailing the processes by which you can configure anonymous access, so that users can access SharePoint content without validation of the users' identities. Anonymous access is disabled by default, which provides an additional layer of security because IIS rejects anonymous access requests before they can ever be processed by SharePoint. To configure the level of access that anonymous users have to content, you must manage three settings:

- Anonymous authentication for the web application
- Permissions assigned to anonymous users for sites, lists, and libraries
- Anonymous access restriction policies for the web application's zones

Enable Anonymous Authentication

You can enable anonymous authentication when you create a web application or after creating a web application. To enable anonymous authentication while creating a web application, simply click Yes for the Allow Anonymous setting on the Create New Web Application page, or, in Windows PowerShell, use the *-AllowAnonymous* switch parameter of the *New-SPWebApplication* cmdlet.

ENABLE OR DISABLE ANONYMOUS ACCESS ON AN EXISTING WEB APPLICATION

1. In the Central Administration Quick Launch, click Application Management.
2. In the Web Applications section, click Manage Web Applications.
3. On the Web Applications Management page, click the name of the web application for which you want to enable or disable anonymous access.
4. On the ribbon, click Authentication Providers.
5. On the Authentication Providers page, click the name of the zone for which you want to enable or disable anonymous access. For example, click Default.

    The Edit Authentication page opens.
6. On the Edit Authentication page, select or clear the Enable Anonymous Access check box, and then click Save.

When you enable anonymous access, SharePoint enables anonymous authentication for the IIS Web site.

> **IMPORTANT** **USE SHAREPOINT TO MAKE THIS CHANGE**
>
> As with other IIS Web site settings, you should not make the change directly in IIS Manager. When you make the change by using SharePoint, the web application properties are modified in the configuration database. Therefore, when you add a new server to the farm or restore a web application, the setting is applied correctly to the new IIS Web site.

When you install the Web Server IIS role, IIS creates the IUSR_*computername* account to authenticate anonymous users in response to a request for web content. The IUSR_*computername* account, where *computername* is the name of the server that is running IIS, gives the user access to resources anonymously under the context of the IUSR account.

Grant Permissions to Anonymous Users

Enabling anonymous access for a web application allows anonymous authentication, but it does not authorize anonymous users, in the context of the IUSR account, to access any content. Therefore, it is not enough simply to enable anonymous access for a web application—you must also grant permissions to anonymous users at the site level.

CONFIGURE ANONYMOUS ACCESS FOR A SITE

1. Click Site Actions, and then click Site Permissions.

   The Permissions page opens.

2. On the ribbon, click Anonymous Access.

   If you are not in the top-level site of a site collection, but rather are in a subsite, and if the top-level site does not allow anonymous access, you will not see the Anonymous Access button on the ribbon. This is because the subsite inherits the permissions from its parent site. Click Stop Inheriting Permissions to block inheritance, and then you can configure anonymous access permissions for the subsite.

   The Anonymous Access page opens.

3. In the Anonymous Users Can Access group, choose one of the following options:

   - **Entire Web Site**   Anonymous users can view content on the entire Web site.

   - **Lists And Libraries**   Anonymous users can view content in certain lists or libraries.

   - **Nothing**   Anonymous users have no access to the site.

4. Click OK.

If you select the Lists And Libraries option, all lists and libraries do not allow anonymous access by default. You must therefore assign anonymous access permissions to specific lists and libraries.

CONFIGURE ANONYMOUS ACCESS TO A LIST OR LIBRARY

1. Navigate to a list or library for which you want to configure anonymous access.

2. On the ribbon, click the List or Library tab.

3. Click the List Permissions or Library Permissions button.

   The Permissions page opens.

4. Click Stop Inheriting Permissions.

5. Click Anonymous Access.

   The Anonymous Access page opens.

6. In the Anonymous Users Can list, select the check boxes for the permissions you want to assign to anonymous users.

   In a document library, anonymous users can, at most, view items. Anonymous users cannot be granted add, edit, or delete item permission.

7. Click OK.

As you've learned, anonymous access involves configuration at both the web application and site levels. You must enable anonymous authentication for the web application, which in turn enables anonymous authentication for the IIS Web site, and then you must specify what content anonymous users can access. You will learn more about configuring permissions and security on sites, lists, and libraries, including the concept of inheritance, in Chapter 4.

> **NOTE USE SITE DESIGN TO MANAGE ANONYMOUS USERS' ACCESS**
>
> You should not configure anonymous access at the per-list and library level. It is difficult to manage access at that level, and it is very difficult to provide anonymous users access to those lists and libraries because the home page is not accessible to anonymous users. Therefore, you should strive to design your site structure so that content that should be accessed by anonymous users is in separate sites from content that requires authenticated access, so that you can manage anonymous access at the site level.

Anonymous Access Restrictions

Farm administrators can enforce permissions related to anonymous access across all sites in a web application by using anonymous access restrictions.

CONFIGURE ANONYMOUS ACCESS RESTRICTIONS

1. On the Web Applications Management page of Central Administration, select the web application that you want to configure.

2. On the ribbon, click Anonymous Policy.

   The Anonymous Access Restrictions page opens, as shown in Figure 3-7.

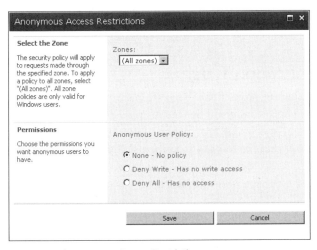

FIGURE 3-7 Anonymous Access Restrictions

3. In the Zones list, select the zone to which the policy will apply.

   To apply to the policy to all access to the web application, select All Zones.

4. In the Permissions section, click one of the following options:

   - **None**   No policy is defined. Anonymous access will be determined by permissions granted to sites, lists, and libraries.

   - **Deny Write**   Anonymous users will be unable to modify content. This policy overrides access granted on content within the web application, effectively ensuring that if a site collection administrator has granted any permissions at all to anonymous users, the maximum level of access will be Read.

   - **Deny All**   This policy overrides all permissions granted on content within a web application. Anonymous users will not have access.

5. Click Save.

The two policies that override site content permissions are primarily used in the following two scenarios:

- **Temporarily Disable Access**   You want to prevent anonymous users temporarily from writing or accessing content, but you do not want to change permissions on content.

- **Restrict Anonymous Access Through A Zone**   You want to restrict anonymous access using one zone, or URL, that is otherwise allowed using another zone. For example, if a web application can be accessed using HTTP using the URL *http://partners .contoso.com*, and can also be accessed using HTTPS with the URL *https://partners .contoso.com*, you might want to ensure that anonymous access is only possible using HTTPS. To do this, you must enable anonymous authentication for the web application; then grant permissions to anonymous users on sites, lists, or libraries in the web application; and then configure anonymous access restrictions to deny all access through the zone associated with the HTTP URL. You will learn more about zones in Lesson 3.

Understand Authentication Types

Authentication—verification of a user's credentials—is performed by a software component called an *authentication provider*. Authentication providers support one or more *authentication methods*. For example, the integrated Windows authentication provider supports both the NTLM and the Negotiate (Kerberos or NTLM) methods. An authentication method defines the protocols and data sources by which the provider performs authentication. In Lesson 1, you learned that there are two types of authentication in SharePoint Server 2010:

- **Classic Mode Authentication**   Classic Mode Authentication is the same type of authentication that was used in Microsoft Office SharePoint Server 2007. Classic Mode Authentication uses Windows authentication provider, which relies on Active Directory to authenticate users.

- **Claims Based Authentication**   Claims Based Authentication is a new feature in SharePoint 2010. Claims Based Authentication can use the Windows authentication provider—just as can Classic Mode Authentication—as well as Forms Based Authentication (FBA) and SAML token providers. You will learn more about Claims Based Authentication later in this lesson.

Each of the providers supports multiple authentication methods. Table 3-1 summarizes the authentication types, providers, and methods. You will learn about each provider and method later in this lesson.

TABLE 3-1 Authentication Options for SharePoint Web Applications

TYPE	PROVIDER	METHODS
Classic Mode Authentication	Windows	Anonymous, Basic, Digest, NTLM, Negotiate (Kerberos or NTLM)
Claims Based Authentication	Windows	Anonymous, Basic, Digest, NTLM, Negotiate (Kerberos or NTLM)
	FBA	LDAP, SQL database, Other DB, Custom
	SAML	ADFS 2.0, Windows Live ID, Third Party

Configure Classic Mode Authentication

Classic Mode Authentication is one of the two types of authentication supported by SharePoint 2010. If you do not require claims, and if you will use only Windows authentication, you can create a web application that uses Classic Mode Authentication.

Classic Mode Authentication supports one authentication provider—Windows—and several methods of Windows authentication: NTLM, Kerberos, Basic, Digest, and Anonymous. You can configure the authentication method when you create the web application or after a web application has been created.

Create a Web Application with Classic Mode Authentication

As you learned in Lesson 1, when you create a web application, you can specify authentication settings on the Create New Web Application page, shown in Figure 3-8.

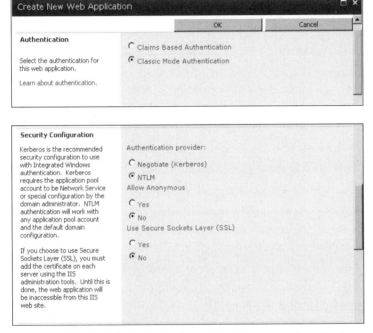

FIGURE 3-8 Classic Mode Authentication settings for a new web application

You can also specify authentication settings when you create a new web application by using Windows PowerShell.

CREATE A NEW WEB APPLICATION WITH CLASSIC MODE AUTHENTICATION

The following example shows the use of the *New-SPWebApplication* cmdlet to create a new web application:

```
New-SPWebApplication -Name <Name> -Port <Port> -HostHeader <HostHeader>
-AuthenticationMethod <AuthenticationMethod> [-AllowAnonymousAccess]
[-SecureSocketsLayer] -URL <URL> -ApplicationPool <ApplicationPool>
-ApplicationPoolAccount <ApplicationPoolAccount> -DatabaseName <DatabaseName>
```

Where:

- *<Name>* is the name of the new web application.
- *<Port>* is the port on which the web application will be created in IIS.
- *<HostHeader>* is the host header, in the format *server.domain.com*.

  Note that the *Get-Help* documentation for the cmdlet states that the format for *<HostHeader>* is *http://server.domain.com*. The documentation is incorrect.

- *<AuthenticationMethod>* is the Windows authentication method, which can be *NTLM* or *Kerberos*.

  If you specify *Kerberos*, it is actually the *Negotiate (Kerberos or NTLM)* method that is used.

- The *-AllowAnonymousAccess* switch parameter, if specified, enables anonymous authentication.
- The *-SecureSocketsLayer* parameter, if specified, enables SSL for the web application.

  As you learned in Lesson 1, you must also use IIS Manager to create the certificate in the server's certificate store and bind the certificate to the IIS Web site.

- *<URL>* is the public URL for the web application's default zone.
- *<ApplicationPool>* is the name of the application pool.
- *<ApplicationPoolAccount>* is the managed account that the application pool will use.

  This parameter is required if you are specifying an *<ApplicationPool>* that does not already exist. Use the *Get-SPManagedAccount* cmdlet as shown in the following example. If the *<ApplicationPool>* already exists, do not include this parameter.

- *<DatabaseName>* is the name for the first content database for the web application.

For example, the following command creates the Contoso partner portal web application with configuration similar to the web application that was created by using Central Administration in Lesson 1:

```
New-SPWebApplication -Name "Contoso Partner Portal" -Port 443
-HostHeader "partners.contoso.com" -AuthenticationMethod "NTLM" -SecureSocketsLayer
-URL "https://partners.contoso.com:443" -ApplicationPool "SharePoint Extranet Applications"
-ApplicationPoolAccount (Get-SPManagedAccount "CONTOSO\SP_WebApps")
-DatabaseName "SharePoint_Content_Partners"
```

The command creates a new application pool. If the application pool already exists, you would not include the *-ApplicationPoolAccount* parameter and value.

Configure a Web Application with Classic Mode Authentication

After a web application is created, you can modify authentication settings on the Edit Authentication page, shown in Figure 3-9.

You can access the Edit Authentication page from the Web Applications Management or the Authentication Providers pages of Central Administration.

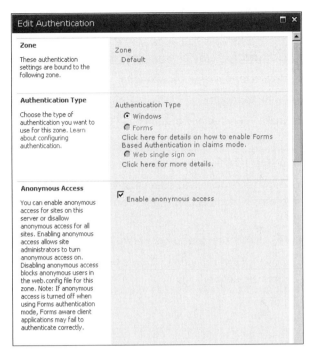

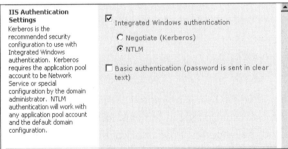

FIGURE 3-9 Edit Authentication page for Classic Mode Authentication

CONFIGURE AUTHENTICATION SETTINGS FROM THE WEB APPLICATIONS MANAGEMENT PAGE

1. In the Central Administration Quick Launch, click Application Management.

2. In the Web Applications section, click Manage Web Applications.

3. Select the web application that you want to modify.

4. On the ribbon, click Authentication Providers.

5. Click the link to the zone that you want to modify.

   By default, each new web application has a single zone, called Default. You will learn more about zones later in this chapter.

   The Edit Authentication page appears.

6. Make your changes, and then click Save.

CONFIGURE AUTHENTICATION SETTINGS FROM THE AUTHENTICATION PROVIDERS PAGE

1. In the Central Administration Quick Launch, click Security.

2. In the Web Applications section, click Specify Authentication Providers.

3. Click the Web Application picker to select the web application that you want to modify.

4. Click the link to the zone that you want to modify.

5. On the Edit Authentication page, make your changes, and then click Save.

Windows Authentication Methods

Windows authentication is available in both classic-mode and claims-based authentication. However, when a web application is using classic-mode authentication, only the Windows authentication provider is supported.

Windows authentication supports the following authentication methods:

- Integrated Windows authentication, which can use either NT LAN Manager (NTLM) or Negotiate (Kerberos or NTLM) authentication methods.

- Basic.

- Anonymous.

- Digest.

- Client certificates.

NTLM

Introduced more than a decade ago, NTLM is the most established form of authentication in Microsoft products.

When a user logs on to his or her computer, the user is prompted for a user name and password. The user name is sent to the domain controller, but the password is never sent over the network. Instead, there is an encrypted challenge/response protocol through which a hash of the password is passed through a one-way hashing algorithm (the challenge) by both the client and the domain controller. The client sends the result (the response) to the domain controller. If the result matches what the domain controller obtained as a result, the password entered by the user must have been correct, and the user is authenticated.

It gets more complicated when a user connects to a server, such as a SharePoint server. If the SharePoint server is a member server—not a domain controller—it has no way of knowing the user's password. So when the user connects to the server, the server has to pass the authentication request up to a domain controller. If the domain controller responds to the server that the user is valid, the authentication succeeds.

Although NTLM is not the most efficient authentication method, and is slightly less secure than Kerberos, it is often chosen as the authentication method for SharePoint web applications because it is easy to set up—it just works, out of the box.

Kerberos

Kerberos is the default authentication method for Windows clients and servers in an Active Directory domain.

Kerberos uses a process that involves encrypted tickets to verify authenticity. When a user logs on and authenticates with the domain, the domain controller's Key Distribution Center (KDC) issues the user a *ticket-granting-ticket* (TGT) that effectively represents that the user has been authenticated. For the lifetime of the TGT (10 hours by default), the user no longer needs to be authenticated.

When the user wants to connect to a service, such as a SharePoint web application that uses Kerberos authentication, the client application returns to a domain controller's KDC, presents the TGT, which confirms that the client has already been authenticated, and requests from a domain controller a service ticket for the specific service to which the client will connect. The client then goes to the service and presents the service ticket.

Because the entire process is encrypted with keys unique to each player (the client, the service, and the domain), the service is able to examine the service ticket and determine that it is being presented by an authenticated client. The service ticket contains the client's identity and roles; the session is established.

This is a very simplistic—but accurate—explanation of Kerberos. If you are interested in more details about Kerberos, see the resources listed in the "Additional Resources About Kerberos Authentication" section.

One of the benefits of Kerberos is that when the client connects to the service, the service does not have to round-trip the authentication to a domain controller, as in NTLM. Instead, the client's ticket for the service ensures the client has been authenticated. This results in improved authentication performance for Kerberos as compared to NTLM.

Another benefit is that Kerberos tickets can be *delegated*—that is, forwarded or *proxied* between tiers. For example, a client connecting to a website provides a Kerberos ticket, and the website can pass the ticket to a back-end data source that can authenticate the user for data access. The web tier does not need to know the user's password to achieve this "double-hop" authentication. The web tier also does not need permissions to the back-end data source—it is all done using the authentication of the client.

To secure this "double-hop" authentication, you can configure Kerberos *constrained delegation*. Constrained delegation restricts which services are allowed to delegate user credentials by specifying, for each application pool or service, the services to which a Kerberos ticket can be forwarded. If you choose to configure constrained delegation, you should configure and test Kerberos with unconstrained delegation and resolve any issues you might encounter prior to configuring constrained delegation.

Kerberos is considered by many organizations to be a preferable authentication mechanism because of the following advantages:

- More secure than NTLM. Kerberos protocols ensure mutual authentication, which prevents what are called "man in the middle" attacks whereby a rogue service could pretend to be a domain controller and intercept authentication requests from clients. Kerberos tickets also contain timestamps that reduce the likelihood of "replay attacks" in which an authentication token can be intercepted and used at a later date for malicious purposes.

- More scalable than NTLM. Kerberos supports authentication across trusted realms and, because it is an industry standard, is supported by platforms other than Windows.

- Supports delegation. Delegation and constrained delegation were explained earlier. Delegation allows a service to impersonate a user without knowing the user's password. Windows Server 2003 and later support constrained delegation as well, which adds a further level of security to the implementation of Kerberos in a Windows enterprise.

- Reduced load on domain controllers. Kerberos requires fewer trips to a domain controller for authentication than NTLM.

The disadvantage of Kerberos is that it requires additional steps to configure. You will learn the fundamental steps to configure Kerberos later in this lesson.

Negotiate (Kerberos or NTLM)

To use Kerberos authentication for a SharePoint web application, select the Negotiate (Kerberos or NTLM) authentication method. The Negotiate authentication method attempts to use Kerberos authentication. But if Kerberos authentication is not supported in the deployed environment, or if the client does not support Kerberos, authentication falls back to NTLM.

> **NOTE KERBEROS-ONLY ISN'T AN OPTION**
> There is no option to use Kerberos as the only authentication method for Windows authentication.

IIS passes the Negotiate security header when Windows Integrated authentication is used to authenticate client requests. The Negotiate security header lets clients select between Kerberos authentication and NTLM authentication. The Negotiate process selects Kerberos authentication unless one of the following conditions is true:

- One of the systems that is involved in the authentication cannot use Kerberos authentication.

- The calling application does not provide enough information to use Kerberos authentication.

If the Negotiate process cannot use the Kerberos protocol, the Negotiate process selects the NTLM protocol.

Configure Kerberos Authentication

To configure Kerberos authentication, you must use *service principal names* or *SPNs* for your SharePoint services, web applications, and SQL Server. This section will summarize the process. For a detailed walkthrough of creating a SharePoint farm with Kerberos authentication, see the TechNet article "Configure Kerberos authentication (SharePoint Server 2010)" at *http://technet.microsoft.com/en-us/library/ee806870.aspx*.

Earlier in this lesson, you learned that when a client wants to connect to a web application that uses Kerberos authentication, the client requests a service ticket from a domain controller's KDC. The request indicates the service to which the client will connect by specifying the service's *service principal name* or *SPN*.

The SPN is made up of three components. The first is the *service class* for the request, which is always *HTTP*—the *HTTP* service class includes both the HTTP and HTTPS protocols. The second is the host name, and the third is the port (if not port 80) of the web application. Together, these three components comprise the SPN of the web application.

For example, a request to *http://intranet.contoso.com* on port 80 equates to an SPN of *HTTP/intranet.contoso.com*. Note that the SPN syntax uses a single forward slash between the service class and host name portions of the name. A request to *https://partners.contoso.com* on port 443 equates to an SPN of *HTTP/partners.contoso.com:443*. A request to *http:// sp2010-wfe1:9999* for Central Administration equates to an SPN of *HTTP/sp2010-wfe1:9999*.

A security principal—a user or computer account in Active Directory—can have one or more associated SPNs. SPNs are an attribute of security principals in Active Directory. That means an account, such as an application pool account, can have multiple SPNs—for example, both *HTTP/intranet.contoso.com* and *HTTP/partners.contoso.com:443*.

When a domain controller's KDC receives the service ticket request from a client, it looks up the requested SPN. The KDC then creates a *session key* for the service and encrypts the session key with the password of the account with which the SPN is associated. The KDC issues a service ticket, containing the session key, to the client. The client presents the service ticket to the service. The service, which knows its own password, decrypts the session key and authentication is complete.

If a client submits a service ticket request for an SPN that does not exist in the identity store, no service ticket can be established and the client will throw an *access denied* error.

For this reason, each component of a SharePoint infrastructure that uses Kerberos authentication requires at least one SPN. For example, the intranet web application app pool account must have an SPN of *HTTP/intranet.contoso.com*.

Configure Service Principal Names for a Service or Application Pool

Note that it is the app pool—not the server—that is associated with the SPN because the app pool is the security context within which the service—the web application in this case—is running. It also makes sense if you consider that each SPN can be associated with only one security principal, and if a web app is load balanced—running on several servers—it is the one app pool account that is constant across all servers and therefore must have the SPN.

For each web application, you should assign two SPNs—one with the fully qualified domain name for the service, and one with the NetBIOS name of the service. Therefore, the intranet web application pool account should also be assigned an SPN of HTTP/intranet.

In many environments, a single application pool can be used by multiple web applications. The app pool account should be given a pair of SPNs for each of its web applications that use Kerberos authentication.

You can use ADSI Edit to add SPNs to an account. To configure an SPN for a service or application pool account, you must have domain administrative permissions or a delegation to modify the *servicePrincipalName* property.

CONFIGURE SPNS USING ADSI EDIT

1. Start ADSI Edit.
2. In the console tree, right-click ADSI Edit, and then click Connect To.
3. In the Connection Settings dialog box, click OK.
4. In the console tree, expand Default Naming Context, then expand the domain, and then expand the nodes representing the OUs in which the account exists. Click the OU in which the account exists.
5. In the Details pane, right-click the service or application pool account, and then click Properties to open the Properties dialog box.
6. In the Attributes list, double-click servicePrincipalName to open the Multi-Valued String Editor dialog box.
7. In the Value To Add field, type the SPN, and then click Add.

   Repeat step 7 for additional SPNs. Remember that an app pool account should have two SPNs, in the form HTTP/site.domain.com and HTTP/site, for each web application that uses Kerberos authentication in the app pool. Remember also to add the port number if the site runs on a port other than port 80—for example, HTTP/site.contoso .com:9999 and HTTP/site:9999.
8. Click OK twice.

You can also use the command-line tool Setspn.exe to add SPNs to an account.

CONFIGURE SPNS USING SETSPN

The following example shows the use of the SetSPN command to add an SPN to an account:

```
setspn <domain\user> -s <SPN>
```

Where:

- *<domain\user>* identifies the security principal to which you want to add an SPN.
- <SPN> is the service principal name that you want to add.

For example, to add SPNs for the intranet web application to the app pool account, you can type the following commands:

```
setspn CONTOSO\SP_WebApps -s HTTP/intranet.contoso.com
setspn CONTOSO\SP_WebApps -s HTTP/intranet
```

The most useful facts to know about SetSPN are the following:

- The *-s* parameter adds an SPN to an account after verifying that a duplicate SPN does not already exist. Duplicate SPNs can cause authentication problems, and it is recommended that you use each SPN only once in a forest. The *-s* parameter is new in Windows Server 2008. Previously, you used the *-a* switch, which adds an SPN but does not check for duplicates. It is recommended that you use *-s* now that it is available, but some documentation might refer to *-a*.
- The *-L* switch lists the SPNs associated with a specific user or computer account.
- The *-Q* switch lists the accounts associated with a specific SPN.

You can type **setspn.exe /?** for more information about SetSPN.

Configure Service Principal Names for SQL Server

To configure Kerberos authentication for SQL Server, you will need to add SPNs to the SQL Server service account—for example, CONTOSO\SVC_SQL. By default, SQL Server communication is over port 1433, so the two SPNs for a SQL Server running on a server named SQLSERVER01 would be the following:

- MSSQLSvc/sqlserver01:1433
- MSSQLSvc/sqlserver01.contoso.com:1433

 Quick Check

- When you configure Kerberos authentication for a web application, what change must be made in Active Directory?

Quick Check Answer

- An SPN must be added to the user account of the application pool identity.

Verify Kerberos Authentication to a Web Application

After you have configured your environment to support Kerberos authentication for a web application, you can validate that Kerberos is being used to authenticate a user. By opening the website you will generate an entry in the Windows Security event log. Examine the Security event log on the web server. The audit event generated by the user's logon will show the security ID of the user and the Logon Process, which should be Kerberos, as shown in Figure 3-10.

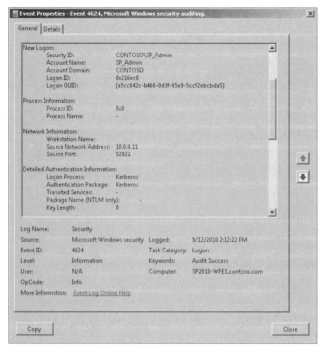

FIGURE 3-10 A Kerberos logon event

Alternately, you can use Klist.exe. KList is a command-line utility included in the default installation of Windows Server 2008 and Windows Server 2008 R2 which can be used to list and purge Kerberos tickets on a given computer. To verify Kerberos with KList, open the website on a client, and then use KList on the client to enumerate its tickets. You will see the ticket with the SPN of the web application, as shown in Figure 3-11.

FIGURE 3-11 KList enumeration of Kerberos tickets

Connect to Back-End Systems

In Chapter 8, "Implementing Enterprise Service Applications," you will learn to connect SharePoint to back-end data systems. For example, you might use Excel Services to present information in a database outside of SharePoint, or you might use Business Data Connectivity Services to create a SharePoint list that displays items stored in another system.

There are several ways to configure connection to a back-end or external system, including the Secure Store Service, the Claims To Windows Token Service, and Kerberos delegation. This chapter has examined authentication to a web application. If you need to support authentication to back end systems, be sure to read the details in Chapter 8.

Additional Resources about Kerberos Authentication

If you want to configure your entire SharePoint environment to support Kerberos, there are numerous additional steps to perform. You can learn more about configuring Kerberos by reading the following articles:

- "Configure Kerberos authentication (SharePoint Server 2010)," *http://technet.microsoft.com/en-us/library/ee806870.aspx*.
- "Kerberos (Windows Server 2008 and Windows Server 2008 R2 Technical Library)," *http://technet.microsoft.com/en-us/library/cc753173(WS.10).aspx*.
- "Kerberos Authentication Technical Reference (Windows Security Collection)," *http://technet.microsoft.com/en-us/library/cc739058(WS.10).aspx*.
- "Windows Authentication," *http://technet.microsoft.com/en-us/library/cc755284(WS.10).aspx*.
- "Kerberos Explained," *http://technet.microsoft.com/en-us/library/bb742516.aspx*.
- "How to use SPNs when you configure Web applications that are hosted on Internet Information Services," *http://support.microsoft.com/kb/929650*.
- "Setspn," *http://technet.microsoft.com/en-us/library/cc731241(WS.10).aspx*.
- "Microsoft Kerberos (Windows)," *http://msdn.microsoft.com/library/aa378747*.
- "Ask the Directory Services Team: Kerberos for the Busy Admin," *http://blogs.technet.com/b/askds/archive/2008/03/06/kerberos-for-the-busy-admin.aspx*.
- "Configure Kerberos authentication for the claims to Windows token service (SharePoint Server 2010)," *http://technet.microsoft.com/en-us/library/ee806887.aspx*.

You can also download the white paper "Configuring Kerberos authentication for SharePoint 2010 Products" at *http://technet.microsoft.com/en-us/library/ff829837.aspx*.

Additional Windows Authentication Methods

Although NTLM or Negotiate (Kerberos or NTLM) are the most commonly used authentication methods, Classic Mode Windows authentication also supports anonymous, basic, and digest authentication methods.

Anonymous

Anonymous authentication enables users to connect to a web application without providing credentials. You can enable anonymous authentication on either the Create New Web Application or Edit Authentication pages.

Anonymous authentication was detailed earlier in this lesson. You learned that anonymous authentication does not provide anonymous users with permission to content within a web application. Anonymous access must be granted at the securable object. You can grant anonymous users permission to an entire site or to specific lists and libraries. You can then restrict access at the web application by applying anonymous access restriction policies, which override permissions.

Basic

Like Integrated Windows authentication, Basic authentication relies on a set of credentials for the user in Active Directory. However, Basic authentication enables a web browser to submit credentials when making an HTTP request, and the credentials are sent as Base64 clear text, unencrypted, to the server. Credentials used in Basic authentication are easily compromised. If you choose to use Basic authentication, you should always enable Secure Sockets Layer (SSL) encryption.

> **NOTE** **WHEN NTLM AND KERBEROS AREN'T SUPPORTED**
> Certain browsers and connection scenarios, such as users behind some proxy servers, will not support NTLM and Kerberos. In these cases, you might need to resort to Basic authentication.

You cannot select Basic authentication when you create a SharePoint web application. Instead, you must do so after creating the web application.

ENABLE BASIC AUTHENTICATION

1. In the Central Administration Quick Launch, click Application Management.
2. In the Web Applications section, click Manage Web Applications.

    The Web Applications Management page opens.
3. Click the name of the web application for which you want to enable or disable anonymous access.
4. On the ribbon, click Authentication Providers.

    The Authentication Providers page opens.
5. Click the name of the zone for which you want to enable or disable anonymous access. For example, click Default.

    The Edit Authentication page opens.
6. In the IIS Authentication Settings section, shown earlier in Figure 3-9, select the Basic Authentication check box.
7. Click Save.

8. Close the Authentication Providers page.

9. Start Command Prompt using the Run As Administrator option, and then type **IISRESET**.

If you select Negotiate (Kerberos) and Basic Authentication, clients should attempt authentication in the following order: Kerberos, NTLM, Basic authentication.

Digest

Digest authentication provides the same functionality as Basic authentication, but with increased security. User credentials are encrypted instead of being sent over the network in plaintext. User credentials are sent as an MD5 message digest in which the original user name and password cannot be deciphered. Digest authentication uses a challenge/response protocol that requires the authentication requestor to present valid credentials in response to a challenge from the server. To authenticate against the server, the client has to supply an MD5 message digest in a response that contains a shared secret password string.

Digest authentication for SharePoint is not particularly common. To implement digest authentication, you will have to select Windows authentication in Central Administration, then configure the IIS Web site for Digest authentication.

Understand Claims Based Authentication

Consider the following summary of Claims Based Authentication:

> *Claims Based Authentication is a flexible framework based on Security Assertion Markup Language (SAML) tokens, and built on the Windows Identity Foundation (WIF). Tokens contain assertions about a user's identity that are generated by trusted authentication providers, which include Windows authentication—just as in Classic Mode Authentication—as well as Forms Based Authentication (FBA) and standard SAML tokens issued by trusted authorities such as Windows Live ID or Active Directory Federated Services 2.0 (ADFS 2.0). By extending the reach of trusted authentication providers, Claims Based Authentication enables authentication across Windows-based systems and systems that are not Windows based. Claims Based Authentication becomes particularly powerful when tokens contain other attributes of a user, such as demographic or organizational information. These attributes can originate within the user's organization, other organizations, or the Internet.*

Doesn't that sound really complex? Don't give up; read on.

Review Authentication in a Windows Domain

If you are not already familiar with Claims Based Authentication, the preceding description of Claims Based Authentication may sound complex. But the concepts related to Claims Based Authentication can be pretty straightforward if you start from the perspective of an authentication scheme that you already understand: authentication within a Windows domain. Let's review the basics of Windows authentication as a basis from which to understand Claims Based Authentication.

When you require access to a system, such as a file server, the system must know who you are before you can be granted access to resources. It would not be manageable to maintain a list of user names and passwords on each system. Therefore, you create a Windows domain by implementing Active Directory Domain Services (AD DS). Within a domain, all systems trust the authentication mechanism of the domain—Kerberos—to validate the identity of a user. So, when you access a file server, the file server does not have to authenticate you. Instead, you bring to the server a Kerberos service ticket that identifies you. The ticket has been created using processes that include encryption using keys known only by the server and the domain. So the server knows that the service ticket is valid. It looks at the ticket to know who you are. The server accepts the ticket's assertion as to your identity because the server trusts the source of the ticket—the AD DS domain's Kerberos KDC. The server does not have to perform authentication—it trusts an external authentication provider.

The Kerberos service ticket does not just identify you. It also contains a list of your domain security group memberships. Again, because the ticket comes from a trusted authority, the server uses that list of groups. The server builds a token that contains your identity—your user account's security identifier, or *SID*—and the SIDs of the groups to which you belong. The token is then used by the local security subsystem to determine whether you have access to a file by comparing the SIDs on the file's access control list to the SIDs in your token. This security token represents you to the local server.

In the past, when a developer wanted to create a secure website, the developer had to build an authentication component. With SharePoint, in Classic Mode Authentication, your Windows security token is translated into an object that represents you within SharePoint—an object called an *SPUser* object. You can think of the *SPUser* object in a SharePoint web application as the conceptual equivalent of your Windows security token—it represents you during your interactions with the web application.

Claims Authentication to a SharePoint Web Application

A *claim* is a set of *assertions*—information about a user. At the most basic conceptual level, a Kerberos service ticket is a claim that, among other things, asserts the identity and group memberships of a user. When you access a SharePoint web application that uses Claims Based Authentication, the web application accepts a claim and translates that claim into the *SPUser* object which, as you know, represents you during your interactions with the web application.

This is the first difference between Classic Mode Authentication and Claims Based Authentication. In Classic Mode Authentication, the web application relies on IIS to pass your Windows security token to the web application. In Claims Based Authentication, the web application relies on the farm's Security Token Service (STS) to deliver a token that contains claims, including claims about your identity.

In Classic Mode Authentication, IIS relies on Active Directory to actually perform authentication. IIS can receive credentials using several methods, including NTLM, Kerberos, Basic, and Digest. In the case of NTLM, Basic, and Digest authentication, IIS authenticates the credentials against Active Directory. In the case of Kerberos authentication, the service ticket contains credentials that have already been authenticated.

In Claims Based Authentication, the STS also does not actually perform authentication. Instead, it relies on a trusted authority to do so. The authority can be Active Directory, or it can be one of a number of other authentication providers. If the Claims Based Application uses the Windows authentication provider, the STS performs essentially the same function as IIS does in Classic Mode Authentication. If Kerberos is available, the service ticket is processed and turned into a set of claims about the user's identity and group memberships. If NTLM, Basic, or Digest authentication are used, the STS authenticates the credentials against Active Directory and then the NT token is translated into a set of claims about the user's identity and group memberships.

The resulting claims are provided to the web application as a token which, as you know, is translated into an *SPUser* object within the web application.

By this point in the discussion, you should understand that a component called an *STS* is doing the work of building tokens that contain claims. You should also have an understanding that if only Windows authentication is used, there is conceptually little difference between Classic Mode Authentication and Claims Based Authentication. But the story is just beginning.

What if you want to make a web application available to partners, but you do not want to add accounts for partner users to your AD DS domain? In the past, a web developer would have to write a custom component to authenticate users and to administer user identities. Now, however, you can use the Forms Based Authentication provider to authenticate users against credentials stored in AD DS; in Active Directory Lightweight Directory Services (AD LDS); in a database such as a SQL Server database; or in an LDAP data store such as Novell eDirectory, Novell Directory Services (NDS), or Sun ONE. Or you can use SAML to authenticate users against credentials stored in Active Directory Federated Services 2.0 (ADFS 2.0), by Windows Live ID, or by a custom trusted source.

Claims Based Authentication thus allows SharePoint web applications to be extended to more diverse sets of users, across domains, forests, and non-Windows environments. You can change the authentication provider or the methods of authentication without having to change the web application itself.

Trust

How are claims actually built? When you attempt to access a web application that uses Claims Based Authentication, you are transparently redirected to a sign-in page for the STS, at which you are authenticated. In some cases, such as Windows authentication, you might never even see this transaction if your browser's security settings are configured to authenticate you silently to trusted sites, and if the website is in a trusted zone. The STS authenticates you and provides a token to your browser. Your browser then returns to the original website, submits the token, and the web application then knows who you are.

But if the browser is submitting a token with assertions about your identity, how does the web application know that those assertions come from a trusted source, and that you have not fabricated a false token containing erroneous statements about who you are?

The process uses a series of standards called *WS-** standards that effectively ensure that the token can be used by the web application. To make a long, complicated story very short, the web application has been configured to trust the STS. The trust involves the exchange of certificates that are used to encrypt the token. If the web application is able to decrypt the token with the shared secret, it knows that the token must have been generated by the trusted STS.

Trust is at the heart of any security system. In an AD DS domain, each component of Windows trusts the local security subsystem, which in turn trusts the domain, which in turn trusts other domains in the forest, and that trust can then be extended to other domains or forests. In SharePoint, all web applications and services in a farm trust the Security Token Service of the farm.

Trust and Claims Based Authentication in Action

When you sign in to a Microsoft website such as Microsoft TechNet or MSDN with your Windows Live ID, you are authenticated using Claims Based Authentication. These websites—which do not run on SharePoint—trust Windows Live ID to verify your identity. They redirect you to a Windows Live ID sign-in control for authentication. Windows Live ID issues your browser an encrypted token that contains assertions as to your identity and other attributes. Your browser passes this token to the website, which can decrypt the token.

Claims

When a claim is presented to a web application, the claim contains assertions about the user's identity. It also can contain claims about the user's group memberships. Each of the authentication methods available in Claims Based Authentication can provide the STS with an enumeration of the user's group memberships, which are added to the claim.

But a claim can provide more than just user and group information, and this is where claims become particularly valuable. Let's assume that you want to be able to send email messages to users from a website. How do you determine a user's email address? You can build and maintain a local database of user email addresses, but in an AD DS domain that information is stored in Active Directory, and so a local database would have to be kept in synch with changes made in Active Directory. Or you can add code to query Active Directory each time an email address is needed. Both approaches require additional work by the website developer.

A claim can include a user's email address or any other attribute of the user, such as the user's manager or the manager's email address, department, job title, age, or gender. Because the claims are presented by the user to the web application, the web application does not need to maintain local copies of the attributes, nor does it need to go look up the attributes in an external source. Instead, the STS is configured to collect the attributes and to create claims.

Claims Based Authentication thus reduces the burden on applications themselves to maintain or look up information about users. Attributes in claims can be used for a variety of purposes. You can assign permissions to content that are based on a claim. For example, you can specify that users must have a job title of Vice President or higher to access content. You can also use claims to look up users. For example, if you want to assign a task to a user, but you can only remember the user's manager, the picker control can expose the manager attribute of users who belong to the site. Developers are particularly excited about the possibilities that are presented now that SharePoint 2010 supports claims.

Federation

Let's now assume that certain content in a web application can only be accessed by users who are employees of your company, Contoso, or of a partner company, Litware. How do you make this work? It would be a burden to have duplicate copies of all Litware user accounts in your AD DS domain or in a separate database, and to keep changes in synch. It would be much easier to simply rely on the administrators at Litware to maintain their user accounts, and to trust the authentication performed by Litware.

With Windows domains, you could configure a trust whereby the Contoso domain trusts the Litware domain. However, firewalls can often prevent trusts from being correctly established and maintained, and many organizations have policies that forbid Windows trusts to external organizations.

Claims Based Authentication supports *federation*, which extends the concepts of trust and claims to third parties. For example, you can configure ADFS 2.0 to authenticate users against both domains, without requiring a trust. You then configure SharePoint's STS to trust the STS exposed by ADFS 2.0. From a terminology perspective, SharePoint's STS becomes the *relying party STS* (RP-STS) and the STS of ADFS 2.0 becomes the *identity provider STS* (IP-STS).

When a user attempts to access a website, the user is redirected to the IP STS for authentication. The token issued by the IP STS (ADFS 2.0 in this example) is then presented to the RP STS (SharePoint's STS in this example), which can augment the token with additional claims before giving the client the token that is then submitted to the web application.

Another example of federated identity is Windows Live ID authentication. You can configure SharePoint's STS to trust tokens issued by Windows Live ID, just as some Microsoft sites do.

Claims Authentication

Claims authentication is built on the Windows Identity Foundation (WIF). WIF is a set of .NET Framework classes that are used to implement claims-based identity. Claims authentication relies on standards such as WS-Federation, WS-Trust, and protocols such as SAML. Claims Based Authentication thus enables you to extend both authentication (identification) and the collection of informational attributes about a user to sources beyond your domain.

It's not important that you, as an IT Pro, master all of the concepts, standards, and protocols, and the tools used to create code used to leverage claims. However, you must be able to configure SharePoint to support claims authentication. In the next section, you will learn how to configure SharePoint for Windows-Claims, Forms-Claims, and SAML-Claims authentication.

Now, test yourself: Return to the beginning of this section, "Understand Claims Based Authentication," and read the summary once again. Does it make sense now?

> **MORE INFO** **CLAIMS AUTHENTICATION AND THE WIF**
>
> The following article provide additional detail regarding claims authentication and the WIF: "Claims-based Identity for Windows: An Introduction to Active Directory Federation Services 2.0, Windows CardSpace 2.0, and Windows Identity Foundation (white paper)," at *http://go.microsoft.com/fwlink/?LinkId=198942*. You can also visit the Windows Identity Foundation home page at *http://go.microsoft.com/fwlink/?LinkId=198943*.

Configure Windows-Claims Authentication

Now that you understand Claims Based Authentication, we can turn our attention to the procedures required to create and configure web applications that use Claims Based Authentication. First, we will explore creating a web application that uses the Windows authentication provider for Claims Based Authentication—*Windows-Claims* authentication. You can create a web application that uses Claims Based Authentication by using Central Administration or Windows PowerShell.

CREATE A WEB APPLICATION WITH WINDOWS-CLAIMS AUTHENTICATION USING CENTRAL ADMINISTRATION

1. In the Central Administration Quick Launch, click Application Management.
2. In the Web Applications section, click Manage Web Applications.
3. On the ribbon, click New to open the Create New Web Application page.
4. In the Authentication section, click Claims Based Authentication.
5. In the Claims Authentication Types section, select the Enable Windows Authentication check box.
6. If you want to use NTLM or Kerberos as the authentication method, select the Integrated Windows Authentication check box. Then, in the drop-down menu, select Negotiate (Kerberos) or NTLM.
7. If you want users' credentials to be sent over a network in a nonencrypted form, select the Basic Authentication (Password Is Sent In Clear Text) check box. If you use basic authentication, ensure that SSL is enabled; otherwise, the credentials can be intercepted by a malicious user.
8. Configure other settings for the new web application. See Lesson 1 for more information about the settings you can configure when creating a web application.

To create a web application by using Windows PowerShell, you must first create an object that represents the authentication provider by using the *New-SPAuthenticationProvider* cmdlet.

CREATE AN AUTHENTICATION PROVIDER USING WINDOWS POWERSHELL

The following example shows the use of the *New-SPAuthenticationProvider* cmdlet to create a new Windows authentication provider.

```
$ap = New-SPAuthenticationProvider [-UseWindowsIntegratedAuthentication]
[-DisableKerberos | DisableKerberos:$false]
[-UseBasicAuthentication] [-AllowAnonymous]
```

Where:

- The -*UseWindowsIntegratedAuthentication* switch parameter specifies that the authentication provider will be Windows.

- The -*DisableKerberos* switch parameter, if specified, disables Kerberos authentication. The authentication provider uses NTLM only.

    The -*DisableKerberos:$false* syntax enables authentication.

- The -*UseBasicAuthentication* switch parameter, if specified, enables Basic authentication.

After you create the object representing the authentication provider, you pass the object as the -*AuthenticationProvider* parameter to the *New-SPWebApplication* cmdlet.

CREATE A WEB APPLICATION WITH CLAIMS BASED AUTHENTICATION USING WINDOWS POWERSHELL

The following example shows the use of the *New-SPWebApplication* cmdlet to create a new web application:

```
New-SPWebApplication -Name <Name> -Port <Port> -HostHeader <HostHeader>
-AuthenticationProvider <AuthenticationProvider> [-AllowAnonymousAccess]
[-SecureSocketsLayer] -URL <URL> -ApplicationPool <ApplicationPool>
-ApplicationPoolAccount <ApplicationPoolAccount> -DatabaseName <DatabaseName>
```

Where:

- *<Name>* is the name of the new web application.

- *<Port>* is the port on which the web application will be created in IIS.

- *<HostHeader>* is the host header, in the format *server.domain.com*.

  Note that the *Get-Help* documentation for the cmdlet states that the format for *<HostHeader>* is *http://server.domain.com*. The documentation is incorrect.

- *<AuthenticationProvider>* is an object representing an authentication provider.

  Use the *New-SPAuthenticationProvider* cmdlet to create an object representing an authentication provider, as described earlier.

- The *-AllowAnonymousAccess* switch parameter, if specified, enables anonymous authentication.

- The *-SecureSocketsLayer* parameter, if specified, enables SSL for the web application.

  As you learned in Lesson 1, you must also use IIS Manager to create the certificate in the server's certificate store and bind the certificate to the IIS Web site.

- *<URL>* is the public URL for the web application's default zone.

- *<ApplicationPool>* is the name of the application pool.

- *<ApplicationPoolAccount>* is the managed account that the application pool will use.

  This parameter is required if you are specifying an *<ApplicationPool>* that does not already exist. Use the *Get-SPManagedAccount* cmdlet as shown in the following example. If the *<ApplicationPool>* already exists, do not include this parameter.

- *<DatabaseName>* is the name for the first content database for the web application.

For example, the following command creates the partner portal web application with configuration similar to the web application that was created by using Central Administration in Lesson 1, but with Claims Based Authentication. A Windows authentication provider is constructed that uses only NTLM—Kerberos is disabled—and passed as the authentication provider for the new web application.

```
$ap = New-SPAuthenticationProvider -UseWindowsIntegratedAuthentication
    -DisableKerberos
New-SPWebApplication -Name "Contoso Partner Portal" -Port 443
    -HostHeader "partners.contoso.com" -AuthenticationProvider $ap -SecureSocketsLayer
    -URL "https://partners.contoso.com:443"
    -ApplicationPool "SharePoint Extranet Applications"
    -ApplicationPoolAccount (Get-SPManagedAccount "CONTOSO\SP_WebApps")
    -DatabaseName "SharePoint_Content_Partners"
```

After you have created the web application, create a site collection. When you create a site collection, you must specify the primary site collection administrator. You can use Central Administration or the *New-SPSite* cmdlet, as described in Chapter 2.

Configure Forms Based Authentication

Forms Based Authentication (FBA) is an identity management system that is based on ASP.NET membership and role provider authentication.

If an unauthenticated user attempts to access a web application using FBA, the user is redirected to a logon form, with which the user submits credentials. The credentials are authenticated against an identity store, which can be AD DS; a database such as a SQL Server database; or an LDAP data store such as Active Directory Lightweight Directory Services (AD LDS), Novell eDirectory, Novell Directory Services (NDS), or Sun ONE.

SharePoint Server 2010 uses the standard ASP.NET membership provider interface to authenticate the user, and the standard ASP.NET role manager interface to gather group information about the user. Each ASP.NET role is treated as a domain group by the authorization process in SharePoint Server 2010. The resulting information about the user is converted into claims by the STS, thus FBA is also called *Forms-Claims* authentication.

To configure FBA, you must manage the following settings, each of which is detailed later in this section:

- **The web application's authentication mode** The web application must use Claims Based Authentication. In SharePoint Server 2010, Forms-Based Authentication is available only when you use Claims Based Authentication.

> **NOTE FBA AND CLASSIC MODE AUTHENTICATION**
>
> If you upgrade a SharePoint 2007 web application that uses FBA, the upgraded web application is configured to use Classic Mode Authentication, and FBA will not function. You must convert the web application to Claims Based Authentication, as described later in this lesson.

- **The config file of the Security Token Service (STS) Application** As you have learned, the STS generates and manages claims tokens. The STS uses the FBA authentication provider to authenticate the user on behalf of the relying party—either the web application or Central Administration. It is the STS that actually performs the authentication, so it must know which provider and data source to use.

- **The Web.config file of the web application's IIS site** You must register the membership provider and role manager in the Web.config file. Although the web application does not perform authentication, it does perform other tasks against the users and roles that are provided. For example, when you assign a task or grant permissions to a user or group, the People Picker control must know the sources from which it can find users.

- **The Web.config file of the Central Administration IIS site**   If you want to manage membership users or roles from the SharePoint Central Administration web site, you must register the membership provider and the role manager in the Web.config file of the Central Administration website as well. For example, you might want assign a user as the primary site collection administrator. If Central Administration does not know how to locate and interact with the FBA provider, it will be unable to locate the user and add the user as the site collection owner.

- **Access to the database against which users are authenticated**   The user database must allow SharePoint to authenticate and look up users.

Create a Web Application with Forms-Claims Authentication

Forms Based Authentication is available only to an application that uses Claims Based Authentication. You can create the web application by using Central Administration or Windows PowerShell.

CREATE A WEB APPLICATION WITH FORMS-CLAIMS AUTHENTICATION USING CENTRAL ADMINISTRATION

1. In the Central Administration Quick Launch, click Application Management.
2. In the Web Applications section, click Manage Web Applications.
3. On the ribbon, click New to open the Create New Web Application page.
4. In the Authentication section, click Claims Based Authentication.
5. In the Claims Authentication Types section, select the Enable Forms Based Authentication (FBA) check box.

6. Enter the membership provider name and the role manager name in the boxes. You will learn more about these settings later in this lesson.
7. In the Sign In Page URL section, do one of the following:

- Click Default Sign In Page if you want users to be redirected to a SharePoint's default sign-in page for claims-based authentication.

- Click Custom Sign In Page, and then type the URL of the customized sign-in page to which you want users redirected for Claims Based Authentication for the web application.

8. Configure other settings for the new web application. See Lesson 1 for more information about the settings you can configure when creating a web application.

CREATE A WEB APPLICATION WITH FORMS-CLAIMS AUTHENTICATION USING WINDOWS POWERSHELL

The following example shows the use of the *New-SPAuthenticationProvider* cmdlet to create a new Forms Based Authentication authentication provider.

```
$ap = New-SPAuthenticationProvider –ASPNETMembershipProvider <MembershipProviderName>
-ASPNETRoleProviderName <RoleProviderName>
```

Where:

- *<MembershipProviderName>* specifies the name of the membership provider. The name must be the valid name of an ASP.NET provider defined in the Web.config file of the application.

- *<RoleProviderName>* specifies the name of the membership provider. The name must be the valid name of an ASP.NET membership provider defined in the Web.config file of the application.

After you create the object representing the authentication provider, you pass the object as the *-AuthenticationProvider* parameter to the *New-SPWebApplication* cmdlet, as described earlier in the procedure, "Create a Web Application with Claims Based Authentication Using Windows PowerShell."

For example, the following command creates the partner portal web application with configuration similar to the web application that was created by using Central Administration in Lesson 1, but with Forms-Claims authentication.

```
$ap = New-SPAuthenticationProvider -ASPNETMembershipProvider "MyMembershipProvider"
   -ASPNETRoleProviderName "MyRoleManager"
New-SPWebApplication -Name "Contoso Partner Portal"
   -Port 443 -HostHeader "partners.contoso.com" –AuthenticationProvider $ap
   -SecureSocketsLayer
   -URL "https://partners.contoso.com:443"
   -ApplicationPool "SharePoint Extranet Applications"
   -ApplicationPoolAccount (Get-SPManagedAccount "CONTOSO\SP_WebApps")
   -DatabaseName "SharePoint_Content_Partners"
```

Configure Web.config Files

After you have successfully created a web application that uses Claims Based Authentication, you must manually configure the specifics of the authentication provider by modifying the configuration file of the IIS site, Web.config.

This section details the configuration of Web.config. Do not be concerned if it sounds confusing. It is! In the practice for this lesson, you will configure FBA. The practice will thus give you hands-on experience modifying Web.config files, and a chance to review and reinforce the details presented here.

The following sample illustrates the structure of the Web.config file, focused on the elements that are important to configure for FBA.

```
<configuration>
...
  <SharePoint>
    <PeoplePickerWildcards>
      <clear />
      <add key="AspNetSqlMembershipProvider" value="%" />
      <add key="MyMembershipProvider" value="*"/>
      <add key="MyRoleManager" value="*"/>
    </PeoplePickerWildcards>
  </SharePoint>
  <connectionStrings>
    <add name="MyConnectionString" [define the connection] />
  </connectionStrings>
  <system.web>
...
    <membership>
      <providers>
       <add name="MyMembershipProvider" [define the membership provider] />
      </providers>
    </membership>
    <roleManager>
      <providers>
        <add name="MyRoleManager" [define the role manager] />
      </providers>
    </roleManager>
    ...
  </system.web>
...
</configuration>
```

As you work with the Web.config files, keep the following tips in mind:

- An element can have values—for example, you might see <roleManager enabled="true">, where enabled="true" is a value of the element roleManager. Do not change the existing values within a tag unless you have been instructed to do so.

- If an element does not exist, you can create it. For example, the Web.config file of the STS site does not have a *<system.web>* element. You can create it in the relative position shown in the preceding example.

- Names are used to link configuration elements. The name of the membership provider and role manager you configure for the SharePoint web application must have a matching entry in the *<membership><providers>* and the *<roleManager><providers>* elements, respectively. If the providers connect to a data source, the connection string must be registered in the *<connectionStrings>* element with a name that matches the name that is used in the definition of the providers in the *<membership><providers>* and the *<roleManager><providers>* elements. Keep close tabs on the names that you use to ensure all of the configuration elements are properly associated.

The *<connectionStrings>* element shown in the preceding example defines a connection to the identity store, typically a SQL database or LDAP directory. The following example registers a connection string named *MySQLDatabase* that connects to the database named *aspnetdb* on the server named *SP2010-WFE1.contoso.com* using integrated authentication:

```
<connectionStrings>
    <add name="MySQLDatabase"
        connectionString="server=SP2010-WFE1.contoso.com;
        database=aspnetdb;
        Integrated Security=SSPI" />
</connectionStrings>
```

You define a membership provider to connect the web application to a provider— a software component that performs the authentication. The most popular out-of-box FBA membership provider is the ASP.NET SQLMembershipProvider provider, which uses a membership database on a SQL server that contains information about users, groups (roles), and profile attributes. When you define the provider, you specify values of the provider that determine its exact behavior. For example, you pass a connection string to the provider so that the provider knows which data source to work with.

The following example configures a SQLMembershipProvider named *MyMembershipProvider*, and instructs the provider to access the data source referred to by the connection string named *MySQLDatabase*:

```
<add name="MyMembershipProvider"
    connectionStringName="MySQLDatabase"
    applicationName="/"
    type="System.Web.Security.SqlMembershipProvider, System.Web, Version=2.0.3600.0,
Culture=neutral, PublicKeyToken=b03f5f7f11d50a3a"
    description="Stores and retrieves roles from SQL Server"
    passwordAttemptWindow="5"
    enablePasswordRetrieval="false"
    enablePasswordReset="false"
    requiresQuestionAndAnswer="true"
    requiresUniqueEmail="true"
    passwordFormat="Hashed"/>
```

> **NOTE HOW TO USE THE TYPE TAG**
>
> The *type* tag must be on one line. In this example, it is shown breaking across lines for formatting purposes only.

Next, you define a role manager. The role manager, also called a role provider, is the software component responsible for identifying the roles, or groups, to which a user belongs. The most popular out-of-box role manager is the ASP.NET SQLRoleProvider, which works against the same membership database as the SQLMembershipProvider, but is responsible for determining the user's group memberships.

The following example configures a SQLRoleProvider named *MyRoleManager* that uses the same data source referred to by the connection string name, *MySQLDatabase*:

```
<add name="MyRoleManager"
    connectionStringName="MySQLDatabase"
    applicationName="/"
    type="System.Web.Security.SqlRoleProvider, System.Web, Version=2.0.3600.0,
    Culture=neutral, PublicKeyToken=b03f5f7f11d50a3a"
    description="Stores and retrieves roles from SQL Server"/>
```

The definition of the membership provider and role manager determines how authentication is performed for a web application. The following examples define the membership provider named *MyMembershipProvider* and the role manager named *MyRoleManager* to use the *LDAPMembershipProvider* and *LDAPRoleProvider* providers, respectively, with the *contoso.com* domain as the data source. If these providers were registered in the *Web.config* files instead of the identically named providers shown previously, the web application would authenticate against the domain instead of against a SQL membership database.

```
<configuration>
. . .
  <system.web>
  . . .
    <membership>
      <providers>
      <add name="MyMembershipProvider"
          type="Microsoft.Office.Server.Security.LdapMembershipProvider, Microsoft
          .Office.Server, Version=14.0.0.0, Culture=neutral,
          PublicKeyToken=71e9bce111e9429c"
          server="contoso.com"
          port="389"
          useSSL="false"
          userDNAttribute="distinguishedName"
          userNameAttribute="sAMAccountName"
          userContainer="DC=contoso,DC=com"
          userObjectClass="person"
          userFilter="(ObjectClass=person)"
          scope="Subtree"
          otherRequiredUserAttributes="sn,givenname,cn" />
      </providers>
    </membership>
    <roleManager>
      <providers>
      <add name="MyRoleManager"
          type="Microsoft.Office.Server.Security.LdapRoleProvider, Microsoft.Office
          .Server, Version=14.0.0.0, Culture=neutral, PublicKeyToken=71e9bce111e9429c"
          server="contoso.com"
          port="389"
          useSSL="false"
          groupContainer="DC=contoso,DC=com"
          groupNameAttribute="cn"
          groupNameAlternateSearchAttribute="samAccountName"
          groupMemberAttribute="member"
```

```
            userNameAttribute="sAMAccountName"
            dnAttribute="distinguishedName"
            groupFilter="(ObjectClass=group)"
            userFilter="(ObjectClass=person)"
            scope="Subtree" />
      </providers>
    </roleManager>
    . . .
  </system.web>
  . . .
</configuration>
```

In the case of the LDAP providers, you do not use or need a *<connectionStrings>* element, because all of the configuration of the connection is defined in the provider itself. Each provider, data source, and scenario requires slightly different configuration.

Hopefully you can see how the architecture of Claims Based Authentication allows the configuration of authentication to be separated fully from the web application itself. All you have to do is change the configuration of the IIS Web site's Web.config file and you can completely change the source of authentication.

One additional change to Web.config is often overlooked: the *<PeoplePickerWildards>* element. If you don't configure this element, the People Picker control will only accept exact matches. The People Picker is used in many places in SharePoint, including assigning tasks and assigning security permissions. There is already a *<PeoplePickerWildcards>* element in the Web.config file—you must simply define the wildcard that is used for your membership and role providers, as shown in the following example:

```
<PeoplePickerWildcards>
    <clear />
    <add key="AspNetSqlMembershipProvider" value="%" />
    <add key="MyMembershipProvider" value="*"/>
    <add key="MyRoleManager" value="*"/>
</PeoplePickerWildcards>
```

Two wildcard definitions are added to the default list—one for the membership provider and one for the role manager. The *key* tag must match the name of the provider that you configured by using Central Administration or the *New-SPAuthenticationProvider* cmdlet. For LDAP data sources, the *value* should be an asterisk (*). For SQL data sources, the *value* should be a percent symbol (%).

To properly configure SharePoint for Forms Based Authentication for a web application, you must configure three Web.config files:

- The Web.config file of the forms-based authentication claims-based web application
- The Web.config file of the Central Administration Web application
- The Web.config file of the Security Token Service

EXAM TIP

Remember the three Web.config files that must be changed to successfully configure Forms Based Authentication for a web application.

Assign Permissions to the User Database

SharePoint will authenticate users against the associated directory, which can be a database such as a SQL database, an LDAP directory such as an AD DS domain or an instance of AD LDS, or a custom provider. SharePoint will also use the directory to look up users, such as when you use the People Picker control to grant users or groups permissions, or to assign a task. For these reasons, the database must allow access by the application pool identities used by Central Administration, by the web application, by the Security Token Service Application, and by services.

The exact permissions required will vary based on your environment and the provider and database that you use for FBA. For example, in the environment that is built by this training kit, if you use a SQL database with the ASP.NET SQLMembershipProvider and SQLRoleProvider providers, the SQL database must allow access by the application pool identity of the web application (*SP_WebApps*, for example), the SharePoint farm service account (*SP_Farm*), which is used by Central Administration, and by the SharePoint service applications app pool identity (*SP_ServiceApps*), which is used by the Security Token Service Application and other services.

Validate Configuration

You can test and verify that your configuration is successful by performing the following actions:

- In Central Administration, create a test site collection in the site. When you configure the Site Collection Administrator, click the Browse button. Search for a user in the Select People And Groups dialog box. Search both with an exact match of the user name, which tests the *membership* provider configuration and by typing only the first few characters, which tests the *PeoplePickerWildcards* configuration.

- Sign in to the web application by using credentials in the FBA provider. Be certain to close any existing connections to the web application before doing so, so that any cached connections are purged. After the website has rendered, test *PeoplePickerWildcards* by adding a user from the membership provider and a group from the role manager to the site's Visitors group.

Create a Site Collection for a Claims Based Authentication Web App

As mentioned earlier, you can use Central Administration to create a site collection. You can also use the *New-SPSite* cmdlet, as described in Chapter 2, but an additional step is required to specify a site collection administrator in the *-OwnerAlias* attribute. If a web application uses Windows authentication, you can simply specify the user name—for example, CONTOSO\SP_Admin. With FBA and SAML authentication providers, you must pass the user as an *SPClaimsPrincipal* object. To do this, you must first create the *SPClaimsPrincipal* object, as shown in the following example:

```
$cp = New-SPClaimsPrincipal -Identity "<MembershipProvider>:<SiteOwner>"
-IdentityType FormsUser
```

Where:

- *<MembershipProvider>* is the name of your membership provider
- *<SiteOwner>* is the user name of the user that you want to assign as the site collection owner.

You then pass the object to the *New-SPSite* cmdlet, as in the following example:

```
$cp = New-SPClaimsPrincipal -Identity "MyMembershipProvider:SiteAdministrator"
  -IdentityType FormsUser
New-SPSite -Url "https://partners.contoso.com" -Name "Contoso Partner Portal"
  -OwnerAlias $cp -Template "STS#0"
```

Configure SAML Token Authentication

SAML token-based authentication allows SharePoint web applications to accept claims of identity that are authenticated from an STS other than SharePoint's STS. For example, you might configure a SharePoint web application to use Active Directory Federated Service 2.0 (AD FS 2.0) for authentication.

SAML token-based administration is the most generic and standards-based implementation of a claims-based environment. Earlier in this lesson, you learned how such an environment works: SharePoint is the relying party STS (RP-STS) and the external STS is the identity provider STS (IP-STS). The IP-STS authenticates the user against the user directory associated with the IP-STS, and then issues a token with claims about the user. The IP-STS is the conceptual equivalent of a domain controller in a claims-based environment.

Let's follow an example. A common scenario is that two organizations want to collaborate together on a project, but each organization wants to be in full control of the user accounts in its Windows domain. AD FS is a federated authentication service, so it can be configured to use multiple mechanisms of authentication. Instead of creating a trust between each organization's Windows domain, AD FS is configured to authenticate users against each domain, and to generate a security token for the user that can be used by the collaborative environment's web application. The domains are the authentication provider, but AD FS is the IP-STS. Users sign in to AD FS and AD FS issues a signed SAML token with claims about the user's identity. The RP-STS trusts AD-FS.

Tokens can include any number of claims about a user, such as a user name and groups the user belongs to, as well as descriptive attributes. The party application receives the SAML token and uses the claims inside to decide whether to grant the client access to the requested resource. Therefore, one of the claims in the token must uniquely identify the user: this is called the *identity claim*. The IP-STS does not have to create the identity claim with the user name that is submitted when the user logs on to the IP-STS. For example, AD FS does not have to create the identity claim with a user's domain user name. The IP-STS can instead create the identity claim using another unique identifier. Many implementations of claims use the email address attribute as the identity claim. The RP-STS must know which claim is guaranteed to be unique for tokens created by the IP-STS.

For this reason, configuration of a claims environment using SAML token-based authentication requires cooperation between the administrators of the RP-STS and IP-STS. The following elements must be coordinated:

- In SharePoint 2010 products, each web application that is configured to use a SAML provider is added to the IP-STS server as a separate RP-STS entry. This task is performed by the owner of the IP-STS. Each web application is identified as a *realm*, which is simply the URL namespace associated with the relying party web application, such as *https://portal.contoso.com*.

- Only the owner of the IP-STS knows which value in the token will always be unique per user and therefore can be relied upon as the identity claim. That information must be communicated to the owner of the IP-STS.

- Tokens will be signed using a certificate generated by the IP-STS. That certificate must be transferred from the IP-STS to the RP-STS.

Implementing SAML token-based authentication with SharePoint 2010 products involves the following processes:

1. Export the token-signing certificate from the IP-STS. This certificate is known as the ImportTrustCertificate.

2. Copy the certificate to a server computer in the SharePoint Server 2010 farm.

3. Define the claim that will be used as the unique identifier of the user. Identifying the unique identifier for the user is part of the claims-mapping process. Claims mapping is performed by using Windows PowerShell.

4. Define additional claims mappings. Define other values in the token that will be used by the RP-STS. For example, many tokens include a value that specifies user roles that can be used to permission resources in the SharePoint Server 2010 farm. All claims from an incoming token that do not have a mapping will be discarded.

5. Create a new authentication provider by using Windows PowerShell. This process creates the SPTrustedIdentityTokenIssuer.

   During this process, you submit the ImportTrustCertificate, the identity claim mapping, and additional claim mappings. You must also create and specify a realm—the URL namespace that is associated with the first SharePoint web applications that you are configuring for SAML token-based authentication.

   After the SPTrustedIdentityTokenIssuer is created, you can create and add more realms for additional SharePoint web applications. This is how you configure multiple web applications to use the same SPTrustedIdentityTokenIssuer.

6. For each realm that is added to the SPTrustedIdentityTokenIssuer, you must create an RP-STS entry on the IP-STS.

7. Create a new SharePoint web application and configure it to use the newly created authentication provider. The authentication provider will appear as an option in Central Administration when claims mode is selected for the web application.

You can configure multiple SAML token-based authentication providers. However, you can only use a token-signing certificate once in a farm. All providers that are configured will appear as options in Central Administration. Claims from different trusted STS environments will not conflict.

If you are implementing SAML token-based authentication with a partner company and your own environment includes an IP-STS, we recommend that you work with the administrator of your internal claims environment to establish a trust relationship from your internal IP-STS to the partner STS. The result is a type of chain of trust and authentication. This approach does not require adding an additional authentication provider to your SharePoint Server 2010 farm. It also allows your claims administrators to manage the whole claims environment.

> *NOTE* **SECURITY AND PERFORMANCE ISSUES**
>
> If you use SAML token-based authentication with AD FS on a SharePoint Server 2010 farm that has multiple web servers in a load-balanced configuration, the performance and functionality of client web-page views can be affected. When AD FS provides the authentication token to the client, that token is submitted to SharePoint Server 2010 for each permission-restricted page element. If the load-balanced solution is not using affinity, each secured element is authenticated to more than one SharePoint Server 2010 server, which might result in rejection of the token. After the token is rejected, SharePoint Server 2010 redirects the client to reauthenticate back to the AD FS server. After this occurs, an AD FS server might reject multiple requests that are made in a short time period. This behavior is by design, to protect against a denial of service attack. If performance is adversely affected or pages do not load completely, consider setting network load balancing to single affinity. This isolates the requests for SAML tokens to a single web server.

Multiple Authentication Providers

In SharePoint 2007, if you wanted users to authenticate to a web application using both Windows authentication and Forms Based Authentication, you were required to extend the web application to a second zone. A zone is a URL namespace through which a web application can be accessed. You could then configure one zone to use Windows authentication, such as *http://extranet.contoso.com*, and another zone to use Forms Based Authentication, such as *https://partners.contoso.com*.

In SharePoint 2010, this is no longer necessary. If a web application is configured for Claims Based Authentication, you can use multiple authentication providers in a single zone. You will learn more about zones in Lesson 3.

Choose an Authentication Type

As you've learned, the default authentication type is Classic Mode Authentication, which supports only the Windows authentication provider and its methods, NTLM and Kerberos, as well as the less regularly used Basic and Digest authentication provided by IIS. When you upgrade a web application, it is upgraded to Classic Mode Authentication.

When you create a new web application, the default is Classic Mode Authentication. If you will use FBA or SAML token-based authentication, you must choose Claims Based Authentication. If you will use only Windows authentication, you can choose either Classic Mode Authentication or Claims Based Authentication.

Although many resources recommend that you use Claims Based Authentication by default for all new web applications, it is important that you test the functionality of the web application in a lab environment before deploying it in production. Depending on the scenario, Claims Based Authentication might not be the best choice. Claims Based Authentication is a new feature in SharePoint Server 2010, and the community is only now learning the nuances of its implementation. Search the Internet for known issues related to Claims Based Authentication, such as the following:

- Custom code might need to be updated. Web Parts or other custom code that relies on or uses Windows identities will have to be updated. If the custom code uses Windows identities, use Classic Mode Authentication until the code is updated.

- Search alerts are currently not supported with claims-based authentication.

- There are problems using the audiences feature with some authentication providers.

- LDAP environments can be implemented by using either forms-based authentication or SAML token-based authentication. We recommend that you use forms-based authentication because it is less complex. However, if the environment supports WS-Federation 1.1 and SAML Token 1.1, SAML is recommended. Profile synchronization is not supported with LDAP providers that are not associated with ADFS 2.0.

Convert Web Applications to Claims Authentication

If you create a web application with Classic Mode Authentication, you can convert the web application to Claims Based Authentication. This is also important if you upgrade a SharePoint 2007 web application that uses Forms Based Authentication to SharePoint 2010. By default, an upgraded application is configured for Classic Mode Authentication. Classic Mode Authentication does not support FBA, so the application will not be accessible by FBA users until it is converted to Claims Based Authentication.

Before you convert to Claims Based Authentication, you should be aware of considerations related to Claims Based Authentication, as discussed in the previous section.

CONVERT A WEB APPLICATION TO CLAIMS BASED AUTHENTICATION

In SharePoint 2010 Management Shell, type the following:

```
$w = Get-SPWebApplication "http://<WebApplicationURL>/"
$w.UseClaimsAuthentication = 1
$w.Update()
$w.ProvisionGlobally()
```

Where:

- <WebApplicationURL> is the URL of the web application that you want to convert to Claims Based Authentication.

After converting the web application, you must migrate users and permissions to account for the new authentication scheme.

MIGRATE USERS AND PERMISSIONS

In SharePoint 2010 Management Shell, type the following:

```
$w = Get-SPWebApplication "http://<WebApplicationURL>/"
$w.MigrateUsers(True)
```

Where:

- *<WebApplicationURL>* is the URL of the web application for which you want to migrate users and permissions.

This process can take quite some time to complete. Be sure to test it in a lab environment so that you can budget appropriate service windows within which to perform the migration in the production environment.

> **BEST PRACTICE   TESTING A CONVERTED WEB APPLICATION**
>
> You cannot convert a web application from Claims Based Authentication to Classic Mode Authentication. Therefore, you must be certain to test the full functionality of a converted web application in a lab environment before converting the production web application. Validate the functionality of both user and administrative tasks. Also, back up the web application prior to converting to Claims Based Authentication.

> **MORE INFO   AUTHENTICATION METHODS**
>
> The following article provides additional details regarding authentication methods: "Plan authentication methods (SharePoint Server 2010)" at *http://technet.microsoft.com/en-us/ library/cc262350.aspx*.

PRACTICE   Configure Authentication

Practices are designed to guide you through important procedures. The instructions in the Training Kit are high-level instructions that will challenge you to think carefully and to apply the procedures that are covered in this lesson, and elsewhere in the Training Kit. If you need assistance, consult the detailed, step-by-step instructions in the Practice Answers on the companion media.

In this practice, you will configure authentication for the Contoso Partner Portal web application. First, you will enable anonymous access. Then, you will re-create the application configured to use Claims Based Authentication. You will create a database of users as an identity store for the SQLMembershipProvider, and you will configure Forms Based Authentication for the web application.

Prepare for the Practice

Before you perform this practice, you must ensure that your lab environment has been built according to the instructions found in the Introduction to this Training Kit. You must also have performed the practice in Lesson 1 of this chapter. If you are currently logged on to SP2010-WFE1, log off before beginning the exercises.

EXERCISE 1   Configure Anonymous Access

In this exercise, you configure anonymous access to the Contoso Partner Portal that you created in the practice of Lesson 1.

1. Log on to SP2010-WFE1 as **CONTOSO\SP_Admin** with the password **Pa$$w0rd**.
2. In Central Administration, enable anonymous authentication for the Contoso Partner Portal web application.
3. Open a new tab of Internet Explorer, and then browse to ***https://partners .contoso.com***.

    An error page opens: *There is a problem with this website's security certificate.* Continue to the website.

    The site is loaded, compiled, and cached for first-time access, and then the site opens.

    If an error appears, refresh the page. It is possible that the client timed out while the site was being loaded by IIS.
4. Enable anonymous access to the entire website.
5. Close the tab of Internet Explorer that displays the Partners site, start a new instance of Internet Explorer, and then browse to ***https://partners.contoso.com***.

    You must use a new instance to clear the cache of the authenticated sign-in.
6. Observe that the Welcome control in the upper-right corner of the page reads, "Sign In."

    You are not yet authenticated to the site.
7. Click Site Actions, and then observe that you do not have access to administrative pages as an anonymous user.
8. Close the instance of Internet Explorer that displays the Partners site.

EXERCISE 2   Delete a Web Application

In this exercise, you delete the Contoso Partner Portal site. In the following exercises, you will re-create the application so that it uses Claims Based Authentication.

- Delete the Contoso Partner Portal site. Be sure to delete the content databases and the IIS sites.

EXERCISE 3   Create a Web Application with Claims Based Authentication

In this exercise, you create a web application for collaboration with partners of Contoso. The web application will use Claims Based Authentication with the Windows authentication provider.

- Use Central Administration to create a web application collaboration with partners. Use the following specifications and guidance:
    - Authentication: Claims Based Authentication
    - Name: Contoso Partner Portal
    - Port: 443
    - Host header: partners.contoso.com
    - Authentication provider: Negotiate (Kerberos)
    - Anonymous authentication: No
    - Secure Sockets Layer (SSL): Yes
    - URL: *https://partnerss.contoso.com:443*
    - Application pool: SharePoint Extranet Applications
    - Application identity: CONTOSO\SP_WebApps
    - Content database name: SharePoint_Content_Partners

EXERCISE 4   Create a Site Collection Using Central Administration

In this exercise, you use Central Administration to create a site collection at the root of the new web application.

1. Use Central Administration to create a site collection. Use the following specifications and guidance:
    - Web application: *https://partners.contoso.com*
    - Title: Contoso Partner Portal
    - Description: Sites for collaboration with partners
    - URL: *https://partners.contoso.com/*
    - Template: Team Site
    - Primary site collection administrator: CONTOSO\SP_Admin

2. Open a new tab of Internet Explorer, and then browse to **https://partners.contoso.com**.

    An error page opens: *There is a problem with this website's security certificate*. Continue to the website.

    The site is loaded, compiled, and cached for first-time access, and then the site opens.

    If an error appears, refresh the page. It is possible that the client timed out while the site was being loaded by IIS.

EXERCISE 5   Configure Forms Based Authentication

In this exercise, you configure the Contoso Partner Portal to use Forms Based Authentication. You then examine the Web.config files for the web application, Central Administration, and STS, in which you will identify the locations that you must modify to configure the authentication provider.

You will not complete the configuration of FBA because that requires establishing an external database of users. The Suggested Practice at the end of this chapter gives you the opportunity to complete the process.

1. In the Central Administration, configure the Contoso Partner Portal web application using the following specifications and guidance:

   - Authentication provider #1: Integrated Windows authentication with the Negotiate (NTLM or Kerberos) method

   - Authentication provider #2: Forms Based Authentication

   - ASP.NET membership provider: MyMembershipProvider

   - ASP.NET role manager: MyRoleManager

EXERCISE 6   Configure Web.config Files

In this exercise, you examine the Web.config files for the web application, Central Administration, and STS, in which you will identify the locations that you must modify to configure the authentication provider for FBA. You will not actually complete the configuration of FBA because FBA requires an external database of users. The Suggested Practice, at the end of this chapter, gives you the opportunity to complete the process.

1. Open the Web.config file of the Contoso Partner Portal IIS Web site.

2. Search for the *<connectionStrings>* element.

   This file does not have an existing *<connectionStrings>* element. In a production environment, a Web.config file might already have a *<connectionStrings>* element, in which case you would simply register the new connection string by inserting an *<add>* element.

   The *<connectionStrings>* section must be a child element of *<configuration>*, which is the root element of Web.config. In other words, *<connectionStrings>* must be a first-level element. It is common practice to place it immediately before the *<system .web>* element begins.

3. Search for the beginning of the *<system.web>* element.

   Be certain that the *<system.web>* element that you find is a first-level element—a child of *<configuration>*. Some *<system.web>* elements are lower-level children of other elements.

4. Inside the *<system.web>* element, find the *<membership>* element. Inside the *<membership>* element, find the *<providers>* element.

   The *<providers>* element contains child *<add>* elements that define each membership provider. You can register a new provider in this element.

   The *name* attribute of the *<add>* element must match the name that you configured as the ASP.NET Membership Provider in the web application. If the provider uses a connection string, the *connectionStringName* attribute must match the *name* of the connection string that you added to the *<connectionStrings>* element.

5. Inside the *<system.web>* element, find the *<roleManager>* element. Inside the *<roleManager>* element, find the *<providers>* element.

   The *<providers>* element contains child *<add>* elements that define each role provider. You can register a new provider in this element.

   The *name* attribute of the *<add>* element must match the name that you configured as the ASP.NET Membership Provider in the web application. If the provider uses a connection string, the *connectionStringName* attribute must match the *name* of the connection string that you added to the *<connectionStrings>* element.

6. Find the *<PeoplePickerWildcards>* element.

   The *<PeoplePickerWildcards>* element defines, for each custom authentication provider, the wildcard that can be used when searching for a user in the People Picker. Without a wildcard definition, the People Picker will locate only the user that is an exact match to the search criteria. With a wildcard defined, you can enter the first characters of the user's name and the search will locate all matching users.

   Each wildcard is defined by an *<add>* element in the *<PeoplePickerWildcards>* element. You can register the wildcards for your membership provider and role provider in this element.

   The *keys* must match the name of the membership and role providers that have been configured for the web application. For a SQL database, the wildcard value is %. For an LDAP directory, the wildcard value is *.

Lesson Summary

- If you want to enable anonymous users to access content in a SharePoint website, you must first enable anonymous authentication for the web application zone. Then a site collection administrator can enable anonymous access to an entire site—and to the objects in the site that inherit permissions from the site—or to individual lists and libraries. Finally, a farm administrator can enforce anonymous access restrictions, which are policies applied to a web application zone that prevent anonymous users from changing or even accessing content.

- SharePoint supports two authentication types: Classic Mode Authentication and Claims Based Authentication.

- In Classic Mode Authentication, users are authenticated by Windows—NTLM, Kerberos, Basic, or Digest authentication—and the resulting security token is passed by IIS to SharePoint. SharePoint translates the token to an *SPUser* object, which represents the user and his or her groups to the web application.

- In Claims Based Authentication, an unauthenticated user is redirected to the Security Token Service, which authenticates the user then provides the user with a token that contains claims about the user's identity, and can contain claims about the user's roles and other attributes. The web application trusts the token that was generated and signed by the STS, and translates the claims to an *SPUser* object.

- Windows Authentication and its methods are supported by both Classic Mode Authentication and Claims Based Authentication.

- Forms Based Authentication is an authentication provider supported by Claims Based Authentication. A user is redirected to a form and submits credentials, typically a user name and password. An authentication method validates the credentials. The authentication method can be the ASP.NET SQLMembershipProvider, which uses a SQL database of users as a directory; an LDAPMembershipProvider, which uses an LDAP directory such as an AD DS domain or instance of AD LDS as a directory; or a custom membership provider. FBA can also use a role manager to provide a list of the groups to which a user belongs. The user identity and roles are converted by the STS to a token.

- SAML token-based authentication uses Security Assertion Markup Language (SAML) tokens issued by an IP-STS external to SharePoint, such as AD FS 2.0. The trusted identity provider is registered with the SharePoint farm by importing the trust certificate of the IP-STS. Web applications can then be configured to use the trusted identity provider.

- When you upgrade a SharePoint 2007 web application that uses FBA, the application is configured to use Classic Mode Authentication, which does not use FBA, so the application will be inaccessible to FBA users. You must convert the application and then migrate users and permissions—tasks that you perform by using Windows PowerShell.

Lesson Review

You can use the following questions to test your knowledge of the information in Lesson 2, "Configure Authentication." The questions are also available on the companion media in a practice test if you prefer to review them in electronic form.

1. You have just configured a web application to use the Negotiate (NTLM or Kerberos) authentication method of the Windows authentication provider. What else must you do to configure Kerberos authentication?

   A. Use Setspn.exe.

   B. Add an SSL binding to the IIS Web site.

   C. Register a trusted identity provider.

   D. Configure the Web.config file of the web application.

2. You have just configured a web application to use the Negotiate (NTLM or Kerberos) authentication method of the Windows authentication provider. How can you verify that the Kerberos protocol is being used? (Choose all that apply.)

   A. Browse to the website. If the website opens, Kerberos authentication is working properly.

   B. Browse to the website, then examine the Security event log of the client.

   C. Browse to the website, then examine the Security event log of the server.

   D. Use Klist.exe on the server.

   E. Use Klist.exe on the client.

   F. Use Setspn.exe.

3. WebApp1 contains a single site collection. You want to allow site collection administrators to be able to grant anonymous users read-only access to content in WebApp1, based on business requirements known to the administrators. What do you do? (Choose all that apply. Each correct answer is a part of the solution.)

   A. In the Site Permissions page of the top-level website in the site collection, enable anonymous access with the Entire Site option.

   B. Configure anonymous access restrictions on all zones with the Deny Write option.

   C. Enable anonymous access on the web application.

   D. In the Site Permissions page of the top-level website in the site collection, enable anonymous access with the Lists and Libraries option.

4. You have created a web application that uses Classic Mode Authentication and the NTLM authentication method. You want to provide access to users at a partner organization. Their accounts will be kept in a SQL database. What must you do to provide this access? (Choose all that apply. Each correct answer is a part of the solution.)

   A. Modify firewall settings to open port 389 to inbound TCP traffic.

   B. Create SQL logins for each partner user.

    C. Modify Web.config files.

    D. Convert the web application to Claims Based Authentication.

    E. Use Central Administration to configure the membership provider and the role provider of the web application.

5. You have just configured WebApplication1 to use Forms Based Authentication by modifying the authentication provider. When you attempt to authenticate to the website, an error appears. What else do you have to do? (Choose all that apply. Each correct answer is a part of the solution.)

    A. Modify the Web.config file of Central Administration.

    B. Modify the Web.config file of the Secure Store Service.

    C. Modify the Web.config file of the Security Token Service Application.

    D. Modify the Web.config file of the web application.

    E. Assign permissions to application pool identities.

Lesson 3: Configure Authentication Zones and Alternate Access Mappings

In Lesson 1, you learned to create and configure a web application, including the steps used to configure secure communication over SSL. In Lesson 2, you explored the management and configuration of authentication methods, including anonymous authentication. In some environments, users will access a SharePoint web application with a single protocol and URL—for example, *https://partners.contoso.com* will authenticate with a single provider, such as Windows authentication, and will be subject to a single set of policies.

But what if you want external users to access a web application using one URL and protocol, such as *https://partners.contoso.com*, and to be authenticated with Forms Based Authentication, but you want internal users to access the web application with a different URL and protocol, such as *http://extranet.contoso.com*? What if you want to enhance security and performance by implementing off-box SSL termination or a reverse proxy?

In these scenarios, you need zones and alternate access mappings. These concepts can be challenging to understand, and even more challenging to implement, because of the loose association between web applications, IIS sites, zones, intermediate devices, and alternate access mappings. In this lesson, you will learn to manage these components of a SharePoint implementation.

After this lesson, you will be able to:

- Describe the purpose of internal and public URLs.
- Describe the relationship between access mappings, zones, and IIS Web sites.
- Extend a web application to a new zone.
- Configure zone properties.
- Configure access to web applications in complex access scenarios.

Estimated lesson time: 90 minutes

Requesting SharePoint Content: Access Mappings, Zones, and URLs

Earlier in this Training Kit, you learned the high-level processes related to requests for content from SharePoint. Let's return to this process by following an example. A user wants to access the home page of the Contoso intranet. The user enters the URL *http://intranet.contoso.com* in a browser. The *public URL* of the Contoso Intranet Web application is *http://intranet.contoso.com*—the URL requested by the user. The client queries DNS to resolve the host name intranet.contoso.com to the IP address, 10.0.0.21, which happens to be an IP address bound to a network interface of a server named *SP2010-WFE1*. The request, *http://intranet.contoso.com*, is sent to 10.0.0.21 over the standard port for HTTP, port 80. The host header of the request contains intranet.contoso.com, the host name and domain name of the user's request.

Now, let's dig deeper into some of the processes that connect the user to the requested content. On SP2010-WFE1, IIS receives the user's request over port 80 and must determine which IIS Web site will service the request. IIS examines the bindings of each site and identifies the Contoso Intranet site as the correct site, because the site is bound to port 80 and the host header, *intranet .contoso.com*. IIS passes the request to SharePoint. The *internal URL* of the Contoso Intranet Web application is the URL of the website as it is received by IIS and passed on to SharePoint. In this simple example, the internal URL is also *http://intranet.contoso.com*—the same URL is passed, unchanged, from the user to IIS to SharePoint. But you will soon learn that it is not always so simple.

Access Mappings

So far, this example illustrates, in more depth, the processes used to fulfill requests for SharePoint content in the most simple environment. Let's now turn our attention to the architectural components and concepts that enable SharePoint to determine which web application should respond to the request.

SharePoint must now determine which SharePoint web application will service the request. SharePoint does not maintain a one-to-one mapping with an IIS Web site. SharePoint web applications and IIS Web sites are two separate entities, although they maintain a close relationship.

Therefore, the fact the Contoso Intranet IIS Web site received the request is not sufficient for SharePoint to know that the Contoso Intranet SharePoint web application must continue processing the request. Instead, SharePoint must examine the URL of the request that has been passed to it by IIS. Again, in this simple example, the URL is *http://intranet.contoso.com*.

SharePoint compares this URL to its access mappings. An *access mapping* associates a URL to a zone of a specific SharePoint web application. SharePoint sees that the URL, *http://intranet.contoso.com*, is associated with the default zone of the Contoso Intranet Web application. SharePoint can then continue processing the request in the context of the Contoso Intranet Web application, and return the requested content to the user.

Zones

In the previous paragraph, a new concept was introduced: the zone. A *zone* is a logical path through which users gain access to a web application. The public face of the zone— the property by which a zone is accessed—is the URL. The zone has other properties that determine how the web application is accessed. For example, the authentication provider is defined for the zone, as are policies including anonymous access restrictions and user policy.

> **NOTE** **WHERE ZONES FIT IN**
> You can think of the *zone* conceptually as the entryway to a building. The URL is the
> address or directions you used to get to the specific entryway—and, of course, a building
> can have several entryways. The web application is the building you are about to enter.
> And, at the entryway, your identity is verified (authentication) and policies can be put
> in place. For example, you might be asked to forfeit your cell phone and camera before
> entering the building.

When you create a web application, you also create a zone for the web application named *Default*, also referred to as the default zone. When you configure the authentication providers for the new web application, the configuration is actually applied to the default zone, not to the web application as a whole. The *Public URL* setting that you specify when you create the new web application is used to create access mappings that apply the URL as both the public URL and the internal URL associated with the default zone. As you saw earlier, the public and internal URLs are often the same.

A web application can include as many as five zones. The default zone is required, is created automatically, and can be modified. But you cannot delete the default zone. It is deleted automatically when you delete the web application. The four additional zones are optional, can be created, modified, and deleted, and are named *intranet*, *extranet*, *Internet*, and *custom*.

To define an additional zone, you simply create an access mapping that associates a unique URL to one of the four additional zones, and then users can access the web application through the new URL. For example, you could add a URL, *http://company.contoso.com*, to the Contoso Intranet Web application as the URL for the zone named *intranet*. Users could then access the Contoso Intranet Web application using either *http://company.contoso.com* or *http://intranet.contoso.com*. Of course you would need to be certain that there was a DNS host record to resolve the names to the IP address of the server, and you would need to add a host header binding to the IIS Web site so that the site would respond to requests to *company.contoso.com* as well as to *intranet.contoso.com*.

The most important thing to know about a zone at this point in the discussion is that after you have defined an additional zone, the content that users access through the new URL is the same content they access through the default zone. Zones are simply different logical paths to the same web application—an association between the protocol, scheme, hostname, and port of an inbound request from a client, and the web application that will respond to the request.

> **NOTE MULTIPLE ZONES**
>
> To continue our conceptual metaphor, you can think of different zones as different entryways into the same building. Each entryway requires a different set of directions to get there, and each zone requires a different URL.

URLs of SharePoint Site Collections and Content

Let's take a short digression to examine the answer to the question, "What happens next?" Let's assume one user browses to *http://intranet.contoso.com*, the home page of the Contoso intranet, shown in Figure 3-12, and clicks the link to the Company Calendar. You can see in Figure 3-12 that the URL to the Company Calendar is *http://intranet.contoso.com/Lists/CompanyCalendar/calendar.aspx*.

FIGURE 3-12 URL of a hyperlink in a web application

What if another user accesses the same Contoso intranet application by entering the URL, *http://company.contoso.com*? When that user clicks the link to the same Company Calendar, the URL will be *http://company.contoso.com/Lists/CompanyCalendar/calendar.aspx*.

How is it that two different users can submit two URLs and access the same content?

Conceptually, SharePoint itself considers the address of the Company Calendar to be *<WebApplicationURL><SiteCollectionURL>Lists/CompanyCalendar/calendar.aspx*, where *<WebApplicationURL>* is the Public URL of the zone, such as *http://intranet.contoso.com:80*, and *<SiteCollectionURL>* is the URL of the site collection relative to the web application. For example, the intranet site collection is at the root of the web application, with the relative URL */.* The URL of content within a site collection is always stored as a value relative to the site collection itself. For example, SharePoint considers the URL of the company calendar to be *Lists/CompanyCalendar/calendar.aspx*.

SharePoint renders the home page of the intranet and generates the hyperlink to the Company Calendar by replacing the variables with their values. For the user that accesses the Contoso intranet through the default zone, the resulting hyperlink target URL is *http://intranet.contoso.com/Lists/CompanyCalendar/calendar.aspx*. SharePoint removes the port, 80, because it is the default port for HTTP. If the Public URL included a non-standard port, it would be included in the link to the Company Calendar. For the user that accesses the Contoso intranet through the intranet zone, the resulting hyperlink target URL is *http://company.contoso.com/Lists/CompanyCalendar/calendar.aspx*.

By abstracting the URL of the web application and the relative URL of the site collection, SharePoint allows a user to access content through more than one URL, or zone. It also enables you to move content easily. If you create a new web application with the public URL *http://portal.contoso.com:80*, and you move the content database from the intranet web application to the portal web application, the URL to the Company Calendar will immediately be generated as *http://portal.contoso.com/Lists/CompanyCalendar/calendar.aspx*. The site collection relative URL, and the relative URL of the Company Calendar did not change—only the web application hosting the site collection changed. Similarly, if you change the external URL of the extranet zone from *http://company.contoso.com* to *http://portal.contoso.com*, the URL of the Company Calendar would be rendered with the new hostname.

Access Mappings

Now that you understand the fundamental concepts of access mappings and zones, let's explore in more detail how you manage each.

You have learned that an *access mapping*, also called an *alternate access mapping*, associates a URL to a zone of a specific SharePoint web application. Behind the scenes, in the SharePoint object model, an access mapping is called an *alternate URL*—it is an *SPAlternateURL* object in a collection called *SPAlternateURLCollection* that is a member of the web application. Wouldn't it have been easier if they just called these *alternate URLs*?

You can manage URLs from the Alternate Access Mappings page of Central Administration.

MANAGE ALTERNATE ACCESS MAPPINGS

1. In the Central Administration Quick Launch, click Applications Management.

2. In the Web Applications section, click Configure Alternate Access Mappings.

   The Alternate Access Mappings page, shown in Figure 3-13, opens.

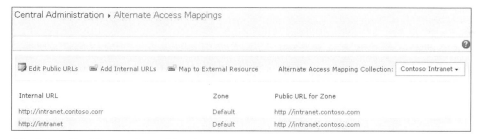

FIGURE 3-13 The Alternate Access Mappings page

From here, you can do the following:

- Click the Alternate Access Mappings Collection selector to pick the web application that you want to modify.

- Click Edit Public URLs to add, modify, or delete the public URL of each zone.

- Click Add Internal URLs to add an internal URL to a zone.

- Click Map To External Resource to configure a URL that maps to a resource outside of SharePoint.

- Click an internal URL to edit or delete the internal URL.

It is easy to understand why the public URL and the internal URL are often the same. A user enters the public URL, *http://intranet.contoso.com*, and IIS receives the request with the same URL and passes the request to SharePoint, which inspects the request and extracts the URL as the internal URL.

It gets more interesting when you answer the question, "Why would the internal URL be *different* than the public URL?" We will answer the question with two common scenarios:

- Single-label host names and fully qualified host names
- Off-Box SSL Termination

In the process of exploring these scenarios, you will learn the purpose of the internal URL and of the public URL.

Single-Label Host Names and Fully Qualified Host Names

You have configured the Contoso Intranet Web application with the URL *http://intranet.contoso.com*. This URL is the URL of the web application—a property in and of itself—and it is both the public URL and the internal URL of the web application's default zone. Let's assume you want to allow users to get to the intranet by typing *http://intranet* or with the current URL, *http://intranet.contoso.com*.

This scenario is supported by two access mappings: You add *http://intranet* as an additional internal URL to the default zone. When a request for *http://intranet* is passed to SharePoint by IIS, SharePoint will identify the URL as the internal URL of the default zone of the Contoso Intranet Web application, and will be able to serve the website to the user.

ADD INTERNAL URLS

1. On the Alternate Access Mappings page, click Add Internal URLs.

    The Add Internal URLs page opens.

2. Confirm that the Alternate Access Mapping Collection list displays the web application that you want to modify.

    If it does not, click the list, then click Change Alternate Access Mapping Collection, and then click the name of the web application that you want to modify.

3. In the URL Protocol, Host And Port box, type the internal URL that you want to add.

    The URL should include the protocol and host name, and the port—for example, *http://intranet:80*. Although you can omit the port if it is a standard port, it is recommended that you use the port for clarity and documentation.

4. In the Zone list, select the zone with which to associate the internal URL and click Save.

The internal URL—*http://intranet* in this example—allows SharePoint to determine which SharePoint web application is being accessed, and through which of that web application's zones. However, the request has to be passed by IIS to SharePoint before that can happen. When you add an internal URL, SharePoint does not add a corresponding host header binding to the IIS Web site. You must manually add the host name of the internal URL as a host header binding to the IIS Web site on each server that will respond to the internal URL.

This is not applicable if you are not using host headers—for example, if you have a dedicated IP address bound to the IIS Web site.

ADD A BINDING TO AN IIS WEB SITE

1. In IIS Manager, in the console tree, expand the server, then expand Sites, and then click the site to which you want to add a binding.

2. In the Actions pane, click Bindings to open the Site Bindings dialog box.

3. Click Add to open the Add Site Binding dialog box.

4. In the Type box, select the protocol—http or https.

5. In the Host Name box, type the host name.

6. Click OK and then click Close.

> **BEST PRACTICE** **MINIMIZING THE MANAGEMENT BURDEN**
>
> When you add an internal URL to a zone for a web application that uses host headers, you must add a binding to the IIS Web site. If you add a new server to the farm, SharePoint will create the IIS Web site but will not add the additional bindings. And, if you ever have to restore the web application, SharePoint will not re-create the bindings. In these ways, the management burden is increased. It is therefore recommended that you minimize the number of instances in which a zone has more than one internal URL.

After an internal URL has been created, you can modify or delete the URL. On the Alternate Access Mappings page, click the URL in the Internal URL column. If you modify or delete an internal URL, be certain to modify bindings on the IIS Web site accordingly.

In our scenario, users can now request *http://intranet*, which has been added as an internal URL to the default zone, as shown in Figure 3-13. The zone now has two internal URLs and one public URL, *http://intranet.contoso.com*.

Let's consider what happens when a user requests *http://intranet*. The request arrives at the web server. The host header binding enables IIS to pass the request to the Contoso Intranet IIS Web site. The website's SharePoint processes receive the request and examine the URL to determine that the request is for the Contoso Intranet Web application. It is now time for SharePoint to render the content of the intranet home page to the user. Remember, from the example presented earlier, that the home page has a link to the company calendar. SharePoint thinks about the link in relative terms. SharePoint considers the URL for the company calendar to be */Lists/CompanyCalendar/calendar.aspx*. When SharePoint renders the link, it adds the public URL of the web application—more specifically, of the zone—to the URL. Therefore, the link that SharePoint renders for the company calendar is *http://intranet.contoso.com/Lists/CompanyCalendar/calendar.aspx*. SharePoint does not render the link as *http://intranet/Lists/CompanyCalendar/calendar.aspx*.

In this scenario, there is no problem. When a user clicks the link to the company calendar, the user can access the calendar with the *http://intranet.contoso.com* URL. In fact, all URLs will be rendered with the fully qualified domain name of the host—with the public URL. The first thing that a user clicks will take the user out of the *http://intranet* URL namespace into the *http://intranet.contoso.com* namespace. Again, no problem is caused—access is still possible. You have simply given users an alternate, shorter URL with which to get to the intranet home page.

Off-Box SSL Termination

The previous scenario was straightforward. Let's explore a slightly more complex scenario. You have configured the Contoso Partner Portal to use SSL with the URL *https://partners .contoso.com*. This is both the public URL and the internal URL of the web application's default zone.

You decide that you want to reduce the performance burden that SSL places on the web server by installing a device that performs off-box SSL termination. This is a device that is placed on the network, logically, between the user and the web server. The device receives the request using SSL over port 443, decrypts the request, and forwards it to the web server, unencrypted, over http with port 80.

In this configuration, users continue to browse to the public URL *https://partners.contoso .com*. DNS resolves the IP address as the network interface of the off-box SSL terminator. The device receives the packet, does its magic, and then forwards the request to IIS as *http://partners.contoso.com*. IIS passes the request to SharePoint, and the internal URL is *http://partners.contoso.com*.

This scenario is addressed with one access mapping. To support this configuration, you must define the zone so that the public URL is *https://partners.contoso.com*, and the internal URL is *http://partners.contoso.com*.

SharePoint must understand that the URL, *http://partners.contoso.com*, is associated with the default zone of the Contoso Partner Portal web application, so that SharePoint can retrieve the requested content. The internal URL is the mapping that is important for SharePoint to process inbound requests. For this scenario to work, the internal URL of the zone must be *http://partners.contoso.com:80*, although you can optionally leave out the port if the URL uses the standard port for the protocol.

It is also important that SharePoint knows that, to the user, the web application is known as *https://partners.contoso.com*, because SharePoint must render hyperlinks and other URLs so that they will be accessible to the user. Consider, again, the link to the company calendar. If SharePoint rendered the link using the internal URL, it would be *http://partners.contoso.com/ Lists/CompanyCalendar/calendar.aspx*, and the user would not be able to click the link and connect to the content successfully.

That is why the public URL is important. The public URL is also referred to as the *outgoing URL* or the *response URL*. In this example, the public URL for the default zone is *https:// partners.contoso.com:443*. It is the public URL that is used to ensure that URLs are rendered correctly for users. Because SharePoint knows that the request arrived with an internal URL associated with the default zone, and that the public URL for the default zone is *https:// partners.contoso.com:443*, SharePoint renders the link to the Company Calendar as *https://portal.contoso.com/Lists/CompanyCalendar/calendar.aspx*. The user is therefore able to click the link and navigate to the company calendar.

> **IMPORTANT MANAGING URLS IN MULTIPLE ZONES**
>
> Never configure an internal URL in one zone that is the same as the public URL of a different zone. This can cause SharePoint to render URLs incorrectly to users accessing the site with the URL as its public zone.

To support the preceding off-box SSL termination scenario, if you have created the web application using SSL as *https://partners.contoso.com*, the public URL is already correct. Add an internal URL, *http://partners.contoso.com*. The resulting Alternate Access Mapping (AAM) collection for the Contoso Partner Portal application is shown in Figure 3-14.

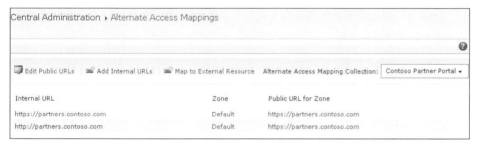

FIGURE 3-14 Access mappings to support off-box SSL termination for the Contoso Partner Portal

The second access mapping is the one that supports the scenario. In this case, the first access mapping is a special mapping that cannot be deleted. For each web application, one access mapping represents the default zone. You can recognize this mapping because when you click the URL on the Alternate Access Mappings page, the Delete button is disabled—you cannot delete the mapping. The public URL and the internal URL of this mapping are the same. You cannot change one without changing the other. We recommend that you do not change this mapping in any way. Instead, add other internal URLs to the default zone, and extend the web application to create new zones.

Load Balancing with Request Overwrites

A load balancer is a service or device that distributes inbound requests to more than one web server. The web server that services the request returns the content to the user. For example, let's say a user requests *http://intranet.contoso.com/SitePages/Home.aspx*. The public URL of the zone is thus *http://intranet.contoso.com*. The load balancer, which can be the Network Load Balancing (NLB) service provided by Windows Server 2008 or a dedicated hardware device, receives the request. Two web servers, named *SP2010-WFE1* and *SP2010-WFE2*, host the intranet web application. The load balancer uses rules, which can be as simple as a round-robin algorithm, to determine the server that will serve the request. The request is distributed to one of the servers.

Many load balancers use a shared IP address that receives the request, and then the load balancer forwards the request to the IP address of one of the servers. If this mechanism is used, the URL sent to IIS is the same URL received by the NLB service. There is no need to change access mappings or to create additional zones.

Some load balancers overwrite the request received from the client and submit the request to the web server. For example, let's say a load balancer receives a request for *http://intranet.contoso.com/SitePages/Home.aspx*. It changes the URL of the request to address a specific server. The new URL is *http://intranet02.contoso.com/SitePages/Home.aspx*.

The request is received by SP2010-WFE2, which hosts the intranet web application. The IIS Web site must be bound to *intranet02.contoso.com* on SP2010-WFE2. Similarly, the IIS Web site must be bound to *intranet01.contoso.com* on SP2010-WFE1. IIS passes the request to SharePoint as *http://intranet02.contoso.com/SitePages/Home.aspx*. SharePoint must return the content to the user. To achieve this, the zone must be mapped to the public URL *http://intranet.contoso.com* and there must be two internal URLs: *http://intranet01.contoso.com* and *http://intranet02.contoso.com*.

> **NOTE FORWARDED REQUESTS FOR AN IP ADDRESS**
>
> Many load balancers forward a request to the specific IP address of a web server without actually changing the URL. This process would not require a different internal URL.

Review Internal and Public URLs

To summarize, each web application zone has one or more internal URLs. When an inbound request is received by IIS and passed to SharePoint, the URL is examined and matched to an internal URL to determine which web application is being accessed, and through which zone. In simple environments, the internal URL of a zone will be the same as the public URL.

The internal URL will be different from the public URL of a zone if a device or service changes the URL that the user requests. For example, an SSL termination service or device changes the protocol of the request from HTTPS to HTTP. A user requests *https://partners.contoso.com* over port 443 and an SSL termination device forwards the request to *http://partners.contoso.com* over port 80. Or, a load balancer uses request overwrites to forward the requests to a web server.

> **EXAM TIP**
>
> The internal and external URLs of an access zone are different when the URL entered by a user is different than the URL received by IIS and SharePoint. This occurs when there is a device, such as an off-box SSL terminator or reverse proxy, between the user and the web server, and when that device overwrites or changes the URL entered by the user.

Public URLs

You can also modify the public URLs of a web application. Remember that the primary purpose of the public URL is to enable SharePoint to render content correctly to users. SharePoint uses the public URL as the URL of the web application as it renders hyperlinks and other URLs.

EDIT THE PUBLIC URLS OF A WEB APPLICATION

1. On the Alternate Access Mappings page, click Edit Public URLs.

2. On the Edit Public Zone URLs page, confirm that the Alternate Access Mapping Collection list displays the web application that you want to modify.

   If it does not, click the list, then click Change Alternate Access Mapping Collection, and then click the name of the web application that you want to modify.

3. Enter, edit, or delete the URLs that users use to access the web application.

4. Click Save.

> **NOTE   DELETING THE DEFAULT ZONE**
>
> You cannot remove the public URL associated with the default zone, which must always be defined. The default zone is deleted when you delete the web application itself.

Manage Zones

A zone, as you've learned, is a logical path to a web application and, technically, is the result of an access mapping that associates a URL and a web application. Five zones are available for each SharePoint web application: *default*, *intranet*, *Internet*, *extranet*, and *custom*.

> **BEST PRACTICE   MAKING THE BEST USE OF THE TYPES OF ZONES**
>
> The names of the additional four zones (*intranet*, *extranet*, *Internet*, and *custom*) bear no technical meaning. There is no difference in configuration between the *Intranet* and the *Extranet* zones—both are simply a logical path—a public URL and an "entryway"—to a web application. The names of zones are for guidance only. Therefore, it is a best practice but not a requirement to extend a web application to the *Extranet* zone if the purpose of the zone will be to support access through your extranet. The zones also have no relationship to Internet Explorer security zones. It is a common misconception that the names of the zones connote technical considerations.
>
> The Default zone, however, is—as its name suggests—the default. If SharePoint cannot determine zone-specific policies to apply to an inbound request, it uses the policies associated with the default zone. You will learn more about policies and zones later in this lesson.

You can create and delete a zone in a web application in two ways: You can define an alternate access mapping, or you can extend and unextend the web application. You will learn both methods in this section, but it is highly recommended that when you want to create or delete a zone, you always extend or unextend the web application, respectively.

Define an Alternate Access Mapping

Let's start with the method that is not recommended: defining an Alternate Access Mapping (AAM).

You learned how to add internal and public URLs earlier in the lesson, in the procedures "Add Internal URLs" and "Edit the Public URLs of a Web Application." If you add a URL to a zone that was previously undefined, you create the zone. The URL you specify as the internal or Public URL of an undefined zone is also added as the public or internal URL, respectively, so that the zone has both the required public URL and the required first internal URL.

Conversely, if you clear the public URL of a zone, or if you delete the last internal URL of a zone, you delete the zone.

It is not recommended to create and delete zones in this fashion. The following are best practices that relate to access mappings and zones:

- Do not add an internal URL associated with a zone that does not yet exist. Doing so creates a zone without an associated website. Instead, extend the web application.

- Do not add a public URL to a zone that does not yet exist. Doing so creates a zone without an associated website. Instead, extend the web application.

- Do not delete the last internal URL associated with a zone. Doing so deletes the zone without deleting the associated website. Instead, unextend the web application.

- Do not remove the public URL associated with a zone. Doing so deletes the zone without deleting the associated website. Instead, unextend the web application.

Extend a Web Application

The second, and recommended method to create a new zone in SharePoint 2010 is to *extend* a web application. When you extend a web application, you create a new zone and an associated IIS Web site.

EXTEND A WEB APPLICATION

1. In the Central Administration Quick Launch, click Application Management.
2. In the Web Applications section, click Manage Web Applications.
3. Select the web application to extend.
4. On the ribbon, click Extend.
5. On the Extend Web Application To Another IIS Web Site page, click Create A New IIS Web Site.
6. In the Name box, type a name that is easily recognizable in IIS Manager, such as **Contoso Partners Extranet**.

7. In the Port box, type the port number. If you are using HTTP, this is usually port 80; HTTPS is usually 443.

8. In the Host Header box, type the host header, which is usually the FQDN of the zone, such as **extranet.contoso.com**.

    You should configure the host header even if you plan to bind the IIS Web site to a unique IP addresses. The host header becomes the internal URL of the site.

9. Configure the settings in the Security Configuration section. See the section, "Security Configuration," earlier in this chapter for more information.

10. In the Public URL section, in the URL box, type the external URL of the zone, such as **http://extranet.contoso.com:80**.

11. In the Zone list, select the zone to which you want to extend the web application, and then click OK.

When you extend a web application, an IIS Web site is created. The IIS Web site for the zones will share the application pool of the web application's other zones. Do not change the application pool associated with a zone.

The Case for Extending Web Applications

Why is it not recommended to create a zone by defining an access mapping, and why is it recommended to do so by extending the web application? You will learn several reasons in this lesson. The first is that the access mappings you create manually are not added to the IIS site underlying the web application. You must therefore manually change the bindings of the IIS site on each web server in the farm to add the new URL as a host header binding. If you add a new server to the farm, SharePoint will create the IIS site on the new server, but will not add the URLs that you added as access mappings. Similarly, if you delete the web application and IIS site, and then restore the web application from a SharePoint backup, SharePoint will re-create the IIS site but will not re-create the bindings.

These problems illustrate one of the separations between SharePoint and IIS: Changes made directly to IIS are not stored in the SharePoint configuration database; therefore, you cannot manage the settings by using SharePoint.

More important, when you create a zone by defining an access mapping in SharePoint, the only thing you have accomplished is to provide access to the web application with a different URL. Earlier in this lesson, you learned that a number of settings can be scoped to a zone, including authentication providers, anonymous access, and policy. These settings can only be applied if an IIS Web site is associated with the zone.

When you extend a web application, you create an IIS Web site associated with the zone. SharePoint configures the IIS Web site with bindings—for example, with a host header binding for the URL of the new zone. This allows SharePoint and IIS to stay in synch with each other. When you extend a web application to a zone, the configuration of the extended web application is stored in the SharePoint configuration database. Therefore, if you add a new server to the farm, SharePoint can create the IIS site and configure it automatically. Similarly, if you delete a web application and then restore it from backup, SharePoint can configure the IIS site.

> **IMPORTANT** **EXTEND THE WEB APPLICATION TO CREATE A NEW ZONE**
>
> To create a new zone, it is recommended that you extend the web application. If you create a zone by adding an access mapping, you cannot use the zone to configure authentication, anonymous access, or user policy uniquely for the zone.

Remove a Zone

To remove a zone properly, you should undo the process you used to create the zone. If you created the zone by defining an alternate access mapping, remove the URLs associated with the zone and the zone will be deleted. If a web application has been extended to the zone, you should delete the extended zone using the procedure that follows.

REMOVE AN EXTENDED ZONE

1. On the Central Administration Quick Launch, click Application Management.
2. In the Web Applications section, click Manage Web Applications.
3. Select the web application for which you want to delete an extended zone.
4. On the ribbon, click the down arrow on the Delete button, and then click Remove SharePoint From IIS Web Site.

> **IMPORTANT** **BE VERY CAREFUL**
>
> Be careful that you choose the correct command. Do not choose the Delete Web Application command or click the Delete button itself, because both actions will result in the deletion of the entire web application.

5. In the Select IIS Web Site And Zone To Remove list, select the zone that you want to remove.

> **IMPORTANT** **DON'T DELETE THE DEFAULT ZONE**
>
> By default, the default zone selected. If you delete the default zone, the web application will be broken. Be certain that you select a zone other than the default zone.

6. If you also want to delete the IIS Web site associated with the zone, click Yes in the Delete IIS Web Sites section.
7. Click OK.

Multiple Zones

Why might you want more than one zone? Zones are also used to scope certain settings for access to a web application, including authentication providers, anonymous access, and policy. If you want to provide access to the content of a web application with more than one variation of these settings, you must use more than one access zone. In this section, you will explore several common scenarios, and you will learn how to address those scenarios by configuring multiple zones.

Problems Resulting from Multiple Zones

Before we proceed, however, let's consider the type of problems that can arise whenever more than two zones are in use. Let's illustrate the problems with examples.

Both John and Jane access the Contoso Partner Portal. John is an internal employee, and accesses the site through the URL *http://extranet.contoso.com*. Jane is a partner, and accesses the site through the URL *https://partners.contoso.com*. Jane wants to send John a link to a the company calendar, which SharePoint renders to her as *http://extranet.contoso.com/Lists/CompanyCalendar/calendar.aspx* because *http://extranet.contoso.com* is the public URL of the default zone. She copies the link to the calendar and sends it to John. John cannot access the site through the URL namespace, *http://extranet.contoso.com*, so the link is inaccessible to John.

SharePoint renders the URLs of content with the public URL of the zone through which the site was accessed. Unfortunately, this is true only of links and URLs that SharePoint generates, such as navigation links in the Quick Launch. However, if a link is hard-coded on a page, it is not altered. For example, if Jane pastes a link to the company calendar into an announcement on the home page, she pastes it as *http://extranet.contoso.com/Lists/CompanyCalendar/calendar.aspx*. When John accesses the site, the URL is not altered to reflect the fact that he is accessing the home page as *https://partners.contoso.com*. The link is effectively broken for John.

> **NOTE** **A CAUTION ABOUT ABSOLUTE URLS**
>
> Absolute URLs—URLs that are hard-coded on a page—cannot be mapped. Be careful about using absolute URLs in the content of a web application that is accessed through more than one URL.

When you are faced with the choice of extending a web application—of creating a new zone—consider the impact on users and applications that will access the web application using a different URL namespace.

With those caveats, let's explore scenarios that can be implemented by creating additional zones. In each of these scenarios, you use the procedure described earlier, "Extend a Web Application," to create an additional zone.

Multiple Authentication Providers

A web application can be configured to only one authentication type—either Classic Mode Authentication or Claims Based Authentication. So if you have two solutions that cannot work in the same mode—for example, custom code that uses Windows identities and therefore cannot work in Claims Based Authentication, and another solution that relies on claims—you must separate the solutions into two different web applications.

Within a web application configured for claims authentication, however, you can have more than one authentication provider. For example, different users can be authenticated by either Windows, forms, or SAML token authentication within a single web application, with a single zone. For example, you can support both Windows and Forms Based Authentication (FBA) on the default zone.

This is a significant improvement over previous versions of SharePoint. In SharePoint 2007, you were required to extend a web application into additional zones to implement different types of authentication for users coming from different networks or authentication providers. This could lead to practical business problems because the different users accessed the content through different URLs.

The fact that Claims Based Authentication can support multiple authentication providers with a single zone reduces a significant design driver for multiple zones.

However, you can still specify different authentication providers on each zone and, in some cases, it will be required. If a zone is configured for forms-based authentication, the zone supports only one provider for FBA. It is not common to require multiple FBA providers, but if some users must be authenticated using the SQLMembershipProvider against a SQL database, and others must be authenticated using the LDAPMembershipProvider against an instance of Active Directory Lightweight Directory Services (AD LDS) or some other LDAP source, those users must access the site through two different zones, and therefore two different URLs. Alternately, you could write a custom FBA provider that abstracts the authentication provided by the two different sources.

Anonymous Access Enabled

Let's examine a scenario in which all content on the Contoso Intranet Web application can be accessed by authenticated users, based on permissions assigned to the content, using the URL *http://intranet.contoso.com*. However, you also want a subset of intranet content to be accessible by anonymous users—such as customers who are visiting Contoso and are connected to the Contoso network—using the URL *http://visitors.contoso.com*.

To support this scenario, you extend the Contoso Intranet Web application to a new zone—perhaps to the zone named *intranet*—with the public URL, *http://visitors.contoso.com*, to the web application. Each zone that has an extended web application supports its own authentication settings. On the zone named *intranet* associated with *http://visitors.contoso.com*, you enable anonymous access. Anonymous access remains disabled on the zone named *default* that is associated with *http://intranet.contoso.com*.

When a user enters a URL that begins with *http://visitors.contoso.com*, the request is received by SharePoint and SharePoint can map the request to the intranet zone of the Contoso Intranet Web application. This zone will accept anonymous connections.

Anonymous Access Restrictions

Anonymous user policy is also set per zone. You might want to allow anonymous users to access both *http://intranet.contoso.com* and *http://visitors.contoso.com*, but enforce read-only access through the zone associated with the URL *http://visitors.contoso.com*.

Reverse Proxy

A reverse proxy is a service that acts as a connector between end users and the web server. A user makes a request, and the reverse proxy receives the request. The reverse proxy filters and translates the request, and then forwards the request to the web server. SharePoint is compatible with many reverse proxy services and devices.

Although each reverse proxy product varies in functionality, they all have the following common characteristics:

- The reverse proxy can authenticate the user and perform inbound filtering based on characteristics of the request packet, and then forward only eligible requests to the web server.
- The reverse proxy can change the URL (host name or port) of the URL requested by the user. For example, a user requests *http://portal.contoso.com* and a reverse proxy receives the request and forwards the request to *http://partners.contoso.com*.
- The reverse proxy can receive requests using one port or protocol, and then forward the requests using another port or protocol. In this way, a reverse proxy can perform off-box SSL termination.
- The reverse proxy can forward the request to a different port than the port on which the request was originally received, and can change the HTTP host header field, thereby masking the internal name of a server or application from external users.

> *NOTE* **FOREFRONT AND THE REVERSE PROXY**
>
> Microsoft Forefront Unified Access Gateway (UAG), formerly Intelligent Application Gateway (IAG), is a very powerful reverse proxy and is the preferred reverse proxy offered by Microsoft. Microsoft Forefront Threat Management Gateway (TMG), formerly Internet Security and Acceleration Server (ISA), can also perform some reverse proxy functionality, but its primary purpose is to serve as an outbound proxy, and to protect users from Internet-based malware.

In reverse proxy scenarios, the URL of a request is directed to the reverse proxy. The URL sent by the reverse proxy to the web server is typically a different host name or port. For example, a user requests the home page of the Contoso Extranet web application, *https://portal.contoso.com/SitePages/Home.aspx*. The public URL of the Contoso Extranet web application—the URL as known to users—is thus *https://portal.contoso.com*. A reverse proxy that handles SSL encryption receives the request over port 443, and translates the request—for example, to *http://extranet.contoso.com/SitePages/Home.aspx* to the web server over port 80. The internal URL of the Contoso Extranet web application—the URL of the web application as known to SharePoint—is thus *http://extranet.contoso.com*. Typically, this URL is not directly accessible to the user—the user would not be able to resolve or connect to the site using the URL *http://extranet.contoso.com*—port 80 would be blocked by the firewall sitting between the user and the reverse proxy.

HTTPS and HTTP

Earlier you learned to configure a single zone so that it could be accessed by users over SSL using off-box termination. The intermediate device forwarded requests to HTTP port 80 on the web server, but users did not access the web application directly using HTTP.

What if you want to provide access to a web application to users on your internal network with the URL *http://intranet.contoso.com* but you want access from outside the network to use SSL, and thus the URL *https://intranet.contoso.com*?

In this configuration—when you want to support user access through *both* HTTP and HTTPS protocols, you must have two zones. Extend the web application. One zone—typically the default zone—is configured for SSL and the other zone without SSL. Do not simply add the SSL binding to the IIS Web site that is also bound to HTTP.

Different Policies

You will learn about web policies in Chapter 4. In short, a policy can grant a user or group permissions to content in a web application that override any permissions associated with a specific site, list, library, folder, item, or document. For example, you can specify a policy for the default zone of the Contoso Intranet that grants the Level 3 Help Desk group Full Control permission to content so that they can support users who are attempting to post content to the intranet. This policy applies when the Contoso Intranet Web application is accessed with the URL *http://intranet.contoso.com*, which is the external or public URL associated with the default zone representing the corporate network. You might want to prevent such broad application of Full Control permission when users in the Level 3 Help Desk group access the Contoso Intranet Web application over the Internet. If the Contoso Intranet Web application is extended to the Internet zone as *http://portal.contoso.com*, the web policies associated with the Internet zone are separate, so you can forego granting the Level 3 Help Desk group Full Control policy. Access using the external Internet zone's external URL, *http://portal.contoso.com*, is not subject to the same web policies as the default zone.

The web application also specifies many settings that apply to the web application, rather than the zone through which the web application is accessed, such as the features that are available in the web application.

Guidance and Recommendations for Zones and Access Mappings

You have explored common scenarios that require more than one zone, and you know some of the common problems that might arise when you have multiple zones. You also know that the best practice for creating an additional zone is to extend a web application. You should also be familiar with the following best practices and recommendations:

- Configure the default zone as the most secure zone. Typically, this means that, if you plan to use SSL for any zone, you should use it for the default zone. If you plan to enable anonymous authentication on one but not all zones, do not enable anonymous authentication on the default zone. When SharePoint cannot determine which policies to apply to an inbound request, it applies the policies associated with the default zone.

- System-generated alerts, such as those related to quotas and site collection usage, are sent using the URLs associated with the default zone. Therefore, you should configure a web application's default zone external URL as the most-often used URL. This consideration should be secondary to the primary recommendation in this list.

- You have learned that you can manually modify host header bindings on the IIS Web site from the IIS Manager, but this is not recommended. Any changes you make using the IIS Manager will not be recorded in the configuration database of the farm, and will not be replicated to other servers in the farm.

- Do not modify the host header binding that SharePoint applies to an IIS site. If SharePoint Server 2010 tries to provision an IIS Web site on another computer in the farm for the same web application and zone, the original host header binding is used instead of the modified binding. If you want to modify an existing binding for an IIS Web site, remove the web application from the zone and then re-extend the web application into the zone with the host header you want to use.

- Do not add the public URL of a zone as a binding to the IIS site of another zone. For example, if the public URL of the extranet zone is *http://extranet.contoso.com*, do not add the host header *extranet.contoso.com* to the IIS site of the default zone. Such manual configuration is not replicated to other IIS servers in the farm. It is not recommended to use the same IIS Web site for multiple zones, unless you are specifically told to do so by Microsoft.

- Host-named site collections cannot use alternate access mappings. Host-named site collections are automatically considered to be in the default zone, and the URL of the request must not be modified between the end user and the server. You will learn more about host-named site collections later in this training kit.

- One zone must be configured to use Windows authentication. The crawler uses NTLM to authenticate. If no zone supports NTLM, content will not be indexed, and therefore a search will never produce results from the web application.

- A URL should never be used as the internal URL of two different zones. The public URL of one zone should never be used as the internal URL of a different zone. If you put these rules together, a URL can only be used once within a web application: either as the public URL of a zone or as the internal URL of a zone. A URL can only be used twice when the URL is both the public and internal URL of a single zone.

Lesson Summary

- Each SharePoint web application is created with a zone named *default* that cannot be deleted. Four additional zones can be defined: *intranet*, *Internet*, *extranet*, and *custom*.

- A zone is defined by one public URL and one or more internal URLs. Each URL includes a protocol, scheme, host name, and port. For example, the public URL of the Contoso intranet is *http://intranet.contoso.com:80*, although the port, 80, can be omitted when you use the standard port for the HTTP protocol (80) or HTTPS protocol (443).

- The internal URL of an access mapping associates the internal URL of a request—the URL as it is received by SharePoint—to a web application zone. The internal URL is also called the *incoming URL*.

- The public URL of a web application allows SharePoint to render content to the user with URLs—for example, target URLs of hyperlinks—with a protocol and host name that are valid for the user, which might be different than the internal URLs of the web application itself. The public URL is also called the *external URL*, *load-balanced URL*, or *outgoing URL*.

- Each zone can specify unique configuration, such as anonymous authentication and restrictions, user policy, and SSL.

- If the internal URL of a request SharePoint has received from IIS is *http://intranet .contoso.com*, SharePoint knows that the request is associated with the zone named *Default* for the Contoso Intranet Web application. SharePoint then performs authentication as configured for the zone, and after the user has been authenticated, SharePoint parses the full URL of the request to determine the site collection and content database that must be accessed. Finally, SharePoint authorizes the user's access, based on a combination of the user's permissions to content and any policies that are enforced on the web application or zone, and then fulfills the request, returning the home page of the Contoso intranet to the user.

PRACTICE   Configure Access Mappings and Zones

Practices are designed to guide you through important procedures. The instructions in the Training Kit are high-level instructions that will challenge you to think carefully and to apply the procedures that are covered in this lesson, and elsewhere in the Training Kit. If you need assistance, consult the detailed, step-by-step instructions in the Practice Answers on the companion media.

In this practice, you configure common access and authentication scenarios that require the configuration of access mappings and zones.

Prepare for the Practice

Before you perform this practice, you must ensure that your lab environment has been built according to the instructions found in the Introduction to this Training Kit. You must also have performed the practice in Lesson 2 of this chapter. If you are currently logged on to SP2010-WFE1, log off before beginning the exercises.

EXERCISE 1 Modify Access Mappings

In this exercise, you

1. Log on to SP2010-WFE1 as **CONTOSO\SP_Admin** with the password **Pa$$w0rd**.

2. Add **http://intranet** as an internal URL to the default zone of the Contoso Intranet Web application.

3. Add **http://intranet** as a host header binding to the Contoso Intranet IIS Web site.

4. Confirm that you can open the site with the URL ***http://intranet***.

   The first time you open a site, IIS loads, compiles, and caches the site. This can take a while. If the site takes too long to load, an error appears. Refresh the page.

5. Observe that the URL to the home page in the address bar is *http://intranet.contoso .com/SitePages/Home.aspx*.

   A redirector loads the home page of the site. The redirector uses the public URL of the web application zone.

EXERCISE 2 Configure Windows-Claims Authentication

In this exercise, you configure authentication for the Contoso Partners Web application so that Windows Authentication is the only authentication provider. This exercise is intended to ensure that the web application is correctly configured for this practice.

- Verify that the Contoso Partner Portal Web application is configured with the following authentication settings:
  - NTLM authentication: Enabled
  - Forms Based Authentication: Disabled

EXERCISE 3 Extend a Web Application

In this exercise, you enable users to access the Contoso Partners Web application using *http://extranet.contoso.com* from the internal network and *https://partners.contoso.com* from the extranet. To do this, you extend the web application to a new zone for intranet users, with the URL *http://extranet.contoso.com*. Your information security manager has recommended that you use the host name *extranet* for your internal users so that it is clear to them that content in the web application is for external consumption.

1. Extend the Contoso Partner Portal to a new zone. Use the following specifications and guidance:

   - IIS Web site name: Contoso Partners Extranet
   - Port: 80
   - Host header: extranet.contoso.com
   - Authentication: NTLM
   - Public URL: *http://extranet.contoso.com:80*
   - Zone: Intranet

   It might seem counterintuitive to use the *intranet* zone for a zone with the URL *extranet*. Remember that the names of the zones (intranet, extranet, Internet, and custom) have no technical meaning. Furthermore, in this scenario, the zone is for internal users to access the Contoso Partner Portal. Access is from the intranet, using HTTP. The site is an external-facing site on which to collaborate with partners, thus the user-facing name of the zone is *extranet*.

2. Open a new tab in Internet Explorer, and browse to ***https://partners.contoso.com***. Sign in as **CONTOSO\SP_Admin**.

   The first time you open a site, IIS loads, compiles, and caches the site. This can take a while. If the site takes too long to load, an error appears. Refresh the page.

3. Open a new tab in Internet Explorer, and browse to ***http://extranet.contoso.com***.

   The Contoso Partner Portal site opens.

   The first time you open a site, IIS loads, compiles, and caches the site. This can take a while. If the site takes too long to load, an error appears. Refresh the page.

EXERCISE 4 Configure Authentication on a Zone

In this exercise, you enable anonymous users to access the root site collection of the Contoso Partner Portal as a landing page from which you can provide links to other sites that require authentication. So that users on non-Windows systems can authenticate to the portal, you will enable Basic authentication as well.

1. Enable anonymous authentication for the default zone of the Contoso Partner Portal Web application.

2. Enable Basic authentication for the default zone of the Contoso Partner Portal Web application.

EXERCISE 5 Configure Anonymous Access Restrictions

In this exercise, you enforce a security policy of your SharePoint governance plan that requires authenticated access to change any content. You do this by configuring an anonymous access restriction policy on the zone through which anonymous users are allowed to authenticate.

- Apply a Deny Write anonymous access restriction policy to the default zone of the Contoso Partner Portal Web application.

    You could apply the policy to all zones, but in this scenario, anonymous authentication is allowed only for the default zone.

EXERCISE 6 Complete and Validate Anonymous Access

In this exercise, you validate that users must be authenticated to access the Contoso Partner Portal site using the URL *http://extranet.contoso.com*, and that anonymous users can access the site using the URL *https://partners.contoso.com*.

1. Close all instances of Internet Explorer so that cached connections are eliminated.

2. Start Internet Explorer and browse to ***http://extranet.contoso.com***. Sign out of the site.

    A Windows Internet Explorer message opens: *The webpage you are viewing is trying to close the window.*

    Click Yes.

    Question: Why did the window close?

3. Start Internet Explorer and browse to ***https://partners.contoso.com***. When the Windows Security dialog box appears, click Cancel to log on as an anonymous user.

    A 401 Unauthorized error page opens.

    Question: Why can you not access the site as an anonymous user?

4. Refresh the page and sign in as **CONTOSO\SP_Admin** with the password **Pa$$w0rd**. Give anonymous users access to the entire site.

5. Close Internet Explorer. Start Internet Explorer and browse to ***https://partners.contoso.com***.

6. When the Contoso Partner Portal site opens, observe the Sign In control in the upper-right corner. You are connected as an anonymous user.

EXERCISE 7 Create the CHAPTER 03 Snapshot

The CHAPTER 03 snapshot captures the state of the environment at the end of Chapter 03. Perform this procedure for each of the following virtual machines: SP2010-WFE1, CONTOSO-DC.

1. Shut down the virtual machine.

2. Unmount any ISO image currently mounted to the CD/DVD drive. Use the "Unmount an ISO Image" procedure in the Lab Environment Build Guide on the companion media.

3. Create a snapshot named CHAPTER 03. Use the "Create a Snapshot" procedure in the Lab Environment Build Guide on the companion media.

Lesson Review

You can use the following questions to test your knowledge of the information in Lesson 3, "Configure Authentication Zones and Alternate Access Mappings." The questions are also available on the companion media in a practice test if you prefer to review them in electronic form.

> **NOTE ANSWERS**
>
> Answers to these questions and explanations of why each answer choice is right or wrong are located in the "Answers" section at the end of the book.

1. You have created a SharePoint-based timecard application, *http://timecards.contoso .com*. You want users to be able to browse to the application using either *http:// timecards.contoso.com* or *http://timecards*. What steps must you take? (Choose two. Each correct answer is a part of the solution.)

    A. Modify the IIS Web site.

    B. Modify the Web.config file.

    C. Modify the managed paths.

    D. Modify the Alternate Access Mappings.

    E. Extend the web application.

2. You have created a web application with the URL *http://server1*. Users can access the application from systems connected to the corporate network, and can authenticate with Windows authentication. You want to allow users to access the application from external systems with the URL *https://server1.contoso.com*. What do you do? (Choose all that apply. Each correct answer is a part of the solution.)

    A. Extend the web application to a new IIS Web site.

    B. Enable SSL for the web application.

    C. Add a binding to an IIS Web site.

    D. Install a certificate on the web server.

3. You have created a web application with the URL, *http://partners.contoso.com*. You want users to access the web application as *https://partners.contoso.com*, through a device that will offload the processing of SSL. What do you do?

    A. Add a host header, *https://partners.contoso.com*, to the IIS Web site.

    B. Add an SSL binding to the IIS Web site.

    C. Modify Alternate Access Mappings in Central Administration.

    D. Extend the web application to create a new zone.

4. You have created a web application, *http://intranet.contoso.com*. Users access the intranet and make changes to content while connected to the corporate network. You want to provide access to the site from outside the corporate network, but you want to ensure that users accessing the site from outside cannot change content. What do you do? (Choose all that apply. Each correct answer is a part of the solution.)

   A. Extend the web application to the extranet zone.

   B. Configure user policy on the extranet zone.

   C. Set the content database to read-only.

   D. Specify permissions on the top-level site collection that allow only read access.

   E. Configure a Deny Write anonymous access restriction.

5. You have created a web application with the URL *http://server1*. The application uses Windows authentication. You want to allow anonymous connections through the URL *https://server1.contoso.com*. What must you do? (Choose all that apply. Each correct answer is a part of the solution.)

   A. Enable anonymous authentication on the default zone.

   B. Add an SSL binding to the IIS Web site.

   C. Modify Alternate Access Mappings in Central Administration.

   D. Extend the web application to create a new zone.

   E. Modify anonymous access restrictions.

   F. Modify the authentication provider.

Chapter Review

To further practice and reinforce the skills you learned in this chapter, you can perform the following tasks:

- Review the chapter summary.
- Review the list of key terms introduced in this chapter.
- Complete the case scenarios. These scenarios set up real-world situations involving the topics of this chapter and ask you to create a solution.
- Complete the suggested practices.
- Take a practice test.

Chapter Summary

- The logical components that allow SharePoint to receive and process a request for content are the web application itself, its five zones, the alternate access mappings associated with each zone, the IIS Web site associated with each zone, and the bindings on the website.
- A user submits a request using the public URL of the web application zone. The request can be modified by an intermediary device, such as an off-box SSL terminator or a reverse proxy, before being forwarded to the front-end web server. The request received by IIS is matched to an IIS Web site based on the site's bindings, which often are based on a host header or, in the case of SSL, a dedicated IP address. The request is then passed to SharePoint, which examines the request's URL and, by identifying a matching the URL with the internal URLs in the web application's Alternate Access Mappings (AAM) collection. The matching URL identifies the zone with which the request will be processed. The zone determines the authentication and policies applied to the request.
- Authentication is managed by one of three authentication providers: Windows, forms based authentication, and SAML-token based authentication. In Classic Mode Authentication, only Windows is supported, but in Claims Based Authentication, all three providers are supported, and you can use multiple providers in a single zone.
- You can also enable anonymous authentication on a zone. However, a site collection administrator must also enable anonymous access and assign anonymous users permissions to content within a site. You can use enforce restrictions on the maximum access granted to anonymous users on a per-zone basis.
- As you design your environment, you must be aware of which settings are scoped to a web application, to individual zones, and to IIS Web sites. This will help you determine the logical architecture that will meet your requirements.

Key Terms

The following terms were introduced in this chapter. Do you know what they mean?

- bindings
- Web.config

- application pool
- Classic Mode Authentication
- Claims Based Authentication
- Secure Sockets Layer (SSL) and Transport Layer Security (TLS)
- Kerberos delegation
- Service principal name (SPN)
- Claim
- SAML token
- IP-STS
- RP-STS
- Zone
- Alternate access mapping

Case Scenario: Troubleshooting Web Application Configuration

In this case scenario, you apply what you've learned about subjects of this chapter. You can find answers to these questions in the "Answers" section at the end of this book.

You have recently begun working at Contoso, Ltd. The previous SharePoint administrator, who is no longer with the company, created an intranet web application. Users can access the web application by typing *http://intranet.contoso.com* or *http://intranet*. You have been told the intranet was configured so that users could type either URL to make it easier for users.

But users are complaining. They report that if they access the site as *http://intranet*, they have to click the Sign In link in the upper-right corner of the page before they can see certain content. If they access the site as *http://intranet.contoso.com*, they see all of their content immediately.

1. What can cause SharePoint to display a Sign In link? Why are users seeing the Sign In link?

2. What might the previous administrator have done that would cause different behavior for *http://intranet* than *http://intranet.contoso.com*?

3. You want to fix this problem, so that users can access the web application using either *http://intranet* or *http://intranet.contoso.com* and immediately see all of their content. You also want to correct configuration that was made by the previous administrator. Describe the tasks you will perform to resolve the situation.

Suggested Practices

To help you successfully master the exam objectives presented in this chapter, complete the following tasks.

Manage Web Applications

Do all the practices in this section. Be certain that you have created a snapshot of your virtual machines prior to performing these practices. When you have completed the practices, revert to the snapshot.

Practice 1: Configure Network Load Balancing

Network Load Balancing (NLB) allows you to distribute requests across multiple web front-end servers (WFEs). NLB can improve performance, and provides redundancy so that if a web server fails, other WFEs can continue to service requests. Windows Server 2008 R2 supports Network Load Balancing. Add the NLB feature to SP2010-WFE1. Even though you have only one server in the farm, you can configure NLB with the cluster IP address—the address that will be exposed to end users—and the IP address of the server. For example, you can configure the cluster IP address as 10.0.0.20/255.255.255.0. Add the IP address of SP2010-WFE1 (10.0.0.21) as a member of the cluster. Finally, change the DNS records for one or more websites to resolve to the IP address of the cluster. Test the configuration by browsing to a website. If it renders, NLB has been configured successfully. Because Windows Server 2008 R2 NLB does not overwrite the inbound request—instead, it sends the request to the IP address of a member—you do not need to configure any zones or access mappings to support this scenario.

Practice 2: Configure Forms Based Authentication

In the practice of Lesson 2, you began to configure Forms Based Authentication (FBA). You configured the web application for FBA, and you examined the Web.config file of the IIS Web site, but you did not change the three Web.config files that are necessary to configure FBA. You also did not create a SQL database to test the functionality of FBA. FBA is one of the most complex configurations in SharePoint. It is highly recommended that you gain hands-on experience with the process. Use resources on Microsoft TechNet and elsewhere on the Internet to configure Forms Based Authentication. Be certain to create a snapshot before you begin, so that you can revert to a known-good state when you have finished this suggested practice.

Take a Practice Test

The practice tests on this book's companion media offer many options. For example, you can test yourself on just the lesson review content, or you can test yourself on all the 70-667 certification exam objectives. You can set up the test so that it closely simulates the experience of taking a certification exam, or you can set it up in study mode so that you can look at the correct answers and explanations after you answer each question.

> **MORE INFO**   **PRACTICE TESTS**
>
> For details about all the practice test options available, see the "How to Use the Practice Tests" section in this book's Introduction.

Administering and Securing SharePoint Content

Most organizations store a variety of content in SharePoint—content that supports scenarios as diverse as a public-facing Internet website and a highly collaborative, confidential project. Content in SharePoint is partitioned into site collections, which are stored in content databases. The content is secured using a flexible and powerful permissions model, so that a user can only access content at a level that has been granted by an administrator. In this chapter, you will learn two of the most important sets of concepts and tasks that you must master to successfully implement SharePoint: how to manage site collections and content databases, and how to ensure that site content is secure.

Exam objectives in this chapter:

- Manage operational settings.
- Manage accounts and user roles.
- Manage Web Applications.
- Manage site collections.

Lessons in this chapter:

Before You Begin

To complete the lessons in this chapter, you must have done the following:

- Performed the practice in Chapter 1.

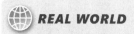
REAL WORLD

Dan Holme

One of the most common complaints I hear from customers is, "I wish I'd known sooner." This complaint arises when they discover that the structure of their SharePoint content—their web applications, site collections, and content databases—just isn't right. They discover that the out-of-box defaults for SharePoint—a single Web application with a single content database and a single site collection—is rarely appropriate to support their requirements for information management and security. They also express this complaint when they discover that the way they have managed users, groups, and permissions doesn't provide manageability that meets their needs. Well, this is your opportunity to "know it sooner." In this chapter, you will learn critical concepts and skills required to configure site collections, content databases, and security. But in addition, I've infused the discussion with important design considerations and guidance. Even if you're experienced with SharePoint, be sure to read this chapter to ensure that you are thoroughly familiar with the nuances of SharePoint's logical structure, and how it supports your governance—and most important, your security—requirements.

Lesson 1: Manage Site Collections and Content Databases

In Chapter 1, "Creating a SharePoint 2010 Intranet," you learned that site collection is a group of SharePoint websites—a top-level website and, optionally, child websites—that share common ownership and administrators, as well as common settings, such as quotas, locks, and site use confirmation and deletion. When you create a site collection, you must assign a site collection administrator. All other site collection properties can be left to their default values, or can be configured to your specifications.

A site collection is hosted in one content database. The content from all sites in the site collection is stored in that content database. A site collection cannot span more than one content database. The content database is the core component of storage management, including backup and restore.

In this lesson, you will learn more about site collections and content databases, including the details about their properties. You will learn to administer site collections and content by using both Central Administration and Windows PowerShell. And you will explore the reasons that it might be important for you to design your SharePoint farm with multiple site collections and content databases.

> **After this lesson, you will be able to:**
> - Create and delete site collections.
> - Configure site collection settings, including ownership and administration, quotas, and site locks.
> - Create and configure content databases.
> - Move site collections between content databases.
> - Configure managed paths.
> - Identify the factors that determine how many site collections and content databases should be created, based on your governance requirements.
>
> **Estimated lesson time: 90 minutes**

Manage Site Collections

Site collections can be created, deleted, and viewed by using Central Administration, Windows PowerShell, or Stsadm. This section details the procedures for Central Administration and Windows PowerShell. You can learn more about Stsadm site collection operations on Microsoft TechNet.

Create Site Collections

You can use Central Administration to create a site collection, or you can use Stsadm with the *createsite* operation. Chapter 1 includes the procedure to create a site collection by using Central Administration. In Chapter 2, "Administering and Automating SharePoint," you used Windows PowerShell to create a site collection with the *New-SPSite* cmdlet. Central Administration and the Windows PowerShell cmdlet are revisited in more detail later in this chapter.

CREATE A SITE COLLECTION USING CENTRAL ADMINISTRATION

1. In the Central Administration Quick Launch, click Application Management.

2. In the Site Collections section, click Create Site Collections to open the Create Site Collection page.

3. In the Web Application section, ensure that you are focused on the web application in which you want to create a site collection.

   If necessary, click the Web Application picker, shown in Figure 4-1, and then click Change Web Application. The Select Web Application dialog box opens. Click the correct web application.

FIGURE 4-1 The Web Application picker control

4. In the Title box, type a title for the site collection.

5. Optionally, type a description in the Description box.

6. In the Web Site Address section, in the URL drop-down list, select the path to use for your URL. You can select the root path (/) or a wildcard inclusion path such as */sites/*.

   If you select a wildcard inclusion path, you must also type the site name to use in the website's URL.

> **NOTE ONLY WILDCARD MANAGED PATHS APPEAR**
>
> Only the wildcard managed paths that have already been defined will be available in the drop-down menu. The *sites* managed path is created by default when you create a web application. See the section "Managed Paths" later in this lesson for more information about managed paths.

7. In the Template Selection section, select the site definition you want to apply to the top-level site of the new site collection—for example, Team Site on the Collaboration tab.

Click the Custom tab to create an empty top-level website and apply a template later.

8. In the Primary Site Collection Administrator section, in the User Name box, type the user name of the site collection administrator using the *DOMAIN\username* syntax.

9. Optionally, in the Secondary Site Collection Administrator section, in the User Name box, type the user name of the secondary site collection administrator using the *DOMAIN\username* syntax.

10. Click OK.

   The site collection is created, and the Top-Level Site Successfully Created page opens.

11. Click OK.

CREATE A SITE COLLECTION USING WINDOWS POWERSHELL

The syntax of a typical *New-SPSite* command is as follows:

```
New-SPSite -Url "<URL for the new site collection>"
-ContentDatabase <Content Database Name> -Name "<Name for Top-Level Site>"
-Template <Template> -OwnerAlias "<domain\user>" [-OwnerEmail "<e-mail address>"]
[-SecondaryOwnerAlias "<domain\user>"] [-SecondaryOwnerEmail "<e-mail address>"]
```

Where:

- *<URL>* is the URL of the site collection you want to create.
- *<Content Database Name>* is the name of the content database within which the site collection should be created. This parameter is optional.
- *<Name>* is the name of the top-level website. The name will appear in the title and heading of the top-level website.
- *<Template>* specifies the site definition for the top-level site—for example, BLANKINTERNET#0, the Publishing Site, or STS#0, the Team Site. Use the *Get-SPWebTemplate* cmdlet to enumerate the available templates.
- The required *-OwnerAlias* parameter's *<domain\user>* value defines the primary site collection administrator.
- The optional *-SecondaryOwnerAlias* parameter is used to define the secondary site collection administrator.
- The *-OwnerEmail* parameter specifies the email address of the primary site collection administrator. The *-SecondaryEmail* parameter specifies the email address of the secondary site collection administrator. These parameters are optional but highly recommended. Without them, SharePoint cannot send email notifications regarding site quotas, site use confirmation, and deletion.

Note that when you create a site collection by using Central Administration, the email addresses of site collection administrators are automatically populated by looking them up in the Active Directory accounts of the administrators. When you use Windows PowerShell to create a site collection, you must specify the email addresses.

For example, the following command creates a site collection at the root of the intranet web application and creates a top-level site with the Publishing site definition.

```
New-SPSite -Url "http://teams.contoso.com" -ContentDatabase "SharePoint_Content_Teams"
-Name "Contoso Departments, Teams, and Projects" -Description "Collaboration sites for
Contoso departments, teams, and projects" -Template "STS#0" -OwnerAlias
"CONTOSO\SP_Admin" -OwnerEmail "SP_Admin@contoso.com"
```

A close examination of the parameters of this command reveals that when you create a site collection—an *SPSite* object—you also create the top-level website—an *SPWeb* object—in the site collection. The *-Name* and *-Description* parameters configure the display name and description of the website, respectively. The top-level site can be configured to use a template, also called a site definition, by using the *-Template* parameter.

Although the site collection and top-level website are two different objects that are created simultaneously, and cannot exist without each other, you can optionally create one or more additional websites within the site collection, typically referred to as *subsites* or *child sites*.

Self-Service Site Creation

The name *self-service site creation* confuses many SharePoint administrators. The ability of users to create a subsite—a child website—within a site collection is controlled by the *Create subsites* permission, which is part of the *Full Control* permission set. Any user who has the *Create subsites* permission can create a subsite within a site collection. However, as you learned in Chapter 3, "Managing Web Applications," the self-service site creation feature actually enables the creation of site *collections*, not subsites. Self-service site creation enables users to create site collections without the assistance of a farm administrator.

In Chapter 3, you learned that you can enable self-service site creation using one of two different interfaces in Central Administration:

- On the Manage Web Applications page, select a Web Application, and then click Self-Service Site Creation on the ribbon.

- On the Application Management page, in the Site Collections section, click Configure Self-Service Site Creation.

Despite the fact that one of the links to enable and configure self-service site creation appears in the Site Collections section of Central Administration, it is important to remember that it is scoped to a web application. If self-service site creation is enabled for a web application, users can create new site collections from the top-level site at the root of the web application.

CREATE A SITE COLLECTION USING SELF-SERVICE SITE CREATION

1. Open the self-service site creation page for the web application. The URL of the page is *http://<Web application URL>/_layouts/scsignup.aspx*.

    When you enable self-service site creation, an announcement is added to the Announcements list indicating the availability of self-service site creation. From the website at the root of the web application, click All Site Content, then click Announcements, then click the announcement entitled Self-Service Site Creation. Then click the link in the Body section of the Announcements dialog box to the scsignup.aspx page.

> **BEST PRACTICE   LINK TO SELF-SERVICE SITE CREATION**
>
> If you enable self-service site creation, add a link to the Self-Service Site Creation page in a location that is easy for users to access.

2. In the Title box, type the title of the top-level website in the new site collection.

3. Optionally, in the Description box, type a description for the top-level website.

4. In the Web Site Address section, if more than one wildcard managed path has been defined, select a managed path from the drop-down list.

    When you create a web application, only one managed path is defined: */sites/*. See the "Managed Paths" section later in this lesson for more information.

5. In the URL Name box, type the site name, which comprises the final element of the URL for the site collection and top-level website.

6. In the Template Selection section, select the site definition you want to apply to the top-level site of the new site collection—for example, Team Site on the Collaboration tab.

   Click the Custom tab to create an empty top-level website and apply a template later.

> **NOTE** **AVAILABLE TEMPLATES ARE BASED ON FEATURES AND CONFIGURATION OF THE SITE**
>
> The available templates will vary based on the features that are enabled and custom templates that have been installed. If you do not see a template that you believe should be available, ensure that appropriate features have been enabled and that the template you desired has been made available. Both of these settings are found on the Site Settings page: feature availability is configured using the Manage Site Features and Site Collection features commands; template availability is configured using the Page Layouts And Site Templates command that appears when a site uses the Publishing Site site definition.

7. In the Additional Site Collection Administrators box, enter the names of additional site collection administrators. The first-listed user will be assigned as the secondary site collection owner, and will receive email notifications related to quotas and site use confirmation and deletion.

8. Click Create.

   The Set Up Groups For This Site page opens. See Lesson 2 for more information about creating site groups.

9. After you have configured site groups, click OK.

View Site Collections

If you want to view all site collections in a web application, you can use Central Administration or Windows PowerShell.

VIEW ALL SITE COLLECTIONS USING CENTRAL ADMINISTRATION

To view all site collections in a web application, use the following procedure:

1. In the Central Administration Quick Launch, click Application Management.

2. On the Application Management page, in the Site Collections section, click View All Site Collections.

   The Site Collection List page opens. It displays relative URLs of site collections in the selected web application.

   If you want to change the selected web application, click the Web Application picker, and then click Change Web Application. The Select Web Application dialog box opens. Click the name of a web application.

3. To display information about a site collection, in the URL column, click the relative URL of the site collection.

Details are shown on the right side of the page.

VIEW ALL SITE COLLECTIONS USING WINDOWS POWERSHELL

The following example shows the use of the *Get-SPSite* cmdlet to enumerate selected properties of all site collections in a web application:

```
Get-SPWebApplication "<WebApplicationURL>" | Get-SPSite -Limit ALL | Format-List
-Property URL,ContentDatabase,Owner,SecondaryContact
```

Where:

■ *<WebApplicationURL>* is the URL of the web application for which you want to list site collections.

Unfortunately, the *SPSite* object does not expose all of the properties that you configured when using the *New-SPSite* cmdlet. For example, the email address of the primary site collection administrator, and the name, description, and template used for the top-level website are not properties of the resulting *SPSite* object.

Some of these properties are members of the *SPWeb* object for the top-level website. Others are exposed by the *SPSiteAdministration* object. *SPSiteAdministration* is an object that exposes properties of site collections and top-level websites to farm administrators. The following cmdlet exposes site collection properties by using the *Get-SPSiteAdministration* cmdlet:

```
Get-SPSiteAdministration |
Select URL,Title,Description,RootWebTemplate,OwnerLoginName,OwnerEmail
```

In fact, of the properties that you configure when creating a site collection, only the content database name is not immediately available to the *Get-SPSiteAdministration* cmdlet. In the practice for this lesson, you will use the following cmdlet to report all of the attributes that you use when configuring a new site collection by using Central Administration or the *New-SPSite* cmdlet:

```
Get-SPWebApplication "http://teams.contoso.com" | Get-SPSite -Limit ALL |
ForEach {$_ | Get-SPSiteAdministration |
Select URL,Title,Description,RootWebTemplate,OwnerLoginName,OwnerEmail ;
$_ | Select ContentDatabase}
```

This one-liner retrieves all site collections for a specified web application. It then iterates through each site collection. For each site collection, the associated *SPSiteAdministration* object returns most of the properties, and the site collection object itself is piped to the *Select-Object* cmdlet to return the content database name.

Delete Site Collections

If a site collection is no longer needed, you might want to delete it. For example, if you created a team site to track progress on a specific project, and the project has ended, you might decide to delete the site collection after a certain amount of time has passed. Your governance plan should guide decisions regarding the life cycle of site collections so that out-of-use content does not remain indefinitely in your SharePoint farm.

When you delete a site collection, you permanently destroy all configuration, user information, and content in the site collection. This includes all site configuration settings; user role and security information; and all websites, lists, and document libraries. It is therefore recommended that you create a backup of a site collection before deleting it. Chapter 11, "Implementing Business Continuity," covers backup procedures. Again, your governance plan should specify whether backups are made of site collections prior to deletion, and the lifespan of such backups.

DELETE A SITE COLLECTION USING CENTRAL ADMINISTRATION

1. In the Central Administration Quick Launch, click Application Management.

2. In the Site Collections section, click Delete A Site Collection.

3. On the Delete Site Collection page, click the Site Collection picker, and then click Change Site Collection.

4. In the Select Site Collection dialog box, click the Web Application picker, and then click Change Web Application.

   The Select Web Application dialog box opens.

5. Click the name of the web application that contains the site collection that you want to delete.

   The Select Site Collection dialog box opens. It displays relative URLs of site collections in the web application that you selected.

6. Click the relative URL of the site collection that you want to delete, and then click OK.

7. On the Delete Site Collection page, read the Warning section and verify that the site collection information is correct.

8. Click Delete.

DELETE A SITE COLLECTION USING WINDOWS POWERSHELL

The following example shows the use of the *Remove-SPSite* cmdlet to delete a site collection:

```
Remove-SPSite -Identity "<URL>" [-GradualDelete]
```

Where:

- *<URL>* is the URL of the site collection you want to delete.

- The optional *-GradualDelete* parameter specifies that you use gradual deletion, which reduces the load on the system during the deletion process.

> **MORE INFO**   **CREATING AND DELETING SITE COLLECTIONS**
>
> The following articles provide further details about creating and deleting site collections:
>
> - "Create a site collection (SharePoint Server 2010)" at *http://technet.microsoft.com/en-us/library/cc263165.aspx*
>
> - "Delete a site collection (SharePoint Server 2010)" at *http://go.microsoft.com/fwlink/?LinkID=192706&clcid=0x409*

Configure Site Collections Using Central Administration

After creating the site collection, you should configure site collection settings. The following settings are among those that are configured at the site collection scope:

- Ownership and administration
- Storage limits and warnings
- Locks
- User and group management
- Features

Site Collection Ownership and Administration

The first setting you should configure is site collection ownership. As you learned in Chapter 2, site collection owners—the primary and secondary site collection administrators of a site collection—receive quota and auto-deletion notices. In addition, they have all the rights associated with site collection administrators.

You can assign site collection owners by using Central Administration, Stsadm, or Windows PowerShell. Central Administration and the Windows PowerShell cmdlet are detailed in the following sections. You can learn more about Stsadm site collection operations on Microsoft TechNet.

ASSIGN SITE COLLECTION OWNERS USING CENTRAL ADMINISTRATION

To assign site collection owners, perform the following procedure:

1. In SharePoint 2010 Central Administration Quick Launch, click Application Management.

2. On the Site Collection Administrators page, in the Site Collection section, confirm that the site collection for which you want to assign ownership is selected.

   If not, click the Site Collection picker, and then click Change Site Collection. Use the Select Site Collection page to select the site collection:

   - Confirm that the Web Application list displays the web application that contains the site collection for which you want to assign ownership.

     If not, click the Site Collection picker, and then click Change Site Collection. On the Select Site Selection page, click the site.

   - In the URL list, click the site collection and then click OK.

3. In the Primary Site Collection Administrator box, type the name of the primary owner, using the format **DOMAIN\username**.

4. In the Secondary Site Collection Administrator box, type the name of the secondary owner, using the format **DOMAIN\username**.

5. Click OK.

ASSIGN SITE COLLECTION OWNERS USING WINDOWS POWERSHELL

The following example shows the use of the *Set-SPSite* cmdlet to assign the site collection owners:

```
Set-SPSite -Identity "<SiteCollection>" -OwnerAlias "<DOMAIN\User>"
-SecondaryOwnerAlias "<DOMAIN\User>"
```

Where:

- *<SiteCollection>* is the URL of the site collection to which you want to add a site collection administrator.

- *<DOMAIN\User>* is the name of the user whom you want to add as a site collection owner.

- The *-OwnerAlias* parameter defines the primary site collection administrator.

- The *-SecondaryOwnerAlias* parameter defines the secondary site collection administrator.

After assigning one or two site collection owners, you should determine which additional users require ownership of the site collection. These users should be assigned the site collection administrators role. As you learned in Chapter 2, site collection administrators have full control of all websites in a site collection. They have access to all content in all sites in that site collection, even if they do not have explicit permissions to that content. Site collection administrators also can configure all settings of the site collection.

ASSIGN SITE COLLECTION ADMINISTRATORS USING CENTRAL ADMINISTRATION

To assign site collection administrators, perform the following procedure:

1. At the top-level site of a site collection, click Site Actions, and then click Site Settings.

2. In the Users And Permissions section, click Site Collection Administrators.

3. Add or remove users from the semicolon-delimited list of site collection administrators.

Any site collection administrator can change the list of site collection administrators. There can be one or more site collection administrators. The primary and secondary owners of the site collection are automatically site collection administrators, and there is no way to segregate owners (which have both site collection administration and contact roles) from site collection administrators. If a site collection has only one or two site collection administrators, those same users are the primary and secondary owners of the site collection as well.

ASSIGN SITE COLLECTION ADMINISTRATORS USING WINDOWS POWERSHELL

Use the *Set-SPUser* cmdlet's *-IsSiteCollectionAdmin* parameter to assign the site collection administrator role to a user in a site collection. Use the following syntax:

```
Set-SPUser -Identity "<DOMAIN\Username>" -IsSiteCollectionAdmin
```

Where:

- *<DOMAIN\Username>* is the identity of the user account. The account must have been added previously to the site collection. Use the *New-SPUser* cmdlet to add a user to a site collection.

When you use Windows PowerShell to add a second site collection administrator, the user is not automatically made a site collection owner.

> **MORE INFO   ASSIGNING SITE COLLECTION ADMINISTRATORS**
>
> You can learn more about managing site collection administrators in the TechNet article, "Add or remove site collection Administrators (SharePoint Server 2010)" at *http://go.microsoft.com/fwlink/?LinkID=192707.*

Quotas

One of the important site collection settings is the quota, which specifies the storage limit values for the maximum amount of data that can be stored in a site collection. Data includes the following:

- Documents stored in document libraries
- List items
- Attachments
- Previous versions of documents, items, and attachments, if versioning is enabled
- Configuration
- Content in the Recycle Bins

When you configure a quota for a site collection, it applies to the collected data within all sites in the site collection. Quotas define the following:

- A storage limit, in megabytes. If you enable and define a storage limit, when the storage limit is reached, users are prevented from adding data to the site, and an email is sent to the site collection owners—the primary and secondary site collection administrators.
- A storage warning level, in megabytes. When site collection storage reaches the storage warning level, an email message is sent to site collection owners, but users can continue to add data to the site. The warning enables owners to proactively address the problem by deleting site content or increasing the storage limit. The storage warning level is optional, but if it is defined it must be a value less than the storage limit.

Quotas also define the resource utilization limits for Sandboxed Solutions. Sandboxed Solutions are discussed in Chapter 10, "Administering SharePoint Customization."

CONFIGURE A QUOTA FOR A SITE COLLECTION USING CENTRAL ADMINISTRATION

To configure a quota for a site collection, perform the following procedure:

1. In Central Administration, click Application Management.
2. On the Application Management page, in the Site Collections section, click Configure Quotas And Locks.

   The Site Collection Quotas And Locks page opens.

3. If you want to change the selected site collection, in the Site Collection section, in the Site Collection picker, click Change Site Collection. Use the Select Site Collection page to select a site collection.

4. In the Site Quota Information section, in the Current Quota Template list, select Individual Quota.

5. Select the Limit Site Storage To A Maximum Of check box, and then type the maximum value in megabytes.

6. If you want to send site storage notification email messages to the site collection owners, select the Send Warning E-Mail When Site Storage Reaches check box, and then type the warning value in megabytes.

CONFIGURE A QUOTA FOR A SITE COLLECTION USING WINDOWS POWERSHELL

The following example shows the use of the *Set-SPSite* cmdlet to configure a quota:

```
Set-SPSite -Identity "<Site>" -MaxSize <StorageLimit> -WarningLevel <WarningLevel>
```

Where:

- *<Site>* is the URL of the site collection whose storage limits you want to change.
- *<StorageLimit>* is the new storage limit for the site collection, in megabytes.
- *<WarningLevel>* is the new warning level for the site collection, in megabytes.

Quota Templates

You can imagine that it can become burdensome to configure the storage limits for each individual site collection—for example, configuring each department in your organization. To facilitate management of storage limits, you can create quota templates. A *quota template* specifies a storage limit and warning level. You can then apply a quota template to a site collection, and the template's limits are applied to the site collection. For example, you could create a single template for departmental team sites, specifying a quota of 500 MB. When you create a site collection for a departmental team site, you simply apply the quota template and the settings in the quota are applied to the site collection.

CREATE, MODIFY, OR DELETE A QUOTA TEMPLATE

To create, modify, or delete a quota template, perform the following procedure:

1. In the Central Administration Quick Launch, click Application Management.

2. On the Application Management page, in the Site Collections section, click Specify Quota Templates to open the Quota Templates page, shown in Figure 4-2.

   You can create, modify, or delete a quota template from the Quota Templates page.

3. Perform one of the following steps:

   - If you want to delete a quota template, select the template in the Template To Modify list, and then click Delete. A confirmation prompt opens. Click OK. The template is deleted. Skip to step 6.

- If you want to modify a quota template, select the template in the Template To Modify list.

- If you want to create a new quota template, click Create A New Quota Template and then, in the New Template Name box, type a name for a new quota template.

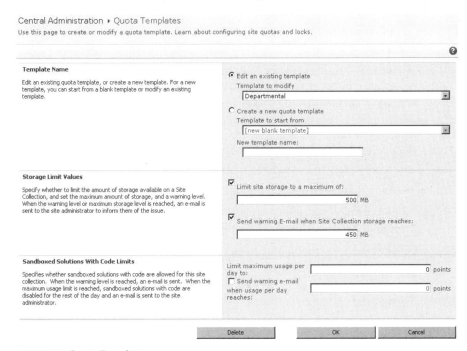

FIGURE 4-2 Quota Templates page

4. In the Storage Limit Values section, specify the values that you want to apply to the template.

- If you want to modify the amount of data that can be stored in the database, select the Limit Site Storage To A Maximum Of check box, and type the new storage limit, in megabytes, in the text box.

- If you want an email message to be sent to the site collection administrator when a storage threshold is reached, select the Send Warning E-Mail When Site Collection Storage Reaches check box, and then type the threshold, in megabytes, in the box.

5. In the Sandboxed Solutions With Code Limits section, set the values for a template for Sandboxed Solutions.

- If you want to limit the resource usage of Sandboxed Solutions in the site collection, select the Limit Maximum Usage Per Day To check box, and then type the daily resource usage limit, in points, in the text box.

- If you want an email message to be sent to the site collection administrator when a resource usage threshold is reached, select the Send Warning E-Mail When Usage Per Day Reaches check box, and then type the daily resource usage warning limit, in points, in the box.

See Chapter 10 for more detail about Sandboxed Solutions.

6. Click OK.

After you create a quota template, it can be applied to one or more site collections. When a quota template is applied to a site collection, the quota template's storage limit and storage warning level properties are applied to the site collection.

APPLY A QUOTA TEMPLATE TO A SITE COLLECTION

To apply a quota template to a site collection, perform the following procedure:

1. In the Central Administration Quick Launch, click Application Management.

2. On the Application Management page, in the Site Collections section, click Configure Quotas And Locks to open the page shown in Figure 4-3.

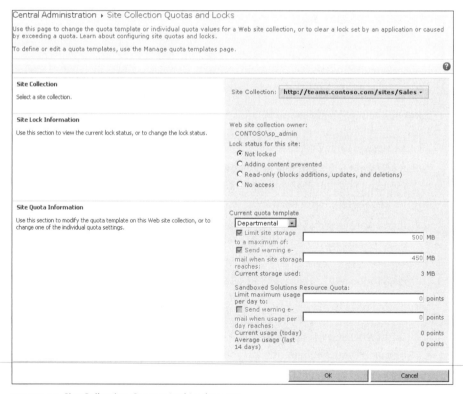

FIGURE 4-3 Site Collection Quotas And Locks page

3. If you want to change the selected site collection, in the Site Collection section, click the Site Collection picker, and then click Change Site Collection. Use the Select Site Collection page to select a site collection.

4. In the Site Quota Information section, click the Current Quota Template list, and then select the new quota template to apply.

5. Click OK.

It is important to understand the architecture of quotas. Quota templates are defined at the farm level. When a quota template is applied to one or more site collections, the properties of the template are applied to the site collection.

If you update a quota template, the new settings apply to any new site collections to which the quota is applied. However, when you update a quota template, the change does not apply to existing site collections. This is not obvious in Central Administration—if you open the Site Collection Quotas And Locks page, you will see the new settings of the template, but those settings are not actually applied until you click OK.

Alternately, you can use Windows PowerShell's *Set-SPSite* cmdlet. The *-QuotaTemplate* parameter can be used to reapply the template and thereby to apply its new settings.

> *MORE INFO* **PLANNING BROWSER SUPPORT**
>
> The following article provides additional details regarding storage limits and quotas: "Manage site collection storage limits (SharePoint Server 2010)" at *http://go.microsoft.com/ fwlink/?LinkID=192708*.

 Quick Check

- When you apply a quota template, SharePoint limits the size of which of the following objects: Web application, site collection, or site?

Quick Check Answer

- Quotas apply to a site collection.

Site Collection Locks

You can apply locks to prevent users from accessing or modifying content in a site collection. Locks are particularly useful when you want to prevent changes to content without changing the permissions on the content itself. Table 4-1 describes the locking options that are available in Microsoft SharePoint Server 2010.

TABLE 4-1 Site Collection Locks

OPTION	DESCRIPTION
Not Locked	Unlocks the site collection and makes it available to users.
Adding Content Prevented	Prevents users from adding new content to the site collection. Updates and deletions are still allowed.
Read-only (Blocks Additions, Updates, And Deletions)	Prevents users from adding, updating, or deleting content.
No Access	Prevents access to content completely. Users who attempt to access the site receive an access-denied message.

LOCK OR UNLOCK A SITE COLLECTION USING CENTRAL ADMINISTRATION

To lock or unlock a site collection, perform the following steps:

1. In Central Administration, click Application Management.

2. On the Application Management page, in the Site Collections section, click Configure Quotas And Locks to open the Site Collection Quotas And Locks page.

3. If you want to change the selected site collection, in the Site Collection section, in the Site Collection picker, click Change Site Collection. Use the Select Site Collection page to select a site collection.

4. On the Site Collection Quotas And Locks page, in the Site Lock Information section, select one of the following options:

    - **Not Locked**   Unlocks the site collection and makes it available to users.

    - **Adding Content Prevented**   Prevents users from adding new content to the site collection. Updates and deletions are still allowed.

    - **Read-Only (Blocks Additions, Updates, And Deletions)**   Prevents users from adding, updating, or deleting content.

    - **No Access**   Prevents access to content completely. Users who attempt to access the site receive an access-denied message.

5. If you select Adding Content Prevented, Read-Only (Blocks Additions, Updates, And Deletions), or No Access, type a reason for the lock in the Additional Lock Information box.

6. Click OK.

LOCK OR UNLOCK A SITE COLLECTION USING WINDOWS POWERSHELL

The following example shows the use of the *Set-SPSite* cmdlet with the *-LockState* parameter to lock or unlock a site.

```
Set-SPSite -Identity "<SiteCollection>" -LockState "<State>"
```

Where:

- *<SiteCollection>* is the URL of the site collection that you want to lock or unlock.
- *<State>* is one of the following values:
  - **Unlock**   Unlocks the site collection and makes it available to users.
  - **NoAdditions**   Prevents users from adding new content to the site collection. Updates and deletions are still allowed.
  - **ReadOnly**   Prevents users from adding, updating, or deleting content.
  - **NoAccess**   Prevents access to content completely. Users who attempt to access the site receive an access-denied message.

User and Group Management

In Lesson 2, you will learn to manage users and groups in SharePoint 2010. The users and groups that are allowed to access content within a site collection are defined at the site collection itself. The permissions assigned to a user and group are configured at the site, list, library, folder, item, or document, but the user list and the groups list is a property of the site collection. See Lesson 2 for more information about user and group management.

Features

Site collections also impose functional boundaries. Features can be activated or deactivated at the site collection level. A feature must be enabled at the site collection level before websites in the site collection can take advantage of the feature. If a feature is deactivated at the site collection scope, it cannot be enabled at the website scope. You will learn more about features in Chapter 10, "Administering SharePoint Customization."

Other Settings in the Site Collections Section of Central Administration

The Site Collections settings in Central Administration tend to cause confusion for several reasons. First, site collection settings do not use the new user interface featuring the ribbon. With a ribbon, you can select an object—such as a web application—and then configure a setting. For site collection settings, you select the setting first, then you must select the web application and then the site collection for which you want to configure the setting, and only then can you configure the setting itself.

Second, two settings listed in the Site Collections section of the Application Management page of Central Administration are not scoped to site collections at all: Self-Service Site Creation and Site Use Confirmation And Deletion. Although both of these settings affect site collections, they are scoped to web applications and affect all site collections in a web application. Self-Service Site Creation can also be configured using the Manage Web Applications page of Central Administration and using the Security page of Central Administration. Site Use Confirmation And Deletion can only be configured from the Site Collections section of the Application Management page.

The configuration of self-service site creation is described in Chapter 3, and the creation of sites using self-service site creation is detailed earlier in this lesson. Site Use Confirmation And Deletion is also covered in Chapter 3.

Configure Site Collections Using Site Settings

After you create a site collection and top-level site, you can configure some administrative settings from Central Administration, as you learned earlier in this lesson. You can configure additional settings on the Site Settings page of the top-level website.

CONFIGURE SITE COLLECTION SETTINGS USING THE SITE SETTINGS PAGE

To configure site collection settings by using the Site Settings page, perform one of the following two procedures:

- From the top-level website of a site collection, click Site Actions, and then click Site Settings.
- From a subsite in a site collection, click Site Actions, then click Site Settings, and then, in the Site Collection Settings section of the Site Settings page, click Top-Level Site Settings.

The Site Settings page of the top-level site, shown in Figure 4-4, provides links to commands that affect both the top-level website and the site collection itself. The commands that appear can vary based on the version of SharePoint that is installed. The links are security-trimmed. If you are a site collection owner or a user with Full Control permission to a site, but you are not a site collection administrator, you will see commands that configure the top-level website settings, shown on the right side of Figure 4-4. If you are a site collection administrator, you will see additional commands that configure the site collection, shown on the left side of Figure 4-4.

Within the settings that can be configured for the site collection and top-level website, additional options appear to a site collection administrator that do not appear for a site owner. For example, a site owner can enable or disable RSS feeds for a site. (By default, RSS feeds are enabled.) A site collection administrator can disable RSS feeds for the entire site collection. If feeds are disabled for the site collection, they are disabled for every site in the site collection and site owners cannot enable feeds.

Many of these settings will be described later in this Training Kit.

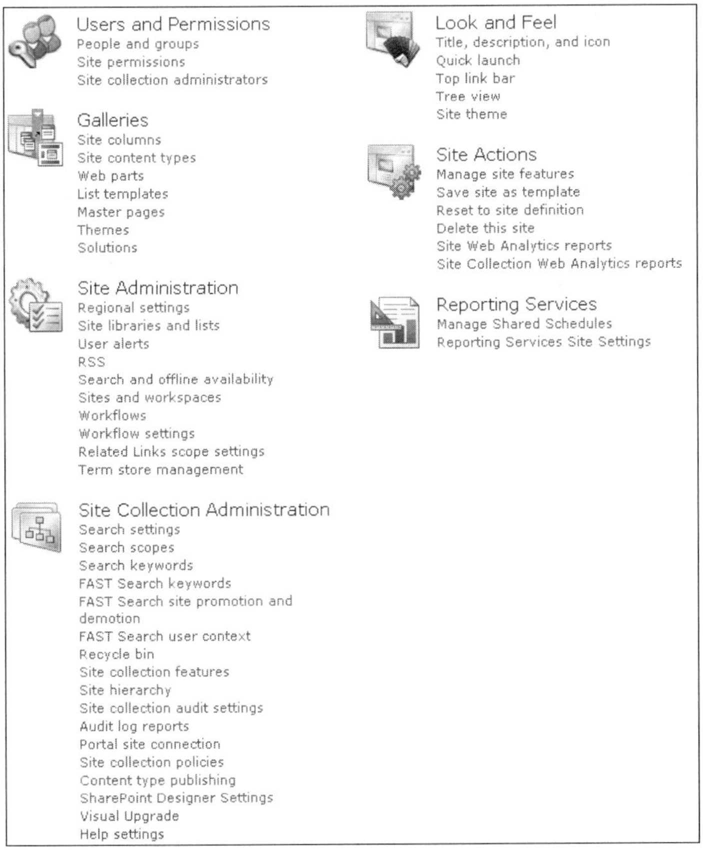

 Users and Permissions
People and groups
Site permissions
Site collection administrators

 Galleries
Site columns
Site content types
Web parts
List templates
Master pages
Themes
Solutions

 Site Administration
Regional settings
Site libraries and lists
User alerts
RSS
Search and offline availability
Sites and workspaces
Workflows
Workflow settings
Related Links scope settings
Term store management

 Site Collection Administration
Search settings
Search scopes
Search keywords
FAST Search keywords
FAST Search site promotion and demotion
FAST Search user context
Recycle bin
Site collection features
Site hierarchy
Site collection audit settings
Audit log reports
Portal site connection
Site collection policies
Content type publishing
SharePoint Designer Settings
Visual Upgrade
Help settings

 Look and Feel
Title, description, and icon
Quick launch
Top link bar
Tree view
Site theme

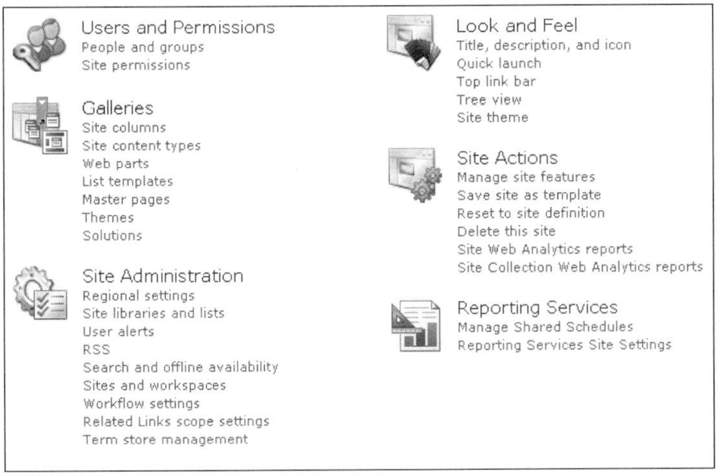

 Site Actions
Manage site features
Save site as template
Reset to site definition
Delete this site
Site Web Analytics reports
Site Collection Web Analytics reports

 Reporting Services
Manage Shared Schedules
Reporting Services Site Settings

 Users and Permissions
People and groups
Site permissions

 Galleries
Site columns
Site content types
Web parts
List templates
Master pages
Themes
Solutions

Site Administration
Regional settings
Site libraries and lists
User alerts
RSS
Search and offline availability
Sites and workspaces
Workflow settings
Related Links scope settings
Term store management

 Look and Feel
Title, description, and icon
Quick launch
Top link bar
Tree view
Site theme

 Site Actions
Manage site features
Save site as template
Reset to site definition
Delete this site
Site Web Analytics reports
Site Collection Web Analytics reports

 Reporting Services
Manage Shared Schedules
Reporting Services Site Settings

FIGURE 4-4 The Site Settings page, as seen by a site collection administrator (top) and a user with Full Control permission of a site (bottom)

Multiple Sites vs. Multiple Site Collections

A site collection can contain one or more websites. Below the top-level site, you can create additional sites, referred to as *subsites*, *subwebs*, or *child sites*.

Figure 4-5 shows subsites in the *teams* site collection for HR, Marketing, Finance, and Engineering. The URL for HR would be *http://teams.contoso.com/HR*. The figure also shows subsites in the *clients* site collection for Litware and Fabrikam. The URL for Litware would be *http://clients.contoso.com/Litware*. The site hierarchy can be even deeper, but be aware of the 260-character URL length limit. In Figure 4-5, each web application contains a single site collection in a single content database.

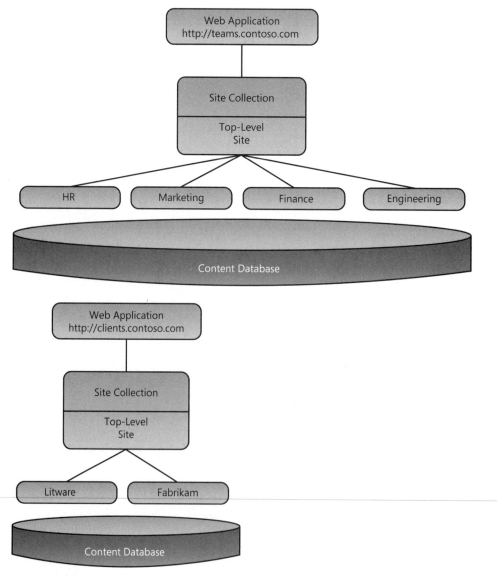

FIGURE 4-5 Subsites

In this section, you will explore some of the factors that determine whether this design is appropriate based on your governance requirements.

Site Collections and Governance Controls

As you've learned in this lesson, a number of governance controls, including content ownership, quota configuration, locks, user and group management, feature availability, and settings such as RSS feeds are configured at and scoped to a site collection. Governance objectives often drive organizations to create multiple site collections that configure unique properties for each site collection.

For example, distinct users might have ownership of the Finance and Engineering websites—an administrator of Engineering might not have full control of content on the Finance website. Additionally, because site collection owners and administrators are defined at the site collection level, a user who requires ownership of Finance—including the ability to configure all conceivable settings—must be made a site collection administrator of the intranet site collection itself.

In the *teams* application, different quotas might be assigned to HR and to Engineering, which works with large documents and projects. Each of these governance controls—quotas and self-service site creation, respectively—require separate site collections.

As another example, users and groups in the *clients* site collection are part of the site collection *http://clients.contoso.com*. Any user management activities—for example, adding users to groups—will take place at the site collection, at which point users and groups representing all clients will be visible. It is not possible to segregate the user and group list, because it is a part of the site collection, not the subsites.

For example, Contoso has two clients: Litware and Fabrikam. If the client project sites Litware and Fabrikam are created as subsites of the root site collection, *http://clients.contoso.com*, their URLs will be *http://clients.contoso.com/Litware* and *http://clients.contoso.com/Fabrikam*, respectively. If a user needs access to the Litware site, the user is added to the site collection, as is a user who needs access to the Fabrikam site. If a group is defined for permissions to content in the Fabrikam site, the group is defined in the groups list of the site collection, and then the group is given permission to content in the Fabrikam site.

Because the list of users and the list of groups is defined at the site collection level, users and groups from both clients are visible, and it is possible for a user from Litware to be accidentally added to the Fabrikam group. Client users and groups are not separated, because all users and groups belong to the site collection itself. To separate users and groups, you must have each client in its own site collection.

Site Collections and Content Databases

Out-of-box data recovery (backup and restore) tools require that you back up and restore a content database. This statement is somewhat oversimplified, and in Chapter 11, "Implementing Business Continuity," you will learn about backup and restore. But in the end, at some level, you are working with an entire content database during backup and at some phase of the recovery process.

The time required to back up or restore a content database should be within the service level defined by your SharePoint governance plan. A large content database can take so long to back up or restore that you might fail to achieve your service level objective.

Because of this relationship between content databases and storage management, governance and service level agreements (SLAs) often drive an organization to create multiple site collections so that site collections can be distributed across content databases. The only way to store sites in separate content databases is to put sites in separate site collections.

For example, if the Finance and Engineering websites are in a single site collection, they are therefore in a single content database. If your SLA with Finance mandates a backup every two hours, but your SLA with Engineering requires a nightly backup, you must also back up the Engineering website every two hours because backup is performed at the site collection level. If the Engineering website is large, this could impact the ability to complete a backup within the specified window. It is therefore likely that you will put each website in a separate content database so that you can back up and restore each database according to your SLA. For each website to be in a separate database, it must be in a separate site collection.

Multiple Site Collections and Content Databases

At this point in the discussion, you should understand that creating your entire SharePoint logical structure as subsites within a single site collection is unlikely to serve you effectively. You are likely to require multiple site collections to support your governance and storage management requirements.

In fact, it could be argued that you should make each departmental site on the Contoso intranet a separate site collection in a separate content database to provide maximum granularity for configuring governance settings. Additionally, from a storage management perspective, you could achieve maximum granularity by hosting each department's site collection in a separate content database.

Now that you understand the reasons for supporting multiple site collections and multiple content databases, you are ready to learn how to build a more governable SharePoint intranet. Figure 4-6 illustrates an intranet site in which each department's website is a top-level website in a department-specific site collection, and each department's site collection is in a dedicated content database.

In the next sections, you will discover how to create site collections in separate content databases to implement designs that are closer to that shown in Figure 4-6. At the end of the lesson, we will revisit design considerations in greater depth.

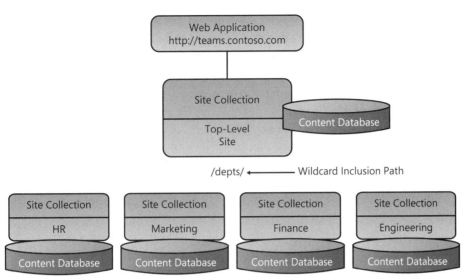

FIGURE 4-6 The teams.contoso.com web application with each department in a separate site collection and content database

Managed Paths

To create a new site collection within a web application, you need a managed path at which to create the site collection.

A *managed path* is a portion of the URI namespace where the site collections exist. A managed path is not directly mapped to content within the web application. Instead, it is used by SharePoint as a namespace (path) node where site collections can be created. The managed path is a node in the URI namespace at which a site collection begins.

An *explicit* inclusion path defines a specific managed path that can be used to create only a single site collection, at the exact URL specified. When you create a web application, SharePoint defines an explicit inclusion path named *root*, which is at the root of the web application (/). For example, the root path for the teams web application shown in Figure 4-6 is *http://teams.contoso.com/* and a single site collection can be created at that exact URL.

A *wildcard* inclusion path such as *http://teams.contoso.com/sites/* indicates that child URLs of the path are managed paths at which site collections are hosted. So, for example, *http://teams.contoso.com/sites/MyTeam* is a managed path at which a site collection can be created. A wildcard inclusion path such as *sites/* allows for unlimited number of site collections to be created directly under the provided path.

It is important to note that a site collection (and therefore a website) cannot be created at the URL of a wildcard inclusion path. For example, you cannot create a site collection or any content at the address *http://teams.contoso.com/sites*.

Two paths are created by default when you create a new web application: the explicit path at the root and a wildcard inclusion path, *sites/*. However, you can define explicit or wildcard inclusion paths with other descriptive names such as *depts* (for departments), *teams*, *clients*, or *projects*. In Figure 4-6, the departmental sites for the HR and Engineering departments are site collections under a wildcard inclusion path, *depts*.

Managed paths allow a SharePoint server to receive a request in the form of a URI and to determine which part of the URI corresponds to a site collection by looking at the list of managed paths for a given web application. SharePoint can then identify the content database that hosts the site collection, and then can retrieve the requested content based on the remaining portion of the URI.

This means that SharePoint has to compare each request to each defined path. So Microsoft supports a maximum of 20 path definitions per web application. A wildcard inclusion path is counted as one path definition, although technically numerous managed paths can be immediately beneath it in the URI namespace.

 Quick Check

- What is the difference between an explicit inclusion managed path and a wildcard inclusion managed path?

Quick Check Answer

- You can create one site collection at the URL of an explicit inclusion managed path. If you add a wildcard inclusion managed path, such as */depts*, you can create multiple site collections below the URL of the managed path, such as */depts/Finance* and *depts/Sales*.

ADD MANAGED PATHS FOR A WEB APPLICATION USING CENTRAL ADMINISTRATION

1. In the Central Administration Quick Launch, click Application Management.
2. On the Application Management page, click Manage Web Applications.
3. Click the web application for which you want to manage paths.
4. On the ribbon, click Managed Paths.
5. On the Define Managed Paths page, in the Add A New Path section, type the path you want to include.
6. Click Check URL to confirm the path name.
7. Use the Type drop-down menu to identify the path as either Wildcard inclusion or Explicit inclusion.
   - The Wildcard inclusion type includes all URLs that are immediately subordinate to the specified URL.
   - The Explicit inclusion type includes only the URL that is indicated by the specified path.

8. Click Add Path.

9. When you have finished adding paths, click OK.

REMOVE MANAGED PATHS FOR A WEB APPLICATION USING CENTRAL ADMINISTRATION

1. In the Central Administration Quick Launch, click Application Management.

2. On the Application Management page, click Manage Web Applications.

3. Click the web application that you want to manage paths.

4. On the ribbon, click Managed Paths.

5. On the Define Managed Paths page, in the Included Paths section, select the check box next to the path that you want to remove.

6. Click Delete Selected Paths.

> **IMPORTANT** **DELETION IS IMMEDIATE**
>
> You will have no additional opportunity to confirm this deletion.

7. When you have finished removing paths, click OK.

ADD A MANAGED PATH USING WINDOWS POWERSHELL

The following example shows the use of the *New-SPManagedPath* cmdlet to add a managed path to a web application:

```
New-SPManagedPath [-RelativeURL] "</RelativeURL>" -WebApplication <WebApplication>
```

Where:

- </RelativeURL> is the relative URL for the new managed path. The type must be a valid partial URL, such as *site* or *sites/teams/*.

- <WebApplication> is the URL of the web application to which the managed path will be added.

REMOVE A MANAGED PATH BY USING WINDOWS POWERSHELL

The following example shows the use of the *Remove-SPManagedPath* cmdlet to remove a managed path from a web application:

```
Remove-SPManagedPath [-Identity] <ManagedPathName> -WebApplication <WebApplication>
```

Where:

- <ManagedPathName> is the name of the managed path to delete.

- <WebApplication> is the URL of the web application that hosts the managed path to delete.

Content Databases

When you create a web application, you specify the name of the initial content database. You can later create additional content databases for the web application.

ADD A CONTENT DATABASE USING CENTRAL ADMINISTRATION

1. In the Central Administration Quick Launch, click Application Management.

2. In the Databases section, click Manage Content Databases.

3. On the Manage Content Databases page, in the Web Application section, ensure that you are focused on the web application in which you want to create a site collection.

   If necessary, click the web application picker, and then click Change Web Application. Click the correct web application.

4. Click Add A Content Database.

5. In the Database Name box, type a name for the database, such as **SharePoint_Content_Intranet_IT**.

   Use the naming standards of your organization to determine the name.

6. Click OK.

ADD A CONTENT DATABASE BY USING WINDOWS POWERSHELL

The following example shows the use of the *New-SPContentDatabase* cmdlet to create a new content database:

```
New-SPContentDatabase -Name <ContentDbName> -WebApplication <WebApplicationName>
```

Where:

- *<ContentDbName>* is the name of the content database that you want to create.

- *<WebApplicationName>* is the name of the web application to which the new database is attached.

Add a Site Collection to a Content Databases

After you create a content database, you can create site collections in that content database.

When you use Central Administration to create a site collection, Central Administration automatically determines which content database will contain the site collection. You cannot easily specify a content database in Central Administration.

Instead, each content database is evaluated to determine which content database has the most available sites, based on the content database's Maximum Sites property and the current number of sites in the content database. The content database with the most available sites is used to host a new site collection. It's important to mention that the size of the content database is not taken into consideration. In the event that more than one content database has the same number of available sites, the content database with the lowest GUID is selected as a tiebreaker.

As you can see, the lack of fine-grained control in Central Administration can be problematic when you are trying to manage the association of site collections to content databases.

You can use the *-ContentDatabase* parameter of the *New-SPSite* cmdlet to create a site collection in a specific content database.

Move a Site Collection Between Content Databases

You cannot move site collections between content databases by using Central Administration. However, you can use Windows PowerShell to move site collections between content databases and thereby to optimize storage management for your site collections.

The following example shows the use of the *Move-SPSite* cmdlet to move a site collection between content databases:

```
Move-SPSite <http://ServerName/Sites/SiteName> -DestinationDatabase
<DestinationContentDb>
```

Where:

- *<http://ServerName/Sites/SiteName>* is the name of the site collection.
- *<DestinationContentDb>* is the name of the destination content database.

Designing Sites, Site Collections, and Content Databases

A simple view of the logical infrastructure of a typical intranet or collaboration web application was shown earlier in Figure 4-6. At the root of the web application is a site collection with a top-level site that serves as the home page, and may contain general content that applies across divisions.

Under a managed path, each division, department, or team gets a unique site collection. The URL to a divisional site is Web application \ [managed path \] site, for example, *http://intranet.contoso.com/depts./HR*.

The division's site collection scopes the ownership, user and group definitions, quotas, features, and other configurations for the site. You will typically need far more site collections than you would anticipate, because governance designs typically require more than one set of configurations at the site collection level.

Optionally, you can put each division's site collection in a dedicated content database to manage storage, backup, and restore. Keep in mind, however, that there are performance-related scalability guidelines that might prevent you from putting every division in a separate site collection in particularly large or complex implementations.

Figure 4-6 illustrates a design approach that is diametrically opposite to the single site collection, multiple site design shown in Figure 4-5. Neither design is appropriate for every organization, or even every collaboration scenario within an organization. When designing your sites and site collections, governance requirements such as security (ownership) and storage management (quotas and locks) will determine the balance between sites and site collections. When designing a strategy for content databases, consider your service level objectives. Include the recovery time objective (how quickly your deleted or corrupted content is brought back online) and your recovery point objective (how far back in time your historical backups are maintained).

For performance reasons you must also consider the following scalability boundaries. In fact, several scalability guidelines apply to SharePoint Server 2010:

- 300 content databases per web application are supported.

  Additionally, the RAM and performance of your SQL Server limits the total number of content databases that should be hosted on that server.

- 200 GB per content database are supported.

  Content database sizes up to 1 terabyte are supported only for large, single-site repositories and archives with non-collaborative I/O and usage patterns, such as Records Centers. Larger database sizes are supported for these scenarios because their I/O patterns and typical data structure formats have been designed for, and tested at, larger scales.

- 100 GB per site collection are supported. If a content database contains only one site collection, the site collection can be up to 200 GB.

- 250,000 Web sites per site collection are supported.

- Up to 2,000 subsites per site view.

> **MORE INFO** **SOFTWARE BOUNDARIES**
>
> The following article provides additional details regarding software boundaries: "SharePoint Server 2010 Capacity Management: Software Boundaries and Limits" at *http://go.microsoft.com/fwlink/?LinkID=192711.*

As you can see, determining the optimal design for your SharePoint farm, web applications, site collections, and content databases is both an art and a science.

Practices are designed to guide you through important procedures. The instructions in the Training Kit are high-level instructions that will challenge you to think carefully and to apply the procedures that are covered in this lesson, and elsewhere in the Training Kit. If you need assistance, consult the detailed, step-by-step instructions in the Practice Answers on the companion media.

In this practice, you will create a web application similar to the one shown in Figure 4-6. You will use Central Administration and Windows PowerShell to create and configure site collections and content databases.

Prepare for the Practice

Before you perform this practice, you must ensure that your lab environment has been built according to the instructions found in the Introduction to this Training Kit.

1. Apply the snapshot CHAPTER 01 to CONTOSO-DC.

2. Apply the snapshot CHAPTER 01 to SP2010-WFE1.

3. Start CONTOSO-DC.

    Wait for the virtual machine to complete startup, at which time the Press Ctrl+Alt+Del prompt appears.

4. Start SP2010-WFE1.

EXERCISE 1   Create a Web Application

In this exercise, you create a new web application for departments, teams, and projects.

1. Log on to SP2010-WFE1 as **CONTOSO\SP_Admin** with the password **Pa$$w0rd**.

2. Start Command Prompt.

3. Use Dnscmd.exe to create a new host (A) record on the DNS server (*contoso-dc .contoso.com*) for *teams.contoso.com* that resolves to the IP address 10.0.0.21. Then close Command Prompt.

4. Start SharePoint 2010 Management Shell using the Run As Administrator option.

5. Use the *New-SPWebApplication* cmdlet to create a web application for departments, teams, and projects. Use the following specifications and guidance:

    ■ Name: Contoso Teams

    ■ Port: 80

    ■ Host header: *http://teams.contoso.com*

    ■ URL: *http://teams.contoso.com:80*

    ■ Application pool: SharePoint Web Applications

    ■ Content database name: SharePoint_Content_Teams

EXERCISE 2   Create a Site Collection Using Central Administration

In this exercise, you use Central Administration to create a site collection at the root of the new web application.

1. Open Central Administration.

2. Create a site collection. Use the following specifications and guidance:

   - Web application: *http://teams.contoso.com*

   - Title: Contoso Departments, Teams, and Projects

   - Description: Collaboration sites for Contoso departments, teams, and projects

   - URL: *http://teams.contoso.com/*

   - Template: Team Site

   - Primary site collection administrator: CONTOSO\SP_Admin

EXERCISE 3   Configure Managed Paths

In this exercise, you add a wildcard inclusion path, *depts*, for department site collections in the teams.contoso.com web application. You also remove the default wildcard inclusion path, *sites*.

   - In Central Administration, configure the managed paths for *teams.contoso.com*. Remove the default wildcard inclusion path, *sites*, and add a wildcard inclusion path, *depts*.

EXERCISE 4   Create a Site Collection by Using Self-Service Site Creation

In this exercise, you enable self-service site creation for the web application, and then use the feature to create a new site collection.

1. In Central Administration, enable self-service site creation for the teams.contoso.com web application. Specify that a secondary site collection administrator is required.

2. In a new tab of Internet Explorer, browse to **http://teams.contoso.com**. Open the announcement that indicates that self-service site creation is enabled. Copy the link to the self-service site creation page, and then paste the address into the address bar.

3. On the self-service site creation page, create a new site collection. Use the following specifications and guidance:

   - Title box: Information Technology

   - Description: Information Technology department team site

   - URL: *http://teams.contoso.com/depts/IT*

   - Template: Team Site

   - Secondary site collection administrator: CONTOSO\AprilM

4. When the Set Up Groups For This Site page opens, accept the defaults.

EXERCISE 5   Create a Content Database Using Central Administration

In this exercise, you use Central Administration to create a content database for the IT departmental team site.

- ■ Switch to Central Administration, and then create a content database. Use the following specifications and guidance:
  - Web application: *http://teams.contoso.com*
  - Database server: SP2010-WFE1.contoso.com
  - Database name: SharePoint_Content_Teams_IT

EXERCISE 6   Move a Site Collection to a Different Content Database

In this exercise, you use Windows PowerShell to move a site collection to another content database.

1. In Central Administration, on the Manage Content Databases page, observe that the new content database contains no sites.

2. Switch to SharePoint 2010 Management Shell, and then use the *Move-SPSite* cmdlet to move the *http://teams.contoso.com/depts/IT* site collection to the SharePoint_Content_Teams_IT content database.

   An error appears.

   Question: What is the cause of the error?

3. Solve the problem that caused the error in the previous step.

   Tip: You must run another instance of SharePoint 2010 Management Shell as CONTOSO\Administrator with the password **Pa$$w0rd** to use the *Add-SPShellAdmin* cmdlet.

   When you have solved the problem, close the new instance of SharePoint 2010 Management Shell that you opened, and then switch back to the instance of SharePoint 2010 Management Shell that you used in step 1.

4. Use the *Move-SPSite* cmdlet to move *http://teams.contoso.com/depts/IT* site collection to the SharePoint_Content_Teams_IT content database. Add the parameter that will suppress confirmation prompts.

   Be sure to read the informational message that is returned by the cmdlet and follow the instructions that it provides.

5. Switch to Internet Explorer, and then refresh the pages shown in both tabs.

   Because IIS has been reset, it will take a few minutes for the sites to be compiled, cached, and loaded.

6. In Central Administration, on the Manage Content Databases page, observe that the new content database now contains one site.

EXERCISE 7 Create Site Collections in Specific Content Databases Using Windows PowerShell

In this exercise, you create content databases and site collections for several departments in the teams.contoso.com web application.

1. Switch to SharePoint 2010 Management Shell.

2. Use the *New-SPContentDatabase* cmdlet to create a content database named **SharePoint_Content_Teams_HR** for the teams.contoso.com web application.

3. Use the *New-SPSite* cmdlet to create a site collection. Use the following specifications and guidance:

   - URL: *http://teams.contoso.com/depts/HR*
   - Content database: SharePoint_Content_Teams_HR
   - Name: HR
   - Description: HR department team site
   - Template: default Team Site template
   - Primary site collection administrator: CONTOSO\SP_Admin
   - Primary site collection administrator email address: SP_Admin@contoso.com

4. In Notepad, create a Windows PowerShell script that uses variables and iteration to create unique content databases and site collections for the following three departments: Finance, Marketing, and Sales. Use the specifications and guidance provided in the previous step, modified to be specific to each department. Save the script to your desktop with the name **CreateDeptSites.ps1**.

5. Run the script.

EXERCISE 8 View All Site Collections

In this exercise, you use Central Administration and Windows PowerShell to view selected attributes of all site collections.

1. In the Central Administration, view the details of each site collection in the teams.contoso.com web application.

2. In SharePoint 2010 Management Shell, type the following command and then press Enter:

```
Get-SPWebApplication "http://teams.contoso.com" | Get-SPSite -Limit ALL |
ForEach {$_ | Get-SPSiteAdministration |
Select URL,Title,Description,RootWebTemplate,OwnerLoginName,OwnerEmail ;
$_ | Select ContentDatabase}
```

3. Compare the output of the command to the following results:

```
Url            : http://teams.contoso.com
Title          : Contoso Departments, Teams, and Projects
Description    : Collaboration sites for Contoso departments, teams, and projects
RootWebTemplate : STS
```

```
OwnerLoginName  : CONTOSO\sp_admin
OwnerEmail      : SP_Admin@contoso.com

ContentDatabase : SPContentDatabase Name=SharePoint_Content_Teams

Url             : http://teams.contoso.com/depts/Finance
Title           : Finance
Description     : Finance department team site
RootWebTemplate : STS
OwnerLoginName  : CONTOSO\sp_admin
OwnerEmail      : SP_Admin@contoso.com

ContentDatabase : SPContentDatabase Name=SharePoint_Content_Teams_Finance

Url             : http://teams.contoso.com/depts/IT
Title           : Information Technology
Description     : Information Technology department team site
RootWebTemplate : STS
OwnerLoginName  : CONTOSO\sp_admin
OwnerEmail      : SP_Admin@contoso.com

ContentDatabase : SPContentDatabase Name=SharePoint_Content_Teams_IT

Url             : http://teams.contoso.com/depts/Marketing
Title           : Marketing
Description     : Marketing department team site
RootWebTemplate : STS
OwnerLoginName  : CONTOSO\sp_admin
OwnerEmail      : SP_Admin@contoso.com

ContentDatabase : SPContentDatabase Name=SharePoint_Content_Teams_Marketing

Url             : http://teams.contoso.com/depts/Sales
Title           : Sales
Description     : Sales department team site
RootWebTemplate : STS
OwnerLoginName  : CONTOSO\sp_admin
OwnerEmail      : SP_Admin@contoso.com

ContentDatabase : SPContentDatabase Name=SharePoint_Content_Teams_Sales
```

4. If the structure or details of the teams.contoso.com web application in your farm are different than what is shown in the preceding code, make appropriate changes to your farm. Check the work that you performed in previous exercises. If necessary, review the Practice Answers to verify that you performed all steps accurately, and that your CreateDeptSites.ps1 script is correct.

Lesson Summary

- Site collections contain a top-level website and zero or more subsites.
- The content and configuration of a site collection is stored in one content database. A content database can host zero or more site collections for a single web application.

- Site collection settings include ownership and administration (the site collection administrators), storage limits (quotas), site collection locks, users and groups, and feature availability.

- Settings of web applications, including self-service site creation and site use confirmation and deletion, affect all site collections within a web application.

- By using Windows PowerShell, you can create a site collection in a specific content database, and you can move a site collection between content databases.

- A managed path is a node in the URI namespace at which a site collection exists. SharePoint uses managed paths to parse a request so that SharePoint can determine which site collection contains the requested content, and thereby determine which content database must be accessed to retrieve the content.

- Each web application defines explicit and wildcard inclusion paths. An explicit inclusion path is a URL that can be a managed path. A wildcard inclusion path specifies a path under which the next element of the URL can be a managed path.

- Governance requirements determine how many site collections and content databases are necessary to support information management needs within a specific web application. However, you must be aware of scalability boundaries: you cannot have an indefinite number of paths, site collections, or content databases within a web application, nor can you store an unlimited amount of data within a site collection or content database.

Lesson Review

You can use the following questions to test your knowledge of the information in Lesson 1, "Manage Site Collections and Content Databases." The questions are also available on the companion media in a practice test if you prefer to review them in electronic form.

> **NOTE ANSWERS**
>
> Answers to these questions and explanations of why each answer choice is right or wrong are located in the "Answers" section at the end of the book.

1. Three users are listed as site collection administrators for the Finance site: LolaJ, AprilM, and PatC. You discover that Lola and April are receiving email notifications about site collection storage limits, but you want Lola and Pat to receive the confirmations. What can you do to achieve this goal?

   A. Configure outgoing email settings.

   B. Use the Specify Quota Settings page in Central Administration.

   C. Change the order of users in the site collection administrators group by using the Site Settings page.

   D. Use the Configure Site Collection Administrators page in Central Administration.

2. You discovered several new sites under *http://teams.contoso.com/sites/* and you want to prevent users from creating new sites in *http://teams.contoso.com*. What can you do?

   A. Use the Manage Web Applications page of Central Administration.

   B. Use the Site Settings page of the *http://teams.contoso.com* website.

   C. Use the *scsignup.aspx* page of the *http://teams.contoso.com* website.

   D. Configure a site lock on the *http://teams.contoso.com* site collection.

3. The content database SharePoint_Content_Intranet is approaching 100 GB, and you want to split its content into a second content database named SharePoint_Content_Intranet_B. What can you do?

   A. Use the *Move-SPSite* cmdlet.

   B. Use the Stsadm *splitdatabase* operation.

   C. Use the Manage Content Databases page of Central Administration.

   D. Use the Configure Content Deployment Paths And Jobs page of Central Administration.

Lesson 2: Secure SharePoint Sites and Content

Security is a priority for SharePoint administrators whose organizations store security-sensitive content in SharePoint lists and libraries. SharePoint 2010 provides a set of security features and capabilities that support a flexible, granular assignment of permissions to users and groups. Additionally, the SharePoint user interface is security-trimmed, so users will not see links to content to which they do not have access. SharePoint also audits all content access, so you can generate reports that document compliance with your governance and security requirements. In this lesson, you explore the concepts, skills, and processes you use to administer security in SharePoint 2010.

> **After this lesson, you will be able to:**
> - Describe the SharePoint 2010 security model.
> - Administer SharePoint group settings and membership.
> - Use Active Directory Domain Services (AD DS) users and groups within SharePoint's security model.
> - Secure SharePoint sites, lists, libraries, folders, items, and documents.
> - Understand permission inheritance in the SharePoint hierarchy.
> - Manage permission levels.
> - Apply user policy to a web application.
> - Audit access to SharePoint content.
>
> **Estimated lesson time: 90 minutes**

Overview of SharePoint Site Security

When a user requests content from a SharePoint site, the request is in the form of a URI, such as *http://teams.contoso.com/depts/IT/SitePages/home.aspx*. Whether the user can access the content or change the content depends on the user's effective permissions on the object referenced by the URI. In the end, it is the individual user's permissions to an object referenced by a specific URI that determines access.

In SharePoint 2010 you will find a flexible model for managing such access—for organizing users and authorizing them to access content for specific tasks. The model consists of users and groups; permissions and permission levels; and securable objects such as sites, lists, and libraries.

Users and Groups

As you learned in Chapter 3, user accounts are defined in the authentication providers of a web application, which can include Active Directory Domain Services (AD DS). Groups can be Windows security groups or a SharePoint group, such as Site Owners, Site Members, or Site Visitors. Groups are created and managed at the site collection level.

Although SharePoint allows you to assign permissions directly to individual users, it is recommended that you organize users into groups for manageability. For example, you can add the user accounts of all Sales staff into a single group called Sales. You can then assign a single permission to the group for access to the Sales team site, and thereby grant all Sales staff access to the site. When a new employee is added to the Sales staff, you add the user to the Sales group and thereby grant the user access to the Sales team site and to all other resources for which you have assigned permissions to the Sales group.

When you use groups to manage access to SharePoint content, you reduce administrative overhead. Later in this lesson, you will learn more about groups and the features that SharePoint provides to facilitate managing group membership. You will also learn how and when to integrate groups from AD DS with SharePoint.

Because it is inefficient to manage permission assignments to individual user accounts, you should assign permissions on a per-user basis only as an exception.

Permissions and Permission Levels

A *permission* allows a specific operation on SharePoint 2010 objects. Permissions are very granular. The *View Items* permission, for example, allows a user to view items in a list or folder, but not to add or remove items. Other permissions include *Edit Items*, *Add Items*, *Delete Items*, *Create Alerts*, *Manage Permissions*, and *Create Groups*.

A *permission level* is a set of permissions that allow users to perform a set of related tasks. When you create a site collection, permission levels are created depending on the site definition—the template—that is selected for the top-level site of the site collection. Several permission levels are created by default for every new site collection, including the following:

- **Read** Allows a user to read documents, items, and pages, but not to make changes to that content. The Read permission level includes the View Items, Open Items, View Pages, and View Versions permissions (among others). It also includes the Create Alerts permission.

- **Contribute** Allows you to read, modify, and delete content. The Contribute permission level includes all of the permissions in the Read permission level plus Edit Items, Add Items, and Delete Items.

- **Full Control** Allows you to make any changes to an object. The Full Control permission level includes all permissions.

Individual permissions can be included in more than one permission level. Permission levels can be customized by any user or group whose permission level includes the Manage Permissions permission. As you'll learn later in this lesson, you can create custom permission levels to support your content access requirements.

Securable Objects and Inheritance

A *securable object* is an object in the SharePoint hierarchy for which you can grant access by assigning a permission level to a user or group. Securable objects include the following: sites, lists, libraries, folders, documents, and items.

By default, permissions assigned to a site, list, library, or folder are inherited by the objects within the container. In fact, by default, all objects in a site collection inherit the permissions assigned to the top-level site in the site collection. You can break inheritance and assign specific, fine-grained permissions to any securable object. You can later reestablish inheritance if your requirements change.

The SharePoint site security model is illustrated in Figure 4-7.

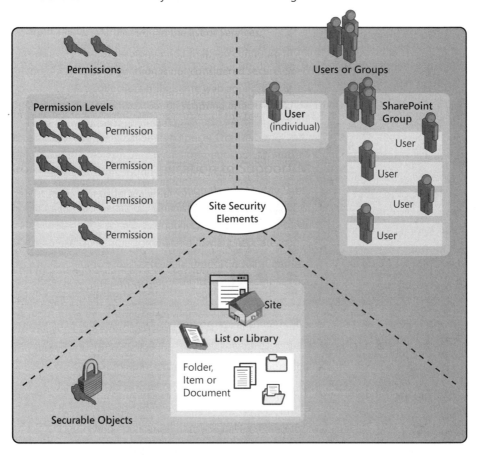

FIGURE 4-7 The SharePoint Site Security model

Administer SharePoint Groups

Now that you understand the big picture of the SharePoint site and content security model, let's turn our attention to the details of managing the first component of the model: groups.

Default Groups and Permission Levels

When you create a site collection, you create a top-level site. Based on the template chosen for the top-level site and the method used to create the site, SharePoint 2010 creates one or more default groups for the site collection, and assigns the groups permissions to the top-level site that are then inherited by all subsites, lists, libraries, folders, documents, and items.

When you use Central Administration to create a site collection with the Team Site template, the following groups are created by most site definitions:

- **Visitors**   This group is assigned the Read permission level.
- **Members**   This group is assigned the Contribute permission level.
- **Owners**   This group is assigned the Full Control permission level.

Other templates create additional groups. For example, the Publishing Site template creates groups that include the following:

- **Viewers**   Members can view pages, list items, and documents.
- **Approvers**   Members can approve new and changed items for publishing.
- **Designers**   Members can modify page designs in the browser and by using SharePoint Designer.
- **Hierarchy Managers**   Members can create and manage folders, lists, and libraries.

When you create a subsite within a site collection, new groups may be created, depending upon the template you select for the new website and whether you choose to inherit permissions from the parent website or to use unique permissions.

Create Groups

Of course, you can create new groups when an existing group does not meet your requirements for access or manageability. You must have the Create Groups permission, which is included in the Full Control permission level, to have the ability to create a group.

CREATE A SHAREPOINT GROUP

1. Click Site Actions, and then click Site Settings.
2. In the Users And Permissions section, click People And Groups.
3. In the Groups Quick Launch, click Groups. Alternately, click More.
   The All Groups list opens.
4. In the toolbar, click New.
5. In the Name box, type a name for the group.
6. In the About Me box, type a description of the group.
   Although the About Me description is optional, it is highly recommended that you document the purpose of the group so that users and administrators can easily identify the purpose of the group in the site.
7. In the Group Owner box, type the name of the group owner.
   The group owner can be an individual user or a group. The owner can be allowed to modify group membership.
8. In the Group Settings section, configure the visibility of group membership and who is allowed to modify group membership.

9. In the Membership Requests section, configure the behavior of membership requests.

   To enable membership requests, you must have configured the outgoing email server of the farm or the web application.

10. In the Give Group Permission To This Site section, select the permission levels that you want to assign to the new group.

    A group can be created without associated permission levels.

    Above the list of permission levels, SharePoint displays the site to which permissions will be granted. Confirm that the site that is displayed is correct, so that you do not unintentionally grant access to another site.

11. Click Create.

View SharePoint Groups

When you create a group, the group is defined at the site collection level. All user and group accounts are defined and managed at the site collection level. However, if you assign permissions to the group, the permissions are associated with the specific site from which you created the group.

VIEW SHAREPOINT GROUPS

1. Click Site Actions, and then click Site Settings.
2. In the Users And Permissions section, click People And Groups.
3. In the Groups Quick Launch, click Groups. Alternately, click More.

   The All Groups list opens.

One of the elements of the SharePoint administrative experience that confuses many site administrators is that the list of groups is filtered based on the context from which you view groups. For example, if you click Site Actions, and then click Site Permissions, you see a list of groups that have permissions to the site. This may not be all groups in the site collection.

If you click Site Actions, then click Site Settings, and then click People And Groups in the Users And Groups section, the page that opens shows you the membership of one group—the default group of the site, typically Site Members—and the Quick Launch displays a partial list of groups that have access to the site. To see all groups, you must click the Groups heading in the Quick Launch, or click More in the Groups section of the Quick Launch.

Modify Group Properties

To modify a group, you must be a site collection administrator or a group owner.

MODIFY A SHAREPOINT GROUP

1. Click Site Actions, and then click Site Settings.
2. In the Users And Permissions section, click People And Groups.

3. In the Groups Quick Launch, click Groups. Alternately, click More.

    The All Groups list opens.

4. Click the name of the group.

5. Click the Settings button, and then click Group Settings.

    As an alternate to steps 4 and 5, you can click the Edit icon next to the group name in the All Groups list.

Modify Group Membership

After you have created groups to meet your security requirements, you can add or remove members.

You can add users or groups from your membership and role provider to a SharePoint group. Keep in mind that you cannot add a SharePoint group as a member of another SharePoint group.

ADD A MEMBER TO A SHAREPOINT GROUP

1. Click Site Actions, and then click Site Settings.

2. In the Users And Permissions section, click People And Groups.

3. In the Groups Quick Launch, click Groups. Alternately, click More.

    The All Groups list opens.

4. Click the name of the group.

5. Click the New button arrow, and then click Add Users.

    Alternately, click the New button.

    The Grant Permissions page opens.

6. In the Users/Groups box, type the names of users or groups that you want to add to the group.

    Add users or groups by their user login name and group name, respectively. Separate multiple users or groups with a semicolon.

    Alternately, you can type a user's or group's display name, but you must enter it exactly as it is known to SharePoint or as it appears in Active Directory. That is typically more difficult to enter correctly than the user login name or group name.

    Alternately, click the Browse button. The Select People And Groups page opens. You can search for a user or group, then select the user or group, and then click Add. Click OK when you have finished selecting users and groups.

7. Optionally, click Check Names.

    SharePoint confirms the correct entry of a user or group by underlining the name.

    If a name cannot be resolved, it is displayed in italics. You can click the name and a menu will appear that allows you to select a close match, to remove the name, or to search for the user or group.

8. In the Send E-Mail section, select or clear the Send Welcome E-Mail To The New Users check box. If you choose to send a welcome message, you can optionally enter a message in the Personal Message box. The message will be appended to the standard SharePoint welcome message.

9. Click OK.

REMOVE A MEMBER OF A SHAREPOINT GROUP

1. Click Site Actions, and then click Site Settings.

2. In the Users And Permissions section, click People And Groups.

3. In the Groups Quick Launch, click Groups. Alternately, click More.

   The All Groups list opens.

4. Click the name of the group.

5. Select the check box in the row of the member that you wish to remove.

   You can click the Select All Users icon in the list header to select or clear all members.

6. Click the Actions button, click Remove Users From Group, and then click OK to confirm.

The Actions menu allows you to send an email message to selected members of a group. If you have a SIP client installed, you can also call selected members of a group.

The Default Group

The Members group of a site is, by default, the default group of a site—a concept that is important to understand. When a user belongs to the default group of a site, the user's membership in the site becomes visible in several places. First, the site will be listed on the user's My Site, on the user's Memberships page. This link allows a user to navigate quickly from his or her My Site to the sites to which the user belongs. Second, in Microsoft Office client applications, the user's site memberships are listed as shortcuts for Open and Save commands.

It is somewhat unfortunate that the Members group of a site plays two roles: it grants Contribute permission level to the site and it acts as the default group that defines membership. If a user is a member of the Visitors or Owners groups, the user's membership does not appear on his or her My Site or in Microsoft Office client applications. At times you might want a user to be a member of a site with a permission level other than Contribute.

It is therefore recommended that you create a custom group for a site, and define that group as the default group. For example, create a group called Site Membership. Do not associate any specific permission level with the group. Add a user to the Site Membership group when you want to expose the site to a user's My Site or Office client applications. Then, as a second step, add the user to a group that assigns the appropriate permission level to the site or its content.

DESIGNATE A GROUP AS THE DEFAULT GROUP

1. Click Site Actions, and then click Site Settings.

2. In the Users And Permissions section, click People And Groups.

3. In the Groups Quick Launch, click Groups. Alternately, click More.
   The All Groups list opens.

4. Click the name of the group.

5. Click the Settings button, click Make Default Group, and then click OK
   to confirm.

SharePoint Group Management Features

When you create a group in SharePoint 2010, or modify the properties of an existing group,
you can implement several features to reduce administrative overhead of group membership
management.

Delegate Membership Management

In some cases, you might want to delegate the management of group membership to one
or more users that are the business owners of a specific process. For example, if a team
site relates to a single project, you can create a group and assign the group an appropriate
permission level, and then you can delegate the ability to add or remove group members to
the project managers. The project managers can then grant users access by adding users to
the group without requiring intervention of an administrator.

To achieve this delegated membership management model, you need to do the following:

- Create a membership management group. For example, create a group called Project
  Site Access Managers. Do not assign the group any permission levels to the SharePoint
  site itself.

- Assign ownership of site groups to the membership management group. For example,
  modify the properties of a group such as the Project Site Members group, which
  has the Contribute permission level. In the Group Owner box, enter the name of the
  membership management group, Project Site Access Managers.

- Allow group owners to change group membership. In the Group Settings section,
  under Who Can Edit The Membership Of The Group?, select Group Owner.

An example is shown in Figure 4-8.

FIGURE 4-8 Delegating membership management to the Project Site Access Managers
group

Enable Requests for Membership

You can enable requests for group membership, so that when a user desires access to a group, the user can make a request that generates an email notification to group managers, who then can approve or reject the request. Optionally, you can enable SharePoint to auto-accept requests for membership.

Configure the Membership Requests section of the group's settings page, shown in Figure 4-9. You should consider using a group email address, so that requests can be processed by whichever group manager is able to respond.

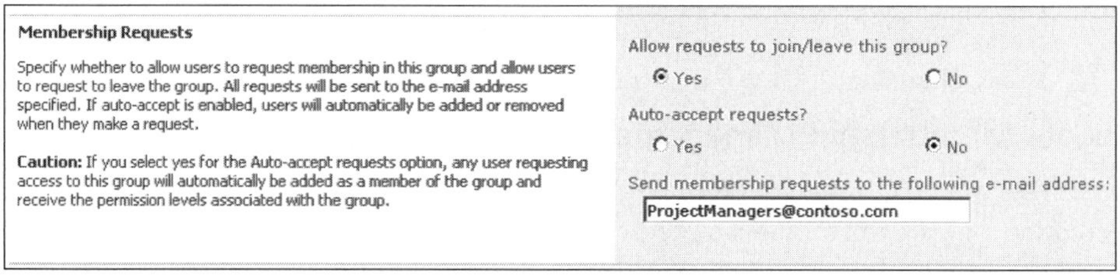

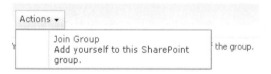

FIGURE 4-9 Membership Requests settings for a SharePoint group

After you have enabled access requests, users can navigate to the group settings page and they can then request membership by clicking the Actions button, shown in Figure 4-10.

FIGURE 4-10 Request to join a group

You will need to provide a link directly to the group settings page or users without access to the groups list cannot navigate to it. To determine the URL of the group settings page, follow these steps:

1. Click Site Actions, and then click Site Settings.

2. In the Users And Permissions section, click People And Groups.

3. In the Groups Quick Launch, click Groups. Alternately, click More.

   The All Groups list opens.

4. Click the name of the group.

5. Observe the URL in the address bar.

The URL will follow this example: http://*URL*/_layouts/people.aspx?MembershipGroupId=*ID*, where *URL* is the URL to the site or to the top-level site in the site collection, and *ID* is the unique ID of the SharePoint group.

When a user requests access, if auto-accept is enabled, the user is immediately added to the group. Otherwise, an email message is sent to the address that you configured for membership requests. A manager that receives the email can follow the instructions and links in the message to accept or reject the membership request.

Enable Requests for Site Access

Requests for membership are enabled on a per-group basis. You can also enable access requests for an entire site.

By default, access requests are enabled for a team site, and requests are emailed to the address of the primary site collection administrator. To enable or disable site access requests, from the Site Permissions page, click Manage Access Requests.

When access requests are enabled, and a user attempts to open a site to which she does not have access, SharePoint displays an error page with a link to request access. Users can also request additional access from the home page of a site by clicking the user menu in the upper-right corner of the page. A notification is sent to the address that is configured for the site, and the administrator can determine whether to grant the user access, and then can add the user to an appropriate site group.

Control Membership Visibility

By default, only the members of a group can see the list of the group's members. In certain scenarios, you may want the membership of the group to be visible to everyone. In the Group Settings section of a group's settings page, shown in Figure 4-8, you can specify either Group Members or Everyone. In this context, *Everyone* means users who have access to the site.

Active Directory and SharePoint Groups

User accounts in Active Directory or another authentication provider are granted access to SharePoint either directly or by adding the users to groups that they have been granted permission levels to a securable object. You have four ways to structure the integration between users and groups in Active Directory and groups and permission levels in SharePoint:

- User accounts in Active Directory are assigned permission levels for SharePoint securable objects. This model is the least manageable—it is rarely appropriate to assign a permission level directly to an individual user, because it is highly likely that either another user will require similar access, or that a user that is currently assigned a certain permission level will require different access in the future.

- User accounts in Active Directory are added as members of a SharePoint group that has been assigned permission levels for SharePoint securable objects. In this model, you can use all of the group management features of SharePoint discussed earlier, including delegated membership management and access requests. Additionally, SharePoint administrators and group owners can view the membership of a group directly in the relevant site collection in SharePoint. Finally, users who are added to the default group of a site will see the site listed in their membership list on their My Sites, and in Microsoft Office client applications.

When you add an Active Directory distribution group to a SharePoint group, the group is expanded and each user is added, individually, to the SharePoint group. You must then manually maintain the synchronization between the SharePoint group and the Active Directory group.

- User accounts in Active Directory are added to security groups in Active Directory, which are assigned permission levels for SharePoint securable content. Using this model centralizes all group management within Active Directory. When a user is added to or removed from a security group, or moved between security groups, the user's access to SharePoint content is changed. However, a SharePoint administrator cannot view group membership within SharePoint, and you cannot use any of the group management features of SharePoint to reduce administrative overhead.

  Additionally, if you ever decide to use an authentication provider other than Active Directory instead of, or in addition to Active Directory, you must then assign new permission levels to appropriate groups in the new authentication provider.

- User accounts in Active Directory are added to security groups in Active Directory, which are added to SharePoint groups, which are then assigned permission levels for SharePoint securable content. This model centralizes group management in Active Directory, but you can also add an individual user to the SharePoint group and thereby grant the user access without requiring that the user belong to the group in Active Directory. This model allows Active Directory administrators to maintain the definition of roles, and to add, move, and remove members, and it allows SharePoint administrators the ability to maintain access to resources within SharePoint.

  You must be careful when adding an Active Directory security group to a SharePoint group when the Active Directory group contains deeply nested security groups, distribution lists, or contact objects. These can cause the nesting to break.

Each of these four options has advantages and disadvantages. No one option is likely to be the answer for every scenario. For each business scenario, you should consider the following criteria:

- Centralized group management in Active Directory, typically by Active Directory administrators
- Control of access to SharePoint content from SharePoint site itself, typically by SharePoint administrators
- Visibility of group membership, or lack thereof, within SharePoint
- Visibility of site membership in users' My Sites and Microsoft Office client applications
- Delegation of group membership management to non-technical business owners or managers of a site
- SharePoint group management features, including access requests

To Nest or Not to Nest?

You should carefully consider your security and group management requirements to determine whether it is best to nest an Active Directory group into a SharePoint group, or to put user accounts directly into a SharePoint group.

When you nest an Active Directory group into a SharePoint group, you centralize management of a role in Active Directory, and the group may have access to other resources, but you lose visibility of the SharePoint group's real membership, and you cannot take advantage of SharePoint group management features such as delegated group membership management and access requests.

The advantages of adding users directly into a SharePoint group are exactly the opposite: you can take advantage of SharePoint's group management features, but you may end up with groups in SharePoint that are redundant with groups in Active Directory.

Generally speaking, when you want to grant access to large numbers of users to a SharePoint site, you are best served by nesting an Active Directory group into the SharePoint group, because you are probably less concerned about the visibility of the membership within SharePoint, or about group membership management features. However, consider a small team site for a project. In this scenario, it is more likely that you want to delegate membership management to the business owner or manager of the project; and that the business owner will want to know who has access to what content in SharePoint. So, for a small team site, you are generally better served by adding users directly to SharePoint groups.

MORE INFO USING SECURITY GROUPS

The following article provides additional details regarding security groups: "Choose security groups (SharePoint Server 2010)" at *http://technet.microsoft.com/en-us/library/cc261972.aspx*.

Configure Permission Levels

As you learned in the "Overview of SharePoint Site Security" section, permission levels—also called *roles*—are sets of permissions that allow users to perform a set of related tasks. A permission level, such as Read, Contribute, Full Control, and Design enable a user access to perform specific tasks on SharePoint content. Table 4-2 lists the permissions associated with the default permission levels for team sites.

TABLE 4-2 Default Permission Levels for Team Sites

PERMISSION LEVEL	DESCRIPTION	PERMISSIONS
Limited Access	Allows access to shared resources on the Web site so that the users can access an item within the site. Designed to be combined with fine-grained permissions to give users access to a specific list, document library, item, or document, without giving them access to the entire site. Cannot be customized or deleted.	■ Browse User Information ■ Use Client Integration Features Open
Read	Allows read-only access to the Web site.	■ View Items ■ Open Items ■ View Versions ■ Create Alerts ■ View Application Pages ■ Use Self-Service Site Creation ■ View Pages ■ Browse User Information ■ Use Remote Interfaces ■ Use Client Integration Features ■ Open
Contribute	Create and edit items in the existing lists and document libraries.	Read permissions, plus: ■ Add Items ■ Edit Items ■ Delete Items ■ Delete Versions ■ Browse Directories ■ Edit Personal User Information ■ Manage Personal Views ■ Add/Remove Personal Web Parts ■ Update Personal Web Parts

PERMISSION LEVEL	DESCRIPTION	PERMISSIONS
Design	Create lists and document libraries and edit pages in the website.	Contribute permissions, plus: ■ Manage Lists ■ Override Check Out ■ Approve Items ■ Add and Customize Pages ■ Apply Themes and Borders ■ Apply Style Sheets
Full Control	Allows full control of the scope.	All permissions

SharePoint creates permission levels based on the templates that are applied to sites in a site collection, but you can also create custom permission levels to support your business and security requirements.

Permission levels are defined at the site collection level. After you define a permission level, you can assign the role to a group for a securable object anywhere in the site collection—assuming, of course, that you have stopped inheritance on the object. You can define a permission level three ways:

- You can modify one of the default permission levels. For example, you might want to modify the Read permission level so that users cannot create alerts.

- You can copy an existing permission level and then modify the copy. For example, you might want to create a permission level that is equivalent to Contribute, but does not allow users to delete items or to view previous versions.

- You can create a new permission level from scratch. For example, you might want to create a permission level that allows managers to check in documents that have been checked out by other users.

MODIFY A PERMISSION LEVEL

1. Click Site Actions, and then click Site Permissions.

2. On the ribbon, click Permission Levels.

3. On the Permission Levels page, click the name of the permission level that you want to modify.

   You cannot modify the Full Control or Limited Access permission levels. However, you can modify the permissions that are included in these permission levels by modifying the permissions that are allowed in a web application. See the "Manage User Permissions" section for more information.

4. Select or clear the permissions that you want to include or exclude from the permission level in the List Permissions list.

5. Optionally, modify the name or description of the permission level.

6. Click Submit.

COPY A PERMISSION LEVEL

1. Click Site Actions, and then click Site Permissions.
2. On the ribbon, click Permission Levels.
3. On the Permission Levels page, click the name of the permission level that you want to copy.
4. Click Copy Permission Level to open the Copy Permission Level page.
5. In the Name box, type a name for the permission level.
6. Optionally, in the Description box, type a description of the permission level.
7. Select or clear the permissions that you want to include or exclude from the permission level in the List Permissions list.
8. Click Create.

CREATE A NEW PERMISSION LEVEL

1. Click Site Actions, and then click Site Permissions.
2. On the ribbon, click Permission Levels to open the Permission Levels page.
3. On the toolbar, click Add A Permission Level to open the Add A Permission Level page.
4. In the Name box, type a name for the permission level.
5. Optionally, in the Description box, type a description of the permission level.
6. Select or clear the permissions that you want to include or exclude from the permission level in the List Permissions list.
7. Click Create.

DELETE A PERMISSION LEVEL

1. Click Site Actions, and then click Site Permissions.
2. On the ribbon, click Permission Levels.
3. On the Permission Levels page, select the check box on the row of the permission level that you want to delete.
4. On the toolbar, click Delete Selected Permission Levels.

> **MORE INFO** **PERMISSION LEVELS**
>
> The following articles provide additional details regarding permission levels:
>
> - "Determine Permission Levels and Groups (SharePoint Server 2010)" at *http://technet.microsoft.com/en-us/library/cc262690.aspx*.
> - "User permissions and permission levels (SharePoint Server 2010)" at *http://technet.microsoft.com/en-us/library/cc721640.aspx*.
> - "Configure custom permissions (SharePoint Server 2010)" at *http://technet.microsoft.com/en-us/library/cc263239.aspx*.

Manage User Permissions

The permissions that are available to add to a permission level are configured at the web application level. By default, every web application allows all SharePoint permissions to be added to permission levels in site collections of the web application. In most scenarios, you will not need to modify the permissions that are available within a web application. Instead, you can simply manage the permission levels that are created within site collections.

It is conceivable, however, that you might want to prevent a permission from being available within a web application. For example, if you want to ensure that users cannot change branding—the look and feel of a site—you can remove the Apply Style Sheets and Apply Themes And Borders permissions from the web application. After doing so, even users with Full Control will not be able to make such changes, because the Full Control permission level will no longer include those two permissions.

CONFIGURE USER PERMISSIONS

1. In the Central Administration Quick Launch, click Application Management.
2. In the Web Applications section, click Manage Web Applications.
3. Select the web application that you want to modify.
4. On the ribbon, click User Permissions.
5. On the User Permissions For A Web Application page, select or clear the permissions that you want to make available to permission levels within the site collection.
6. Click Save.

Understand Inheritance

As you learned earlier, you can assign permission levels for a SharePoint securable object: a site, list, library, folder, item, or document. By default, permissions are assigned to the top-level site in a site collection and all content within the site inherits its permissions from the top-level site. When permissions are inherited, you cannot modify them.

Inheriting permissions is the easiest way to manage a group of websites. When possible, you should design a site collection so that all permissions can be assigned at the top-level site, so that you can avoid assigning permissions at the site, list, or library levels. This reduces administrative overhead and improves manageability of security and access control for the following reasons:

- Users can easily understand their level of access because it is consistent throughout a site.
- You can manage permissions more easily because permissions are set at only a single level in the securable object hierarchy.
- You can audit access by reporting access at only one level in the securable object hierarchy.
- SharePoint performance is maximized because there are fewer permissions to evaluate.

Using fine-grained permissions can complicate permissions management. In addition, when inheritance is broken, a user with Manage Permissions permission can edit the object's permissions, which could compromise security or prevent users from accessing content.

However, in many cases, you may have to assign fine-grained permissions at the site level, or even at the list or library levels. And in some scenarios, you may have to manage access at the folder, item, or document level.

You can break inheritance and assign specific permissions to any securable object, and you can later reestablish inheritance if your requirements change.

When you block inheritance, the only permissions that apply to the site are the explicit permissions. Any changes to the parent site no longer affect the subsite for which inheritance is blocked. This is somewhat different from the permissions model for the NTFS file system, for example, in which the effective permissions on a folder are a combination of inherited and explicit permissions. In SharePoint, the effective permissions for a securable object are *either* the inherited *or* the explicit permissions.

When you reestablish inheritance, you lose all explicitly defined permission levels, and access to the object is defined only by the permissions applied to the parent container.

> **BEST PRACTICE** **PERMISSIONS INHERITANCE**
>
> In SharePoint 2010, you can assign a permission level to a single document or list item. However, when you assign permissions at such granular levels, it becomes more difficult to manage and troubleshoot access. It is therefore recommended that you organize content within sites, lists, and libraries based on common access requirements, and to assign permissions to those containers.

Implement SharePoint Roles and Role Assignments

Now that you understand how SharePoint can use user accounts, AD DS groups, and SharePoint groups, and how to manage permission levels, you are ready to assign permission levels to SharePoint content. Permission levels are also referred to as *roles*. *Role assignment* is the process of granting a role to a user or group.

Manage Permissions for a Site, List, Library, Folder, Item, or Document

When you create a new site, permissions are inherited by default from the parent site. If you do not wish to use this inheritance model, click More Options in the Create dialog box. Then, under User Permissions, click Use Unique Permissions. This option is shown in Figure 4-11.

You can also manage permissions for a subsite, list, library, folder, item, or document at a later time by using the permissions page for the object.

- **Site Permissions**   Click Site Actions, and then click Site Permissions.
- **List Permissions**   On the list's ribbon, click the List tab, and then click List Permissions. Alternately, click the List tab, click List Settings, and then click Permissions For This List.

- **Library Permissions** On the library's ribbon, click the Library tab, and then click Library Permissions. Alternately, click the Library tab, click Library Settings, and then click Permissions For This Document Library.

- **Folder Permissions** Expand the folder's menu, and then click Manage Permissions.

- **Item Permissions** Expand the item's menu, and then click Manage Permissions. Alternately, click View Properties, and then click Manage Permissions.

- **Document Permissions** Expand the document's menu, and then click Manage Permissions. Alternately, click View Properties page, and then click Manage Permissions.

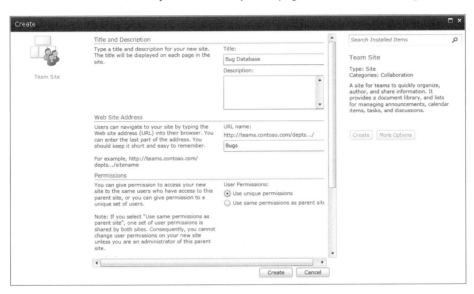

FIGURE 4-11 The Create dialog box

After you have opened the permissions page for the securable object, you can then manage the permission levels assigned for that object.

STOP INHERITING PERMISSIONS FOR A SITE

1. Click Stop Inheriting Permissions.

2. In the confirmation dialog box, click OK.

When you block permissions inheritance, SharePoint converts the previously inherited permissions into explicit permissions assigned to the object. The result is that effective permissions remain the same. However, because the permissions are now explicitly assigned to the object, you can remove permissions that you do not want, and you can add new permissions.

ASSIGN A ROLE (GRANT PERMISSIONS)

1. Click Grant Permissions.

2. In the Select Users box, enter the users or security groups.

3. In the Grant Permissions section, perform one of the following steps:
   - Select Add Users To A SharePoint Group (Recommended), and then select the site group from the drop-down list. The users or groups you selected in step 3 will be added to the site group you select from the drop-down list, and will thereby inherit the permissions assigned to the site group.
   - Select Grant Users Permission Directly, and then select the permission levels you want to assign to the users or groups you selected in step 3.
4. In the Send E-Mail section, select or clear the Send Welcome E-Mail To The New Users check box. If you plan to send a welcome message, you can optionally enter a message in the Personal Message box. The message will be appended to the standard SharePoint welcome message.
5. Click OK.

If you are assigning permissions for a site, you can click Create Group on the ribbon of the site permissions page. You can then create a new group and assign it permission levels to the site. This procedure is effectively the same as the "Create a SharePoint Group" procedure listed earlier in the lesson. The Create Group button on the ribbon is simply another path to the same command.

After a group has been assigned a role for an object, you can later modify the permission levels assigned to the group. For example, after a project is complete you might want to prevent Site Contributors from making further modifications to the site's content.

MODIFY A ROLE ASSIGNMENT (EDIT PERMISSIONS)
1. Select the check box on the row of the group or user whose role you want to modify.
2. Click Edit User Permissions.
3. On the Edit Permissions page, select or clear the permission levels that you want to assign to the group or user.
4. Click OK.

You can also remove a group's permissions to an object.

REMOVE A ROLE ASSIGNMENT (REMOVE PERMISSIONS)
1. Select the check box on the row of the group or user whose role you want to remove.
2. Click Remove User Permissions.
3. In the confirmation dialog box, click OK.

This procedure does not delete the group itself. Instead, it removes the permission levels that had been assigned to the group for the object.

If you later decide that you want to reestablish inheritance, you can reset permissions on an object to inherit from the parent container. When you reestablish inheritance, all explicit permissions are removed.

REESTABLISH INHERITANCE
1. On the ribbon, click Inherit Permissions.
2. In the confirmation dialog box, click OK.

All explicitly defined roles are removed. The roles assigned to the parent container are applied to the object.

Effective Permissions

When a user has been assigned multiple permission levels—for example, if a user has been assigned permission levels directly and belongs to a group that has been assigned permission levels—the user's effective permissions, also called the user's resultant permissions, are the sum total of all assigned permissions. Unlike NTFS permissions, SharePoint does not support Deny permissions on content (site collections, sites, lists, libraries, folders, documents, or items). All permissions are *Allow* permissions and those permissions combine to determine a user's effective permissions. However, you will learn in the next section that you can apply Deny policies at the web application level.

It can be a challenge to determine what permission levels have been assigned to a user, directly or indirectly, through group membership. SharePoint 2010 makes it easier to get a snapshot of access by using the Check Permissions tool.

When you view the Site Permissions, List Permissions, or Library Permissions page, the Check Permissions tool is displayed on the ribbon. You can use Check Permissions to determine the resultant permissions for a user to confirm that a user has the desired level of access.

VIEW EFFECTIVE PERMISSIONS FOR AN OBJECT

1. On the ribbon, click Check Permissions to open the Check Permissions dialog box.

2. In the User/Group box, type the name of the user or group whose permissions you want to check.

   Alternately, click the Browse button to search for a user or group.

3. Click Check Now.

   Effective permissions for the user are reported, as shown in Figure 4-12.

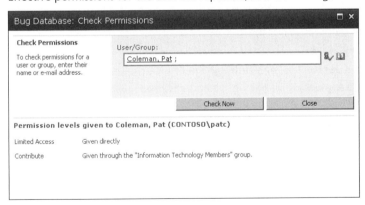

FIGURE 4-12 Check Permissions dialog box

4. Click Close.

Manage Web Policy

You can use one additional pair of tools to manage site and content security: *permission policy levels* and *user policy*. A permission policy level is a collection of permissions—very much like a permission level within a site collection—that is defined at the web application level. A permission policy level can allow or deny each of the granular permissions, such as View Items, Add Items, Create Alerts, or Create Groups.

You assign a permission policy level to a user or group to specify a user policy. User policy scopes access at the web application or for a specific authentication zone of a web application.

The four default permission policy levels are Full Control, Full Read, Deny Write, and Deny All. The policy names are self-explanatory. If a user is assigned a permission policy level for a web application or zone, the permission policy cannot be overridden by permissions assigned within a site collection. The following examples illustrate how permission policies can be used:

- If a user is assigned the Full Control permission policy, the user is effectively a site collection administrator for all site collections in the web application, with full access to all content, whether or not the user has been granted permissions within the site collections themselves.

- If a user is assigned the Full Read permission policy, the user has Read access to all content within the web application, without requiring specific permissions within a site collection. The search indexer—the crawler account—is assigned Full Read permission policy to all SharePoint Web applications by default, so that it has access to index all content.

- If a user is assigned the Deny Write permission policy, the user cannot add, modify, or delete items; cannot create alerts or delete versions; and is restricted from making any change to content within the web application. This is true even if the user has been granted a permission level to content that would otherwise allow access. A Deny Write permission even overrides the Full Control permission level assigned to site content. Web application user policy wins.

- If a user is assigned the Deny All permission policy, the user cannot access any content within a web application.

These examples illustrate two important points about user policy. First, permissions defined in the permission policy level within a user policy take precedence over conflicting permissions assigned to site content. Second, unlike permission levels used within site collections, permission policy levels can include Deny permissions. And when a Deny permission is in effect, it will win over not only a permission level that allows access, but also over a permission policy that has a conflicting Allow permission.

The four default permission policy levels are identical to those that existed in SharePoint 2007. SharePoint 2010 enhances the flexibility of policies by allowing you to create custom permission policies. In fact, you can create a permission policy that allows or denies each of the granular permissions that you can use within a permission level in a site collection.

MANAGE PERMISSION POLICY LEVELS

1. In the Central Administration Quick Launch, click Application Management.
2. In the Web Applications section, click Manage Web Applications.
3. Select the web application for which you want to manage permission policy levels.
4. Click Permission Policy to open the Manage Permission Policy Levels page.
5. Perform one of the following steps:
   - To create a new permission policy level, click Add Permission Policy Level. The Add Permission Policy Level page opens.
   - To modify a permission policy level, click the name of the permission policy level. The Edit Permission Policy Level page opens.
6. In the Name box, type a name for the permission policy level.
7. Optionally, in the Description box, enter a description of the permission policy level.
8. In the Permissions section, select or clear permissions that you wish to include or exclude, respectively, from the permission policy level.
9. Click Save.

DELETE A PERMISSION POLICY LEVEL

1. In the Central Administration Quick Launch, click Application Management.
2. In the Web Applications section, click Manage Web Applications.
3. Select the web application for which you want to manage permission policy levels.
4. Click Permission Policy.
5. On the Manage Permission Policy Levels page, select the check box in the row of the permission policy level you want to delete.
6. Click Delete Selected Permission Policy Levels.
7. In the confirmation dialog box, click OK.

To assign a permission policy level to a user or group, you must create a user policy. The user policy associates the permission policy level with a user or group for a web application or for a specific authentication zone of a web application.

This allows you to create a policy that applies to access based on the vector of access. For example, you might allow users on your intranet certain access to content within a web application, defined by permission levels assigned for the site content. However, you might configure a user policy that specifies that when users access the site through the extranet, they cannot make changes to content—it is read-only because they are accessing the content through a different authentication zone.

CREATE A USER POLICY

1. In the Central Administration Quick Launch, click Application Management.
2. In the Web Applications section, click Manage Web Applications.
3. Select the web application for which you want to assign a user policy.
4. Click User Policy to open the Policy For Web Application dialog box.
5. Click Add Users to open the Add Users page opens.
6. In the Zones list, select the zone for which the policy will apply, or select (All Zones) to apply the policy to the web application for all zones.
7. Click Next.
8. In the Choose Users box, enter the users or groups to whom the user policy will be applied.
9. In the Choose Permissions section, select the check boxes for the permission levels that you want to assign to the users.
10. Click Finish.

MODIFY A USER POLICY

1. In the Central Administration Quick Launch, click Application Management.
2. In the Web Applications section, click Manage Web Applications.
3. Select the web application for which you want to assign a user policy.
4. Click User Policy to open the Policy For Web Application dialog box.
5. Select the check box next to the user name, and then click Edit Permissions Of Selected Users.

    Alternately, click the user name.

    The Edit Users page opens.
6. In the Permission Policy Levels section, select the check boxes for the permission levels that you want to assign to the users.
7. Click Save.

DELETE A USER POLICY

1. In the Central Administration Quick Launch, click Application Management.
2. In the Web Applications section, click Manage Web Applications.
3. Select the web application for which you want to assign a user policy.

4. Click User Policy to open the Policy For Web Application dialog box.

5. Select the check box next to the user name, and then click Delete Selected Users.
   A confirmation dialog box opens.

6. Click OK.

You can also manage user policy in Central Administration by clicking Security in the Quick Launch, and then, in the Users section, clicking Specify Web Application User Policy. This approach is not ribbon-enabled and therefore is not sensitive to context. You must be sure to select the correct web application that you want to modify.

Audit Access to SharePoint Content

SharePoint tracks access to content, and you can generate reports regarding content access by enabling auditing. Auditing is enabled at the site collection level.

ENABLE AUDITING

1. Click Site Actions, and then click Site Settings.

2. In the Site Collection Administration section, click Site Collection Audit Settings.
   The Configure Audit Settings page opens, as shown in Figure 4-13.

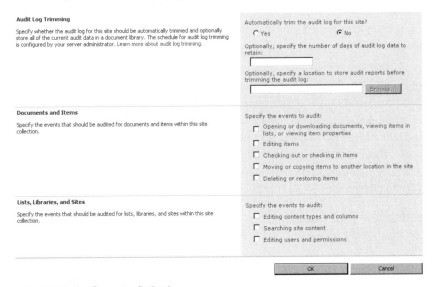

FIGURE 4-13 Configure Audit Settings page

3. In the Documents And Items section and in the Lists, Libraries, And Sites section, select the check boxes of the activities that you want to audit.

   Audit logs can grow rapidly. To reduce the size of audit logs, you can enable trimming. Audit log trimming removes old entries from the logs, and optionally archives those older entries as a report stored in a document library.

4. Optionally, in the Audit Log Trimming section, enable audit log trimming. You can specify the number of days of audit log data to retain, and you can specify a document library within which archived log data is saved after it is trimmed from the audit logs.

VIEW AUDIT LOG REPORTS

1. Click Site Actions, and then click Site Settings.

2. In the Site Collection Administration section, click Audit Log Reports to open the View Auditing Reports page.

3. To view a report, click the report name, and then specify a location in which to save the report.

    To create a custom report, click Run A Custom Report. On the Customize page, you can filter audit logs for data based on users, groups, activities, lists or libraries, and timeframes.

PRACTICE   Manage SharePoint Site Security

Practices are designed to guide you through important procedures. The instructions in the Training Kit are high-level instructions that will challenge you to think carefully and to apply the procedures that are covered in this lesson, and elsewhere in the Training Kit. If you need assistance, consult the detailed, step-by-step instructions in the Practice Answers on the companion media.

In this practice, you will create and secure a website for users collaborating on the marketing strategy for Contoso, Ltd. Initially, marketing staff and senior managers will need to add and edit content on the site. You want to allow the project's managers, Kevin Cook and Toni Poe, to manage group membership so that you do not have to be involved with granting access to additional team members. You also want to enable Kevin to check in a document that has been checked out by another user, so that if a user is unavailable for an extended period of time and forgets to check a document in, other users can regain the ability to make changes to the document.

Prepare for the Practice

Before you perform this practice, you must ensure that your lab environment has been built according to the instructions found in the Introduction to this Training Kit. You must also have performed the practice in Lesson 1 of this chapter. You must be logged off of SP2010-WFE1 before beginning the exercises.

EXERCISE 1   Create a Site Collection

In this exercise, you delete the existing team site for the Marketing department. You will then re-create the site collection for use in this practice.

1. Log on to SP2010-WFE1 as **CONTOSO\SP_Admin** with the password **Pa$$w0rd**.

2. In Central Administration, delete the following site collection: *http://teams.contoso.com/depts/Marketing*.

3. Create a new site collection. Use the following specifications and guidance:
   - Title: Marketing
   - Description: Marketing department team site
   - URL: *http://teams.contoso.com/depts/Marketing*
   - Template: Team Site
   - Primary Site Collection Administrator: CONTOSO\SP_Admin

EXERCISE 2   Manage Default Groups

In this exercise, you manage membership and properties of the default site groups.

1. Open a new tab in Internet Explorer and browse to ***http://teams.contoso.com/depts/marketing***.
2. Add CONTOSO\KevinC to the Marketing Owners group.
3. Add the Marketing security group in Active Directory to the SharePoint Marketing Members site group.

EXERCISE 3   Create a Subsite

In this exercise, you create a subsite to support collaboration between the marketing team and senior managers around the marketing strategy for the upcoming year.

- Create a subsite. Use the following specifications and guidance:
  - Title: Marketing Strategy
  - URL: *http://teams.contoso.com/depts/Marketing/MarketingStrategy*
  - Template: Team Site
  - Permissions: Use Unique Permissions
  - Navigation Inheritance: Use the top link bar from the parent site
  - Allow SharePoint to set up groups for the site. Accept all defaults.

EXERCISE 4   Grant Access to a Site

In this exercise, you grant marketing staff and senior managers access to the Marketing Strategy site.

- Navigate to the Site Permissions page, and then use the Grant Permissions button to add the following groups to the Marketing Strategy Members group: Marketing, Senior Managers.

EXERCISE 5   Delegate Group Membership Management

In this exercise, you delegate the management of group membership in the Marketing Strategy site to select users.

1. Create a new group. Use the following specifications and guidance:
   - Group name: Marketing Strategy Membership Managers
   - Group description: Users who can manage the membership of the site's Members group

- Group owner: SP_Admin, the SharePoint Administrator And Setup User account
- Permissions: none

2. Add the following users to the Marketing Strategy Membership Managers group: CONTOSO\KevinC, CONTOSO\ToniP.

3. Configure the Marketing Strategy Members so that the new Marketing Strategy Membership Managers group can add and remove members.

EXERCISE 6   Create a Permission Level

In this exercise, you create a permission level that allows a user to check in a document that has been checked out by another user.

- At the top-level site of the Marketing site collection, *http://teams.contoso.com/depts/marketing*, create a permission level. Use the following specifications and guidance:
  - Name: Override Check Out
  - Description: Users can check in a document that has been checked out by another user. Users can also discard checkout.
  - Permissions: Override Check Out

EXERCISE 7   Create a Role and a Role Assignment

In this exercise, you create a group for users who are allowed to override checkout. You then grant the group permission to override checkout for the site.

1. Create a group. Use the following specifications and guidance:
    - Name: Checkout Managers
    - Description: Users who can manage check out
    - Permissions: Override Check Out

2. Add the following user to the group: CONTOSO\KevinC.

EXERCISE 8   Examine Effective Permissions

In this exercise, you examine the effective permissions of a user on the Marketing Strategy site.

- Determine the effective permissions of CONTOSO\KevinC on the Marketing Strategy site.

EXERCISE 9   Create the CHAPTER 04 Snapshot

The CHAPTER 04 snapshot captures the state of the environment at the end of Chapter 4. Perform this procedure for each of the following virtual machines: SP2010-WFE1, CONTOSO-DC.

1. Shut down the virtual machine.

2. Unmount any ISO image currently mounted to the CD/DVD drive. Use the "Unmount an ISO Image" procedure in the Lab Environment Build Guide on the companion media.

3. Create a snapshot named CHAPTER 04. Use the "Create a Snapshot" procedure in the Lab Environment Build Guide on the companion media.

Lesson Summary

- SharePoint site and content security results from assigning permission levels that consist of granular permissions to users and groups for securable objects.

- SharePoint groups can contain users from Active Directory or from other authentication providers, and can contain security groups from Active Directory. SharePoint groups cannot be members of other SharePoint groups.

- By default, permissions are inherited from the parent container, up to the top-level site of a site collection.

- It is a best practice to configure all access at the top-level site of a site collection, but it is often necessary to control access at more granular levels.

- You can block inheritance and specify explicit permissions. Later, you can reinstate inheritance, at which time all explicit permissions are removed.

- Although SharePoint creates groups and permission levels based on the template that is applied to a website, you can create your own groups and permission levels to support your requirements.

- Permission policies can be assigned to a user or group at the web application level to create a user policy. Permissions in a user policy can be Allow or Deny policies. The permissions defined in a user policy take precedence over any conflicting permissions within a site collection.

Lesson Review

You can use the following questions to test your knowledge of the information in Lesson 2, "Secure SharePoint Sites and Content." The questions are also available on the companion media in a practice test if you prefer to review them in electronic form.

> **NOTE ANSWERS**
>
> Answers to these questions and explanations of why each answer choice is right or wrong are located in the "Answers" section at the end of the book.

1. In the Marketing site, there are subsites for marketing projects. In one subsite, Project A, you want to ensure that users who can modify content cannot delete content. What do you do?

   A. Configure user policy to deny the Delete Items permission to the Domain Users group.

   B. Copy the Contribute permission level and remove the Delete Items permission. Assign the new permission level to the Project A Members group.

   C. Add the Deny Delete Items permission to the Project A site.

   D. Configure the content database as read-only.

2. You want to allow managers of the Project A site to check in documents that were checked out by another user, in case a user forgets to check in a document before going on vacation. What can you do? (Choose all that apply.)

   A. Create a custom permission level that includes only the Override Check Out permission, and assign it to the managers.

   B. Assign managers the Contribute permission level.

   C. Assign managers the Full Control permission level.

   D. Assign managers the Design permission level.

3. You want to prevent users in the site's Members group from changing one page in a Pages library without preventing changes to other pages in the library. What can you do?

   A. Add a user policy that denies the Edit Items permission.

   B. Remove users from the site's Members group, and add users to the site's Visitors group.

   C. Stop inheritance on the library, and remove the site's Members group.

   D. Stop inheritance on the page, and remove the site's Members group.

Chapter Review

To further practice and reinforce the skills you learned in this chapter, you can perform the following tasks:

- Review the chapter summary.
- Review the list of key terms introduced in this chapter.
- Complete the case scenarios. These scenarios set up real-world situations involving the topics of this chapter and ask you to create a solution.
- Complete the suggested practices.
- Take a practice test.

Chapter Summary

- Site collections contain a top-level website and zero or more subsites. A site collection is stored in a content database, which can also contain other site collections.
- Site collections and content databases support governance requirements including security, backup and restore, and storage management.
- Managed paths are nodes in the URI namespace that contain SharePoint content—a SharePoint site collection.
- SharePoint's security model is a flexible and powerful combination of users and groups, permission levels made up of granular permissions, and securable objects. By default, an object inherits its permissions from its parent container, so all objects inherit permissions from the top-level site.
- You can manage groups, permission levels, and role assignments to support a model of site content security that is aligned with your requirements.
- You can use Web policy to apply overriding permissions for all content in a Web application, or for an authentication zone of a Web application.

Key Terms

The following terms were introduced in this chapter. Do you know what they mean?

- Site collection
- Content database
- Managed path
- Permission level
- Securable object
- Inheritance
- Permission policy level
- User policy

Case Scenario: Configure Site Collections and Content Databases

In the following case scenario, you will apply what you've learned about subjects of this chapter. You can find answers to these questions in the "Answers" section at the end of this book.

You are tasked to redesign a web application, partners.contoso.com, that supports extranet collaboration with ten partners. It is expected that partner websites will not contain more than 5 GB of content. You will be expected to back up all partner websites nightly. For each partner website, a user from Contoso and a user from the partner need to be given full ownership of the content and configuration. The websites currently exist, but during a review of permissions you discovered that the partner user administrators were able to view user information about other partners, and it is important that the user information for each partner is partitioned so that partners cannot identify each other.

1. Based on what you have discovered about the partners.contoso.com web application, how many site collections and content databases must be currently in place?

2. How many site collections should you create to support the requirements of the application?

3. How many content databases should you create to support the requirements of the application?

4. Your Compliance group must have full control access to all content in all partner sites. What can you use to ensure that the access is granted, and that a site collection administrator cannot block access to content?

Suggested Practices

To help you successfully master the exam objectives presented in this chapter, complete the following tasks.

Practice 1: Configure and Apply Quota Templates

In Lesson 1, you learned to configure and apply quota templates. Create a quota template named Department (Standard) with a storage limit of 50 MB, and a quota template named Department (Large) with a storage limit of 100 MB. Apply the Department (Standard) quota to the HR team site collection, *http://teams.contoso.com/depts/HR*. Upload large documents to the site's Shared Documents document library until you have filled the quota and cannot upload additional content. Observe the behavior of the SharePoint site when the quota has been reached. Apply the Department (Large) template to the site collection. Attempt to upload additional content to the site. If you are blocked from doing so, identify and remediate the problem.

Practice 2: Explore Site Settings

In Lesson 1, you learned that some site collection settings are configured by using Central Administration, and others by using the Site Settings page of the top-level website in the site collection. Add a user account that is not a site collection administrator to the Information Technology Owners group in the *http://teams.contoso.com/depts/IT* site. Sign in to the site as CONTOSO\SP_Admin. Open the Site Settings page. Examine the settings that are available. Sign in to the site as the user that you added to the Owners group. Examine the settings on the Site Settings page. Explore the differences between the settings that are available to SP_Admin, a site collection administrator, and those that are available to a site owner. Drill into the settings to identify the settings that are available to both users, but offer different options based on whether the setting is scoped to the site collection or only to the top-level website.

Practice 3: Security

In Lesson 2, you learned that you can configure fine-grained permissions on lists, libraries, folders, documents, and items. Open the Shared Documents library Marketing Strategy site that you created in the practice for Lesson 2. Configure permissions on the library so that the Marketing Visitors group cannot access the library. Create a folder called Brainstorming. Configure permissions on the folder so that the Marketing Strategy Members group can add and modify documents, but cannot delete documents. Configure auditing for changes to content. Upload a document to the document library, then change the document, and then delete it. View the audit reports and identify the events related to the changes you made.

Take a Practice Test

The practice tests on this book's companion media offer many options. For example, you can test yourself on just the lesson review content, or you can test yourself on all the 70-667 certification exam objectives. You can set up the test so that it closely simulates the experience of taking a certification exam, or you can set it up in study mode so that you can look at the correct answers and explanations after you answer each question.

> **MORE INFO** **PRACTICE TESTS**
>
> For details about all the practice test options available, see the "How to Use the Practice Tests" section in this book's Introduction.

CHAPTER 5

Service Applications and the Managed Metadata Service

Certain functionality is required across web applications in a SharePoint farm, including authentication, search, taxonomy, connectivity to back-end data sources, and user profiles. Users don't connect directly with these services. Instead, a user-facing web application accesses the functionality it requires from a middle tier of shared services, in which each service provides a specific type of functionality to one or more web applications in the farm or, possibly, to web applications in remote farms.

So, for example, when a user performs a search by using a query web part in a web application, the query web part connects to search services to return results to the user. Searches performed in other web applications can connect to the same search service, to other search services in the farm, to search services in a remote farm, or to federated search services such as Bing.

SharePoint has several architectural models for services: Different services are implemented different ways. However, the most high-profile, functional services such as those already mentioned are implemented using the Service Application Framework (SAF) introduced in SharePoint 2010.

In Lesson 1, you will learn about the SAF and its components. You will learn to deploy services—service instances and service applications—so that the functionality of a service can be consumed by web applications in the farm or in remote farms. You will also learn to manage administration and configuration of service applications.

In Lesson 2, you will explore, in depth, the Managed Metadata Service, which is an important service application that supports information architecture by providing a centrally managed term store and shared content types.

Exam objectives in this chapter:
- Manage site collections.
- Configure service applications.

Lessons in this chapter:

Before You Begin

To complete the lessons in this chapter, you must have done the following:

- Performed the practice in Chapter 1.

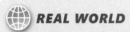 **REAL WORLD**

Dan Holme

In Microsoft Office SharePoint Server 2007, services were provided using Shared Service Providers (SSPs). SSPs were monolithic units that provided multiple services, including search, user profiles, InfoPath forms, and the business data catalog. During the product life cycle of Microsoft Office SharePoint Server (MOSS) 2007, enterprises discovered that SSPs did not scale well to meet the needs of complex enterprises. Microsoft created an entirely new model—the Service Application Framework—for delivering services in SharePoint 2010. The SAF promises to remove the vast majority of "pain points" that were encountered in MOSS 2007. Additionally, Microsoft introduced new services—including the Managed Metadata Service—that deliver valuable functionality that was missing entirely in previous versions of SharePoint. Unfortunately, terminology and concepts related to the SAF can be confusing.

This chapter aims to equip you with a solid understanding of the SAF, so that you can digest and understand sometimes vague and conflicting documentation and messages. If you can successfully master the fundamental concepts of the SAF, you will be equipped to deliver services effectively within and between SharePoint farms.

Lesson 1: Administer Service Applications

The Service Application Framework (SAF) is the architectural model by which important shared services—including search, metadata, business data connectivity, and user profiles— are deployed, managed, backed up, restored, and shared across farms. In this lesson, you will study the concepts, terminology, and skills required to master the administration of service applications in SharePoint 2010. In later lessons and chapters, you will explore, in depth, many of the specific service applications available in SharePoint Server 2010.

After this lesson, you will be able to:

- Start and stop a service instance.
- Deploy a service application.
- Create an application connection (proxy).
- Create and modify an application connection group (proxy group).
- Manage service application associations of a web application.
- Delegate administration of a service application.
- Share a service application between farms.

Estimated lesson time: 90 minutes

Service Instance

When you install SharePoint Server 2010, services are installed that provide functionality for search, taxonomy, user profiles, rendering of Excel worksheets, and more. Each service—more accurately referred to as a *service instance*—that is installed on a server consists of one or more of the following components:

- Binary files such as DLLs
- Configuration files
- Settings in the farm configuration database
- Registry-based configuration
- Windows services
- Timer jobs
- Web pages with which to manage the service

You can identify the service instances installed on a SharePoint server with Central Administration and with Windows PowerShell.

VIEW SERVICE INSTANCES USING CENTRAL ADMINISTRATION

To view service instances using Central Administration, open the Services On Server page by performing the following steps:

1. In the Central Administration Quick Launch, click System Settings.

2. In the Servers section, click Manage Services On Server.

3. On the Services On Server page, click the Server list, and then click Change Server.

4. On the Select Server page, click the name of the server for which you want to view services.

   By default, only configurable services are displayed.

5. Click the View menu, and then click All.

VIEW SERVICE INSTANCES USING WINDOWS POWERSHELL

The following example shows the use of the *Get-SPServiceInstance* cmdlet to return all service instances on a server:

```
Get-SPServiceInstance -Server <Server Name>
```

Where:

- *<Server Name>* is the name of the server for which you want to list service instances. If the *-Server* parameter is omitted, the cmdlet returns all service instances in the farm.

Although services are installed on every server in the farm, most services are not started by default. Some services are started when you run the SharePoint 2010 Products Configuration Wizard, or when you use equivalent Windows PowerShell commands to create a farm or add a server to the farm. Remaining services must be started by using Central Administration or Windows PowerShell.

START A SERVICE INSTANCE USING CENTRAL ADMINISTRATION

To start a service instance using Central Administration, perform the following steps:

1. In the Central Administration Quick Launch, click System Settings.

2. In the Servers section, click Manage Services On Server.

3. Click the Server menu, and then click Change Server.

4. On the Services On Server page, click the Server list, and then click Change Server.

5. On the Select Server page, click the name of the server on which you want to start the service.

   By default, only configurable services are displayed. To view all services, click the View menu, and then click All.

6. Click Start on the row of the service that you want to start.

You can stop a service instance by clicking Stop on the row of the started service instance.

START A SERVICE USING WINDOWS POWERSHELL

The following example shows the use of the *Start-SPServiceInstance* cmdlet to start a service instance:

```
Start-SPServiceInstance -Identity <SPServiceInstancePipeBind>
```

Where:

- *<SPServiceInstancePipeBind>* is a service instance—for example, an object retrieved by using the *Get-SPServiceInstance* cmdlet—or a GUID of the service instance that you want to start.

You can use the *Stop-SPServiceInstance* cmdlet to stop a service.

Before you work with a service instance with Windows PowerShell, you must either bind to the specific service with which you want to work, or provide the GUID of the service instance. The following example assigns a service instance to a variable, and then uses the *Start-SPServiceInstance* cmdlet to start the service instance:

```
$ServerName = "SP2010-WFE1.contoso.com"
$ServiceName = "Managed Metadata Web Service"
$ServiceInstance = Get-SPServiceInstance –Server $ServerName |
    Where { $_.TypeName -eq $ServiceName }
Start-SPService $ServiceInstance
```

You can modify the first two lines of the script to specify the server and service name with which you want to work. The third line of the script uses the *Get-SPServiceInstance* cmdlet to retrieve all service instances on the specified server, and pipes the resulting collection to the *Where-Object* cmdlet, which filters the collection to the service instance that matches the specified service instance name.

The *Status* property of a service instance specifies whether the service is *Disabled* or *Online*. While the service is being started, the *Status* property will be *Provisioning*. While the service is being stopped, the *Status* property will be *Unprovisioning*.

Some service instances require additional configuration when you start the service. For example, you must provide the farm account's user name and password when you start the User Profile Synchronization Service, as you will learn in Chapter 6, "Configuring User Profiles and Social Networking."

Few services—the User Profile Synchronization Service is one—can be run only on one server in the farm. You can run most SharePoint services on more than one server. This allows you to provide redundancy for a service, so that if a service instance fails on one server, requests for the service can be handled by a service instance on another server. Multiple service machine instances also enable you to scale a service out—to service clients from a greater number of servers. Later in this lesson, you will learn how clients are directed, in round-robin format, to multiple online service instances.

A server running a service instance is often referred to as an *application server*, particularly if the server is not providing web applications to users.

Service Applications

The Service Application Framework (SAF) is an important architectural feature of SharePoint 2010. The SAF provides a model by which services can be deployed, provided, consumed, and managed. A service application represents a deployed—that is, an accessible—instance of a service. The service application framework provides a way for consumers in the farm to access the functionality of a centralized service, and the service application can manage the configuration and behavior of a service.

For example, the Search Service Application is the deployed instance of search services in the farm. The service application provides a management interface in Central Administration. You can use the management interface of the Search Service Application to specify the configuration of content crawling, indexing, and query behavior, and the configuration is propagated to the distributed service instances of the SharePoint Server Search service. When a user performs a search—for example, by using a query web part—the web part is connected to the Search Service Application and the request is redirected by a built-in round-robin algorithm to an available SharePoint Server Search service instance.

Examples of other service applications are:

- The Managed Metadata Service, which provides a centralized term store to support taxonomy and folksonomy, and syndicates content types across site collections. Any web application that connects to the Managed Metadata Service can contain a managed metadata column that exposes the terms in a term set, or an enterprise keywords column that allows the entry of multiple keywords from any term set or user-generated terms.

- The Business Connectivity Service, which enables SharePoint to connect to external data sources.

- The User Profile Service, which synchronizes user profile attributes from Active Directory and other sources.

- The Secure Token Service, which provides authentication services to applications and services that use claims-based authentication.

> **NOTE CONFUSING TERMINOLOGY**
>
> The terminology around SharePoint services can be confusing—the Managed Metadata Service, for example, is the default name of the service application, whereas the service is called the Managed Metadata Web Service. Excel Services is the default name of the service *application,* whereas the *service* is named Excel Calculation Services. Keep in mind that the service instance is the process running on one or more servers in the farm, whereas the service application is a logical, farm-level component that exposes the service instance to web applications and manages the configuration of the service instance.

Service Application Endpoint

The SharePoint services we've discussed so far are web services, built upon Windows Communication Foundation (WCF). When you deploy a service application and start the associated service instance on a server, SharePoint provisions the web service and a corresponding virtual directory within the SharePoint Web Services IIS Web site on that server, as shown in Figure 5-1.

FIGURE 5-1 SharePoint service virtual directories

Each virtual directory is named with the GUID of the service. You can use the *Get-SPServiceInstance* cmdlet to determine the GUID of a service. If you explore the virtual directory, you will see that SharePoint services reside in the *C:\Program Files\Microsoft Office Servers\14.0\WebServices* folder. As shown in Figure 5-2, services are now WCF services (.svc files), rather than ASP.net web services (.asmx files).

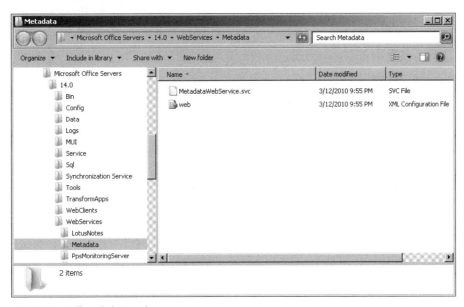

FIGURE 5-2 A SharePoint service

The virtual directory and associated files comprise the *service application endpoint*. A web application will communicate with the service application endpoint to obtain the functionality of the service.

Some of the services listed on the Services On Server page are wrappers for Windows services. For example, the Microsoft SharePoint Foundation Timer service instance is a wrapper for the SharePoint 2010 Timer Windows service. Some services, including the Document Conversions service, are service instances that do not implement the SAF.

> **NOTE MAJOR SERVICES IMPLEMENT THE SAF**
>
> The variety of implementations of the service model in SharePoint can be confusing at times, so keep in mind that the services that provide high-profile, user-facing functionality—search, metadata, user profiles, and business connectivity services, for example—are implemented using the SAF, in which there is both a service application and one or more service instances.

Service Scalability and Redundancy

SharePoint service instances can run on more than one server. When a web application interacts with a service application, the Application Discovery and Load Balancer Service Application service—also called the Topology service—distributes requests to a running instance of the service. The distribution uses a simple round-robin algorithm, although some services provide their own load balancing scheme—for example, Excel Services—and the request distribution can be extended by developers to include more nuanced rules.

Thus, by starting service instances for a service on more than one server in the farm, you provide reliability. If an instance of a service fails, the Topology service will detect the failure and will route requests to other running instances. Additionally, as you add service instances, you scale the performance of the service.

Create a Service Application

You can deploy a service application by using the Farm Configuration Wizard, Central Administration, or Windows PowerShell. You used the Farm Configuration Wizard to deploy service applications in Chapter 1, "Creating a SharePoint 2010 Intranet." The following procedures illustrate the process of creating a service application, with the Managed Metadata Service service application as an example.

CREATE A MANAGED METADATA SERVICE APPLICATION USING CENTRAL ADMINISTRATION

To create a Managed Metadata Service application, perform the following steps:

1. In the Central Administration Quick Launch, click Application Management.
2. In the Service Applications section, click Manage Service Applications.
3. In the ribbon, click New, and then click Managed Metadata Service.

    The Create New Managed Metadata Service page opens.
4. In the Name box, type a name for the service application.

5. In the Database Server box, type the name of the SQL server on which the database for the Managed Metadata Service application will be created.

6. In the Database Name box, type the name of the Managed Metadata Service application database to create.

7. In the Application Pool section, specify an existing application pool in which to run the service, or create a new application pool by specifying a name and a managed account for the application pool identity.

   To optimize performance of your farm, it is recommended to run all service applications in a single, shared application pool. If you have a significant business driver for process isolation, you can achieve physical isolation of a service application by choosing or creating a different application pool.

8. Click OK.

Each service application has a Windows PowerShell cmdlet with which you can create the service application.

CREATE A MANAGED METADATA SERVICE APPLICATION USING WINDOWS POWERSHELL

The following example shows the use of the *New-SPMetadataServiceApplication* cmdlet to create a new Managed Metadata Service service application:

```
New-SPMetadataServiceApplication -Name <Name> -DatabaseName <Database Name>
-ApplicationPool <Application Pool>
```

Where:

- *<Name>* is the name of the new Managed Metadata Service service application.

- *<Database Name>* is the name of the database for the new service application.

- *<Application Pool>* is the name of an application pool that will host the new service application.

Additional parameters are available to configure settings such as the content type hub. Use the *Get-Help* cmdlet with the *–detailed* parameter for more information.

For example, the following command creates a Managed Metadata Service service application for the Research and Development term store:

```
New-SPMetadataServiceApplication -Name "Managed Metadata Service - Research and
Development" -DatabaseName "SharePoint_Service_Metadata_Research" -ApplicationPool
"SharePoint Web Services Default"
```

You can delete service applications by using Central Administration or by using the *Remove-SPServiceApplication* cmdlet. Use the *Get-Help* cmdlet to learn more about *Remove-SPServiceApplication*. Some service applications have a specific *Remove-SP** cmdlet. Type **Get-Command Remove*SP*Application** for a list of these service applications.

When you create a service application, the related service instance is not started on any server in the farm. You must, therefore, ensure that you have started the service instance on one or more servers. As you learned earlier in this lesson, you can start the service by using Central Administration or Windows PowerShell.

Service Application Connections (Proxies)

A service application's application connection, also called its *proxy*, is a virtual entity that creates the connection point for the web application. If a web application needs functionality provided by a Managed Metadata service application, for example, the web application must be connected to the service application's application connection. The application connection controls the interaction between the web application and the service application. The application connection can apply permissions or configuration that gives web applications a subset of functionality of the service application. For example, the application connection for the Managed Metadata Service determines whether web applications subscribe to content types published in the content type hub.

When you create a service application by using the Farm Configuration Wizard or Central Administration, a new application connection is created automatically. If you create a service application by using Windows PowerShell, you must also create an application connection. Each service application has a cmdlet that creates an application connection.

CREATE AN APPLICATION CONNECTION (PROXY) USING WINDOWS POWERSHELL

The following example shows the use of the *New-SPMetadataServiceApplicationProxy* cmdlet to delete a site:

```
New-SPMetadataServiceApplicationProxy -Name <Name> -ServiceApplication <Service
Application Name>
```

Where:

- *<Name>* is the name for the new application connection.
- *<Service Application Name>* is the name of the Managed Metadata Service service application with which the new application connection will be associated.

Additional parameters are available to configure settings such as content type subscription and whether the new connection should be added to the farm's *default* connection group. Use the *Get-Help* cmdlet with the *–detailed* parameter for more information.

For example, the following command adds an application connection to the service application that was created in the previous section:

```
New-SPMetadataServiceApplicationProxy -Name "Managed Metadata Service - Research and
Development" -ServiceApplication "Managed Metadata Service - Research and Development"
```

Service Application Connection Groups (Proxy Groups)

A web application uses the service application connection to communicate with the service application. You can configure a web application to connect to only the service application connections that it requires. Typically, a web application requires more than one service application, and several web applications require the same service applications. To make it easier for you to manage the associations between a web application and the service application connections it requires, you can create a logical grouping of service application connections (proxies) called an *application connection group*, or *proxy group*. You can then configure a web application to connect to the group. The other web applications that require the same services can connect to the same group.

When a web application connects to an application connection group, the application is connected to all of the application connections that are members of that group, and thereby to all of the services provided by those connections.

The Farm Configuration Wizard sets up all service applications and creates a single application connection group, named *default*, that is available and can be used by any web application in the farm. By default, all new web apps are connected to the *default* connection group. So, by default, all web applications in the farm are connected to all service applications in the farm.

This default provides maximum functionality and ease of setup. However, one of the most important features of SharePoint 2010's service application model is that you are not limited to this "all apps connect to all services" topology. You can—and most likely should—modify the service applications that are in the default group, so that it includes only those service applications that you want consumed by all new web applications by default.

You can use the Service Application Associations page of Central Administration to edit application connection groups, including the default group.

EDIT A SERVICE APPLICATION CONNECTION GROUP USING CENTRAL ADMINISTRATION

To add or remove service application connections in an application connection group, perform the following steps:

1. In the Central Administration Quick Launch, click Application Management.
2. In the Service Applications section, click Configure Service Application Associations.
3. On the Service Application Associations page, click the View menu, and then click Web Applications.
4. In the list of web applications, in the Application Proxy Group column, click the name of the service application connection group that you want to change.
5. To add a service connection to the group, select the check box next to the service application that you want to add to the connection group.

    To remove a service application connection from the connection group, clear the check box next to the service application that you want to remove from the connection group.
6. Click OK.

You can also create custom application connection groups that provide exactly the services required by web applications in the farm. Unfortunately, there is no place in the Central Administration user interface where you can create a new application connection group. You must do so by using Windows PowerShell.

CREATE A NEW SERVICE APPLICATION CONNECTION GROUP

The following example shows the use of the *New-SPServiceApplicationProxyGroup* cmdlet to create a new service application proxy group:

```
New-SPServiceApplicationProxyGroup -Name <Name>
```

Where:

- *<Name>* is the name of the new service application proxy group.

For example, the following command creates a proxy group named *ResearchAndDevelopment*:

```
New-SPServiceApplicationProxyGroup -Name ResearchAndDevelopment
```

After you create an application connection group, you can define the application connections that belong to the group. Again, this is not easy in the user interface. The new application connection group will not appear in the Service Application Associations page until after you have assigned a web application to the application connection group. The procedures for associating a web application with an application connection group are in the next section.

You can use Windows PowerShell to add application connections to the application connection group.

ADD A SERVICE APPLICATION CONNECTION TO AN APPLICATION CONNECTION GROUP

The following example shows the use of the *Add-SPServiceApplicationProxyGroupMember* cmdlet to create a new service application proxy group:

```
Add-SPServiceApplicationProxyGroupMember [-Identity] <Proxy Group Name> -Member <Proxy>
```

Where:

- *<Proxy Group Name>* is the name of a service application connection group.
- *<Proxy>* is the GUID of an application connection or a variable representing an application connection. *<Proxy>* can also be an array of connection objects or GUIDs.

For example, the following command adds the application connection named *Managed Metadata Service – Research And Development* to the application connection group named *ResearchAndDevelopment*:

```
$proxy = Get-SPMetadataServiceApplicationProxy "Managed Metadata Service - Research And
Development" Add-SPServiceApplicationProxyGroupMember "ResearchAndDevelopment" -Member
$proxy
```

To remove a service application connection from an application connection group, use the *Remove-SPServiceApplicationProxyGroupMember* cmdlet.

Connections for Multiple Instances of a Service Application

Some service applications, including Managed Metadata and Search, can support multiple instances within a single application connection group. Web applications associated with the connection group will consume services from all instances of these service applications. In Figure 5-3, you can see two instances of a Managed Metadata Service service application.

Most service applications, however, can only exist once in an application connection group. For these service applications, if you have connections to more than one instance in the connection group, you must mark one instance as the default. In Figure 5-3, you can see the Set As Default link. Web applications will not consume services from the other instances of that service application.

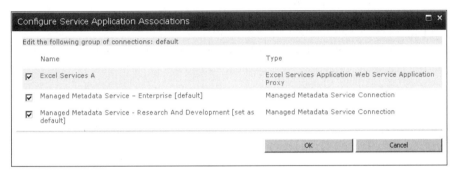

FIGURE 5-3 Multiple instances of a service application

Application Associations

A web application is associated either with one application connection group, or with a custom collection of application connections. You specify the association when you create a web application. Figure 5-4 shows the Service Application Connections section of the Create New Web Application page.

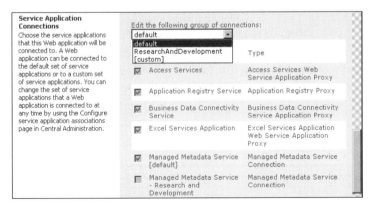

FIGURE 5-4 The Service Application Connections section of the Create New Web Application page

If you choose an existing application connection group, the web application will connect to all service application connections in the group. If you choose *[custom]*, you can select the specific application connections that the web application requires.

> **NOTE** **UNDERSTAND THE [*CUSTOM*] GROUP**
>
> The *[custom]* group is not a connection group per se. It simply indicates that the web application has its own defined collection of service application connections. If you select *[custom]* for two different web applications, each web application can have a different set of connections.

You can manage associations of existing web applications by using Central Administration or Windows PowerShell.

CONFIGURE APPLICATION ASSOCIATIONS USING CENTRAL ADMINISTRATION

To configure application associations, perform the following steps:

1. In the Central Administration Quick Launch, click Application Management.
2. In the Service Applications section, click Configure Service Application Associations.
3. In the Web Application / Service Application column, click an application.
4. In the Edit The Following Group Of Connections list, select the application connection group with which you want to associate the application.
5. If you selected *[custom]* in the previous step, you can select or clear check boxes for each application connection.
6. Click OK.

You can also configure the custom service application connection group of a web application by selecting a web application, and then clicking Service Connections on the Web Application Management page. You cannot change service applications connection groups using this page.

CONFIGURE APPLICATION ASSOCIATIONS USING WINDOWS POWERSHELL

You must modify the *ServiceApplicationProxyGroup* property of a web application to associate the web application with a proxy group. The following example associates the web application *http://research.contoso.com* with the *ResearchAndDevelopment* proxy group.

```
$web = Get-SPWebApplication "http://research.contoso.com"
$web.ServiceApplicationProxyGroup = Get-SPServiceApplicationProxyGroup
("ResearchAndDevelopment")
$web.Update()
```

To set a web application back to using the *[default]* group, use the following commands:

```
$web = Get-SPWebApplication "http://research.contoso.com"
$web.ServiceApplicationProxyGroup = Get-SPServiceApplicationProxyGroup("")
$web.Update()
```

Assign Administrators of a Service Application

Farm administrators always have rights to manage all service applications. Those rights cannot be removed. SharePoint 2007 did not make it easy to delegate the administration and configuration of an individual service, but in SharePoint 2010 you can delegate the administration of service applications.

Service application administrators are delegated by members of the Farm Administrators group. The administrators of a service application can configure settings for a specific service application in a farm. However, these administrators cannot create service applications, access any other service applications in the farm, or perform any farm-level operations, including topology changes. For example, the service application administrator for a Search service application in a farm can configure settings for that Search service application only.

ASSIGN ADMINISTRATORS OF A SERVICE APPLICATION USING CENTRAL ADMINISTRATION

To assign administrators of a service application, perform the following steps:

1. In the Central Administration Quick Launch, click Application Management, and then, in the Service Applications section, click Manage Service Applications.

2. Click the row of a service application.

   Do *not* click the name of a service application. Most service application names are links to the service application's management application.

3. In the ribbon, click Administrators.

When you assign a service application administrator, and the user is not already a member of the Farm Administrators group, the user is added to the Delegated Administrators group in Central Administration. This gives the user the ability to access the Central Administration website. If for some reason a user cannot access Central Administration even though you have assigned the user an administrative role for a service application, verify that the user has been made a member of the Delegated Administrators group.

MANAGE MEMBERSHIP OF THE DELEGATED ADMINISTRATORS GROUP

To manage the membership of the Delegated Administrators group, perform the following steps:

1. In Central Administration, click Site Actions, and then click Site Permissions to open the Permissions page.

2. Click the Delegated Administrators link.

3. To add a user, click New.

   To remove a user, select the check box next to the user, click Actions, and then click Remove Users From Group.

Restrict Access to a Service Application

By default, a web application that is associated with a service application connection—either through an application connection group or through a custom set of application connections—has full access to the functionality provided by the service application.

This is because the Local Farm identity has Full Control permission, by default, to a service application connection. The Local Farm identity is a special identity—like a group—that represents all service application and application pool accounts in the farm.

However, you can modify application connection permissions to restrict access to a service application, such that even if a web application is associated with the application connection, the web application has limited or no access to the service application. To restrict access to a service application, you must perform the following steps:

1. Add a specific service account to the service application.

2. Grant permissions to specific service or application pool accounts.

3. Remove the Full Control permission that is assigned to the Local Farm identity.

You can perform these tasks by using Central Administration or by using Windows PowerShell 2.0.

Restrict Access to a Service Application Using Central Administration

To restrict access to a service application by using Central Administration, you must perform the following steps:

1. Retrieve the web application service account.

2. Add the web application service account to the service application.

3. Remove the local farm ID from the service application.

RETRIEVE A WEB APPLICATION SERVICE ACCOUNT USING CENTRAL ADMINISTRATION

To retrieve a web application service account by using Central Administration, perform the following steps:

1. In the Central Administration Quick Launch, click Security.

2. In the General Security section, click Configure Service Accounts.

3. On the Service Accounts page, select the web application name from the first drop-down list.

    The service account is shown in the Select An Account For This Component list. Record the service account name because you will use it in the next procedure.

4. Click Cancel to exit the Service Accounts page without making any changes.

GRANT PERMISSIONS FOR A SERVICE APPLICATION TO A WEB APPLICATION USING CENTRAL ADMINISTRATION

To grant permissions for service accounts to access a service application by using Central Administration, perform the following steps:

1. In the Central Administration Quick Launch, click Application Management.

2. In the Service Applications section, click Manage Service Applications.

3. On the Manage Service Applications page, click the row that contains the service application for which you want to assign permissions.

4. In the ribbon, click Permissions.

5. In the Connection Permissions dialog box, type the service account name that you retrieved in the previous procedure, and then click Add.

6. In the middle pane, click the newly added service account name.

7. Select the check box for the permission level that you want to assign to the service account.

   Because the Local Farm identity that represents all application pool and service accounts is assigned Full Control permission by default, you must remove the permission assigned to Local Farm.

8. In the middle pane, click Local Farm, and then click Remove.

9. Verify that the Connection Permissions page now lists only the service account that you want to access the service application, and that the service account has the required permissions on the service application. Click OK.

Restrict Access to a Service Application Using Windows PowerShell

The process to restrict access to a service application by using Windows PowerShell is more complex than performing the same task by using Central Administration. In Windows PowerShell 2.0, you must perform the following high-level procedures, some of which gather and store information for input into later procedures.

RESTRICTING ACCESS TO A SERVICE APPLICATION USING WINDOWS POWERSHELL

To restrict access to a service application by using Windows PowerShell, perform the following steps:

1. Retrieve the local farm ID:

   ```
   $farmID = Get-SPFarm | select id
   ```

2. Retrieve the web application service account:

   ```
   $webapp = Get-SPWebApplication http://intranet.contoso.com
   $username = $webApp.ApplicationPool.UserName
   ```

3. Create a new claims principal that contains the web application service account:

   ```
   $principal = New-SPClaimsPrincipal $username -IdentityType WindowsSamAccountName
   ```

4. Retrieve the security object of the service application:

   ```
   $serviceapplicationname = "Managed Metadata Service"
   $spapp = Get-SPServiceApplication -Name $serviceapplicationname
   $spguid = $spapp.id
   $security = Get-SPServiceApplicationSecurity $spguid
   ```

   In the preceding example, the service application is named "Managed Metadata Service." Change this value to match the name of the service application for which you want to modify access permissions. The name assigned to the *$serviceapplicationname* variable must match the display name of the service application exactly, including capitalization.

5. Add the web application service account to the security object of the service application:

```
$rights = "Full Control"
Grant-SPObjectSecurity $security $principal -Rights $rights
```

The rights will generally be "Full Control," but can vary based on the service application and your requirements. To determine what rights are available for a service application, run the following code:

```
$serviceapplicationname = "Managed Metadata Service"
$spapp = Get-SPServiceApplication -Name $serviceapplicationname
$rightslist = Get-SPServiceApplicationSecurity $spapp
$rightslist.NamedAccessRights
```

6. Remove the local farm ID from the security object of the service application:

```
Revoke-SPObjectSecurity $security $farmID
```

7. Assign the updated security object to the service application:

```
Set-SPServiceApplicationSecurity $spapp -ObjectSecurity $security
```

8. Display and review updated permissions:

```
(Get-SPServiceApplicationSecurity $spapp).AccessRules
```

RESTORE FARM-WIDE ACCESS TO A SERVICE APPLICATION USING WINDOWS POWERSHELL

To restore access to a service application for all web and service applications in the farm, run the following script:

```
$serviceapplicationname = "Managed Metadata Service"
$farmID = Get-SPFarm | select id
$claimProvider = (Get-SPClaimProvider System).ClaimProvider
$principal = New-SPClaimsPrincipal -ClaimType `
   "http://schemas.microsoft.com/sharepoint/2009/08/claims/farmid"
   -ClaimProvider $claimProvider -ClaimValue $farmid
$spapp = Get-SPServiceApplication -Name $serviceapplicationname
$spguid = $spapp.id
$security = Get-SPServiceApplicationSecurity $spguid
Grant-SPObjectSecurity -Identity $security -Principal $farmID -Rights "Full Control"
Set-SPServiceApplicationSecurity $spguid -ObjectSecurity $security
```

In the preceding example, the service application is named "Managed Metadata Service." Change this value to match the name of the service application for which you want to modify access permissions. The name assigned to the *$serviceapplicationname* variable must match the display name of the service application exactly, including capitalization.

RESTORE FARM-WIDE ACCESS TO A SERVICE APPLICATION USING CENTRAL ADMINISTRATION

To restore access to a service application for all web and service applications in the farm, you must first run the following Windows PowerShell command:

```
$farmID = Get-SPFarm | select id
```

Copy the ID that the command displays to your clipboard. Then, perform the following steps:

1. In the Central Administration Quick Launch, click Application Management.
2. In the Service Applications section, click Manage Service Applications.
3. On the Manager Service Applications page, click the row that contains the service application for which you want to assign permissions.
4. In the ribbon, click Permissions.
5. In the Connection Permissions dialog box, paste the ID of the farm account you obtained by running the Windows PowerShell command, and then click Add.
6. In the middle pane, click the local farm account name.
7. Select the Full Control check box and then click OK.

Share Service Applications across Farms

Some service applications can be shared across SharePoint farms. Other service applications can be shared only within a single farm. The following out-of-box service applications can be shared across farms:

- User Profile
- Managed Metadata
- Search
- Business Connectivity Services
- Secure Store
- Web Analytics

Deploy Cross-Farm Service Applications

To share a service application between two farms, you must perform the following high-level steps:

1. Configure the trust between the two farms. This involves an exchange of certificates.
2. In one farm, publish one or more service applications. This creates a URL for the published service application.
3. In the other farm, connect to the published service applications. When you connect to a service application in the remote farm, you specify the URL of the service application.

If the publishing and consuming farms are in two different Active Directory domains, some service applications require a trust relationship between the two domains:

- **User Profile** The Active Directory domains of the publishing and consuming farms must trust each other.
- **Business Data Connectivity and Secure Store** The domain of the publishing farm must trust the domain of the consuming farm.

Configure Trust between Farms

Before a service application can be shared from a publishing farm to web applications in a consuming farm, an administrator of the consuming farm must provide two trust certificates to the administrator of the publishing farm: a root certificate and a Security Token Service (STS) certificate. Additionally, an administrator of the publishing farm must provide a root certificate to the administrator of the consuming farm. By exchanging certificates, each farm acknowledges that the other farm can be trusted.

The process of establishing trust consists of the following steps, which must be performed on both the consuming and publishing farms:

1. Export certificates.

    A. On the consuming farm, export the root certificate.

    B. On the consuming farm, export the STS certificate.

    C. On the publishing farm, export the root certificate.

2. Transfer the exported certificate (*.cer) files to the other farm.

3. Import certificates and establish trust.

    A. On the publishing farm, import the root certificate of the consuming farm and establish a trusted root authority.

    B. On the publishing farm, import the STS certificate of the consuming farm and establish a trusted service token issuer.

    C. On the consuming farm, import the root certificate of the publishing farm and establish a trusted root authority.

You can export certificates only by using Windows PowerShell. You can import certificates and establish trust by using either Central Administration or Windows PowerShell. The procedures for each step are described below.

EXAM TIP

Keep track of the certificates that are exported and imported from each farm—the publishing farm and the consuming farm. Also keep track of which steps can be performed only by using Windows PowerShell.

EXPORT THE ROOT CERTIFICATE

The following example shows how to export the root certificate:

```
$rootCert = (Get-SPCertificateAuthority).RootCertificate
$rootCert.Export("Cert") | Set-Content <Path\Filename.cer> -Encoding byte
```

Where:

-   *<Path\Filename.cer>* is the path and filename to which to export the root certificate.

EXPORT THE STS CERTIFICATE

The following example shows how to export the STS certificate from the consuming farm:

```
$stsCert = (Get-SPSecurityTokenServiceConfig).LocalLoginProvider.SigningCertificate
$stsCert.Export("Cert") | Set-Content <Path\Filename.cer> -Encoding byte
```

Where:

- *<Path\Filename.cer>* is the path and filename to which to export the STS certificate.

The administrator of the consuming farm must perform both procedures, and must copy the resulting certificate (*.cer) files to the administrator of the publishing farm. The administrator of the publishing farm must export the root certificate of the publishing farm, and copy the resulting certificate (*.cer) file to the administrator of the consuming farm.

The administrators of the publishing and consuming farms then import each other's root certificate, and use the certificate to establish a trust relationship. This can be done by using Central Administration or Windows PowerShell.

ESTABLISH TRUST USING CENTRAL ADMINISTRATION

To establish trust by using Central Administration, perform the following procedure after exporting certificates and copying them to the farm.

1. In the Central Administration Quick Launch, click Security.
2. In the General Security section, click Manage Trust to open the Trust Relationship page.
3. Click New to open the Establish Trust Relationship page.
4. Enter a name that describes the purpose of the trust relationship.
5. Browse to and select the Root Authority Certificate for the trust relationship.

   This must be the Root Authority Certificate that was exported from the other farm by using Windows PowerShell.
6. If you are performing this task on the publishing farm, select the Provide Trust Relationship check box. Type in a descriptive name for the token issuer and browse to and select the STS certificate that was copied from the consuming farm. Click OK.

If you use Windows PowerShell to establish the trust relationship, you must import the root certificate to establish a trusted root authority. This must be done on both farms. Then you must import the STS certificate to establish a trusted service token issuer. This must be done on the publishing farm.

IMPORT THE ROOT CERTIFICATE AND CREATE A TRUSTED ROOT AUTHORITY

The following example shows how to import the root certificate and create a trusted root authority:

```
$trustCert = Get-PfxCertificate <Path\Filename.cer>
New-SPTrustedRootAuthority <Farm Name> -Certificate $trustCert
```

Where:

- *<Path\Filename.cer>* is the path and filename of the root certificate to import.
- *<Farm Name>* is a descriptive name of the farm from which the root certificate was exported. This becomes the display name of the trusted farm.

The administrator of the publishing farm must also import the STS certificate that was copied from the consuming farm and use the imported certificate to create a trusted service token issuer.

IMPORT THE STS CERTIFICATE AND CREATE A TRUSTED SERVICE TOKEN ISSUER

The following example shows how to import the STS certificate and create a trusted service token issuer:

```
$stsCert = Get-PfxCertificate <Path\Filename.cer>
New-SPTrustedServiceTokenIssuer <Farm Name> -Certificate $stsCert
```

Where:

- *<Path\Filename.cer>* is the path and filename of the STS certificate to import.
- *<Farm Name>* is a descriptive name of the farm from which the STS certificate was exported. This becomes the display name of the trusted service token issuer.

Publish a Service Application

On the farm in which the service application is located, an administrator must explicitly publish the service application. Service applications that are not explicitly published are available to the local farm only.

An administrator must also give the consuming farm permission to the Application Discovery and Load Balancing Service Application on the publishing farm. After doing this, give the consuming farm permission to the published service applications that it will be consuming.

PUBLISH A SERVICE APPLICATION USING CENTRAL ADMINISTRATION

To publish a service application, perform the following steps:

1. In the Central Administration Quick Launch, click Application Management.
2. In the Service Applications section, click Manage Service Applications.
3. Click the row of the service application that you want to publish.

   Do *not* click the name of a service application. Most service application names are links to the service application's management application.
4. On the ribbon, click Publish to open the Publish Service Application page.
5. In the Connection Type drop-down list, select the protocol for the connection—http or https.
6. Select the Publish This Service Application To Other Farms check box.

7. Copy the Published URL into your clipboard. This URL will be entered by an administrator of the consuming farm.

   The URL will be similar to the following: *urn:schemas-microsoft-com:sharepoint:service: 9c1870b7ee97445888d9e846519cfa27#authority=urn:uuid:02a493b92a5547828e21386 e28056cba&authority=https://ua_powershell:32844/Topology/topology.svc.*

8. Optionally, enter a description and a link to a web page that will be visible to administrators of remote farms.

9. Click OK.

PUBLISH A SERVICE APPLICATION USING WINDOWS POWERSHELL

The following example shows the use of the *Publish-SPServiceApplication* cmdlet to publish a service application:

```
Publish-SPServiceApplication -Identity <ServiceApplicationGUID>
```

Where:

- *<ServiceApplicationGUID>* is the GUID of the service application that you want to publish. If you do not know the GUID of the service application, use the following example to publish a service application by name. Change the value assigned to the variable *$spapp* so that it matches the display name of the service application you want to publish exactly, including capitalization.

  ```
  $serviceapplicationname = "Managed Metadata Service"
  Get-SPServiceApplication -Name $serviceapplicationname |
      Publish-SPServiceApplication
  ```

After you publish the service application, you must retrieve the URL for the published service application.

RETRIEVE INFORMATION ABOUT PUBLISHED SERVICE APPLICATIONS

The following example shows the use of the *Get-SPTopologyServiceApplication* cmdlet to retrieve the URL for the Topology service application:

```
Get-SPTopologyServiceApplication
```

You can also use the *Uri* property of a service application object to determine the published URL of the application.

Connect to Remote Service Applications

After the publishing farm has published the service application, an administrator of the consuming farm can connect to that service application from the consuming farm by specifying the published URL of the service application.

CONNECT TO A SERVICE APPLICATION ON A REMOTE FARM USING CENTRAL ADMINISTRATION

To connect to a service application on a remote farm by using Central Administration, perform the following steps:

1. In the Central Administration Quick Launch, click Application Management.

2. In the Service Applications section, click Manage Service Applications.

3. On the ribbon, click the Connect button down arrow, and then click the type of service application to which you want to connect.

4. On the Connect To A Remote Service Application page, in the Farm Or Service Application Address box, type the URL.

   You can enter either the URL of the published service application or the URL of the remote farm's topology service application.

   The Connect To A Remote Service Application page opens. It displays the service applications that match the URL that you typed in Step 4. If you entered the URL of a published service application, only the corresponding service application is listed. If you entered the URL of the remote farm's topology service, all published service applications are listed.

5. Click the row of the service application to which you want to connect.

6. Optionally, select the check box to add the service application connection to the farm's default application connection group.

7. Click OK.

8. You are prompted to change the connection name. Type a new name into the Connection Name text box or leave the default name, and then click OK.

9. Click OK to complete the procedure.

CONNECT TO A SERVICE APPLICATION ON A REMOTE FARM USING WINDOWS POWERSHELL

The following example shows the use of the *New-SPMetadataServiceApplicationProxy* cmdlet to connect to a service application on a remote farm:

```
New-SPMetadataServiceApplicationProxy –Name <Name> -URI <Service Application URL>
```

Where:

- *<Name>* is the name for the new application connection.
- *<Service Application URL>* is the published URL of the Managed Metadata Service service application with which the new application connection will be associated.

After you have used Central Administration or Windows PowerShell to connect to a published service application on a remote farm, you must add the service application connection to an application connection group on the consuming farm, or web applications must use a custom application connection group to connect directly to the application connection. The procedures for doing this are identical to the procedures used to add an application connection from a local service application to an application connection group. See the section "Service Application Connection Groups (Proxy Groups)" earlier in the chapter for details.

Service Application Design

Service application design is an art and a science. Keep in mind the following rules regarding the logical design of service applications:

- You can have more than one instance of most service applications in a farm.
- Each service application has one application connection.
- A service application's connection can belong to more than one application connection group.
- An application connection group contains connections for one or more service applications.
- A web application is associated either with one application connection group or with a custom group of application connections for the services it requires.
- An application connection group can contain connections for more than one instance of a specific service application.

    For some service applications, such as Search and Managed Metadata, you can add connections for more than one instance to an application connection group, and associated web applications will consume the services of each instance. For most service applications, however, you can have only one instance—the instance configured as default—and web applications will consume the service from only the default instance.

- You can restrict access of a web application to a service application.
- Some service applications can be shared across farms.

You can use these rules to determine the logical design of your SharePoint services—that is, the relationships between web applications and the service applications they require. After you have determined the logical design of your service applications based on the services that are required by web applications in the farm, you can then determine the physical design of service instances to support performance and redundancy requirements.

- A service instance can run on one or more servers in the farm.
- A server can run service instances for multiple, different services, or can be dedicated to a single service.

PRACTICE Administer Service Applications

Practices are designed to guide you through important procedures. The instructions in the Training Kit are high-level instructions that will challenge you to think carefully and to apply the procedures that are covered in this lesson, and elsewhere in the Training Kit. If you need assistance, consult the detailed, step-by-step instructions in the Practice Answers on the companion media.

In this practice, you will deploy a Managed Metadata Service service application. You will begin with a snapshot, created in Chapter 1, in which the Farm Configuration Wizard had not been run, and therefore only the default service applications had been deployed.

You will now deploy the first new service application to the farm. In Lesson 2, you will use the Managed Metadata Service service application to manage taxonomy and content type publishing.

Prepare for the Practice

Before you perform this practice, you must ensure that your lab environment has been built according to the instructions found in the Introduction to this Training Kit.

1. Apply the snapshot SHAREPOINT INSTALLED AND CONFIGURED to CONTOSO-DC.

2. Apply the snapshot SHAREPOINT INSTALLED AND CONFIGURED to SP2010-WFE1.

3. Start CONTOSO-DC.

   Wait for the virtual machine to complete startup, at which time the Press Ctrl+Alt+Del prompt appears.

4. Start SP2010-WFE1.

5. Log on to SP2010-WFE1 as **CONTOSO\SP_Admin** with the password **Pa$$w0rd**.

6. Start SharePoint 2010 Management Shell using the Run As Administrator option.

7. Type the following command, and then press Enter:

   ```
   & 'C:\70667TK\Practice Files\05_01\05_00_Setup.ps1'
   ```

   A script will run that creates the web applications, content databases, and site collections necessary for the exercises in this chapter.

8. Close SharePoint 2010 Management Shell.

EXERCISE 1 **Register a Managed Account for the Service Applications Application Pool**

In this exercise, you register CONTOSO\SP_ServiceApps as a managed account so that it can be used to create an application pool for service applications.

■ Register CONTOSO\SP_ServiceApps as a managed account. The password of the account is Pa$$w0rd.

EXERCISE 2 **Create a Managed Metadata Service Application Using Central Administration**

In this exercise, you create a Managed Metadata service application to support requirements for taxonomy, folksonomy, and centrally managed content types.

■ Create a Managed Metadata service application. Use the following specifications and guidance:

- Name: Managed Metadata Service – Enterprise.

- Database server: SP2010-WFE1.contoso.com.

- Database name: SharePoint_Service_Metadata_Enterprise.

- Application pool: A new pool named SharePoint Service Applications that uses the managed account CONTOSO\SP_ServiceApps as its identity.
- Report Syndication Import Errors: No.

You will select this option in Lesson 2.

- Add This Service Application To The Farm's Default List: Yes.

EXERCISE 3   **Start the Managed Metadata Web Service Service Instance**

In this exercise, you start the service instance of the Managed Metadata Web Service on SP2010-WFE1.

- Start the Managed Metadata Web Service on SP2010-WFE1.

EXERCISE 4   **Examine Service Application Connection Groups and Application Associations**

In this exercise, you examine the farm's default connection group and verify that web applications in the farm are associated with the connection group.

- Examine the members of the service application connection group named *default*.
- Examine the association of the Contoso Intranet web application. Observe that if you change the association to *[Custom]*, you can specify the individual service application connection(s) with which the application is associated. Do not make any changes, however. Verify that the Contoso Intranet web application is associated with the application connection group named *default*.

Lesson Summary

- A service instance is a process that is added to servers in the farm. A service instance can run on one or more servers in the farm.
- A service application is a deployed instance of a service. A service application allows web applications in the farm to share a service. Some service applications can be shared across farms.
- An application connection, also called a *proxy*, provides the communication interface between a web application and a service application.
- An application connection group, also called a *proxy group*, contains the application connections of one or more service applications. SharePoint creates an application group named *default*, and you can define additional application connection groups. A service application connection can be a part of more than one application connection group. Some service applications can support connections to more than one instance of the service application within a single application connection group.

- Allows you to associate a web application with all the application connections that belong to the group. A web application is associated with one, and only one, application connection group, or the application has a custom group of associations with the application connections of the specific services that the application requires.

- The service application framework gives you granular control over which services are deployed and how they are shared:

    a. You can deploy only the service applications that are needed to a farm.

    b. Web applications can be configured to use only the service applications that are needed, instead of all the services that have been deployed.

    c. You can deploy multiple instances of the same service in a farm and assign unique names to the resulting service applications.

    d. You can share service applications across multiple web applications within the same farm.

Lesson Review

You can use the following questions to test your knowledge of the information in Lesson 1, "Administer Service Applications." The questions are also available on the companion media in a practice test if you prefer to review them in electronic form.

> **NOTE   ANSWERS**
>
> **Answers to these questions and explanations of why each answer choice is right or wrong are located in the "Answers" section at the end of the book.**

1. You want to deploy the first instance of Excel Services in your farm. What must you do? (Choose all that apply. Each correct answer is a part of the complete solution.)

    A. Install Microsoft Office Excel 2010 on the SharePoint server.

    B. Start the Excel Calculation Services service on at least one server.

    C. Create an Excel Services Application.

    D. Create a web application called Excel Services.

2. You want to share taxonomy managed in Farm A with web applications in Farm B. What must you do? (Choose all that apply. Each correct answer is a part of the complete solution.)

    A. Publish the Managed Metadata Services application in Farm A.

    B. Start the Managed Metadata Web Service on at least one server in Farm B.

    C. Publish the Managed Metadata Web Service in Farm B.

    D. Create a connection in Farm A.

    E. Create a connection in Farm B.

    F. Start the Managed Metadata Web Service on at least one server in Farm A.

Lesson 2: Configure the Managed Metadata Service Application

The Managed Metadata Service (MMS) application plays a critical role in enterprise content management because it supports the two primary components of information architecture: taxonomy and content types. In this lesson, you learn how to use the Managed Metadata Service to manage enterprise metadata, and then you learn how to syndicate content types.

> **After this lesson, you will be able to:**
> - Describe the roles of the MMS.
> - Configure terms (taxonomy) and keywords (folksonomy).
> - Configure content type syndication.
>
> **Estimated lesson time: 60 minutes**

Metadata and Information Architecture

Metadata is, broadly speaking, one or more attributes or properties of an item. The *author* and *modified date* attributes of a document are each, and collectively, metadata. Metadata is implemented in SharePoint as columns, and columns can be one of several data types, including text, numeric, date/time, and hyperlink. The process of applying an attribute to content is often called *tagging*. For these reasons, you will hear a number of synonyms of *metadata*, including *attributes*, *properties*, *columns*, *fields*, *keywords*, and *tags*. But the term you'll hear most in relation to the metadata management in SharePoint is *term*. A term is a word or phrase that can be used as an attribute of an item or document.

Information architecture categorizes information into a coherent structure, typically by creating a hierarchical structure based on metadata that allows the information to be described, managed, located, and understood. A fundamental component of an information architecture is a *taxonomy*—a structured collection of terms that is centrally defined and tightly managed. A closely related concept is *folksonomy*, which refers to user-generated tags. Terms can be managed and controlled in a variety of ways, allowing an enterprise to expose a managed taxonomy while allowing user-generated tags (folksonomy). A taxonomy and folksonomy that are designed and managed to support the requirements of a business can allow information architecture to grow organically and to change over time.

SharePoint 2010 introduces the Managed Metadata Service, which centralizes the management of terms and provides features to support taxonomy, folksonomy, and the life cycle of terms. Each Managed Metadata Service application—a farm can have more than one—contains a *term store*, which is a hierarchical collection of centrally managed terms that you can define and then use as attributes for items and documents across your SharePoint site collections, web applications, and farms.

Within the term store are term sets and terms. A *term set* is a collection of related terms. You can associate a column of an item or document with a term set. When the user edits the properties of the item or document, the user is able to select one of the terms in the term set.

For example, Figure 5-5 shows a term set named *Departments* that contains several terms, including *Information Technology*. The term set and terms are stored and managed centrally as part of the Managed Metadata Service application.

FIGURE 5-5 A term set

After the term set has been defined, you can create a column that exposes the term set as metadata for an item or document. Figure 5-6 shows a user picking a department from the *Departments* term set to populate a column named *Contoso Department* for a document.

FIGURE 5-6 Using managed metadata

The relationship between the term set and the column that exposes the terms in the term set is the most important functional component of the Managed Metadata Service application. This relationship enables an organization to define terms centrally, and to restrict users to a set of predefined terms across site collections, web applications, and even farms. The term *managed metadata* refers to the fact that terms and term sets can be created and managed independently from the columns that expose the terms in a term set.

An organization might have tens or hundreds of thousands of terms in hundreds or thousands of terms sets. Some of those term sets might be available across the enterprise, whereas others might be restricted to a subset of web applications, and yet others might be shared with other farms or organizations. The Managed Metadata Service application wraps the functional relationship between a term set and metadata columns with features that provide management of terms, including a variety of security settings that determine who can see, use, and modify terms.

One or more term sets is contained within a *term group*. The term group is the security container. The term group's *Contributors* role is assigned to users who will manage the term sets and terms within the group. If your organization has a tightly managed information architecture in which a single individual or team manages terms, you might need only one term group. If, on the other hand, you delegate term management, you need multiple term groups. For example, you might delegate management of the *Departments* term set to human resources managers, and management of terms related to products to the managers of the marketing organization. To support this example, you create two term groups and assign appropriate managers the *Contributors* role for the term group.

A Managed Metadata Service application maintains a database that contains the term store for the service application. The term store contains terms in a hierarchical structure consisting of term groups, term sets, and terms. Web applications that connect to the service application will have the opportunity to use any of the terms in the term store. Figure 5-7 portrays the hierarchy of objects in the term store of a Managed Metadata Service application.

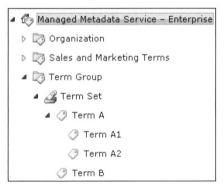

FIGURE 5-7 Term store hierarchy

Using Terms

Once you have terms—whether in managed taxonomies or user-driven folksonomies—users can begin tagging—assigning terms (metadata) to content. Tags are everywhere in SharePoint Server 2010. You can tag items, documents, pages, and sites from the SharePoint Web interface, or by using SharePoint-aware applications such as Microsoft Office 2010.

SharePoint refers to tagging with several terms, each of which are somewhat ambiguous and are therefore used differently in different contexts. *Content tagging* or *social tagging* is the addition of terms to content to describe what it is, what it contains, and what it does. This is in contrast to *expertise tagging*, which is the association of terms with a person, to describe what the person does, what projects they work on, and what skills they have.

Tags in SharePoint can be public or private. They can be assigned manually by a user, or automatically.

One of the primary reasons to tag content is to make it easier to locate by browsing or by searching. SharePoint uses tags to provide metadata-driven navigation and filtering and to produce a tag cloud control. Tags can be used as search refiners, and tags can be used by the routing rules of the Content Organizer to route content to the appropriate location.

Information Architecture and the Managed Metadata Service Application

The Managed Metadata Service offers features that are important for implementing an enterprise information architecture:

- Managed metadata separates the management of terms themselves from the columns that use the terms.

- You can delegate term management to librarian roles, represented by the term group's contributor and group manager roles.

- You can support multiple languages. After you have installed a language pack, you can add installed languages as a working language for a term set. Then you can select a term and specify the default label and other labels for each working language. Unlike the default language, you are not required to have a label for every term in a working language.

- Managed terms encourage more consistent use of terminology. Terms are available across content types, site collections, web applications, and even farms. Terms are findable thanks to the term suggestions and term picker that are inherent in the managed metadata control. Finally, terms are used more accurately because they are presented within the context of their term set and can be found using synonyms and abbreviations.

- Terms are dynamic. As soon as a keyword or term is added to the term store, it is available to all enterprise keyword or managed metadata columns in all web applications that connect to the Managed Metadata Service application. Changes to terms, including new labels, synonyms, and merged terms, cascade through the system.

- Managed metadata can be used to refine search results and provide metadata-based navigation, allowing users to locate content more efficiently.

> **MORE INFO**   **MANAGED METADATA**
>
> The following article provides additional details regarding managed metadata: "Managed metadata overview (SharePoint Server 2010)" at *http://technet.microsoft.com/en-us/library/ ee424402*.

Create and Use Terms: The Big Picture

Now that you have an understanding of the role of terms and the Managed Metadata Service application, let's take a look at managing and using terms, from beginning to end, at a very high level. We will focus on the main tasks involved with creating and using terms. Then, we will return to the structural components of the Managed Metadata Service to explore each in detail.

Create Terms in a Term Store

You can deploy a Managed Metadata Service application by using the Farm Configuration Wizard, Central Administration, or Windows PowerShell. You learned how to create a Managed Metadata Service application in Lesson 1.

A service application is a deployed instance of a SharePoint web service. The web service runs on one or more SharePoint servers. The service application typically determines the behavior of the service, and provides an administrative interface with which to configure the service. When you deploy a service application such as the Managed Metadata Service, the associated web service does not start automatically on any one server. You must manually start the service on the servers that you want running the service. You learned how to start service instances of a service in Lesson 1.

After you have created the Managed Metadata Service, you can use the Term Store Management Tool as the administrative interface with which to manage terms in the term store.

OPEN THE TERM STORE MANAGEMENT TOOL

To open the Term Store Management Tool, perform the following steps:

1. In the Central Administration Quick Launch, click Application Management.
2. In the Service Applications section, click Manage Service Applications.
3. Click the Managed Metadata Service link.

    You can click the link of either the service application or the service application connection. Both will open the same Term Store Management Tool. Alternately, you can click the row of the service application or application connection, and then click Manage.

    The Term Store Management Tool opens.

4. Confirm that the tool is focused on the metadata application that you want to administer.

    In the Available Service Applications list, select the correct metadata application.

A farm administrator must assign term set administrators. In fact, depending on the method you use to create a new Managed Metadata Service application, you might not be a term set administrator even though you created the application and even if you are a member of the Farm Administrators group. However, as a farm administrator, you can administer all service applications, and therefore you can give yourself permission to the term store.

ASSIGN TERM STORE ADMINISTRATORS

To grant permission to manage the term store, perform the following steps:

1. Open the Term Store Management Tool.
2. In the Term Store Administrators box, type the names of term set administrators, separated by semicolons.
3. Click Save.

The top-level containers within the term store are term groups. A term group, as you have learned, is a security container. The term group's *Contributors* role defines the users that can manage term sets and terms within the term group.

CREATE A TERM GROUP

To create a term group, perform the following steps:

1. Open the Term Store Management Tool.
2. Expand the term store.
3. Point at the term store and then click the drop-down arrow that appears.
4. Click New Group.
5. Type the name for the term group, and then press Enter.
6. Optionally, configure properties of the term group, and then click Save.

    For example, you can assign users to the *Contributors* role. These users will be able to access the Term Store Management Tool in Central Administration to manage term sets and terms within the term group.

Within a term group, you can create term sets.

CREATE A TERM SET

To create a term set, perform the following steps:

1. Open the Term Store Management Tool.
2. Expand the term store.
3. Point at the term group within which you want to create a term set, click the drop-down menu of the term group, and then click New Term Set.
4. Type a name for the term set, and then press Enter.
5. Optionally, configure properties of the term group, and then click Save.

    For example, you can configure a term set to be an open or closed term set. If a term set is open, you can allow users to add terms to the term set when tagging items or documents. If a term set is closed, which is the default value, only term group Contributors and Managers and term store Administrators can add terms to the term set, and they must use the Term Store Management Tool to do so.

Within a term set, you can create terms.

CREATE A TERM

To create a term, perform the following steps:

1. Open the Term Store Management Tool.
2. Expand the term store.
3. Expand the term group and the term set within which you want to create the term.

4. Point at the term set or term beneath which you want to create the term, and then click the drop-down arrow that appears.

5. Click Create Term.

6. Type the term, and then press Enter.

After you have created a term set, you can begin to use the terms in the term set as tags for items and documents. To do this, you must add a managed metadata column to a list, library, or content type.

The managed metadata column type is new to SharePoint Server 2010. When you create a managed metadata column, you specify a single term set from which the column's valid values come. Create a new content type or modify an existing content type, and add the managed metadata column to the content type.

ADD A MANAGED METADATA COLUMN TO A SITE AS A SITE COLUMN

To add a managed metadata column as a site column, perform the following steps:

1. Open the site in which you want to use a managed metadata term set.

2. Click Site Actions, and then click Site Settings.

3. In the Galleries section, click Site Columns.

4. Click Create.

5. In the Column name box, type a name for the column.

6. In the list of column types, click Managed Metadata.

7. In the Group section, select a column group or create a new column group.

8. In the Term Set Settings section, expand the term store, expand the term group that contains the term set, and then click the term set. You might need to search for a managed term set first in the Use A Managed Term Set box.

> **IMPORTANT A MANAGED METADATA COLUMN IS RELATED TO ONE TERM SET**
>
> A managed metadata column can be associated with only one term set, and all terms in the term set will be available as values for the column. If a term set does not meet your needs, you must either modify the term set or create a new term set with the terms you require.

9. Optionally, configure other settings for the column.

    For example, you can specify that the column allows multiple values. Also, if the term set is an open term set, you can configure the column to allow fill-in choices.

10. Click OK.

After you have created a site column associated with a term set, you can add that site column to a content type, or directly to a list or library.

ADD A MANAGED METADATA SITE COLUMN TO A SITE CONTENT TYPE

To add a managed metadata site column to a site content type, perform the following steps:

1. Click Site Actions, and then click Site Settings.

2. In the Galleries section, click Site Content Types.

3. Click the site content type to which you want to add managed metadata.

4. Click Add From Existing Site Columns.

5. In the Select Columns From list, select the column group that contains the managed metadata column.

6. In the Available Columns list, click the managed metadata column, then click Add.

7. Click OK.

Apply Terms to Items or Documents

After adding a managed metadata column to a list, library, or content type, users can apply terms from the term set as values for the column.

The new and edit forms of an item or document will display the *managed metadata control* for a managed metadata column, and the user interacts with this control to enter the column's value. Earlier in this chapter, Figure 5-6 shows a managed metadata control.

The managed metadata control enables the user either to type a value or to select a value by hierarchically navigating the term set that is associated with the column. If the user begins typing a value, the AJAX-driven control displays all terms in the associated term set that begin with the characters the user has typed. The name of the term set and the term's position in the hierarchy are indicated along with the term itself.

If the column's definition allows multiple values, the user can select more than one term. If the term set is an open term set and the column's configuration allows fill-in values, the user can create a new term in the term set's hierarchy.

It is important to note the following about the managed metadata control:

■ The control consists of a text box, a browse button, and a term selection page.

■ You can type a term into the text box.

■ As you type, the control provides suggestions. If the highlighted suggestion is appropriate, you can press Enter. Alternately, you can select any suggestion by using the arrow keys to select the suggestion and then pressing Enter, or by clicking the suggestion.

■ If you type a term that does not exist in the term store, your entry is displayed in red with a red, dashed underline. You cannot save the change until you correct the entry.

■ You can click the Browse For A Valid Choice button. The term selection page opens, as shown in Figure 5-8. The term selection page shows all terms in the term set. To select a term, click the term, then click Select, and then click OK.

FIGURE 5-8 The term selection page

- If the term set has an email address in the term set's *Contact* property, the term selection page displays a Send Feedback link. The link is a simple *<mailto:>* hyperlink that opens the user's email client with the *To:* address prepopulated with the term set contact's email address.

- If the term set is an open term set, the Add New Item link appears. Click the term set or term underneath which you want to add a term. Click the Add New Item link, and a new, blank term appears. Type the label for the term, and then press Enter.

Now that you have learned both the concepts and high-level functionality of the Managed Metadata Service, let's review some important points about terms:

- Terms are stored in a term set, within a term group.

- There can be multiple term sets and term groups within the term store of a Managed Metadata Service application.

- Typically, terms are tightly managed; therefore, term sets are closed by default, meaning that only term group managers and contributors can add, modify, or delete terms in the term set.

- A managed metadata column exposes all terms from only one term set.

Keywords

Often, enterprises want to allow the generation of a folksonomy, within which terms are created by users adding tags to content and people. Terms in a folksonomy are typically unmanaged—users can tag content or people with whatever words and phrases they want to apply.

Folksonomy in SharePoint Server 2010 is supported by *keywords*. Keywords are terms that are stored in a single, non-hierarchical term set called the *keyword set*. When content is tagged and a term does not exist, it is added to the keyword set.

Keywords and terms are not really very different. Both are terms that can be used to tag content. Both are stored in the term store. The primary differences are:

- Term sets are typically closed. The keyword set is typically open—users can add keywords to the keyword set when they tag content with words or phrases that do not already exist in the keyword set.

- Terms are typically highly managed. They have numerous properties, about which you will learn later in this lesson. Terms are structured within term sets and term groups, and can be reused across term sets and term groups. Keywords, on the other hand, are unmanaged—they are simply words or phrases used to tag content, and do not support a wide range of additional properties.

- Keywords are added to content in an enterprise keywords column, which is rendered as an enterprise keywords control. Terms in term sets are added to content in managed metadata columns that are rendered as managed metadata control.

Allow Users to Tag Content with Keywords

Content can have one or more managed metadata columns, each exposing terms from a different term set. When you want users to tag content freely by using enterprise keywords, you simply add the predefined enterprise keywords site column to a list, library, or content type.

ADD AN ENTERPRISE KEYWORDS COLUMN TO A SITE CONTENT TYPE

To add an enterprise keywords column to a site content type, perform the following steps:

1. Click Site Actions, and then click Site Settings.
2. In the Galleries section, click Site Content Types.
3. Click the site content type to which you want to add an enterprise keywords column.
4. Click Add From Existing Site Columns.
5. In the list of columns, click Enterprise Keywords, and then click Add.

   A message appears.
6. Click OK to add the column.
7. Click OK to close the content type.

Tag Content Using Keywords

After adding an enterprise keywords column to a list, library, or content type, users with permission to modify the content type can apply terms from the keyword set to content, and can add new terms that become part of the keyword set.

The EditForm.aspx page of an item or document will display the *managed keyword control* for enterprise keyword columns.

It is important to note the following about the control:

- The control consists of a text box, a browse button, and a term selection page.
- As you type, the control provides suggestions. If the highlighted suggestion is appropriate, you can press Enter. Alternately, you can select any suggestion by using the arrow keys to select the suggestion and then pressing Enter, or by clicking the suggestion.
- You can type a word or phrase that does not already exist as a keyword, and it will be added to the keyword set. This is the default behavior of the enterprise keywords column; however, SharePoint can be configured to prevent adding new keywords to the keyword set.

Keywords are typically created by users when they tag content with a word or phrase that is not already in the keyword set. However, if you want to add a keyword directly to the keyword set, you can do so by using the following procedure.

ADD A KEYWORD BY USING THE TERM STORE MANAGEMENT TOOL

To add a keyword by using the Term Store Management Tool, perform the following steps:

1. Open the Term Store Management Tool.
2. Expand System, and then expand Keywords.
3. Point at the Keywords, and then click the drop-down arrow that appears.
4. Click New Keyword.
5. Type the keyword, and then press Enter.

Manage Terms

Now that you have followed the high-level procedures by which terms and keywords are created and incorporated into items and documents, we can turn our attention to how to administer managed metadata, from the bottom up, starting with the terms themselves.

Term Properties

Terms are more than simply a word or phrase. They are an object with a variety of properties. The properties appear on the properties page of the term.

MODIFY A TERM

To modify the properties of a term, follow this procedure:

1. Open the Term Store Management Tool.
2. Click the term.
3. Modify one or more properties of the term.
4. Click Save.

The properties that you can modify include the following:

- **Available For Tagging**   By default, terms are available to be used for tagging. Why would you create a term and then not make it available? Terms themselves are hierarchical within a term set. That is, a term can have one or more terms as child objects. For example, you might have terms for teams or departments within the IT group. If you have a term hierarchy within a term set, you might want nodes that have child terms to be unavailable for tagging.

- **Language**   If you have a language pack installed, and the term store has the language specified as a working language, you can select each language and modify the Default Label and Other Labels.

- **Description**   Use a description to help users understand when to use the term, and to disambiguate amongst similar terms.

- **Default Label**   The default label for the term for the selected language. The default label is what is referred to as the *term*. However, as you are learning, the term is more than just the label. In fact, behind the scenes, everything is managed with unique identifiers.

- **Other Labels**   Synonyms and abbreviations for the term for the selected language. When other labels are configured for a term, users can enter any of the synonyms or abbreviations in a managed metadata control, and their entry will be changed into the default label for the term. The other labels even appear as suggestions when a user begins to type into a managed metadata control.

- **Member Of**   A term can be reused in multiple locations. The Member Of list is a list of locations in which the term exists.

- **Source**   When a term exists in more than one location, the term's properties can be edited in only one—its source. The permissions that apply to the source location affect who can modify the term's properties.

- **Sort Order**   By default, terms are sorted alphabetically within the parent term set or term. However, you can manually specify the sort order.

CONFIGURE A CUSTOM SORT ORDER FOR A TERM SET

To specify a custom sort order for a term set, perform the following steps:

1. Click the Custom Sort tab.
2. Click Use Custom Sort Order.
3. Modify the sort order.

Term Tasks

You can use the drop-down menus in the term store hierarchy of the Term Store Management Tool to perform the following actions related to terms:

- **Create Term**   Create a new term in a selected term set, or as a child of a selected term. Terms within a term set can also be arranged in a hierarchy.
- **Copy Term**   Create a new term that is a copy of an existing term. The source term's properties are copied to the new term, and then the new term is a unique object with no relationship or linkage to its original source.
- **Move Term**   Move a term to another location in the term hierarchy.
- **Delete Term**   Remove a term from the term store.
- **Deprecate Term**   Disable the term so that it no longer can be used as a valid term but stays part of the system.
- **Merge Term**   To merge terms, select a source term, then choose Merge Term, and then select a target term. The result is that the source term and its synonyms are added as synonyms of the target term.
- **Reuse Term**   A term can be placed in more than one location in the taxonomic hierarchy. To use a term in a new location—within a term set or as a child of another term—select the target location, then choose Reuse Term, and then select the source term. The source term will be added as a kind of link to the selected target location. Changes to a term's properties affect every instance of the term. The term's *Source* property defines the location in the hierarchy in which the term can be modified, and the permissions on that location determine which users can modify the term. The term's source can be changed to any of its locations by a user who currently has permission to modify the term.

Enterprise Keywords

As you learned in a previous topic, keywords are stored in a flat, non-hierarchical term set called the *keyword set*. Keywords have only one property: *Available For Tagging*. And you can perform only three actions. The first two are *New Keyword* and *Delete Keyword*, which are self-explanatory.

The third action is *Move Keyword*. This allows you to take a keyword and move it into a term set, where it becomes a managed term and acquires all of the additional properties associated with terms. This process is how an organization can organically grow a folksonomy and migrate resulting terms into a taxonomy.

Manage Term Sets

You have learned that a term set is a collection of related terms. Let's now explore the properties and management tasks of term sets.

Term Set Properties

A term set has a *Term Set Name* and a *Description*, as well as an *Available For Tagging* property. A term set also has the following properties:

- **Contact**   An email address for a contact for the term set. If an email address is entered in the *Contact* property, the managed metadata control displays a *Submit Feedback* link in the term picker. A user who wants to submit feedback or request a change to the term set can click the link and an email message is started with the *To* address populated by the value of the term set contact.

- **Submission Policy**   The submission policy determines whether users can add terms to the term set from the managed metadata control. If a submission policy is *open*, the managed metadata control displays an *Add New Item* link. So if a user wants to tag content with a term that is not already in the term set for a managed metadata column, the user can add a new term on the fly. This allows for folksonomy within the context of a managed term set. The newly added term will be available to other managed metadata columns that reference the same term set.

> **NOTE   ENABLE USERS TO ADD TERMS**
> For a user to add a new item to a term set, the term set must have an open submission policy, the managed metadata column must allow fill-in choices, and the user must have permission to change an item or document that contains the managed metadata column.

- **Owner, Stakeholders**   These two properties—as well as *Contact*—are informational only. They are used to document individuals or groups who are associated with the term set. These two properties do not assign any permissions whatsoever to the term set.

Term Set Tasks

From a design perspective, the most important point to remember is that a term set is used as the source of terms for a managed metadata column. A managed metadata column can use only one term set, and all terms that are available for tagging within that term set can be applied as values to the column.

Therefore, anytime you need a column with managed metadata, you should check to see whether a term set already exists that meets your needs exactly—that has the appropriate labels and properties—and, if not, create a new term set. Remember that terms can be reused in more than one term set.

Earlier in the lesson, you learned the procedure to create a term set. The term set's drop-down menu allows you to perform the following actions on the term set:

- **Delete Term Set**   Delete the term set and its terms.
- **Move Term Set**   Move a term set to another term group.

- **Copy Term Set**   Create a new term set with the same properties as the source term set. All terms in the source term set are added, as reused terms, to the new term set. This allows you to create variations on a term set for scenarios in which a managed metadata column needs to contain a superset, subset, or other variation of terms that are already in use in another term set.

Manage Term Groups

You have learned that a term group is a collection of one or more term sets. A term group has a *Group Name* and a *Description*. Most importantly, the term group defines two roles:

- **Contributors**   Contributors have full permission to edit terms and term set hierarchies within the term group.

- **Group Managers**   Contributor permissions plus the ability to import term sets. Group Managers can also add users to the Contributors role.

You can create a term group from the term store, by following the procedure listed earlier in this lesson. The term group's drop-down menu allows you to perform the following actions on the term group:

- **Delete Term Group**   Delete the term group.

- **Import Term Set**   Import a term set using a comma-separated values (.csv) file. A sample import file can be found in the root of the term store. In Term Store Management, in the properties pane, click the term store, and then click View A Sample Import File.

> **MORE INFO   IMPORTING TERMS**
>
> The following article provides additional details regarding the procedure for importing terms: "Managed metadata input file format (SharePoint Server 2010)" at *http://technet.microsoft.com/en-us/library/ee424396.aspx*.

Manage the Term Store

Each Managed Metadata Service application has one term store. Metadata service applications cannot share term stores. The term store properties define the following:

- **Term Store Administrators**   Term store administrators have full control over the term store. Term Store Administrators can perform all actions of group managers, can create and delete term groups, and can assign users to the group managers role. Term store administrators can also modify the default and working languages of a term set.

- **Default Language**   Each term store must have a default language specified and every term must have a label defined in the default language.

- **Working Languages**   After you have installed a language pack, you can add installed languages as a working language for a term set. Then you can select a term and specify the default label and other labels for each working language. Unlike the default language, you are not required to have a label for every term in a working language.

Terms are not added to a term store by default when you add a language pack. There is no automatic translation service. You must manually configure the labels for terms in each language that you want a term set to expose.

When a term has labels in multiple languages, the language of the site determines which labels are visible. For example, if the *Department* term set has terms defined in both French and English, an English-language team site will allow users to use English terms from the term set in a managed metadata column, and a French team site will allow users to use French terms from the term set.

To create a term store, you must create a Managed Metadata Service application. The steps for this procedure are listed earlier in this lesson. You also learned earlier in the lesson that a farm administrator must assign term store administrators.

To delete a term store, you must delete the Managed Metadata Service application.

DELETE A MANAGED METADATA SERVICE APPLICATION

To delete a Managed Metadata Service application, perform the following steps:

1. In the Central Administration Quick Launch, click Application Management.
2. In the Service Applications section, click Manage Service Applications.
3. Click the service application to delete.
4. In the ribbon, click Delete to open the Delete Service Application page.
5. Optionally, select the Delete Data Associated With The Service Applications check box.
6. Click OK.

Local Term Sets

Term sets can be global or local. A *global term set* is what we have been examining thus far—a term set that is maintained using the Term Store Management Tool and available to all web applications that connect to the Managed Metadata Service application.

A *local term* set is maintained in the term store, but it is created and managed within a site collection, rather than within the Term Store Management Tool. The resulting term set is available to all sites in the site collection, but not to other site collections. Using a local term set has advantages over legacy methods for tagging data—for example, choice and lookup fields—because the local term set is maintained by the Managed Metadata Service, so you can define synonyms and manage terms just as you would a global term set. Users who are site collection administrators have permissions to create local term sets.

To create a local term set, add a managed metadata column to a list, library, or content type. When asked to specify the term set for the column, click Customize Your Term Set.

Term Store Design

Now you have explored each component in the term store hierarchy, shown earlier in Figure 5-7. Let's review the characteristics of each component from the perspective of term store design.

- One or more *terms* are contained in a *term set*. Terms can also be created as child objects of other terms.

- A *term set* is a group of related terms, and is the scope of a managed metadata column. When you add a managed metadata column to a content type, list, or library that will use tags, you specify the term set that will be used in the column. Each managed metadata column can use terms from only one term set, and all terms in the term set are available.

- One or more *term sets* are contained in a *term group*.

- A *term group* is a security container that manages who can modify term sets and terms. You can specify, for a term group, who has permission to modify the term sets and terms in the term group.

- One or more *term groups* are contained in a *term store*.

- A *term store* is the database that contains the terms for a Managed Metadata Service application.

- The *keyword set* is a flat, non-hierarchical term set that is used to apply terms to enterprise keyword columns. The managed keyword control displayed by an enterprise keyword column exposes terms from the keyword set as well as all other term sets that are available to the web application.

Because permissions to modify terms are applied at the term group level, and because SharePoint 2010 supports multi-tenancy for the Managed Metadata Service application, most organizations will need only one term store, in one Managed Metadata Service application.

Many organizations will need only one term store, in one Managed Metadata Service application. You might need an additional term stores for several reasons. The following sections explore these reasons. Remember that you must deploy an additional Managed Metadata Service application to create an additional term store. A farm can have zero or more Managed Metadata Service applications, and web applications can connect to zero or more Managed Metadata Service applications in the farm.

Scalability Guidelines

You will require an additional Managed Metadata Service application and term store if you exceed the following performance-related scalability guidelines of a term store:

- No more than 1,000 term sets per term store
- No more than 30,000 terms per term set
- No more than 1,000,000 terms per term store

Administrative Separation

Additionally, you will require an additional term store if you want to completely isolate the administration of a term store or the terms within a term store. As you have learned, the term store's administrators have full control of the term store—they can create, delete, and manage terms and assign term group contributors and managers. If you require a term store with a unique set of administrators, you must create an additional Managed Metadata Service application.

Term Isolation

You must also create an additional Managed Metadata term store if you want to completely hide terms from a part of your organization. Let's assume that the Research and Development (R&D) department wants to maintain a separate term store to contain terms related to R&D and to products under development. They do not want terms to be visible in any way outside of the R&D web applications. This is not possible to support within a single term store.

End users can only see terms from term sets that are used by managed metadata columns. However, if you use an enterprise keywords column, end users can potentially see terms from all term sets. When a user starts typing a keyword, the AJAX-driven suggestions are derived from all term sets.

Furthermore, any user that can add a column to a list, library, or content type can see all term sets in the Managed Metadata Service application in the control that is used to select the term set for a managed metadata column.

To address the requirement for complete isolation of terms, you can deploy a second Managed Metadata Service application for the R&D term store. A farm can have more than one Managed Metadata Service application and a web application can connect to more than one Managed Metadata Service application proxy. You can connect the web applications used by the R&D department to both the R&D Managed Metadata Service and to the enterprise-wide Managed Metadata Service. Term sets from both term stores can be used to tag content within the R&D Web applications. Other web applications will connect only to the enterprise-wide Managed Metadata Service application, and will have no visibility into the R&D term store.

A separate Managed Metadata Service application creates a completely partitioned term store. Separate term stores create security isolation of data. Farm administrators give web applications visibility into appropriate term stores when they connect web applications to MMS service applications.

An alternative to separate term stores hosted by separate Managed Metadata Service applications is to implement *multi-tenancy*. Multi-tenancy is beyond the scope of this book, but in sum it allows a single database to be partitioned between consumers of a service.

Cross-Farm Scalability

Another important driver towards multiple term stores is the fact that separate Managed Metadata Service applications and term stores provide various levels of service scalability. Web applications in the farm and from other farms connect to the term store, so if, for example, you need a term set to span multiple farms, but other term stores are used only within one farm—and perhaps contain terms that you do not want visible to enterprise keyword fields in the other farm—then you should create a separate metadata application and term store to publish to both farms.

> **MORE INFO**   **DESIGNING MANAGED METADATA SERVICE APPLICATIONS**
>
> The following article provides additional details regarding the design of Managed Metadata Service applications: "Plan terms and term sets (SharePoint Server 2010)" at *http://technet.microsoft.com/en-us/library/ee519604.aspx.*

Content Type Syndication

It is common that sites in different site collections require similar content types. For example, the Legal department at Contoso creates a template for non-disclosure agreements (NDAs), and a content type for NDAs that uses the template and declares all new NDAs as records. Each of Contoso's business units have SharePoint site collections with document libraries in which NDAs will be maintained. The content type can be published, in a manner of speaking, from the Legal department to all Contoso business units.

Sharing content types across site collections, web applications, and farms was quite challenging in SharePoint 2007. The Managed Metadata Service makes it easy in SharePoint 2010.

Each Managed Metadata Service application has a Content Type Hub property that specifies the URL of a site collection from which to publish content types. All other web applications that connect to the Managed Metadata Service receive copies of the content type from the content type hub, and updates made at the hub can be propagated.

You must take several steps to publish content types. These steps are described in the following sections.

Specify the Content Type Hub

Each Managed Metadata Service application has a Content Type Hub property that specifies the URL of a site collection from which to publish content types.

CONFIGURE THE CONTENT TYPE HUB OF A MANAGED METADATA SERVICE APPLICATION

To configure the content type hub of a Managed Metadata Service application, perform the following steps:

1. In the Central Administration Quick Launch, click Application Management.
2. In the Service Applications section, click Manage Service Applications.
3. Click the row of the Managed Metadata Service application.

    Do not click the name of the service application. The name is a link that opens the Term Store Management Tool.

4. In the ribbon, click Properties.

5. In the Content Type Hub box, type the URL of the site collection from which the service application will consume content types.

6. Select the Report Syndication Import Errors From Site Collections Using This Service Application check box.

   When a web application tries to import the content types from its Managed Metadata Service applications, and encounters an error, the error is always logged to that web application. This option creates a second error associated with the content type hub site collection, so that import errors from all subscriber sites are centralized and can be viewed in one place: the hub.

7. Click OK.

Configure Web Applications to Consume Content Types

Although the Managed Metadata Service application controls whether content types are published, and from which site collection, the application connection controls whether web applications using that connection subscribe to the content types that are being published.

CONFIGURE CONTENT TYPE SUBSCRIPTION FOR A MANAGED METADATA SERVICE
APPLICATION CONNECTION

1. In the Central Administration Quick Launch, click Application Management.

2. In the Service Applications section, click Manage Service Applications.

3. Click the row of the Managed Metadata Service application connection.

   Do not click the name of the service application connection. The name is a link that opens the Term Store Management Tool.

4. In the ribbon, click Properties.

5. Select the Consumes Content Types From The Content Type Gallery check box.

6. Click OK.

Publish a Content Type

After a site collection has been designated as a content type hub, content types in the site collection can be published to the Managed Metadata Service application, and thereby made available to other web applications that use that Managed Metadata Service application.

PUBLISH A CONTENT TYPE

1. In the content type hub site collection, click Site Actions, and then click Site Settings.

2. Click Site Content Types.

3. Click the content type that you want to publish.

4. Click Manage Publishing For This Content Type.

5. Click Publish.

6. Click OK.

The same Manage Publishing For This Content Type command can be used to republish, or update, a content type, and to unpublish a content type.

Run the Timer Jobs

Two timer jobs are responsible for content type syndication: The *Content Type Hub* job finds new content types in the designated content type hub. The *Content Type Subscriber* job—there is one for each web application in the farm—imports content types from the content type hub of each Managed Metadata Service application to which the web application subscribes. If you do not want to wait for content type syndication jobs to run, you can run them manually.

MANUALLY RUN TIMER JOBS FOR CONTENT TYPE SYNDICATION

To manually run timer jobs for content type syndication, perform the following steps:

1. In Central Administration, click Monitoring.
2. Click Review Job Definitions.
3. Click Content Type Hub.
4. Click Run Now.
5. Wait a few moments for the job to complete.

    Optionally, you can click Content Type Hub to return to the job definition. Refresh the page and monitor the *Last Run Time* property. When it updates to the current time, the job is complete.

6. Click Content Type Subscriber on the row for the subscriber web application.
7. Click Run Now.
8. Wait a few moments for the job to complete.

    Optionally, you can click Content Type Subscriber to return to the job definition. Refresh the page and monitor the *Last Run Time* property. When it updates to the current time, the job is complete.

Design Content Type Syndication

Earlier in this lesson, we proposed that many organizations will require only one term store, and therefore only one Managed Metadata Service application. However, when you factor content type syndication into your design, the equation can change. Each Managed Metadata Service application can publish content types from only one content type hub. If you want content types from multiple site collections to be published, you must create additional Managed Metadata Service applications, each with a unique content type hub. Web applications in the farm can connect to each of the Managed Metadata Service applications from which they require content types.

In such a model, additional Managed Metadata Service applications are providing only content type syndication functionality. Managing unique term stores is not inherently required, so the additional term stores can remain empty.

Alternately, you can create a single site collection that serves as the content type hub for the enterprise, and each organization that wants to define content types can do so within that site collection. The site collection is, in effect, dedicated to content type publishing, and does not contain any user-facing pages, lists, or libraries.

Figure 5-9 shows a Managed Metadata Service application that provides enterprise-wide taxonomy and folksonomy, as well as content types that are managed in a centrally defined, dedicated site collection. A second Managed Metadata Service application is used to publish content types that are managed by the legal department, but contains no terms. A third Managed Metadata Service application contains terms that the R&D department wants to isolate from the rest of the organization. And a fourth Managed Metadata Service application contains terms and content types that are published to a farm that is shared with a partner organization.

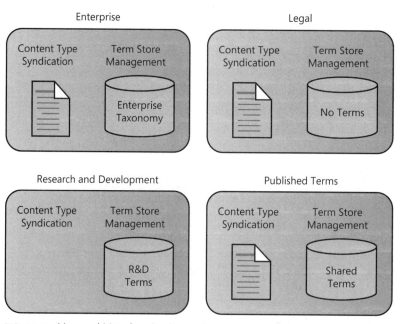

FIGURE 5-9 Managed Metadata Service applications

PRACTICE Implement the Managed Metadata Service Application

Practices are designed to guide you through important procedures. The instructions in the Training Kit are high-level instructions that will challenge you to think carefully and to apply the procedures that are covered in this lesson, and elsewhere in the Training Kit. If you need assistance, consult the detailed, step-by-step instructions in the Practice Answers on the companion media.

In this practice, you will deploy a Managed Metadata Service application.

Prepare for the Practice

Before you perform this practice, you must ensure that your lab environment has been built according to the instructions found in the Introduction to this Training Kit. You must also have performed the practice in Lesson 1 of this chapter. You must be logged off of SP2010-WFE1 before beginning the exercises.

EXERCISE 1   Delegate Permission to Administer the Term Store

When you create the Managed Metadata Service application by using the Farm Configuration Wizard, you are an administrator of the application, but you are not an administrator of the term store itself, by default. You created the Managed Metadata service application manually, but in this exercise, you verify that you have the ability to administer the term store.

1. Log on to SP2010-WFE1 as **CONTOSO\SP_Admin** with the password **Pa$$w0rd**.

2. Verify that your account, CONTOSO\SP_Admin, is assigned the Term Store Administrators role for the Managed Metadata Service – Enterprise service application.

EXERCISE 2   Add Terms to the Term Store

In this exercise, you create term groups, term sets, and terms.

1. Create a term group named *Organization*, and a term set named *Departments*. Add the following terms to the term set: *Finance, HR, IT, Engineering*, and *Sales*.

2. Create a term group named *Sales and Marketing Terms*. Create a term set named *Customers* and add the following terms to the term set: *Litware, Fabrikam, Tailspin Toys, Worldwide Importers*. Add the following terms as child terms of *Worldwide Importers*: *Europe, Americas, Asia, Africa, Australia*.

EXERCISE 3   Import Terms to the Term Store

In this exercise, you import a term set.

1. Import the following term set into the *Sales and Marketing Terms* term group: C:\70667TK\Practice Files\05_02\ContosoProducts.csv.

2. Open the CSV file with Notepad, examine the format of the file, and compare the file to the resulting imported term set.

EXERCISE 4   Add a Managed Metadata Column to a Site

In this exercise, you add the two managed metadata columns you created to a site.

1. In a new tab of Internet Explorer, browse to ***http://intranet.contoso.com/sites/ SharePoint***.

2. Add a site column. Use the following specifications and guidance:
   - Column name: Contoso Customer.
   - Column type: Managed Metadata
   - Group: Contoso Managed Metadata Columns
   - Term set: Sales And Marketing Terms

3. Add a content type. Use the following specifications and guidance:
   - Content type name: Contoso Proposal
   - Parent content type: Document
   - Group: Contoso Enterprise Wide Content Types
   - Add the *Contoso Customer* site column to the content type

EXERCISE 5   Configure Content Type Syndication

In this exercise, you configure content type syndication.

1. Configure the properties of the Managed Metadata service application to specify the content type hub ***http://intranet.contoso.com/sites/SharePoint***. Configure reporting of syndication errors to the content type hub site collection.

2. Configure the properties of the Managed Metadata service application connection to specify that web applications will subscribe to published content types.

EXERCISE 6   Publish a Content Type

In this exercise, you publish a content type, and you see the content type in another site collection.

1. Switch to the tab of Internet Explorer that shows the *http://intranet.contoso.com/sites/ SharePoint* website. Confirm that the Customer Proposal content type is published.

   The content type cannot yet be unpublished or republished because the Content Type Hub timer job has not yet run.

2. Switch to Central Administration. Run the two timer jobs required to publish content types and for the Teams Web application to receive the content types.

   Verify that the Content Type Hub job has completed before running the Content Type Subscriber job. Ensure that you run the Content Type Subscriber job from the Contoso Teams Web application. Verify that the subscriber job has completed.

3. Browse to the content type gallery of the website ***http://intranet.contoso.com/sites/ SharePoint***. Observe that in the Contoso Enterprise Wide Content Types group, the Customer Proposal appears. Open the content type and observe that you cannot alter columns, information management policies, or workflows for the content type from the subscribing site collection.

EXERCISE 7   Add a Content Type to a Library

In this exercise, you create a document library for proposals and configure the library to use the Contoso Proposal content type.

1. Create a document library named Proposals.

2. Enable management of content types. Delete the default content type, *Document*, and add the content type *Customer Proposal*.

EXERCISE 8   Use a Managed Metadata Control

In this exercise, you add a proposal to the Proposals library and specify the customer by using the Managed Metadata control.

1. Upload a proposal to the Proposals library *C:\70667TK\Practice Files\05_01\Litware Proposal*.

2. In the Contoso Customer managed metadata control, type **LIT** and then wait. Observe that *Litware* is suggested. Press Enter to accept the suggestion. Then delete the text. Click the Browse For A Valid Choice button, and then select Litware.

EXERCISE 9   Create the CHAPTER 05 Snapshot

The CHAPTER 05 snapshot captures the state of the environment at the end of Chapter 5. Perform this procedure for each of the following virtual machines: SP2010-WFE1, CONTOSO-DC.

1. Shut down the virtual machine.

2. Unmount any ISO image currently mounted to the CD/DVD drive. Use the "Unmount an ISO Image" procedure in the Lab Environment Build Guide on the companion media.

3. Create a snapshot named CHAPTER 05. Use the "Create a Snapshot" procedure in the Lab Environment Build Guide on the companion media.

Lesson Summary

- The Managed Metadata Service plays two roles that are important to support an enterprise information architecture. First, it provides a centralized store of terms for taxonomy and folksonomy. Second, it publishes content types from a content type to allow central definition of content types.

- Each Managed Metadata Service application has one term store.

- Within the term store are zero or more term groups. Users can be assigned the Contributors role for a term group, and can then modify term sets and terms within the term group.

- Term sets collect related terms. A managed metadata column exposes all terms in a term set. Terms in a term set can be arranged in a hierarchical structure.

- The Keywords set supports folksonomy. When an Enterprise Keywords column is used, a user can tag content with any term in any term set, and the user can add a new term, which will be added to the Keywords set.

- A site can define a managed metadata column that uses a local term set—a term set available only to the site.

- Content type syndication requires configuration of the Managed Metadata Service application and of the application connection. By default, all content types in the content type hub are configured as published. The Content Type Hub job publishes content types, and the Content Type Subscriber job for each web application retrieves published content types.

Lesson Review

You can use the following questions to test your knowledge of the information in Lesson 2, "Configure the Managed Metadata Service." The questions are also available on the companion media in a practice test if you prefer to review them in electronic form.

> **NOTE ANSWERS**
>
> Answers to these questions and explanations of why each answer choice is right or wrong are located in the "Answers" section at the end of the book.

1. You want to allow sales managers to add customers as terms so that content can be tagged with customer names. You do not want sales managers to change any other collections of terms. What must you create? (Choose all that apply. Each correct answer is part of the complete solution.)

   A. An additional Managed Metadata service application.

   B. A term store.

   C. A term group.

   D. A term set.

   E. A keywords set.

2. You want to share content types that have been created in the legal site collection with the human resources site collection. Both site collections are in a single web application. What must you configure? (Choose all that apply.)

   A. Nothing. Content types can be shared between site collections without additional configuration.

   B. Add the human resources site collection as the content type hub for the Managed Metadata service application.

   C. Add the legal site collection as the content type hub for the Managed Metadata service application.

   D. Create a content deployment job from the legal site collection to the human resources site collection.

   E. Configure the application connection of the Managed Metadata Service application.

Chapter Review

To further practice and reinforce the skills you learned in this chapter, you can perform the following tasks:

- Review the chapter summary.
- Review the list of key terms introduced in this chapter.
- Complete the case scenario. This scenario sets up a real-world situation involving the topics of this chapter and ask you to create a solution.
- Complete the suggested practices.
- Take a practice test.

Chapter Summary

- Many important services are provided using a model in which the service instance, running on one or more servers, is abstracted by a logical component called a *service application*. Service applications can be used by one or more web applications. When a web application requests a service from the service application, the request is fulfilled by one of the service instances.
- Each service application has an application connection, or proxy. The connection defines the communication between a web application and a service application.
- Application connections are collected in an application connection group, or proxy group, that allows a web application to connect to multiple services. A web application can connect to an application connection group or to individual service application connections.
- Some service applications can be shared across farms.
- The Managed Metadata Service is a service application that provides support for taxonomy, folksonomy, and content type syndication.

Key Terms

The following terms were introduced in this chapter. Do you know what they mean?

- Service instance
- Service application
- Service application endpoint
- Proxy or application connection
- Application connection group or proxy group

- Information architecture
- Metadata
- Taxonomy
- Folksonomy
- Content type

Case Scenario: Configure Service Applications and the Managed Metadata Service

In the following case scenario, you will apply what you've learned about subjects of this chapter. You can find answers to these questions in the "Answers" section at the end of this book.

You have a Managed Metadata Service application called *Managed Metadata Service—Enterprise*. It provides terms to all web applications in the farm. It also publishes content types stored in the *http://intranet.contoso.com/Sites/SharePoint* site collection. Contoso is opening a new office in a remote location to support a joint venture with Litware, Inc. The remote office will have a new SharePoint farm. Users from both Contoso, Ltd., and Litware, Inc., will access web applications in the farm.

1. A set of terms will be created to support taxonomy of the joint venture. Terms should be available in the new farm as well as in the SharePoint farms of Contoso and Litware. The security team has directed that the Contoso and Litware farms should not trust each other directly. In which farm should the terms for the joint venture be created? How will all three farms consume terms from the joint venture term set?

2. Three users must be able to manage terms in the joint venture term set. How do you delegate them permission to do so?

3. Contoso and Litware each want to provide definitions of content types to be used in the joint venture farm. How can this be configured?

Suggested Practices

To help you successfully master the exam objectives presented in this chapter, complete the following tasks to configure the Managed Metadata Service.

Practice 1: Configure Open Term Sets

In Lesson 2, you created the Customers term set. Configure the Customers term set as an open term set. Modify the Contoso Customer site column on the SharePoint site (*http://intranet.contoso.com/sites/SharePoint*) so that it allows fill-in choices. Republish the Customer Proposal content type. Then run the Content Type Hub and Content Type Subscriber jobs, as described in the Practice for Lesson 2.

Upload a proposal to the Proposals library (*http://teams.contoso.com/depts/Sales/Proposals*). In the *Contoso Customer* column, add a new customer, *Woodgrove Bank*. Remember that you must click the Browse button of the managed metadata control to add a new term.

In the Term Store Management tool, refresh your view and then confirm that *Woodgrove Bank* now appears in the *Customers* term set.

Practice 2: Configure Enterprise Keywords

Add an Enterprise Keywords column to the Customer Proposal content type. Republish the content type and run the Content Type Hub and Content Type Subscriber jobs. Open the properties of a proposal in the Proposals library and confirm that the Enterprise Keywords column is available. Add the following tags to the document: *SharePoint; Fabrikam*. Save the document.

In the Term Store Management tool, refresh your view and then confirm that SharePoint now appears in the Keywords set. Move the term *SharePoint* to the *Departments* keyword set as a child term of the term *IT*.

Practice 3: Publish a Service Application

If you have sufficient system resources, create a new virtual machine and install a new instance of SQL Server and SharePoint. Create an additional farm in the Contoso domain. Create a trust relationship between the two farms. Publish the Managed Metadata Service - Enterprise service application, and connect to the service application from the new farm. Add terms to the term store of the service application. Demonstrate that you can create a site collection in the new farm and use a managed metadata column from the term store.

Take a Practice Test

The practice tests on this book's companion media offer many options. For example, you can test yourself on just the lesson review content, or you can test yourself on all the 70-667 certification exam objectives. You can set up the test so that it closely simulates the experience of taking a certification exam, or you can set it up in study mode so that you can look at the correct answers and explanations after you answer each question.

> **MORE INFO** **PRACTICE TESTS**
>
> For details about all the practice test options available, see the "How to Use the Practice Tests" section in this book's Introduction.

CHAPTER 6

Configuring User Profiles and Social Networking

In the last few years, social networking has revolutionized the Internet and altered the way millions communicate. It's clear that users enjoy interacting by using these tools and find social networking to be engaging. Whether you're running an intranet portal, extranet, or public-facing website, engaging users and encouraging participation is a key objective, so SharePoint 2010 includes social networking features. The fields provided by user profiles allow you and your colleagues to find the skills and expertise you require. My Sites give users their own space to publish content. In this chapter you will learn how these features can improve productivity and how to set up and configure them in SharePoint 2010.

Exam objectives in this chapter:
- Configure service applications.
- Manage accounts and user roles.
- Manage Web Applications.
- Manage site collections.

Lessons in this chapter:

Before You Begin

To complete the lessons in this chapter, you must build your lab environment according to the instructions found in the Introduction to this Training Kit and have done the following:
- Performed the practices in Chapter 1
- Performed the practices in Chapter 5

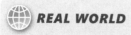

REAL WORLD

Alistair Matthews

Now that social networking is ubiquitous on the Internet, almost everyone is familiar with status updates, tagging, commenting, liking, and other features that you find on Facebook, Twitter, MySpace, and other sites. Most people also understand what a user's public profile is and how to share content such as photos and videos. This makes it much easier for you to sell SharePoint Server 2010 user profiles and My Sites to budget holders—it's social networking in your intranet. If you're using SharePoint to host an Internet site, you're providing a really easy way to enable these features, which most visitors now expect.

When you describe user profiles and My Sites in this way, you'll find you split the audience: those people who enthuse about Facebook and Twitter will be very keen to have these capabilities. They immediately understand how social networking can unite your company, improve communications, and raise productivity. The other part of the audience sees social networking as a waste of time and they will want you to disable it in SharePoint. Who's right? That really depends on the nature of your workers and their jobs. After all, a production-line worker probably cannot work more efficiently just because she has a profile on the intranet. However, for knowledge workers, social networking encourages them to share their expertise. I also contend that social networking tools help users to feel part of a team—but not all customers agree with me!

Lesson 1: Configure User Profiles

A user profile in SharePoint 2010 describes a user to his colleagues and friends and improves communication by enabling users to locate the right collaborators. Because you probably already have rich information stored about users, the User Profile Service Application can synchronize profiles with external sources of user information and ensure that user properties are up to date everywhere.

After this lesson, you will be able to:

- Describe user profiles and how they improve communication in your organization.
- List the functions of the User Profile Service Application.
- Describe the architecture of the User Profile Service Application.
- Configure a User Profile Service Application.
- Create multiple User Profile Service Applications.
- Configure user profile synchronization with Active Directory Domain Services (AD DS), Lightweight Directory Access Protocol (LDAP) directories, databases, and other sources of information about users.
- Filter user profile synchronization.
- Map user profile properties to fields in external sources of information.
- Configure the timer jobs used by a User Profile Service Application.

Estimated Lesson Time: 60 minutes

Social Networking for Business

In its first incarnation, the World Wide Web consisted of simple sites that delivered static content to browsers. As technologies such as ASP and PHP evolved, webmasters could deliver dynamic content that changed depending on dates, user preferences, and other factors. This enabled users to fill in forms and upload files, but the general direction in which information flowed was from the website to the user.

More recently, social networking websites such Facebook and Twitter have provided very little content; instead, users provide their own. This change in paradigm has engaged millions of people and altered how social lives are arranged and how photos, videos, and other materials are shared. The new approach is often referred to as Web 2.0 to differentiate the new participatory sites from traditional web publishing sites. SharePoint administrators and architects should consider Web 2.0 features because they are proven to increase user interaction and communication and to draw users to a site. They can make the difference between a static intranet that users rarely visit and consider irrelevant and a vibrant intranet community that helps users with their jobs.

Web 2.0 is not a precisely defined term, but Web 2.0 sites frequently include some or all of the following features:

- **Profiles**   Each user of a Web 2.0 page has a profile that describes him or her to others. Sometimes all details are displayed to everyone, but often only the user's friends see all the information on the user profile.

- **Friends Lists**   Many sites enable users to befriend each other. A user's friends may, for example, see the user's complete profile and be able to comment on content. They may also receive alerts when their friends make changes to the profile.

- **Tags**   In a Web 2.0 site, users can tag items to indicate that they like or dislike it, agree or disagree, or to add a comment. This enables conversations about any item and immediate participation. It also helps to rate content—if many users like an item, it is likely to be of high quality or highly relevant or insightful. Users who are flooded with information can easily determine which content is most likely to be useful. Tag clouds display links to all the items tagged.

- **Tag Clouds**   A tag cloud displays two things: the tags that exist in a particular set of content and the number of times each tag is used. More popular tags are displayed in a larger font. In this way authors and site visitors can immediately see which topics are often discussed. A tag cloud is often used on a blog to display the subjects the user often writes about, but one could also be used to illustrate subjects in a larger body of content, such as an entire website or portal. Figure 6-1 shows a tag cloud.

- **Authoring**   A Web 2.0 site allows users to contribute, for example, by writing blog entries or editing Wiki pages.

- **Content**   Photos, videos, documents, and other content can be uploaded and shared with friends.

- **Search**   A Web 2.0 site with many contributing users rapidly becomes large and requires an efficient search system to ensure users can find what they need.

Authoring   Content   Contoso   I like it
Internal   My Sites   Search
SharePoint   Social Networking   Tagging
User Profiles   Web 2.0

FIGURE 6-1 Tag cloud

An understanding of Web 2.0 is important for SharePoint administrators and architects for several reasons. First, if you want to use SharePoint 2010 to host a website with Web 2.0 functionality you must know what is possible out of the box. (In fact, SharePoint includes functionality that addresses all of the requirements and is therefore an excellent choice for your Web 2.0 site.) However, even if you use SharePoint to host an intranet or extranet, you should consider this functionality and decide whether it will improve productivity and aid users as they perform their jobs. Some analysts consider such functionality a distraction and harmful to productivity. You should therefore consider the nature of your business and the needs of users in your SharePoint planning documents.

EXAM TIP

Many companies implementing SharePoint 2010 may decide against social networking features and won't provide My Sites for their users. They may even restrict user profiles. Although your organization may have excellent business reasons for this approach, you should not bring a prejudice against My Sites, user profiles, and social tagging into the exam room because questions will arise that test your knowledge of these features. Be clear that a business case against social networking in one organization does not apply universally and is certainly no excuse for a gap in your knowledge.

Social Networking Example Scenarios

The following scenarios illustrate situations in which social networking, far from being a distraction, can improve productivity within an organization. You should consider whether any of these scenarios relate to your own company to decide whether the SharePoint 2010 social networking features are right for you.

A Method to Broaden Communication

In a traditional office environment, workers meet and socialize only with people who work close to them. For example, in a small regional office or retail space, all workers see each other every day and may have sporadic contact with certain members of staff from the local head office, such as roving sales staff and senior managers. This situation may not seem to inhibit business, but it does not help to share knowledge and broaden your skills base.

Imagine, for example, a software consultancy with offices all over Europe. A consultant in France meets and solves a technical problem with an antivirus software product. Subsequently and independently, another consultant in Spain encounters the same problem and spends a few hours solving it. This is time that could have been saved with some communication between offices.

In companies without SharePoint, an email distribution list such as "All Consultants" might have been used for such issues. After trying for a few hours the Spanish consultant might email this distribution list and receive an answer from the French consultant, assuming she was available and not at a customer site. With SharePoint, by contrast, the French consultant might have written a blog entry or published a document on her My Site on the subject. When the Spanish consultant sees the problem, he knows the solution immediately because he has already read the French information.

A Personal Location for Content

SharePoint is an excellent system for creating, managing, and editing content of all kinds. It excels at collaborative authoring and at modeling authoring procedures with workflows and approvals. However, quality control requires most companies to implement strict authoring procedures with multiple review stages and approval criteria. This approach is essential for documents intended for customers, who have high expectations.

Now consider a worker who has taken it upon herself to research thoroughly a business problem. She has her manager's approval because the problem applies broadly. She wants to publish her research internally so the whole company can benefit and improve working practices. The problem is that the company has no intranet location for such publishing—all the SharePoint document authoring sites relate to specific projects and have complex and expensive review procedures.

The worker's My Site is an excellent location for this kind of internal publishing. My Sites enable a less formal and more flexible kind of publishing that benefits the entire company.

A Method to Keep in the Loop

Companies rightly value participation and a sense of team membership in their work force. They spend a lot of money to foster an atmosphere of cooperation and common ownership. For example, team bonding exercises and office away days are popular although they are expensive. Without good communication within your company, workers can, by contrast, feel isolated and alone, particularly if they work at small offices or from home. Although they are experts in their own projects, they may have little or no idea what the rest of the company is doing.

On SharePoint My Sites, you can include activity streams. These show the recent actions of all the user's colleagues. For example, all the following actions are shown in an activity stream:

- A colleague creates, edits, or deletes a document.
- A colleague writes a new blog entry or edits a Wiki page.
- A colleague writes comments, tags, or rates another user's content.
- A colleague makes changes to his or her own My Site.

Activity streams therefore create a snapshot of the company's activities, or at least those of each user's colleagues. Because the user configures his own list of colleagues, this activity stream can encompass a large cross section of the organization. You can use it to generate a "buzz" around hot topics and projects, engage workers in projects that only indirectly affect them, and encourage knowledge sharing.

User Profiles and the User Profile Service Application

Like the profiles with which you may be familiar from Internet social networking sites, user profiles in SharePoint 2010 display information about each user. For example, profiles may include contact information, site memberships, and expertise. Many organizations have repositories of information about their workforce already in place, so SharePoint 2010 makes it easy to keep those repositories synchronized.

What Is a User Profile?

A SharePoint 2010 farm is a rich authoring environment in which users constantly write, edit, read, comment on, and otherwise interact with documents, web pages, pictures, videos, and all types of content. SharePoint is designed to scale up to handle content for the largest global companies with hundreds of thousands of users. In such a situation it's easy for a single user to become an anonymous entity with two results:

- Each user feels like a tiny cog in the machine with a minimal contribution. She cannot identify the changes she has added and is not encouraged to help.

- Each user can find little information about his colleagues and co-workers. He may become friendly with those in his own office but never make contact with remote users who may be able to help him.

A user profile addresses these problems. It describes a user and her skills and expertise and it differentiates a user from her colleagues. The user's profile is that user's identity within the SharePoint system. When a user creates content, such as a blog entry, it is linked to her profile. This means that the user is clearly identified as the author and she can clearly define her own contribution. Other users can see who has authored, edited, or commented on content and find out more details, such as which team that user works in. User profiles are therefore a key component that encourages productivity in your community of users.

User profiles are also essential to enable users to locate each other with People Search. Suppose you're working on a project and require a particular skill that you don't have. Traditionally, you would ask around the office but you may have difficulty locating the right person for the job. SharePoint user profiles include skills and expertise and, crucially, the SharePoint crawler indexes some user profile properties. This means you can search for and locate someone with the skill you need no matter what his location in the enterprise. Once again, you can see how user profiles increase communication within your organization and optimize productivity. In SharePoint 2010, People Search also works on a phonetic basis, which can be very useful if, for example, you search for a user but misspell his name. Figure 6-2 illustrates People Search results.

User profiles also underpin SharePoint audiences, which enable you to target content toward specific groups of users. For example, you can create an audience called "Board Members" that contains only directors of the company. Site administrators can then target a Web Part to this audience. For example, they can include an Excel spreadsheet in a dashboard web page, but target it to the "Board Members" audience. Non-directors would not see this Web Part. The membership of an audience can be defined in two ways:

- The membership of Windows security groups and distribution lists. For example, if you have a security group called "Board Members" in the AD DS, the user profile service can import the same membership into a SharePoint audience.

- Properties in user profiles. For example, you could define an audience called "Board Members." Users are automatically a member of this audience if they have the value *Director* in their *SPS-JobTitle* user profile property.

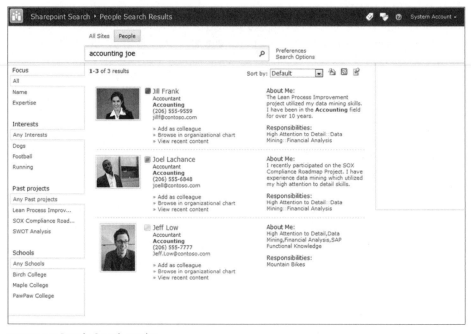

FIGURE 6-2 People Search results

NOTE **USER PROFILES AND MY SITES**

User Profiles and My Sites are closely related, but you can use user profiles without a My Site to go with each one. A My Site is a personal space in which a user can create her own content and publish it to colleagues without completing the approval procedures that may be required in production sites such as project sites. For example, a My Site is a good place for a user to maintain a blog.

This is rich and valuable functionality but you may decide it is not appropriate for your SharePoint system—perhaps because of storage space restrictions—or you may be directed by management to disable it. In such cases user profiles on their own are sufficient to maintain a user's unique identity and users can edit some properties.

Planning User Profile Properties

SharePoint includes a default set of properties in user profiles but you can add or remove properties to match your organization's requirements. When you plan user profiles, your first task is to fix the properties required. You can view the default list of user profile properties here: *http://technet.microsoft.com/en-us/library/ee721054.aspx.*

The properties available can be categorized as follows:

- **General Information**   These include phone numbers, address details, description fields such as "About Me," graphics field such as "Picture URL," and so on.
- **Memberships**   These include SharePoint site memberships and SharePoint group memberships. Other people can understand the role a user takes in the organization from these memberships.
- **Colleagues**   These include managers, peers, and direct reports. From these properties you can understand a user's position in the organization's hierarchy.
- **System properties**   These include *UserProfile_Guid*, *SID*, *SPS-ResouceSID*, and other properties that are essential for SharePoint and AD DS functionality but rarely displayed to the user. You should not remove these from user profiles.

When planning user profiles, you should consider the picture you wish to paint of each user to herself and her colleagues. Start with the system properties that are essential and add to these properties, those that are critical to your business. For example, if you run a consultancy it is important to store the qualifications for each consultant so that you can book the right person for each job. Full contact information is usually critical and you may need to add properties such as an instant messaging address to the default set. Ensure that this list of properties supports all the People Searches you expect from users.

When you have a critical set of properties, add to this list properties that enrich the user profile, such as the *PictureURL*, which is one of the default set. It doesn't enable People Search or underpin SharePoint functionality, but it adds a vital personal touch to a user's SharePoint experience. When a user has a *PictureURL* set, his own photograph appears next to all of his comments, documents, and other content. Some users prefer to use a cartoon version of themselves, which can sometimes add humor. Other properties, such as interests, hobbies, or birthdays can also be added to this list. These details may seem trivial but you can use them to engage users and increase participation.

In most SharePoint 2010 farms, you synchronize user profiles with some external source of information about users. This source is often AD DS, but it may also be a database or a line-of-business application, such as SAP. Therefore, to the list of user profile properties, you must add any external properties that do not match.

> **NOTE** **MAPPING USER PROFILE PROPERTIES**
>
> A property in a user profile may match that in an external source but have a different name. For example, there is a default user profile field called CellPhone. In a human resources database you may have a field called Mobile. These are clearly functionally identical and you should avoid duplication. You can do this by adding a property mapping. This will ensure that changes to the *CellPhone* property synchronize with the Mobile database field. It is not necessary to add a *Mobile* property to user profiles.

Each property in a user profile may or may not be indexed by the SharePoint crawler. This is an important consideration in your planning to ensure the People Search works as you expect it to. Therefore, when you have a complete list of properties for user profiles, decide whether to index each and document your decision.

User Profile Subtypes

Because your organization has different user roles, you shouldn't expect all users to have the same set of properties in their user profiles. For example, permanent employees may need employee numbers and tax information to be stored. Contractors and short-term staff may not need such information.

In SharePoint 2010 you can create multiple user profile subtypes to optimize the storage of user information and cater to users with very different needs. When multiple subtypes exist, you can select, for each profile property, which subtypes include that property, as shown in Figure 6-3.

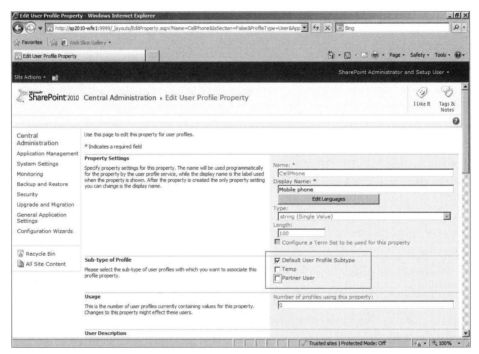

FIGURE 6-3 Associating the *CellPhone* property with a user profile subtype

User Profile Policies

A user profile can contain a large range of properties, some of which may be of a sensitive nature. For example, you may wish to include each user's home phone number in user profiles, but not publish this to the entire company. Instead, only each user's manager should see the home phone number. In this way you can ensure that users are contactable but prevent intrusions into their privacy.

For each user profile property you can set any of the available policy settings and a default visibility. The five policy settings are:

- **Enabled**   This property can be completed in a user profile. Who can read it depends on the visibility setting.

- **Required**   This property must contain data either provided by the user or taken from a synchronized source.

- **Optional**   This property may or may not contain data.

- **Disabled**   Only administrators of the User Profile service application can see this property. It cannot be displayed to the user or the user's colleagues.

- **User Override**   Users can override the default visibility.

The default visibility for each profile property must be one of the following:

- **Everyone**   Every user who can access a site collection connected to the current user profile service application can view this property for all users.

- **My Colleagues**   Only users listed in a user's My Colleagues list can view this property. This list can be configured by the user.

- **My Team**   Only users listed in the user's immediate team can view this property. The My Team list is a subset of the My Colleagues list.

- **My Manager**   Only the user's immediate manager can see the contents of the property.

- **Only Me**   This property is only visible to the user and no one else.

In a small company in which all users know each other, you may decide to make all user profile properties visible to everyone. However, as organizations grow and users no longer work with the whole company, privacy becomes more important and the user profile policy must be more carefully planned and more restrictive. As you restrict access to user profile properties, ensure that users can still locate each other and view business-critical information. Also, ensure that properties used to define audiences are required—otherwise, users may not see content targeted at them.

The Business Case for User Profiles

Earlier in the chapter, you saw how the social networking features of SharePoint Server 2010 can increase productivity. The following sections focus exclusively on user profiles and illustrate how they underpin communications in SharePoint user communities.

Publishing Relationships

When you publish the company structure to the entire organization you clearly define each user's role and responsibilities. In SharePoint user profiles the following relationships are included by default:

- **Manager**   Each user has only one manager to whom he or she reports.

- **Peers**   These users all report to the same manager.

- **Colleagues**   This list is configured by the user and includes everyone the user works with.
- **Team Members**   This list is also configurable but smaller than Colleagues.

In addition to organizational relationships, user profiles can include site memberships and distribution list memberships.

Locating Users

User profiles are required for the SharePoint People Search feature to work. This enables you to locate a colleague by searching on user profile properties such as the following:

- **User name, full name, or last name**   If you have met a colleague but remember nothing more than her name, you can locate all the user profile information by searching in an Enterprise Search Center site. In SharePoint Server 2010, this search also works on a phonetic basis, which helps if you misspell the name.
- **Skills and expertise**   If you have a problem to solve, you can locate someone with the right skills quickly and easily.
- **Colleagues or team members**   Easily identify the coworkers of a user you know. This may be helpful when a user is on vacation.

The user profile properties indexed by the SharePoint crawler are configurable, so a wide range of other searches can be supported. Enabling users to locate each other in this way, instead of relying on word of mouth, removes frequent barriers to productivity.

Supporting Audiences

Audiences in SharePoint 2010 enable you to target content. Your SharePoint farm will certainly contain a huge quantity of content—it is inevitable that each user will only be interested in a portion of it. You can create an audience based on the membership of AD DS security groups or distribution lists, which works well when these closely reflect user roles. However, you can also define audiences based on the values in user profile properties. For example, you could create:

- An audience that includes all users who have "Databases" in their skill set.
- An audience that includes all users whose manager is Kevin McDowell.
- An audience that includes all the members of the "Windows Deployment Project" site.

Having created an audience, you can target items in lists, document libraries, and asset libraries to that audience. To do this, a site administrator must enable audience targeting on the list. When a user creates a new item or uploads a new document, he can select the target audience by using a people picker control. Users only see the documents targeted at audiences of which they are members. You can also target Web Parts at one or more audiences. This is an excellent way to create dashboards with relevant, targeted information.

The Role of the User Profile Service Application

The User Profile service application underpins user profiles and supports related functionality. This service application is required for all of the following features of SharePoint 2010:

- **User Profiles** All the properties that identify and describe a user within the SharePoint farm, its site collections, and subsites.

- **Organization Profiles** In SharePoint 2010, you can also support profiles that describe one or more organizations. The organization's teams and divisions, for example, can be described in a profile.

- **Profile Synchronization** The User Profile service application is responsible for exchanging user information with AD DS, databases, line-of-business applications, and other external sources of user information.

- **Audiences** The User Profile service application compiles audience membership based on security group membership, distribution group membership, or the values of user profile properties.

- **My Sites** Within the User Profile service application configuration, you can configure the location of the My Site host site collection and the path to personal sites.

- **Social Tags and Notes** Functional user profiles are required for users to add tags and notes to content—for example, to add comments to a blog entry. The Managed Metadata service application is also necessary for this functionality.

As you can see, at least one user profile service application is necessary for a large range of the most interactive SharePoint functionality. You should consider it essential in the vast majority of farms. It is easy to deploy the user profile service application—in most cases, you configure this service application when you run the Initial Farm Configuration Wizard. You should do this the first time you open the Central Administration site, immediately after installing SharePoint. For more details, see Chapter 1, "Creating a SharePoint 2010 Intranet."

As for the other service applications, Farm Administrators can delegate the administration of the User Profile service application to a dedicated security group. This approach conforms with the principal of least privilege and ensures that any security breaches have minimal impact. However, it is likely that in most organizations an administrator's responsibilities will include other service applications and perhaps other parts of the SharePoint farm.

The User Profile service application is available in SharePoint Server 2010 Standard and Enterprise editions but is not a part of SharePoint Foundation 2010.

Prerequisites for a Functional User Profile Service Application

Before you can run the User Profile service application successfully, the following must be in place:

- Managed Metadata service application

  The Managed Metadata service application stores and manages terms and keywords. Users can choose to add these to documents, items, and assets whenever a Managed

Metadata column is included in the content type. Terms are hierarchical and created by administrators; keywords are stored with no hierarchy and created by users themselves. The Managed Metadata service also makes it possible to share content types in site collections and web applications.

- A database server

  The User Profile service application uses three databases to store user profiles, tags and notes, and configuration data. More details of these databases are described in the following sections. You must have a functional database server to run this service application, but you can use the same database server that hosts content databases and other SharePoint databases, as long as it has sufficient hardware resources to cope with the relatively light load involved.

- Timer jobs in SharePoint

  The User Profile service application uses SharePoint timer jobs for many tasks. More details of these jobs are described in the following sections. If there is a problem with timer jobs, the User Profile service application cannot function.

- External source of information for user profiles

  Strictly speaking, it is not necessary to import user profile data into SharePoint from an external source—users can add data manually. However, because almost all organizations have user information already stored—in AD DS, a human resources database, a line-of-business application, or some other store—and because it is critical to keep all these stores up to date, you should almost always use user profile synchronization.

- A server farm installation

  If, during installation, you chose to install SharePoint 2010 in a standalone configuration, user profile synchronization is not available. Again, remember that users can manually add their own data but, for the reasons given in the previous point, most administrators require synchronization with their existing stores.

- Microsoft Forefront Identity Manager

  SharePoint Server 2010 uses components of Forefront Identity Manager to synchronize user profiles. These components are installed automatically when you install SharePoint, although they are not visible in All Programs unless you install Forefront as well. In the list of Windows Services you can see Forefront Identity Manager Service and Forefront Identity Manager Synchronization Service. These services may be disabled until you configure profile synchronization.

- Local administration rights for the SharePoint farm account

  To start the User Profile Synchronization Service, the SharePoint farm account must be a member of the local Administrators group on the server where the service runs.

- Synchronization rights in the AD DS domain for the user synchronization account

You can choose any account for the User Profile service application to run under. It is also a good idea to use a dedicated account for this purpose. The account you use must have permission to replicate changes in each AD DS domain that you want to import from. You will assign these rights in Exercise 3 of the Practice.

Extra User Profile Service Applications

A single User Profile service application can be used throughout your SharePoint system to publish user profiles and synchronize them with one or more other stores. Most companies use this configuration because they want user profiles to be visible universally. Remember that you can restrict access to sensitive information by configuring user profile policies if you have security concerns.

However, like other service applications, you can also partition user profiles into two or more User Profile service applications within a single farm. You might consider this architecture in the following two scenarios:

- Your business model requires you to keep sections of your company separate and prevent users in one section from obtaining information about users in another. Although this is rare, security protocols and legislation occasionally require it.

- You host SharePoint services for two or more tenant companies. In such a configuration, it is vital to separate each tenant organization.

Later in this chapter, you will see the configuration steps required to partition User Profile service applications.

The Architecture of the User Profile Service Application

The User Profile service application works in a similar way to the other service applications. For example, you can share a single User Profile service application between all the site collections in a SharePoint farm and even connect to it from multiple farms. In the following sections you will learn about timer jobs and databases that are unique to the User Profile service application.

User Profile Service Application Timer Jobs

The User Profile service application creates and executes several timer jobs to complete tasks such as user profile synchronization and maintaining social tags and notes. You can examine these in the Central Administration site. To review the list of timer jobs, perform the following steps:

1. Log on as a Farm Administrator.
2. Start SharePoint 2010 Central Administration.
3. In the Central Administration Quick Launch, click Monitoring.
4. In the Timer Jobs section, click Review Job Definitions.

   All the timer jobs associated with the User Profile service application have names that begin with User Profile Service.

Table 6-1 contains the complete list of user profile timer jobs.

TABLE 6-1 User Profile Service Application Timer Jobs

TIMER JOB	DESCRIPTION	SCHEDULE
User Profile Service - Activity Feed Cleanup Job	Users can add activity feeds to their My Site to show changes made by their colleagues. This job removes items that are older than 14 days.	Daily
User Profile Service - Activity Feed Job	This job compiles the activity feeds.	Hourly
User Profile Service - Audience Compilation Job	This timer job compiles audiences that are based on user profile properties.	Weekly
User Profile Service - My Site Suggestions Email Job	This job sends emails to users who do not update their My Site very often. These emails include colleague and keyword suggestions	Monthly
User Profile Service - Social Data Maintenance Job	This job aggregates social tags and ratings.	Hourly
User Profile Service - User Profile Change Cleanup Job	This job cleans changes that are older than 14 days from the user profile change log. It also migrates user rights from one user to another, such as when a user account is renamed.	Daily
User Profile Service - User Profile Change Job	This job processes changes to existing user profiles.	Hourly
User Profile Service - User Profile Incremental Import Job	This timer job imports user profiles from external sources such as the AD DS or a database. This job only imports profiles that have been added since the last import.	1 minute
User Profile Service - User Profile Language Synchronization Job	This timer job responds when new language packs are installed. It localizes strings related to the User Profile service application.	1 minute
User Profile Service Proxy - Social Rating Synchronization Job	This timer job ensures that social rating tags are kept synchronized between the social tagging database and content databases.	Hourly
User Profile to SharePoint Full Synchronization	This timer job imports user profiles from external sources such as the AD DS or a database. This job imports all profiles whether they have been recently added or not.	Hourly
User Profile to SharePoint Quick Synchronization	This timer job synchronizes data from user profiles to a site when users are added as members of that site.	5 minutes

In general, it is not recommended to alter the schedule and settings for these timer jobs. However, you may need to reconfigure in the following circumstances:

- If you want to use activity feeds on My Sites. The User Profile Service - Activity Feed Job is disabled by default. For more information about activity feeds, see Lesson 2.

- If you want to increase or decrease a frequency. For example, you may decide to send suggestion emails more often than once a month.

- If you must troubleshoot the User Profile service application.

User Profile Service Application Databases

When you deploy a User Profile service application, SharePoint creates three databases to support it:

- **The Profile Database**   This stores user profiles and all the properties you have configured and synchronize with external stores.
- **The Synchronization Database**   This stores the configuration details for external sources of information, their location, and property mappings.
- **The Social Tagging Database**   This stores tags and notes created by users against SharePoint and external content. Each tag or note is associated with a profile ID.

When you create the User Profile service application you must configure the database server and database name for all three databases. For each you can also name a failover database server, if one is available on your network. It is possible to separate each of these databases onto a dedicated database server; however, in most cases these databases will be placed on the same server, which will also host other SharePoint databases such as the Managed Metadata term store database. This is because:

- It is unlikely that the load placed on the database server by the three User Profile service application databases will be high enough to justify dedicated hardware.

- All three databases must be available for full user profile functionality. Therefore, you do not decrease the impact of database failures much by separating them onto separate servers.

Configuring the User Profile Service Application

Now that you understand the User Profile service application, you can configure and implement it. Before you perform these procedures in a production environment, you must carefully investigate your requirements and completed detailed planning documents. Have these documents in hand as you step through each procedure.

Configuring the User Profile Service Application

For simple configurations, you can use the Initial Farm Configuration Wizard to set up the User Profile Service Application. You should do this immediately after you have installed SharePoint 2010 and run the SharePoint 2010 Product Configuration Wizard.

RUN THE INITIAL FARM CONFIGURATION WIZARD

1. In the Central Administration Quick Launch, click Configuration Wizards.

2. Under Farm Configuration, click Launch The Farm Configuration Wizard.

3. Click Start The Wizard.

4. Under Service Account, configure the SharePoint service application account as you have planned.

5. Under Services, ensure that the User Profile Service Application check box is selected, along with the other service applications you want to configure.

6. Click Next.

    Your service applications are created and configured.

7. On the next page, fill in the details if you wish to configure a site collection and then click OK. Otherwise, click Skip.

8. Click Finish.

Manually Configuring a User Profile Service Application

To create a My Site configuration that is secure, or to deploy the User Profile service application without My Sites, you must configure the User Profile service application manually. It is recommended that you always use this method and never rely on the Initial Farm Configuration Wizard described in the previous section.

NOTE **THE MANAGED METADATA SERVICE APPLICATION**

In the following procedures, it is assumed that the Managed Metadata service application has been set up already. For more information on this service application, see Chapter 5, "Service Applications and the Managed Metadata Service."

CREATE THE USER PROFILE SERVICE APPLICATION IN CENTRAL ADMINISTRATION

> **IMPORTANT** **THE SHAREPOINT FARM ACCOUNT AND LOCAL ADMINISTRATIVE PRIVILEGES**
>
> For the following procedures to work, the SharePoint Farm Account must be a member of the local Administrators group on the server where the User Profile Synchronization Service runs.

To create the user profile service application in Central Administration, complete the following steps:

1. In the Central Administration Quick Launch, click Application Management.
2. Under Service Applications, click Manage Service Applications.
3. Click New, and then click User Profile Service Application.
4. In the Create New User Profile Service Application dialog box, in the Name box, type a suitable name, such as **Contoso User Profile Service Application**.
5. In the Application Pool section, configure the properties that you planned.
6. In the Profile Database section, configure server, database name, authentication, and failover server properties for the profile database.
7. In the Synchronization Database section, configure the server, database name, authentication, and failover server properties for the synchronization database.
8. In the Social Tagging Database section, configure server, database name, authentication, and failover server properties for the Social database.
9. In the Profile Synchronization Instance section, select the server that will run the Profile Synchronization service.

> **NOTE** **MY SITE PROPERTIES**
>
> My Site Properties in the User Profile service application, such as the personal site path, have not been covered here. You will see how to configure those properties in Lesson 2.

10. In the Default Proxy Group section, if this is the first User Profile service application you have created, select Yes. For subsequent User Profile service applications, select No.
11. Click Create, and when prompted click OK.

CREATE THE USER PROFILE SERVICE APPLICATION IN WINDOWS POWERSHELL

The following example shows the use of the *New-SPProfileServiceApplication* cmdlet to create a new User Profile service application:

```
New-SPProfileServiceApplication -Name <ServiceName> -ApplicationPool <AppPool>
-ProfileDBServer <DBServer>
-ProfileDBName <ProfileDBName> -ProfileDBFailoverServer <FailoverDBServer>
-SocialDBServer <DBServer>
```

```
-SocialDBName <SocialDBName> -SocialDBFailoverServer <FailoverDBServer>
-ProfileSyncDBServer <DBServer>
-ProfileSyncDBName <SyncDBName> -ProfileSyncDBFailoverServer <FailoverDBServer>
-PartitionMode
```

Where:

- *<ServiceName>* is the name you have chosen for your service application, such as Contoso User Profile Service Application.

- *<AppPool>* is the name of, GUID of, or reference to an existing application pool.

- *<DBServer>* is the name of a database server where the databases will be created.

> **NOTE   SEPARATING DATABASES**
>
> You can give the same *<DBServer>* value for all three databases if you want to host them on the same database server, or you can give different values if you want to separate them onto dedicated database servers.

- *<FailoverDBServer>* is the name of the failover server that provides fault tolerance for the databases.

- *<ProfileDBName>* is the name of the profile database to create.

- *<SocialDBName>* is the name of the social tagging database to create.

- *<SyncDBName>* is the name of the synchronization configuration database to create.

> **NOTE   THE *–PARTITIONMODE* SWITCH**
>
> You should only use the *–PartitionMode* switch when you want to partition user profiles into more than one User Profile service application—for example, to support multiple tenants.

When you use Windows PowerShell to create a User Profile service application, you must manually create the service application proxy to go with it by using the *New-SPProfileServiceApplicationProxy* cmdlet:

```
New-SPProfileServiceApplicationProxy -Name <ServiceProxyName> -ServiceApplication
<UserProfileServiceApp>
-DefaultProxyGroup
```

Where:

- *<ServiceProxyName>* is the name you have chosen for your service application proxy, such as Contoso User Profile Service Application Proxy.

- *<UserProfileServiceApp>* is the name of, GUID of, or reference to an existing User Profile service application. You can usually provide a reference by using a pipe from the previous cmdlet.

START THE USER PROFILE SERVICE AND THE USER PROFILE SYNCHRONIZATION SERVICE

To start the user profile services by using the Central Administration site, complete the following steps:

1. In the Central Administration Quick Launch, click System Settings.
2. Under Servers, click Manage Services On Server.
3. Ensure that the server where the user profile services should run is selected in the Server box.
4. Locate the User Profile Service and next to it, click Start.
5. Locate the User Profile Synchronization Service and next to it, click Start.

6. In the Select User Profile Application drop-down list, select the User Profile Service Application you just created.
7. Enter and confirm the password for the Service Account.
8. Click OK.
9. Start Command Prompt.
10. Type **iisreset** and then press Enter.

Synchronizing User Profiles with External Sources

In some situations, such as a new web-facing Internet site, you may have no existing information about your users. Site visitors must register and fill in new details about themselves in their user profiles. In such cases, the User Profile service application is used with synchronization.

However, if you already store information about users, you should import that data into SharePoint and ensure that it is kept up to date both within SharePoint and its original location. To enable this, the User Profile service application can synchronize user profiles with external stores. Almost all organizations already store user information before they deploy SharePoint Server 2010, so this configuration is prevalent.

You can synchronize user profiles with the following stores:

- **AD DS**   This is the primary source of information about users for many companies. AD DS on Windows Server 2003 SP2 and later is supported.

- **LDAP Directories**   Third-party directory services, such as SunOne and IBM Tivoli, can also be used as a source, if they are LDAP-compliant.

- **Databases and Line-of-Business Applications**   A human resources application, for example, may store user information in a database such as Microsoft SQL Server. Line-of-business applications such as SAP or Siebel contain rich data about users. To synchronize such sources with SharePoint user profiles, you can use a Business Connectivity Services (BCS) connection.

> **NOTE   BUSINESS CONNECTIVITY SERVICES**
> BCS is a highly functional feature of SharePoint Server 2010 that enables you to import and synchronize external data into SharePoint lists. For more information about BCS, including how to create connections, see Chapter 8, "Implementing Enterprise Service Applications."

Configuring Synchronization

The precise steps you take to configure synchronization depend on the type of source you will synchronize with. For example, when you synchronize with an AD DS forest, you can automatically discover a domain controller or manually specify one. However, the process is similar for all sources, so a general description of the steps has been outlined in this section.

If you want to synchronize user profiles with a database or line-of-business application, you must first configure a BCS connection. It is also a good idea to test the connection by creating an external content type and external list that displays the user information. When you are satisfied that the connection works well, the external content type and list can be deleted. When you create the connection in the follow procedure, select Business Data Connectivity in the Type drop-down list.

CONNECT TO A STORE OF USER INFORMATION

1. In the Central Administration Quick Launch, click Application Management.
2. Under Service Applications, click Manage Service Applications.
3. Click the User Profile Service you want to synchronize.
4. Under Synchronization, click Configure Synchronization Connections.
5. Click Create New Connection.

6. In the Name box, type an appropriate name for the connection, such as **Connection to Contoso AD DS Forest**.

7. In the Type box, select Active Directory, or whichever type is appropriate for your remote store.

8. If you are connecting to AD DS, in the Forest Name text box, type the name of your AD DS forest.

9. Enter the credentials of an account that has the directory sync right in AD DS.

10. Click Populate Containers.

11. Select all the containers that include SharePoint users that you want to synchronize.

12. Click OK.

Using Connection Filters

When you connect to AD DS or an LDAP directory, you can select the containers from which to import users. Therefore, it is not necessary to import all users, and you can omit containers without SharePoint users, such as the Computers container in AD DS.

Sometimes, however, single containers in the source directory contain a mix of accounts you wish to import and those you wish to exclude. You can define a flexible set of filters on each connection. When an account matches the filter, the User Profile service application does not import it into a user profile or keep it synchronized.

DEFINE A FILTER

Define a filter by completed the following steps:

1. In the Central Administration Quick Launch, click Application Management.

2. Under Service Applications, click Manage Service Applications.

3. Click the User Profile Service you want to filter.

4. Under Synchronization, click Configure Synchronization Connections.

5. Point to the connection you want to filter and click Edit Connection Filters in the drop-down list.

6. In the Attribute drop-down list, select an attribute in the external source on which to base your filter, such as Division.

7. Select an operator—for example, Equals.

8. In the Filter text box, type a value—for example, **IT**.

9. Click Add.

   The new filter appears at the top of the page. You can repeat steps 6 through 9 to add other filters and choose whether they should all match (AND) or only one needs to match (OR) to exclude an account. For AD DS, you can specify filters for both user accounts and groups.

10. Click OK.

Mapping User Profile Properties

Frequently a property in a user profile is functionally identical to one in an external source but has a different name. For example, the *CellPhone* property that appears in the default list of user profile properties is clearly the same as the Mobile field in AD DS. Regardless of the different names, these properties should be synchronized. You can configure a mapping between such properties in the synchronization configuration so that the User Profile service application propagates any changes.

CONFIGURE A MAPPING

To configure a mapping, complete the following steps:

1. In the Central Administration Quick Launch, click Application Management.
2. Under Service Applications, click Manage Service Applications.
3. Click the User Profile service application you wish to configure.
4. Under People, click Manage User Properties.
5. Scroll down the list of properties to locate the Contact Information category.
6. Under Contact Information locate the property you wish to map, such as the Mobile Phone property.
7. Point to the property name and click Edit in the drop-down list.

> **NOTE NAME AND DISPLAY NAME**
>
> Notice that the property name shown to users is not always the same as the name SharePoint uses to store a property. For example, the *CellPhone* property has a display name of Mobile Phone.

8. Scroll down to locate the Property Mapping for Synchronization section. By default no mappings are present.
9. Under Add New Mapping, select the Source Data Connection that contains a functionally identical property.
10. In the Attribute drop-down list, select the attribute in the source store that you want to map to. For example, in AD DS, the *CellPhone* property should map to the Mobile field.
11. Click Add.
12. Scroll to the bottom of the page and click OK.

Running Synchronizations

When you have completed your synchronization configuration, you should ensure that synchronization runs. You can manually start synchronization, but under ordinary circumstances, a timer job ensures that user profiles are synchronized automatically on a configurable schedule.

A manual or scheduled synchronization can be one of two types:

- **Full**   All user profiles are synchronized, whether or not they have changed. Use this type with care because it can involve heavy network traffic and server load.
- **Incremental**   Only profile changes are synchronized. Network traffic and server load is minimized.

Incremental synchronizations are sufficient to propagate changes in most circumstances, but an occasional full synchronization may be required. For the first synchronization, both types are functionally equivalent and all profiles are propagated.

INITIATING A SYNCHRONIZATION MANUALLY

To start an immediate synchronization, complete the following steps:

1. In the Central Administration Quick Launch, click Application Management.
2. Under Service Applications, click Manage Service Applications.
3. Click the User Profile Service Application you wish to synchronize.
4. Under Synchronization, click Start Profile Synchronization.
5. Select Start Incremental Synchronization or Start Full Synchronization.
6. Click OK.

EDITING THE SYNCHRONIZATION SCHEDULE

To edit the incremental synchronization timer job schedule, complete the following steps:

1. In the Central Administration Quick Launch, click Application Management.
2. Under Service Applications, click Manage Service Applications.
3. Click the User Profile Service Application you wish to synchronize.
4. Under Synchronization, click Configure Synchronization Timer Job.

> **NOTE**   **THE CONFIGURE SYNCHRONIZATION TIMER JOB LINK**
>
> The Configure Synchronization Timer Job link you clicked is a simple shortcut to the User Profile Service Application – User Profile Incremental Synchronization timer job. You can view and edit this and all other timer jobs in the Monitoring section of Central Administration.

5. Under Recurring Schedule, specify the frequency and times when the synchronization will run.
6. Click OK.

PRACTICE   Configure User Profiles

Practices are designed to guide you through important procedures. The instructions in the Training Kit are high-level instructions that will challenge you to think carefully and to apply the procedures that are covered in this lesson and elsewhere in the Training Kit. If you need assistance, consult the detailed, step-by-step instructions in the Practice Answers on the companion media.

In this practice, you configure user profiles and the User Profile Service Application. You will also synchronize user profiles with the AD DS.

Prepare for the Practice

Before you perform this practice, ensure that your lab environment has been built according to the instructions found in the Introduction to this Training Kit.

1. Apply the snapshot CHAPTER 05 to CONTOSO-DC.

2. Apply the snapshot CHAPTER 05 to SP2010-WFE1.

3. Start CONTOSO-DC.

   Wait for the virtual machine to complete startup, at which time the Press Ctrl+Alt+Delete prompt appears.

4. Start SP2010-WFE1.

5. Log on to SP2010-WFE1 as **CONTOSO\SP_Admin** with the password **Pa$$w0rd**.

EXERCISE 1   Add the SharePoint Farm Account to the Local Administrators Group

For the User Profile Synchronization Service to start, the CONTOSO\SP_Farm account must be a member of the local Administrators group on the SharePoint server. In this exercise, you assign that membership.

- Use Server Manager to open the Local Users and Groups tool.
- Add the CONTOSO\SP_Farm account to the Administrators group.

EXERCISE 2   Register a Managed Account for User Profile Synchronization

In this exercise, you register CONTOSO\SP_UserSync as a managed account so that it can be used to synchronize AD DS accounts with SharePoint user profiles.

- Register CONTOSO\SP_UserSync as a managed account. The password of the account is Pa$$w0rd.
- Log off SP2010-WFE1.

EXERCISE 3   Grant the User Profile Synchronization Account Replicating Directory Changes Permission

In this exercise, you assign the Replicating Directory Changes permission to the CONTOSO\SP_UserSync account.

- Log on to SP2010-WFE1 as CONTOSO\Administrator.
- Start Active Directory Users And Computers and enable Advance Features.
- Open the Properties for the contoso.com domain and click the Security tab.
- Add the CONTOSO\SP_UserSync to the list.
- Assign the following permissions to the CONTOSO\SP_UserSync account:
  - Replicating Directory Changes
  - Replicating Directory Changes All

- Replicating Directory Changes In Filtered Set
- Replication synchronization
- Close Active Directory Users And Computers and log off SP2010-WFE1.

EXERCISE 4 Configure the User Profile Service Application

In this exercise, you create and configure a new User Profile service application.

- Create a User Profile service application. Use the following specifications and guidance:
  - Name: User Profile Service Application – Enterprise.
  - Application pool: Use a pool called SharePoint User Profile App Pool that runs under the CONTOSO\SP_UserSync account.
  - Database server for all three databases: SP2010-WFE1.
  - Profiles database name: SharePoint_Service_User_Profiles_Enterprise.
  - Synchronization database name: SharePoint_Service_User_Sync_Enterprise.
  - Social tagging database name: SharePoint_Service_User_Social_Enterprise.
  - Profile synchronization instance server: SP2010-WFE1.
  - Use the Default Proxy Group.

EXERCISE 5 Start the User Profile Services

In this exercise, you start the User Profile Service and the User Profile Synchronization Service.

- Go to the list of Services on Server SP2010-WFE1.
- Start the User Profile Service.
- Reboot the server SP2010-WFE1 and log on as CONTOSO\SP_Admin.
- Start the User Profile Synchronization Service. Use the following specifications and guidance:
  - User Profile Application: User Profile Service Application – Enterprise.
  - Password for the SharePoint Farm Account: Pa$$w0rd.
- Start Command Prompt, and then run the *iisreset* command.

EXERCISE 6 Configure Synchronization with the AD DS

In this exercise, you add a connection to the AD DS forest for synchronizing user profiles.

- Go to the list of service applications and manage the User Profile Service Application – Enterprise.
- Configure a new synchronization connection. Use the following specifications and guidance:
  - Connection Name: To AD DS
  - Type: Active Directory
  - Forest name: contoso.com

- Automatically discover the domain controller.
- Account name: CONTOSO\SP_UserSync
- Import all the accounts in the People organizational unit only.

■ When the connection is complete, log off SP2010-WFE1.

EXERCISE 7 Configure User Accounts to Import

In this exercise, you set some properties on AD DS user accounts to text user profile synchronization.

■ Log on to SP2010-WFE1 as CONTOSO\Administrator.

■ Open Active Directory Users And Computers.

■ Open the People organizational unit.

■ For April Meyer, set the Mobile property to 0123456789.

■ For Julian Isla, set the Job Title property to Contractor.

■ Log off SP2010-WFE1.

EXERCISE 8 Map a User Profile Field to the AD DS

In this exercise, you map the *CellPhone* user profile property to the AD DS *Mobile* property.

■ Open Central Administration and navigate to the Service Applications list.

■ Manage User Profile Server Application – Enterprise.

■ In Manage User Properties, edit the Mobile Phone property.

■ Add a new mapping. Use the following specifications and guidance:

- Source Data Connection: To AD DS
- Attribute: mobile
- Direction: Import

EXERCISE 9 Configure a Connection Filter

In this exercise, you filter the connection to AD DS so that contractors are not given a user profile.

■ In Central Administration, manage the User Profile Service Application – Enterprise.

■ Open the Configure Synchronization Connections list.

■ Point to the To AD DS connection and click Edit Connection Filters in the drop-down list.

■ Add a user filter. Use the following specifications and guidance:

- Attribute: title
- Operator: Equals
- Filter: Contractor

EXERCISE 10   Synchronize with the AD DS

In this exercise, you initiate a synchronization and observe the results.

- In Central Administration, go to Manage Service Applications.
- Manage the User Profile Service Application – Enterprise.
- Notice that there are zero profiles and the Profile Synchronization Status is Idle.
- Start a profile synchronization.
- Refresh the page after a few seconds. Notice that Profile Synchronization Status is Synchronizing.
- Every few minutes, refresh the page until the Profile Synchronization Status is Idle again.
- Notice the number of user profiles is now greater than zero.
- Go to Manage User Profiles and find the profile for April Meyer.
- Observe the value of the Mobile Phone property.
- Search for the profile for Julian Isla and note the result.

Lesson Summary

- Social Network features such as social tagging provide rich functionality to SharePoint users that can increase productivity or, in some situations, encourage users to waste time. Evaluate these features carefully and only implement them if you expect them to improve productivity.
- User profiles publish information about your users, such as their role in the company. You can implement user profiles without enabling other social networking features and without encouraging time-wasting. You should use them in almost all SharePoint farms.
- You can configure the properties in user profiles, create user profile subtypes, and use policies to govern who can see what properties.
- The User Profile service application manages profiles, compiles audiences, and manages My Sites.
- You can synchronize user profiles with external stores of user information such as AD DS, an LDAP directory, a line-of-business system, or a human resources database.

Lesson Review

You can use the following questions to test your knowledge of the information in Lesson 1, "Configure User Profiles." The questions are also available on the companion CD in a practice test if you prefer to review them in electronic form.

1. You configure the User Profile service application to synchronize information about
   users with a human resources database application. Sometime later an HR worker
   calls you to say that all properties in SharePoint user profiles seem to be working well,
   except for the Office field, which is blank for all users. How can you resolve this issue?
   (Choose all that apply. Each correct answer is part of the complete solution.)

   A. Create a Business Connectivity Services connection and an external content type
      for the human resources database.

   B. Create a user profile synchronization connection to the human resources database.

   C. Add a filter to the user profile synchronization connection that filters on the Office
      field.

   D. Add a mapping to the user profile synchronization connection that links the Office
      field to the equivalent field in the human resources database.

   E. Initiate a full synchronization on the user profile synchronization connection to the
      human resources database.

2. You use Windows PowerShell to create a new User Profile service application by using
   the *New-SPProfileServiceApplication* cmdlet. The command completes successfully.
   The User Profile services start correctly. However, an error appears when you try to
   open the service application in Central Administration to configure synchronization.
   What could be the problem? (Choose all that apply.)

   A. You have not loaded the SharePoint snap-in to Windows PowerShell.

   B. You have not created a proxy to go with your new service application.

   C. The SharePoint farm account does not have local administrator rights.

   D. You have not performed an IISReset after starting the User Profile services.

   E. You have not enabled self-service site creation on the relevant web application.

Lesson 2: Configure My Sites

In Lesson 1 we considered social networking on the Internet and its potential for business. Although user profiles are essential for social networking, on their own they do not enable typical Web 2.0 functionality, such as personal content publishing and tagging. To complete your social networking functionality in SharePoint you must provision My Sites. Just as its name implies, a My Site is a space that a user controls for his or her own content, tags, activity streams, and other features. We will examine My Sites in this lesson.

> **After this lesson, you will be able to:**
> - Describe the functionality that a My Site makes available to users.
> - Decide whether to implement My Sites in your organization, and for which users.
> - Configure a web application to host My Sites.
> - Create a site collection to host My Sites.
> - Choose to partition My Sites across two or more site collections.
> - Configure a User Profile Service Application to support My Sites.
> - Configure your own My Site.
> - Configure timer jobs to enable activity feeds.
> - Manage social tags and notes.
>
> **Estimated Lesson Time: 40 minutes**

Giving Users Their Own Sites

The objective that My Sites address is to give each user his or her own space in the SharePoint Server 2010 farm. For reasons of security and availability, there must be some limits on what users can do with their spaces, but the restrictions will usually be much less prohibitive than elsewhere in the farm. By providing My Sites you encourage participation, broaden communication, and, if you are successful, create a global community that shares knowledge and business acumen. Your community may even be able to improve their social lives!

 REAL WORLD

Alistair Matthews

My Sites provide a hugely powerful new tool to users and they can become very enthusiastic. This is exactly what you hope for with any system deployment project, but it can also cause problems. At one of my customer deployments, for example, a user uploaded a video to his My Site and, because it was funny, it sparked a trend—everyone was posting videos, and some users were posting several, usually without the same wit! The content database for the My Site web application rapidly grew beyond our estimates. Eventually we had to move it to a larger disk array.

You cannot always anticipate this level of enthusiasm in your users. I would suggest that you plan your content database with a significant size contingency, because disk space is a lot cheaper than it used to be. Most important, make sure you monitor the size of the database so that you can respond early to unforeseen circumstances like this.

A Typical My Site

To understand the potential that My Sites represent, it is necessary to know what a typical My Site consists of. This may vary because users can add Web Parts and developers can add features, but in general, a My Site includes:

- My Profile

    This is the user profile with which you became familiar in the previous lesson. It displays contact information, role, skills, pictures, and other properties that administrators configure. This is the only part of My Site that you can synchronize with external stores.

- My Content

    This is a set of document libraries and media libraries in which a user can publish her own content. The principal advantage to providing this library is that restrictions usually applied to content creation—such as permissions, approval requirements, and workflows—are not needed. Instead each user takes responsibility for his own content. A user can place unofficial documents, research, humorous content, and other materials here. It is a good place for relevant information that would be inappropriate in team sites, project sites, or other locations in SharePoint. My Content includes a Personal Documents library for private content and a Shared Documents library for public content.

- Tags and Notes

    You can use this tool to tag or post notes on websites within or outside of the SharePoint farm. You can use such tags to highlight a page to your colleagues, comment on it, or to remind yourself about it.

- Colleagues

    This list is configured by the user and can include people from all departments she regularly or occasionally works with. This list is like a Friends list on an Internet social networking site—visitors to the My Site can use this list to understand the user's role and contact other colleagues she has met.

- Memberships

    This includes site memberships, security group memberships, and distribution list memberships. Again, this information describes the user's role and responsibilities to My Site visitors.

- Activity Streams

  An activity stream is an automatically compiled list of a user's actions and those of his colleagues. Tags, notes, documents, items, and status updates appear in this list. An activity stream illustrates at a glance what you and your colleagues are currently working on. It can generate a "buzz" around a project or topic and interest people outside the immediate team.

> **MORE INFO** **CUSTOMIZING MY SITES**
>
> Users can customize the content that appears on their My Site and also add, remove, and edit Web Parts to alter what is displayed. You should consider the Web Parts that appear in the Web Part gallery to enable this. See Chapter 10, "Administering SharePoint Customization," for more information about managing Web Parts.
>
> Developers can also customize the site template that SharePoint uses to create each My Site. For example, they can add company branding, extra pages, or extra Web Parts to all My Sites by creating SharePoint features. For more information about customizing the My Site template, see *http://blogs.msdn.com/b/spsocial/archive/2010/04/08/customizing-my-sites-in-microsoft-sharepoint-2010.aspx*.

Planning My Sites

Before you deploy My Sites within your SharePoint Server 2010 farm, you should consider and document the following issues.

PREREQUISITES

The following should be in place and fully functional before you deploy My Sites:

- User Profile Service Application

  My Sites cannot function at all without the User Profile service application. As well as the user profiles themselves, tags, notes, and activity streams are all managed by this service application.

- User Profile Synchronization

  Like user profiles, My Sites can be used without synchronization with AD DS or another store. However, because almost all organizations already store user information in some electronic form, you should almost always set up user profile synchronization.

- A web application to host My Sites

  Like all SharePoint sites, My Sites must be placed in a web application. It is also recommended that you separate My Sites into a dedicated web application for enhanced security and to prevent contention with business-critical sites. Furthermore, this web application requires:

  - Self-service site creation.
  - A managed path for personal sites.

- A site collection to host My Sites.

  All My Sites will be created within this site collection. This site collection must be based on the My Site Host template.

- Search Service Application

  My Sites can function with the Search service. However, users will not be able to search for people based on the properties, memberships, and skills listed in their profiles.

- Managed Metadata Service Application

  Social tagging requires the Managed Metadata service application to be functional.

PLANNING THE WEB APPLICATION AND CONTENT DATABASE

When you enable My Sites, you can use an existing web application. In this case, My Site content is stored in an existing content database. You should ensure that this extra content does not increase the size of the database beyond the limits imposed by disk space, backup time, and restore time.

However, it is recommended as a best practice to create a web application dedicated to My Sites, and this architecture implies a dedicated content database. This approach has the following advantages:

- You must enable self-site creation for My Sites. If they are in a dedicated web application you need not enable this property for other site collections.

- My Site content frequently has different backup requirements. For example, you may consider My Site content to be less business-critical than project or product content. In this case you may decide to back up this content database less often and restore it after other content databases.

- My Site content frequently has different availability requirements. Again, if you consider My Sites to be non-critical, you can place this database on disk sets that are not fault tolerant, or a non-clustered database server. Disk space on such hardware is likely to be cheaper per megabyte and, if you anticipate a lot of personal content, that can reduce pressure on the budget.

> **CAUTION** **BUSINESS-CRITICAL MY SITES**
>
> Although many administrators consider My Sites to be non-critical, as described in the preceding bullet points, this is not always the case. You should think carefully about your own users and working methods before you make this decision.
>
> For example, consider a SharePoint farm deployed in a technical consultancy. Each consultant uses My Site to store all documents related to her own projects so that she has full control over her own content. Such My Sites are certainly business-critical and the impact of their loss or a delay in restoring them after a failure could be substantial and financial. You should certainly invest in fault-tolerant storage and backup for these My Sites just as you would for other SharePoint content.

You must also consider the likely total size of My Site content when you plan the content database. If you already have a store of personal content, such as home folders on a file server, you can use it to estimate the size of the content database. However, consider the following questions:

- Are users placing all their documents on the file server? Users frequently store materials on their local hard drives. The extra functionality available in My Site will encourage them to store everything there and increase the size of their content.

- Are videos and images likely to be shared in My Sites? This functionality is familiar from Internet social networking sites and users may expect it. High-resolution videos and images imply heavy use of disk space.

- Are users likely to blog regularly? Although individual blog entries without attachments do not take up much space, if all users write regular entries, and they are prolific, storage requirements can increase rapidly.

- How long does content remain relevant? By encouraging users to delete old and irrelevant content you can limit the growth of the content database.

Just as for any other site collection, you can specify a quota template when you create the site collection that hosts My Sites.

GEOGRAPHICALLY DISTRIBUTED MY SITES

In a global organization, it is a good idea to store My Sites close to the users that own them, so that access to your own site is rapid and responsive. In SharePoint 2010 you can use multiple User Profile service applications and multiple My Site hosts to enable this. The following components are required:

- **Multiple User Profile service applications**   Each User Profile service application specifies a single My Site host for all the user profiles it contains. Therefore, you should create one service application for each SharePoint server that hosts My Sites.

- **Multiple My Site Host Site Collections**   You may decide, for example, to place a My Site host at each regional headquarters.

- **Audiences**   Create audiences that examine a location value, such as Office or Country, in the user profile. Use these audiences to target My Sites, so that the host where users create their My Site is the one closest to them.

You must also configure each User Profile service application to trust all the My Site hosts. You will learn how to configure these components later in this lesson.

Social Tagging

In a paper-based office, it's very common to write a note and stick it to a document when you pass it to a colleague. People do this, for example, to add review instructions, to highlight passages, to indicate a level of importance or a level of sensitivity, or to share a joke. Some computer applications have implemented similar functionality. For example, in Microsoft Word, you can add comments throughout a document. However, there's no general tool to do this for any kind of content. You cannot add a comment to a JPEG image file, for example. You have to open a Word document to see the comments, so the commenter has to tell you that they exist, unless you happen to open the document again.

On social networking websites, by contrast, users are familiar with commenting on just about all content. Because this ability is built into the architecture of the site it does not rely on the specifications of each type of content.

Rich social tagging is a new and very functional feature in SharePoint Server 2010. You can use it to comment on all SharePoint content and web pages outside of SharePoint. In this section you will learn how tagging can enrich your users' experience.

What Can User Do with Tags?

SharePoint users can add several different kinds of tags to content and several Web Parts that display tags in different ways.

SOCIAL TAGS

With social tags you can mark items of interest. For example, you can organize all the content you need to consult to write a document. You can also use tags to highlight content to other users, such as members of your project team.

A social tag is a word or phrase. It is stored with the identity of the user who created it and the URL of the item he tagged. It is kept in the User Profile service application social tagging database.

Users create their own tags, so they are not like keywords in the Managed Metadata service, which are created by administrators. They are more like managed metadata terms, which are created by users, but you do not need a managed metadata column in the content type to apply a tag to an item.

TAG CLOUDS

You are probably familiar with tag clouds from Internet blogs: a tag cloud displays the most popular tags used on a set of information. In the tag cloud, large text indicates frequently used tags and smaller text indicates rarely used tags. SharePoint Server 2010 includes a Tag Cloud Web Part that you can include in any site, including your My Site. This display shows at a glance what topics a set of content covers, what it concentrates on, and what subjects are mentioned in passing.

See Figure 6-1 for a tag cloud example.

NOTE BOARD

The Note Board is another SharePoint Web Part in which users can add spontaneous comments to any SharePoint 2010 page. The idea is to let users express their thoughts immediately without having to move to a separate tool such as email or instant messaging. Other users can see these comments both on the note board control itself and in activity streams. Anonymous comments are not permitted. Figure 6-4 shows the Note Board tool.

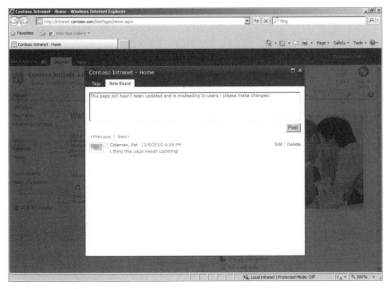

FIGURE 6-4 The Note Board

RATINGS

Users can rate content by giving it a score from 1 to 100. Content with many high ratings is likely to be of high quality, so this is an excellent way to attract attention to useful and eloquent content. Ratings are community-driven and rely on the participation of many visitors to be most effective.

Ratings consist of the score itself, a user identity, the URL of the rated item, and the date and time the item was rated. They are stored in a separate table within the social tagging database in the User Profile service application. Because a rating is stored separately from the item, users do not need write permission on an item to rate it. To use ratings, the Rating feature must be enabled on the Site Collection.

BOOKMARKLETS

You can add a comment to a web page outside the SharePoint organization by creating a *bookmarklet*. They are similar to tags for internal content. Bookmarklets work by adding a JavaScript control to the user's favorites in the browser.

When users click the favorite, their Tags and Notes page in their My Site opens and they can type their text. Tags on external content are saved in the social tagging database and are visible to users' teams and colleagues.

Planning Social Tagging

Consider the following issues before you enable social tagging in your organization:

SECURITY AND PRIVACY

When a user tags a site or document, the URL of that content is displayed to all that user's colleagues and team members on the My Site. Permissions are still enforced, so a user cannot access a tagged item unless he has permission to it. However, access to a sensitive document's URL may occasionally represent a security breach—for example, if the document's URL includes its title and the title is "Immanent Redundancies"!

For these reasons, administrators can configure a list of sites in which content cannot be tagged. Plan this list very carefully.

PERFORMANCE AND CAPACITY

Unless you have an existing tagging system, it is difficult to estimate the total disk space that tags, bookmarklets, and ratings will occupy. Each tag is small and requires very little storage space. However, if tagging becomes popular with your users, you might find that the storage space required begins to rise rapidly.

You should keep a careful eye on the size of the User Profile service application's social tagging database in the months after deploying My Sites. Also, be prepared to scale up storage for this database. For example, if you place it in a RAID 5 array, you can respond to high demand by adding extra spindles.

ASSIGNING PERMISSIONS

Throughout this lesson, we have assumed that all users should be able to create a My Site and use tags, but this might not be the case in your organization. For example:

- You grant access to users from a partner organization, through an extranet, to your SharePoint organization. You have created user accounts in AD DS for these partner users but you do not want to enable them to create My Sites. You would like them to be able to tag content.

- You have temporary workers, such as contractors, that have restricted access to your network and SharePoint for a limited time. My Sites for such workers would usually be a waste of resources and their tags may or may not be desirable.

In SharePoint 2010 you have permissions that restrict social networking features. Assign these from the User Profile service application. Table 6-2 shows the three permissions that are available.

TABLE 6-2 Social Networking User Permissions

PERMISSION	DESCRIPTION	DEFAULT AUTHORIZATION
Use Personal Features	Grants the right to edit a user's own profile, edit the list of colleagues, and edit memberships	All Authenticated Users
Create Personal Sites	Grants the right to create a My Site	All Authenticated Users
Use Social Features	Grants the right to add tags, ratings, and bookmarklets	All Authenticated Users

As you can see, these permissions are assigned by default to all authenticated users, but you can create a much more restrictive set of authorizations to match your plan.

Administrators also have a range of permissions available. Table 6-3 shows these permissions.

TABLE 6-3 Social Networking Administrator Permissions

PERMISSION	DESCRIPTION	DEFAULT AUTHORIZATION
Manage Profiles	Grants the right to edit any user profile property in the User Profile service application.	SharePoint Farm Account
Manage Audiences	Grants the right to create, edit, delete, and compile audiences.	SharePoint Farm Account
Manage Permissions	Grants the right to assign these permissions for the User Profile service application.	SharePoint Farm Account
Retrieve People Data for Search Crawlers	Grants the right to access user profile properties for compiling indexes. You should assign this right to your Search Service crawler account.	SharePoint Farm Account
Manage Social Data	Grants the right to delete tags, ratings, and bookmarklets for any user profile in the User Profile service application.	SharePoint Farm Account

IMPORTANT **PERMISSIONS FOR THE SHAREPOINT SEARCH CRAWLER**

Notice the Retrieve People Data for Search Crawler permission in Table 6-3. This is designed to enable the SharePoint Search crawler to access the user profile data with being granted read permission. If your Search crawler account does not have this permission, profiles are not indexed and People Search does not work.

Strictly speaking, by the principle of least privilege, this permission should be assigned to the user account that you run your crawler under and only that account. Therefore, you should remove the SharePoint Farm Account.

For more information about Search and the crawler account, see Chapter 7, "Administering SharePoint Search."

Configuring My Sites

The following tasks are completed by administrators to deploy and configure My Sites in a SharePoint farm. A healthy My Site deployment requires a healthy User Profile service application, so you should have already completed the procedures in Lesson 1 before you take the following steps. Most of the tasks described are completed only once, but some, such as managing social tags, become part of day-to-day SharePoint administration.

> **CAUTION** **MY SITES AND THE INITIAL FARM CONFIGURATION WIZARD**
>
> After you complete your SharePoint installation and the SharePoint 2010 Products Configuration Wizard, you often run the Initial Farm Configuration Wizard. This tool will configure both the User Profile service application and My Sites for you, if you select User Profile Service Application in the list of Services.
>
> However, it is not recommended that you configure My Sites by using this tool, because the resulting configuration is not considered secure. Specifically, the wizard places the My Site Host site collection in the same web application as the Central Administration site. Conceivably, in such a situation scripting attacks could be used by a My Site owner to get Farm Administrator privileges.

Configuring a Web Application to Support My Sites

As a best practice, the web application that hosts My Sites should be dedicated to the task. This configuration enables administrators to manage the content for My Sites separately from other content. It also avoids enabling self-service site creation, which is required for My Sites, on other site collections for which it is inappropriate.

You learned how to create web applications in Chapter 1, so these procedures assume that you have already created one. You must enable self-service site creation and add a managed path for personal sites.

ENABLING SELF-SERVICE SITE CREATION

You must perform the following procedure after both the web application and the site collection for My Sites have been created.

1. In the Central Administration Quick Launch, click Application Management.
2. Under Web Applications, click Manage Web Applications.
3. Click the web application that you have created for My Sites.
4. On the Ribbon, click Self-Service Site Creation.
5. Click On.

> **NOTE** **SECONDARY CONTACTS**
>
> Because each user takes charge of his or her own My Site, secondary contacts are not necessary and you should not select the Require Secondary Contact check box.

6. Click OK.

ADDING A MANAGED PATH FOR PERSONAL SITES

1. In the Central Administration Quick Launch, click Application Management.

2. Under Web Applications, click Manage Web Applications.

3. Click the web application that you have created for My Sites.

4. On the Ribbon, click Managed Paths.

5. In the Path text box, type the path where you intend to place My Sites—for example, **personal**.

6. In the Type drop-down list, select Wildcard Inclusion.

7. Click Add Path and then click OK.

Configuring a Site Collection to Support My Sites

You learned how to create a site collection in Chapter 1, so the procedure will not be repeated here. The only configuration requirement for the site collection is that it be based on the My Site Host template.

Configure a User Profile Service Application to Support My Sites

1. In the Central Administration Quick Launch, click Application Management.

2. Under Service Applications, click Manage Service Applications.

3. Click the User Profile service application.

4. Under My Site Settings, click Setup My Sites.

5. Under Preferred Search Center, enter a path to a Search Center site.

> **NOTE** **LINK TO A SEARCH CENTER**
>
> The path that you enter in the Preferred Search Center text box is the location that users are forwarded to when they execute a search in a My Site. For more information about Search Centers and search scopes, see Chapter 7.

6. In the My Site Host Location text box, type the path to the Site Collection you have created to host My Sites.

7. Under Personal Site Location, in the Location text box, type the managed path you added to the web application.

8. Under Site Naming Format, select a naming scheme for My Site URLs.

9. Under Language Options, choose whether users are permitted to set the language of their My Site.

10. Under Read Permission Level, pick user accounts and security groups that should be able to browse My Sites. By default, all authenticated users receive this right.

11. Under My Site Email Notifications, type a sender's address for emails from My Sites.

12. Click OK.

Other Administrative Tasks

For full and secure My Site functionality, you must also enable timer jobs and assign permissions to users and administrators. Sometimes, in day-to-day administration, it is also necessary to manage tags that users have added to content.

ENABLING ACTIVITY STREAMS

The activity streams that display user actions to team members and colleagues are compiled by a SharePoint timer job. You must enable this timer job manually:

1. In the Central Administration Quick Launch, click Monitoring.

2. Under Timer Jobs, click Review Job Definitions.

3. Scroll down to locate the User Profile Service Application – Activity Feed Job timer job. You may need to move to page 2 or 3 to locate this job.

4. Notice that the timer job is disabled.

5. Click that timer job.

6. Under Recurring Schedule, configure times when the activity streams should be compiled.

7. Click Enable.

ASSIGNING USER PERMISSIONS

Restrict access to My Site functionality and tagging by assigning permissions by following these steps:

1. In the Central Administration Quick Launch, click Application Management.

2. Under Service Applications, click Manage Service Applications.

3. Click the User Profile service application.

4. Under People, click Manage User Permissions.

5. Click NT AUTHORITY\Authenticated Users and then click Remove.

6. Click All Authenticated Users and then click Remove.

7. Type the name of the user or group you wish to assign permission to, such as **CONTOSO\Domain Users**.

8. Click the Check Names button.

9. Click Add.

10. Select the Use Personal Features check box for users or groups who should be able to edit their own profiles.

11. Select the Create Personal Site check box for users or groups who should be able to create a My Site.

12. Select the Use Social Features check box for users or groups who should be able to tag content.

13. Click OK.

ASSIGNING ADMINISTRATOR PERMISSIONS

Restrict permissions for administrators by completing the following steps:

1. In the Central Administration Quick Launch, click Application Management.

2. Under Service Applications, click Manage Service Applications.

3. Click a blank area on User Profile service application line. Do not click the name itself.

4. On the Ribbon, click Administrators.

5. Type the name of the user or group you wish to assign permission to, such as **CONTOSO\Domain Admins**.

6. Click the Check Names button.

7. Click Add.

8. Select the Manage Profiles check box for users or groups who should be able to edit any profiles.

9. Select the Manage Audiences check box for users or groups who should be able to edit audiences.

10. Select the Manage Permissions check box for users or groups who should be able to assign User Profile service application permissions.

11. Select the Retrieve People Data For Search Crawlers check box for SharePoint search crawler accounts.

12. Select the Manage Social Data check box for users or groups who should be able to edit any tags.

13. Click OK.

MANAGE SOCIAL TAGS

Not all tags and notes are welcome—sometimes users write off-topic comments, sometimes they are rude, and sometimes they do not consider company policies. If a user makes a comment on your content, you cannot delete it yourself and the user may be unwilling to retract it. Any administrator with the Manage Social Data permission, however, can delete any comment. Do this by completing the following steps:

1. In the Central Administration Quick Launch, click Application Management.

2. Under Service Applications, click Manage Service Applications.

3. Click the User Profile service application.

4. Under My Site Settings, click Manage Social Tags And Notes.

5. In the Type drop-down list, select Tags Or Notes.

6. In the User people picker control, enter the name of the user who made the comment you wish to find. You can enter multiple names in this box.

7. If you know the URL of the view where the comment appears, enter it in the URL box.

8. Enter a Date Range.

9. Enter words that the tag or note contains.

> **NOTE MULTIPLE SEARCH CRITERIA**
>
> The search will only return notes or tags that satisfy all the criteria you enter. If you do not find the tag or note you were expecting, try fewer criteria.

10. To delete any inappropriate comment, select its check box on the left and then click Delete.

Creating Your Own My Site

When the administrators have completed the deployment of the User Profile service application and My Sites, users can begin creating their sites and populating them with content. Users can do this without involving administrators, but it is a good idea to try the process at least once to ensure that it works. Also, each administrator is likely to have his or her own site!

To create a My Site, follow these steps:

1. Go to any SharePoint page.

2. In the top right, click your user name and then click My Site.

> **NOTE MY SITE LINKS**
>
> From this page users can click the links in any order. In this case we'll start with My Profile.

3. Click My Profile and then click Edit My Profile, beneath the picture placeholder.

4. Configure the properties as you require them. Notice that for many properties you can select who can see the value.

5. At the bottom of the page, click Save And Close.

6. Click My Content. Default document libraries are created.

7. Add documents to your personal and shared document libraries.

8. Click My Profile and then click the Colleagues tab.

9. Click Add Colleagues.

10. In the Colleagues people picker, type the name of a user you work with.

11. Click Check Names.

12. Click OK.

13. In the Suggested Colleagues box, select other coworkers and then click Add.

14. Click the Memberships tab. Sites and distribution lists that you are a member of are displayed.

PRACTICE **Configure My Sites**

Practices are designed to guide you through important procedures. The instructions in the Training Kit are high-level instructions that will challenge you to think carefully and to apply the procedures that are covered in this lesson and elsewhere in the Training Kit. If you need assistance, consult the detailed, step-by-step instructions in the Practice Answers on the companion media.

In this practice, you configure a web application and site collection to host My Sites. You also configure the User Profiles Service Application and create a My Site for an example user account.

Prepare for the Practice

Before you perform this practice, ensure that your lab environment has been built according to the instructions found in the Introduction to this Training Kit. You must also have performed the practice in Lesson 1 of this chapter. You must be logged off of SP2010-WFE1 before beginning the exercises.

EXERCISE 1   Create a New Web Application

In this exercise, you create a new web application and set up DNS records to support it.

- Log on to SP2010-WFE1 as **CONTOSO\SP_Admin** with the password **Pa$$w0rd**.
- Use Central Administration to create a new web application. Use the following specifications and guidance:
  - Name: MySites
  - Port: 80
  - Host Header: my.contoso.com
  - URL: *http://my.contoso.com*
  - Create a new application pool
  - Application Pool Name: SharePoint MySite Application
  - Application Pool User Account: CONTOSO\SP_WebApps
  - Database Server: SP2010-WFE1
  - Database Name: SharePoint_Content_MySites
- Create a new DNS A record in the contoso.com forward lookup zone. This record should resolve my.contoso.com to 10.0.0.21.

EXERCISE 2   Configure Your New Web Application to Support My Sites

In this exercise, you make the configuration changes that are necessary to support My Sites on the web application you just created.

- For the MySites web application that you created in Exercise 1, make the following configuration changes:
  - Enable self-service site creation.
  - Add a wildcard inclusion managed path for the relative path **personal**.

EXERCISE 3   Create a New Site Collection to Host My Sites

In this exercise, you create a new site collection to host My Sites for users.

- Use Central Administration to create a new Site Collection. Use the following specifications and guidance:
  - Web Application: *http://my.contoso.com*
  - Title: Contoso My Sites
  - Description: This site collection hosts your My Site
  - URL: *http://my.contoso.com/*
  - Template: My Site Host
  - Primary Site Collection Administrator: CONTOSO\SP_Admin

EXERCISE 4   Configure My Sites in the User Profile Service Application

In this exercise, you configure the User Profile service application that you created in Lesson 1 to support My Sites.

- Use Central Administration to manage the User Profile Service Application – Enterprise service application that you created in Lesson 1.
- Set up My Sites for this service application. Use the following specifications and guidance:
  - My Site Host: *http://my.contoso.com/*
  - Personal Site Location: personal
  - Site Naming Format: User name (do not resolve conflicts)
  - My Site E-mail Notifications From Address: mysite@contoso.com

EXERCISE 5   Configure a My Site

In this exercise, you create a My Site for Pat Coleman and populate it with content.

- In Internet Explorer, browse to ***http://intranet.contoso.com***.
- Grant permissions to the CONTOSO\Domain Users group to view the site.
- Log off of SP2010-WFE1.
- Log on to SP2010-WFE1 as **CONTOSO\PatC** with the password **Pa$$w0rd**.

- Use Internet Explorer to browse to ***http://intranet.contoso.com***.
- Use the link to Pat Coleman's My Site.
- Edit Pat Coleman's profile. Make changes to the text fields of your choice.
- For Pat Coleman's picture use the PatColeman.jpg file found on the CD in the Practice Files\06_02 folder.
- Enter a status of your choice in the What's Happening text box.
- Under My Content, create a blog and a first blog entry for Pat Coleman.

EXERCISE 6   Use Tags to Highlight Content

In this exercise, you use tags and notes.

- Check the tags and notes lists on Pat Coleman's Tags And Notes tab.
- Go to the Contoso Intranet homepage and use the I Like It tool.
- Add the tags **Contoso** and **Internal** to the Contoso Intranet homepage.
- Add a note to the page to indicate that it requires an update.
- Return to Pat Coleman's profile and refresh the Tags And Notes tab.
- Add the SharePoint Tags And Notes Tool to the Internet Explorer Favorites menu.
- Return to the Contoso Intranet homepage.
- Click Tags And Note Board on your favorites menu and examine the tags and notes listed.
- Close all windows and log off of SP2010-WFE1.

EXERCISE 7   Create the CHAPTER 06 Snapshot

The CHAPTER 06 snapshot captures the state of the environment at the end of Chapter 6. Perform this procedure for each of the following virtual machines: SP2010-WFE1, CONTOSO-DC.

1. Shut down the virtual machine.
2. Unmount any ISO image currently mounted to the CD/DVD drive. Use the "Unmount an ISO Image" procedure in the Lab Environment Build Guide on the companion media.
3. Create a snapshot named CHAPTER 06. Use the "Create a Snapshot" procedure in the Lab Environment Build Guide on the companion media.

Lesson Summary

- My Sites enable complete Web 2.0 social networking functionality within a SharePoint Server 2010 intranet, extranet, or Internet solution.
- My Sites give users a space to publish content with fewer restrictions than may apply elsewhere in the SharePoint hierarchy.
- My Sites require a fully functional User Profile service application. In most cases, profile synchronization is also needed.

- My Sites are full SharePoint sites within a dedicated Site Collection based on the My Site Host template.

- You can create several My Site host servers for different groups of users. For example, you can distribute My Site hosts around a global environment so that they are close to the users they serve.

- Social Tagging encourages participation and can improve communication and collaboration within your production teams.

Lesson Review

You can use the following questions to test your knowledge of the information in Lesson 2, "Configure My Sites." The questions are also available on the companion media in a practice test if you prefer to review them in electronic form.

> **NOTE ANSWERS**
>
> Answers to these questions and explanations of why each answer choice is right or wrong are located in the "Answers" section at the end of the book.

1. You have deployed My Sites in your organization. Feedback from users is good. However, some users have complained that they do not receive updates about their colleagues' tags, notes, and statuses. What could be the problem? (Choose all that apply.)

   A. You did not enable self-service site creation on the web application that hosts My Sites.

   B. You did not create a managed path for personal sites in the web application that hosts My Sites.

   C. You did not configure user profile synchronization with AD DS.

   D. You did not enable the User Profile Service Application – Activity Feed Job timer job and schedule it to run regularly.

   E. The SharePoint Search crawler account does not have the Retrieve People Data For Search Crawlers permission on the User Profile service application.

2. You have deployed My Sites successfully and users are regularly tagging SharePoint pages. One day you receive a call from a user who wants to highlight a page on a rival company's website and comment on it to his colleagues. How can he make such comments? (Choose all that apply.)

   A. By using SharePoint tags

   B. By using SharePoint notes

   C. By using SharePoint terms

   D. By using SharePoint keywords

   E. By using the SharePoint Tags And Note Board bookmarklet

Chapter Review

To further practice and reinforce the skills you learned in this chapter, you can perform the following tasks:

- Review the chapter summary.
- Review the list of key terms introduced in this chapter.
- Complete the case scenarios. These scenarios set up real-world situations involving the topics of this chapter and ask you to create a solution.
- Complete the suggested practices.
- Take a practice test.

Chapter Summary

- User profiles identify each user to their colleagues within the SharePoint farm.
- My Sites give each user a space for content and enable tags and notes.
- User profiles can be used without My Sites, but do not enable full Web 2.0 functionality.
- Both user profiles and My Sites require the User Profile service application to be fully functional.
- User profile synchronization is not strictly required but most organizations find it essential.
- Tagging promotes a community of users, increases communication, and fosters a sense of belonging among your workforce.

Key Terms

The following terms were introduced in this chapter. Do you know what they mean?

- Social networking
- User profile
- User profile subtype
- User profile policy
- Audience
- My Site
- User Profile service application
- User profile synchronization
- Tag

- Note
- Tag Cloud
- Bookmarklet
- Activity Streams

Case Scenario: Configuring User Profiles and Social Networking

In the following case scenario, you will apply what you've learned about subjects of this chapter. You can find answers to these questions in the "Answers" section at the end of this book.

You run a SharePoint Server 2010 farm for an engineering consultancy. The consultancy employs permanent consultants and engages freelance consultants for busy periods and projects requiring extra skills. You want to enable My Sites for all these users but your requirements differ for the two groups: permanent staff My Sites are considered mission-critical, freelancers' My Sites are low priority. All users have AD DS accounts.

1. You want to ensure that permanent consultants' My Sites are highly resilient to hardware failures and quickly restorable in the event of a disaster. You want to spend less on storage for freelance consultants' My Sites and prevent high disk consumption. How can you configure SharePoint to support this?

2. You want to prevent freelance consultants from using social tags but permanent staff should be able to tag any content. How can you configure SharePoint to support this?

Suggested Practices

To help you successfully master the exam objectives presented in this chapter, complete the following tasks.

Practice 1: Configure Synchronization with Other Sources of User Data

In Lesson 1, you configured user profile synchronization with AD DS, but this is probably not the only source you will come across in your own work. SharePoint can also synchronize with other LDAP directory services, databases, and line-of-business applications. To practice synchronizing with a database that contains user information:

1. Create a database with suitable fields. Ideally, use a copy of a real user database from your own organization if you have permissions. Alternatively, you can use the Adventure Works sample database (*http://msftdbprodsamples.codeplex.com*) or make up your own data.

2. Create a BCS connection to the database. Although an external content type and external list are not required, it is often helpful to create them to test the connection and ensure that the connection works as expected. Once you are satisfied, you can delete the external content type and external list.

3. On your User Profile service application, create a new synchronization connection of the type **BDC**.

4. Run a synchronization as you did in Chapter 1.

Practice 2: Configure Segmented My Sites

Often you may wish to distribute My Sites across multiple web applications and site collections. For example, you might have a global organization and need to place My Sites close to the users that own them. Your lab environment may not enable you to practice this with multiple SharePoint servers or even with multiple virtual servers because of memory limitations. However, you can take the following steps, which simulate most aspects of this process, in a single-server SharePoint farm. These steps assume you have completed both lessons and their practices:

1. Configure a second web application, with a separate content database, to host My Sites. In a single-server farm, use a distinct port number or host header for this application.

2. Configure a new site collection within the new web application based on the My Site Host template.

3. Enable self-service site creation and a managed path for personal sites on the new web application.

4. Set up a second User Profile service application.

5. Configure both My Site host site collections as trusted locations in the opposite User Profile service application.

6. Create audiences to target users to the right My Site host for their location.

Take a Practice Test

The practice tests on this book's companion media offer many options. For example, you can test yourself on only the lesson review content, or you can test yourself on all the 70–667 certification exam objectives. You can set up the test so that it closely simulates the experience of taking a certification exam, or you can set it up in study mode so that you can look at the correct answers and explanations after you answer each question.

> **MORE INFO** **PRACTICE TESTS**
>
> For details about all the practice test options available, see the "How to Use the Practice Tests" section in this book's Introduction.

CHAPTER 7

Administering SharePoint Search

A ny company that works with content quickly generates a large body of work, and this body of work continues to expand as projects are completed, new products are brought to market, and the company expands. In most cases, this content is also created in a wide variety of formats: Office documents may be the most common, but PDF files, photos, videos, Silverlight applications, and other media are also popular, and your company may also use specialized file types, such as Computer-Aided Design (CAD) projects. The depth and breadth of the content you store can become dizzying even for a relatively small company. Faced with this challenge, how can you enable users to rapidly locate all the documents relevant to their task on any given day? Enterprise search is the tool that addresses this problem and SharePoint Server 2010 is equipped with two search engines. In this chapter, you will understand SharePoint Search and learn how to configure it.

Exam objectives in this chapter:
- Configure indexing and search.
- Configure SharePoint farms.
- Configure service applications.

Lessons in this chapter:

Before You Begin

To complete the lessons in this chapter, you must build your lab environment according to the instructions found in the Introduction to this Training Kit and:

- Performed the practices in Chapter 1
- Performed the practices in Chapter 5
- Performed the practices in Chapter 6

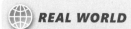 **REAL WORLD**

Alistair Matthews

In some companies it has become critical for users to be able to access information instantaneously, often because the customer is waiting on the phone. If customer service representatives are slow with their responses, it not only annoys the customer they are speaking to, but it also lengthens the queue of people waiting to speak to someone. This is one of the most common sources of irritation in the modern relationship between customer and provider.

One of our clients ran a concierge call center–customers would phone from any city in the world wanting to know what restaurant to eat at, what show to see, or what hotel to stay at. We set up SharePoint Search to index both information from appropriate Internet feeds and the shared expertise of all the staff in the center, which was considerable. We proved that SharePoint Search could easily satisfy the intense demands of a call center, but such a situation requires a carefully tuned implementation and a good understanding of the right architecture.

Lesson 1: Configure Search

In any company with a large volume of content, the SharePoint administrator must understand fully the formats, locations, and technologies that store all items, documents, and files. Although SharePoint will probably become your principal content store, in many cases you must interoperate with file shares, websites, Line-Of-Business (LOB) applications, databases, and so on. SharePoint can index all of these locations so that users can search your entire enterprise in a single operation. This is the essence of an enterprise search system. In this lesson you will learn how to plan for and deploy a comprehensive search solution in SharePoint.

After this lesson, you will be able to:

- Describe how enterprise search capabilities improve productivity.
- Understand capabilities that FAST Search Server 2010 for SharePoint adds to native SharePoint search.
- List the components of the Search user interface.
- Describe how index and query servers collaborate to provide search.
- Outline the steps in the crawling process.
- Outline the steps in the query process.
- Deploy a Search service application.
- Configure content sources.
- Configure search scopes.

Estimated Lesson Time: 45 minutes

Why Do You Need Search?

Much like social networking, search is a set of functions that have been developed on the Internet by Google, Bing, Yahoo!, and other providers. In the early days of the Internet, it became clear that the large variety of content and huge number of sites made it difficult to locate what you needed. Search engines became one of the most important tools—without them it was impossible for users to navigate the breathtaking depth of content. As the Internet grew, search providers had to scale their engines to satisfy both the huge volume of web pages and the huge demand for their services. Today, Internet search engines are so efficient and scalable that users take their capabilities for granted, and think nothing of locating a single rarely visited page about, for example, Qing dynasty architecture from among all the public websites that exist. The more you think about this, the more miraculous it seems.

More recently it has become clear that most companies and other organizations also generate large amounts of content and that similar challenges arise despite the smaller scale. Ten thousand documents represent a tiny fraction of the size of the Internet, but it's still impossible for a user to look through them all. A search solution is therefore essential to most companies.

Search efficiency is also a key consideration. Recent research indicates that a typical information worker spends up to nine hours a week searching for information. If you can help users to find that information in seconds rather than minutes, you can immediately boost productivity by 20 percent or more.

SharePoint Server 2010 has a Search technology built on best practices developed for Internet search. It can scale up to index any volume of content and respond rapidly to millions of users. It can also index content stored in many different systems, not just SharePoint, so users can literally search every document and record the enterprise has if you choose to enable it. When you deploy your search solution in a SharePoint farm, your aim is to accelerate users' access to content and therefore increase productivity.

Characterizing Your Content

SharePoint has a search solution that is powerful and complex. Before you can deploy it, you must have a thorough and in-depth understanding of the content. You need to catalog and classify this content against several different criteria.

Start the process by identifying all the locations in your organization where any kind of electronic content is stored. The following list is intended to illustrate typical possibilities but it is by no means exhaustive, and more locations may exist in your case:

- **SharePoint**   Any lists, document libraries, asset libraries, and sites in SharePoint can be indexed. Some companies may have replaced many of the stores listed here with SharePoint sites.

- **File shares**   File shares were the most popular location to store shared files. Although SharePoint document libraries are more functional, you may have to continue to support these for political, historical, or budgetary reasons.

- **Websites**   If your Internet-facing public site is not hosted on SharePoint, that does not mean SharePoint cannot index it. SharePoint can index any HTTP server.

- **Intranet and extranet sites**   Because intranet and extranet sites also use HTTP, SharePoint can index their content.

- **LOB applications**   You can use Business Connectivity Services (BCS) to connect to LOB applications such as SAP and Siebel. Through such connections, SharePoint can index LOB content.

- **Databases**   BCS connections can also import database records into SharePoint external lists. SharePoint can index these records.

- **Exchange Public Folders**   Many organizations use Public Folders in Microsoft Exchange for discussions and knowledge-sharing. SharePoint server can index these so that SharePoint search results can include them.

- **Lotus Domino servers**   If your company uses Lotus Notes for email and other functions, content stored on Domino servers can be included in your SharePoint indexes.

- **Other types of store**   SharePoint can index any store as long as a protocol handler exists for it. Third parties provide protocol handlers for their own technologies and developers can create custom protocol handlers for unusual stores. Protocol handlers are discussed in more detail later in this lesson.

For each of the technologies in the preceding list, investigate how many locations there are. For example, how many file shares exist? For each of these locations, list the number of documents, records, or web pages and the total size of all content. In this way, you build a detailed analysis of enterprise content.

For each of the preceding storage technologies, you must also investigate the different types of file or record it stores. Some technologies have a single type—for example, databases only store database records, although many can now store files as Binary Large Objects (BLOBs). In a file share, by contrast, any type of computer file may appear. Consider the following types of files and records when planning your solution:

- **SharePoint list items**   Any list item stored in SharePoint can be indexed regardless of its content type.
- **Office documents**   All Microsoft Office documents can be indexed, including OneNote files.
- **Web pages**   HTML files may exist in websites, SharePoint lists, file shares, or other locations.
- **XML files**   XML files are widely used for storing information in a semi-structured way.
- **Media assets**   Many media files present challenges to the SharePoint crawler. For example, if a speaker says the word "SharePoint" in an MP3 file, the crawler cannot index it. However, MP3 and other files support other metadata fields. SharePoint can index this data, so you should encourage your users to complete such fields.
- **LOB records**   The format of records and files in LOB applications varies widely. However, if you can import LOB records into external lists, SharePoint can include them in the index.
- **Database records**   SharePoint can index these records if they appear in external lists.
- **Third-party file formats**   SharePoint can index any file or records type as long as an IFilter exists for it. An IFilter is a software component that describes a file format to SharePoint. Third parties provide IFilters for their own technologies and developers can create custom IFilters for unusual files. IFilters are discussed in more detail later in this lesson.

After you have considered the different stores and file types that you must index, you should also thoroughly investigate security requirements for your enterprise content to ensure that rapid access does not compromise sensitive materials. In fact, SharePoint Search is very good at ensuring security:

1. When the crawler indexes any file or record, it also records the Access Control List (ACL) for the file and stores it in the search database.
2. When the user makes a query, all results that satisfy the query terms are returned.
3. Before results are displayed, security trimming removes those results to which the user does not have at least Read permission.

However, you should not consider this security trimming to be foolproof. In particular, consider the following issues:

- Who has access to the index files and search database? Any user account with such access may be used to identify and locate sensitive files.

- Are ACLs properly implemented in the content sources? For example, if you index a file share used exclusively by a small department, can you be sure that department adheres to the principle of least privilege?

- Do LOB, databases, and other stores support ACLs? Some third-party stores have limited or non-existent authorization regimes.

- Do your third-party protocol handlers record ACLs properly? If you have a custom protocol handler, for example, has the developer included code to record ACLs during a crawl?

> **CAUTION HIGHLY SENSITIVE CONTENT**
>
> If you consider the preceding questions carefully, it is perfectly possible to index sensitive materials without enabling unauthorized access. However, some content may be so sensitive or so valuable that the highest levels of protection are required. Consider leaving such materials out of your index. Because there are likely to be a relatively small number of these documents, you may consider searching for these documents less important than protecting them.

The Consequences of Not Indexing

In a company with no enterprise search solution, you rely on your users' knowledge of their own content and its locations, and you should not underestimate their capabilities. However, memories of old projects fade and people move to other departments and other careers. Their replacements may not hear about a document that can solve their problems or complete their knowledge. A common consequence in such situations is that users reinvent the wheel by writing documents that already exist in some obscure store.

The same problem can arise when you have an enterprise search solution, but it is not encyclopedic. For example, you might leave some documents out of the index because they are security-sensitive or because a department did not inform you of their existence. If users regard the search solution as all-knowing and do not receive a result for a query, they assume such a document does not exist. You should try to achieve an index of your entire enterprise if it is possible. If non-indexed documents must exist, you should remind authorized users that they will not show up in search results.

SharePoint Products and Technologies for Search

Some search functionality is included in all editions of SharePoint. However, the capabilities vary widely from a simple site search tool in SharePoint Foundation 2010 to industry-leading encyclopedic enterprise search in FAST Search Server 2010 for SharePoint. The available editions include:

- **Microsoft SharePoint Foundation 2010**   SharePoint Foundation does include a search tool, but it is limited to the local site. This is perfect for a website, for example, and enables visitors to search all pages in the site, but it is not an enterprise search solution.

- **Microsoft SharePoint Server 2010**   SharePoint Server includes all the tools you need to build an enterprise search solution that scales to around 100 million documents.

- **Microsoft Search Server 2010 Express**   Search Server Express is a free download that you can use to build a scalable enterprise search tool to index your enterprise. Advance content management features are not included. This is a good option to consider if you want to add enterprise search to a non-SharePoint document management system or LOB application.

- **Microsoft FAST Search Server 2010 for SharePoint**   FAST Search Server adds the most advanced features and highest scalability to SharePoint search. Up to 500 million documents can be indexed, and tools such as thumbnail document previews, visual best bets, and precise refinements are included. Use FAST for the most powerful, largest, and useable enterprise search solutions.

Use Table 7-1 to make a direct comparison of the search capabilities in SharePoint, Search Server, and FAST. The following sections offer a more detailed discussion of each capability.

TABLE 7-1 Search Capabilities and SharePoint Editions

CAPABILITY	SHAREPOINT SERVER 2010	SEARCH SERVER 2010 EXPRESS	FAST SEARCH SERVER 2010
Enterprise Scale Search	Yes	Yes	Yes
Extreme Scale Search	No	No	Yes
Basic Sorting	Yes	Yes	Yes
Advanced Sorting	No	No	Yes
Best Bets	Yes	Yes	Yes
Visual Best Bets	No	No	Yes
Search Scopes	Yes	Yes	Yes
Query Suggestions and "Did you mean?"	Yes	Yes	Yes
Metadata-Driven Refinement	Yes	Yes	Yes
Deep Refinement	No	No	Yes
People and Expertise Search	Yes	Yes	Yes
Phonetic and Nickname Search	Yes	Yes	Yes
Mobile Search	Yes	Yes	Yes
Windows 7 Search	Yes	Yes	Yes
Click-Through Relevancy	Yes	Yes	Yes

CAPABILITY	SHAREPOINT SERVER 2010	SEARCH SERVER 2010 EXPRESS	FAST SEARCH SERVER 2010
Relevancy Tuning	Yes	Yes	Yes
Tunable Relevance with Multiple Rank Profiles	No	No	Yes
Duplicate Detection	Yes	Yes	Yes
Federated Search	Yes	Yes	Yes
Search Connector Framework	Yes	Yes	Yes
Business Intelligence Indexing Connector	No	No	Yes
Advanced Content Processing	No	No	Yes
Contextual Search	No	No	Yes
Extensible Search	No	No	Yes
Rich Web Indexing	No	No	Yes
Similar Results	No	No	Yes

SharePoint and Search Server Express Capabilities

The following list describes each of the search capabilities in SharePoint Server and Search Server Express in more detail:

- **Enterprise Scale Search**   SharePoint and Search Server can scale up to index around 100 millions documents and records with query responses returned in under 1 second. This is enough for all but the very largest organizations.

- **Basic Sorting**   Users can sort results on a few fields, such as the modified date.

- **Best Bets**   Administrators can create best bets for commonly searched terms. For example, for the query "Disciplinary Procedure," you could create a best bet that links to the company handbook.

- **Search Scopes**   By providing search scopes you enable users to search subsets of your enterprise content. For example, you could create a search scope that included all documents on the Internet-facing website or all documents that were tagged with the term "Technical."

- **Query Suggestions**   As you type, SharePoint suggests common search queries. If you mistype or misspell a query, SharePoint provides "Did you mean?" results. Related queries can also be shown in the results page.

- **Metadata-Driven Refinement**   The search results page includes the new refinements panel that lets you narrow your search rapidly. For example, by clicking a link you can narrow your search to return only Word documents or only documents by a particular author.

- **People and Expertise Search**   When user profiles are in place and populated with data, you can find colleagues by using a dedicated scope and properties such as Ask Me About and Department.

- **Phonetic and Nickname Search**   If you are introduced to someone, you may misspell his or her name in a search. SharePoint returns all People Search results that sound the same. For example, if you search for "John," a user called "Jon Jaffe" would be returned.

- **Mobile Search**   Search SharePoint from your Windows Phone or other smart phones.

- **Windows 7 Search**   When you use the Windows 7 desktop search tool, you can receive results from your enterprise index.

- **Click-Through Relevancy**   Results that are popular receive a boost in relevancy so that they appear closer to the top of result lists.

- **Relevancy Tuning**   Administrators can tune the relevancy algorithm. This algorithm determines which results appear at the top of result lists.

- **Duplicate Detection**   If your enterprise has multiple versions of the same document, SharePoint lists them as a single result to reduce clutter.

- **Federated Search**   Include results from external search engines on your results page. This could be a non-SharePoint location, such as Bing, or another SharePoint Search Center in your own organization.

- **Search Connector Framework**   You can use the protocol handlers and IFilters to index many different types of stores and files. SharePoint includes IFilters and protocol handlers for many common technologies, and you can use BCS connections to extend the crawler's reach further. Developers can also create custom IFilters and protocol handlers for unusual or unique technologies. In this way, you can create an index for all the content in your entire organization.

FAST Search Capabilities

When you add FAST Search Server 2010 to your SharePoint search solution, you can make use of the following extra capabilities:

- **Extreme Scale Search**   100 million documents in an index is large enough for most organizations. Occasionally, organizations need larger indexes to maintain query response times that are less than 1 second. With FAST, you can index up to around 500 million documents.

- **Advanced Sorting**   You can sort search results based on any managed property.

- **Visual Best Bets**   Best bets in FAST can include a graphic or rich media element.

- **Deep Refinement**   The refinement panel in a FAST results page is richer with links to extra refinements. Each refinement link also includes the exact number of documents it returns.

- **Tunable Relevance with Multiple Rank Profiles**   In FAST, the relevancy given to each result is determined by a rank profile. A rank profile consists of the weight given to content freshness, proximity, context, and other factors. You can define multiple rank profiles and assign different profiles to different groups of users.

- **Business Intelligence Indexing Connector**   If you use Excel Services or SharePoint Reporting Services, the Business Intelligence Indexing Connector generates richer results for workbooks and reports. For example, descriptions are richer, and extra properties unique to workbooks and reports appear in the refinement panel.

- **Advanced Content Processing**   FAST can automatically extract terms and keywords from a document and save the terms and keywords in the document's metadata. This is extremely useful if users are not in the habit of completing document properties fully.

- **Contextual Search**   You can tailor search results based on the user context or audience.

- **Extensible Search**   With FAST it is easy to create custom search applications such as research and development portals and knowledge bases for support personnel.

- **Similar Results**   Each result has a Similar Results link. When users click this link, they see results that did not satisfy the query but are close in content to the result.

SharePoint Search Architecture

The SharePoint enterprise search solution is built on a wide variety of components that index content, accept queries, and display results. In this section, you will learn about these components and how to place them in your SharePoint farm. You will also examine the processes by which SharePoint indexes content and responds to user queries.

The Search User Interface

Search tools appear in many locations in the SharePoint user interface. For example, you can create a dedicated search center—this is a SharePoint site that is based on the Enterprise Search Center template. However, the search box appears on all pages in the Team Site template and enables users to run searches from that site directly, without navigating to a search center first.

All parts of the search user interface are built from specialist Web Parts. Administrators can customize search and results pages by customizing the position and properties of these Web Parts just like they can for any other Web Part page. Table 7-2 lists and describes these Web Parts.

TABLE 7-2 Search Web Parts

WEB PART	DESCRIPTION
Search Box	Users enter query terms into this Web Part. They can also select a search scope and click the Search button.
Advanced Search Box	Users enter standard queries and can also query managed properties and parameters.
People Search Box	This Web Part is like the Search Box except that it only searches the People scope.

WEB PART	DESCRIPTION
Dual Chinese Search	Used to search dual Chinese documents and items simultaneously.
Search Core Results	This Web Part shows the main results list.
People Search Core Results	This Web Part is like the Search Core Results Web Part except that it only displays results from the People scope.
Refinement Panel	This Web Part displays a range of links that users can click to refine their search rapidly. This Web Part is at the left of the standard results page.
People Refinement Panel	This Web Part is like the Refinement Panel except that it displays refinements for user profiles only.
Search Best Bets	This displays the Best Bet results administrators have created for common search terms. These results are usually at the top of the results page.
Related Queries	Displays "Did You Mean" queries and other common queries that are close to the search terms the user entered.
Search Paging	Enables users to browse to later pages of search results.
Search Statistics	Displays the approximate total number of results and the time taken to return results.
Federated Results	Displays results from federated locations, such as Internet search engines or other SharePoint farms.
Top Federated Results	Displays the top ranked results from a federated location.

These Web Parts appear throughout the SharePoint user interface and become very familiar to users. Figure 7-1 shows the Search Box Web Part on a Team Site page.

FIGURE 7-1 The Search Box Web Part

For a dedicated search site, you can use the Enterprise Search Center template. Figure 7-2 shows the home page for such a site. Notice the Search Box Web Part and the search scopes.

Most of the Web Parts in the Table 7-2 display results, statistics, or other information on results pages. Figure 7-3 shows a typical results page. You can see the Core Results, Best Bets, Refinement Panel, and other Web Parts.

You can also place these Web Parts on any customized Web Part page within SharePoint. For example, you can add the People Search Box to an HR team site so that staff can rapidly locate personnel in any department.

FIGURE 7-2 An Enterprise Search Center home page

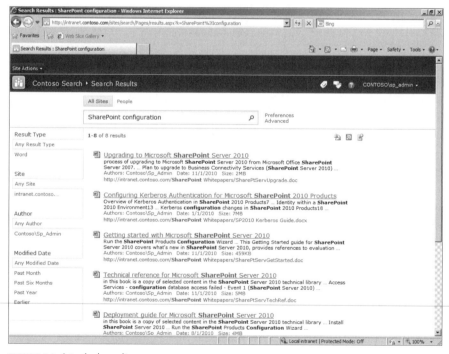

FIGURE 7-3 A typical results page

Server Roles

SharePoint Server 2010 includes a Search service application that you must create and configure to enable search in your farm. As for the Managed Metadata and User Profile service applications, you can have one Search service application that handles all indexing and queries or multiple service applications to partition indexes. This lesson assumes that you will create one global Search service application in your farm. For more details about multiple Search service applications, see Lesson 3.

A single Search service application contains several server roles. You can run all these roles on a single server or distribute them onto several servers to scale out your search solution.

- **Crawl Servers**   A Crawl Server builds and stores the index file. The crawler runs on the Crawl Servers and runs queries against web front-end servers and other content sources to build a picture of the content. SharePoint Sever 2010 is the first version of SharePoint in which you can create more than one Crawl Server in a SharePoint farm.

- **Query Servers**   When the index is complete, it is distributed to all the Query Servers. When users submit queries, they are sent to a Query Server to return results.

- **Database Servers**   The index is a file and is not stored in a database. However, the Search service application does create and use the following three databases that must be placed on a SQL Server:

  - The Search Administration Database. This stores the search configuration.

  - The Search Property Database. This stores managed properties, history data, and other crawl information.

  - The Crawl Database. This stores ACLs, the values of managed properties, and other metadata.

IFilters and Protocol Handlers

SharePoint Search is design to be modular and extensible. New or unusual storage technologies and file types can, at least in theory, be indexed by the SharePoint crawler as long as it can communicate with the store and understand the contents of the files. Two types of software component enable this:

- **Protocol Handlers**   These communicate with the information store so that the crawler can obtain its content. For example, the File Protocol Handler communicates with Server Message Block (SMB) file servers so that the crawler can access Windows file shares and index the files in them.

- **IFilters**   These describe the structure of a file type to the crawler so that it can diagnose and index the words within it. For example, Word documents with .doc and .docx extensions are supported by an IFilter.

SharePoint Server 2010 and Search Server 2010 Express include a wide range of Protocol Handlers and IFilters out-of-the-box, so you may frequently find that all your enterprise content can be crawled without modifying the default components. However, sometimes you must add extra Protocol Handlers and IFilters. Third parties provide these for common storage technologies and file types. Developers can also create custom IFilters and Protocol Handlers.

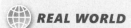 **REAL WORLD**

Alistair Matthews

Lots of organizations use PDF files, but an IFilter is not included in SharePoint Server 2010 by default. In fact, Microsoft does not provide one at all. This is the most common reason to add an extra IFilter to SharePoint.

Three vendors—Adobe, Foxit, and TET—do provide PDF IFilters, so you must decide which you prefer. A very detailed comparison is available at the following location: *http://blogs.msdn.com/b/opal/archive/2009/03/10/pdf-ifilter-battle-second-round.aspx*

It's simple to install and use any of these IFilters, but make sure that you use the 64-bit version—it is the only one that works with SharePoint 2010.

The Search Process

It is important to understand fully how SharePoint crawls content and runs queries so that you can architect an efficient and highly available search solution. This knowledge will also help you with troubleshooting.

SharePoint crawls content on a schedule that administrators configure. Because crawling is a resource-intensive process, it is important to make sure that it does not consume resources and deny service to users. You can do so by scheduling the crawl at off-peak hours, but if your users work around the clock, extra hardware and dedicated servers may be required.

HOW SHAREPOINT CRAWLS CONTENT

A crawl server indexes all the content sources you have configured to create the index file and populate search databases. The crawl usually runs at scheduled times, but administrators can also manually initiate crawls. For each content source you define, you can schedule two types of crawls:

- **Full Crawl**   All items in the content source are indexed.
- **Incremental Crawl**   Only items that have changed since the last crawl are indexed.

Incremental crawls conserve resources and are sufficient to ensure an up-to-date index. However, you should also schedule occasional full crawls, perhaps once a week, to double-check every item.

When a crawl runs, SharePoint completes the following steps:

1. The crawler obtains the first start address from the content database.

2. The crawler invokes the appropriate protocol handler for the address.

3. The protocol handler identifies all the nodes in the content source. For example, on a file share, a node would be a file. In a SharePoint list, a node would be an item.

4. For each node, the protocol handler invokes the appropriate IFilter.

5. The IFilter extracts properties, metadata, and ACLs from the node. The crawler adds these to the crawl database.

6. The content of the node is broken into words.

7. Noise words such as *the* and *to* are removed.

8. The words are added to the index.

9. The crawler moves to the next node.

10. When all the nodes in the first start address have been crawled, the crawler moves to the next start address.

11. When all the start addresses in the content source have been crawled, the index is complete. The Crawl Server copies the index file to all query servers in batches.

> **NOTE THE SEARCH SERVICE ACCOUNT**
>
> The crawler runs in the security context of the search service account. This should be a managed account and you select it when you set up the Search service application. You must select an account that has write permission to the location on all query servers where the index is stored; otherwise, the index cannot be propagated.

> **NOTE SCHEDULING CRAWLS**
>
> If you have lots of high-specification hardware, you can index very often without reducing responsiveness for users. However, because the crawl is resource-intensive, scheduling crawls at off-peak hours is popular. When you plan your crawl schedules you must weigh the importance of an up-to-date index against the possible impact of crawls during office hours. In some companies, users are productive around the clock, so crawls must always be concurrent with high demand.
>
> If you choose to index every 24 hours, for example, be aware that new nodes will not reach the index for several hours. Users can be confused if they cannot locate a document they know has just been created, so it's a good idea to inform users about this issue and explain that the very latest nodes may not appear in search results.

THE QUERY PROCESS

When a user submits a query, the rapid response seems to imply a simple process. However, because SharePoint is an advance enterprise search engine, the process has several stages:

1. The user enters query terms and clicks the Search button.

2. Extra information, such as the user's identity and location, are added to the query terms.

3. The complete query is forwarded to a query server.

4. The query server runs the query against the index and the crawl database.

5. For each result, the query server obtains the ACL stored in the crawl database.

6. The query server removes all the results that the user does not have read access to. This process is called *security trimming*.

7. The results are returned to the web server and displayed to the user.

> **NOTE** **PROPERTY SEARCHES**
>
> By using the Advanced Search tool or entering advanced query syntax, users can query only managed properties. For example, they could search for all documents authored by Pat Coleman. Because managed properties are stored in the crawl database, such queries are run against the database server only and the index itself is not needed.

Configuring Search

Now that you understand how search works in SharePoint 2010, you can configure it to match your plans by following these procedures.

Deploying a Search Service Application

As for managed metadata and user profiles, you must begin your search configuration by creating and configuring the Search service application. Continue your configuration by creating content sources and search scopes.

START THE INTIAL FARM CONFIGURATION WIZARD

> **CAUTION** **RESULTS OF THE INITIAL FARM CONFIGURATION WIZARD**
>
> When you use the Initial Farm Configuration Wizard to deploy the Search service application, you are not asked about many aspects of its configuration. For example, you cannot specify a location for the crawl database and it is automatically placed on the same database server as the content databases. This may not match your deployment plan. For the most flexible Search service application deployment, use Central Administration or Windows PowerShell as described in later procedures.

1. In the Central Administration Quick Launch, click Configuration Wizards.

2. Under Farm Configuration, click Launch The Farm Configuration Wizard.

3. Click Start The Wizard.

4. Under Service Account, configure the SharePoint service application account as you have planned.

5. Under Services, ensure that the Search Service Application check box is selected, along with the other service applications you want to configure.

6. Click Next.

   Your service applications are created and configured.

7. On the next page, fill in the details if you wish to configure a site collection and then click OK. Otherwise, click Skip.

8. Click Finish.

DEPLOY A SEARCH SERVICE APPLICATION MANUALLY

A farm administrator can create and configure a Search service application by completing the following steps:

1. In the Central Administration Quick Launch, click Application Management.

2. Under Service Applications, click Manage Service Applications.

3. Click New, and then click Search Service Application.

4. In the Create New Search Service Application dialog box, in the Name box, type a suitable name, such as **Contoso Search Service Application**.

5. Under FAST Service Application, select None.

> **NOTE** **FAST SERVICE APPLICATIONS**
>
> In this procedure, you are deploying a native SharePoint Search service application, so you select None here. For more information about FAST deployment, see Lesson 2.

6. In the Search Service Account box, select the user account that the Search service application uses to authenticate with content sources.

7. Under Application Pool for Search Admin Web Service, configure the properties that you planned. For example, if you planned to use a single application pool for all service applications, select it from the list.

8. Under Application Pool for Search Query and Site Settings Web Service, configure the properties that you planned.

9. Click OK.

10. When the process is complete, click OK.

DEPLOY A SEARCH SERVICE APPLICATION IN WINDOWS POWERSHELL

When you use Windows PowerShell to configure search, you must issue several commands. Start by issuing the *New-SPEnterpriseSearchServiceApplication* cmdlet to create a new Search service application:

```
$SearchApp = New-SPEnterpriseSearchServiceApplication -Name <ServiceName>
-ApplicationPool <AppPool>
```

Where:

- *<ServiceName>* is the name you have chosen for your service application, such as Contoso Search Service Application.

- *<AppPool>* is the name of, GUID of, or reference to an existing application pool.

Next you must create a service application proxy to enable web applications to connect to the new service application:

```
$SearchAppProxy = New-SPEnterpriseSearchServiceApplicationProxy -Name <ProxyName>
-Uri $SearchApp.Uri.AbsoluteURI
```

Where:

- *<ProxyName>* is the name you have chosen for your service application proxy, such as Contoso Search Service Application Proxy.

> **NOTE THE –URI PARAMETER**
>
> The *–Uri* parameter specifies the URI of the Search service application you created in the previous command. The easiest way to provide this path is to save the Search service application in a variable—in this case *$SearchApp*—and call its *Uri.Absolute.URI* property.

You must also create a new Search Administration Component. Do this by issuing the *Set-SPEnterpriseSearchAdministrationComponent* cmdlet:

```
$SearchServiceInstance = Get-SPEnterpriseSearchServiceInstance -Local
Set-SPEnterpriseSearchAdministrationComponent -SearchApplication $SearchApp
-SearchServiceInstance $SearchServiceInstance
```

Defining Content Sources

When you use Central Administration to create a Search service application, a default content source called Local SharePoint Sites is also created. It includes all SharePoint sites that are hosted on the local server. You should review the settings for this content source to ensure that it matches your plans. You can either adjust the properties or delete the Local SharePoint Sites content source and create content sources from scratch. To create a content source, complete the following steps:

1. In the Central Administration Quick Launch, click Application Management.

2. Under Service Applications click Manage Service Applications.

3. Click the Search service application you created earlier.

4. On the Quick Launch, under Crawling, click Content Sources.

5. Click New Content Source.

6. In the Name text box, type a descriptive name, such as **Internet Site Content Source**.

7. Under Content Source Type, select the storage technology for this content source.

8. Under Start Addresses, type one or more URLs where content is stored.

> **NOTE** **CONTEXT-SENSITIVE USER INTERFACE**
>
> The options you must configure on this page depend on the Content Source Type that you selected. The rest of this procedure assumes you selected SharePoint Sites as an example.

9. Under Crawl Settings, choose whether to crawl subsites under the start address or just the top-level site in the site collection.

10. Under Crawl Schedules, in the Full Crawl drop-down list, select an existing schedule or click Create Schedule.

11. In the Incremental Crawl drop-down list select an existing schedule or click Create Schedule.

12. Under Content Source Priority select Normal or High Priority.

13. Under Start Full Crawl, select the box to initiate a full crawl immediately.

14. Click OK.

Defining Search Scopes

Administrators should plan and create search scopes so that users can search through portions of the enterprise content. For example, you could create a search scope for documents created by engineers, or documents in the intranet site collection.

To define a search scope, complete the following steps:

1. In the Central Administration Quick Launch, click Application Management.

2. Under Service Applications click Manage Service Applications.

3. Click the Search service application you created earlier.

4. On the Quick Launch, under Queries and Results, click Scopes.

> **NOTE** **DEFAULT SEARCH SCOPES**
>
> Notice that there are two search scopes by default: the All Sites scope, which includes all enterprise content, and the People scope, which includes all user profiles and enables People Search.

5. Click New Scope.

6. In the Title text box, type a descriptive name for the scope, such as **Engineer's Documents**.

7. In the Description text box, type a description of the scope and its contents.

8. Optionally, to forward users to a dedicated results page, specify a target results page URL under Target Results.

9. Click OK.

10. Click the scope you just created.

11. Under Rules, click New Rule.

> **NOTE CONTEXT-SENSITIVE USER INTERFACE**
>
> The options you must configure in this page depend on the Scope Rule Type that you select. The rest of this procedure assumes you select Property Query as an example.

12. Under Scope Rule Type, select Property Query.

13. In the Add Property Restrictions drop-down list, choose a property to test, such as JobTitle.

14. In the = text box, type a value, such as **Engineer**.

15. Under Behavior, choose whether to include matching results in the scope, exclude matching results from the scope, or require that all results in the scope match this rule.

16. Click OK.

17. On the Quick Launch, click Search Administration.

18. Under System Status, next to Scopes Needing Update, click Start Update Now.

> **IMPORTANT SEARCH CENTER SITES**
>
> The Search service application is now functional and indexing is working. However, before users can make queries, you must create a search site. To do this, create a site in an existing or new site collection based on the Basic Search Center or Enterprise Search Center template. For more information about creating sites, see Chapter 4, "Administering and Securing SharePoint Content."

PRACTICE Configure Search

Practices are designed to guide you through important procedures. The instructions in the Training Kit are high-level instructions that will challenge you to think carefully and to apply the procedures that are covered in this lesson and elsewhere in the Training Kit. If you need assistance, consult the detailed, step-by-step instructions in the Practice Answers on the companion media.

In this practice, you configure a Search service application for the SharePoint farm. You will also ensure that the Search service account has the correct rights, crawl the content, and make sample queries.

Prepare for the Practice

Before you perform this practice, you must ensure that your lab environment has been built according to the instructions found in the Introduction to this Training Kit.

1. Apply the snapshot CHAPTER 06 to CONTOSO-DC.

2. Apply the snapshot CHAPTER 06 to SP2010-WFE1.

3. Start CONTOSO-DC.

   Wait for the virtual machine to complete startup, at which time the Press Ctrl+Alt+Delete prompt appears.

4. Start SP2010-WFE1.

5. Log on to SP2010-WFE1 as **CONTOSO\SP_Admin** with the password **Pa$$w0rd**.

EXERCISE 1 Add Some Documents

To demonstrate search functionality, SharePoint must have some content to index. In this exercise, you copy some documents to a SharePoint document library.

- Browse to the SharePoint site at ***http://intranet.contoso.com***.

- Add a new Document Library named SharePoint Whitepapers.

- Add all the documents in the following folder to the new Document Library: C:\70667TK\Practice Files\07-01*.*

EXERCISE 2 Register a Managed Account for the Search Service

In this exercise, you register the SP_Crawl account as a managed account.

- Register CONTOSO\SP_Crawl as a managed account. The password of the account is Pa$$w0rd.

EXERCISE 3 Grant Local Group Membership to the Search Service Account

In this exercise, you ensure that the SP_Crawl account has the necessary rights and group membership.

- Use Server Manage to administer local groups.

- Add the CONTOSO\SP_Crawl account to the WSS_WPG group.

EXERCISE 4 Configure the Search Service Application

In this exercise, you create and configure a Search service application for your farm.

- Use Central Administration to create a new Search service application. Use the following specifications and guidance:

  - Name: Search Server Application – Enterprise

  - FAST Service Application: None

  - Search Service Account: CONTOSO\SP_Crawl

  - Application Pool For Search Admin Web Service: SharePoint Service Applications

  - Application Pool For Search Query And Site Settings Web Service: SharePoint Service Applications

EXERCISE 5   Define Content Sources

In this exercise, you configure content sources for the new Search service application.

- In Central Administration, examine the list of Content Sources for the new Search service application.
- Edit the Local SharePoint Sites content source.
- Ensure that *http://intranet.contoso.com* is included in the list of Start Addresses.
- Configure a full crawl to run once a week on Sunday at 1:00 A.M.
- Configure an incremental crawl to run every day at 12:00 A.M.

EXERCISE 6   Define Search Scopes

In this exercise, you configure a new search scope that includes only Word documents.

- Create a new search scope. Use the following specifications and guidance:
  - Title: Word Documents
  - Description: Search all Word documents in the enterprise.
- Add a new rule to the search scope. Use the following specifications and guidance:
  - Search Rule Type: Property Query
  - Query: FileExtension = doc
  - Behavior: Include
- Add a second new rule to the search scope. Use the following specifications and guidance:
  - Search Rule Type: Property Query
  - Query: FileExtension = docx
  - Behavior: Include

EXERCISE 7   Initiate a Crawl

In this exercise, you run a full crawl to index the SharePoint farm.

- Open the list of Content Sources.
- Initiate a full crawl on the Local SharePoint Sites content source.
- When the crawl is complete, examine the crawl history.

EXERCISE 8   Create an Enterprise Search Center

In this exercise, you create a new Site Collection based on the Enterprise Search Center template.

- Create a new site collection. Use the following specifications and guidance:
  - Web Application: *http://intranet.contoso.com*
  - Title: Contoso Search
  - Description: Use this site to search all Contoso content.

- Web Site Address: *http://intranet.contoso.com/sites/search*
- Template: Enterprise Search Center
- Primary Site Collection Administrator: CONTOSO\SP_Admin
- Restart the SP2010-WFE1 image.

EXERCISE 9   Query the Index

In this exercise, you run queries against your new search solution.

- Use Internet Explorer to browse to ***http://intranet.contoso.com/sites/search***.
- Search for SharePoint content.
- Browse to ***http://intranet.contoso.com***.
- Edit the Site Collection Search Settings.
- Enable custom scopes and forward users to *http://intranet.contoso.com/sites/search/pages* for results.
- Set the Dropdown Mode to Show Scopes Dropdown.
- Go to the list of Site Scopes and click Display Groups.
- Edit the Search Dropdown group.
- Add the Word Documents scope to the Search Dropdown group.
- Return to the intranet home page and refresh the page.
- Search for SharePoint in the Word Document scope.
- Log off of SP2010-WFE1.

Lesson Summary

- The search technologies developed and proven on the Internet are applicable in enterprises and can accelerate knowledge workers' access to the content they need.
- SharePoint Server 2010 and Search Server 2010 can index content throughout your organization in many file types and storage technologies to create a true enterprise search solution.
- FAST Search Server 2010 for SharePoint adds the richest search functionality to your solution, including thumbnails, extra refinements with precise numbers, and greatest scalability.
- SharePoint Search maintains security by storing the ACLs associated with each node and security trimming search results.
- The SharePoint Search user interface is constructed from Web Parts so that you can easily customize it to user requirements.
- SharePoint Search is provided by the Search service application. As for the other service applications, you can configure a single Search service application for your enterprise or deploy multiple instances to smaller groups of users.

- You can configure existing SharePoint servers to perform search functions or dedicate servers to Index, Query, and Search Database roles.

- SharePoint include IFilters for common file types and Protocol Handlers for common storage technologies. To extend the reach of the crawler you can use BCS connections or add third-party IFilters and Protocol Handlers.

- Although the Initial Farm Configuration Wizard can deploy the Search service application, it is recommended that you plan the deployment carefully and perform it manually by using Central Administration or Windows PowerShell.

- Define content sources for all the locations where you keep content. Content sources include schedules on which full and incremental searches are run.

- Define search scopes to enable users to search subsets of your content.

Lesson Review

You can use the following questions to test your knowledge of the information in Lesson 1, "Configure Search." The questions are also available on the companion media in a practice test if you prefer to review them in electronic form.

> **NOTE   ANSWERS**
>
> Answers to these questions and explanations of why each answer choice is right or wrong are located in the "Answers" section at the end of the book.

1. You are deploying Search for your SharePoint farm. You want to create a single search solution for all users and all content in your enterprise. You use SharePoint for document management and to host your intranet. You use an LOB system to manage production and customer relationships, and you use Lotus Notes for email and discussion groups. Your public website is written in PHP and hosted on an Apache server. Which of the following configuration tasks should you complete? (Choose all that apply.)

   A. Create an account for the Search service and register it as a managed account.

   B. Ensure that the account you created is a member of the WSS_WPG group on SharePoint servers.

   C. Ensure that the account you created is a member of the WSS_Admin_WPG group on SharePoint servers.

   D. Create a single Search service application.

   E. Create a Search service application for each planned content source.

   F. Define four content sources for SharePoint, the LOB application, Lotus Notes, and the public website.

   G. Create an Enterprise Search Center site.

2. You have configured the Search service application, and users can successfully run queries in an Enterprise Search Center. A user complains that PDF files she knows to exist in a file share are not returned in search results. Which of the following actions could solve this problem? (Choose all that apply.)

A. Add a content source for the file share to the Search service application.

B. Add a start address for the file share to an existing content source in the Search service application.

C. Install a Protocol Handler for file shares.

D. Install a Protocol Handler for PDF documents.

E. Install an IFilter for file shares.

F. Install an IFilter for PDF documents.

Lesson 2: Refine Search

The search functionality included in SharePoint Server 2010 is powerful and incisive. Many organizations may find that a simple Search service application with a single Enterprise Search Center suits their purposes very well. However, many find that their specific needs require a more unusual configuration. In SharePoint, you can make many adaptations to target your solution to the unique needs of your workers. In this lesson, you will see the need for and nature of these adaptations and learn how to configure them.

After this lesson, you will be able to:

- Describe how keywords, best bets, and managed properties help users to find the content they need more quickly.
- Understand federated search and diagnose situations in which it is useful.
- Understand how to target search pages to users' needs.
- Configure keywords, best bets, and managed properties.
- Federate your Search service application with SharePoint and other search tools.
- Customize the search tools to target user needs.
- Understand refinements that are only possible in FAST Search Server 2010 for SharePoint.

Estimated Lesson Time: 40 minutes

The Need for Adaptation

As you learned in Lesson 1, SharePoint provides an encyclopedic search solution that can index your entire enterprise. It is natural to assume that such an all-encompassing tool suits all businesses out of the box, but this is not the case. In fact, one size does not fit all and each company has unique needs that derive from its unique business. SharePoint search can adapt to all these needs. Consider the following examples.

Partner Organizations

By specializing within an industry, many enterprises aim to excel in a small but complex field. However, this strategy requires the involvement of other companies to deliver a complete project to a customer, so a number of critical partnerships must be developed. Close day-to-day communication between your own users and partner users is essential. Sharing knowledge is a key to success.

Each company in the partnership may have its own enterprise search solution. You should consider whether to integrate these solutions to enable users to locate documents from throughout the partnership. SharePoint can accommodate this requirement by federating search results with SharePoint Search Centers and other standards-based search tools in each partner.

Design Companies

For a graphic design company, the look and feel of content is uniquely important and often outweighs the words. Consider, for example, a designer who works for two clients and has prepared terms and conditions documents for both. Later she searches for those documents.

These documents are likely to be similar in syntax and in the vocabulary used. In standard SharePoint search results, it may be difficult to tell them apart. However, as soon as you open the documents, one look is enough to differentiate them, because the branding and layout are entirely different.

FAST Search Server 2010 can include graphical thumbnails of all items in a results list. The designer in this case can locate the document she needs without opening each one, because the thumbnail makes the look and feel of each document clear.

Technical Consultancies

When you have a large body of content in your index, many results are returned for each query. You are probably aware of how important it is on the Internet to get your website among the top results in search engines such as Google and Bing. Similarly, in an enterprise search, it is important to get relevant results to the top.

SharePoint has a complex and customizable algorithm that determines the order of results and tries to place the most relevant results near the top. For example, popular items, which users frequently click in the core results Web Part, are considered likely to be relevant and boosted up the order. However, your own company may have unique circumstances that require you to modify relevancy calculations.

Consider an engineering company that specializes in jet engine parts. Certain words, such as *turbine*, *fairing*, and *bearing*, have a particular meaning that is rarely used in other industries. Documents containing such specific terms are likely to be relevant to technicians and should appear close to the top of search results. You can create keywords for each of these terms so that matching documents appear at the top of results.

Ways to Refine Search Results

SharePoint Server 2010 Search can be tuned to target the unique requirements described in the preceding situation and many other circumstances. Administrators and architects must have a thorough understanding of the options available to ensure that users get to the content they need in the smallest number of clicks. The following sections describe these refinement options.

Keywords and Best Bets

Keywords and best bets enable administrators to influence the results that are returned to a user for a given query:

- **Keywords** A keyword declares a term to be of particular importance to the SharePoint query engine. If the user enters a keyword as part of a query, documents that contain that keyword receive a boost in the relevance calculation and appear at the top of the results. A keyword can be either a single word or a phrase, and you can also enter any number of synonyms. You can optionally enter a definition for future reference.

- **Best Bet** A best bet is a way to direct users to the result that is most likely to satisfy their needs. For example, when users enter the query "Vacation booking procedure" they may receive 50 results, but it is most likely they want to read the entry in the company handbook. Best bets appear at the top of the search results, before the Core Results Web Part, as shown in Figure 7-4. To create a best bet you must first create a keyword for the term or phrase. You can then add any number of best bets, each with a title and description—which SharePoint will display in the results page—and a URL to the relevant document.

FIGURE 7-4 Best bets in an enterprise search center results page

> **IMPORTANT** **RESPONDING TO COMMON QUERIES**
>
> Before you deploy your search solution, you must carefully plan all aspects, including keywords and best bets. However, you must be aware the users may not behave as predicted and you might have to respond. You can spot what users do by enabling and examining SharePoint query logging.

If you notice, for example, that many users search for "Office Help," that may indicate a need for more training resources. You could add an Office online training course to your intranet to satisfy this need, but you need to make it easy to find. Use a keyword and corresponding best bet to alert users to the course's existence.

Managed Properties

SharePoint indexes a wide range of properties for each item by default. For an appointment item in a SharePoint Calendar list, for example, the subject and notes properties are crawled. Other properties, such as the GUID, are not likely to be searched for, so SharePoint leaves them out of the index. In the case of files, the content is always indexed with certain important properties. For example, when the crawler indexes a Word document, it crawls the main body of the document as well as the author and title properties in its metadata. The properties that SharePoint indexes are called *managed properties*.

Often the default set of managed properties are sufficient and requires no modification. However, consider the following cases:

- **A custom content type** A user or developer has created a custom content type in a list, perhaps by adding extra fields to an existing type, such as a new content type called Product that contains a Part Number field. It's very important for the users to be able to locate Products by searching for the Part Number. You must add the Part Number field as a managed property.

- **An external content type** A BCS connection has imported database items into SharePoint with unique fields. For example, you have connected to an HR database by using BCS and have a new external list that includes all the employees in your company. HR staff must be able to locate an employee by searching for his or her Employee Number. Again, you must add the Employee Number field as a managed property.

> *NOTE* **ADDING MANAGED PROPERTIES**
>
> Managed properties are simple to add but the Search service must have indexed an example before you can add them. For example, after the Product content type is created, you must create the first Product in the list and run an incremental crawl. Only then will you be able to add a managed property for the Part Number field because SharePoint has recorded its existence. For more information about this procedure, see the next section in this lesson. For more information about content types, see Chapter 5, "Service Applications and the Managed Metadata Service."

You can narrow searches to examine specific managed properties by using property search syntax. For example, to return all items that have the *ProductRange* property set to *Adventure*, use this query:

ProductRange:Query

Note that there are no spaces between the words and the colon.

MORE INFO **SHAREPOINT SEARCH SYNTAX**

For more information about the syntax you can use in SharePoint queries, see "Building Search Queries" at *http://msdn.microsoft.com/en-us/library/ee556426.aspx*.

Federated Search

If your SharePoint Search solution has an index that contains all the content users ever need, all queries can be run against that index. As you have seen, because of the wide support in SharePoint for different stores and node types, this is a common scenario. However, sometimes you must have more than one index and you would like users to receive results from many indexes at the same time. This is when federated search is useful. Consider these example scenarios:

- **Multiple SharePoint Search service applications**   In a global organization, you may want to provide, for example, a European search center and a North American search center so that users receive rapid responses from local servers. To enable this you create one Search service application for each continent. You expect users to find local results most relevant but you want to display results from remote continents as well. You can federate the European search center with the North American search center to achieve this.

- **SharePoint Search and other search solutions**   Let's say you use SharePoint to provide search but a partner organization uses Google Search Appliance to index content. Again you'd like users to see results from both. Because both SharePoint and Google Search Appliance support the OpenSearch standard, you can add Google Search Appliance as a federated location in SharePoint.

- **SharePoint Search and Internet search engines**   Perhaps a specialist search engine dedicated to your industry has been set up on the Internet. You want to present these results to users along with SharePoint results. If the specialist search engine supports OpenSearch, you can add it as a federated location in the Search service application.

MORE INFO   **THE OPENSEARCH STANDARD**

OpenSearch is a new standard that enables search solutions from different vendors to share results. You can find out more at *http://www.opensearch.org*.

When you federate one search solution with another, user queries are sent to both indexes and results are displayed in the same page. In SharePoint, federated results are displayed in the federated results Web Parts, so users can clearly differentiate them from results from the local index. After you have added a federated location, make sure you remember to add these Web Parts to the results page or users will not see federated results.

A federated location also includes a trigger. You can use the trigger to filter which queries are sent to the federated location. The three types of triggers are:

- **Always**   All queries are sent to the federated location.
- **Prefix**   Only queries that start with the string you specify are sent to the federated location.
- **Pattern**   Only queries that match the .NET regular expression you specify are sent to the federated location.

> **MORE INFO   REGULAR EXPRESSIONS**
>
> Regular expressions are an extremely powerful method of pattern matching. For more information about how to formulate a regular expression, see the following page:
> *http://msdn.microsoft.com/en-us/library/hs600312.aspx.*

Custom Search Pages

In Lesson 1, you saw how to provide a search user interface by creating a Basic or Enterprise Search Center site. Although these site templates are hugely functional, you can also add custom search pages to any existing site.

To do this, you first add a web page to any site in which you have write permissions. Then insert the Search Box Web Part on that page. You can either add a second page to display results or add the Search Core Results Web Part to the same page as the Search Box. Edit the properties of the Search Box Web Part to forward requests to the page with the Search Core Results Web Part. This technique enables administrators to place search functionality wherever it is required in SharePoint sites without any custom code.

Customizing the Refinement Panel

The Refinement Panel is a critical tool that lets users drill down into large result sets quickly to find the document they need. It is a Web Part that you can add to any page with the Search Core Results Web Part on it. The links that it displays are dependent on filters that are defined in the Web Parts properties. You can add extra filters to the default set to customize the behavior of the Refinement Panel.

> **NOTE   EDITING REFINEMENT PANEL FILTERS**
>
> Refinement Panel Filters are defined in XML code, which you can see in the properties of the Web Part. Some experience with XML is required to define your own filters. It is also helpful to use an XML Editor such as Visual Studio for this purpose, although the task can be completed with any text editor.

FAST Search Server 2010 for SharePoint Refinements

SharePoint Server 2010 has advanced enterprise search built in, and many companies will find it satisfies all their search requirements. The refinements listed in the preceding section can all be made without FAST. However, you should remember that FAST enables extra refinements that are not possible in SharePoint Server 2010:

- **Advanced Sorting**   Users can sort results by more fields.
- **Visual Best Bets**   Best bet links can include graphics and rich media.
- **Multiple Rank Profiles**   You can tune relevance calculation differently for different groups of users.
- **Similar Results**   Each result has a link to similar results that have similar content but do not match the user's initial search.

For more details about these refinements, see Lesson 1. If you need any of the preceding refinements, you should plan to deploy FAST. For more information about the topology of a FAST farm and deployment, see Lesson 3.

Configuring Refinements

Use the following procedures to configure search refinements in SharePoint Server 2010.

Keywords and Best Bets

Keywords and best bets enable the administrator to influence results supplied to users. Results that match a keyword are boosted in relevance and therefore appear at the top of results pages. Best bets are links presented to the user in a separate Web Part when he searches for a keyword.

> **NOTE   KEYWORD AND BEST BET ADMINISTRATION**
>
> Keywords and best bets are configured by site administrators at the site collection level. You do not need to be a farm administrator or have access to Central Administration to configure these properties.

ADD A KEYWORD

1. In Internet Explorer, open the site collection you wish to configure.
2. Click Site Actions and then click Site Settings.
3. Under Site Collection Administration, click Search Keywords.
4. Click Add Keyword.
5. Under Keyword Information, in the Keyword Phrase text box, enter the word or phrase for your keyword.
6. In the Synonyms text box, enter terms or phrases with the same meaning as the keyword phrase. Separate synonyms with a semicolon.

7. In the Keyword Definition rich text box, define the keyword for users. In this text, you can use fonts, bullet points, links, and other formatting.

8. In the Contact people picker, enter a user account that users should contact to change this keyword.

9. Under Publishing, you can enter Start, End, and Review Dates for the keyword. These dates are useful if the keyword is relevant for a limited time period.

10. Click OK.

ADD A BEST BET

For each keyword you configure, you can optionally add a best bet:

1. In Internet Explorer, open the site collection you wish to configure.

2. Click Site Actions and then click Site Settings.

3. Under Site Collection Administration, click Search Keywords.

4. Click the keyword you wish to edit.

5. Under Best Bets, click Add Best Bet.

6. In the Add Best Bet dialog box, in the URL box, enter a link to the destination users should visit.

7. In the Title text box, enter the title for the best bet link as you want it to appear at the top of search results.

8. In the Description text box, enter text to help users understand the keyword and best bet destination.

9. Click OK.

10. On the Edit Keyword page, click OK.

Managed Properties

If you want the SharePoint crawler to index unusual or custom fields or metadata for items or files, you must configure managed properties for those fields. To add a managed property, complete the following steps.

> **IMPORTANT** **NEW FIELDS AND MANAGED PROPERTIES**
>
> Before you can add a managed property for a new field, the crawler must have indexed an item with that field. For a custom content type, for example, you must define the fields, define the content type, add an item of the new content type, and initiate a crawl before you can complete these steps. For more information about configuring content types, see Chapter 5. For more information about initiating crawls, see Lesson 1 in this chapter.

ADD A MANAGED PROPERTY

1. In the Central Administration Quick Launch, click Application Management.

2. Under Service Applications, click Manage Service Applications.

3. Click the Search Service Application you wish to configure.

4. In the Quick Launch, under Queries and Results, click Metadata Properties.

5. Click New Managed Property.

6. Under Name and Type, in the Property Name text box, enter a name. This should closely match the field name, but spaces are not permitted.

7. In the Description text box, enter a descriptive text.

8. Select the type of information this Managed Property contains.

9. For fields that can have multiple values, such as lists, select the check box.

10. Under Mappings To Crawled Properties, click Add Mapping.

11. In the Crawled Property Selection dialog box, in the Crawled Property Name text box, enter the name of the field.

12. Click Find.

13. Click a crawled property in the list and then click OK.

14. At the bottom of the page, click OK.

Federating Search Results

If you want to federate search results with another SharePoint Search service application or any Open Search index, you must add a federated location in Central Administration. You must also add federated results Web Parts to a search results page.

ADD FEDERATED LOCATIONS

1. In the Central Administration Quick Launch, click Application Management.

2. Under Service Applications, click Manage Service Applications.

3. Click the Search Service Application you want to configure.

4. In the Quick Launch, under Queries and Results, click Federated Locations.

> **NOTE** **DEFAULT FEDERATED LOCATIONS**
>
> SharePoint Server 2010 includes five federated locations by default so you may not need to create your own. For example, the Internet Search Results location forwards queries to the Bing search engine. To add these locations to search results pages, use the federated results Web Parts as described in the next section.

5. Click New Location.

6. In the Location Name text box, type a descriptive name. This name is used by administrators and is not displayed to users.

7. In the Display Name text box, type a descriptive name. This name is the one users see.

8. In the Description text box, describe the destination.

9. In the Author text box, type the user or company users should see as responsible for this location.

10. In the Version text box, type a version number.

11. Under Trigger, specify Always or the prefix or regular expression trigger that you planned.

12. Expand Location Information.

13. Select the Location Type.

> **NOTE CONTEXT-SENSITIVE USER INTERFACE**
>
> The subsequent fields depend on the location type that you select. This procedure assumes that you have selected OpenSearch 1.0/1.1.

14. At the bottom of the page, click OK.

ADD FEDERATED RESULTS WEB PARTS

To add the Federated Results Web Part to a Enterprise Search Center results page, complete the following steps.

1. In Internet Explorer, open the Enterprise Search Center site you wish to configure.

2. Enter any search terms and click the Search button. SharePoint displays the results page.

3. Click Site Actions, and then click Edit Page.

4. Locate the Web Part Zone where you want to display federated results. Often, this is the Right Zone.

5. In your selected Web Part Zone, click Add A Web Part.

6. In the list of Web Part Categories, click Search.

7. In the Web Parts list, click Federated Results, and then click Add.

8. Next to the new Federated Results Web Part, click the down arrow and then click Edit Web Part.

9. In the Properties sheet for the Federated Results Web Part, in the Location drop-down list, select the federated location you created in the previous procedure.

10. Click OK.

11. In the ribbon, click Save And Close.

Subsequently, when a user runs a query, results from the federated location are displayed in a separate Web Part on the right of the page.

Creating Custom Search Pages

Use the following steps to add a custom search page to a SharePoint site. In this case, the Search Box Web Part and the Search Core Results Web Part are added to the same page.

1. In Internet Explorer, navigate to the page where you want the new search page.

2. Click Site Actions, and then click View All Site Content.

3. Click Create.

4. In the Filter By list, click Page.

5. Click Web Part Page, and then click Create.

6. In the Name box, type **SearchPage** or whatever page name you planned.

7. Choose a Layout Template.

8. In the Document Library drop-down list, select Site Pages or whatever page library you planned.

9. Click Create.

10. Locate the Web Part Zone where you want to place the Search Box.

11. Click Add A Web Part.

12. In the Web Part Categories list, click Search.

13. In the Web Parts list, click Search Box and then click Add.

14. In the new Search Box Web Part, click the down arrow and then click Edit Web Part.

15. In the Search Box properties, expand the Scopes Dropdown section.

16. In the Dropdown Mode list, select Show Scopes Dropdown. This enables users to choose the search scope.

17. Expand the Miscellaneous section.

18. In the Target Search Results Page URL text box, type the address of the page you just added, such as **http://intranet.contoso.com/SitePages/SearchPage.aspx**.

19. In the Search Box properties, click OK.

20. Locate the Web Part Zone where you want to place the Search Core Results Web Part.

21. Click Add A Web Part.

22. In the Web Part Categories list, click Search.

23. In the Web Parts list, click Search Core Results and then click Add.

> *NOTE* **ENABLING FULL FUNCTIONALITY**
>
> The preceding procedure creates a page that displays only core results. For other functionality, such as best bets and federated results, add other search Web Parts to the page.

PRACTICE **Refine Search Configuration**

Practices are designed to guide you through important procedures. The instructions in the Training Kit are high-level instructions that will challenge you to think carefully and to apply the procedures that are covered in this lesson and elsewhere in the Training Kit. If you need assistance, consult the detailed, step-by-step instructions in the Practice Answers on the companion media.

In this practice, you improve Search performance by adding managed properties, best bets, and keywords. You will also create your own search page on the intranet site.

Prepare for the Practice

Before you perform this practice, you must ensure that your lab environment has been built according to the instructions found in the Introduction to this Training Kit. You must also have performed the practice in Lesson 1 of this chapter. You must be logged off of SP2010-WFE1 before beginning the exercises.

EXERCISE 1   Add a Custom Content Type and a Custom Field

Before you can register a managed property to enable users to search on a custom field, the crawler must have indexed an example of that field. In this exercise, you create a custom field and content type. Later in this practice, you will register the field as a managed property.

- Log on to SP2010-WFE1 as **CONTOSO\SP_Admin** with the password **Pa$$w0rd**.
- Browse to **http://intranet.contoso.com**.
- Add a new site column to the site. Use the following specifications and guidance:
  - Column Name: Technology
  - Type: Single Line of Text
  - Group: Custom Group
- Add a new content type to the site. Use the following specifications and guidance:
  - Name: Technical Announcement
  - Description: Use for technological announcements
  - Select Parent Content Type From: List Content Types
  - Parent Content Type: Announcement
  - Group: Custom Content Types
- Add the Technology column to the Technical Announcement Content Type.

EXERCISE 2   Add an Item

In this exercise, you configure the Announcements list and create an item for SharePoint to crawl.

- Enable management of content types for the Announcements list on the intranet site.
- Add the Technical Announcement content type to the Announcements list.
- Create a new Technical Announcement item in the Announcements list. Use the following specifications and guidance:
  - Title: Search Center Available
  - Body: IT has deployed a new Search Center for the Contoso Intranet
  - Technology: SharePoint

EXERCISE 3   Initiate a Crawl

In this exercise, you initiate a full crawl for the Local SharePoint Sites content source.

- Start Central Administration.
- Open the Search Service Application – Enterprise and examine the list of Content Sources.
- Initiate a Full Crawl for the Local SharePoint Sites content source.

EXERCISE 4   Configure Managed Properties

In this exercise, now that SharePoint has crawled an example of the Technology field, you register the field as a managed property.

- Examine the Metadata Properties for the Search service application.
- Add a new managed property. Use the following specifications and guidance:
  - Name: Technology
  - Type: Text
  - Mappings: ows_Technology(Text)
- Initiate a second Full Crawl for the Local SharePoint Sites content source.
- Close Central Administration.

EXERCISE 5   Configure Keywords and Best Bets

In this exercise, you configure a keyword and a best bet for the word *SharePoint*.

- Browse to the intranet.contoso.com site.
- Add a new Search keyword. Use the following specifications and guidance:
  - Keyword Phrase: SharePoint
  - Synonyms: SharePoint Server 2010; SharePoint Foundation 2010
  - Keyword Definition: Advanced collaboration software from Microsoft.
- Add a best bet to the SharePoint keyword. Use the following specifications and guidance:
  - URL: *http://intranet.contoso.com/SharePoint%20Whitepapers*
  - Title: SharePoint Whitepapers
  - Description: This library contains a range of technical documents about SharePoint.

EXERCISE 6   Add a Custom Search Page to the Contoso Intranet

In this exercise, you customize the Contoso intranet site by adding a custom search page.

- In Internet Explorer, browse to the ***http://intranet.contoso.com*** site.
- Add a new Web Part Page to the site. Use the following specifications and guidance:
  - Name: CustomSearch.aspx

- Layout Template: Full Page Vertical
- Document Library: Site Pages
- Add a Search Box Web Part to the new Web Part page. Set the following properties:
  - Scopes Dropdown Mode: Show Scopes Dropdown
  - Target Search Results Page URL: *http://intranet.contoso.com/SitePages/ CustomSearch.aspx*
- Add a Search Core Results Web Part to the new Web Part page.
- Add a Search Best Bets Web Part to the new Web Part page.
- Finish editing the Web Part Page.

EXERCISE 7   Query the Index

In this exercise, you test the new search page that you created in Exercise 6. You will also use the keyword and best bet and run a property search.

- Open your new CustomSearch site page.
- Search for SharePoint in All Sites.
- Examine the Best Bet and Core results returned.
- Enter the query **Technology:SharePoint**.
- Why is only one result returned?

Lesson Summary

- Different organizations in different industries have very different search requirements. Therefore, SharePoint search is highly customizable and tunable.
- If you create a keyword, search results that match receive a boost in relevance and appear close to the top of results lists.
- By adding a best bet, you can direct users to a URL that is most likely to meet their needs.
- You can search for any property of SharePoint items or document metadata if you create managed properties for each metadata field.
- By creating federated search locations, you can forward queries to other indexes, such as other SharePoint Search service applications, third-party indexes, and Internet locations to broaden the reach of searches.
- You can add search functionality to any SharePoint page by using the Search Web Parts.
- FAST Search Server 2010 for SharePoint includes a range of extra refinements.
- Ensure that you monitor user queries—you may be able to improve performance and accelerate users' access to documents they need.

Lesson Review

You can use the following questions to test your knowledge of the information in Lesson 2, "Refine Search." The questions are also available on the companion media in a practice test if you prefer to review them in electronic form.

> **NOTE   ANSWERS**
>
> Answers to these questions and explanations of why each answer choice is right or wrong are located in the "Answers" section at the end of the book.

1. A site administrator calls you to explain that she has added a new custom column called ProjectNumber to the Project content type in the Portal site collection yesterday. She would like users to be able to search on this column. An incremental crawl ran successfully overnight. When you try to add a managed property, you cannot find a field called ProjectNumber and there is no such column in the Crawled Columns list. What could be the problem?

   A. You must run a full crawl before the column appears in the Crawled Columns list.

   B. The site administrator must create an item with the ProjectNumber field and the item must be crawled before the column appears in the Crawled Columns list.

   C. The site administrator must delete and re-create the lists in which Project content type is used.

   D. The site administrator does not have the dbowner role on the crawl database.

   E. You do not have the dbowner role on the crawl database.

2. You are planning a SharePoint Search implementation. Users have asked to see thumbnails of all results so that they can identify documents by their branding and layout without opening each result. The board has approved this requirement as mission-critical. What should you recommend in your planning document?

   A. Create a managed property for the Thumbnail field in the Search service application.

   B. Use a keyword to boost thumbnail results relevance.

   C. Use best bets to display thumbnails in results pages.

   D. Modify the Refinements Panel XML to display thumbnails.

   E. Purchase and implement FAST Search Server 2010 for SharePoint.

Lesson 3: Manage Enterprise Search Topology

Now that you have a good understanding of Search in SharePoint 2010 and can implement and refine search tools for small- and medium-sized farms, you should consider how to architect a search solution for large enterprises. SharePoint Search solutions can scale up to around 100 million indexed items but, to keep the index fresh and query responses rapid, system architects need to understand and implement many servers that host different types of search components. You will examine how architects plan large search systems in this lesson. You will also see how and why to use multiple Search service applications and learn more about FAST Search Server 2010 for SharePoint.

After this lesson, you will be able to:

- Plan a server topology for a global SharePoint Server 2010 system.
- Understand when to dedicate servers to the index, query, database, and other roles.
- Support the largest numbers of users and documents.
- Create multiple search service applications for a globally distributed environment.
- Separate multiple tenant companies into separate Search service applications.
- Separate Internet-facing and intranet-facing search solutions.
- Understand the architecture of FAST Search Server 2010 for SharePoint.
- Install and configure FAST Search Server 2010 for SharePoint.
- Deploy FAST Service Applications.

Estimated Lesson Time: 35 minutes

Planning a Large-Scale Search Architecture

SharePoint Server 2010 has numerous improvements in the search architecture that make it more versatile and scalable than earlier versions. These include:

- **A more granular architecture** This enables architects to, for example, scale crawl and query functions separately.
- **An index file that can be partitioned** This enables a more manageable index without the very large file sizes that can affect backup and restore.
- **Crawl servers no longer store the entire index** This reduces hardware requirements for Crawl Servers.
- **Multiple crawl servers** This enables architects to improve index freshness by crawling multiple sources simultaneously.
- **A larger scaling limit** This enables architects to scale their solution to 100 million documents or more.

This versatility places an extra burden on the system architect: To deploy search successfully in a large farm, you must understand each component and server role thoroughly. You must also comprehend your organization's need and priorities to create a search tool that users will value.

This section describes the process of planning a search solution for a large organization and the decisions the architect must make.

> **NOTE SCALING SEARCH SERVICE APPLICATIONS**
>
> All of the architectures described in this section are possible with a single Search service application. You can scale to the largest corpus sizes with such a solution. Later in this chapter you will learn about situations that require multiple Search service applications.

Profiling Requirements

As with any large IT project, you must begin by examining and understanding the needs of your company. To do this, interview key stakeholders such as users, administrators, and board members. Find out what problems they have and identify which problems can be solved by the search solution you are planning.

When you plan a search solution, the following requirements are critical:

- Corpus size

    The corpus is the complete body of items and documents that SharePoint will index. It can include all SharePoint items, all files in file shares, all Exchange public folder items, all databases to which you connect through the BDC, and so on. Plan your content sources and for each determine the number of items and the total size of the content. Then sum the results to determine the size of the corpus.

    The corpus size determines the type of architecture you select. For example, if you have fewer than 20 million documents, you can deploy search within an existing SharePoint farm. Above that number, you should consider creating a dedicated SharePoint farm for the Search service application.

- Crawl Time

    This is the amount of time the crawler takes to complete a full crawl. It depends on the number of content sources, the response time from each content source, and the volume of data in each content source. By testing the responsiveness of each content source you can estimate this value.

    With slow content sources and large corpuses the crawl time can grow to several hours. Crawls that are supposed to complete during off-peak hours may continue into office hours and affect users. In extreme cases, a crawl may not complete before the next is scheduled to begin.

- Freshness

    This is the maximum time it takes for new items and changes to appear in the index and therefore be available to search. Many companies, for example, run crawls overnight, so documents may not appear in the index until 24 hours after creation.

If freshness is a priority for you, you should consider running more frequent crawls. In such cases, ensure that your hardware is powerful enough to do this without reducing responsiveness. You can avoid contention by dedicating servers to the Index role and separating them from user queries. However, some resources, such as network bandwidth, may still be overtaxed in this architecture.

You should also educate your users about the freshness they can expect.

- Query Latency

  This is the time it takes for the Search solution to return results to a user. The faster results are returned, the more productive users will be and the more they will use your search tool. In many companies it is considered critical to keep this value below 1 second.

  If latency is a high priority, budget for dedicated query servers with large amounts of RAM.

- Availability

  This is the percentage of time that a system is available. In SharePoint search planning, you should consider the availability of a crawl separately from the availability of a query.

  If Crawl Servers fail and crawls cannot proceed, there may be minimal impact on users until the freshness of the index falls to very long time scales. By contrast, if Query servers fail, there is an immediate impact: searches return errors.

  High availability requires a larger budget: multiple servers with fault-tolerant disks ensure that redundant hardware can take over after a failure.

Planning Logical Topology

The logical components of a search solution are as follows:

- **Crawlers** A crawler is a process that connects to content sources and crawls nodes. Crawlers run on SharePoint Servers with the Crawl Server role.

- **Index Partitions** An index partition is a portion of the index that the crawler creates. Each index partition can contain up to 10 million items, so for small and medium-sized corpuses, a single index partition is often sufficient. Although crawlers create the index partitions, the partitions are stored on servers with the Query Server role.

- **Crawl Databases** A crawl database stores ACLs, the values of managed properties, and other metadata. This database must be located on a SQL Server.

- **Search Property Databases** A search property database stores managed properties, history data, and other crawl information. This database must be located on a SQL Server.

- **Search Administration Databases** A search administration database stores the search configuration. This database must be located on a SQL Server.

- **Query Components** A query component is a mirror of a single index partition. You can use query components to provide redundancy and increase performance for an index partition. Query components are located on servers with the Query role.

Your plan for each of these components depends on the priorities that you identified for your search solution. Table 7-3 shows recommendations for each priority.

TABLE 7-3 Planning Logical Components

PRIORITY	ARCHITECTURE SUGGESTIONS
A low crawl time	Use a large number of crawlers so that content sources can be crawled concurrently.
Good index freshness	Ensure rapid crawling by using many crawlers.
Low query latency	Split the index into several partitions. (You will place these on separate servers to provide load balancing.)
High crawl availability	Use many crawlers and add crawl databases and search property databases.
High query availability	Partition the index several times and plan to use two query components to mirror each index partition.

In the next section, you will see how to distribute these logical components on physical hardware.

Planning Physical Topology

The physical components of any system architecture include the servers and their components such as CPUs, RAM, and hard disk arrays. Because advanced, fault-tolerant hardware is expensive, the amount you invest in hardware is proportional to the importance of the availability of the system. If the search solution is considered to be mission-critical, as it is in many global organizations, you will have an extensive budget for hardware.

In a SharePoint farm three server roles are directly relevant to search:

- **Crawl Servers** A crawl server hosts one or more crawlers. Because crawling is a CPU- and memory-intensive process, processing speed and RAM are high priorities on crawl servers. Because the complete index is not stored on a crawl server, a large amount of disk space is not usually required. However, high-speed disk arrays accelerate crawls. In SharePoint 2010, you can create many crawl servers to provide redundancy and concurrent crawls.

- **Query Servers** A query server stores index partitions and query components and responds to user queries. For large indexes, lots of disk space is required but a single index can be partitioned between drives on the same server or even across multiple query servers. Provide redundancy and extra capacity by using multiple query servers.

- **Database Servers** A database server hosts the crawl, search property, and search administration databases. You can reduce contention by splitting the crawl and search property databases onto dedicated SQL servers and by placing transaction logs for each database onto dedicated spindles. The location of the search administration database is less critical because it does not receive as many queries. Provide redundancy for database servers by using server clusters.

Table 7-4 suggests appropriate physical architectures to match the priorities and logical components listed in Table 7-3.

TABLE 7-4 Planning Physical Components

PRIORITY	ARCHITECTURE SUGGESTIONS
A low crawl time	Use multiple dedicated crawl servers. Use two crawlers on each crawl server. Use servers with powerful CPUs and lots of RAM.
Good index freshness	Use the same architecture as above. Pay careful attention to scheduling to ensure that indexing does not contend for resources with user queries.
Low query latency	Use multiple query servers. For each index partition, use two query components on separate query servers. Ensure that there is enough memory to store at least 33 percent of the index in memory.
High crawl availability	Use multiple crawl servers and two crawlers on each crawl server. Add extra crawl databases on database servers to provide redundancy.
High query availability	Use multiple query servers, index partitions, and query components. Use clustered or mirrored database servers for crawl and search property databases.

You can use such techniques to support corpuses with up to 100 million items or documents and many hundreds of queries per second. This capacity should be sufficient for most global organizations. However, the largest search deployments will require FAST Search Server 2010.

Using Multiple Search Service Applications

In the preceding section, you saw how to scale a single Search service application up to the largest sizes. You can also create multiple Search service applications in a single SharePoint farm, but this should not be considered a scalability solution. Instead, use more than one Search service application when you want to create two or more indexes of separate content. The following sections describe three common situations in which this is required.

Supporting Multiple Tenants

In a multi-tenant SharePoint farm, you host SharePoint services for many tenant companies in return for subscription fees. For small companies that cannot afford to employ SharePoint experts, this model has many advantages. When you design the farm, your priority is to provide each tenant with a secure, discrete system. Your aim is to make it appear that each tenant has its own farm.

When you deploy search, it is essential to separate each tenants corpus from all the others. For example, when a user from Litware Inc. runs a search for "upcoming products," she should not see any results that describe Northwind Traders' confidential products in development.

Although security trimming can help with such requirements, the most secure way to ensure this separation is to provide a separate Search service application for each tenant. This ensures that the Litware index is entirely separate from the Northwind Traders index and inappropriate results will never be displayed.

Supporting Globally Distributed Search

In a large global organization, Wide Area Network (WAN) links between countries or continents are often slow or intermittent. Queries sent across such links can be very slow. Crawling a content source on the other side of a WAN link can have an impact on crawl times and freshness. Both are expensive if WAN charges are calculated per megabyte.

Consider, for example, a company with a large office in Europe and a second large office in Asia. Administrators want a search solution that is rapid and responsive. In addition, because of the language barrier, users are most often interested in results from their own office. For example, a Japanese user regularly reads results from Asia but only occasionally finds European results helpful.

In this situation, consider deploying separate Search service applications for Europe and Asia. Use service application proxies to ensure that users are directed to their local query servers. This ensures that neither crawls nor queries cross the slow WAN link.

You might also consider federating the European and Asian search centers. If you do this, European users see Japanese results in a separate Federated Results Web Part, perhaps to the right of the Core Results Web Part. In this way you optimize the use of the WAN link while providing a global search solution.

Hosting Internet and Intranet Sites

If you use SharePoint to host both Internet and intranet sites, you usually wish to provide search functionality to both, but it is essential that confidential internal documents are not displayed to Internet users. Conversely, internal users may find Internet pages helpful.

Here you should consider a Search service application for the Internet site and a second Search service application for the intranet portal. You should also federate but in one direction only: add the Internet search page as a federated location in the intranet Search service application.

Adding FAST Search Server 2010 for SharePoint

In Lesson 1 you learned about the extra capabilities that FAST Search Server for SharePoint 2010 adds to the native SharePoint search functionality. For large or specialized organizations, FAST provides compelling reasons to upgrade and improves productivity. If your organization has purchased FAST you must carefully plan the deployment. Bear in mind that FAST farm architectures are not like native SharePoint search architectures and require a very different approach. In this section, you will see how to architect and deploy a FAST farm.

FAST Architecture

You cannot install FAST on the same servers as SharePoint; instead, you must create a separate FAST farm. SharePoint servers act as a front end for user queries and run two important Search service applications. Figure 7-5 illustrates how the SharePoint farm and the FAST farm integrate.

The SharePoint farm remains the interface between users and the search solution. For example, Enterprise Search Center sites and other search pages run here. To use FAST you must also add two Search service applications to the SharePoint farm: the FAST Query Search service application and the FAST Content Search service application.

In the FAST farm itself a range of components run to retrieve and process content, match queries, and administer the system. In a small deployment or lab environment you can deploy all components on a single server. However, in most cases the components are distributed across servers for load balancing and fault tolerance. It is this multi-server architecture that enables the extreme scaling that is characteristic of FAST.

FAST components also use SQL Server databases. For example, the FAST Administration component uses a FAST Search Administration database to store the configuration of the system.

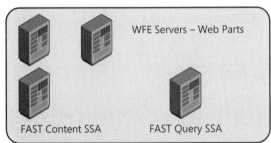

WFE Servers – Web Parts

SharePoint Farm

FAST Content SSA   FAST Query SSA

Administration
Search Cluster
Query Processing
Web Analyzer
Item Processing

FAST Farm

FAST Search Admin DB
FAST SSAs Admin DB
Property DB (Query SSA)
Crawl DB (Query SSA)

SQL Servers

FIGURE 7-5 FAST and SharePoint server topology

FAST Service Applications

When you deploy FAST Search, the SharePoint farm remains the users' sole point of contact with the search solution. For example, to submit queries, users enter information into Web Parts in SharePoint sites, just as they do for native SharePoint Search. In addition, all the non-search functions in the SharePoint farm, such as document managements, record management, and social networking, remain within SharePoint. However, you must add two new service applications to the SharePoint farm:

- **The FAST Query Search Service Application**   The Query SSA acts as a gateway between SharePoint and the FAST farm. It receives all queries and forwards them to FAST query processing. It also returns results. The Query SSA also contains all the crawl and query components for People Search. When you search for users or expertise the FAST farm is not involved at all.

> *IMPORTANT*   **QUERY SSA AND THE FAST FARM**
>
> You must use only a single Query SSA for each FAST farm. However, like any SharePoint service application, you can scale the Query SSA out over several application servers to provide extra capacity and fault tolerance.

- **The FAST Content Search Service Application**   The Content SSA enables FAST to crawl content from a wide variety of sources. This is the default indexing connector for FAST. The Content SSA can retrieve content from almost any content source, including SharePoint sites, websites, file shares, and so on. The Content SSA does not process content—that is completed in the FAST farm.

FAST Farm Components and Server Topology

The servers in the FAST farm run several different components that you can distribute to provide fault tolerance, handle larger corpuses, and decrease query time. These components include:

- **Item Processing**   This component processes items during crawls. Items are received from the Content SSA, document formats are parsed, and crawled properties are mapped to managed properties. Linguistic processing, such as word breaking and noise word removal, also takes place in the Item Processing component.

- **Web Analyzer**   This component improves relevancy ranking by analyzing content in two ways. First, the Web Analyzer examines the search click-through logs to discover each item's popularity. Those that are clicked often receive a relevancy boost. Second, the Web Analyzer examines hyperlink structures. Those items that are linked to from many other pages receive a similar boost.

- **Search Cluster**   The search cluster stores the complete index and matches queries to items. This is the heart of the FAST search solution; it is designed to be extremely scalable. When the index is large you can split it across many indexing columns, each of which is placed on a separate server. You can also create backup indexing columns for fault tolerance. Search rows consist of query matching servers that run queries against the index. The search row always has the same number of servers as there are columns in the index.

- **Query Processing**   This component processes queries before they are run in the search cluster. For example, noise words are removed. Query processing also makes changes to results lists before they are returned to the user. For example, security trimming takes place in this component.

- **Search Administration**   This component contains all the functionality necessary to configure and administer the FAST Search system.

> **NOTE   THE ADMINISTRATION USER INTERFACE**
>
> To configure FAST, administrators use the Central Administration site or Windows PowerShell. However, these user interface components call the Search Administration component in the FAST farm to enact the changes made.

Configuring FAST Search Server 2010 for SharePoint

If you decide to deploy a FAST Search Server 2010 for a SharePoint farm, use the following procedures to install it and the Search service applications.

Before you install FAST it is recommended that you create a domain user for FAST administration tasks. Place this user into the FASTSearchAdministrators group in the AD DS domain and ensure that it has sysadmin privileges on the SQL Servers.

INSTALL FAST

1. Insert the FAST Search Server disk in the drive. The welcome screen is displayed.
2. Click Install Software Prerequisites.
3. Click Next.
4. Accept the license terms, and then click Next.
5. When the prerequisite installation is complete, click Finish.
6. Restart the server.
7. In the FAST welcome screen, click Install FAST Search Server 2010 For SharePoint.
8. Select an installation location, and then click Next.
9. When the installation is complete, click Finish.
10. Click Start, click Microsoft FAST Search Server 2010 For SharePoint, and then click FAST Search Server 2010 For SharePoint Configuration Wizard.
11. Select the installation type according to your architect plan, and then click Next.
12. Enter the user name and password of the FAST Administration user you created earlier, and then click Next.
13. Enter the certificate password, and then click Next.
14. Enter the fully qualified domain name of the FAST server and a base port.
15. Enter a database connection string for the database instance that will store the FAST databases, and then click Next.

16. Select the type of SharePoint farm so that the Web Analyzer can optimize click-through relevancy, and then click Next.

17. Restart the server.

DEPLOY THE FAST SERVICE APPLICATIONS

As you have seen, two SSAs in the SharePoint farm provide essential integration with the FAST farm: Content SSA and Query SSA. Use the following procedure to create these SSAs.

Much of the information required in the following procedures is contained in the install_info.txt file, which you can find in the FAST installation folder on a FAST server. Ensure that you have a copy of this file in hand before you begin these procedures.

1. In the Central Administration Quick Launch, click Application Management.

2. Under Service Applications, click Manage Service Applications.

3. On the ribbon, click New and then click Search Service Application.

4. In the Service Application Name text box, type an appropriate name for the FAST Content SSA.

5. Under FAST Service Application, select FAST Search Connector.

> **IMPORTANT** **SSA INSTALLATION ORDER**
>
> You must install a FAST Search Connector—the Content SSA—before you install a FAST Search Query SSA.

6. Configure a service account and application pool for the Content SSA according to your plan.

7. In the Content Distributors text box, type the fully qualified domain name and port of the content distributors. You can find this value in the install_info.txt file.

8. Type a name for the content collection.

9. Click OK.

10. On the ribbon, click New and then click Search Service Application.

11. In the Service Application Name text box, type an appropriate name for the FAST Query SSA.

12. Under FAST Service Application, select FAST Search Query.

13. Configure an application pool for the Search Admin Web Service according to your plan.

14. Configure an application pool for the Search Query and Site Settings Web Service according to your plan.

15. In the Query Service Location text box, type the correct value, which you can find in the install_info.txt file.

16. In the Administration Service Location text box, type the correct value, which you can find in the install_info.txt file.

17. In the Resource Store Location text box, type the correct value, which you can find in the install_info.txt file.

18. Enter the user name and password for the administration account you created earlier.

19. Click OK.

PRACTICE Build a Fault-Tolerant Search Topology

Practices are designed to guide you through important procedures. The instructions in the Training Kit are high-level instructions that will challenge you to think carefully and to apply the procedures that are covered in this lesson and elsewhere in the Training Kit. If you need assistance, consult the detailed, step-by-step instructions in the Practice Answers on the companion media.

In this practice, you will build a more fault-tolerant search topology by adding extra crawl and property databases, an extra crawler, and an extra index partition with mirrored query components. This practice simulates building redundancy and extra capacity into the system.

> **NOTE REAL-WORLD FAULT TOLERANCE**
>
> Your virtual server environment for this Training Kit contains only a single server, so you cannot build redundancy to server failures into the search topology. And because the SP2010-WFE1 image has only a single virtual hard drive, you cannot spread databases, temporary files, and index files onto dedicated spindles as you would in the real world. However, this practice does illustrate the steps required to build such a robust topology on real servers. Bear in mind, as you complete this practice, that you should not ordinarily place multiple index partitions on a single server or place databases and index files on the same hard drive.

Prepare for the Practice

Before you perform this practice, you must ensure that your lab environment has been built according to the instructions found in the Introduction to this Training Kit. You must also have performed the practice in Lesson 2 of this chapter. You must be logged off of SP2010-WFE1 before beginning the exercises.

EXERCISE 1 Create Folders for Index and Temporary Files

In this exercise, you create folders that will hold the extra index partition and temporary crawl files.

- In the root of the C: drive, create a folder called Search Files.
- Within Search Files, create three folders called:
  - Index Partition 2 Files

- Crawler 2 Temp Files
- Query Component 2 Files

EXERCISE 2   Create a New Crawl Database

In this exercise, you create a second crawl database.

- In Central Administration, manage the following service application:
  - Search Service Application – Enterprise
- Modify the Search Application Topology.
- Add a new Crawl Database. Use the following specifications and guidance:
  - Database Server: SP2010-WFE1
  - Database Name: SharePoint_Service_Search_Crawl_2

EXERCISE 3   Create a New Property Database

In this exercise, you create a second property database.

- Add a new Property Database to the search topology. Use the following specifications and guidance:
  - Database Server: SP2010-WFE1
  - Database Name: SharePoint_Service_Search_Property_2

EXERCISE 4   Create a New Crawler

In this exercise, you add a new crawler to the SP2010-WFE1 server.

- Add a new Crawl Component to the search topology. Use the following specifications and guidance:
  - Server: SP2010-WFE1
  - Associated Crawl Database: SP2010-WFE1\SharePoint_Service_Search_Crawl_2
  - Temporary Location of Index: C:\Search Files\Crawler 2 Temp Files

EXERCISE 5   Create a New Index Partition

In this exercise, you create a new index partition for the Search service application.

- Add a new Index Partition and Query Component to the search topology. Use the following specifications and guidance:
  - Server: SP2010-WFE1
  - Associated Property Database: SP2010-WFE1\SharePoint_Service_Search_Property_2
  - Location of Index: C:\Search Files\Index Partition 2 Files

EXERCISE 6   Create a New Query Component and Apply Topology Changes

In this exercise, you create a second mirror query component in the index partition you created in Exercise 5. You will also apply all your changes.

- Add a Mirror to the Query Component New 1. Use the following specifications and guidance:
  - Server: SP2010-WFE1
  - Location of Index: C:\Search Files\Query Component 2 Files
- Apply your topology changes.

> **NOTE APPLYING TOPOLOGY CHANGES**
>
> **This process may take several minutes.**

EXERCISE 7 Run a Full Crawl

In this exercise, you run a full crawl with the new search topology.

- Initiate a full crawl on the Local SharePoint Sites content source.
- While the crawl takes place, examine the contents of the following folders:
  - C:\Search Files\Crawler 2 Temp Files
  - C:\Search Files\Index Partition 2 Files
  - C:\Search Files\Query Component 2 Files
- When the crawl is complete, close Internet Explorer.
- Log off of SP2010-WFE1.

EXERCISE 8 Create the CHAPTER 07 Snapshot

The CHAPTER 07 snapshot captures the state of the environment at the end of Chapter 7. Perform this procedure for each of the following virtual machines: SP2010-WFE1, CONTOSO-DC.

1. Shut down the virtual machine.
2. Unmount any ISO image currently mounted to the CD/DVD drive. Use the "Unmount an ISO Image" procedure in the Lab Environment Build Guide on the companion media.
3. Create a snapshot named CHAPTER 07. Use the "Create a Snapshot" procedure in the Lab Environment Build Guide on the companion media.

Lesson Summary

- You can dedicate application servers in SharePoint farms to query and crawl roles for granular control over performance.
- More than one query server can be used to ensure rapid responses and fault tolerance.
- More than one crawl server can be used to ensure fault tolerance, enable very large indexes, and crawl several content sources concurrently.

- When planning your architecture, the predicted corpus size and desired crawl time, index freshness, query latency, and availability should be evaluated.
- These requirements determine the logical components you use, including crawlers, index partitions, databases, and query components.
- These logical components are distributed across physical query, crawl, and database servers.
- You can also create multiple search service applications to create separate indexes.
- FAST Search Server 2010 for SharePoint requires a separate FAST farm in addition to the SharePoint farm.
- FAST Query and Content Search service applications must be added to the SharePoint farm to support FAST.
- The FAST farm has an extremely flexible and scalable architecture—each component can be distributed across multiple servers.

Lesson Review

You can use the following questions to test your knowledge of the information in Lesson 3, "Manage Enterprise Search Topology." The questions are also available on the companion media in a practice test if you prefer to review them in electronic form.

> **NOTE ANSWERS**
>
> Answers to these questions and explanations of why each answer choice is right or wrong are located in the "Answers" section at the end of the book.

1. You have asked a colleague to plan an installation of FAST Search Server 2010 for SharePoint for your existing SharePoint farm. His plan includes three Content SSAs and three Query SSAs in the SharePoint farm, plus three index columns in the FAST farm Search Cluster to scale out to the expected corpus size. How should you correct his plan? (Choose all that apply.)

   A. Inform him that only one Query SSA is possible for each FAST Farm.

   B. Inform him that only one index column is possible in each FAST Farm.

   C. Inform him that multiple servers within a single Content SSA can be used to scale to large corpus sizes.

   D. Inform him that multiple servers within a single Query SSA can be used to scale to large corpus sizes.

   E. Inform him that multiple index columns within a single Search Cluster can be used to scale to large corpus sizes.

2. You have a SharePoint farm that will provide services to five tenant companies. You are planning Search services for the farm. Which of the following configurations will ensure that each tenant can only view results from its own company?

   A. Create five site collections, one for each company. Create a single Search service application with five crawlers and five query servers.

   B. Create five site collections, one for each company. Create a single Search service application with five crawl servers and five query servers.

   C. Create five site collections, one for each company. Create a single Search service application with one server that takes the crawl and query roles. Create five separate sites based on the Search Center template.

   D. Create five site collections, one for each company. Create five Search service applications, each indexing a different company site collection. Create five separate sites based on the Search Center template connected to the appropriate Search service application.

   E. Install FAST Search Server 2010 for SharePoint. Create five separate index columns in the FAST farm Search Cluster.

Chapter Review

To further practice and reinforce the skills you learned in this chapter, you can perform the following tasks:

- Review the chapter summary.
- Review the list of key terms introduced in this chapter.
- Complete the case scenarios. These scenarios set up real-world situations involving the topics of this chapter and ask you to create a solution.
- Complete the suggested practices.
- Take a practice test.

Chapter Summary

- Search is a mission-critical service in many organizations of all types because it has a direct, positive effect on user productivity.
- SharePoint Server 2010 includes an advanced search engine out of the box that can satisfy the requirements of most organizations.
- The largest organizations or specialized companies may benefit from the extra capabilities in FAST Search Server 2010 for SharePoint.
- SharePoint can index a large variety of content stored in many technologies around your company.
- SharePoint provides Search Center and Enterprise Search Center site templates for centralized search tools. You can also add search Web Parts to any page in SharePoint.
- SharePoint search is implemented in a Search service application.
- Many components, such as best bets, keywords, and managed properties, can be used to turn search performance to the needs of your users.
- Use federation to integrate your index with others from elsewhere in your organization or from other companies.

Key Terms

The following terms were introduced in this chapter. Do you know what they mean?

- Search Service Application
- Index
- Index Partition
- Query Component
- Content Sources

- Crawler
- Crawl Server
- Query Server
- Keywords
- Best Bets
- Visual Best Bets
- Managed Properties
- Search Scopes
- Security Trimming
- Refinement Panel
- People Search
- Relevancy
- IFilter
- Protocol Handler
- Corpus
- Federated Search
- OpenSearch
- Index Freshness
- Query Latency

Case Scenario: Optimizing an Enterprise Search Solution

In the following case scenario, you will apply what you've learned about the subjects of this chapter. You can find answers to these questions in the "Answers" section at the end of this book.

You have been running a search solution in SharePoint Server 2010 for an international electronics company for six months. You have recently completed a survey of stakeholders to obtain their feedback and find out whether you can improve the solution.

1. The board has requested that whenever users search for "Electronic" or "Electrical," they see a link to the company's Internet-facing site. This site is not hosted on SharePoint. How can you configure Search to permit this?

2. Search administrators tell you that they often see the query "circuit board etching" in the search logs. When you ask users about it they tell you that this is an important phrase in electronic design but they also mention that they often have to scroll to the second or third page of results to find results on this specific term. Results on integrated circuits are placed at the top. How can you configure Search to prioritize "circuit board etching" results?

3. One team in your company works with a special content type called Electrical Component. This has a custom column called Component Type that stores values such as *resistor*, *capacitor*, *integrated circuit*, and so on. This team complains that when they search for *resistor* they do not see all the examples of resistors in their list. They have noticed that only those with *resistor* in the Description or Title columns are returned. How can you solve this issue?

Suggested Practices

To help you successfully master the exam objectives presented in this chapter, complete the following tasks.

Practice 1: Configure SharePoint to Index Exchange Public Folders

When you create a Search service application in SharePoint, a content source called All SharePoint Sites is created automatically. This includes all sites, lists, and libraries in the SharePoint farm. If you want SharePoint to index a database, you must connect to it by using BCS. Then you can add a content source for the database. This is a procedure that you will need to complete in many organizations because databases are ubiquitous:

1. Create a database with suitable fields. Ideally, use a copy of a real user database from your own organization if you have permissions. Alternatively, you can use the Adventure Works sample database or make up your own data.

2. Create a BCS connection to the database. For more information about configuring all aspects of BCS, see Chapter 8, "Implementing Enterprise Service Applications."

3. Create a BCS external content type for each database record type that you want to index. It is important to set the Title field carefully for each of these external content types. This will ensure that search results are descriptive and explanatory.

4. Add a new content source to index the external content types. Select the Line Of Business Data content source type.

5. Run a full crawl for your new content source.

6. When the crawl is complete, search for words that you know to appear in the database. Do you receive results?

Practice 2: Configure Federation with a Second Search Service Application

In Lesson 2 you saw how federated search can integrate your index with an index from elsewhere in your company or from a third party. For example, you can use federation to display Internet search engine results, such as those from Google or Bing, alongside your internal intranet results. In Lesson 3, you learned about situations in which multiple Search service applications exist in a single company. You can use federation to share results between these service applications if it is appropriate. Practice federating between Search service applications by completing the following steps:

1. Create a new site collection and upload some sample content into it.

2. Create a second Search service application in your existing SharePoint farm.

3. Configure content sources so that the new service application indexes only the new site collection.

4. Create a new Search Center site in the new site collection.

5. Ensure that the new site collection is connected to the new Search service application.

6. Run a full crawl in the new Search service application.

7. Use the new Search Center to run a query against the new index. You now have a complete, separate search solution. In the next steps you will federate this with the original Search service application.

8. In the new Search service application, add a federated location that points to the original search service application.

9. In the new Search Center site, add the Federated Results Web Part to the results page.

10. Run searches to test your configuration.

Take a Practice Test

The practice tests on this book's companion media offer many options. For example, you can test yourself on just the lesson review content, or you can test yourself on all the 70-667 certification exam objectives. You can set up the test so that it closely simulates the experience of taking a certification exam, or you can set it up in study mode so that you can look at the correct answers and explanations after you answer each question.

> **MORE INFO** **PRACTICE TESTS**
>
> For details about all the practice test options available, see the "How to Use the Practice Tests" section in this book's Introduction.

CHAPTER 8

Implementing Enterprise Service Applications

In the preceding chapters you have seen the core functionality of Microsoft SharePoint Server 2010 that makes it such an excellent content management system for the enterprise and the web. This module covers several features that you can use to interact with non-SharePoint software and extend the reach of the SharePoint platform. In each case, you extend SharePoint by adding new service applications to your farm. Several service applications are available to increase the integration between SharePoint and Microsoft Office software. Excel, Access, Visio, and InfoPath all have dedicated service applications, and you can use Office Web Applications to make Office tools available to those who do not have the Office Suite installed on their computers. Furthermore, you can use Business Connectivity Services (BCS) to integrate SharePoint with databases, web services, and Line Of Business (LOB) applications.

Exam objectives in this chapter:

- Configure service applications.
- Configure SharePoint farms.

Lessons in this chapter:

Before You Begin

To complete the lessons in this chapter, you must build your lab environment according to the instructions found in the Introduction to this Training Kit and have done the following:

- Performed the practices in Chapter 1
- Performed the practices in Chapter 5
- Performed the practices in Chapter 6
- Performed the practices in Chapter 7

 **REAL WORLD**

Alistair Matthews

This chapter includes some fairly disparate topics but they all have a common theme: integrating SharePoint with other software. All the lessons you'll see involve adding one or more service applications to the farm to extend the reach of SharePoint. In Lesson 1, for example, you'll see how to use BCS to import data from databases and other systems. When you do this, users can make changes to the data–it will synchronize with the external system automatically. In all the other lessons, you'll see how to integrate SharePoint with Office applications more closely.

Of course, integrating software packages is one of the thorniest subjects that face a systems administrator. Often, major systems get integrated by developers writing custom code. Most, but not all, of these developers are highly skilled, and budget constraints can limit the effectiveness of data exchange. I've often found myself scripting fixes or laboriously altering data after such integration projects went wrong.

That's why I'm grateful for the out-of-the-box integration tools that are included with SharePoint 2010. I think BCS in particular will save organizations a lot of time and money and will save me a lot of worry.

Lesson 1: Implement Business Connectivity Services

SharePoint does not exist in a software vacuum—in fact almost all organizations have other content-storage systems. Unless you can integrate these with SharePoint, you can end up having to duplicate work and manually synchronize changes. When users forget to make changes in multiple locations great confusion can arise! Business Connectivity Services (BCS) make it simple to connect SharePoint to other systems and automatically synchronizes changes. Best of all, this integration rarely requires any developer time—instead, administrators and power users can set up connections.

After this lesson, you will be able to:

- Understand how BCS can integrate SharePoint with other business systems.
- Describe the architecture of BCS in SharePoint 2010.
- Create BCS connections to databases and LOB systems by using SharePoint Designer.
- Create external content types that represent external entities within SharePoint.
- Create external lists and enable users to interact with external data.
- Choose a BCS Web Part for a business scenario.

Estimated Lesson Time: 45 minutes

Connecting SharePoint to Other Business Systems

In a new organization or in a limited project, you might work exclusively with SharePoint and not concern yourself with other systems. However, almost all existing organizations have existing systems that store documents and information and that will coexist with SharePoint in the long-term. Most SharePoint consultants or administrators will therefore need to integrate SharePoint with other business systems sometime in their careers.

A Typical Scenario: Tailspin Toys

To illustrate some typical integration challenges let's consider a fictitious toy manufacturer called Tailspin Toys. The IT department has been asked to deploy SharePoint for the following reasons:

- To provide document-management facilities to the entire organization.
- To host the Internet-facing website for TailspinToys.com.
- To enable users to interact socially.

You planned and deployed your SharePoint system. Users responded positively and the board rates the deployment as a success. However, several issues have arisen that negatively affect user productivity:

- Tailspin Toys uses SAP to manage resources and manufacturing. The board would like changes in SAP, such as stock levels, to be automatically imported to SharePoint for use in dashboards and reports.

- The HR department uses a Microsoft SQL Server database to store employee information. HR personnel would like the employee ID and other properties in the HR database to be available in SharePoint user profiles.

- Tailspin Toys developed their own system for customer relationship management. The board would like information about customers to be imported regularly into SharePoint.

This kind of systems integration has traditionally required developers to write extensive custom code. However, by using the SharePoint BCS, Tailspin Toys can solve all these problems. The next section describes BCS and how it addresses the issues identified.

Business Connectivity Systems

In SharePoint 2007, you could use the Business Data Connector (BDC) to import data from other systems into SharePoint. Although versatile, the BDC did not permit you to make changes to the data in SharePoint and was complex to configure. In SharePoint 2010, by contrast, BCS enables users to change data and will synchronize those changes with the external systems. Furthermore, you can configure BCS without any developer skills by using Microsoft SharePoint Designer 2010. BCS can connect to the following systems:

- **Databases**   BCS can connect to several different relational database servers including Microsoft SQL Server and Oracle.

- **Line-Of-Business Systems**   BCS can connect to Line-Of-Business (LOB) systems such as SAP and Siebel. Because these applications are widely used to support many business functions, BCS can broaden the reach of your SharePoint sites in your organization. For example, you could use such connections as the basis of dashboards that display key business intelligence.

- **Web Services**   BCS can connect to any application that publishes data in a Web service. Many third-party applications and websites include such Web services.

- **WCF Services**   Windows Communication Foundation (WCF) is a Microsoft .NET technology that developers use to create multi-tier distributed applications. BCS can connect to any application that publishes data through WCF services.

BCS supports the following operations, as long as they are permitted by permissions and the external system in question:

- **Create**   New records, created in SharePoint external lists, are created in the external system the next time synchronization occurs.

- **Read**   Any record imported into SharePoint can be read by users with the correct authorization.

- **Update** Changes to existing records, made in SharePoint external lists, are propagated to the external system on the next synchronization.

- **Delete** When a user deletes an item in a SharePoint external list, the item is also removed from the external system.

> **NOTE BCS CONNECTIONS AND USER PROFILES**
>
> As you saw in Chapter 6, "Configuring User Profiles and Social Networking," the User Profile service application can import user details through a BCS connection. If you have information about users stored in a LOB application or an HR database, this can enrich users' profiles considerably.

You should now be able to see how BCS addresses the Tailspin Toys scenario:

- By making a BCS connection to SAP, you can import live data about products and stock levels into a SharePoint external list. You could use the SharePoint Chart Web Part to display this information in graphic forms in dashboards. None of this requires custom coding or developer time.

- By making a BCS connection to the HR database, you can import personnel information such as the employee ID into SharePoint user profiles. To do this you simply configure the User Profile service application.

- If the Tailspin Toys customer relationship management system includes Web or WCF Services that publish data, SharePoint administrators can connect to it by using a BCS connection and import data. Even if there are no Web or WCF Services in the system, developers can usually add them.

These examples illustrate the broad power that BCS represents for systems integration. Many integration tasks that traditionally would require long and expensive development projects can now be accomplished by administrators or even by power users.

BCS Architecture

Before you begin using BCS, you must understand the following key components:

- **External System** As described in the previous section, SharePoint supports various external systems, including LOB systems, databases, and Web services.

- **External System Instances** In your organization, you might connect to several different databases. Each of these is an external system instance. For each instance you must define connection information—such as a database connection string—and authentication information so that SharePoint can log on to the external system.

- **External Content Types** External content types are very similar to SharePoint content types that you saw in Chapter 5, "Service Applications and the Managed Metadata Service." Both are collections of columns of different types. However, the columns in an external content type are set by the external system instance. For example, if you connect to a database, you will probably create an external content type for each table in the database, and the columns in the external content type will match the columns in the database table.

- **External Lists** Just as external content types are similar to content types, external lists are similar to SharePoint lists, which you saw in Chapter 4, "Administering and Securing SharePoint Content." SharePoint users can view and edit the data in an external list in their browser but their changes are synchronized with the external system instance.

You create and configure all of the preceding components by using SharePoint Designer 2010. This tool enables administrators and power users to make many kinds of customizations to the SharePoint environment. For example, you can create new sites, pages, content types, lists, libraries, and workflows. In this module, we will concentrate on SharePoint Designer's BCS functionality. Figure 8-1 shows the SharePoint Designer console.

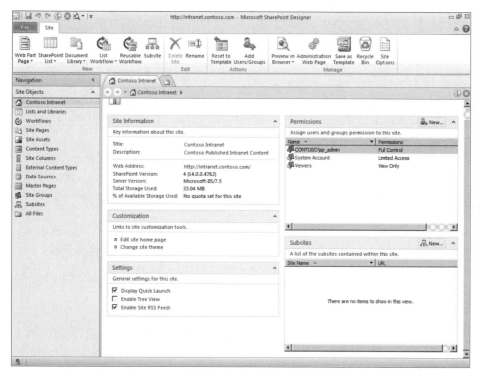

FIGURE 8-1 SharePoint Designer

NOTE **OBTAINING SHAREPOINT DESIGNER 2010**

SharePoint Designer 2010 is a free tool that you can download from the following location: *http://www.microsoft.com/downloads/en/details.aspx?FamilyID=d88a1505-849b-4587-b854-a7054ee28d66&displaylang=en.*

SharePoint BCS is built from a range of components that run on web front-end servers, application servers, database servers, and client computers. Figure 8-2 shows the architecture in detail.

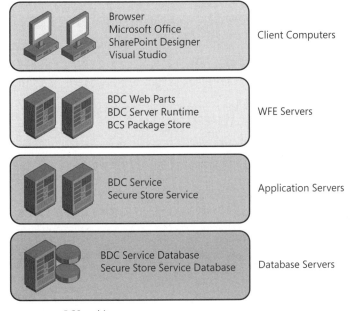

FIGURE 8-2 BCS architecture

For each computer in the architecture, the BCS components are as follows:

- Web Front-End Servers:
  - **BCS Web Parts**   Six Web Parts are provided to display, filter, and interact with external data. You can add these to any SharePoint page to add business intelligence functionality.
  - **BDC Server Runtime**   The server runtime is the component that connects to external systems, imports new data, and exports changes made in SharePoint.
  - **BCS Package Store**   The package store holds the configuration details on external system instances, external content types, and external lists in memory on front-end servers. The server runtime uses this store to make connections.
- Application Servers:
  - **BDC Service**   This shared service publishes the details of external system instances, content types, and lists to all web front-end servers in the farm. You can either run this shared service on a dedicated application server or, in a smaller farm, host it with other shared services.
  - **Secure Store Service**   This shared service is used by BCS to securely store authentication details so that SharePoint can robustly connect to external systems. For example, a user's credentials are often different in SharePoint and in the

external system. By mapping sets of credentials the Secure Store service removes this barrier.

- Database Servers:
  - **BDC Service Database**   This database stores the complete BCS configuration, including the properties of external content types, external lists, and connection details.
  - **Secure Store Service Database**   This database stores configuration details for the Secure Store service.
- Client Computers:
  - **Browser**   Users interact with external lists by using Internet Explorer or another browser, just as they do with other SharePoint lists and libraries.
  - **Microsoft Office Suite**   Workspace, Word, and Outlook users can interact directly with external systems through the BCS Office Integration Client Runtime.
  - **SharePoint Designer**   Administrators, power users, and developers can configure external system instances, external content types, and external lists by using SharePoint Designer.
  - **Visual Studio**   Advanced BCS customization tasks, such as the creation of a new external system type, may require custom code. Developers can use application templates in Visual Studio for help writing such code.

Connecting to External Data

To set up a fully functional connection to an external system, you must complete the following stages:

- Add and configure a Business Data Connectivity service application.
- Add and configure a Secure Store service application.
- Add a BCS external content type and define operations.
- Add external lists and forms.
- Assign permission to the external list.

Each of these stages is described in the following procedures, which illustrate how to connect to a SQL Server database. When you connect to a LOB system or Web service, some options and choices differ but the overall steps are the same.

ADD AND CONFIGURE A BUSINESS DATA CONNECTIVITY SERVICE APPLICATION

Use the following procedure to create a BDC service application:

1. In the Central Administration Quick Launch, click Application Management.
2. Under Service Applications, click Manage Service Applications.
3. On the ribbon, click New and then click Business Data Connectivity Service.
4. In the Name text box, type a suitable name for the service application.
5. Under Database, in the Database Server text box, type the name of the database server where you want to create the BDC database.

6. In the Database Name text box, type a name for the database.

7. In the Application Pool section, set details for the application pool to match your plan and click OK.

8. When the BDC service application creation is complete, click OK.

9. On the Central Administration Quick Launch, click System Settings.

10. Under Servers, click Manage Service on Server.

11. In the Server box, select the server that you want to host the Business Data Connectivity Service.

12. In the Service list, next to Business Data Connectivity Service, click Start.

ADD AND CONFIGURE A SECURE STORE SERVICE APPLICATION

The BCS server application relies on the Secure Store service application to manage authentication details for external systems. You may already have a Secure Store service application in your farm for other purposes. If not, use the following procedure to add and configure this service application:

1. In the Central Administration Quick Launch, click Application Management.

2. Under Service Applications, click Manage Service Applications.

3. On the ribbon, click New and then click Secure Store Service.

4. Under Database, in the Database Server text box, type the name of the database server where you want to create the Secure Store database.

5. In the Database Name text box, type a name for the database.

6. In the Application Pool section, set details for the application pool to match your plan.

7. Under Enable Audit, specify whether to use audit logging for the Secure Store service application and the number of days to keep logs. Auditing is recommended for the security-sensitive service. Click OK.

8. When the Secure Store service application creation is complete, click OK.

9. On the Central Administration Quick Launch, click System Settings.

10. Under Servers, click Manage Service on Server.

11. In the Server box, select the server that you want to host the Secure Store Service.

12. In the Service list, next to Secure Store Service, click Start.

CREATE A BCS EXTERNAL CONTENT TYPE AND DEFINE OPERATIONS

Use this procedure to connect to an external system, configure the connection, and add the external content type:

1. Click Start, All Programs, SharePoint, and then click Microsoft SharePoint Designer 2010.

2. Under Open SharePoint Site, click Open Site.

3. In the Site Name text box, type **http://intranet.contoso.com** and then click Open.

4. In the Navigation pane on the left, click External Content Types.

5. On the ribbon, in the New section, click External Content Type.

6. Under External Content Type Information, next to Name, click New External Content Type and then type a name. This is the name the system will use for the external content type.

7. Next to Display Name, click New External Content Type and then type a name. This is the name that will be display to users.

8. Next to External System, click the link.

9. Click Add Connection.

10. In the Data Source Type list, select SQL Server and then click OK.

11. In the SQL Server Connection dialog box, give details of the database to connect to, and then click OK.

> **NOTE** **USING THE SECURE STORE SERVICE APPLICATION TO CONNECT**
>
> When SharePoint connects to the database server, it must provide credentials and authenticate on the user's behalf. If the same credentials are used on the database server and the SharePoint server, you can select Connect With User's Identity at this point. Otherwise you must create a Secure Store application to store credentials and map them to SharePoint users. Then you can select the Secure Store application ID here.

12. The database appears in the Data Source Explorer pane. You can expand nodes to explore the structure of the database.

13. Locate the table, view, or stored procedure that you want to import into SharePoint.

14. Right-click the object and then click Create All Operations.

15. In the All Operations dialog box, click Next.

16. Configure each data source element in the database. The necessary steps depend on the columns in the database column or view and the data types.

17. Click Next.

18. The next page enables you to add Filter Parameters. Click Finish.

ADD EXTERNAL LISTS AND FORMS

Now that you have created an external system instance and an external content type, you must add an external list and create default forms so that users can read and edit the external data.

1. In SharePoint Designer, on the ribbon, click Create Lists and Form.

2. If the Save Confirmation dialog box appears, click Yes.

3. In the Create List and Form dialog box, in the List Name text box, type a display name for the external list.

4. Optionally, in the List Description text box, type a description to help users understand the external list.

5. If you want SharePoint to create a default InfoPath form, check the box. Otherwise, SharePoint will create an ASP.NET form to display and edit the items.

6. Click OK.

ASSIGN PERMISSIONS TO THE EXTERNAL LIST

To ensure security you must carefully control authorization on the external list. This controls the operations that users can complete. To assign permissions, use the following steps:

1. In the Central Administration Quick Launch, click Application Management.

2. Under Service Applications, click Manage Service Applications.

3. Click the BDC service application that contains your external list.

4. On the ribbon, in the View section, ensure that External Content Types is selected.

5. Select the box to the left of the external content type you wish to administer.

6. On the ribbon, click Set Object Permissions.

7. In the People Picker dialog box, type the name of a user account or security group.

8. Click the Check Names button, and then click Add.

9. Select the permissions you wish to assign to the selected user or group.

10. Add other users and groups and set their permissions according to your security requirements.

11. Click OK.

> **NOTE** **PERMISSIONS FOR EXTERNAL CONTENT TYPES**
>
> You must ensure that at least one user has Set Permissions permission, so that he or she can assign permissions to other users. As a best practice, ensure that this permission is available to a group of power users or administrators. A user must have Edit and Execute permissions to have full create, read, update, and delete functionality for an external content type.

When these procedures have been completed, users can access the external list in SharePoint just as they can a normal SharePoint list. Any changes made in SharePoint will be propagated to the external system.

Using BCS Web Parts

The BCS Web Parts enable all users with permission to edit pages to add business intelligence functionality to their Web Part pages. The following procedure describes how to add the Business Data List Web Part to a page:

1. In Internet Explorer, browse to the page you want to edit.

2. On the ribbon, click the Page tab, and then click Edit Page.

3. Place the cursor where you would like to add the Web Part.

4. On the ribbon, click the Insert tab.

5. On the ribbon, click Web Part.

6. In the list of Categories, click Business Data.

7. In the list of Web Parts, click Business Data List.

8. Click Add.

9. In the new Business Data List Web Part, click Open The Tool Pane.

10. Scroll to the right to access the Web Part properties sheet.

11. Under Business Data List, in the Type text box, type the name of the external content type you want to display. Alternatively you can click the Select External Content Type button and select the type from a list.

12. At the bottom of the properties sheet, click OK.

13. On the ribbon, click Page, and then click Save & Close.

14. The external list is displayed on your page.

PRACTICE   **Configure a BCS Connection**

Practices are designed to guide you through important procedures. The instructions in the Training Kit are high-level instructions that will challenge you to think carefully and to apply the procedures that are covered in this lesson and elsewhere in the Training Kit. If you need assistance, consult the detailed, step-by-step instructions in the Practice Answers on the companion media.

In this practice, you will create a simple database in SQL Server. You create a Business Data Connectivity service application and then use SharePoint Designer to connect to the database and create an external content type. You will also demonstrate that users can modify data in SharePoint and that their changes propagate to the database.

Prepare for the Practice

Before you perform this practice, ensure that your lab environment has been built according to the instructions found in the Introduction to this Training Kit.

1. Apply the snapshot CHAPTER 07 to CONTOSO-DC.

2. Apply the snapshot CHAPTER 07 to SP2010-WFE1.

3. Start CONTOSO-DC.

    Wait for the virtual machine to complete startup, at which time the Press Ctrl+Alt+Delete prompt appears.

4. Start SP2010-WFE1.

5. Log on to SP2010-WFE1 as **CONTOSO\SP_Admin** with the password **Pa$$w0rd**.

EXERCISE 1   Install SharePoint Designer 2010

In this exercise, you install SharePoint Designer 2010. You must have downloaded the tool from the following location before you begin the exercise: *http://www.microsoft.com/downloads/en/ details.aspx?FamilyID=d88a1505-849b-4587-b854-a7054ee28d66&displaylang=en.*

1. Double-click SharePointDesigner.exe.

2. Accept the license terms and perform a default installation.

EXERCISE 2   Create the Fourth Coffee Products Database

In this exercise, you set up the Fourth Coffee products database to use as an example of an external system:

1. Use SQL Server Management Studio to create a new database called Fourth_Coffee_Products.

2. Use SQL Server Management Studio to open the following SQL script: C:\70667TK\ Practice Files\08_01\FourthCoffeeProducts.sql.

3. Execute the script.

4. Examine the contents of the new database. This is the sample data for this practice.

EXERCISE 3   Create a Business Data Catalog Service Application

In this exercise, you add a new Business Data Catalog service application to your SharePoint farm:

1. In Central Administration Quick Launch, click Application Management.

2. Add a new Business Data Connectivity service. Use the following specifications and guidance:

   - Name: Business Data Connectivity – Enterprise

   - Database Server: SP2010-WFE1

   - Database Name: SharePoint_Service_BDC

   - Application Pool: Use an existing pool.

   - Application Pool: SharePoint Service Applications.

3. Start the Business Data Connectivity Service on the SP2010-WFE1 server.

EXERCISE 4   Create a Secure Store Service Application

In this exercise, you add a new Secure Store service application to support the BDC service application you created in Exercise 2:

1. Add a new Secure Store service application. Use the following specifications and guidance:

   - Name: Secure Store – Enterprise

   - Database Server: SP2010-WFE1

   - Database Name: SharePoint_Service_Secure_Store

- Application Pool: Use an existing pool.
- Application Pool: SharePoint Service Applications.

2. Start the Secure Store Service on the SP2010-WFE1 server.
3. Restart the SP2010-WFE1 server.

EXERCISE 5 Create and Configure an External Content Type

In this exercise, you use SharePoint Designer to configure a SharePoint BCS external system that connects to a simple SQL Server database. You will also create an external content type and external list to display data from the database:

1. Log on to SP2010-WFE1 as **CONTOSO\SP_Admin** with the password **Pa$$w0rd**.
2. Use SharePoint Designer to open the *http://intranet.contoso.com* site.
3. Create a new external content type. Use the following specifications and guidance:
   - Name: FourthCoffeeProduct
   - Display Name: Fourth Coffee Product
4. For the External System, add a new connection. Use the following specifications and guidance:
   - Data Source Type: SQL Server
   - Database Server: SP2010-WFE1
   - Database Name: Fourth_Coffee_Products
   - Connect with User's Identity
5. Locate the Products Table in the Fourth_Coffee_Product database and create all operations for it.
6. For the Product Name parameter, select Show In Picker.
7. Create the lists and forms for the FouthCoffeeProduct external content type. Use the following specifications and guidance:
   - List Name: Fourth Coffee Products
   - List Description: This is the product catalog from our partner, Fourth Coffee

EXERCISE 6 Assign Permissions to the External Content Type

In this exercise, you ensure that users have sufficient permission to view and edit external data:

1. Start the Central Administration website and open the Business Data Connectivity – Enterprise service application.
2. Set permissions for the FourthCoffeeProduct external content type. Use the following specifications and guidance:
   - CONTOSO\SP_Admin; Edit, Execute, Selectable in Clients and Set Permissions.
   - CONTOSO\Domain Users; grant Edit and Execute.

EXERCISE 7   Access and Edit External Data

In this exercise, you access and edit data in the SharePoint external list:

1. Start SQL Server Management Studio and locate the Fourth_Coffee_Products database.

2. Select the first 1,000 records from the dbo.Products table.

3. Examine the results and note the SalePrice value for Nicaraguan Fair-Trade Coffee.

4. Open the ***http://intranet.contoso.com*** site in Internet Explorer.

5. Browse to the Fourth Coffee Products external list.

6. Change the Sale Price of Nicaraguan Fair-Trade Ground Coffee to $4.90.

7. Create a new product. Use the following specifications and guidance:

   - ProductID: 0006

   - ProductName: Fourth Coffee Special Espresso Blend

   - Description: This blend is perfect for after dinner

   - CatalogNumber: Frth0006

   - CostPrice: 2.50

   - SalePrice: 4.50

8. Switch to SQL Server Management Studio.

9. Select the first 1,000 records from the dbo.Products table.

10. Examine the results.

11. Close all windows and applications.

12. Log off of SP2010-WFE1.

Lesson Summary

- Because so many organizations have data in existing LOB, database, and other systems, SharePoint must import data for use in sites, dashboards, and applications.

- Business Connectivity Services can connect to a wide variety of external systems and integrate them with SharePoint.

- BCS can enable users to perform create, read, update, and delete operations in SharePoint. All changes are synchronized with the external system.

- You use SharePoint Designer to make connections to external systems and create external content types to match the external data structure.

- BCS includes a range of components that run on web front-end servers, application servers, database servers, and client computers.

- You can add BCS data functionality to any SharePoint page by using the BCS Web Parts to display and edit external data.

Lesson Review

You can use the following questions to test your knowledge of the information in Lesson 1, "Implement Business Connectivity Services." The questions are also available on the companion media in a practice test if you prefer to review them in electronic form.

> **NOTE ANSWERS**
>
> Answers to these questions and explanations of why each answer choice is right or wrong are located in the "Answers" section at the end of the book.

1. You are planning a BCS deployment to integrate a SharePoint farm with a SAP system. You are deciding whether to use a dedicated application server or share BCS application servers with the Search service application. You want to estimate the extra load that BCS will place on the application servers. Which of the following components run on application servers? (Choose all that apply.)

   A. The BDC Server Runtime

   B. The BDC Service

   C. The BCS Web Parts

   D. The BCS Package Store

   E. The Secure Store Service

   F. The BDC Service Database

2. Your manager asks you to investigate a custom server application used by the Sales department. Sales would like to be able to update customer leads when they are away from the office and have intermittent connections from their laptops to the company intranet. Your boss suggests they could use SharePoint and Office Workspace to make these changes, which would propagate to the Sales application through BCS. Which of the following features would enable SharePoint BCS to connect if sales leads were available in the Sales application? (Choose all that apply.)

   A. An ASP.NET-based user interface that users view in a browser.

   B. A user interface built on InfoPath forms.

   C. A Web service that publishes sales leads.

   D. A WCF Service that publishes sales leads.

   E. An Access database that stores sales leads.

   F. A SQL Server database that stores sales leads.

Lesson 2: Implement InfoPath Forms Services

Anytime you want to collect information from a user in most computer systems, you make the user complete and submit a form. Usually, this consists of various named and labeled fields of different types, such as text, multiple choice, numeric, true or false, and so on. You'll be familiar with forms in desktop applications, websites, smart phone applications, and just about every piece of software you use. They are closely analogous to paper-based forms, such as a vacation request, but have extra capabilities. For example, they can display live, up-to-the-minute data from a database to help users make decisions. Microsoft Office InfoPath 2010 provides the richest environment for creating and publishing forms. When you use InfoPath with SharePoint, you can enrich item forms, add forms to workflows, rapidly create user surveys, and complete many other global information gathering tasks.

After this lesson, you will be able to:

- Understand the components and capabilities of InfoPath forms.
- Describe the components of InfoPath 2010.
- Administer InfoPath Forms Services in SharePoint 2010.
- Modify default SharePoint forms by using InfoPath.
- Publish new forms created in InfoPath.
- Create forms-driven applications.

Estimated Lesson Time: 45 minutes

SharePoint and InfoPath

It is important to be clear that you don't need to use InfoPath to work with forms in SharePoint 2010. In fact, when you create a new content type, either in the browser or in SharePoint Designer, and create a new item of that type, SharePoint will display a default form with all the editable fields. If you want to make changes to this form, you can do so with SharePoint Designer, although many such tasks will require knowledge of HTML or even ASP.NET and so qualify as developer tasks.

InfoPath, by contrast, enables administrators and power users to make highly functional forms, as shown in Figure 8-3, without writing any code. For example, you can:

- Connect to a database and display records or query results on your form.
- Populate a drop-down list with items from a SharePoint list.
- Show or hide parts of a form based on criteria. For example, if the form records a help desk request, you can show the Feedback field only when the Status field contains the value *Complete*.
- Style the form and add a corporate look and feel.

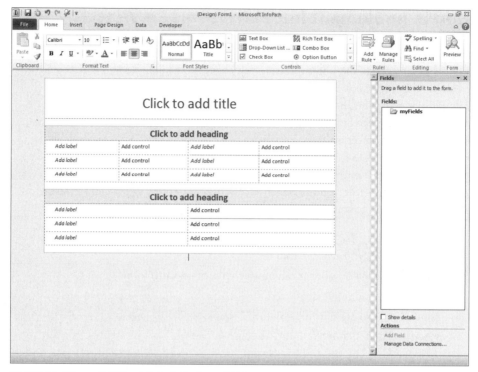

FIGURE 8-3 Microsoft Office InfoPath Designer 2010

Adding InfoPath Forms to SharePoint 2010

Because InfoPath forms are a type of content, SharePoint 2010 is an ideal location to store them, just like documents, multi-media files, web pages, and all the other formats you have seen in this book. You can use InfoPath in two principle ways within SharePoint:

- By creating native InfoPath forms and storing them in document libraries.

    Like a Word document, an InfoPath form consists of a template and the contents. In Word, the content is the text. In InfoPath the content is the values of all the fields. When you store a Word document in SharePoint, you can promote some text within the content to be a property of the document so that its value can be displayed in the Document Library's list views and be indexed. Similarly, with InfoPath forms, individual fields can be promoted to the form's metadata.

    An InfoPath form template can also be used as the default form for a document library. When users click the New Item button, the form is displayed in their browser and they can complete the fields.

- By using InfoPath to edit default forms.

    When you create a content type by defining and combining columns, SharePoint creates a default, fully functional form for the content type. In SharePoint 2010, you can edit this default form in InfoPath. This powerful technique enables administrators and power users to add advanced functionality to default forms without writing any code. It is also an easy way to add corporate branding to forms or just brighten them up.

InfoPath forms within SharePoint can be used to create highly functional custom business applications without any input from developers. Multiple forms, lists, document libraries, workflows, and pages can be combined to support the business processes in your organization. Such applications are known as *SharePoint Composites*.

> **NOTE INFOPATH FORMS IN THE BROWSER**
>
> If InfoPath is installed on the user's computer it will display any InfoPath form that the user creates or edits. However, the user does not require InfoPath to use InfoPath forms in SharePoint: When a user without InfoPath opens an InfoPath form, a page called FormServer.aspx renders an HTML and JScript version and the user sees it in the browser.

An InfoPath Scenario

To examine the InfoPath capabilities further, consider the following scenario: You are an administrator in a large organization. The IT department runs a help desk that offers first- and second-line support to all users. You've been asked to create a help desk application with which users can register help desk requests and support personnel can record the actions they took to solve each request. The following functional requirements have been requested:

- Dynamic Categories

    When users fill in their request, they select a category such as hardware, software, telephones, and so on. IT would like to be able to add new categories to the system without editing and republishing the form.

    To satisfy this requirement, you could create a SharePoint list that contains the categories. In InfoPath, you could configure the Categories drop-down list to populate its list from the SharePoint list. This means that when IT adds a new category to the SharePoint list, it automatically appears in the InfoPath form for new requests.

- Dynamic Frequently Asked Questions

    When users create a help desk request, IT would like the form to display solutions from the FAQ. When users select a category, IT would like the form to display solutions for that category. In this way, users receive targeted help and may be able to solve their own problems.

    To satisfy this requirement, you could create the FAQ as a SharePoint list with Question and Answer columns. Each question should also be categorized using the same list of categories as the help desk requests. In InfoPath, controls exist to display a field from a SharePoint list and you can filter these controls in response to user input.

- Calculated Fields

    IT would like users to receive an estimated time when a member of the support staff might address their request. Each request takes, on average, about 15 minutes to solve, although some take significantly longer.

    You can satisfy this request by using a calculated field in InfoPath. By counting the number of requests in the queue and multiplying by 15, InfoPath can make a simple estimate for the user.

- Corporate Branding

    The board has requested that the new company logo and the Internet site look and feel be used in the Help Desk application.

    To satisfy this requirement, use the InfoPath form designer to add graphics files to the form and set fonts and colors to match the corporate look and feel.

InfoPath Forms Architecture

In SharePoint 2010, the following components support InfoPath Forms Services:

- **ASP.NET Modules** Various ASP.NET pages and controls render InfoPath forms for browsers to display. This includes the FormServer.aspx page and IIS modules.

- **InfoPath Forms Services HTTP Handler** This HTTP handler receives and responds to data requests from InfoPath forms.

- **Form Converter** The InfoPath form designer generates form templates in .xsn files. These are based on XML using a specific schema. The Form Converter creates ASP.NET pages and controls from this XML so that the ASP.NET modules can render them.

- **Page Generator** This component communicates with external data sources, such as databases. It also handles the session state and handles data posted back to the server from the client.

Publishing Locations for InfoPath Forms

The architect of InfoPath Forms Services is designed to enable users to create their own forms while ensuring server stability and availability. This is always a trade-off: when you give users a powerful tool for customization you often open the host system to instability. In this case, for example, a poorly developed form may interrupt SharePoint services and prevent users from accessing their data.

To encourage customization by users and ensure server stability, SharePoint provides two locations for form templates:

- In SharePoint Lists and Document Libraries

    Users with appropriate permissions can upload InfoPath form templates to any SharePoint document library to be used to collect data or as the basis of a more complex application. These forms do not require administrators to approve them, so they encourage customization. However, to prevent poorly written forms from impacting SharePoint stability they are run in a restricted process called a *sandbox*. Forms run in the sandbox are prevented from taking dangerous actions. For example, they cannot write to a database or access resources in another site collection. Their use of server resources is also strictly controlled to prevent resource contention.

Sandboxed forms enable a surprisingly large portion of InfoPath functionality. Users can develop their own solutions without involving the IT department. Administrators can be sure that such solutions will not impact availability.

- In Central Administration

  Sometimes the sandbox prevents functionality that is required in an InfoPath form. Perhaps the most common example is the requirement to read from an external database. For such cases, SharePoint provides a farm forms library—forms published here run outside the sandbox and are not restricted. You can see this forms library in Central Administration.

  Without the sandbox, a poorly written form might cause instability. To prevent this, these forms require approval by administrators. You should only grant approval when a form has been thoroughly tested.

Administering InfoPath Forms Services

There is no service application to create or configure for InfoPath Forms Services. Instead, InfoPath support is built into core SharePoint functionality. However, a SharePoint State service application is required to support InfoPath forms and you must configure InfoPath Forms Services to ensure security and support form designers. This section describes these tasks.

CREATE A STATE SERVICE APPLICATION

The State Service is a shared SharePoint service that enables InfoPath forms, Visio diagrams, and other SharePoint components to store information across many browser page requests. It must be running for InfoPath forms to be rendered in the browser. You can enable it by selecting the appropriate check box in the Initial Farm Configuration Wizard. Alternatively, you can use Windows PowerShell cmdlets to create the service, its database, and its service application proxy:

```
$serviceApp = New-SPStateServiceApplication -Name "<StateServiceName>"
New-SPStateServiceDatabase -Name "<StateServiceDatabase>"
-ServiceApplication $serviceApp -DatabaseServer "<DBServerName>"
New-SPStateServiceApplicationProxy -Name "<ApplicationProxyName>"
-ServiceApplication $serviceApp -DefaultProxyGroup
```

Where:

- *<StateServiceName>* is the name you have chosen for your service application, such as "Contoso State Service Application."
- *<StateServiceDatabase>* is the name for the database stored in SQL Server.

- <DBServerName> is the name of the SQL server.
- <ApplicationProxyName> is the name you have chosen for your service application proxy.

UPLOAD AND ACTIVATE FORM TEMPLATES

Users can manage their own forms in lists and libraries. The sandbox restricts these forms so that administrators need not become involved. However, if a user asks to run a form outside the sandbox, an administrator must upload it in Central Administration and then activate the form to the site collection in which it will be used.

> **IMPORTANT** **TESTING FORMS**
>
> Forms published in Central Administration are not restricted by the sandbox. Before you complete the following steps, ensure that you have thoroughly tested the form and that you are satisfied that it cannot cause any damage.

1. In Central Administration Quick Launch, click General Application Settings.
2. Under InfoPath Forms Services, click Upload Form Template.
3. In the File Name text box, type the full path to the form template file or use the Browse button to locate it.
4. To check the form for errors, warnings, and other issues, click Verify.
5. If the verification completes to your satisfaction, click OK.
6. If the form is a new version of one that is already in use, you can use the options in the Upgrade section to manage how existing instances are handled.
7. Click Upload.
8. In the list of form templates, point to the new form, and then, in the drop-down list, click Activate to a Site Collection.
9. In the Site Collection box, select the site collection in which the form will be used.
10. Click OK.

MANAGE FORM TEMPLATES

Forms in the Central Administration forms library can be deactivated, removed, and quiesced. Use the quiesce option when forms govern long-running processes. Users cannot create new instances of quiesced forms but they can edit existing instances to complete a business process. When all instances are complete, you can safely remove or upgrade the form. The following process describes how to quiesce a form. The steps for deactivation and removal are very similar.

1. In Central Administration Quick Launch, click General Application Settings.
2. Under InfoPath Forms Services, click Manage Form Templates.
3. Point to the form you want to quiesce, and then, in the drop-down list, click Quiesce Form Template.

4. Under Quiesce, type a number of minutes to wait. To quiesce the form immediately, type **0**.

5. Click Start Quiescing.

CONFIGURE INFOPATH FORMS SERVICES

In Central Administration, farm administrators can also set a range of global values to govern InfoPath forms behavior:

1. In the Central Administration Quick Launch, click General Application Settings.

2. Under InfoPath Forms Services, click Configure InfoPath Forms Services.

3. Under User Browser-Enabled Form Templates, select the Allow Users To Browser-Enable Form Templates and Render Form Templates That Are Browser-Enabled By Users check boxes. If a form is not browser-enabled, a user must have InfoPath to open and edit it.

4. Under Data Connection Timeouts, set the default number and maximum number of milliseconds for timeouts.

5. Under Data Connection Response Size, set a maximum number of kilobytes for database query responses.

6. Under HTTP Data Connections, select whether to require SSL for any authentication request using HTTP. This option ensures that credentials are encrypted.

7. Under Embedded SQL Authentication, choose whether to embed credentials in SQL requests. Because these credentials are stored in plain text within SharePoint, you may consider this a security risk.

8. Under Authentication To Data Sources, choose whether to allow forms to use the credentials that may be stored in data connection files.

9. Under Cross-Domain Access For User Form Templates, choose whether user form templates can access data from foreign domains.

10. Under Thresholds, set values to prevent form templates from over-consuming server resources.

11. Under User Sessions, set values to reset user sessions, in minutes, that overuse server resources.

12. Click OK.

MANAGE DATA CONNECTION FILES

Many InfoPath forms require a connection to a data source. For example, you can use a database table to populate a drop-down list or a SharePoint list to display links in the form. In InfoPath, you can use a wizard to make these connections. If you want to reuse the connection information you can save it as a data connection file—an XML file with a .xml or .udcx file extension. In SharePoint Central Administration, you can create a library of connection files to make it simple for form authors to connect to data.

The following example describes how to upload a connection file and categorize it:

1. In Central Administration Quick Launch, click General Application Settings.
2. Under InfoPath Forms Services, click Manage Data Connection Files.
3. Click Upload.
4. In the File Name text box, type the full path to the data connection file or use the Browse button to locate it.
5. In the Category text box, type a name for the category of this data connection.

> **NOTE DATA CONNECTION CATEGORIES**
> The categories assigned to data connection files are simply to group similar connections together and should help InfoPath users choose the right connection.

6. Under Web Accessibility, choose whether this connection file should be accessible through HTTP. If you select this box users can download the connection file to their client computers. If you leave this check box cleared, the data connection can only be used by administrator-approved forms.
7. Click Upload.

ENABLE THE WEB SERVICE PROXY FOR INFOPATH FORMS SERVICES

The Web Service Proxy for InfoPath Forms Services is used to surmount certain authentication issues that arise when an InfoPath form is rendered in a browser and accesses data from a Web service. Users that have InfoPath installed on their computer never face these issues.

If your SharePoint farm uses NTLM authentication, InfoPath forms are rendered in the browser, and InfoPath forms must authenticate with a Web service to access data, you must enable the Web Proxy by completing the following steps:

1. In Central Administration Quick Launch, click General Application Settings.
2. Under InfoPath Forms Services, click Configure InfoPath Forms Services Web Service Proxy.
3. Under Enable InfoPath Forms Services Web Service Proxy, select Enable.
4. If you want sandboxed forms to use the Web Proxy, under Enable InfoPath Forms Services Web Service Proxy For User Forms, click Enable, and then click OK.

Creating Sandboxed InfoPath Forms

Although the sandbox restricts the actions that an InfoPath form can complete, the vast majority of InfoPath functionality is available for forms published in SharePoint lists. If a user has created a form that can run in the sandbox, you should encourage that user to publish it in a list or library and not go to the trouble of obtaining administrator approval for publishing in Central Administration. In this way, you reduce the administrative workload and the total cost of ownership. You also make it easier for users to alter forms when requirements change.

The following procedures illustrate how to work with sandboxed forms.

PUBLISH A FORM TEMPLATE IN A DOCUMENT LIBRARY

Use this procedure to create a new InfoPath form and publish it to a new document library:

1. Click Start, All Programs, Microsoft Office, and then click Microsoft InfoPath Designer 2010.
2. Under Available Form Templates, click SharePoint Form Library.
3. Under SharePoint Form Library, click Design Form.
4. Add controls, labels, and formatting to the form as required.

> **NOTE USING THE FORMS DESIGNER**
>
> The InfoPath Designer is a rich and easy-to-use environment for creating forms. However, complete instructions for form design are beyond the scope of this procedure. You may find the designer to be self-explanatory, but for more information go to *http://office.microsoft.com/en-gb/infopath-help/.*

5. When the form is complete, on the ribbon, click the File tab and then click Save.
6. Type a name in the Form Name text box and then click Save.
7. Click the File tab, click Publish, and then click SharePoint Server.
8. In the Publishing Wizard, type the URL of the SharePoint site where you would like to publish your form. Click Next.
9. Select Form Library and then click Next.
10. Select Create a New Form Library and then click Next.
11. Type a name for your new form library and optionally type a description, and then click Next.
12. If you want form fields to be promoted to library columns, click Add to add them to the column list. Any field that you want to appear in SharePoint views or to be indexed by the SharePoint crawler must be in this column list. Click Next.
13. Review the summary information, and then click Publish.
14. When the form has been published, click Close. Users can now start to create forms from your template in the new forms library.

MODIFY A DEFAULT SHAREPOINT FORM

In SharePoint 2010, you can use the InfoPath Designer 2010 to modify any item form in a SharePoint list or library. For example, when you create a custom content type, you define columns of different types and combine them. SharePoint creates a fully functional but plain form for viewing and editing the new content type. To brand this default form or add advanced functionality, you can use InfoPath to modify it:

1. In Internet Explorer, browse to the list that contains your content type.
2. On the ribbon, click the List tab.

3. On the ribbon, in the Customize List section, click Customize Form. InfoPath Designer starts and displays the default form.

4. Add controls, labels, and formatting to the form as required.

5. When the form is complete, click the File tab, and then click Quick Publish.

6. When the form has been published, click OK. When users create a new item in the list, your modified form will display the data.

PRACTICE Configure InfoPath Forms Services

Practices are designed to guide you through important procedures. The instructions in the Training Kit are high-level instructions that will challenge you to think carefully and to apply the procedures that are covered in this lesson and elsewhere in the Training Kit. If you need assistance, consult the detailed, step-by-step instructions in the Practice Answers on the companion media.

In this practice, you configure InfoPath Forms Services in your SharePoint farm and create and use an administrator-approved InfoPath form. You also modify a default item form in the InfoPath Designer.

Prepare for the Practice

Before you perform this practice, ensure that your lab environment has been built according to the instructions found in the Introduction to this Training Kit. You must also have performed the practice in Lesson 1 of this chapter. You must be logged off of SP2010-WFE1 before beginning the exercises.

EXERCISE 1 Configure InfoPath Forms Services

In this exercise, you configure InfoPath Form Services in your farm to wait longer for data connection time-outs:

1. Log on to SP2010-WFE1 as **CONTOSO\SP_Admin** with the password **Pa$$w0rd**.

2. Use Central Administration to configure InfoPath Forms Services. Use the following specifications and guidance:

   - Default Data Connection Timeout: 15000 milliseconds
   - Maximum Data Connection Timeout: 25000 milliseconds
   - All other settings: Default

EXERCISE 2 Configure the SharePoint Server State Service

In this exercise, you create and configure that State service application by using Windows PowerShell:

1. Start the SharePoint 2010 Management Shell.

2. Get a list of all the State Service Applications in the farm.

3. Execute a command that creates a new State service application called "State Service Application – Enterprise". Store the service application in a variable called *$serviceApp*.

4. Execute a command that creates a new State service database. Use the following specifications and guidance:

   - Database Name: "SharePoint_Service_State"
   - Service Application: $serviceApp
   - Database Server: "SP2010-WFE1"

5. Execute a command that creates a new State service application proxy. Use the following specifications and guidance:

   - Name: "State Service Application Proxy"
   - Service Application: $serviceApp
   - Add the new proxy to the Default Proxy Group.
   - Get a list of all the State Service Applications in the farm for a second time.

EXERCISE 3   Install Office 2010

To complete the remaining exercises in this practice, and the exercises in Lessons 3 and 4, you must have Office 2010 installed on the SP2010-WFE1 image. These instructions assume that you have downloaded the evaluation version of Office Professional Plus, but you could also install a licensed version:

1. Locate and double-click the ProfessionalPlus.exe file or insert the Office 2010 disk.
2. Enter your license key and accept the license agreement.
3. Perform a default installation.

EXERCISE 4   Create an Administrator-Approved InfoPath Form

In this exercise, you create a simple Vacation Request InfoPath form and prepare it for administrator approval:

1. Use InfoPath Designer 2010 to create a new Blank Form template.
2. Use **Vacation Request** for the form title.
3. Add a text box control, label it **Full Name**, and rename its field **FullName**.
4. Add a Date Picker control, label it **Start Date**, and rename its field **StartDate**.
5. Add a second Date Picker control, label it **End Date**, and rename its field **EndDate**.
6. Edit the Advanced Form Options to use the Domain security level.
7. Save the form template to the Desktop as **VacationRequest.xsn**.
8. Publish the form. Use the following specifications and guidance:

   - Site: *http://intranet.contoso.com*
   - Administrator-Approved Form Template
   - Location for the Form Template: C:\70667TK\Practice-Files\08_02\VacationRequest
   - Add the FullName and StartDate fields as SharePoint site columns.

EXERCISE 5   Approve the New Form

In this exercise, you approve the form you created in the last exercise:

1. Use Central Administration to verify the form template you just created.
2. Use Central Administration to upload the form template to the farm form library.
3. Activate the VacationRequest.xsn form template to the *http://intranet.contoso.com* site collection.

EXERCISE 6   Use an Administrator-Approved Form in a Library

In this exercise, you use the new administrator-approved form in the Contoso intranet site:

1. Use Internet Explorer to browse the ***http://intranet.contoso.com*** site.
2. Examine the contents of the Form Templates library. The VacationRequest template you created in Exercise 3 should appear.
3. Create a new Form Library in the site called **Vacation Requests**.
4. Add the VacationRequest content type to this Form Library.
5. Create and save a Vacation Request for yourself.

EXERCISE 7   Modify an Existing Form Template

In this exercise, you use InfoPath to modify the default form for a SharePoint list:

1. In Internet Explorer, browse to the Tasks list in the intranet site.
2. Customize the form for the Tasks list.
3. Apply the SharePoint – Berry theme to the Tasks list.
4. Publish the modified form.
5. Create a new task and notice the change to the Task form.
6. Close all windows and applications.
7. Log off of SP2010-WFE1.

Lesson Summary

- InfoPath is a rich and easy-to-use forms development tool.
- No custom-coding skills are required to create rich and highly customizable InfoPath forms.
- SharePoint is an ideal platform to publish and store InfoPath forms and is tightly integrated with InfoPath functionality.
- InfoPath forms can display data from SharePoint lists and libraries and connect to other data sources such as databases.
- It's very easy to style and brand forms in the InfoPath designer.
- You can use SharePoint to store native InfoPath forms or use InfoPath to modify default SharePoint forms.
- Users do not require InfoPath installed on their computers to access and use InfoPath forms because SharePoint can render them in the browser.

- InfoPath forms published in SharePoint lists and libraries are run in a sandbox—a process that prevents them from impacting SharePoint reliability.

- InfoPath forms can also be run outside the sandbox but administrators must approve such forms in Central Administration.

Lesson Review

You can use the following questions to test your knowledge of the information in Lesson 2, "Implement InfoPath Forms Services." The questions are also available on the companion media in a practice test if you prefer to review them in electronic form.

> **NOTE ANSWERS**
>
> Answers to these questions and explanations of why each answer choice is right or wrong are located in the "Answers" section at the end of the book.

1. A user in the Finance department wants to conduct a survey from the entire company to assess the effectiveness of the department. She has created an InfoPath form with all the necessary fields and she wants to know how she can use SharePoint to store responses. The form simply collects information such as names, ratings, comments, and opinions about various services offered by Finance. What do you tell her?

    A. She must use the InfoPath publishing wizard to prepare the form for administrator approval. An administrator must approve the form before she can use it in a SharePoint form library.

    B. She must replicate the form in SharePoint Designer.

    C. She must upload the form to the Forms Library in the Finance SharePoint site and use it as the content type for a new Forms Library.

    D. She must work with a SharePoint developer to complete the form functionality.

2. You have created a new content type that describes your company's products. You have used this content type in a new SharePoint list called Products. You used InfoPath Designer 2010 to modify the default form for this content type and add links to catalog documents and component ordering sites. When users who do not have InfoPath installed try to open a product, they receive an error. Users with InfoPath can use the form without problems. Which of the following could cause this problem? (Choose all that apply.)

    A. No State Service is available in the SharePoint farm.

    B. A farm administrator has configured InfoPath Forms Services to disallow browser-enabled form templates.

    C. A farm administrator has disabled cross-domain access for user form templates.

    D. The users are not browsing with Internet Explorer.

    E. The details in the data connection file you used are incorrect.

Lesson 3: Implement Excel Services

The vast majority of documents stored in SharePoint are created in Office applications. In fact, it is extremely unusual to find SharePoint used with any other productivity suite. Microsoft has worked closely with customers to enhance Office users' experience of SharePoint by creating a range of services for specific applications. In this lesson, you will see how to use Excel Services to provide extra server-side functionality for spreadsheets. You can build data-driven dashboards and analytical solutions that work with live data. In subsequent lessons, you will see the extra integration provided for Access and Visio.

> **After this lesson, you will be able to:**
> - Create and configure an Excel Services service application.
> - Describe the architecture of Excel Services in SharePoint 2010.
> - Plan an Excel Services deployment for your SharePoint farm.
> - Describe Excel integration that does not require Excel Services.
> - Describe functionality that Excel Services adds to SharePoint 2010.
> - Publish an Excel spreadsheet to Excel Services.
> - Use the Excel Web Access Web Part.
> - Enable parameter input in the Excel Web Access Web Part.
>
> **Estimated Lesson Time: 30 minutes**

Excel and SharePoint

Excel users have been collaborating on their spreadsheets for many years. Traditionally, an author could share a spreadsheet with her colleagues by emailing it to them or by saving it to a file share. You'll probably be familiar with the kind of issues that can arise to slow productivity or compromise security in such scenarios:

- Multiple users can work on a spreadsheet simultaneously. When the final user saves a version, changes saved by earlier users are frequently lost.

- In a file share, permissions are used to control access, but when email is used to distribute a spreadsheet, it is very hard to ensure that it does not reach inappropriate eyes.

- If you restrict access to a spreadsheet in a file share, it is hard to publish portions of it. For example, consider a spreadsheet that includes company salaries. You should restrict access to board members and HR staff, but some information, such as a graph showing remuneration trends, might be appropriate for wider distribution. You would have to distribute this by pasting it into a separate file.

Collaboration with SharePoint

Even without Excel Services, SharePoint provides a much more functional collaboration environment for Excel users. For example, versioning in document libraries prevents users from making concurrent changes and losing previous data. This system works in the following way:

- A user cannot edit a document unless he or she checks it out of SharePoint. At this point the user downloads the latest version of the document.
- While the document is checked out, no other user can make changes.
- When the user is finished, he or she uploads the new version to SharePoint and checks the document back in.
- Other users can now check out the document and download the latest changes before making modifications.

This system ensures that no concurrent changes are possible and that users always have the latest version of the file before they begin editing. Such systems are characteristic of any modern collaboration tool.

Also remember that Excel spreadsheets are fully indexed by the SharePoint Search crawler. This means that you can search spreadsheet content as well as its metadata.

None of the preceding functionality is specific to Excel; however, SharePoint 2010 also includes import and export tools for Excel:

- **The Import Spreadsheet List Template**   This tool enables you to create a SharePoint list by importing data from an Excel spreadsheet. In a SharePoint site, the user creates a new list as usual but selects the Import Spreadsheet list template and specifies the ranges of cells to import. SharePoint creates columns and data types to match the content but you may have to check that the most appropriate data types have been used. No connection between the Excel spreadsheet and the SharePoint list is maintained and changes in one application will not appear in the other.

- **The Export to Excel Tool**   This tool enables you to populate a new spreadsheet with data from a SharePoint list. When you browse a list, on the ribbon List tab, you can click the Export To Excel button, as shown in Figure 8-4. This downloads a query (.iqy) file that Excel can open and display the data. In this case there is a one-way link from SharePoint to Excel. You can see changes in the SharePoint list in Excel by clicking the Refresh button. Changes in Excel do not reach the SharePoint list.

FIGURE 8-4 The Export to Excel Tool

Collaboration with SharePoint and Excel Services

As you have seen, you can do a lot with Excel in SharePoint 2010 even without Excel Services configured. However, two situations are not well covered:

- **Users without Excel** In Lesson 2, you saw how InfoPath Forms Services can render InfoPath Forms in the browser so that users who don't have InfoPath installed can view and edit a form. In a similar way, Excel Services can render a spreadsheet in the browser. It is therefore an excellent way to publish spreadsheet data more widely and helps users of other browsers, operating systems, and devices.

- **Partial access to spreadsheets** Consider the salaries spreadsheet mentioned earlier in this lesson. You'd like to publish the graph that shows salary trends without enabling users to see each other's salaries. By using Excel Services, you can publish a graph, data range, or pivot table like this without enabling users to see the underlying data.

A spreadsheet rendered in the browser by Excel Services does not include the full functionality you find in Excel itself. However, it is excellent for data display and you can enable some interaction. By setting up a parameter, you can enable users to enter information to use in a spreadsheet graph or calculation.

Any data rendered by Excel Services is linked to an original spreadsheet. Therefore, when you update the spreadsheet with new data, changes are automatically displayed to browsers. The original spreadsheet can be stored in SharePoint, a file share, or an HTTP website.

Business Intelligence and Dashboards

Business intelligence has been a hot topic in IT for many years. It describes how IT can help decision makers to understand how a company is performing by providing rich, live analysis of business data. Because many businesses use Excel spreadsheets to store a large proportion of the data that makes the company tick, you can see that Excel Services can provide a powerful business intelligence tool.

In business intelligence, a dashboard is a display that shows critical data from a variety of sources. You can easily create dashboards in SharePoint: create a Web Part page and add to it data displays and graphs from Excel spreadsheets. Excel Services enables you to do this by using two Web Parts:

- **The Excel Web Access Web Part** The Excel Web Access Web Part can display any data range, graph, or pivot tool from any spreadsheet published through Excel Services.

- **The Chart Web Part** The Chart Web Part can create many chart types including bar charts, pie charts, line graphs, and others. It can take data from many sources including Excel Services. Use this Web Part to make a chart from Excel data when the original spreadsheet does not include the chart you need.

Excel Services Architecture

The architecture of Excel Services is shown in Figure 8-5.

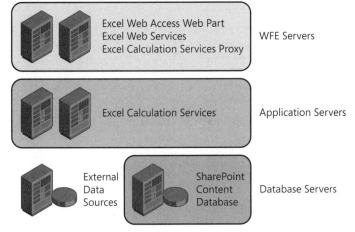

FIGURE 8-5 Excel Services Architecture

The components shown perform the following functions:

- **Excel Web Access**   This is the Web Part that renders spreadsheets into HTTP and JScript for display in the browser.
- **Excel Web Services**   This component publishes Excel spreadsheet data in the form of Web services. Developers can call these services from custom code.
- **Excel Calculation Services Proxy**   This component is the service application proxy that connects the SharePoint Web Front-End servers to the Excel Calculation Service on one or more application servers.
- **Excel Calculation Services**   This component is the heart of the architecture. The Excel Calculation Service opens spreadsheets, makes calculations, updates external data, and maintains session state.

- **SharePoint Content Database**   When a spreadsheet is published from a SharePoint document library, the Excel Calculation Service must connect to the main SharePoint content database to open it.

- **External Data Sources**   When a spreadsheet is stored outside SharePoint, SharePoint must connect to the external store. These stores can be file shares or websites.

Configuring Excel Services

Before you can publish spreadsheets through Excel Services, you must create an Excel Services Service Application. You can also configure a range of settings to ensure security and stability. Use the following procedures to make these changes:

CREATE AN EXCEL SERVICES SERVICE APPLICATION IN CENTRAL ADMINISTRATION

Excel Services are implemented as a service application. You might have created this service application when you ran the Initial Farm Configuration Wizard. However, if you did not select the Excel Services check box in that wizard, you must manually create the service application in the following way:

1. In Central Administration Quick Launch, click Application Management.
2. Under Service Applications, click Manage Service Applications.
3. Click New, and then click Excel Services Application.
4. In the Name text box, type an appropriate name for the service application.
5. Under Application Pool, select the existing application pool or create a new pool according to your planned architecture.
6. Choose whether to add this service application to the default proxy list.
7. Click OK.

CREATE AN EXCEL SERVICES SERVICE APPLICATION IN POWERSHELL

Alternatively, you can create the Excel Services service application by using the following Windows PowerShell cmdlet:

```
New-SPExcelServiceApplication -Name "<ExcelServiceName>" -ApplicationPool <AppPool>
```

Where:

- *<ExcelServiceName>* is the name you want to use for your new Excel Services service application.

- *<AppPool>* is a variable that contains the application pool you want to add this service application to.

CONFIGURE EXCEL SERVICES

Administrators can control many aspects of the behavior of Excel Services. For example, you can restrict memory usage on the application server and require encryption for extra security. To configure your Excel Services service application, follow these steps:

1. In Central Administration, click Application Management.

2. Under Service Applications, click Manage Service Applications.

3. Click the Excel Services service application you want to configure, and then click Manage.

4. Click Global Settings.

5. Under Security, choose the file access method. Excel Services will either impersonate the current user or authenticate as the Application Pool account, when it connects to a spreadsheet stored outside SharePoint.

6. Under Security, choose whether to require encryption for the client to front-end server communication.

7. Under Security, choose whether to permit spreadsheets to be displayed across different HTTP domains.

8. Under Load Balancing, choose a load balancing scheme for Excel Calculation Services. When Excel Services runs on more than one application server, this scheme distributes the processing load across those servers to maximize performance.

9. Under Memory Utilization, set values to limit the amount of memory in megabytes that is used by Excel Calculation Services on the application servers.

10. All Excel spreadsheets accessed through Excel Services are cached on the application servers to improve performance. Under Workbook cache, you can configure the location of this cache and its maximum size.

11. Under External Data, set the maximum lifetime in seconds of connections to file shares and websites. Older connections are reopened. To manage authentication, you can also specify the identity of a Secure Store application that contains user account mapping details.

12. Click OK.

> **IMPORTANT EXCEL SERVICES SERVER APPLICATION ACCESS TO THE CONTENT DATABASE**
>
> To be able to work, Excel Services must create tables in the SharePoint Content Database. For this reason, you must ensure that you create a login for the user account used by the Application Pool in which Excel Services runs. Grant the dbowner role and the public role to this account for the content database.

Using Excel Services

Now that there is a properly configured Excel Services service application, users can publish spreadsheets in Excel Services, start to use data in dashboards, and so on. The following procedures illustrate how to complete these tasks.

PUBLISH A SPREADSHEET TO EXCEL SERVICES

The following procedure illustrates how to publish a workbook sheet and a chart from a spreadsheet to Excel Services:

1. Use Excel 2010 to open the spreadsheet.
2. Click File, and then click Save & Send.
3. Click Save To SharePoint.
4. Under Save To SharePoint, click Publish Options.
5. In the drop-down list, select Sheets.
6. Select the check box next to the Sheet you want to publish.
7. In the drop-down list, select Items in the Workbook.
8. Select the check box next to the Chart you want to publish.
9. Click OK, and then click Save As.
10. Save the spreadsheet to a local folder, such as the My Documents folder.
11. Start Internet Explorer and browse to the SharePoint site where you want to publish the spreadsheet.
12. Browse to a document library or create a new document library.
13. Click Add Document.
14. Use the Browse tool to locate the Excel spreadsheet you just created.
15. Click OK.
16. In the list of documents, point to the spreadsheet and drop down the list.
17. Click View In Browser. Excel Service renders the spreadsheet in Internet Explorer.

USE THE EXCEL WEB ACCESS WEB PART

To create dashboards and other business intelligence user interfaces, you must add the Excel Web Access Web Part to a SharePoint page. Use the following steps to complete this task:

1. In Internet Explorer, browse to the page where you want to display Excel information.
2. On the ribbon, click the Page tab, and then click Edit.
3. Place the cursor on the page where you want the Excel information to appear.
4. On the ribbon, click Insert, and then click Web Part.
5. In the list of Categories, click Business Data.
6. In the list of Web Parts, click Excel Web Access, and then click Add. The Web Part is added and displays the title "Select a Workbook".
7. Click Click Here To Open The Tool Pane.
8. In the Tool Pane on the right of the page, next to the Workbook text box, click the Browse button.
9. Browse to locate the workbook you want to display. Select the workbook and then click OK.

10. If you want to display a specific item from the workbook, such as a chart or pivot table, type the item's name in the Named Item text box.

11. At the bottom of the Tool Pane, click OK. The Web Part displays the information you selected.

<hr/>

PRACTICE **Configure Excel Services**

Practices are designed to guide you through important procedures. The instructions in the Training Kit are high-level instructions that will challenge you to think carefully and to apply the procedures that are covered in this lesson and elsewhere in the Training Kit. If you need assistance, consult the detailed, step-by-step instructions in the Practice Answers on the companion media.

In this practice, you create and configure an Excel Services service application for the Contoso SharePoint farm. You also use Excel Services to publish a simple Excel spreadsheet and display it on a web page.

Prepare for the Practice

Before you perform this practice, ensure that your lab environment has been built according to the instructions found in the Introduction to this Training Kit. You must also have performed the practice in Lesson 2 of this chapter. You must be logged off of SP2010-WFE1 before beginning the exercises.

EXERCISE 1 Grant Database Permissions to the Service Application

In this exercise, you ensure that the web application pool service account has the correct access to the intranet content database.

1. Log on to SP2010-WFE1 as **CONTOSO\SP_Admin** with the password **Pa$$w0rd**.

2. Open SQL Server Management Studio and browse to the Users container in the SharePoint_Content_Intranet database.

3. Add CONTOSO\SP_ServiceApps as a user of the database. Grant this user the dbowner role.

4. Close SQL Server Management Studio.

EXERCISE 2 Create an Excel Services Service Application

In this exercise, you create the Excel Services Service Application that is required for Excel spreadsheet publishing:

1. Use Central Administration to manage service applications.

2. Add a new Excel Services Application. Use the following specifications and guidance:
   - Name: Excel Services – Enterprise
   - Use an existing application pool
   - Application Pool: SharePoint Service Applications

EXERCISE 3   Configure the Excel Services Service Application

In this exercise, you configure the Excel Service Application to restrict the size of the workbook cache and extend the connection lifetime for external data. You will also ensure that the Excel Calculation Service is started:

1.   Open the Excel Services service application you created in Exercise 2.

2.   Amend the following Global Settings. Leave all other settings at the default values:

   ■   Maximum Size of Workbook Cache: 20,000 MB

   ■   External Data Connection Lifetime: 2,500 milliseconds

EXERCISE 4   Export a SharePoint External List to a Spreadsheet

In this exercise, you create a custom SharePoint list, populate it with simple data, and then export the list to an Excel Spreadsheet:

1.   In Internet Explorer, browse to the *http://intranet.contoso.com* site.

2.   Create a new Custom List called Sales Figures.

3.   Rename the Title column to be called Representative Name.

4.   Add a Currency column called Q1 Sales.

5.   Add a new item to the list. Use the following values:

   ■   Representative Name: Michael Raheem

   ■   Q1 Sales: $32,000

6.   Add a second new item to the list. Use the following values:

   ■   Representative Name: Henrik Jensen

   ■   Q1 Sales: $28,500

7.   Add a new item to the list. Use the following values:

   ■   Representative Name: Kelly Rollin

   ■   Q1 Sales: $42,000

8.   Export the list to Excel.

9.   In the new spreadsheet, insert a 3-D Clustered Column chart. Use the first two columns in the spreadsheet for the data source.

10.   Save the spreadsheet in the Documents library as **SalesFigure.xlsx**.

EXERCISE 5   Publish a Spreadsheet to Excel Services

In the exercise, you publish the new spreadsheet to Excel Services:

1.   Click the Save & Send shortcut on the File tab.

2.   Use the Publish Options to select items Chart 1 and Table_owssvr_1 for publishing.

3.   Save the spreadsheet and close Excel.

4.   Use Internet Explorer to upload the spreadsheet to the Shared Documents library in the Contoso intranet.

5.   View the spreadsheet in the browser.

EXERCISE 6 Use the Excel Web Access Web Part to Display Data

In this exercise, you add a chart to the intranet home page. The chart will display sales data for Contoso sales representatives.

1. In Internet Explorer, browse to the Contoso intranet homepage.

2. Below the SharePoint Documents Web Part, insert an Excel Web Access Web Part.

3. Configure the new Web Part to display the SalesFigures.xlsx spreadsheet in the Shared Documents library.

4. Close all windows and applications.

5. Log off of SP2010-WFE1.

Lesson Summary

- Excel and SharePoint integration is close even without Excel Services. For example, you can export a list to an Excel spreadsheet to use the data for calculation.

- Version control governs and organizes documents collaboration for all types of content, including Excel spreadsheets.

- Excel Services displays Excel spreadsheets in the browser. This helps users without Excel and also enables you to publish spreadsheet data without granting access to an entire Excel file.

- Spreadsheets rendered in the browser by Excel Services do not include full functionality. However, you can make such spreadsheets interactive by including parameters. Users can alter these parameters and view how they affect calculations, pivot tables, and charts.

- Use the Excel Web Access Web Part and the Chart Web Part to build business intelligence dashboards in a SharePoint portal.

Lesson Review

You can use the following questions to test your knowledge of the information in Lesson 3, "Implement Excel Services." The questions are also available on the companion media in a practice test if you prefer to review them in electronic form.

> **NOTE** **ANSWERS**
>
> Answers to these questions and explanations of why each answer choice is right or wrong are located in the "Answers" section at the end of the book.

1. Users have been successfully publishing Excel spreadsheets in the Contoso intranet site collection for some time. Today a user calls to ask why she cannot publish a spreadsheet in the Finance site collection. She has uploaded the file to a Document

Library but when she clicks View In Browser, she receives an error. Which of the following actions may solve this problem?

A. Create an Excel Services service application in your SharePoint farm.

B. Start the Excel Shared Service on at least one application server in the farm.

C. Choose round-robin load balancing in the Excel Services Global Settings.

D. Advise the user that she must use the Excel Web Access Web Part to display the spreadsheet in the browser.

E. Grant the Excel Services user account the dbowner role on the Finance content database.

2. You have yet to implement Excel Services in you SharePoint farm. The board has requested that you migrate the Employees spreadsheet, which lists employees and various data about them, including salaries, into a SharePoint site. Which of the following actions should you complete? (Choose all that apply.)

A. Create a new Excel Services service application and configure its properties.

B. Grant the Excel Services user account the dbowner role on the appropriate content database.

C. Start the Excel Shared Service on at least one application server in the SharePoint farm.

D. Use the Import Spreadsheet list template to create a new list and import data from the Excel Spreadsheet.

E. Restrict access to the new list by applying permissions carefully.

Lesson 4: Implement Access Web Services

Microsoft Access is the most widely used desktop database application—many thousands of organizations across the world use it to manage data. Even in organizations with server database systems such as SQL Server, Access remains popular because users can create databases and entire applications without involving DBAs and developers. Because Access is part of the Microsoft Office Suite, you'll find it installed on the majority of client computers. For these reasons, Microsoft has added extra functionality to SharePoint Server 2010 to support Access in the form of a dedicated service application. Where the Access Web Services service application is available, Access users can publish their databases and applications as sites in SharePoint without learning advanced SharePoint customization skills. In this lesson, you will see how to set up and configure Access Web Services and how to publish databases.

> **After this lesson, you will be able to:**
> - Describe how Access is integrated with SharePoint without Access Web Services.
> - Describe how Access Web Services improves SharePoint integration with Access.
> - Create and configure an Access Web Services service application.
> - Create and use an Access Web Database site.
>
> **Estimated Lesson Time: 30 minutes**

Access and SharePoint

Access users create databases by creating tables to store structured data. For each table they define named columns and they define a data type for column. Each row of data is called a *record*. To enter and edit data records, Access users can type into the table itself or define forms. When data exists in the tables, users can write queries to interrogate the data and reports to analyze it. By using multiple tables, forms, queries, and reports, Access users can create sophisticated and highly functional applications. It is this versatility that accounts for the popularity of the database package.

All these objects are saved in a single file with an .mdb extension. Introduced in Access 2007, Access 2010 uses the new file type that has an .accdb extension. This file type supports extra features, such as multi-valued fields and attachments to records and you should use it whenever possible. The .accdb format does not support the following three features:

- **Earlier versions of Access**   If any user does not have at least Access 2007, do not use the new format.
- **Replication**   If you want to replicate data to another Access database, do not use the new format.
- **User-level security**   If you need to restrict access to certain parts of the database for certain users, do not use the new format. SharePoint permissions, NTFS permissions, and file share permission apply to the entire file but you cannot apply more granular restrictions.

You can upload an Access file to SharePoint and receive the benefit of its collaboration features even when you do not have Access Web Services set up. For example, by enabling versioning and document check-in, you can prevent user changes from being overwritten with concurrent changes just as you saw in the case of Excel in the previous lesson. If you enable this configuration, you should bear in mind the following use cases:

- **Read**   All users with Read permission can download a copy of the database to their local computers, even when the file is checked out by another user.

- **Edit Design**   If a user wants to modify a table, form, query, or report, that user must check the file out, make the changes, and then check it back into SharePoint.

- **Edit Data**   If users want to add, edit, or delete records, they must also check the file out.

Notice that while the file is checked out, no other user can make modifications. This is a barrier to collaboration and means that this system is only appropriate when a fairly small team is collaborating on a database. In a server-based database like SQL Server, by contrast, individual records can be edited without locking the entire database. This means that each user can edit different records simultaneously.

Access Web Services Enhancements

Access Web Services is designed to connect Access to SharePoint and make it easier to create Access-like applications within SharePoint sites. When you have Access Web Services, users can publish their Access applications to SharePoint—tables, forms, queries, and reports can all be uploaded and converted to SharePoint objects. Each database table, for example, is implemented as a SharePoint list. A SharePoint site implemented in this way is called a *web database*.

> *NOTE* **ACCESS WEB SERVICES AND SHAREPOINT EDITIONS**
>
> Access Web Services is only available in SharePoint Server 2010 Enterprise edition.

This approach has many advantages that cannot be realized by simply uploading an Access file to a SharePoint library. Table 8-1 lists these advantages.

TABLE 8-1 Comparing Access Databases in SharePoint Libraries with Web Databases

ISSUE	ACCESS DATABASE IN SHAREPOINT LIBRARY	WEB DATABASE
Concurrent Edits	Only one user can check a database out and make changes at a time.	Different users can alter separates records simultaneously.
Visibility	Access must be installed on your local computer if you want to read or edit data.	Any user with a web browser can read and edit data. Access is not required.

ISSUE	ACCESS DATABASE IN SHAREPOINT LIBRARY	WEB DATABASE
Permissions	Permissions can be applied only to the file as a whole. You cannot restrict access to individual objects such as tables or forms.	You can set granular permissions on lists, forms, and other objects.
Design Skills	Access skills are required to create databases and applications.	No extra skills are required to create web databases. Anyone with Access skills can publish a web database.

 REAL WORLD

Alistair Matthews

The main reason Access Web Services is a powerful tool is that Access skills are very common among the general Office user community. Almost all the users you come across in companies that have the Office Suite have at least used Access, even if it was only for data entry. However, you may be surprised by the number of users who have created their own Access databases in the past and often included some pretty advanced queries, forms, and reports. Now such users can create highly functional SharePoint sites on their own, without involving IT or any developers and, most important, without learning a whole new set of skills specific to SharePoint. You will not even have to tell them what a content type is!

IMPORTANT **THE NEW ACCESS FILE FORMAT**

If you want to create a web database from an Access database, it must be saved in the new Access 2007 format with an .accdb file extension. If you have an .mdb file, you must open it in Access 2010 and use Save As to create a new database in the new format.

Access Web Services also includes some web database templates that you can use as the basis of your new application. In this case, you can publish a web database without creating it in Access 2010. After creating the application, you can make modifications to adapt it to your precise needs. For example, you could add a new column in a table. The templates are as follows:

- Assets Web Database
- Charitable Contributions Web Database
- Contacts Web Database
- Issues Web Database
- Projects Web Database

Implementing and Configuring Access Web Services

Before users can start to create web databases, you must set up the Access Web Services service application. This is implemented as a service application just like Excel Services, Search, User Profiles, and several of the other SharePoint 2010 services that you have seen.

CREATE AN ACCESS WEB SERVICES SERVICE APPLICATION IN CENTRAL ADMINISTRATION

In the Central Administration site, you can create an Access Web Services service application by following these steps:

1. In Central Administration Quick Launch, click Application Management.
2. Under Service Applications, click Manage Service Applications.
3. On the ribbon, click New, and then click Access Services.
4. In the Name text box, type an appropriate name for the services application.
5. Under Application Pool, select an existing application pool or create a new one according to your plan.
6. Under Add To Default Proxy List, choose whether to connect this service application to the default proxy group. If you clear this check box, you must manually connect this service application to proxies.
7. Click OK.

CREATE AN ACCESS WEB SERVICES SERVICE APPLICATION IN POWERSHELL

Alternatively, you can use Windows PowerShell cmdlets to create the service application:

```
New-SPAccessServiceApplication –Name "<AccessServiceName>" –ApplicationPool <AppPool>
```

Where:

- *<AccessServiceName>* is the name you want to use for your new Access Web Services service application.
- *<AppPool>* is a variable that contains the application pool you want to add this service application to.

CONFIGURING ACCESS WEB SERVICES

You can tune the behavior of Access Web Services. For example you can control the maximum number of rows and columns returned for each query to ensure that large databases do not overburden the application server. To configure the Access Web Services service application, follow these steps:

1. In Central Administration, click Application Management.
2. Under Service Applications, click Manage Service Applications.
3. Click the Access service application you want to configure, and then click Manage.
4. Under Lists and Queries, use the Maximum Columns Per Query text box and the Maximum Rows Per Query text box to limit the size of query responses.
5. Under Lists and Queries, use the Maximum Sources Per Query text box to limit the number of lists that a single query can interrogate.
6. Under Lists and Queries, use the Maximum Calculated Columns Per Query text box to limit the number of calculated fields that can be interrogated in a single query. Calculated fields can place extra load on the Access service application.
7. Under Lists and Queries, use the Maximum Order By Clauses Per Query text box to limit the levels of ordering in each query. Ordering results by several different fields can overload the application server.
8. Under Lists and Queries, choose whether to allow outer joins. Outer joins are not always necessary for functional databases and consume extra processing time.
9. Under Lists and Queries, choose whether to allow non-remotable queries.
10. Under Lists and Queries, set the Maximum Records Per Table. This value helps to prevent the database from growing beyond control.
11. In Maximum Application Log Size, set a limit on the number of records in the Access Services log.
12. Under Sessions Management, use the Maximum Request Duration text box to set a limit on request time. Requests that take longer than this time return an error.
13. Under Session Management, use the Maximum Sessions Per User text box and the Maximum Sessions Per Anonymous User text box to prevent users from overloading the server.
14. Data returned in queries is cached in memory on the application server to maximize performance. Use the Cache Timeout text box to ensure that out-of-date information is not returned.
15. Under Sessions Management, use the Maximum Session Memory text box to prevent memory contention with other service applications and processes.
16. Under Memory Utilization, use the Maximum Private Bytes text box to limit Access Services memory usage.
17. Under Template, restrict the Maximum Template Size to prevent users from uploading very large database templates.
18. Click OK.

Using Access Web Services

Now that you have deployed and configured Access Web Services, users can start creating and using web databases.

CREATE AN ACCESS WEB SERVICES WEB DATABASE

In this example procedure, Access 2010 is used to create a new web database from the Projects template:

1. In Internet Explorer, browse to the site collection where you want to create the web database.
2. Click Site Actions, and then click More Options.
3. In the list of Categories, click Web Databases.
4. Click Projects Web Database, or whichever template is closest to your requirements.
5. In the Title text box, type a suitable title for your database.
6. In the URL Name text box, type a path to your database.
7. Click Create. SharePoint creates the site and renders the Getting Started page.
8. Explore the tabs, create new customers and new projects, and view reports.

PRACTICE   Configure Access Web Services

Practices are designed to guide you through important procedures. The instructions in the Training Kit are high-level instructions that will challenge you to think carefully and to apply the procedures that are covered in this lesson and elsewhere in the Training Kit. If you need assistance, consult the detailed, step-by-step instructions in the Practice Answers on the companion media.

In this practice, you enable Access Web Services and then create a web database by using the Projects web database template. You also use the browser and Access to edit data.

Prepare for the Practice

Before you perform this practice, ensure that your lab environment has been built according to the instructions found in the Introduction to this Training Kit. You must also have performed the practice in Lesson 3 of this chapter. You must be logged off of SP2010-WFE1 before beginning the exercises.

EXERCISE 1   Create an Access Web Services Service Application

In this exercise, you create a new Access Web Services service application by using Central Administration:

1. Log on to SP2010-WFE1 as **CONTOSO\SP_Admin** with the password **Pa$$w0rd**.
2. In Central Administration, open the Manage Service Applications page.

3. Create a new Access Services service application. Use the following specifications and guidance:
   - Name: Access Services – Enterprise
   - Use an existing application pool
   - Application Pool: SharePoint Service Applications

EXERCISE 2   Configure Access Web Services

In this exercise, you configure the new Access Web Services service application to restrict the size of result sets and increase the maximum template size:

1. Configure the Access Services – Enterprise service application. Use the following specifications and guidance:
   - Maximum Columns Per Query: 25
   - Maximum Rows Per Query: 1,000
   - Maximum Template Size: 50 MB
   - Leave all other fields at their default values
2. Start the Access Database Service on the SP2010-WFE1 server.
3. Close Central Administration.

EXERCISE 3   Create a Web Database

In this exercise, you use the Products template to create a new web database:

1. Use Internet Explorer to open the Contoso intranet site.
2. Create a new site in the site collection by using the Projects Web Database template. Use the following specifications and guidance:
   - Title: Contoso Projects
   - URL Name: contosoprojects

EXERCISE 4   Edit the Data in the Browser

In this exercise, you test the new web database by adding a record in the browser:

1. In Internet Explorer, add a new customer to the Contoso Projects database. Use the following specifications and guidance:
   - First Name: Jean-Phillipe
   - Last Name: Bagel
   - Email Address: jpbagel@tailspintoys.com
   - Company: Tailspin Toys
2. Add a second new customer to the Contoso Projects database. Use the following specifications and guidance:
   - First Name: Soren
   - Last Name: Francker

- Email Address: sorenf@lucernepublishing.com
- Company: Lucerne Publishing

EXERCISE 5   Edit the Data in Access

In this exercise, you test the database by adding data in Access 2010:

1. Open the web database in Access 2010.
2. Add a third record to the Customers table. Use the following specifications and guidance:
   - First Name: Manoj
   - Last Name: Svamala
   - Email Address: manoj.svamala@fabrikam.com
   - Company: Fabrikam Inc
3. Synchronize your changes with the SharePoint server.
4. Close Access and refresh the web database in Internet Explorer.
5. Examine the Customers table.
6. Close all applications and windows.
7. Log off of SP2010-WFE1.

Lesson Summary

- Access Services enables Access users to create access-like databases on SharePoint servers for their whole team to use.
- Users without Access installed on their local computer can read and edit a Access Services web database in the browser.
- Users with Access can use it to edit a web database and then synchronize their changes with the web database.
- To create a web database from an Access database, the Access database must be saved in the new file format with the .accdb file extension.
- Access Web Services includes five template web databases. You can use these as starting points and adapt them to your requirements.
- Microsoft Access skills are very common within the Office user community. Access Web Services enables users with Access skills to create functional SharePoint sites without learning SharePoint skills.

Lesson Review

You can use the following questions to test your knowledge of the information in Lesson 4, "Implement Access Web Services." The questions are also available on the companion media in a practice test if you prefer to review them in electronic form.

NOTE ANSWERS

Answers to these questions and explanations of why each answer choice is right or wrong are located in the "Answers" section at the end of the book.

1. A group of users in the Marketing department has created a web database in a SharePoint site to manage their sales leads. They can add information, edit existing records, and query the database. However, an error is generated when they try to view any reports. What action may solve this problem?

   A. Re-create the web database by using one of the provided web database templates.

   B. Install Microsoft SQL Server 2008 R2 on at least one server in the SharePoint farm.

   C. Install Microsoft SQL Server 2008 R2 Reporting Services Add-in for SharePoint Technologies 2010.

   D. Create an Access Web Services service application in the SharePoint farm.

   E. Start the Access Database Service on at least one application server in the SharePoint farm.

2. A user calls you to say that he is unable to create a web database from an Access database he uses with his team. Other web databases have been created and used by other teams. Which of the following actions may solve this issue? (Choose all that apply.)

   A. Ensure that the user has the latest version of Access.

   B. Ensure that the user has saved the database in the .accdb format.

   C. Ensure that the Access Web Services service application exists in the SharePoint farm.

   D. Ensure that the database is not larger than the Maximum Template Size value in the Access Web Services configuration.

   E. Ensure that the user's account has permission to create sites in the site collection.

Lesson 5: Implement Visio Services

If you have ever used Visio to draw technical diagrams, you'll be familiar with its versatility and capabilities. It is a popular and powerful way to create a huge range of illustrations and it is quick to use. SharePoint provides the same document management facilities for Visio diagrams as for other file types but Microsoft has provided extra integration in the form of Visio Services. When you implement Visio services, Visio authors can publish web diagrams to SharePoint. Users without Visio can view these diagrams in the browser. Visio Services lets you publish diagrams to a much broader audience.

> **After this lesson, you will be able to:**
> - Describe how Visio users can use SharePoint without Visio Services.
> - Describe functionality that Visio Services adds to SharePoint 2010.
> - Plan secure but functional data access for Visio Services.
> - Create and configure a Visio Graphics Services service application.
> - Publish Visio Web Drawing files to users without Visio.
> - Use the Visio Web Access Web Part.
>
> **Estimated Lesson Time: 30 minutes**

Visio and SharePoint

Visio diagrams are just another file type and form of content. Therefore, SharePoint's content management facilities can be used to publish them, just as they can for Word documents, Excel spreadsheets, and other file types. A team of Visio users can save a diagram to a SharePoint library and use the versioning and checkout features to organize their separate contributions. Any user with Visio installed on her local computer, often as part of the Office suite, can open and edit these files.

> **NOTE THE VISIO VIEWER**
>
> One way to broaden the reach of Visio diagrams is to use the Visio Viewer. This free ActiveX control can be downloaded and installed on client computers. Once present, the viewer enables users to examine Visio diagrams in their web browser. They can pan, zoom, change pages, and view shape properties. You can download the Visio Viewer at *http://www.microsoft.com/downloads/en/details.aspx?FamilyID=f9ed50b0-c7df-4fb8-89f8-db2932e624f7&displaylang=en*.

It is not always possible to install the Visio Viewer on client computers. Change management policies may restrict the installation of ActiveX controls and users may have other browsers and operating systems. Also bear in mind that some users are wary of installing extra software because it takes time and clutters the hard disk.

You can overcome these difficulties by installing and configuring Visio Services on your SharePoint farm. Visio Services can render any Visio Web Drawing in the browser. All the work is done on the SharePoint front end and application servers and no extra software is required on the client.

Visio Services is implemented as a service application, similar to Excel Services and Access Web Services. It is included in SharePoint Server 2010 Enterprise edition only. It includes a shared service called the Visio Graphics Service that runs on the application servers you choose and a Web Part to add Visio diagrams to SharePoint pages and dashboards.

> **IMPORTANT VISIO WEB DRAWING FORMAT**
>
> Visio 2010 can save diagrams in a variety of formats, including native binary and XML formats (.vsd and .vdx files). To publish a diagram through Visio Services, you must save it in Visio Web Drawing format, with a .vdw extension. You must use Visio Professional or Premium editions to create these Visio diagrams.

In the browser, a rich range of Visio display functionality is available for examining drawings, as shown in Figure 8-6. For example, users can:

- Zoom and pan to investigate a complex drawing.
- View shape data.
- View hyperlinks.
- Change pages.
- Download the diagram to open it in Visio.

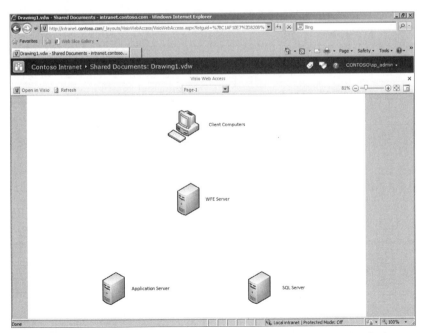

FIGURE 8-6 A Visio Web Drawing rendered by Visio Services and displayed in the browser

Visio Web Services also supports data-connected drawings. These use a data source, such as a database server, to enrich the drawing. Visio Services keeps these data connections live and updates the drawing when the source changes. This is an excellent tool for presenting live data to users and can enrich business-critical applications such as dashboards and portals.

Plan Visio Services Connections

Connections to data sources provide the largest planning challenge to the administrator of Visio Services. However, because this functionality significantly broadens the usefulness of diagrams, you should understand these challenges and ensure that your implementation supports users' needs.

You can connect Visio Web Drawings to data stored in the following technologies:

- SharePoint Lists in the SharePoint farm where the drawing is published
- Excel spreadsheets published in the SharePoint farm where the drawing is published
- SQL Server databases on SQL Server 7.0 or later servers
- OLE DB or ODBC compliant databases

To view any Visio drawing in his browser, a SharePoint user must have read permission to the document library in which it is stored. This applies to all diagrams, including those that do not use data connections.

If a data connection is used in a drawing, authorization becomes more complex, because the user must be authenticated on SharePoint and the data source, and he must have permissions to access the data as well as the diagram. Table 8-2 describes the conditions that you must satisfy.

TABLE 8-2 Authentication and Authorization Requirements for Visio Data Connections

DATA SOURCE	AUTHENTICATION	AUTHORIZATION
SharePoint List	The list must be stored in the same SharePoint farm as the Visio drawing.	The user who views the diagram must have read permission in the connected list.
Excel Spreadsheet in SharePoint Library	The spreadsheet must be stored in the same SharePoint farm as the Visio drawing. Excel Services must be installed and configured.	The user who views the diagram must have read permission in the connected spreadsheet.
SQL Server	The connection can use Windows Authentication or SQL Server Authentication.	The user account that is used to make the connection must have read permission on the connected database table.
OLE DB or ODBC Database	The credentials are contained in a database connection string stored in the Visio Web Drawing.	The user named in the connection string must have read permission on the connected database table.

Configuring Visio Services

If you have SharePoint Server 2010 Enterprise edition, you can enable Visio Services by creating and configuring a service application as described in the following procedures. Often, when the Initial Farm Configuration Wizard is run, the Visio Services check box is selected—if so, the Visio Services service application is created automatically and you need only to configure it.

CREATE A VISIO SERVICES SERVICE APPLICATION IN CENTRAL ADMINISTRATION

If Visio Services was not created by the Initial Farm Configuration Wizard, you can use the following steps in Central Administration to configure it:

1. In Central Administration Quick Launch, click Application Management.
2. Under Service Applications, click Manage Service Applications.
3. Click New, and then click Visio Graphics Service.
4. In the Visio Graphics Service Application Name text box, type an appropriate name for your service application.
5. Under Application Pool, select an existing application pool or create a new one according to your plan.
6. Under Create A Visio Graphics Service Application Proxy, choose whether to connect this service application to the default proxy group. If you clear this check box, you must manually connect this service application to proxies.
7. Click OK.

CREATE A VISIO SERVICES SERVICE APPLICATION IN WINDOWS POWERSHELL

Alternatively, you can use Windows PowerShell cmdlets to create the service application:

```
$visioService = New-SPVisioServiceApplication -Name "<VisioServiceName>"
-ApplicationPool <AppPool>
New-SPVisioServiceApplicationProxy -Name "<VisioProxyName>"
-ServiceApplication $visioService
```

Where:

- *<VisioServiceName>* is the name you want to use for your new Visio Services service application.
- *<AppPool>* is a variable that contains the application pool you want to add this service application to.
- *<VisioProxyName>* is the name you want to use for the proxy that connects this service application to the web applications.

CONFIGURE VISIO SERVICES

The Visio Services service application includes a range of tuning settings to maximize the performance of the service and minimize contention with other processes that run on the application servers. Tune your service application by using the following steps:

1. In Central Administration, click Application Management.
2. Under Service Applications, click Manage Service Applications.

3. Click the Visio service application you want to configure, and then click Manage.

4. Click Global Settings.

5. Under Maximum Drawing Size, use the text box to limit the size of a web drawing in megabytes that users can publish through Visio Services. Large drawings place a correspondingly large load on server memory and processing power.

6. Under Minimum Cache Age, type the minimum number of minutes that a rendered drawing remains in the cache. Because rendering the drawing requires significant processing resources on the application server, careful configuration of the cache can significantly improve performance.

7. Under Maximum Cache Age, type the maximum number of minutes that a rendered drawing remains in the cache.

8. Under Maximum Recalc Duration, type a time-out in seconds for data refresh operations on data-connected diagrams.

9. Under External Data, type a Secure Store Service application ID to use for the Unattended Service Account. This account is used to connect to external data sources when other methods fail.

10. Click OK.

Using Visio Services

The following procedures illustrate how users interact with Visio Services.

PUBLISH AND VIEW A VISIO WEB DRAWING

To publish a Visio Web Drawing file to SharePoint the user must save the drawing as a .vdw file and upload it to a document library. Users with permission to read the file can then use the View In Web Browser tool:

1. Open the diagram to be published in Visio 2010.

2. Click File, click Save & Send, and then click Save To SharePoint.

3. Under File Types, click Web Drawing, and then click Save As.

4. Browse to a suitable location, and then click Save.

5. In Internet Explorer, browse to a SharePoint document library.

6. On the ribbon, click the Documents tab, and then click Upload Document.

7. Use the Browse tool to locate your web drawing file, and then click Open.

8. Click OK.

9. Point to the web drawing in the document library, drop down the list, and then click View In Web Browser. The Visio Web Access tool opens and displays the drawing.

USE THE VISIO WEB ACCESS WEB PART TO DISPLAY A WEB DRAWING

Visio Services also enables users to add a Visio diagram to any Web Part page by using the Visio Web Access Web Part. After you have published the web diagram in SharePoint, display it in a web page by taking the following steps:

1. In Internet Explorer, browse to the page where you want to display the Visio drawing.

2. On the ribbon, click the Page tab, and then click Edit.

3. Place the cursor on the page where you want to display the diagram.

4. On the ribbon, click Insert, and then click Web Part.

5. In the list of Categories, click Business Data.

6. In the list of Web Parts, click Visio Web Access, and then click Add. The new Web Part is added to the page and displays the "Select a Web Drawing" message.

7. Click Click Here To Open The Tool Pane.

8. Scroll to the top right of the page to access the Visio Web Access tool pane.

9. Next to the Web Drawing URL box, click the browse button.

10. Locate the web drawing in the SharePoint hierarchy, and then click OK.

11. At the bottom of the tool pane, click OK. The Web Part displays the drawing. You can zoom, pan, and change pages.

PRACTICE Configure Visio Services

Practices are designed to guide you through important procedures. The instructions in the Training Kit are high-level instructions that will challenge you to think carefully and to apply the procedures that are covered in this lesson and elsewhere in the Training Kit. If you need assistance, consult the detailed, step-by-step instructions in the Practice Answers on the companion media.

In this practice, you set up Visio Services in your SharePoint farm. You also create a diagram in Visio 2010 and publish it to a SharePoint document library.

Prepare for the Practice

Before you perform this practice, ensure that your lab environment has been built according to the instructions found in the Introduction to this Training Kit. You must also have performed the practice in Lesson 4 of this chapter. You must be logged off of SP2010-WFE1 before beginning the exercises.

EXERCISE 1 Create a Visio Services Service Application

In this exercise, you create a new Visio Services service application using Central Administration:

1. Log on to SP2010-WFE1 as **CONTOSO\SP_Admin** with the password **Pa$$w0rd**.

2. In Central Administration browse to the Manage Service Applications page.

3. Create a new Visio Graphics Service. Use the following specifications and guidance:

   - Name: Visio Services – Enterprise
   - Use an existing application pool
   - Application Pool: SharePoint Service Applications

EXERCISE 2   Configure Visio Services

In this exercise, you configure the Visio Services drawing cache. Because drawings change frequently in your company, you want to cache rendered drawings for longer:

1. Configure the Visio Services service application you created in Exercise 1. Use the following specifications and guidance:

   ■ Minimum Cache Age: 15 minutes

   ■ Maximum Cache Age: 120 minutes

2. Start the Visio Graphics Service on the SP2010-WFE1 server.

EXERCISE 3   Install Visio 2010

In this exercise, you install Visio 2010 on the SP2010-WFE1 image. These steps assume you have downloaded the Visio 2010 evaluation executable.

1. Start the evaluation installation and enter your product key.

2. Accept the license agreement.

3. Perform a standard installation.

EXERCISE 4   Create and Publish a Visio Web Drawing

In this exercise, you create a simple Visio web drawing and publish it to the Contoso intranet:

1. Start Visio 2010 and choose the Network template category.

2. Create a new drawing based on the Basic Network Diagram template.

3. Add shapes to the diagram to describe a simple SharePoint farm with front-end servers, database servers, application servers, and client computers.

4. Save the drawing as a web drawing in the Documents library.

5. Close Visio 2010.

6. Upload your Visio web drawing to the *http://intranet.contoso.com/ shared%20documents library*.

7. View the web drawing in the browser.

8. Experiment with the zoom, page, and shape information tools.

EXERCISE 5   Use the Visio Web Part

In this exercise, you display the web drawing on the Contoso intranet homepage by using the Visio Web Access Web Part:

1. Browse to the Contoso intranet home page.

2. Add a Visio Web Access Web Part to the page.

3. Configure the Web Part to display the SharePointFarm web drawing you uploaded to the Shared Documents library.

4. Save the page.

5. Close all windows and applications.

6. Log off of SP2010-WFE1.

Lesson Summary

- Visio Services can render Visio drawings in the web browser for users who do not have Visio 2010 or the Visio Viewer ActiveX control.

- You must use Visio 2010 and save your drawing with a .vdw extension to publish it through Visio Services.

- Users can zoom, pan, and view shape data in the browser but cannot edit the drawing.

- You can publish data-connected Visio drawings. Any change in the data source will automatically be reflected in the rendered Visio drawing.

- You must carefully plan your authentication method when web drawings include data connections.

- With the Visio Web Access Web Part, you can include a Visio diagram on any SharePoint page.

Lesson Review

You can use the following questions to test your knowledge of the information in Lesson 5, "Implement Visio Services." The questions are also available on the companion media in a practice test if you prefer to review them in electronic form.

> **NOTE   ANSWERS**
>
> Answers to these questions and explanations of why each answer choice is right or wrong are located in the "Answers" section at the end of the book.

1. You have deployed Visio Services in your SharePoint farm. Users are successfully publishing Visio drawings in SharePoint libraries. A user calls you to say that she has published a Visio drawing that includes a data connection to a SharePoint list. When she views the drawing in the browser, she receives an error. She does not receive an error when she opens the diagram in Visio. Which of the following issues might cause this problem? (Choose all that apply.)

    A. The user has created the drawing in Visio 2007 or earlier.

    B. The user has saved the drawing in .vsd format.

    C. The user does not have permission to the SharePoint list to which the drawing connects.

    D. The SharePoint list to which the drawing connects is in a different SharePoint farm.

    E. The Visio Graphics shared service has not been started on at least one SharePoint application server.

Lesson 6: Implement Office Web Applications

Many of the lessons in this chapter have focused on ways to integrate more closely with Microsoft Office Suite products. Excel Services and Visio Services, for example, enable users without those products to view Excel spreadsheets and Visio drawings in their browsers, with some interactivity. Office Web Applications are an alternative tool that you can use to provide browser access to Office documents and they enable a slightly different, complementary set of features. Although Office Web Applications do not provide the advanced functionality of the Office desktop software, you will find that their capabilities make them extremely useful in an environment with different browsers and operative systems. In this lesson, you will see how Office Web Applications work, when they are useful, and how to administer the system.

> **After this lesson, you will be able to:**
> - Identify scenarios in which Office Web Applications help.
> - Describe the architecture of Office Web Applications.
> - Plan a deployment of Office Web Applications.
> - Deploy Office Web Applications.
> - Configure the associated service applications.
> - Configure sites and site collections for Office Web Applications.
> - Test Office Web Applications from various clients.
>
> **Estimated Lesson Time: 25 minutes**

The Role of Office Web Applications

By now, you've seen how SharePoint Server 2010 Enterprise provides extra integration with InfoPath, Excel, Access, and Visio. The first thing to understand is how Office Web Applications differ from, and enhance, those service applications.

Office Web Applications are described as "an online companion" to Word, Excel, PowerPoint, and OneNote. They enable users to access and edit documents from wherever they are and whatever computer or device they are using. Table 8-3 compares the Office Web Applications with other SharePoint Office integration features.

TABLE 8-3 Comparing Office Integration Features

APPLICATION	SHAREPOINT SERVICE APPLICATION	OFFICE WEB APPLICATIONS
Word	None	Enables users to view and edit Word documents in the browser.

APPLICATION	SHAREPOINT SERVICE APPLICATION	OFFICE WEB APPLICATIONS
Excel	Excel Services calculates spreadsheets and renders them in the browser. Parameters enable limited interaction.	Enables users to view *and* edit Excel spreadsheets in the browser. Requires Excel Services.
PowerPoint	None	Enables users to view, edit, and broadcast PowerPoint slide decks in the browser.
Access	Access Web Services enable Access users to publish databases as SharePoint web databases. Fully interactive.	None
OneNote	None	Enables users to view and edit OneNote files in the browser.
Visio	Visio Services renders data-connected web drawings in the browsers. Zoom, pan, and page selection supported.	None

As you can see, Office Web Applications complement other SharePoint Office integration by supported extra applications (Word, PowerPoint, and OneNote) and extending functionality for Excel.

Some other differences should also be noted:

- Excel Services, Access Web Services, and Visio Services are only included in SharePoint 2010 Enterprise edition. Office Web Applications can be added to any edition of SharePoint, including SharePoint Foundation 2010.

- Extra licenses may be required to run Office Web Applications in your organization. In general, organizations with Office desktop licenses and SharePoint licenses do not need extra SharePoint or Office client access licenses. However, you should check licensing requirements before deploying Office Web Applications. For more details, see *http://www.microsoft.com/licensing/*.

- Office Web Applications are also available as part of Windows Live. If you have a Windows Live account, you can create Office documents by going to *http://home.live.com*, logging in, and clicking the Office link.

Microsoft has implemented Office Web Applications by using broadly supported technologies and web standards so that they are available to the broadest range of users. However, it is important to note that the precise functionality you can use depends on the browser and the browser version on your computer or device. For more details, see "Testing Office Web Applications" later in this lesson.

To obtain Office Web Applications, you will need to be a Volume Licensing customer, or have a TechNet or MSDN subscription. Go to the following site, log in, and search for Office Web Applications: *http://msdn.microsoft.com/en-us/*.

Office Web Applications Architecture

The Office Web Applications architecture is designed to support the broadest range of browsers possible and while supplying a rich set of Office functionality. The architecture is shown in Figure 8-7.

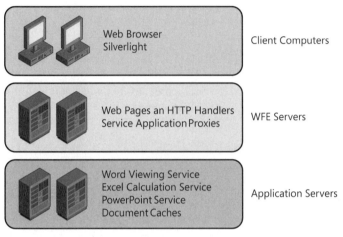

Client Computers

WFE Servers

Application Servers

FIGURE 8-7 The Office Web Applications Architecture

The components in the architecture are described in the following list, grouped by the computer they run on:

- Client Computer
  - Web Browser: A broad range of browsers, such as Internet Explorer, Mozilla Firefox, and Safari are supported and tested. However, some features may not be available in all versions of all browsers.
  - Silverlight: Silverlight is used to implement the richest level of Office Web Application functionality. Without Silverlight, you may find functionality restricted.
- Web Front-End Server
  - Web pages and HTTP handlers: These components render the Office documents in the browser as HTML, JScript, and Silverlight. They are separate web pages and handlers for each application.
  - Service application proxies: These proxies enable the Web pages and HTTP handlers to connect to the appropriate service applications on the application servers.
- Application Servers
  - Word Viewing Service: This service application performs most of the processing involved in displaying Word documents.

- Excel Calculation Service: Office Web Applications uses Excel Services to render Excel spreadsheets.

- PowerPoint Service: This service application performs most of the procession involved in displaying PowerPoint slide decks.

- Caches: Rendered documents are cached in memory on application servers so that subsequent requests for them can be returned quickly.

Office Web Applications also install a SharePoint Feature at the site collection level called Office Web Apps. After you have installed Office Web Applications you must ensure this Feature is enabled on every site collection.

Deploying Office Web Applications

When you have downloaded Office Web Applications from the Volume Licensing site, or obtained a disk, use the following procedures to install and configure it.

INSTALL OFFICE WEB APPLICATIONS

Use the following steps to install the Office Web Applications binaries on an existing SharePoint server farm:

1. Insert the disk or double-click on the downloaded executable.

2. If the User Account Control appears, click Yes.

3. Enter your product key, and then click Continue.

4. Select I Accept The Terms Of This License Agreement, and then click Continue.

5. Click Server Farm.

6. Choose Complete, and then click Install Now. Office Web Applications are installed.

7. When the installation is complete, click Close.

8. In the SharePoint Product Configuration Wizard, click Next.

9. In the dialog box, click Yes.

10. Ensure that Do Not Disconnect From This Server Farm is selected, and then click Next.

11. Ensure that No This Machine Will Continue To Host The Web Site is selected, and then click Next.

12. Review the settings, and then click Next.

13. When the configuration completes, click Finish. The SharePoint Configuration Wizards page in the Central Administration site appears.

14. Click Start The Wizard.

15. Ensure that the Excel Service, PowerPoint Service, and Word Viewing Service check boxes are selected, and then click Next.

16. Click Skip.

When you have completed the preceding procedure, Office Web Applications are installed and integrated into your SharePoint farm. You should check the following in Central Administration:

- The list of service applications includes an Excel Services service application, a PowerPoint service application, and a Word Viewing service application.

- Go to Manage Services on Server and ensure that the following services are started: Excel Calculation Services, PowerPoint Service, and Word Viewing Service.

Also ensure that the Office Web Apps feature is enabled at the site collection level for all the sites where you want to use Office Web Applications.

Testing Office Web Applications

Microsoft used the most widely supported web technologies and standards to create Office Web Applications. For this reason, most web browsers receive good functionality regardless of the operating system on which they run. Although Silverlight is used to provide the richest user experience, it is not required: when Silverlight is not present Office Web Applications renders pages without it.

Microsoft defines three levels of compatibility for Office Web Applications:

- **Supported**   This is the highest level of compatibility. Browsers in this level receive full Office Web Applications functionality when they open documents. This level includes the 32-bit versions of Internet Explorer 7 and 8.

- **Supported with Known Limitations**   Most functionality works well for browsers in this level. This level includes the 64-bit versions of Internet Explorer 7 and 8, Firefox 3.6 and later, and Safari 4.04 and later.

- **Not Tested**   Browsers in this level have not been tested but might receive good functionality anyway. It is up to you to discover what features work if your browser is in this level. Any browser not in the previous two levels, including Google Chrome, is in this level.

If, for example, all your users have the 32-bit version of Internet Explorer 8, you can be confident that Office Web Applications will work in full. However, in most cases you will need to support other browsers and should investigate what functionality is available.

> **NOTE   MICROSOFT BROWSER SUPPORT LEVELS FOR SHAREPOINT 2010**
> You can find out more about the browser support levels, including specific instances of limitations, at *http://technet.microsoft.com/en-us/library/cc288142.aspx*.

You should also thoroughly test Office Web Applications from each browser that you intend to support. One simple way of testing Office Web Applications from a particular browser is to use Windows Live. Office Web Applications are available on the Windows Live site to anyone who has a Windows Live account. If you can, for example, create and edit a Word document in Windows Live, you should be able to complete the same action in SharePoint.

PRACTICE **Configure Office Web Applications**

Practices are designed to guide you through important procedures. The instructions in the Training Kit are high-level instructions that will challenge you to think carefully and to apply the procedures that are covered in this lesson and elsewhere in the Training Kit. If you need assistance, consult the detailed, step-by-step instructions in the Practice Answers on the companion media.

In this practice, you install Office Web Applications on your SharePoint farm and open a Word document for editing.

Prepare for the Practice

Before you perform this practice, ensure that your lab environment has been built according to the instructions found in the Introduction to this Training Kit. You must also have performed the practice in Lesson 5 of this chapter. You must be logged off of SP2010-WFE1 before beginning the exercises.

EXERCISE 1 Install Office Web Applications

In this exercise, you install Office Web Applications:

1. Log on to SP2010-WFE1 as **CONTOSO\SP_Admin** with the password **Pa$$w0rd**.
2. Begin the installation by inserting the disk or double-clicking the downloaded executable.
3. In the Installation Wizard, use the following specifications and guidance:
   - Installation type: Server Farm
   - Complete Installation
4. Run the SharePoint Products Configuration Wizard. Use the following specifications and guidance:
   - Do Not Disconnect From This Server Farm
   - This Machine Will Continue to Host the Central Administration Site

5. Run the Initial Farm Configuration Wizard. Use the following specifications and guidance:

   - Install Excel Services.

   - Install PowerPoint Services.

   - Install Word Viewing Services.

   - Do not create a new site collection.

EXERCISE 2   Start Shared Services

In this exercise, you ensure that the shared services necessary to support Office Web Applications are running:

1. In Central Administration, ensure that the following shared services are started on the SP2010-WFE1 server:

   - Excel Calculation Service

   - PowerPoint Service

   - Word Viewing Service

EXERCISE 3   Upload a Word Document

In this exercise, you create a Word document and upload it to a SharePoint document library:

1. Use Word 2010 to create a new document with the text of your choice.

2. Save the document to your Document library as Web Apps Test.docx.

3. Upload the document to the *http://intranet.contoso.com/shared%20documents* library.

4. Edit the document in the browser.

Lesson Summary

- Office Web Applications are an additional component that you can install in your SharePoint farm to permit users to open and edit Office documents in their browser.

- Office Web Applications are available for Word, Excel, PowerPoint, and OneNote files.

- You may require extra SharePoint or Office Client Access Licenses to use Office Web Application in your organization.

- Office Web Applications are built using broadly supported web technologies and standards. Therefore, you can access this functionality through a wide range of web browsers on different devices and operating systems.

- The precise functionality you can use depends on the browser you use.

- Silverlight provides the richest Office functionality to users but is not required to access Office Web Applications.

- Test the browsers, operating systems, and devices that you must support to ensure that the functionality your users need is available.

Lesson Review

You can use the following questions to test your knowledge of the information in Lesson 6, "Implement Office Web Applications." The questions are also available on the companion media in a practice test if you prefer to review them in electronic form.

> **NOTE** **ANSWERS**
>
> **Answers to these questions and explanations of why each answer choice is right or wrong are located in the "Answers" section at the end of the book.**

1. You have installed Office Web Applications in your SharePoint farm and ensured that the shared services are running. Users in the intranet site collection can edit Word documents in the browser. However, when users in the Finance Web Application try to open a Word Document in the browser, they do not see the shortcut in the SharePoint ribbon. Which of the following issues may cause this problem?

   A. The Word Viewing service application has not been created in the SharePoint farm.

   B. The Word Viewing shared service has not been started on at least one application server.

   C. Users who cannot see the shortcut do not have Word 2010 installed on their computers.

   D. The Office Web Apps Feature has not been enabled on the Finance site collection.

   E. Users who cannot see the shortcut do not have Silverlight installed on their computers.

Chapter Review

To further practice and reinforce the skills you learned in this chapter, you can perform the following tasks:

- Review the chapter summary.
- Review the list of key terms introduced in this chapter.
- Complete the case scenarios. These scenarios set up real-world situations involving the topics of this chapter and ask you to create a solution.
- Complete the suggested practices.
- Take a practice test.

Chapter Summary

- Business Connectivity Services (BCS) enables you to integrate external systems with SharePoint lists.
- BCS can import data into external lists in SharePoint sites where users can edit it. Changes are automatically synchronized with the external system.
- BCS can connect to databases, line-of-business systems, Web services, and WCF Services that publish data.
- InfoPath forms provide rich data-gathering capabilities. Anyone can author forms without requiring developer skills.
- InfoPath forms can be stored in SharePoint and form the basis of functional custom applications.
- InfoPath can also be used to edit default SharePoint forms for items and content types.
- Excel Services publishes Excel spreadsheets in the browser for those who do not have Excel installed.
- Users can take an Access database and publish it as a web database in a SharePoint site.
- Visio Services display Visio web drawings in the browser for users who do not have Visio installed.
- Office Web Applications enable Word, Excel, PowerPoint, and OneNote users to open and edit documents in the browser.

Key Terms

The following terms were introduced in this chapter. Do you know what they mean?

- Business Connectivity Services
- InfoPath Forms Services
- Excel Services
- Access Web Services
- Visio Services

- Office Web Applications
- External Content Type
- External List
- Secure Store Service
- SharePoint Composites
- Sandbox
- Administrator-Approved Form
- Versioning
- Check In/Check Out
- Web Database
- Web Database Template
- Visio Web Drawing
- Visio Viewer
- Data-Connected Drawings

Case Scenario: Configuring User Profiles and Social Networking

In the following case scenario, you apply what you've learned about subjects of this chapter. You can find answers to these questions in the "Answers" section at the end of this book.

Your organization uses SharePoint to host its Internet site and a line-of-business application to store information about its product line. You want the SharePoint website to automatically display details of new products as they are added the the line-of-business application. You want to ensure that no changes can be made to this data on the SharePoint site.

1. You want to import product information from the line-of-business application into a SharePoint list. How can you complete this task?

2. You want to ensure that website visitors, some of whom authenticate with SharePoint and have AD DS accounts, cannot alter product data. How can you prevent modifications?

Suggested Practices

To help you successfully master the exam objectives presented in this chapter, complete the following tasks.

Practice 1: Set Up a BCS Connection to the Adventure Works Sample Database

In Lesson 1, you configured BCS to connect to a simple database of coffee products. Real-world scenarios will probably require you to connect to much more complicated database. Microsoft provides the Adventure Works sample database in CodePlex. You can download it and install it on any SQL Server. The sample databases are available from *http://msftdbprodsamples.codeplex.com.* This will enable you to experiment with multiple external content types and external lists:

1. Install the Adventure Works database. The downloadable executable provides a simple wizard to complete this task.

2. Explore the sample database in SQL Server Management Studio. Become familiar with the tables and views included.

3. Create BCS connections, external content types, and external lists for both tables and views.

Practice 2: Build a Business Intelligence Dashboard

In Lessons 3 and 5 you saw how Excel spreadsheets and Visio drawings can be displayed in Web Parts in any SharePoint page. These tools enable you to present business-critical information in easily digestible charts, pivot tables, and drawings. Choose a role in your organization, such as Sales Representative, and build a dashboard that presents all the information that role needs:

1. Create pivot tables and charts within Excel spreadsheets that display the latest sales data. Publish these spreadsheets in a SharePoint document library.

2. On a new SharePoint Web Part page, add Excel Web Access Web Parts to display these pivot tables and charts.

3. Add parameters to the Excel spreadsheets that enable users to alter critical values in the spreadsheet and see the effects.

4. Create Visio diagrams that connect to the Excel spreadsheets and publish them in a SharePoint document library.

5. Use the Visio Web Access Web Part to display these drawings on the dashboard page.

Take a Practice Test

The practice tests on this book's companion media offer many options. For example, you can test yourself on only the lesson review content, or you can test yourself on all the 70-667 certification exam objectives. You can set up the test so that it closely simulates the experience of taking a certification exam, or you can set it up in study mode so that you can look at the correct answers and explanations after you answer each question.

> *MORE INFO* **PRACTICE TESTS**
>
> For details about all the practice test options available, see the "How to Use the Practice Tests" section in this book's Introduction.

CHAPTER 9

Deploying and Upgrading to SharePoint 2010

This training kit introduces you to the fundamental concepts and skills required to install and configure Microsoft SharePoint 2010. This chapter takes that knowledge and applies it to more complex situations and implementations, and to scenarios that are commonplace in the real-world use of SharePoint 2010. This chapter covers a wide range of operational activities, such as upgrading SharePoint 2007 installations to SharePoint 2010, building SharePoint farms consisting of multiple servers, and managing SharePoint deployments and service accounts.

Exam objectives in this chapter:

- Deploy new installations and upgrades.
- Configure SharePoint farms.
- Configure service applications.
- Manage site collections.
- Manage accounts and user roles.
- Deploy new installations and upgrades.
- Optimize the performance of a SharePoint environment.

Lessons in this chapter:

Before You Begin

To complete the lessons in this chapter, you must have done the following:

- Performed the practice in Chapter 1, "Creating a SharePoint 2010 Intranet."

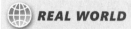 **REAL WORLD**

Dan Holme

In this chapter, you expand your examination of SharePoint to include enterprises that already have SharePoint in place. This chapter introduces upgrade approaches that are documented on Microsoft TechNet, which are relatively simple procedures. What is challenging about an upgrade is not the procedure itself, but the planning and preparation for the upgrade. In this chapter, I present upgrade strategies in a manner that I've found helps my customers to identify the factors that, for them, are most important for decision making. The unfortunate truth, in my experience, is that although Microsoft provides an in-place upgrade approach as an attractive, simple option, most organizations choose to implement a database attach or hybrid upgrade to reduce downtime and to mitigate risk. The good news is that although a database attach may appear to be more complex—and it does require some additional servers—virtual or physical—it can actually be a simpler upgrade method, because it enables a thoughtful, gradual approach to upgrade.

Lesson 1: Upgrade to SharePoint 2010

If you already have a farm running Microsoft Office SharePoint Server 2007 (MOSS 2007), you can upgrade the farm to SharePoint 2010 by using one of several upgrade approaches. Each upgrade approach is characterized by pros and cons related to requirements, effort, and risk. In this lesson, you learn the details of each upgrade strategy. You master the procedures that are required to upgrade to SharePoint 2010—procedures that are addressed by the 70-667 exam—and you learn how to select the best upgrade approach for your organization.

After this lesson, you will be able to:

- Upgrade SharePoint 2007 to SharePoint 2010.
- Plan SharePoint installations and upgrades.
- Perform a pre-upgrade check.
- Identify customizations that might block upgrade.
- Perform an in-place upgrade.
- Perform a database attach upgrade.
- Manage visual upgrade to the SharePoint 2010 user interface.
- Manage the upgrade of services.
- Troubleshoot upgrade problems.

Estimated lesson time: 90 minutes

Understanding Upgrade and Migration Approaches

You can upgrade or migrate to SharePoint 2010 from previous versions of SharePoint and from other platforms by using one of several approaches. Upgrade and migration approaches include:

- **In-place upgrade** You can upgrade your existing farm to SharePoint 2010. This is called an *in-place upgrade*.
- **Database attach upgrade** You can build a new SharePoint 2010 farm, and then copy and mount your content databases to the farm, at which time the content databases are upgraded. This is called a *database attach* upgrade.
- **Migration** You can build a new SharePoint 2010 farm, and then copy data and configuration to the farm. Migration requires significant effort, custom development, or migration tools from third-party independent software vendors (ISVs).

Some upgrade methods combine the preceding options—these are often referred to as *hybrid approaches*. The technical procedures for each upgrade and migration approach will be detailed later in this lesson.

You must consider the following factors when selecting your upgrade or migration path:

- **Version support** An in-place upgrade can be used to upgrade a farm running Windows SharePoint Services version 3.0 or Microsoft Office SharePoint Server 2007 to SharePoint Foundation 2010 or SharePoint Server 2010, respectively. You cannot perform an in-place upgrade for previous versions of SharePoint. Instead, you must either perform multiple version-to-version upgrades or use a migration tool. You must also use a migration tool to migrate content from any other platform—for example, eRoom, DocuShare, or Lotus Notes—to SharePoint 2010.

- **Associated upgrades** Before you can perform an in-place upgrade, you must ensure that hardware meets the requirements of SharePoint 2010, that each server runs Windows Server 2008 (64-bit) or Windows Server 2008 R2, and that the database server runs a compatible version of SQL Server. In more established SharePoint 2007 farms it is common to find 32-bit versions of SharePoint running on 32-bit versions of Windows Server 2003 and SQL Server 2000. Upgrading to meet SharePoint 2010 prerequisites can entail significant effort.

- **Hardware requirements and configuration** An in-place upgrade preserves the farm's physical infrastructure—servers, server and network configuration, and databases. A database attach upgrade and a migration move content to a new SharePoint 2010 farm that requires a separate infrastructure that you must deploy and configure.

- **What is upgraded** An in-place upgrade preserves the configuration of the SharePoint farm. It upgrades the content databases and services. Customizations remain available after an in-place upgrade, although manual steps may be required to upgrade or rework them. A database attach upgrade updates only the content databases, preserving the content of web applications. However, farm configuration and services are not migrated, so you must configure the SharePoint 2010 farm directly and deploy new services. Customizations must also be transferred to the new farm manually. Any missing customizations may cause unintended losses of functionality or user experience issues. A migration copies or moves content and configuration from a source environment to a SharePoint 2010 farm based on the capabilities of your migration tool.

- **Downtime** When you perform an in-place upgrade, the farm is offline while the upgrade is in progress. The upgrade proceeds continuously. Consequently, you must allocate enough time for all content to be upgraded in sequence. Other upgrade and migration paths enable you to migrate content more gradually, thereby reducing downtime. Because database attach and migration are performed on a separate SharePoint 2010 farm, your current farm can remain online, with databases set to read-only.

- **Upgrade speed** If you perform a database attach upgrade, you can upgrade multiple content databases at the same time, which results in faster upgrade times overall than an in-place upgrade.

- **Rollback** A failed in-place upgrade requires you to remove SharePoint 2010, reinstall SharePoint 2007, and recover data and configuration from a backup made prior to the upgrade. If a database attach upgrade or migration fails, the content and service can continue to be provided by the SharePoint 2007 farm.

- **Flexibility**   A database attach upgrade allows you upgrade the databases in any order and at any pace. You can use a database attach upgrade to combine multiple farms into one farm.

- **Database access**   To perform a database attach upgrade, you need direct access to the database servers. Additionally, if you will be backing up, copying, or transferring content databases over the network, you must allocate sufficient time. An in-place upgrade requires no access to database servers.

- **Upgrade testing and validation**   Because an in-place upgrade updates the entire farm, you must be confident that the upgrade will succeed, and that there will be no upgrade blockers. Therefore, it is critical that you fully test the upgrade prior to performing it. The time required to validate the upgrade readiness of a large, complex farm can be significant. A database attach upgrade or migration allows you to test a subset of your farm and then upgrade that subset of content in a granular, iterative process.

- **Services**   An in-place upgrade migrates the services in your SharePoint 2007 shared service provider (SSP) to individual service applications in SharePoint 2010. If you perform a database attach upgrade, you must deploy and configure new services. This can be time consuming. For example, you must deploy search and wait for a full crawl to complete. You must also determine how to migrate more complex services such as user profiles and business data connectivity.

For many organizations, the business processes, downtime, and risk associated with an in-place upgrade are significant drivers toward a database attach upgrade. A database attach upgrade or migration also allows you to restructure content—to move websites, site collections, and web applications to a model that meets your business requirements—and to leave behind content that is no longer necessary. The two major drawbacks of a database attach upgrade are the additional hardware requirements of a separate SharePoint 2010 farm and the potential complexity of configuring new services.

Because migration entails the use of ISV migration tools, migration is not addressed by the 70-667 exam, and will not be covered in this training kit.

Upgrade Requirements

You must ensure that your farm meets the hardware, operating system, database server, and software requirements for SharePoint 2010. These requirements are detailed in Chapter 1. The impact of the requirements is discussed in the following sections.

64-Bit Environment

SharePoint Server 2010 can only run in a 64-bit environment. If you plan an in-place upgrade, your existing farm must be a 64-bit environment.

If your existing farm is currently in a 32-bit environment, you cannot perform an in-place upgrade. In this scenario, you should install a new SharePoint Server 2010 farm and then move your data to that farm by using database attach upgrade.

It is not recommended that you combine an in-place upgrade with a migration to a 64-bit environment. However, if you choose to do so, you must migrate your existing farm to a 64-bit environment before you perform the in-place upgrade. Details for migration to a 64-bit environment are at *http://technet.microsoft.com/en-us/library/dd622865(office.12).aspx*.

If you are migrating to a 64-bit environment, you must identify and remediate 32-bit components that must be recompiled. Some 32-bit applications and custom assemblies—for example, Web Parts and event receivers—must be recompiled to run in a 64-bit environment. Some components can run in both 32-bit and 64-bit environments and do not have to be recompiled. If the existing components were acquired from third parties, check with the third-party vendors about 64-bit compatibility and updated versions.

Operating System

SharePoint Server 2010 can only run on a 64-bit edition of Windows Server 2008 with Service Pack 2 (SP2), or on Windows Server 2008 R2. If you are currently running Office SharePoint Server 2007 on Windows Server 2003, you must first migrate or upgrade the operating system.

If your farm is already running a 64-bit version of Windows Server 2003, you can upgrade to Windows Server 2008 or Windows Server 2008 R2, and then perform an in-place upgrade of the farm.

However, don't combine an operating system upgrade with an upgrade to SharePoint Server 2010. Instead, build a new SharePoint 2010 farm and then move your data to that farm by using database attach upgrade. This migration path allows you to migrate to 64-bit hardware and a compatible, 64-bit operating system. This method also allows you to more easily isolate and remediate issues that arise from the migration of the operating system and the upgrade of SharePoint itself.

SQL Server

SharePoint 2010 requires that the database server runs a 64-bit version of one of the following: Microsoft SQL Server 2008 R2, SQL Server 2008 with Service Pack 1 (SP1) and Cumulative Update 2, or SQL Server 2005 with SP3 and Cumulative Update 3. If your existing farm uses SQL Server 2000, you must upgrade to one of these versions before you can upgrade to SharePoint 2010.

 Quick Check

- Your existing MOSS 2007 farm uses SQL Server 2000 as its database. What is the minimum version of SQL Server that is required to upgrade your farm to SharePoint 2010?

Quick Check Answer

- SQL Server 2005 with SP3 and Cumulative Update 3.

It is not recommended that you combine the actions of upgrading or migrating the SQL Server platform with the migration or upgrade of SharePoint. Instead, upgrade or migrate SQL Server, and then upgrade or migrate SharePoint. The procedure to move all SharePoint databases between SQL Server instances is described on Microsoft TechNet at *http://go.microsoft.com/fwlink/?LinkId=159761*. Refer to SQL Server documentation for guidance regarding upgrading and migrating SQL Server.

SharePoint Version

As mentioned earlier, you can use either an in-place upgrade or a database attach upgrade to upgrade from Windows SharePoint Services version 3.0 or Microsoft Office SharePoint Server 2007 to SharePoint Foundation 2010 or SharePoint Server 2010, respectively. However, you must ensure that your existing farm is updated with Service Pack 2 and the October 2009 Cumulative Update or later. You cannot perform an upgrade without these updates. You can find information about these updates and links to the downloads at *http://go.microsoft.com/fwlink/?LinkID=169179* or at the SharePoint 2007 update center at *http://technet.microsoft.com/en-us/office/sharepointserver/bb735839.aspx*.

Pre-Upgrade Check

The pre-upgrade check is an STSADM operation that you run on your existing farm to identify issues that might affect upgrade and to review recommendations and best practices. The pre-upgrade checker is added to STSADM by Service Pack 2 and the October 2009 (or later) Cumulative Update. To run the pre-upgrade checker, type the following command:

```
"%CommonProgramFiles%\Microsoft Shared\web server extensions\12\BIN\STSADM.exe"
-o preupgradecheck
```

The pre-upgrade check produces a report with the information such as the following:

- A list of all servers and components in the farm and whether the servers meet the following requirements for upgrading: 64-bit hardware and the Windows Server 2008 operating system.

- The alternate access mapping URLs that are being used in the farm.

- A list of all site definitions, site templates, features, and language packs that are installed in the farm.

- Whether there are server-side customizations in the farm that are not supported, such as database schema modifications.

- Whether any orphaned databases or sites are in the farm.

- Whether missing or invalid configuration settings are in the farm, such as a missing Web.config file, invalid host names, or invalid service accounts.

- Whether the databases meet the requirements for upgrade—for example, databases are set to read/write—and any databases and site collections that are stored in Windows Internal Database are not larger than 4 GB.

You can use the information in the pre-upgrade checker report to determine the following:

- Whether to perform an in-place upgrade or a database attach upgrade. For example, if your servers do not meet the requirements for in-place upgrade, or if customizations exist that cannot be upgraded, you need to consider performing a database attach upgrade.

- Whether to upgrade some or all site collections that contain customized sites.

- Which sites need to have customizations redeployed, reapplied, or redone after the upgrade.

You might need to run the pre-upgrade checker more than once. For example, if you discover a blocking issue, you can remediate the problem and then run the pre-upgrade checker again.

> **MORE INFO** **PRE-UPGRADE CHECKER**
>
> Learn more about the pre-upgrade checker from the following resources:
>
> - Pre-upgrade check: STSADM operation (Office SharePoint Server): *http://go.microsoft.com/fwlink/?LinkID=149848*.
>
> - Pre-upgrade scanning and reporting for future releases (Office SharePoint Server): *http://go.microsoft.com/fwlink/?LinkID=148375*.
>
> - Run the pre-upgrade checker (SharePoint Server 2010): *http://technet.microsoft.com/en-us/library/cc262231.aspx*.

Managing Customizations

One frequent cause of failures during upgrade is that the environment has missing or incompatible customized features, solutions, or other elements. These elements include:

- Custom site definitions
- Custom style sheets, including cascading style sheets, and images
- Custom Web Parts
- Custom Web services
- Custom features and solutions
- Custom assemblies
- Web.config changes (such as security)
- Administrator-approved form templates (.xsn files) and data connection files (.udcx files) for InfoPath
- Any other components or files on which your sites depend

You can identify any custom elements on which your sites depend by using the pre-upgrade checker and, for a database attach upgrade, the *Test-SPContentDatabase* cmdlet. For detailed steps, see the "Identify and install customizations" section in "Use a trial upgrade to find potential issues (SharePoint Server 2010)" at *http://technet.microsoft.com/ en-us/library/cc262155.aspx*.

After identifying customizations, you must determine whether to keep, replace or rebuild, or discard the customizations. For details, see "Determine how to handle customizations (SharePoint Server 2010)" at *http://technet.microsoft.com/en-us/library/cc263203.aspx*. Be sure that any custom elements required by sites and services that you upgrade are installed on your SharePoint 2010 farm before you begin a database attach upgrade.

In-Place Upgrade

An in-place upgrade is performed on your existing farm, preserving the hardware and the server and network configuration of your farm. SharePoint binaries, content, services, and configuration are upgraded to SharePoint 2010 as part of a single process.

The following steps outline the procedures that you perform for an in-place upgrade:

1. The SharePoint administrator performs pre-upgrade steps described earlier in this lesson.

2. The SharePoint administrator runs Setup for SharePoint 2010 on the server that runs the SharePoint Central Administration website. Setup detects the previous version of SharePoint and automatically selects an in-place upgrade.

3. The SharePoint administrator runs Setup on the remaining front-end web servers and application servers in the farm.

4. The SharePoint administrator runs the SharePoint Products Configuration Wizard on the server that hosts the Central Administration website. This server, the configuration database, services, and content databases are upgraded sequentially.

5. The SharePoint administrator runs the SharePoint Products Configuration Wizard on all the other servers in the farm.

6. The SharePoint administrator confirms that the upgrade has finished successfully.

7. If visual upgrade is being used, the SharePoint administrator or site owner can migrate sites to the SharePoint 2010 look-and-feel. Visual upgrade is described later in this lesson.

If the upgrade stops or fails before the SharePoint Products Configuration Wizard was completed, you can restart the upgrade from that point by running the SharePoint Products Configuration Wizard again or by using a command-line operation. This process is also known as forcing a software upgrade. Be sure to research and address the problem that caused the failure or stoppage before you restart upgrade. To restart upgrade, perform the following steps:

1. Open Command Prompt using the Run As Administrator option.

2. Navigate to the following directory: *%CommonProgramFiles%*\Microsoft shared\ Web server extensions\14\Bin.

3. Type the following command:

```
psconfig -cmd upgrade -inplace v2v -passphrase <passphrase> -wait
```

Database Attach Upgrade

A database attach upgrade is performed on a new farm, allowing you to migrate to new hardware, and enabling you to maintain your existing farm while you migrate content. When you attach a content database from your existing farm to the new SharePoint 2010 farm, the content is upgraded. You can transfer content databases by backing them up in the existing farm and restoring them into the SharePoint 2010 farm, or by detaching them from the existing farm and attaching them to the new farm.

The following steps outline the procedures that you perform for a database attach upgrade:

1. The SharePoint administrator deploys a new SharePoint Server 2010 farm.

2. The SharePoint administrator installs language packs and transfers all customizations to the SharePoint 2010 farm.

3. The SharePoint administrator deploys and configures services in the SharePoint 2010 farm. Details about service migration are provided later in this lesson.

4. The SharePoint administrator takes one web application offline in the MOSS 2007 farm. This can be done by changing the load balancer or IIS Web site to stop service requests.

5. The SharePoint administrator detaches the content databases for the web application from the existing farm. Use the *deletecontentdb* operation of STSADM to detach a content database.

6. The SharePoint administrator attaches the content databases to the appropriate web application in the new farm, which automatically triggers an upgrade of the content databases.

7. The SharePoint administrator confirms that the upgrade has finished successfully.

8. If visual upgrade is being used, the SharePoint administrator or site owner can migrate sites to the SharePoint 2010 look-and-feel. Visual upgrade is described later in this lesson.

9. The SharePoint administrator configures the new farm to start serving requests for the web application. This can be done by changing the load balancer or DNS to direct requests to the new farm.

10. The SharePoint administrator repeats steps 4 through 9 for each web application in the existing farm.

The preceding steps upgrade one web application at a time. Alternately, you can perform a database attach upgrade with broader scope. You can also take multiple web applications offline—or even take the entire existing farm offline—and attach all content databases to the new farm.

Before you attach a database, you can Windows PowerShell cmdlet *Test-SPContentDatabase* to determine whether any server-side customizations are missing from the target environment. One frequent cause of failures during upgrade is that the environment is missing customized features, solutions, or other elements. Be sure that any custom elements you need are installed on your front-end web servers before you begin the upgrade process. You can use the pre-upgrade checker and, for a database attach upgrade, the *Test-SPContentDatabase* cmdlet to identify custom elements used by the sites in a content database.

To attach the database, use the *Mount-SPContentDatabase* cmdlet. You can open multiple instances of Windows PowerShell and run the *Mount-SPContentDatabase* cmdlet in each instance to upgrade multiple content databases concurrently. This is called *parallel upgrade*, and it can reduce the overall upgrade time for your farm. The maximum number of parallel upgrades that you should perform depends on your hardware.

If the upgrade fails, use the *Upgrade-SPContentDatabase* cmdlet to resume the upgrade of a content database that is already mounted.

Database Attach Upgrade with Read-Only Databases

The standard database attach upgrade results in some downtime while a web application is upgraded. The following steps utilize a read-only copy of content databases in the existing farm to provide some level of access to a web application while it is migrated:

1. The SharePoint administrator deploys a new SharePoint Server 2010 farm.

2. The SharePoint administrator installs language packs and transfers all customizations to the SharePoint 2010 farm.

3. The SharePoint administrator deploys and configures services in the SharePoint 2010 farm. Details about service migration are provided later in this lesson.

4. The SharePoint administrator sets the content databases for one web application in the existing farm to read-only by using SQL Server Management Studio to modify the properties of the databases.

5. The SharePoint administrator uses SQL Server to back up the content databases for the web application.

6. The SharePoint administrator restores a copy of the content databases into the new farm.

7. The SharePoint administrator attaches the restored content databases to the appropriate web application in the new farm. This automatically triggers an upgrade of the content databases.

8. The SharePoint administrator confirms that the upgrade has finished successfully.

9. If visual upgrade is being used, the SharePoint administrator or site owner can migrate sites to the SharePoint 2010 look-and-feel. Visual upgrade is described later in this lesson.

10. The SharePoint administrator configures the new farm to start serving requests for the web application. This can be done by changing the load balancer or DNS to direct requests to the new farm.

11. The SharePoint administrator takes the web application offline in the original farm.

12. The SharePoint administrator repeats steps 4 through 11 for each web application in the existing farm.

In-Place Upgrade with Detached Databases

You can use an in-place upgrade to upgrade your existing farm to SharePoint 2010 while preserving configuration, services, and content. However, during an in-place upgrade, databases are upgraded serially. During the upgrade, the farm is not available.

One hybrid approach reduces downtime by using database attach upgrades to speed up the in-place upgrade. The following steps outline the procedures:

1. The SharePoint administrator takes the existing farm offline. This can be done by changing the load balancer or IIS sites to stop accepting service requests or by turning off all of the components and services on each server computer in the farm.

2. The SharePoint administrator detaches all content databases from the farm.

3. The SharePoint administrator performs an in-place upgrade on the original farm servers, services, and configuration database. The procedures for an in-place upgrade are described earlier.

   At the end of this step, the farm is upgraded, but the detached content databases have not yet been upgraded.

4. The SharePoint administrator attaches the content databases to the appropriate web applications. This automatically triggers an upgrade of the content databases.

Step 4 is the critical step, because you can attach more than one content database at a time and the content databases will be upgraded concurrently, which can reduce the total time required to upgrade the content databases in the farm.

Using a Temporary Upgrade Farm

In each of the approaches outlined earlier, the production farm is responsible for upgrading content databases—during the in-place upgrade or after attaching a content database. You can reduce the performance penalty on your production farm by using a temporary upgrade farm to upgrade content databases.

Install a temporary SharePoint 2010 farm that is separate from your production farms. Detach or back up content databases in your existing farm and attach them to your temporary SharePoint 2010 farm. After the upgrade of the content database is complete, you can attach it to your production SharePoint 2010 farm—whether that farm is a new farm or the result of an in-place upgrade of your existing farm.

Other Upgrade Approaches

Several other approaches to upgrade can reduce downtime:

You can combine the approaches described previously for additional hybrid approaches. For example, you can set all content databases in your original farm to read-only mode and then create a copy of the farm. On the copied farm, detach content databases and perform an in-place upgrade. Then attach content databases to use parallel upgrade to rapidly upgrade all of the content. Switch users to the new farm after the upgrade is completed.

Another option to consider if you are facing an overly long outage window is to use Alternate Access Mapping (AAM) URL Redirection with a database attach approach. This approach uses AAMs on the new farm to temporarily redirect users to the existing farm while you upgrade the content on the new farm. This is an advanced method and should not be used unless other downtime mitigation techniques are not sufficient. For more information, see "Using AAM URL redirection as part of the upgrade process (SharePoint Server 2010) (white paper)" at *http://technet.microsoft.com/en-us/library/ee720448.aspx*.

Visual Upgrade

When you upgrade to SharePoint 2010 by using either in-place or database attach upgrade, the upgraded sites maintain the look of WSSv3 or MOSS 2007. After users have been trained regarding SharePoint 2010's new interface, you can enable it. The ability to control the user interface (UI) and to maintain backward compatibility of the user experience is called *visual upgrade*.

Farm administrators can choose to adopt the new look for all sites during upgrade. If the farm administrator keeps the old UI, a site owner can upgrade her website. A preview feature allows users to preview the look and functionality of the SharePoint 2010 UI and to ensure that customizations do not interfere with new features such as the ribbon. If the preview identifies a problem, the site owner can revert to the SharePoint 2007 UI.

If the preview is successful, the site owner can apply the SharePoint 2010 UI, at which point SharePoint enables functionality that depends on UI elements such as the ribbon. After applying the SharePoint 2010 UI, you cannot revert to the SharePoint 2007 UI unless you restore a backup of the content database that was created before you changed the UI.

During an in-place upgrade of a server farm, you make the choice to use visual upgrade as a step in the SharePoint Products Configuration Wizard. If you are performing an in-place upgrade of a stand-alone farm, you must use Psconfig.exe to make your choice by typing the following command:

```
psconfig.exe -cmd upgrade [-preserveolduserexperience <true|false>]
```

During a database attach upgrade, you can make the choice of preserving the old look and thereby allowing visual upgrade, or updating to the new look as part of the upgrade by using one of the following:

- The *Updateuserexperience* parameter of the *Mount-SPContentDatabase* cmdlet
- The *preserveolduserexperience* parameter of the *addcontentdatabase* STSADM operation

When visual upgrade is available, a site owner can select one of the following three modes:

- **Use the previous user interface**   The site retains the interface from Microsoft Office SharePoint Server 2007.

- **Preview the updated user interface** The site is updated with the SharePoint 2010 look. Site owners and users can evaluate the site's appearance and functionality. When this mode is chosen, features from the SharePoint 2007 interface will not be available.

- **Update the user interface** Finalizes the user interface and enables all SharePoint 2010 functionality that relies on the new UI.

You can change the upgrade mode from the Site Settings page on the Title, Description, and Icon page. You can also modify and report upgrade modes by using Windows PowerShell. Windows PowerShell can also be used to revert a finalized UI back to the SharePoint 2007 UI. At the site collection level, a site collection administrator can prevent site owners from updating the UI, or can apply the SharePoint 2010 UI to all sites in the site collection.

For detailed instructions, see "Manage visual upgrade (SharePoint Server 2010)" at *http://technet.microsoft.com/en-us/library/ff607998.aspx*.

Upgrading Services Using In-Place Upgrade

In MOSS 2007, a Shared Services Provider (SSP) hosts one or more centrally managed, reusable services, such as search, user profiles, InfoPath Forms, and business data connectivity (BDC). One or more web applications consume the services of an SSP, and a web application can connect to only one SSP. In SharePoint 2010, each service is represented by one or more service applications, as you learned in Chapter 5, "Service Applications and the Managed Metadata Service."

Upgrading SSPs Using In-Place Upgrade

When you perform an in-place upgrade from MOSS 2007 to SharePoint 2010, each service in an SSP is upgraded to a distinct service application, each with its own service application proxy. For example, if you have only one SSP named SharedServices1 that includes search, user profiles, and BDC, upgrade will create three service applications: search, user profiles, and business connectivity services (BCS)—the SharePoint 2010 equivalent of the BDC.

The name of the upgraded service application will include the name of the SSP, for example SharedServices1_Search. If you have more than one SSP, each service in each SSP will be upgraded to a distinct service application. Service applications created by upgrading an SSP keep their associations with the web applications that consumed from that SSP.

SSP administrators are added to the SharePoint Central Administration website as delegated administrators. SSP databases are migrated to the appropriate service application databases. Finally, the SSP site is upgraded as a mostly blank site except for the Business Data Catalog profile pages. The site can be deleted after the upgrade if it is not needed for Business Data Catalog pages.

Figure 9-1 illustrates a MOSS 2007 farm with a single SSP on the left, and the same farm after an in-place upgrade on the right.

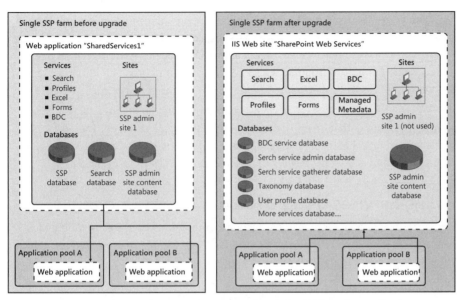

FIGURE 9-1 In-place upgrade of a MOSS 2007 SSP to SharePoint 2010 service applications

Upgrading Search Using In-Place Upgrade

Search is one of the more complex services. In MOSS 2007, an SSP can host one Office SharePoint Server Search service (OSearch). The OSearch service is used to crawl content repositories, index the crawled content, and serve search queries that are issued by end users. An SSP has two databases: the SSP database that contains settings for search—such as content sources and scopes—and the search database that contains crawler internal data such as logs and the property store of metadata from crawled documents. The crawler, hosted on a single index server, crawls content and creates a content index on the file system of the index server. The search service propagates the content index to the file system of the query server, which hosts a single component to host queries.

If an administrator of MOSS 2007 wants to have more than one group of settings—for example, to crawl separate content sources or to store crawled content in separate indexes— the administrator must create more than one SSP and then configure the OSearch service separately in each SSP.

When you perform an in-place upgrade to SharePoint 2010, the OSearch service of each SSP is upgraded to a search service application. Settings are migrated from the SSP to the appropriate search service application. Databases from an SSP are migrated to SharePoint 2010's search administration database, crawl database, and property database.

A crawler is upgraded to a crawl component, and a query server is upgraded to a query component. In SharePoint 2010, the crawl component propagates the content index directly to the index partitions on the query servers—the crawl component does not maintain a copy of the content index. After an in-place upgrade, you can scale search by adding servers and by adding crawl components, query components, crawl databases, and property databases—processes discussed in Chapter 8, "Implementing Enterprise Service Applications." Because of improvements to search performance, topology, and scalability, you might decide that you can consolidate multiple OSearch services in MOSS 2007 to fewer search service applications in SharePoint 2010. You might also decide to use multi-tenancy, discussed later in this chapter.

Search centers—site collections based on a search center site definition—will be upgraded to SharePoint 2010 during an in-place upgrade or database attach upgrade. They will maintain the look of MOSS 2007 until visual upgrade is performed. Read more about visual upgrade of search centers at *http://technet.microsoft.com/en-us/library/ff823735.aspx.*

Upgrading Services Using Database Attach Upgrade

When you perform a database attach upgrade, only content databases are upgraded. Most services must be deployed and configured in the SharePoint 2010 farm. However, you can attach the SSP database to upgrade profile service data.

Upgrading Profiles Using Database Attach Upgrade

If you are using Profile Services in your existing MOSS 2007 farm, you can attach the SSP databases from your old farm, but only the profile information in that database will be upgraded.

Configure the User Profile Service Application (UPA) before performing the database attach upgrade of the SSP database. If you have taxonomy data in your SSP database, configure the Managed Metadata service as well. Ensure that the UPA and Managed Metadata Service Application are in the same proxy group. You must upgrade the SSP database and configure the UPA before you upgrade My Sites.

Upgrading Search Using Database Attach Upgrade

Search databases and settings cannot be upgraded with a database attach upgrade. You must deploy and configure search, and perform a full crawl to rebuild the content index.

Upgrading InfoPath Forms Service Using Database Attach Upgrade

You cannot directly upgrade InfoPath Forms Services when you perform a database attach upgrade to SharePoint 2010. To upgrade InfoPath Forms Services, export any administrator-deployed form templates (.xsn files) and data connection files (.udcx files) from your MOSS 2007 farm by using the following command:

```
STSADM.exe -o exportipfsadminobjects -filename <path to export CAB>
```

Then, import the administrator-deployed form templates and data connection files to your new farm before you attach the content databases. Use the *Import-SPIPAdministrationFiles*

Windows PowerShell cmdlet to import the forms. If the URL of the new server differs from the URL of the previous server, you can run the *Update-SPInfoPathAdminFileUrlWindows* cmdlet to update links that are used in the upgraded form templates.

Upgrading BDC Using Database Attach Upgrade

Data from the Business Data Catalog service is not upgraded to the Business Data Connectivity service when you perform a database attach upgrade. If you want to continue to use the external data that is accessed through one or more application definitions, you must complete the following tasks:

1. In your MOSS 2007 farm, export any application definitions (models) that are required by your solution from the Office SharePoint Server 2007 Business Data Catalog. For detailed steps, see "Export application definition" at *http://technet.microsoft.com/en-us/library/cc816952(Office.12).aspx*.

2. Update the solution to use the object model and features of the Microsoft Business Connectivity Services. This includes updating the application definition file to be compatible with Microsoft Business Connectivity Services. For information about the Business Data Connectivity service object model, see "Microsoft SharePoint 2010 Software Development Kit" at *http://go.microsoft.com/fwlink/?LinkId=166117*.

3. In the SharePoint 2010 farm, configure the Business Data Connectivity service application.

4. After the upgrade, import the updated model into the Business Data Connectivity service. For more information, see "Manage BDC models (SharePoint Server 2010)" at *http://technet.microsoft.com/en-us/library/ee524073.aspx*.

Upgrading Excel Services Using Database Attach Upgrade

Excel Services is not upgraded when you perform a database attach upgrade. You must deploy the Excel Services service application in the SharePoint 2010 farm and configure all settings, including trusted locations and trusted data connections, to match the settings of your MOSS 2007 farm.

Upgrading SSO Using Database Attach Upgrade

SSO has been deprecated and replaced by the Secure Store in SharePoint 2010. When you perform a database attach upgrade, you must deploy and configure this service application so that you can upgrade Excel Services Application and Business Data Catalog data. For more information, see the "Create and configure the Secure Store service application and migrate SSO data to the Secure Store service" section in "Perform post-upgrade steps for a database attach upgrade (SharePoint Server 2010)" at *http://technet.microsoft.com/en-us/library/cec02ed9-c6d7-4a64-87c7-49308076969a*.

Post-Upgrade Steps

After a database attach upgrade, you can modify administrator permissions for services. By default, farm administrators have permissions to all services when you perform a database attach upgrade.

After upgrade, you must also perform the following tasks:

- **Reconfigure timer jobs**   During the upgrade, they are set back to their default times. Be sure to record your timer job schedules before the upgrade so you can reapply the times.

- **Configure blocked file types**   This setting is not upgraded.

- **Configure forms-based authentication**   Web applications that were configured to use forms-based authentication or Web single sign-on (Web SSO) authentication in MOSS 2007 must be converted to claims authentication after upgrading to SharePoint 2010. Then configure the web application zones for forms-based authentication or Web SSO authentication, as appropriate. Then, migrate users and permissions to SharePoint Server 2010. For detailed steps, see "Configure forms-based authentication for a claims-based web application (SharePoint Server 2010)" at *http://technet.microsoft.com/en-us/library/ee806890.aspx*.

- **Upgrade profile properties to taxonomy data and update the photo store**   Multi-value profile properties data from Microsoft Office SharePoint Server 2007 was stored in the Shared Services Provider (SSP) database as part of the Profile Services data. For SharePoint Server 2010, this data must now be converted to taxonomy data and be stored in the managed metadata database. To move and upgrade the data, you must have created a service application for the Managed Metadata service. After that is complete, you can use the *Move-SPProfileManaged MetadataProperty* Windows PowerShell cmdlet to upgrade profile and taxonomy data and move it to the Taxonomy database. This cmdlet reconnects the data to the Managed Metadata and User Profile service applications. You must run this cmdlet for each Managed Metadata property that you want to upgrade; there is no option to specify all properties. Note that the Managed Metadata service does not accept certain characters (such as semicolons, angle brackets, pipes, quotation marks, or tab characters) that were allowable in user profile properties based on choice lists in Office SharePoint Server 2007. If a term or term set uses a character that is no longer accepted, the character is removed and replaced with a space when it is upgraded. You must also update the photo store for profile services. For more information, see "Upgrade profile properties to taxonomy data and update the photo store for Profile Services" at *http://technet.microsoft.com/en-us/library/7d4d75f0-fe37-4ade-809e-d68c730a0745#Taxonomy*.

- **Configure the User Profile Synchronization Service (UPS)**   Settings from the profile synchronization service in MOSS 2007 are not upgraded to SharePoint 2010.

- **Create and configure the Secure Store service application and migrate SSO data to the Secure Store service** The SSO service that was available in Office SharePoint Server 2007 has been replaced with the Secure Store service in SharePoint Server 2010. A direct upgrade path is not available for the data and settings from SSO to the Secure Store service, but you can migrate application definitions from the SSO database to a new Secure Store database by using Windows PowerShell cmdlets. Note that passwords are not upgraded. After you upgrade the application definitions, you can make the Secure Store Service the default SSO provider. For detailed steps, see "Create and configure the Secure Store service application and migrate SSO data to the Secure Store service" at *http://technet.microsoft.com/en-us/library/7d4d75f0-fe37-4ade-809e-d68c730a0745#SecureStore*.

- **Provision a new unattended service account that uses the Secure Store Service to interact with Excel Services** Excel Services Application needs the Secure Store service account to function correctly.

- **Upgrade solutions that depend on the Business Data Catalog** If your Business Data Catalog solution depended on the Web Parts that are provided by Office SharePoint Server 2007 and SharePoint Server 2010 by default (such as the Business Data List Web Part or the Business Data Actions Web Part), you must upgrade your solution to use the upgraded application definitions (called *BDC models*) in the Business Data Connectivity service, because those Web Parts have been upgraded to use the new object model provided by the new service. For detailed steps, see "Upgrading solutions that depend on the Business Data Catalog" at *http://technet.microsoft.com/en-us/library/7d4d75f0-fe37-4ade-809e-d68c730a0745#MigrateBDC*, and "Plan to upgrade to Business Connectivity Services (SharePoint Server 2010)" at *http://technet.microsoft.com/en-us/library/ff607947.aspx*.

- **Consider migrating the Business Data Catalog profile pages to a new location** If you perform an in-place upgrade, the SSP Admin site is upgraded as a site that is mostly empty, except for BDC profile pages.

For detailed information about post-upgrade steps that you must perform after a database attach upgrade, see *http://technet.microsoft.com/en-us/library/cc263286.aspx*. For details about steps you must perform after an in-place upgrade, see *http://technet.microsoft.com/en-us/library/ee704551.aspx*.

> ***MORE INFO*** **UPGRADING MULTIPLE FARMS**
>
> To learn about upgrading more than one farm—for example, a parent farm hosting shared SSPs and child farms—see the following TechNet article: "Upgrade farms that share services (parent and child farms) (SharePoint Server 2010)" at *http://technet.microsoft.com/en-us/library/cc303435.aspx*.

Reviewing and Troubleshooting Upgrade Results

Whether you are building a new SharePoint 2010 farm or upgrading from a SharePoint 2007 environment, always make sure to review the results of the process. The log files created during an installation or upgrade contain valuable information about not only the outcome of the activity, but also the current state of your environment when the installation or upgrade completes. The log files generated by these processes include the following:

- The SharePoint 2010 Setup.exe log file
- The SharePoint 2010 Products and Technology Configuration Wizard (PSConfig.exe) PSCDiagnostics log file
- The SharePoint 2010 Upgrade log files

SharePoint 2010 creates a new log file each time one of these processes is executed, rather than appending the new data to an older log file. You can use tools such as Windows PowerShell and LogParser to facilitate data extraction and reporting. You can also review the Check Update Status page in Central Administration for additional information, and you should run STSADM –o LocalUpgradeStatus on each SharePoint server in the farm to review the individual status of each server. Windows event logs and the logs of associated components such as IIS and SQL Server can also provide insight into the results of the upgrade.

Review each log file associated with the installation or upgrade carefully to identify issues or errors. Search the log files for keywords such as *Error, Warning, Failure,* or *Success*. Look for items that are of significance to your environment. If you find any issues, try to resolve those with the broadest impact or scope first before focusing on small problems or errors.

Additional Upgrade Paths

You cannot upgrade directly from Microsoft Office SharePoint Portal Server 2003 to Microsoft SharePoint Server 2010. The changes between versions are too great, and the hardware requirements differ so much that an in-place upgrade is not possible or supported. You can, however, perform a series of database attach upgrades to first upgrade your content to Microsoft Office SharePoint Server 2007 and then to SharePoint Server 2010.

You can upgrade from SharePoint Foundation 2010 to SharePoint Server 2010 by using either the in-place or database attach upgrade approaches. To upgrade in place, you install SharePoint Server 2010 over SharePoint Foundation 2010 and then perform the additional configurations that SharePoint Server 2010 requires. To upgrade by using the database attach upgrade approach, you create a separate SharePoint Server 2010 farm. Then you copy the content databases to that farm, attach the databases, and upgrade the data.

You can convert from a trial version of SharePoint Server 2010 to a licensed product edition by entering your license in Central Administration. In the Upgrade and Migration section, click Convert Farm License Type and then, in the Enter The Product Key box, type the new product key.

You can upgrade from SharePoint Server 2010 Standard CAL to SharePoint Server 2010 Enterprise CAL. First you must enable enterprise features for the farm by following these steps:

1. In Central Administration, click Upgrade And Migration.

2. In the Upgrade And Patch Management section, click Enable Enterprise Features.

3. Enter the product key and then click OK.

After you have enabled the features for the farm, you can enable the features on existing sites in the farm by performing the following steps:

1. In Central Administration, click Upgrade And Migration.

2. In the Upgrade And Patch Management section, click Enable Features On Existing Sites.

3. On the Enable Features On Existing Sites page, select the Enable All Sites In This Installation To Use The Following Set Of Features check box, and then click OK.

Upgrade Notes

Upgrade and migration is a significant task that should be approached with planning and testing. In addition to the concepts and skills that have been presented in this lesson, consider the following points when you plan and execute your upgrade:

- Before you upgrade, consider cleaning up your existing farm and performing database maintenance and hygiene tasks. For details, see "Clean up an environment before upgrade (SharePoint Server 2010)" at *http://technet.microsoft.com/en-us/library/ ff382641.aspx*.

- Use the SharePoint administrator and setup user account—SP_Admin, for example—to perform upgrade tasks. Ensure that the account has sufficient permissions to perform the upgrade. The account must be a member of the db_owner fixed database role for the databases that you want to upgrade. Alternately, assign the account the sysadmin server role for the duration of the upgrade and then, after the upgrade is complete, remove the account from the role.

- Do not upgrade unless you have validated your upgrade procedures with a trial upgrade in a lab environment. For details, see "Use a trial upgrade to find potential issues (SharePoint Server 2010)" at *http://technet.microsoft.com/en-us/library/cc262155 .aspx*, and "Best practices for testing upgrade (SharePoint Server 2010)" at *http://technet.microsoft.com/en-us/library/ff382640.aspx*.

- Before you perform an in-place upgrade, ensure that you have a full backup and that you have tested recovery of the farm in a lab environment.

Be certain to read the resources in the TechNet resource center, "Upgrade and Migration for SharePoint Server 2010," at *http://technet.microsoft.com/en-us/sharepoint/ee517214.aspx*.

Practices are designed to guide you through important procedures. The instructions in the Training Kit are high-level instructions that will challenge you to think carefully and to apply the procedures that are covered in this lesson and elsewhere in the Training Kit. If you need assistance, consult the detailed, step-by-step instructions in the Practice Answers on the companion media.

In this practice, you perform a database attach upgrade on a newly installed SharePoint 2010 farm. You will begin with a snapshot, created in Chapter 1, in which the Farm Configuration Wizard had not been run, and therefore only the default service applications had been deployed. You will create a web application and upgrade a content database from a MOSS 2007 farm. Finally, you will perform a visual upgrade of the new site.

Prepare for the Practice

Before you perform this practice, you must ensure that your lab environment has been built according to the instructions found in the Introduction to this Training Kit.

1. Apply the snapshot SHAREPOINT INSTALLED AND CONFIGURED to CONTOSO-DC.

2. Apply the snapshot SHAREPOINT INSTALLED AND CONFIGURED to SP2010-WFE1.

3. Start CONTOSO-DC.

    Wait for the virtual machine to complete startup, at which time the Press Ctrl+Alt+Del prompt appears.

4. Start SP2010-WFE1.

5. Log on to SP2010-WFE1 as **CONTOSO\SP_Admin** with the password **Pa$$w0rd**.

6. Disable loopback checking by double-clicking the following registry merge file:

    ```
    C:\70667TK\Practice Files\09_01\DisableLoopbackCheck.reg
    ```

    In the User Account Control window, click Yes. A Registry Editor message prompts you to confirm the change. Click Yes. A Registry Editor message informs you that the change was successful. Click Yes.

EXERCISE 1 Examine a Pre-Upgrade Check Report

In this exercise, you examine a pre-upgrade check report.

■ Open C:\70667TK\Practice Files\09_01\PreUpgradeCheck-20110515-201115-338.htm. Examine the information provided in the report.

EXERCISE 2 Create a Web Application

In this exercise, you create a web application in a newly installed SharePoint 2010 farm by running a Windows PowerShell script.

1. Open SharePoint 2010 Management Shell using the Run As Administrator option.

2. Create a web application by running the following Windows PowerShell script:

    ```
    C:\70667TK\Practice Files\09_01\09_01_Setup.ps1
    ```

The script prompts you for the password of the CONTOSO\SP_WebApps account, which is **Pa$$w0rd**.

The script registers SP_WebApps as a managed account, then creates a new web application called teams.contoso.com in a new application pool named SharePoint Web Applications that uses the SP_WebApps managed account as its identity. The script creates a top-level site collection in the web application, using the Team Site template. Finally, the script creates a DNS host (A) record for teams.contoso.com.

3. Verify that the web application, site collection, and DNS record were created by browsing to *http://teams.contoso.com*.

   It will take some time for IIS to precompile and render the new web application.

EXERCISE 3 Assign SQL Permissions for a Database Attach Upgrade

In this exercise, you assign permissions the sysadmin role to the SP_Admin account so that the account has permissions to restore and upgrade a content database.

1. Open SQL Server Management Studio using the Run As Different User option. Authenticate as **CONTOSO\SQL_Admin** with the password **Pa$$w0rd**. Connect to SP2010-WFE1.contoso.com.

2. In the Object Explorer panel, expand the Security node, and then expand Server Roles. Assign the sysadmin role to CONTOSO\SP_Admin. Then close SQL Server Management Studio.

EXERCISE 4 Restore a Backed-Up SQL Database

In this exercise, you restore a content database from a MOSS 2007 farm. The content database contains the team site for the Finance department's collaboration site.

1. Open SQL Server Management Studio. Connect to SP2010-WFE1.contoso.com.

   Note: After assigning the sysadmin role to the SP_Admin account, there is no need to use the Run As Administrator or Run As Different User options.

2. Restore the database backup, C:\70667TK\Practice Files\09_01\Teams_Finance_Content.bak, to a new database named SharePoint_Content_Teams_Finance.

   Note: If you are unfamiliar with SQL restore procedures, refer to the Practice Answers for this exercise, which you can find on the companion media.

EXERCISE 5 Evaluate a Content Database for Upgrade Readiness

In this exercise, you evaluate the content database to ensure that upgrade is possible.

■ Use the *Test-SPContentDatabase* cmdlet to evaluate the SharePoint_Content_Teams_Finance database for upgrade into the *http://teams.contoso.com* web application.

   Note that the cmdlet reports an error related to a missing setup file for the Web Part, Microsoft.Office.Excel.WebUI.dwp. You can ignore this error. In this scenario, you have already tested upgrade in the lab and you know that the upgrade succeeds despite this error.

EXERCISE 6   Perform a Database Attach Upgrade

In this exercise, you attach the content database and perform an upgrade of the database.

1. Use the *Mout-SPContentDatabase* cmdlet to attach the SharePoint_Content_Teams_ Finance database to the *http://teams.contoso.com* web application.

2. On the Manage Content Databases page in Central Administration, verify that the SharePoint_Content_Teams_Finance database is started.

   Because the content database is a sample that was created in a farm in another domain, it has an invalid site collection administrator.

3. In the *http://teams.contoso.com* web application, replace the primary site collection administrator of the /depts/Finance site collection with **CONTOSO\SP_Admin**.

EXERCISE 7   Manage Visual Upgrade Settings

In this exercise, you perform a visual upgrade of the Finance team site.

1. Open a new tab in Internet Explorer, and then browse to ***http://teams.contoso.com/ depts/Finance***. Authenticate as **CONTOSO\SP_Admin** with the password **Pa$$w0rd**.

2. Examine the site's MOSS 2007 user interface.

3. From the Site Actions menu, preview the SharePoint 2010 user interface.

4. From the Site Settings page, revert to the previous user interface.

5. On the Site Settings page, in the Site Collection Administration section, examine the Visual Upgrade settings that are available to site collection administrators.

6. Finalize the upgrade to the SharePoint 2010 user interface.

Lesson Summary

- You can upgrade to SharePoint Server 2010 from Microsoft Office SharePoint Server 2007 with Service Pack 2 and the October 2009 or later cumulative update.

- You perform an in-place upgrade on your existing farm's hardware. The farm, its settings and configuration, web applications, and services are upgraded. During the upgrade, the farm is not available to users. The only rollback is to restore a backup of the farm.

- You perform a database attach upgrade by attaching a content database from a MOSS 2007 farm to a separate SharePoint Server 2010 farm. Before you perform a database attach upgrade, you must build a farm and deploy services. When you attach a content database to the new farm, the upgrade is performed automatically. You can attach multiple databases to perform parallel upgrade, which can reduce the total upgrade time. During the upgrade, the MOSS 2007 farm can remain online, with databases set to read-only.

- Most MOSS 2007 services cannot be upgraded by performing a database attach upgrade. You can only upgrade user profile data. You must export InfoPath forms from the MOSS 2007 farm and import them to the SharePoint 2010 farm. Other services must be deployed and configured in the SharePoint 2010 farm.

- Several hybrid approaches are available for upgrading farms. The hybrid approaches combine the database attach and in-place upgrade options, as well as a separate farm, to reduce downtime.

- Before performing any upgrade, you must carefully review the configuration of your farm and any customizations you have deployed to ensure that the upgrade is possible. Then you must test your upgrade procedures in a lab environment.

- If you want to migrate content to SharePoint 2010, you can move content manually or use third-party migration tools.

Lesson Review

You can use the following questions to test your knowledge of the information in Lesson 1, "Upgrade to SharePoint 2010." The questions are also available on the companion media in a practice test if you prefer to review them in electronic form.

> **NOTE ANSWERS**
>
> An answer to this question and explanations of why each answer choice is right or wrong are located in the "Answers" section at the end of the book.

1. You have a Microsoft Office SharePoint Server 2007 farm. The farm includes the following servers: A server named SERVER1 running Microsoft SQL Server 2005 and a server named SERVER2 running Microsoft Office SharePoint Server 2007. All servers run the 64-bit edition of Windows Server 2003 Service Pack 2 (SP2). You want to perform an in-place upgrade to SharePoint Server 2010. What must you do?

   A. On SERVER1, upgrade SQL Server 2005 to SQL Server 2008 R2.

   B. On SERVER1, install Windows Server 2003 Service Pack 3 (SP3).

   C. On SERVER1, upgrade to Windows Server 2008 R2.

   D. On SERVER2, upgrade to Windows Server 2008 R2.

2. You have a farm running Microsoft Office SharePoint Server 2007 Service Pack 1 (SP1). All servers in the farm are running the 64-bit edition of Windows Server 2003 Service Pack 2 (SP2). You plan to run the SharePoint Server 2010 Pre-Upgrade Check. What should you do to ensure that you run it successfully?

   A. Install Windows SharePoint Services 3.0 Service Pack 2 (SP2) and SharePoint Server 2007 SP2 on all servers in the farm.

   B. Install Windows PowerShell 2.0 on the server running Central Administration.

   C. In Central Administration, configure content databases as read-only.

   D. Upgrade all SharePoint servers to Windows Server 2008 SP1 or Windows Server 2008 R2.

3. You have a Microsoft Office SharePoint Server 2007 farm. All SharePoint servers have Service Pack 2 (SP2) and a recent cumulative update installed. You need to evaluate the farm's readiness for the upgrade and identify issues that might interfere with the upgrade. What should you do?

A. Install Windows PowerShell 2.0 and run the *Test-SPContentDatabase* cmdlet.

B. Run STSADM – o *preupgradecheck*.

C. Run PSConfig with the *–cmd* upgrade switch.

D. Download and run the SharePoint Administration Toolkit.

Lesson 2: Scale and Manage SharePoint 2010 Farms

In Chapter 1 you learned how to install SharePoint Server 2010. In subsequent chapters, you learned how to create and configure web applications, site collections, sites, content databases, and service applications. At this point in the Training Kit, you have performed all practices on a SharePoint farm consisting of a single SharePoint server and one SQL database server.

Building a SharePoint farm with multiple servers presents you with far more choices, as well as more complexity, than does a single-server farm. This lesson introduces the various roles a server can play in a SharePoint farm, common models for deploying servers in a farm, and the actual processes involved in creating a farm with multiple servers.

In this lesson, you will learn how to add servers to the farm, how to track and block SharePoint installation, and how to configure important features including managed accounts and multiple languages.

After this lesson, you will be able to:

- Install SharePoint servers and farms.
- Describe SharePoint server roles.
- Describe SharePoint server topologies.
- Build a SharePoint farm consisting of multiple servers.
- Script the farm-building process.
- Build a farm that supports multiple languages.
- Configure operational settings in SharePoint 2010.
- Update SharePoint.
- Configure managed service accounts.
- Install and enable additional languages.

Estimated lesson time: 60 minutes

SharePoint Server Roles

A SharePoint 2010 farm can serve small teams of five or fewer users, but can also scale to serve the largest of enterprises and the most heavily visited of websites on the Internet. To enable this scalability and flexibility, SharePoint 2010 supports the distribution of web applications and services across servers. You can consolidate roles to as few as one server. You can assign a single role to a server, thereby dedicating the server to that role. You can assign roles to more than one server to support availability requirements. And you can distribute roles across servers in the farm to achieve performance objectives.

Web applications are provided to users on servers in the farm that have the Microsoft SharePoint Foundation Web Application service running. Servers that host only web applications are often referred to as *web front ends*, or *WFEs*. Services such as search, metadata, user profiles, and Excel services are provided by service instances started on at least one server in the farm. Servers that host services are often referred to as *application servers*. And, of course, database services are provided by instances of Microsoft SQL Server.

Determine Topology

The consolidation or distribution of components determines the farm's topology. The topology of servers and services that is best for your enterprise depends heavily on your business requirements, content, and usage patterns.

A single-server farm runs both SQL Server and SharePoint—and all SharePoint components—on one server. Such a topology offers no protection from downtime of the server, and might suffer performance degradation under periods of heavy use. For these reasons, a single-server farm is often appropriate only for training and development environments, and for sites with low utilization patterns, such as a small, remote office.

SQL Server performance poses a potential bottleneck to the overall performance of a SharePoint farm. For that reason, most organizations choose to run SQL Server on computers that are separate from the web and application servers. A farm with a dedicated server running all SharePoint components, separate from the SQL Server server or cluster, can support higher levels of utilization.

However, a SharePoint farm with only one server running SharePoint offers no redundancy for SharePoint itself. If the server fails, SharePoint sites are not available. For this reason, it is best practice to have at least two servers running SharePoint in a farm, and to run components on both servers that are important to the operations of your organization, based on the service-level agreements (SLAs) specified by your SharePoint governance plan.

As you distribute and load balance web applications and install services on multiple servers, you also gain performance efficiencies. Load balancing distributes requests for content from web applications across servers. SharePoint automatically distributes requests to service applications across the servers that run those services.

Add more servers to the farm based on your performance and availability requirements. Many organizations find that search indexing—performed by the crawl component of the search service—is performance intensive, particularly when crawling shared folders on file servers. For this reason, the crawl role is among the first to be assigned to one or more dedicated servers, so that crawl activity does not interfere with other services and vice versa.

When you add application servers, you should group similar services on an application server. For example, presentation services that render Microsoft Office documents to users— Excel Services, InfoPath Form Services, Visio Services, Access Web Services, and Office Web Applications—share similar usage and performance characteristics, so you can group them on one or more servers that are separate from search servers, for example.

Similarly, if you add servers or clusters running SQL Server as database hosts for farm services and web applications, consider grouping databases with similar data and usage. For example, group search databases on one database server or cluster and group web application content databases on another.

Add a Web or Application Server to the Farm

You can add one or more servers to the farm to achieve redundancy, availability, and performance scalability requirements.

Prepare a Server for Addition to the Farm

Each new server must meet the hardware and software requirements described in Chapter 1 and you should maintain consistent configuration on all servers in the farm. Therefore, the server's operating system should be at the same service pack level and have the same security updates and other hotfixes as existing servers in the farm. Document the location of the SharePoint binaries—the SharePoint program files—and of the log files on the existing farm servers, and use the same locations on the new server.

> **NOTE   THE TRACE LOG**
>
> The location of the trace log must be the same on all servers on the farm. When you add a new server to the farm, the path for the trace log must exist, or you will be prevented from adding the server to the farm. Additionally, if the location does not exist on all servers in the farm, servers cannot log data.

The account you use to install SharePoint must be in the Administrators group of the new server, and in the Farm Administrators SharePoint group. It is recommended that you use the SharePoint administrator and setup user account described in Chapter 1—for example, SP_Admin.

Install SharePoint Prerequisites

Before you can install SharePoint and add the server to the farm, you must install the prerequisite software and configure roles, features, and settings. Use the SharePoint Products Preparation tool, Prerequisiteinstaller.exe, to perform these tasks. As you learned in Chapter 1, you can download the prerequisites to a shared folder and then use a command line or script that directs the Prerequisite Installer to the shared folder as the path for each prerequisite. Chapter 1 also mentioned that you must install two additional hotfixes and disable loopback checking. Perform these steps on each new server in the farm.

Install SharePoint Server

After you have installed the prerequisites, you can install SharePoint Server 2010.

INSTALL SHAREPOINT SERVER

1. From the product media or a shared folder that contains the SharePoint Server 2010 Products installation files, run Setup.exe.

2. On the SharePoint 2010 Start page, click the link to install SharePoint Server 2010.

3. Review and accept the Microsoft License Terms.

4. Select a Server farm installation and then select a complete installation.

5. Accept the default file location where SharePoint Server 2010 will be installed or change the installation path to suit your requirements.

> **BEST PRACTICE** **INSTALL SHAREPOINT ON A SEPARATE DRIVE**
>
> It is recommended that you install SharePoint Server 2010 on a drive that is separate from the operating system files.

6. When Setup finishes, a dialog box prompts you to complete the configuration of your server by running the SharePoint Products Configuration wizard. You can start the wizard immediately, or you can start it later from the Start menu or Windows command prompt.

   Ensure that the server is running with the same service packs, language packs, and updates as other servers in the farm. It is recommended that you install these components before you run the SharePoint Products Configuration Wizard.

Add the Server to the Farm

After you have installed the SharePoint binaries, service packs, language packs, and updates, you can add the SharePoint server to the farm.

ADD A SERVER TO THE FARM USING THE SHAREPOINT 2010 PRODUCTS CONFIGURATION WIZARD

1. On the new server, click Start, All Programs, Microsoft SharePoint 2010 Products, and then click Microsoft SharePoint 2010 Products Configuration Wizard.

   If a User Account Control window opens, click Yes.

2. On the Welcome To SharePoint Products page, click Next.

3. On the Connect To A Server Farm page, click Connect To An Existing Server Farm.

4. Click Next.

5. On the Specify Configuration Database settings page, type the name of the instance of SQL Server in the Database server box and then click Retrieve Database Names.

6. Select the name of the configuration database in the Database Name list and then click Next.

7. On the Specify Farm Security Settings page, type the farm passphrase in the Passphrase box and then click Next.

8. On the Completing The SharePoint Products Configuration Wizard page, click Next.

You can also use Windows PowerShell to add the server to the farm. If you intend to use Windows PowerShell to configure the server, you must have completed the installation of SharePoint binaries described in the "Install SharePoint Server" procedure earlier in this section. In addition, the account that you use—SP_Admin, for example—must be assigned the SharePoint_Shell_Access role on the configuration database, and must be in the WSS_Admin_WPG local group on the server where SharePoint 2010 is installed.

ADD A SERVER TO THE FARM USING WINDOWS POWERSHELL

1. On the Start menu, click All Programs, Microsoft SharePoint 2010 Products, and then click SharePoint 2010 Management Shell.

   You will type the commands in the following steps at the Windows PowerShell command prompt.

2. Type the following command to connect the server to a configuration database:

   ```
   Connect-SPConfigurationDatabase -DatabaseServer "<DatabaseServer>" -DatabaseName
   "<ConfigurationDatabaseName>" -Passphrase "<Passphrase>"
   ```

   where:

   - *<DatabaseServer>* is the name of the server that hosts the configuration database
   - *<ConfigurationDatabaseName>* is the name of the configuration database
   - *<Passphrase>* is the farm passphrase

4. Type the following command to install the Help File Collections:

   ```
   Install-SPHelpCollection -All
   ```

5. Type the following command to install the Security Resource for SharePoint:

   ```
   Initialize-SPResourceSecurity
   ```

6. Type the following command to install the basic services:

   ```
   Install-SPService
   ```

7. Type the following command to install all the features:

   ```
   Install-SPFeature -AllExistingFeatures
   ```

8. Type the following command to install Application Content:

   ```
   Install-SPApplicationContent
   ```

Verify the Addition of the Server

You can verify the addition of the server to the farm by clicking Manage Servers In This Farm in Central Administration. If the server appears, the addition was successful. You can also use Windows PowerShell to verify that the server was added successfully. Type the following command to get a list of servers in the farm.

```
Get-SPFarm | Select Servers
```

If the addition of the server to the farm has failed, examine the log files on the new server in the *%CommonProgramFiles%*\Microsoft Shared\Web Server Extensions\14\LOGS folder.

Configure the Server Role

In Chapter 1 you learned that a SharePoint server can perform one or more roles. The web server role hosts web applications associated with IIS sites that respond to requests for content by a user. Web servers host the web pages and Web Parts that are necessary to render the requested content to the user. The application server role provides services that are consumed by web applications—services such as search, metadata, or Excel Services. These roles can be played by a single server or can be distributed across two or more servers based on your requirements for performance, availability, and redundancy.

After adding the server to the farm, you can start and stop services to configure the server to accommodate the role for which it was intended.

START OR STOP SERVICES ON A SERVER BY USING CENTRAL ADMINISTRATION

1. In the Central Administration Quick Launch, click System Settings.
2. In the Servers section, click Manage Services On Server.
3. Click the Server list to select the server that you want to manage.
4. Use the list of available services to start or stop services on the server.

In Chapter 7, "Administering SharePoint Search," you learned how to configure search topology by deploying additional crawl and query components, index partitions, and search databases. When you have more than one server in your farm, you can choose to distribute these roles across more than one server to improve performance and availability. You can also choose to dedicate a server as an index or query server by starting only the search service and deploying a crawl or query component.

Add a Database Server to the Farm

You can add a database server to the farm if you want to scale the database tier of the farm. New content and service application databases can be created on the new database server. You can further optimize performance by grouping collections of similar databases on separate database servers. For example, content databases can be on one SQL server, search databases on a second SQL server, and other service application databases on a third.

First, you must install SQL Server on the new database server. The version of SQL Server must be the same as other database servers serving the farm. In addition, the underlying operating system, service pack levels, security updates, and hotfixes should be consistent among database servers.

After you install SQL Server, you must create logins for the SharePoint administrator and setup user account—for example, SP_Admin—and the SharePoint farm service account—for example, SP_Farm. These accounts must have logins on the instance of SQL Server and must be assigned the dbcreator and securityadmin server roles.

A database server does not belong to the farm in the same way that a SharePoint web or application server belongs to the farm. The database server is not dedicated to a single farm. In fact, a server running SQL Server can host databases for multiple farms. Therefore, you do not join a database server running to the farm in the same way that you add a server running SharePoint to the farm. Instead, you simply reference the new database server when you create a content or service application database.

Remove a Server from the Farm

You can remove a web server or application server from the farm by uninstalling SharePoint Server 2010. Before you do so, you must ensure that any important components or services on the server exist on other servers in the farm. Otherwise, when you uninstall SharePoint you might damage existing sites or services. You must also stop all service instances that are started on the server by using the Manage Services On Server page in Central Administration. If you are removing a database server from the farm, you must move any farm databases hosted on the server to another database server in the farm.

To remove a SharePoint web or application server, uninstall SharePoint Server 2010 by using Programs And Features in Control Panel. SharePoint program files and data are removed, and IIS sites associated with SharePoint Web applications are rendered inaccessible.

If a web server or application server is no longer available—for example, if the server has failed—you can remove it from the farm by using Central Administration. You can also use this procedure to remove a database server from the farm.

REMOVE A SERVER FROM THE FARM

1. In Central Administration, click System Settings in the Quick Launch, and then click Manage Servers In This Farm.

2. On the Servers In Farm page, locate the row that contains the name of the server that you want to remove, and then click Remove Server.

3. A warning appears. Click OK to remove the server.

The Servers In Farm page refreshes, and the server that you removed no longer appears in the list of servers.

Track the Creation of SharePoint Farms

A SharePoint farm has no information about other SharePoint deployments that might exist in the same enterprise. An enterprise might want to track the creation of SharePoint farms to ensure compliance with licensing and with its SharePoint governance.

To track installation of SharePoint 2010 farms, you must create a container in Active Directory Domain Services (AD DS). The SharePoint Products Configuration Wizard creates an object called a *Service Connection Point*—often referred to as a *marker*—when a new farm is created.

CREATE A CONTAINER FOR SHAREPOINT SERVICE CONNECTION POINTS

1. On a computer that has the AD DS Remote Server Administration Tools (RSAT) installed, open ADSI Edit.

2. On the Action menu, click Connect To and select to the domain that you want to use.

3. In the console tree, expand the connection, expand the domain name, and then click CN=System.

4. Right-click CN=System, click New, and then click Object.

5. In the Create Object dialog box, in the Select A Class box, click Container and then click Next.

6. In the Value box, type **Microsoft SharePoint Products** as the container name and then click Next.

7. Click Finish.

8. Right-click the container (CN=Microsoft SharePoint Products) and then click Properties.

9. Click the Security tab and then click Advanced.

10. Click Add.

11. In the Select Users, Computers, Service Accounts, Or Groups box, type **Authenticated Users** and then click OK.

   If a user cannot write to this container when he installs SharePoint Server 2010, a Service Connection Point will not be created. Consider giving all Authenticated Users the permission so that you can track all installations.

12. In the Permission Entry For Microsoft SharePoint Products dialog box, in the Permissions list, select the Allow check box for Create service Connection Point Objects and then click OK.

The AD DS container within which Service Connection Points are created and deleted is named Microsoft SharePoint Products. The SharePoint Products Configuration Wizard automatically detects the container with this default name. You can use a different name, but then you must create a string registry value named *ContainerDistinguishedName* in the following registry key: HKEY_LOCAL_MACHINE\SOFTWARE\Policies\Microsoft\SharePoint. Configure *ContainerDistinguishedName* with the distinguished name of the container.

The AD DS container must be permissioned so that any user who might use the SharePoint Products Configuration Wizard has permission to create or delete markers. Therefore, you should give all users the ability to create and delete Service Connection Point objects.

You can also use Windows PowerShell to add or update the service connection point for an existing farm in AD DS. Type the following commands:

```
$TopologyURI = Get-SPTopologyServiceApplication | Select URI
Set-SPFarmConfig -ServiceConnectionPointBindingInformation $TopologyURI
```

A service connection point is also created when you install a new SharePoint farm in the domain. When the last server in a farm is removed, the service connection point is deleted.

To delete a service connection point in AD DS by using Windows PowerShell, type the following command in SharePoint 2010 Management Shell:

```
Set-SPFarmConfig -ServiceConnectionPointDelete
```

You can examine a service connection point by using ADSI Edit. In the Microsoft SharePoint Product container, right-click the *serviceConnectionPoint* object and then click Properties. The URL for the server farm's Application Discovery and Load Balancer Service will be listed in the *serviceBindingInformation* attribute. The service connection point contains the URL to the Application Discovery and Load Balancer Service, also known as the *topology* service application.

To determine the service connection point information for the current farm in AD DS, type the following command in SharePoint 2010 Management Shell:

```
Get-SPFarmConfig -ServiceConnectionPoint
```

To list all SharePoint farms in a domain by querying for *serviceConnectionPoint* objects, run the following Windows PowerShell script:

```
#Change DC=Contoso; DC=Com to your target domain name
$Dom = 'LDAP://CN=Microsoft SharePoint Products; CN=System; DC=Contoso; DC=Com'
$Root = New-Object DirectoryServices.DirectoryEntry $Dom
$sel= New-Object DirectoryServices.DirectorySearcher
$sel.SearchRoot=$root
$adobj=$sel.FindAll()
$adobj | ForEach-Object {$_.Properties.servicebindinginformation}
```

Block SharePoint Installation

An enterprise might want to prevent users or administrators from installing unapproved instances of SharePoint. When SharePoint setup (Setup.exe) is run, it examines a registry value to determine whether setup is allowed to proceed. The registry value is a DWORD registry value named *DisableInstall* located in the HKEY_LOCAL_MACHINE\Software\Policies\Microsoft\Shared Tools\Web Server Extensions\14.0\SharePoint registry key. If the value exists and its data is set to 1, installation is blocked and the user performing setup receives the message shown in Figure 9-2. If the data is set to 0 or if the value does not exist, installation proceeds.

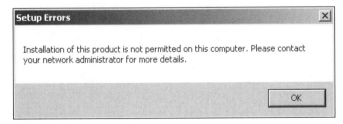

FIGURE 9-2 The error message that appears when SharePoint installation is blocked

To block installation of SharePoint on a server, simply create the registry value and set it to 1. In the practice for this lesson, you will block and then allow SharePoint installation by configuring this value. However, in a production environment, you should use Group Policy—a feature of AD DS—to deploy the registry value to all computers in the domain. For more information about deploying registry values, see "Configure a Registry Item" at *http://technet.microsoft.com/en-us/library/cc753092.aspx*.

Managed Accounts

You learned in Chapter 1 that you must prepare several domain accounts for SharePoint services, most notably the SP_Farm account—the SharePoint farm service account—and the SP_WebApps and SP_ServiceApps accounts—used by application pools for web applications and service applications, respectively. For each application pool you create, you should create a unique account for the app pool identity to facilitate auditing and manageability. If you have multiple farms—such as a production farm and a test farm—you should have separate accounts for each farm. It is clearly possible to have quite a few service accounts in place to support an enterprise SharePoint implementation.

Traditionally, it has been painful to manage service accounts because when you changed a service account's password, you had to update the logon information of each service and application pool that used the account as its identity.

SharePoint 2010 introduces a feature designed specifically to address this challenge: *managed accounts*. A managed account is a user account that is registered with SharePoint. You use the managed account to create web applications and service applications, and for SharePoint services. When a password change is necessary, you make the change in SharePoint. SharePoint updates the password in Active Directory and then updates the logon information of associated services. You can also configure automatic password changes so that SharePoint changes the passwords of managed accounts without administrator interaction.

Register a Managed Account

After you create a user account in the domain, you register the account in SharePoint.

REGISTER A MANAGED ACCOUNT

1. In the Central Administration Quick Launch, click Security.
2. In the General Security section, click Configure Managed Accounts.
3. Click Register Managed Account.
4. In the User Name box, type the name of the account. Use the *DOMAIN\username* syntax.
5. In the Password box, type the password.

    Optionally, you can configure automatic password changes for the managed account when you register the account. Automatic password changes are discussed later in this lesson.
6. Click OK.

When you register the account, you store the user name and password of the account in the farm configuration database. It is encrypted with the farm encryption key, which itself is encrypted with the farm service account password and is stored in a secure key of the registry.

Use the *New-SPManagedAccount* cmdlet to register a managed account by using Windows PowerShell. To delete a managed account, use the *Remove-SPManagedAccount* cmdlet.

Use a Managed Account

After you register a managed account, you can use the account as the identity for a SharePoint service, service application, or web application. For example, when you create a web application, if you assign the web application to a new application pool, you specify the name and identity for the new application pool, as shown in Figure 9-3.

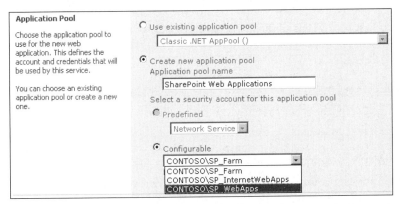

FIGURE 9-3 Selecting a managed account for the identity of a new application pool

Change the Password of a Managed Account

To change the password of a managed account, you do not use Active Directory Users And Computers. Instead, you use the Configure Managed Accounts page in SharePoint Central Administration.

CHANGE THE PASSWORD OF A MANAGED ACCOUNT

1. In the Central Administration Quick Launch, click Security.

2. In the General Security section, click Configure Managed Accounts.

3. Click the Edit icon next to the managed account that you want to change.

4. In the Credential Management section, shown in Figure 9-4, select the Change Password Now check box.

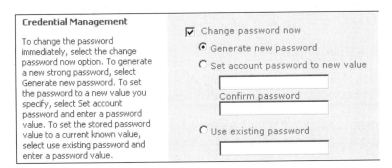

FIGURE 9-4 Changing the password of a managed account

5. Choose one of the following options:

- Generate New Password   Change the password to a randomly generated password. SharePoint ensures that the new password meets the complexity requirements of the password policy.

- Set Account Password To New Value   Specify a new password for the managed account.

- Use Existing Password   Update the managed account password to a value that has previously been set in Active Directory.

6. Click OK.

SharePoint changes the password of the Active Directory user account, and then updates the logon information for each service and application pool that uses the account as its identity.

> **NOTE NO DELEGATION REQUIRED**
>
> You do not need to modify permissions in AD DS to use SharePoint's managed accounts feature. In normal help desk scenarios, a user forgets her password and an administrator uses the Reset Password permission to assign a new password to the user. The Reset Password permission must be assigned to that administrator. However, SharePoint uses the Change Password permission in AD DS, which is assigned to all users by default. The Change Password permission requires that a user knows the old password, and when you register a managed account, you register the account's password. SharePoint can change passwords for managed accounts just as any user can change her password if she knows her current password.

Managed account passwords should be changed only by using the preceding procedure. If an administrator changes the password of an account directly in the domain directory service, the associated SharePoint services and application pools will fail to authenticate. Therefore, you should modify the delegation of managed accounts in AD DS so that AD DS administrators cannot reset the password of a managed account. However, if you do change a managed account's password directly in the domain, you can use the third option shown in Figure 9-4, Use Existing Password, to update SharePoint service and application pool logon information with the account's new password.

Automate Password Changes

SharePoint can eliminate the administrative burden of managing service account passwords by automatically changing passwords based on a configurable schedule.

CONFIGURE AUTOMATIC PASSWORD CHANGES FOR A MANAGED ACCOUNT

1. In the Central Administration Quick Launch, click Security.

2. In the General Security section, click Configure Managed Accounts.

3. Click the Edit icon next to the managed account that you want to change.

4. In the Automatic Password section, shown in Figure 9-5, select the Enable Automatic Password Change check box.

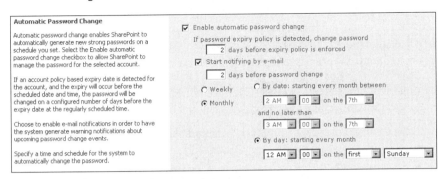

FIGURE 9-5 Configure automatic password changes

5. Configure password change settings to meet your requirements, and then click OK.

The most important setting related to automatic password change is the schedule for the change. You can choose a weekly or monthly schedule. When a managed account password is changed, the services and application pools associated with that account must be reset or restarted, which causes a short interruption of service. It is therefore important that you configure a schedule that aligns with your service level agreement (SLA) for farm maintenance time windows.

If the AD DS password policy that applies to a managed account causes the password to expire before the scheduled automatic password change, SharePoint proactively changes the managed account's password to prevent an unintended disruption of service. When you enable automatic password changes, configure the If Password Expiry Policy Is Detected, Change Password X Days Before Expiry Policy Is Enforced setting.

You can optionally configure SharePoint to notify administrators that the account's password will be changed. Such a notification can remind administrators that there will be a temporary interruption of service, and that service logs will register events related to service shutdown and startup. Select the Start Notifying By E-Mail check box, and then configure the number of days in advance of the password change at which to send the email notification. The email address for notifications is configured on the Password Management Settings page.

CONFIGURE THE EMAIL ADDRESS FOR NOTIFICATIONS

1. In the Central Administration Quick Launch, click Security.

2. In the General Security section, click Configure Password Change Settings.

3. On the Password Management Settings page, in the Notification E-mail Address box, type the email address, and then click OK.

Only one email address is used for all password change notifications. Unfortunately, you cannot specify separate email addresses for each managed account. The email address should be a group inbox that can be accessed by farm administrators.

You should configure automatic password changes for all SharePoint managed accounts. If you do not configure automatic password changes, you must manually change the password of each managed account before its password expires. SharePoint can remind you that a managed account password will expire and that the password must be changed manually.

CONFIGURE NOTIFICATION OF EXPIRING PASSWORDS FOR MANAGED ACCOUNTS

1. In the Central Administration Quick Launch, click Security.

2. In the General Security section, click Configure Password Change Settings.

3. In the Account Monitoring Process Settings section, configure the Days Before Expiry To Send Notification Of Password Expiration Setting.

4. Ensure that a valid email address is specified in the Notification E-mail Address box, and then click OK.

Remember that this setting will send an email notification in advance of a password expiration event only for managed accounts that do not have automatic password change configured. A managed account that has automatic password change configured will generate a notification of the scheduled change based on the setting on the Manage Account page.

Use the *Set-SPManagedAccount* cmdlet to configure the settings of a managed account by using Windows PowerShell. This cmdlet allows you to configure automatic password changes and all of the other settings that are exposed on the Manage Account page in Central Administration.

Change Service and Application Pool Accounts

When you create a service or an application pool for a service application or web application, you assign a managed account as the identity for that service or application pool. SharePoint maintains a mapping of services and application pools and their associated managed accounts. This mapping enables SharePoint to update appropriate services and application pools when you change the password of a managed account.

You can change the assignment of a managed account to a service or application pool by using the Service Accounts page in Central Administration. For example, if you created two application pools and assigned a single managed account to both application pools, you can assign a new managed account to one of the application pools so that there is an isolation of identity and privilege, with each application pool using a separate identity.

CHANGE A SERVICE OR APPLICATION POOL ACCOUNT

1. In the Central Administration Quick Launch, click Security.

2. In the General Security section, click Configure Service Accounts.

3. In the Credential Management section, select the service or application pool from the drop-down list.

4. Review the list of components in the farm that are associated with the selected service or application pool.

5. In the Select An Account For This Component list, select a managed account and then click OK.

> **NOTE** **UNMANAGED ACCOUNTS**
>
> Unfortunately, not all SharePoint accounts are managed accounts. Crawl accounts, user profile synchronization connection accounts, and accounts in the Secure Store are not managed accounts. Therefore, you must manually change the password for these accounts in AD DS and then update the logon information for the accounts in SharePoint.

Support Multiple Languages

By default, the language displayed in Central Administration and in any new site is the language of the version of SharePoint that you installed. You can enable support for multiple languages by installing one or more language packs. A list of language packs is available at *http://technet.microsoft.com/en-us/library/ff463597.aspx*.

To install a language pack, download the language pack from *http://go.microsoft.com/fwlink/?LinkID=192105*. Install the language pack, and then run the SharePoint Products Configuration Wizard on each web server in the farm—it is important that every web server has the same language packs installed.

When you create a new site, you can specify the default language of the site. After you create a site, you can enable additional languages for the site.

CONFIGURE ADDITIONAL LANGUAGES FOR A SITE

1. Click Site Actions, and then click Site Settings.

2. In the Site Administration section, click Language Settings.

3. In the Alternate Language(s) section, select the check box next to each language that you want to enable for the site.

4. Click OK.

After you have enabled multiple languages, the site will render user interface text—menus, ribbon labels, column names, and so on—based on the language detected from the browser's request. A user can change languages by clicking the welcome control in the upper-right corner of the page, as shown in Figure 9-6.

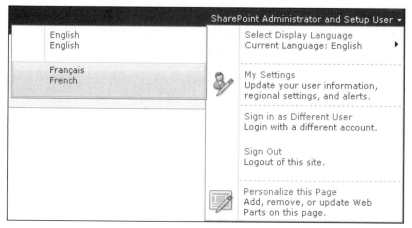

FIGURE 9-6 Select the display language for a site

For more information about deploying language packs, see "Deploy language packs (SharePoint Server 2010)," at *http://technet.microsoft.com/en-us/library/cc262108.aspx.*

PRACTICE **Scale and Manage a SharePoint 2010 Farm**

Practices are designed to guide you through important procedures. The instructions in the Training Kit are high-level instructions that will challenge you to think carefully and to apply the procedures that are covered in this lesson and elsewhere in the Training Kit. If you need assistance, consult the detailed, step-by-step instructions in the Practice Answers on the companion media.

In this practice, you will manage the deployment and configuration of SharePoint in the contoso.com domain. You will block SharePoint installation and you will experience a blocked installation. You will then enable installation tracking and produce a report of farms in the domain. Then you will add a server to the farm. Finally, you will configure automatic password changes for a managed account.

Prepare for the Practice

Before you perform this practice, you must ensure that your lab environment has been built according to the instructions found in the Introduction to this Training Kit. You must perform the practice in Lesson 1 of this chapter.

You also must install and configure an additional server running Windows Server 2008 R2. Create a virtual machine with at least 4 GB of RAM and two processor cores. Install Windows Server 2008 R2. Use the instructions found in the Introduction to this Training Kit and in the Lab Environment Build Guide on the companion media. Configure the server with the following settings:

- Server Name: SP2010-WFE2
- Time Zone: Match the time zone of SP2010-WFE1 and CONTOSO-DC.

- Domain: Join the contoso.com domain.
- IP address: 10.0.0.22
- Subnet mask: 255.255.255.0
- DNS Server: 10.0.0.11

EXERCISE 1   Block SharePoint Installation

In this exercise, you block SharePoint installation by configuring an entry in the registry of SP2010-WFE2. In a production environment, use Group Policy to deploy the registry entry to computers on which you want to block SharePoint installation.

1. Log on to SP2010-WFE2 as **CONTOSO\Administrator** with the password **Pa$$w0rd**.
2. Create the following registry value:
   - Key: HKEY_LOCAL_MACHINE\Software\Policies\Microsoft\Shared Tools\ Web Server Extensions\14.0\SharePoint
   - Type: DWORD (32-bit) VALUE
   - Value Name: DisableInstall
   - Value Data: 1

   Alternately, you can double-click \\SP2010-WFE1\C$\70667TK\Practice Files\09_02\ BlockSharePointInstall.reg, which will enter the correct value in the registry.

EXERCISE 2   Verify That SharePoint Installation Is Blocked

In this exercise, you verify that SharePoint installation is blocked on SP2010-WFE1.

- Run \\SP2010-WFE1\SP2010\Setup.exe.

   A Setup Errors message appears. It indicates that installation of SharePoint is not permitted.

EXERCISE 3   Enable SharePoint Installation

In this exercise, you enable SharePoint installation by configuring an entry in the registry of SP2010-WFE2. In a production environment, you should use Group Policy to deploy the registry entry to computers on which you want to block SharePoint installation.

- Change the *DisableInstall* registry value that you created in Exercise 1 so that its value is 0.

   Alternately, you can double-click \\SP2010-WFE1\C$\70667TK\Practice Files\09_02\ EnableSharePointInstall.reg, which will enter the correct value in the registry.

EXERCISE 4   Configure Tracking of SharePoint Installation

In this exercise, you configure a container for Service Connection Points in Active Directory Domain Services.

1. Log on to CONTOSO-DC as **CONTOSO\Administrator** with the password **Pa$$w0rd**.

2. Open ADSI Edit and create a container named Microsoft SharePoint Products with the distinguished name CN=Microsoft SharePoint Products,CN=System,DC=contoso, DC=com.

3. Assign the Authenticated Users group permissions to create *serviceConnectionPoint* objects.

EXERCISE 5   Add Service Connection Points for Existing Farm Servers

In this exercise, you configure a container for Service Connection Points in Active Directory Domain Services.

1. Log on to SP2010-WFE1 as **CONTOSO\SP_Admin** with the password **Pa$$w0rd**.

2. In SharePoint 2010 Management Shell, type the following two commands.

```
$TopologyURI = Get-SPTopologyServiceApplication | Select URI

Set-SPFarmConfig –ServiceConnectionPointBindingInformation $TopologyURI
```

3. On CONTOSO-DC, in ADSI Edit, in the console tree, open the properties of the *serviceConnectionPoint* object that you just created in the CN=Microsoft SharePoint Products. Locate the value of the *serviceBindingInformation* attribute.

EXERCISE 6   Prepare the Farm and Servers

In this exercise, you configure the firewall on the server running SQL Server to allow inbound connections, and you will delegate SP_Admin permissions to install SharePoint on SP2010-WFE2.

1. On SP2010-WFE1, open Windows Firewall With Advanced Security. Create an inbound rule named **SQL Server (Inbound TCP 1433)** and configure the rule to allow inbound traffic on port 1433.

2. On SP2010-WFE2, add CONTOSO\SP_Admin to the local Administrators group. Then log off of SP2010-WFE2.

EXERCISE 7   Install SharePoint Prerequisites

In this exercise, you install SharePoint prerequisites on SP2010-WFE2.

1. On SP2010-WFE1, copy C:\70667TK\Practice Files\09_02\PrequisiteInstaller.Arguments. txt to the C:\Software\SharePoint 2010 folder.

   The file may already exist from a previous exercise. Replace the existing file.

   Open and examine the file. It is a script that points to the location of SharePoint prerequisites. Close the file.

2. Log on to SP2010-WFE2 as **CONTOSO\SP_Admin** with the password **Pa$$w0rd**.

3. Run \\SP2010-WFE1\SP2010\Prerequisiteinstaller.exe. Restarts may occur. After the Microsoft SharePoint 2010 Products Preparation Tool is complete, open the %TEMP% folder. Open the most recent log file with a name beginning with PrerequisiteInstaller. Scroll to the end of the file. Confirm that prerequisites were installed successfully. If the process is not complete, repeat this step.

EXERCISE 8   Install SharePoint

In this exercise, you install SharePoint on SP2010-WFE2.

- On SP2010-WFE2, run \\SP2010-WFE1\SP2010\Setup.exe. Be sure to choose a Server Farm / Complete installation.

EXERCISE 9   Add a Server to the SharePoint Farm

In this exercise, you add SP2010-WFE2 to the farm.

1. Run the SharePoint 2010 Products Configuration Wizard. Join the new server to the existing farm. The farm passphrase was configured in the practice of Chapter 1: **My Farm Pa$$phrase**.

2. In Central Administration, confirm that the server was added successfully to the farm. Optionally, in SharePoint 2010 Management Shell, run the following command:

```
Get-SPFarm | Select Servers
```

EXERCISE 10   Create and Register a Managed Account

In this exercise, you create and register a managed account for websites that will be accessible over the Internet, so that such sites can be run in an application pool that is isolated from intranet sites.

1. Log on to CONTOSO-DC as **CONTOSO\Administrator** with the password **Pa$$w0rd**. Create a user account in the Service Accounts OU. Use the following configuration:
   - Full Name: **SharePoint Internet Accessible Web Sites**.
   - User Logon Name: **SP_InternetWebApps**.
   - Password: **Pa$$w0rd**.
   - User Must Change Password At Next Logon: No.

2. Log on to SP2010-WFE1 as **CONTOSO\SP_Admin** with the password **Pa$$w0rd**. In Central Administration, register the new account as a managed account.

EXERCISE 11   Configure Automatic Password Change

In this exercise, you configure automatic password change for the new managed account.

- Configure automatic password change for the CONTOSO\SP_InternetWebApps managed account so that its password is changed at 2:00 A.M. on the first Sunday of every month.

Lesson Summary

- You can scale a SharePoint farm by adding a server to the farm, and then assigning roles to the server. The server can host user-facing web applications, one or more service applications, or a combination of web and service applications.
- You can also scale out the database layer of a SharePoint farm by creating databases on additional SQL servers.

- Active Directory *serviceConnectionPoint* objects mark the existence of a SharePoint farm in an AD DS domain. You must create a container for these markers. After you create the container, the SharePoint configuration routine (psconfig.exe) creates a marker for a new farm automatically. You can also create and delete markers by using Windows PowerShell.

- You can manage servers on which SharePoint can or cannot be installed by configuring a registry value. You should use Group Policy to deploy the registry value to computers in an AD DS domain.

- Services and application pools use managed accounts as their identities. A managed account is an AD DS user account that has been registered in the SharePoint farm. SharePoint can change the password of the account in the AD DS domain and then update service or application pool logon information. SharePoint can also schedule automatic password changes on a weekly or monthly basis. The managed accounts feature greatly reduces the administrative burden of maintaining service accounts.

- You can install language packs to allow users to create sites in which SharePoint user interface elements are localized to a language other than the default language of the SharePoint installation. When you create a site, you can specify the language of the site. After you create the site, you can enable alternate languages for the site.

Lesson Review

You can use the following questions to test your knowledge of the information in Lesson 2, "Scale and Manage SharePoint 2010 Farms." The questions are also available on the companion media in a practice test if you prefer to review them in electronic form.

> **NOTE ANSWERS**
>
> An answer to this question and explanations of why each answer choice is right or wrong are located in the "Answers" section at the end of the book.

1. Which of the following are required to join a SharePoint server to a farm? (Choose all that apply.)

    A. A container for service connection points in Active Directory.

    B. The password for the SharePoint farm service account, SP_Farm.

    C. The farm passphrase.

    D. The sysadmin role on the server running SQL Server.

    E. The name of the server hosting the farm configuration database.

2. You want to install SharePoint Server 2010. When you run Setup.exe, you are told that SharePoint installation is not permitted on the server. Which of the following steps will allow you to successfully install SharePoint?

   A. Delete the *DisableInstall* registry value in the HLKM\Software\Policies\Microsoft\ Shared Tools\Web Server Extensions\14.0\SharePoint registry key.

   B. Add a container to Active Directory with the distinguished name CN=Microsoft SharePoint Products,CN=System in the domain naming context of Active Directory Domain Services.

   C. Use the *-cmd* upgrade parameter of Psconfig.exe.

   D. Use the *Set-SPFarm* cmdlet in Windows PowerShell.

3. You create an Active Directory user account named SP_ServiceAccounts and you use that account as the identity for service applications on your SharePoint 2010 farm. You are required to change the password of the account every 30 days. You want to achieve this goal with minimal administrative effort. What should you do?

   A. In Central Administration, open the Password Management Settings page.

   B. In Central Administration, modify the managed account settings.

   C. In Central Administration, add SP_ServiceAccounts to the Delegated Administrators group.

   D. Use the *New-SPManagedAccount* cmdlet in Windows PowerShell.

Chapter Review

To further practice and reinforce the skills you learned in this chapter, you can perform the following tasks:

- Review the chapter summary.
- Review the list of key terms introduced in this chapter.
- Complete the case scenarios. These scenarios set up real-world situations involving the topics of this chapter and ask you to create a solution.
- Complete the suggested practices.
- Take a practice test.

Chapter Summary

- SharePoint supports a variety of upgrade approaches, each of which are based on in-place or database attach upgrades.
- Before upgrading to SharePoint 2010, the SharePoint 2007 farm must have Service Pack 2 and the October 2009 Cumulative Update or later.
- For an in-place upgrade, the farm must also meet all hardware, software, and configuration prerequisites for SharePoint 2010. For a database attach upgrade, the target farm must satisfy all prerequisites.
- You must consider myriad factors to determine the best upgrade approach for your enterprise.
- SharePoint 2010 allows you to add SharePoint servers to the farm and then to deploy web applications and services to the new servers to meet your requirements for performance and availability.
- You can track and block the installation of SharePoint and the creation of SharePoint farms in your enterprise to ensure compliance with licensing and your governance plan.
- SharePoint 2010's managed accounts feature significantly reduces the administrative effort required to maintain service accounts for SharePoint.
- SharePoint 2010 supports multiple languages. You must add a language pack to enable a language other than the default language of the SharePoint installation.

Key Terms

The following terms were introduced in this chapter. Do you know what they mean?

- In-place upgrade
- Database attach upgrade
- Visual upgrade
- Managed account

Case Scenarios

In the following case scenarios, you will apply what you've learned about subjects of this chapter. You can find answers to these questions in the "Answers" section at the end of this book.

Case Scenario 1: Determining an Upgrade Strategy

You have a farm running Microsoft SharePoint Server 2007, Service Pack 1. Farm databases are stored on a server running a 64-bit edition of SQL Server 2005. All servers run the 64-bit version of Windows Server 2003. Servers have four processors and 4 GB of RAM. The SQL server has 8 GB of RAM. You want to upgrade the farm to SharePoint 2010. You want to upgrade the farm to SharePoint 2010. Among the new features you plan to use is SQL mirroring.

1. As you consider an in-place upgrade, describe the changes you must make to the farm before you can perform an in-place upgrade.

2. You have two major concerns related to upgrade. First, you must minimize downtime. Second, you must ensure easy recovery in the event of a failed upgrade. What upgrade approach should you recommend to your management, and for what reasons?

Case Scenario 2: Managing SharePoint Farms in the Enterprise

You want to ensure that your SharePoint governance plan is followed. Your governance plan stipulates that the only instances of SharePoint that are permitted, other than the production farm and the test farm, are installations of SharePoint in instances of virtual machines (VMs) used by developers.

1. You want to ensure that SharePoint installations are blocked on all computers in the domain except for developer virtual machines. Describe how you can meet this goal.

2. You want to generate a report of all SharePoint farms in the domain. Describe how you can meet this goal.

Suggested Practices

To help you successfully master the exam objectives presented in this chapter, complete the following tasks.

Managing SharePoint Farms

Do all the practices in this section. Be certain that you have created a snapshot of your virtual machines prior to performing these practices. When you have completed the practices, revert to the snapshot.

Practice 1: Manage Service Accounts

Create a new web application for the public-facing website of contoso.com. When you create the web application, create a new application pool named SharePoint Public Website. For the application pool identity, assign the SP_InternetWebApps managed account that you created in the practice for Lesson 2. Create a new Active Directory user account called SP_PublicWebSite. Use Central Administration to register the account as a managed account. Use Central Administration to change the identity of the SharePoint Public Web Site application pool to the new SP_PublicWebSite managed account.

Create a new Active Directory user account called SP_ServiceApps if it does not already exist. Use Windows PowerShell to register the account as a managed account. Use Central Administration to configure automatic password change for the new account on the first Sunday of each month. Use Central Administration to deploy a new search service application. When you create the service application, create an application pool named SharePoint Service Applications. For the application pool identity, assign the SP_ServiceApps managed account. Notice that when you assign a managed account, you select the account from a drop-down list of existing managed accounts. You are not prompted for the account's password because the password has already been registered with the farm.

After deploying search, examine the configuration of the default crawl account. The default crawl account is not associated with a managed account. You can identify this fact because you are prompted to configure both the user name and the password for the account. Notice that the SP_ServiceApps managed account is used as the default crawl account. This is problematic, because when the password is changed automatically, SharePoint will update the password of the application pool, but SharePoint will not update the password of the default crawl account.

Create a new Active Directory user account called SP_Crawl if it does not already exist. Assign this account as the default crawl account. Configure a crawl schedule for SharePoint sites. Use the defaults for full and incremental crawl schedules.

Take a Practice Test

The practice tests on this book's companion media offer many options. For example, you can test yourself on just the lesson review content, or you can test yourself on all the 70-667 certification exam objectives. You can set up the test so that it closely simulates the experience of taking a certification exam, or you can set it up in study mode so that you can look at the correct answers and explanations after you answer each question.

> **MORE INFO** **PRACTICE TESTS**
>
> For details about all the practice test options available, see the "How to Use the Practice Tests" section in this book's Introduction.

CHAPTER 10

Administering SharePoint Customization

SharePoint Server 2010 comes with a large number of features and functionality out-of-the-box so many companies will not need to customize it. However, businesses have an almost limitless variety of—and disparate requirements for—their content management systems. Microsoft has therefore built SharePoint with many customizable features so that you can adapt it to needs that are often unique to your organization. And most important, you do not need to be a developer to make most customizations. Instead, you can use the browser, SharePoint Designer 2010, and Office InfoPath 2010 to create forms, pages, workflows, content types, and other unique kinds of content. In this chapter, you will see how to make these customizations and install and administer customizations made by other users and developers.

Exam objectives in this chapter:
- Manage site collections.
- Deploy and manage SharePoint solutions.

Lessons in this chapter:

Before You Begin

To complete the lessons in this chapter, you must build your lab environment according to the instructions found in the Introduction to this Training Kit and have done the following:
- Performed the practices in Chapter 1
- Performed the practices in Chapter 5

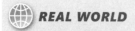
REAL WORLD

Alistair Matthews

Most content management systems—in fact almost all advanced pieces of software—are customizable by developers. This is because the requirements different organizations place on their software are so diverse and frequently unique. Consider Excel spreadsheets as an example—it's not possible for Microsoft to anticipate every feature users throughout the world might need but you can use VBA and Excel macros to add the tool you need.

This is also true of SharePoint—developers have rich and varied opportunities to add custom code. What is new in SharePoint 2010, however, is that users can make their own custom solutions called *SharePoint Composites*. This has huge implications because users can take control of their own sites and adapt them to their own needs without relying on developers.

As an administrator, you will probably find this prospect daunting—uncontrolled customization means instability, rampant use of resources, and messy sites. Well, that is not what happens in SharePoint because Composite solutions are restricted by the sandbox. They cannot access security-related functions, they cannot call web services, and they cannot write directly to the hard disk. In fact, they can't take any dangerous action. Furthermore, their use of resources is strictly controlled by quotas. You can be confident that the sandbox, when properly administered, will run Composites safely. Microsoft is so confident of this that in SharePoint Online you can run Composites in the sandbox, even though many other tenant companies may be hosted on the same SharePoint servers.

Lesson 1: Customize SharePoint

Before you embark on a SharePoint customization project, it is essential to understand that components within SharePoint that can be customized, know what you can achieve with them, and learn the skills required to make the changes. You will be surprised by how much you can do with SharePoint Designer, for example, but some changes must be done by a developer in Visual Studio or another development environment. In this lesson, you will see what changes are possible and who can complete them with which tools. You will also see how to customize the SharePoint user interface, forms, workflows, and other objects.

> **After this lesson, you will be able to:**
>
> - Describe how administrators, power users, and developers can customize SharePoint to satisfy unique requirements.
> - Select the most appropriate tool to complete a customization task.
> - Design a custom SharePoint solution for a business problem.
> - Describe elements of the SharePoint environment that administrators and power users can customize.
> - Understand elements of the SharePoint environment that developers can customize.
> - Customize SharePoint user interface elements.
> - Create a custom workflow.
>
> **Estimated Lesson Time: 60 minutes**

Introduction to SharePoint Customization

Customization is not normally the domain of the SharePoint administrator but belongs to the developer. However, it is an excellent idea for administrators to understand what developers can do. Furthermore, in SharePoint, administrators and even power users can make changes and build complex and powerful applications without involving a developer at all. Such applications are called SharePoint Composites. SharePoint administrators must become deeply involved in the customization process, both administering custom features and making their own changes.

> *NOTE* **RETAINING CONTROL OF SHAREPOINT CUSTOMIZATIONS**
>
> The concept of SharePoint Composites, and the idea of users making their own custom applications, understandably worries many seasoned systems administrators and raises many questions. How can you ensure that resources are not consumed heavily by a Composite? How can you prevent a badly written Composite from interfering with critical services? Can you guarantee security and stability?

In SharePoint 2010, you can be sure that Composites will not reduce stability or cause resource contention, because they run in a restricted environment called the sandbox. Within the sandbox, Composites cannot, for example, access data outside the local site collection, run partially trusted code, or use security-sensitive functions. You can also set resource quotas to prevent contention.

To learn more about the sandbox, see Lesson 2, "Deploy and Manage Solutions and Features."

In this section you will see the techniques you can use to customize SharePoint functionality and the tools you must use in each case. You will also learn more about the roles of administrators, power users, and developers in SharePoint and how they differ from other content management environments you may be used to. You will also study some scenarios that illustrate how custom solutions can be built from multiple custom objects on SharePoint.

SharePoint Customization Techniques

You have already seen some important techniques for customizing SharePoint. For example, in Chapter 5, "Service Applications and the Managed Metadata Service," you saw how to add metadata columns to content. This is an important skill whenever you customize SharePoint because custom projects almost always involve unique types of data with unique fields. For example, if you create a SharePoint list to store information about your products, you might need new site columns to store part numbers, catalog numbers, and dimensions. You can assemble these site columns into a unique content type that describes your products.

When you create a new content type, SharePoint automatically generates a form that you can use to create and edit items. This form is arranged in the order the site columns are defined in the content type and the controls are selected according to the type of data stored in each site column. For example, if you created a "single line of text" column, the form displays a text box into which users can enter data. Perhaps, in a specific case, you'd like to use a drop-down list instead, so that users can select from a limited range of options. This requires you to modify the default form. In SharePoint 2010 you can use either SharePoint Designer or Office InfoPath 2010 to adapt a form to your needs. You can also use these tools to rearrange elements, look up external information, or add branding and graphics to your forms. Figure 10-1 shows the InfoPath Designer editing a default SharePoint form.

Another way to modify the user interface in SharePoint 2010 is to create web pages. You can do this in the browser or use SharePoint Designer. Web pages are usually stored in a Page Library and you can use them as a site homepage and link to other pages or external locations. SharePoint blogs and wikis make it easy for users to create their own pages.

You can also create Web Part pages and populate them with Web Parts. Web Parts are rich web controls that you can assemble into highly functional dashboards and custom displays. For example, the Chart Web Part can analyze data from SharePoint lists or Excel spreadsheets and draw a range of pie charts, bar charts, and other data presentation graphics. Optionally, you can enable users to customize Web Part Pages by adding extra Web Parts and removing those that are not relevant to them.

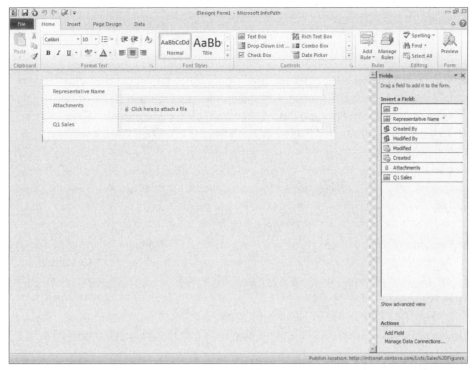

FIGURE 10-1 Editing a default SharePoint form in InfoPath 2010

It is also common to add branding to all the pages in a site and customize layouts. You can do this by modifying or creating a master page. A master page should contain all the common elements that appear on many pages in your site. For example, the SharePoint Quick Launch appears in the master page and therefore is always displayed, even though you do not add it to every page manually. By creating a master page, you can impose a standard look and feel on all the pages, regardless of their authors.

You might also need to model a business process in a SharePoint site. For example, suppose you want to use a SharePoint site to store product documents. To author these documents, your company has developed a sophisticated process, with many stages, that involves authors, editors, technical reviewers, graphic designers, and managers. You can create a workflow that models this process and enforces its specific stages. The workflow can remind users of their tasks by email or by using a Tasks lists. It can also use InfoPath or SharePoint Designer forms to collect information.

By combining these techniques you can create a complete custom application in SharePoint that specifically addresses the needs of your company or a single department.

Notice that none of the techniques mentioned so far requires developer skills. In SharePoint, highly functional custom applications are possible, even when developers are not available or the project budget does not stretch to their time. However, some tasks do need a developer. For example:

- **Custom Web Parts**   If none of the built-in Web Parts satisfies your requirements, developers can create new Web Parts by writing ASP.NET code.

- **Microsoft Silverlight Applications**   Silverlight is a rich web application development tool that developers can use to create highly interactive content and animations. You can display any Silverlight application in a SharePoint page by using the Silverlight Web Part that comes with SharePoint, but a developer or third party must write the application for you.

- **Custom Workflow Activities**   You build workflows from a range of versatile activities that can send emails, log activity, assign tasks, and take other actions. However, you may find that none of the built-in activities can perform the actions you require. In such cases developers can create custom activities for you to include.

- **Custom BCS Connections**   As you saw in Chapter 8, "Implementing Enterprise Service Applications," BCS can connect SharePoint to many external systems for read and write data operations. However, your organization may use an unusual or unique data storage system. In some cases, developers must create custom BCS connection types to enable SharePoint to connect with external systems.

These are just some examples of customization tasks that require development skills.

SharePoint Customization Roles

It is worth considering the roles users take in customizing SharePoint in more detail, because it differs from previous versions and from other systems you may be familiar with.

Traditionally, neither users nor administrators can make any customizations to a system. When custom features are required, a team of developers works with stakeholders to define requirements. They then develop a solution and test it in a lab environment. There is usually a beta deployment, during which users can give their feedback. The final version is then deployed. This is a tried and tested approach that has been formalized in many methodologies such as Agile and Microsoft Solution Framework. However, there are some common problems:

- **Developers command good salaries**   The costs of custom development projects are often high.

- **Developers are busy**   It might be months before one or more developers can be spared to address your needs.

- **Developers and users often misunderstand a requirement**   The challenge here is for the user, who understands the requirement well, to describe it to the developer, who does not have the same in-depth knowledge of the job. Often, such misunderstandings only become clear at the beta stage, when the user realizes that the solution is not what is needed.

In SharePoint Composites, users customize SharePoint by creating their own pages, lists, libraries, forms, and workflows. They can also connect to external systems with BCS. This often reduces the cost of developing a custom solution and avoids the need to wait for developer bandwidth. Also, the people who understand the need create the solution and there is less scope for miscommunication. Furthermore, if requirements change as business processes evolve, users can respond quickly by adapting their own composite.

This approach is analogous to the way Excel or Access have been used in the past. When a department had a custom requirement and good Office skills in house, they created a spreadsheet or Access database to address their needs. SharePoint Composites are similar in that they empower users to solve their own problems. Excel and Access solutions, however, were not very scalable or flexible because they depended on a single file. Multiple users could not make simultaneous or offline changes. With a SharePoint Composite, a solution created by users gets all the familiar SharePoint content management facilities. Users can work simultaneously and use Office Workspace 2010 to synchronize offline changes.

A SharePoint Composite application is limited and developers can add many capabilities to their solutions that are not available in Composites. For example, if your solution must access data outside SharePoint or write data to the file system, developers must be involved. In addition, when you want to create a stable, well-tested, and high-performance application, use a team of developers.

Table 10-1 summarizes how roles have changed in SharePoint 2007 and SharePoint 2010.

TABLE 10-1 Comparing Customization Roles in SharePoint 2007 and SharePoint 2010

ROLE	SHAREPOINT 2007	SHAREPOINT 2010
User	Cannot make customizations.	Probably not skilled enough to make customizations.
Power User	Can make some customizations such as new content types.	Can create sandboxed SharePoint Composites.
Administrator	Can make some customizations such as new content types.	Can create sandboxed SharePoint Composites and control Composite resource usage.
Developer	Can create fully functional custom solutions.	Can create fully functional custom solutions, including those that require .NET code.

SharePoint Customization Tools

You must choose the right tool to make the customization you have in mind. To create a complete Composite, you will often use two or three of the following tools for different tasks:

- **The Browser** Many fundamental changes can be made in the web user interface without a specialized tool. For example, you can create custom site columns, content types, lists and libraries, and Web Part Pages.

- **SharePoint Designer 2010**   In SharePoint Designer, you have the same capabilities as the browser. However, in addition, you can create custom workflows, page layouts, master pages, forms, and BCS connections.

- **Office InfoPath 2010**   InfoPath provides the richest forms environment for SharePoint. If you want to create highly functional forms without writing code, choose InfoPath. InfoPath forms can be used to create and edit list items, set document metadata, and initiate and modify workflows.

- **Visual Studio 2010**   Visual Studio is a developer tool and should be used when custom .NET code is required. Visual Studio provides the highest level of customization for complex and powerful solutions.

Customization Scenarios and Example Approaches

To deepen your understanding of SharePoint customization techniques, consider the following scenarios and solutions.

Help Desk Solution

A global company has a telephone help desk to provide first-line support for computer hardware, software, and telephony. You have been asked to build a site on which users can make help desk requests and receive hints and tips. The following features are required:

- Categorized frequently asked questions.
- When users make a request, they must select a category and receive tips from the FAQ with matching categories.
- When a user creates a new request, a help desk engineer is emailed an alert.
- When engineers solve problems, they mark them as resolved.
- Users are sent an email when their request is resolved.

You could use the following custom objects to build this solution:

- **Site Columns and Content Types**   To store frequently asked questions, create a Question content type with a Category site column. To store requests, create a Request content type with relevant site columns. Include the same Category site column so that users can select from the same list of categories.

- **InfoPath Forms**   You can use InfoPath to build advanced forms. For example, when users select a category for a new request, you can display links to questions in the same category in the FAQ. You can also include calculations, validation, and multiple form views. The forms can also include branding for a consistent look and feel.

- **Workflow**   You can create a workflow to send email notifications to engineers and users.

- **Master Page**   If you want the branding to be visible outside of forms, add it to a custom master page for the solution.

Notice that you can create all of the preceding custom objects in either SharePoint Designer or InfoPath. You can build this entire solution without developer involvement.

Document Authoring Solution

A manufacturing company writes a user manual, a service manual, and a press release for each product that it builds. Each of these documents has a different authoring process. For example, the press release is authored by a member of marketing and reviewed by an engineer, a copy editor, a lawyer, and a manager before publication. You have been asked to create a custom SharePoint solution in which documents can be authored and reviewed and which enforces business processes to ensure quality.

You could use the following custom objects to build this application:

- **Custom content types** You could create a custom content type for each document type. You could plan to store all documents in a single library, create separate libraries for each document type, or create a separate library for each product.

- **A user manual workflow** Because each document type has a different review process, consider creating separate workflows for each. You can associate each workflow with the corresponding content type. The user manual workflow might route the document through reviews by technical authors, content editors, and managers.

- **A service manual workflow** The service manual workflow must model the review process for this document type. For example, it might route the document through reviews by engineers, technical authors, and content editors. The workflow can assign tasks and send alert emails at each stage.

- **A press release workflow** A third workflow can model the review process for press releases.

This is an example of a workflow-driven SharePoint Composite. You can build custom content types and workflows in SharePoint Designer. Once again, this solution does not require the involvement of developers.

HR Integration Solution

As a final example, consider a global company that uses SharePoint for all document management. You have been asked to investigate the possibility of integration between SharePoint and a custom Human Resources (HR) application that was built by a third party. The solution must:

- Import employee information for both read and write operations. Changes in both SharePoint and the HR application must be synchronized automatically.

- Display rich data analysis in charts and other graphical representations.

To determine the best approach for this integration project, you should consider:

- **Data access** You can use BCS to connect SharePoint to the HR application. If you can access HR data through SQL queries, web services, or WCF services, you can create connections in SharePoint designer. However, if data is accessed in some more unusual way, you may need to ask developers to create a custom BCS connection type.

- **Data displays** Exactly what data analysis and displays are required in SharePoint? If managers want common types of charts, for example, the Chart Web Part can probably create the displays you need. However, more unusual or esoteric displays may require a developer to create a custom Web Part or Silverlight application. This is a developer task.

This scenario illustrates the limits of SharePoint Composites. Under certain circumstances, a user-developed Composite created in SharePoint Designer may be enough to satisfy the requirements. However, when needs are more unusual or specific, you will need to involve developers to create custom user interface elements and other functionality.

Customizable Objects

Now that you have a broad understanding of SharePoint Composites and other possible customizations, it is time for a more detailed examination of custom components that you can create. This section describes custom components that can be created by power users, administrators, and developers so that you can architect a complete solution to a specific issue.

User Interface Elements

 **REAL WORLD**

Alistair Matthews

Administrators and developers are often focused, quite rightly, on the functionality of their application. They consider the user interface last and place a low importance on it. When projects go wrong, schedules and budgets come under pressure and the user interface often suffers.

This is a problem I've come across many times in custom applications built on SharePoint and other technologies. The result is a brilliantly designed and implemented application that nobody uses because it appears complex, unhelpful, and sometimes just dull.

The user interface for your application should be simple and logical, and fit closely the users' understanding of their own jobs. Tools and functions should be placed exactly where a user expects and to achieve this you must understand how they work day-to-day. Furthermore, the interface should engage and attract users so that they are encouraged to interact with your application. These factors often make the difference between a successful project and a failure.

SharePoint presents a rich and functional user interface that remains constant and familiar throughout all sites. It is not always necessary to modify the out-of-the-box look and feel, but most companies will want to add branding and often make more extensive changes. You can make such changes by using the following custom components:

- **Web Parts** A Web Part is a control that you can insert into pages in a SharePoint site. SharePoint comes with a wide selection of Web Parts and developers can create more by writing ASP.NET code. Some Web Parts, such as the Chart Web Part and the Content Query Web Part, are highly functional and customizable. When you design a custom solution, evaluate all the built-in Web Parts first to see if they satisfy your needs. If not, consider engaging a developer to create a custom Web Part. Figure 10-2 shows how to add the Content Editor Web Part to a page.

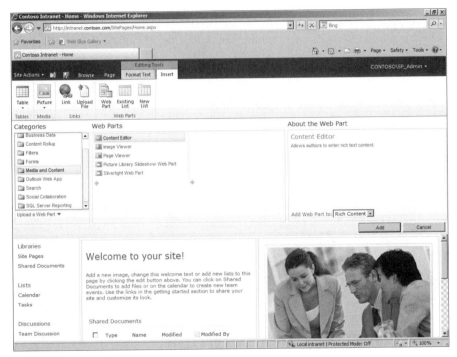

FIGURE 10-2 Adding a Web Part to a Web Part Page

- **Web Part Pages** Create Web Part Pages to present one or more Web Parts to users. A single Web Part Page can display rich information from many locations within SharePoint or from BCS connections. You can use them to implement targeted dashboards at the heart of your applications. When you create a new Web Part Page, you can choose from several general layouts, such as three-column pages, or two-column pages with a header.

  You should also consider enabling personalization for each Web Part Page. When you do this, users can add and remove Web Parts from the default set to adapt the page more closely to their needs. They can also reorder the Web Parts on the page.

- **Master Pages** All sites in SharePoint use Master Pages to display common elements that appear on all pages in a site. For example, the Quick Launch, the top navigation bar, and the ribbon are all in the Master Page and so are shown throughout each SharePoint site. A site administrator can change the Master Page for a site at any time by choosing one from the Master Page Gallery. SharePoint includes several Master Pages out-of-the-box. Administrators and power users can also create new ones in SharePoint Designer by using a WYSIWYG page editor. Master Pages are commonly used to add company logos and branding to SharePoint sites and custom solutions. Figure 10-3 shows the SharePoint Designer editing a Master Page.

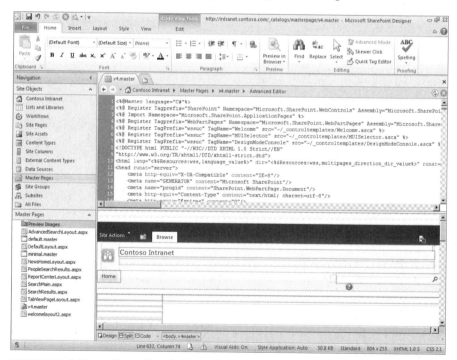

FIGURE 10-3 Editing a Master Page in SharePoint Designer

- **Silverlight Applications** Silverlight is a rich web development tool that can present animations, videos, sounds, and other media within any web page. A large range of custom Silverlight applications are available from Microsoft and third parties, some of which are designed specifically for use in SharePoint sites. Developers can also create custom Silverlight applications in Visual Studio, Expression Blend, or other tools. To place Silverlight content on a SharePoint page, upload the application to a SharePoint media library, then use the Silverlight Web Part to display the application on a Web Part Page.

Content Types and Columns

Whenever you create a custom site or Composite application, you must store data in new forms. For example, the Help Desk application described above must store questions for the FAQ and Help Desk Requests from users. You should model each of these new types of objects with a custom content type. You can use existing site columns, such as Title and Description, in your new content types but you must also define new site columns. In the Help Desk, for example, you might define an Engineer site column to store the name of the technician assigned to each Help Desk Request.

When you design a solution, consider using lookup site columns. These enable you to look up values from other SharePoint lists and libraries. For example, you might have a list of Categories that users regularly add to. When you use a lookup site column for the category value in your Product content type, you enable users to select from the list of categories. New entries in the Categories list automatically appear in the Product form when users create them.

Forms

A form is a page that collects information from a user. Forms are usually a key part of the user interface and are completed by users at all stages of the application flow. In a SharePoint Composite you can use forms:

- **To edit list items** SharePoint creates a default form for all content types; you can modify this form with custom branding and controls.
- **To create InfoPath form documents in Form Libraries** Form libraries can store InfoPath forms that users have completed and submitted.
- **To edit metadata for documents** You can use forms to prompt the user for extra information when they save a document of a given content type.
- **To initiate and modify a workflow** You can use forms to collect required values from a user at the start of or during a workflow.

You can write forms in SharePoint Designer or, for the largest range of features, in Office InfoPath 2010.

> **MORE INFO** **INFOPATH AND INFOPATH FORMS SERVICES**
>
> For more information about using InfoPath forms in SharePoint 2010, see Chapter 8.

Workflows

Many SharePoint Composite applications must support complex business processes that are unique to a single organization. A business process often involves many users in different departments and may take days or months to complete. You can model such processes and enforce compliance by creating workflows.

Consider the following scenario: an insurance company has a standardized procedure for assessing claims and paying policy holders. You have been asked to create a SharePoint Composite that manages this process, collects information at each stage, and alerts workers to claims that require their attention. You could create the following workflow:

- **Step One**   A member of the call center staff completes a form with the details of the claim and saves it in an InfoPath Forms Library. The workflow automatically starts and emails a claims assessor to alert her to the new claim. The workflow creates a Task item to assign the claim to the assessor.

- **Step Two**   The workflow waits for the assessor to consider the claim. The assessor marks the claim as either "Approved" or "Rejected" and marks the task as completed. If the claim is rejected, the call center staff member is notified and must contact the customer. If the claim is Approved the workflow moves to Step 3.

- **Step Three**   If the claim is for more than US$100,000 it must be considered by a Director. The workflow emails a Director and creates a new Task to this effect. The Directory may reject any requests that the claims assessor marked as Approved.

- **Step Four**   If the claim is approved, the call center staff member is notified and must contact the customer.

This is a simple example that illustrates typical actions that a workflow takes to manage a business process. You can create many workflows in a single SharePoint Composite and associate them with lists, libraries, or content types. You can also specify whether the workflow starts automatically (often when a new item is created in a list) or manually. SharePoint can display the progress of each workflow in views or on a status page.

You can write workflows by using a simple editor in SharePoint Designer. You can build up a functional and complex workflow from a broad range of activities. However, sometimes you may wish to take an unusual action in a workflow and find that it is not supported by the editor. In such cases, a developer can create a custom workflow activity in Visual Studio and deploy it to SharePoint.

Site Templates and Site Definitions

You can think of site templates and site definitions as ways to encapsulate many SharePoint customizations into single files called SharePoint solutions. Such files have the .wsp file extension. By creating a solution file that includes all your custom components, such as Web Parts, content types, lists, libraries, master pages, and so on, you make it easy to deploy an application created in one SharePoint farm to another. This technique is commonly used to deploy solutions from development farms to testing and staging farms as well as to production farms when all tests are complete and all bugs are fixed. You could also use it to deploy a solution to several farms in a global environment or to SharePoint farms owned by partners or customers.

Site templates and site definitions are similar because they are both encapsulated in SharePoint solution files, but they differ in who creates them and how they are created:

- **Site Templates**   These can be created by power users and administrators as well as developers. When you have completed a custom SharePoint site that addresses your needs, site administrators can use the Save Site as Template tool. This creates the solution file and saves it in the user solutions gallery. From here you can download the solution file and use it to deploy the solution elsewhere.

> *IMPORTANT*   **SITE TEMPLATES AND BASE TEMPLATES**
>
> Site templates store modifications to base templates. For example, if you build your custom site on the Team Site template, SharePoint assumes that the complete Team Site template is available in the destination farm and adds only your changes to the solution file. This is usually a sound assumption.
>
> However, occasionally conditions are not the same in the destination farm. For example, if the target SharePoint farm uses a different language from that where you created your site template, the base template may not be available. The result is that the new site template does not appear in the list when you try to create a new site based upon it. Therefore, be careful that all base templates and languages are available in the destination farms. Site definitions do not have this limitation.

- **Site Definitions**   These are created only by developers by using the Site Definition project template in Visual Studio. In this case, Visual Studio creates and populates the solution file with all necessary files.

> *MORE INFO*   **DEPLOYING SOLUTION FILES**
>
> For more information about how to deploy solution files, both inside and outside of the sandbox, see Lesson 2, "Deploy and Manage Solutions and Features."

Administrator Customization Tasks

The following procedures show some ways that power users and administrators can customize SharePoint sites without writing any code or using Visual Studio. By using a combination of the following procedures, you can create heavily customized solutions that directly address users' needs. You can also modify and adapt a solution without waiting for a developer.

CREATE AND EDIT A WEB PART PAGE IN THE BROWSER

When you want a web page that includes rich web controls and displays data that is targeted to a team of users, use a Web Part Page. SharePoint includes a broad range of Web Parts that you can assemble into a compelling dashboard and developers can create custom Web Parts. Use the following steps to create a Web Part Page:

1. In Internet Explorer, open the website in which you want to add the page.
2. Click Site Actions and then click More Options.

> **IMPORTANT** **ENSURE THAT YOU CREATE A NEW WEB PART PAGE**
>
> If you click Site Actions and then click New Page, you will not create a new Web Part Page. Although you can add Web Parts to a regular page in SharePoint 2010, advanced functionality such as personalization and Web Part Zones is not available.

3. In the Filter By list, click Page.
4. Click Web Part Page and then click Create.
5. In the Name text box, type an appropriate name for the new page. This name will become the file name and part of the URL.
6. Under Layout, choose the most appropriate layout for the Web Part Page. For example, if you want a single Web Part zone that occupies the whole page, click Full Page Vertical.
7. Under Save Location, choose a library in which to save the new Web Part Page.
8. Click Create. SharePoint creates and displays the new page in Edit Mode.

ADD AND CONNECT WEB PARTS IN THE BROWSER

Now that you have a new, empty Web Part Page, you should add some Web Parts to it to provide the functionality and user interface. In this example procedure, a new List View Web Part and a new InfoPath Form Web Part are added to the page. These Web Parts can be connected so that when an item in the list is clicked, its form is displayed on the same page:

> **IMPORTANT** **INFOPATH FORMS AND LIST ITEMS**
>
> To display an item in the InfoPath Form Web Part you must modify the default form for the list that contains those items by using InfoPath. This ensures that the item opens in an InfoPath form. For details about how to edit item forms in InfoPath, see Chapter 8, Lesson 2, "Implement InfoPath Forms Services."

1. Open a Web Part Page in Internet Explorer.
2. If the page is not in Edit Mode, click the Page tab on the ribbon and then click Edit Page.
3. In the Web Part Zone where you want to add the List View Web Part, click Add A Web Part.
4. In the Categories list, select Lists And Libraries.
5. In the list of Web Parts, click the list that you want to display in the Web Part Page.

6. Click Add.

7. In the Web Part Zone where you want to display the InfoPath Form, click Add A Web Part.

8. In the Categories list, select Forms.

9. In the list of Web Parts, click InfoPath Form Web Part and then click Add.

10. In the new InfoPath Form Web Part, click Click Here To Open The Tool Pane.

11. In the List or Library drop-down list, select the list you selected in step 5.

12. At the bottom of the Web Part properties sheet, click OK.

13. In the title bar of the InfoPath Form Web Part, click the down arrow at the top right, click Connections, click Get Data From, and then click the name of the List View Web Part you added.

14. On the ribbon, click the Page tab and then click Stop Editing.

15. Select an item in the List View Web Part. The details are displayed in the InfoPath Form Web Part.

ADD A SILVERLIGHT APPLICATION TO A WEB PAGE

Silverlight applications provide rich, compelling, and animated user interfaces within web pages. You can use Silverlight applications to enrich any web page. To make it easy to use a Silverlight application on a Web Part Page, SharePoint 2010 includes the Silverlight Web Part:

1. In Internet Explorer, open the Web Part Page where you want to display the Silverlight application.

2. If the page is not in Edit Mode, click the Page tab on the ribbon and then click Edit Page.

3. In the Web Part Zone where you want to add the List View Web Part, click Add A Web Part.

4. In the Categories list, select Media And Content.

5. In the list of Web Parts, click Silverlight Web Part, and then click Add.

6. In the URL box, type the URL to the Silverlight application and then click OK.

7. Click the Page tab on the ribbon and then click Stop Editing. SharePoint displays the Silverlight application in the Web Part Page.

> **NOTE** **STORING SILVERLIGHT APPLICATIONS**
> The URL that you enter in step 6 can point to a Silverlight application stored anywhere on your intranet or the Internet. Often, the Silverlight application has been supplied by a third party or developed by your own team. In such cases you might like to store the application within SharePoint so that you get the full benefit of SharePoint's content management facilities. You can upload a Silverlight application to any SharePoint media library that you have modify access to. Then simply supply the URL of the Silverlight application within the media library to the Silverlight Web Part.

CREATE A NEW MASTER PAGE IN SHAREPOINT DESIGNER

By creating a new master page, you can impose a customized but consistent look and feel on all the pages in a site. In this procedure, a new master page is added by copying a default master page. This copy is then modified. Finally, the new master page is set as the default master page for the site:

1. Click Start, All Programs, SharePoint, and then click Microsoft SharePoint Designer 2010.

2. Under Open SharePoint Site, click Open Site.

3. In the Open Site dialog box, in the Site Name text box, type the URL to the site you want to edit, and then click Open.

4. In the Navigation pane on the left, click Master Pages.

5. Select a master page and then, on the ribbon, click Copy.

6. On the ribbon, click Paste.

7. Right-click the new master page, and then click Rename.

8. Type a name for the new master page.

9. Click the new master page and then, under Customization, click Edit File. The SharePoint Designer master page editor opens.

10. On the View tab, click Design to access the WYSIWYG editor. You can type changes and add or remove interface elements here.

11. On the View tab, click Code to access the ASP.NET code editor. You can use this page to add or remove tags if you are comfortable with HTML editing.

12. When you have completed your changes, click Save.

13. In the Site Definition Page Warning dialog box, click Yes.

14. In the Navigation pane, click Master Pages.

15. Right-click the new master page, and then click Set As Default Master Page.

16. In the Navigation pane, click the name of the site. On the ribbon, click Preview In Browser. The site opens and displays the home page within your new master page.

CREATE A WORKFLOW IN SHAREPOINT DESIGNER

By creating workflows, you can model complex business processes with many steps and activities. You can also coordinate the actions of many team members. In this procedure, a simple example list workflow with only one step is created:

1. Click Start, All Programs, SharePoint, and then click Microsoft SharePoint Designer 2010.

2. Under Open SharePoint Site, click Open Site.

3. In the Open Site dialog box, in the Site Name text box, type the URL to the site you want to edit, and then click Open.

4. In the Navigation pane on the left, click Workflows.

5. On the ribbon, in the New section, click List Workflow.

6. Click the list for which you want to create a workflow.

7. In the Name box, type a name for the new workflow.

8. In the Description box, type a description that will help users and administrators to understand the purpose of the workflow.

9. Click OK. The SharePoint Designer Workflow Editor opens.

10. Click within Step 1.

11. On the ribbon, in the Insert section, click Action and then click Send An Email.

12. To edit the email, in step one, click These Users.

13. In the To text box, enter an email address to send the email to. You can also click the address book icon to the left to select context-sensitive addresses. For example, you can select the User Who Created The Current Item.

14. In the Subject line, type **Thank you for creating a new item**.

15. In the body text box, enter the text of your email.

16. Click OK. You can add other actions, steps, and conditions to build up a complex workflow.

17. When the workflow is complete, click Save on the ribbon.

18. To publish the workflow to users, click Publish.

19. In the Navigation pane, click Workflows and then click your new workflow.

20. Under Start Options, click Start Workflow Automatically When An Item Is Created.

21. On the ribbon, click Save and then click Publish.

22. Open the list in Internet Explorer.

23. Create a new item. The workflow sends an email and takes the other actions you specified.

PRACTICE **Building a Custom SharePoint Site**

Practices are designed to guide you through important procedures. The instructions in the Training Kit are high-level instructions that will challenge you to think carefully and to apply the procedures that are covered in this lesson and elsewhere in the Training Kit. If you need assistance, consult the detailed, step-by-step instructions in the Practice Answers on the companion media.

In this practice, you make a series of simple customizations to a new SharePoint site. You also save your new site as a SharePoint site template for use in later practices.

Prepare for the Practice

Before you perform this practice, ensure that your lab environment has been built according to the instructions found in the Introduction to this Training Kit.

1. Apply the snapshot CHAPTER 05 to CONTOSO-DC.

2. Apply the snapshot CHAPTER 05 to SP2010-WFE1.

3. Start CONTOSO-DC.

   Wait for the virtual machine to complete startup.

4. Start SP2010-WFE1.

5. Log on to SP2010-WFE1 as **CONTOSO\SP_Admin** with the password **Pa$$w0rd**.

EXERCISE 1   Create a New Site

In this lab, you create a new SharePoint site in the IT site collection. During subsequent exercises you will add custom components to the new site:

1. Use Internet Explorer to browse to ***http://teams.contoso.com/depts/IT***.

2. Create a new site. Use the following specifications and guidance:

   - Template: Blank Site

   - Title: Marketing Tools

   - Description: This site is for Marketing personnel to manage sales leads.

   - Website address: *http://teams.contoso.com/depts/IT/Marketing*

EXERCISE 2   Add Site Columns and a Content Type

In this exercise, you create a custom content type and new site columns to go with it:

1. Create a new Site Column in the Marketing site. Use the following guidance and settings:

   - Column Name: Lead Address

   - Type: Multiple Lines of Text

2. Create a new Site Column in the Marketing site. Use the following guidance and settings:

   - Column Name: Contact Name

   - Type: Single Line of Text

3. Create a new Site Column in the Marketing site. Use the following guidance and settings:

   - Column Name: Lead Type

   - Type: Choice

   - Choices: Trade Show, Referral, Web Search

4. Create a new content type in the Marketing site. Use the following guidance and settings:

   - Name: Lead

   - Description: Stores Leads for marketing personnel

   - Select Parent Content Type From: List Content Types

- Parent Content Type: Item
- Columns: Contact Name, Lead Address, Lead Type, Company.

EXERCISE 3 Create a SharePoint List

In this exercise, you create a list to store marketing leads:

1. Create a new list in the Marketing site. Use the following guidance and settings:
   - List Template: Blank List
   - Name: Leads
   - Description: Place your sales leads here
   - Display on the Quick Launch: Yes
   - Content Types: Lead

EXERCISE 4 Create and Edit a Web Part Page

In this exercise, you create a new Web Part Page as the home page for the Marketing site:

1. Create a new document library in the Marketing site. Use the following settings and guidance:
   - Name: Pages
   - Description: Stores marketing site pages
   - Display on Quick Launch: No
   - Document Template: Web Part Page
2. Create a new Web Part Page in the Pages library. Use the following settings and guidance:
   - Name: MarketingHome.aspx
   - Layout Template: Full Page Vertical
3. Set the MarketingHome.aspx page to be the home page for the site.
4. Add a Web Part to the MarketingHome.aspx page that displays the Leads list.

EXERCISE 5 Install SharePoint Designer

In this exercise, you install SharePoint Designer 2010. You must download the tool from the following location before you begin the exercise: *http://www.microsoft.com/downloads/en/details.aspx?FamilyID=d88a1505-849b-4587-b854-a7054ee28d66&displaylang=en.*

1. Double-click SharePointDesigner.exe.
2. Accept the license terms and perform a default installation.

EXERCISE 6 Edit a Master Page

In this exercise, you create and edit the master page for the Marketing site:

1. Use SharePoint Designer to open the Marketing site within the IT site collection.
2. In the list of Master Pages, make a copy of the v4.master file.

3. Rename the new file marketing.master.

4. Edit the marketing.master file.

5. Locate the `</head>` tag in the HTML code.

6. Insert the following lines just before the `</head>` tag:

```
<style type="text/css">
   body
   {
           background-color:#CC6600;
   }
</style>
```

7. Save your changes and close the Page Editor.

8. Set marketing.master to be the default master page for the site.

9. Refresh the Marketing site in Internet Explorer. The new master page imposes a new background color.

EXERCISE 7 Create a Workflow

In this exercise, you create a simple workflow for the Marketing site:

1. In SharePoint Designer, add a new Tasks list to the Marketing site. Use the following settings and guidance:

   - Name: Follow Up Tasks

   - Description: Tasks for converting leads into sales

2. Create a new List Workflow for the Leads list. Use the following settings and guidance:

   - Name: Leads Processing Workflow

   - Description: Creates tasks for marketing staff

3. In the Workflow Editor, add an action to Step 1 that creates a new task in the Follow Up Tasks list.

4. Configure the Leads Processing Workflow to start automatically whenever a new item is created.

5. Save and publish the workflow.

6. In Internet Explorer, create a new item in the Leads list.

7. Browse to the Follow Up Tasks list. The workflow has created a new task for the lead.

EXERCISE 8 Save the Site as a Site Template

In this exercise, you package your changes into a site template and download the SharePoint solution file for later use:

1. In Internet Explorer, browse to the Site Settings for the Marketing site.

2. Use the Save Site as Template tool. Use the following settings and guidance:

   - File Name: MarketingTools

   - Template Name: Marketing Tools

- Template Description: This template includes all the tools used by marketing personnel

3. Browse to the Solutions Gallery in the IT site collection top-level site.

4. Download the MarketingTools solution file to your desktop.

5. Close all windows and log off the SP2010-WFE1 server.

Lesson Summary

- Like many content management systems, developers can customize many aspects of SharePoint 2010 to adapt features to the unique needs of individual companies and organizations.

- Unlike in other systems, power users and administrators can make their own customizations and do not require developer skills to build complex, flexible, and adaptable applications known as SharePoint Composites.

- Enabling users to create their own custom applications means that they can respond to requirements quickly and adapt to changes in business processes rapidly without waiting for developer availability and budgets.

- SharePoint Composites run inside a sandbox, which ensures that poorly designed Composites do not threaten stability and security or use too many resources.

- Some customizations, including site columns, content types, and Web Part Pages, can be completed in the browser without specialized tools.

- SharePoint Designer can complete more extensive customizations, such as master pages and workflows.

- For the most flexible forms within a Composite application, use Office InfoPath 2010 to edit default forms and create new forms.

- Developers use Visual Studio as the most powerful SharePoint customization tool.

- Users can encapsulate a SharePoint Composite application by saving it as a user solution site template. This solution can be deployed to other farms and site collections.

- Developers can encapsulate their solutions as site definitions.

Lesson Review

You can use the following questions to test your knowledge of the information in Lesson 1, "Customize SharePoint." The questions are also available on the companion media in a practice test if you prefer to review them in electronic form.

> **NOTE ANSWERS**
>
> Answers to these questions and explanations of why each answer choice is right or wrong are located in the "Answers" section at the end of the book.

1. You are a SharePoint administrator in a global organization with SharePoint farms in Europe and the United States. The marketing team in France has built a Composite application to manage the development of marketing materials. The United States marketing team has seen this application and asked for it to be deployed in the North American SharePoint farm. The French users have created a user solution file and sent it to you. You have deployed the solution file to the North American SharePoint farm but no marketing materials site template appears and you cannot proceed to create the new site. What could cause this problem?

   A. The sandbox does not allow user solutions created in other farms to run.

   B. A developer must re-create the French marketing solution in Visual Studio and encapsulate it as a site definition.

   C. The marketing solution was based on a SharePoint site template in the French language that is not present in the North American farm.

   D. The marketing solution uses custom Web Parts that are not available in the North American farm.

   E. Microsoft Office InfoPath 2010 has not been deployed to all client computers in the North American farm.

2. You have created a SharePoint Composite solution that the sales department will use to store leads and translate them into sales. The board is impressed with the functionality but has asked you to implement the corporate branding on every page in the Sales site. Which of the following objects should you edit?

   A. The site's default master page.

   B. The sales lead workflow.

   C. All Web Part Pages in the Sales site.

   D. All Web Parts in the Sales site.

   E. The site definition.

Lesson 2: Deploy and Manage Solutions and Features

As you saw in Lesson 1, SharePoint administrators can become involved in the customization process in SharePoint 2010 because you do not need to write code to adapt SharePoint to your needs. However, administrators usually do not make their own customizations, but deploy and manage customizations made by others. Teams of users, for example, may create their own SharePoint Composite to address their particular needs and business processes—administrators may need to restrict the resources available to such Composites to ensure stability. Third-party or in-house developers may create SharePoint solutions in Visual Studio or another development environment—administrators need to deploy such solutions and create new sites, lists, libraries, and pages from them. In this lesson you will study the administrative tasks required to run a customized SharePoint farm.

After this lesson, you will be able to:

- Describe the SharePoint Feature infrastructure and understand the contents of a SharePoint Feature.
- Understand the capabilities, content, and restrictions of sandboxed user solutions.
- List the extra capabilities of farm solutions.
- Deploy and manage SharePoint Features in farms, sites, site collections, and web applications.
- Deploy and manage SharePoint user solutions.
- Deploy and manage SharePoint farm solutions.

Estimated Lesson Time: 40 minutes

Introducing Solutions and Features

SharePoint Features are units of functionality that can be activated and deactivated to target SharePoint to your needs. SharePoint includes a wide range of features out of the box and developers can create their own. Solutions are single files that are used to deploy customizations, and each solution can contain one or more features. In this lesson, you will learn about features and solutions and see a range of procedures that illustrate how to manage them.

Features

The SharePoint feature infrastructure permits developers to create units of functionality that administrators can install and enable or disable piece by piece. Within a single feature, developers can add Web Parts, timer jobs, master pages, workflows, BCS connection types, and any other customization. Customizations that depend on each other will often be in the same feature. SharePoint includes a wide range of features out of the box, such as the Publishing Infrastructure Feature that enables web content management.

Features are deployed with one of four scopes. The feature scope determines where the feature is enabled, who can enable it, and what custom components it can contain:

- **Site** features with the site scope appear in the site-level feature gallery and can be enabled by a site owner. Site features can deploy custom components only within the site where they are enabled. For example, if a site-scoped feature is enabled in the Sales site, a Web Part that it contains cannot be used in any other site, unless the feature is enabled in that site.

- **Site collection** features with the site collection scope appear in the Feature gallery at the site collection level and can be enabled only by site collection administrators. Site collection features can deploy custom components to the entire site collection. For example, if a site collection scoped feature is enabled in the Intranet site collection, a Web Part that it contains appears in the Web Part gallery for all sites in the collection.

- **Web application** features with the web application scope appear in a dedicated list within Central Administration and can only be enabled by farm administrators. Web application features can deploy custom components to all sites and site collections in a web application.

- **Farm** features with the farm application scope appear in the Central Administration farm features gallery and can only be enabled by farm administrators. Custom components in these features are deployed to all sites in the farm. The Manage Farm Features page is shown in Figure 10-4.

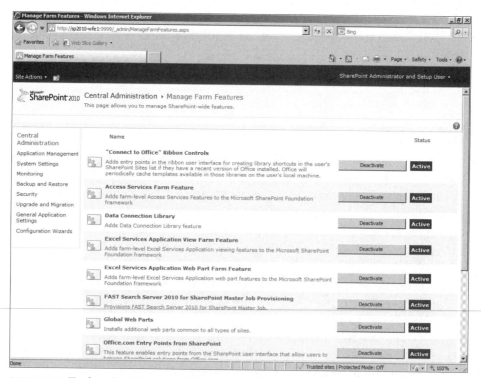

FIGURE 10-4 The farm-level features gallery

You should note that each feature can depend on other features. For example, if a developer creates a features that extends the web content management capabilities of SharePoint, she might choose to make it dependent on the Publishing Infrastructure Feature, which contains all the core web publishing components in SharePoint.

Administrators must know how to enable and disable features at any scope. Occasionally, a developer may supply a SharePoint feature for installation but it is more common to build such a feature into a SharePoint solution file for reasons outlined in the next section. Procedures for installing, enabling, disabling, and removing features are described later in this lesson.

NOTE INSTALLING FEATURES IN MULTI-SERVER FARMS

If you have more than one web front-end server in your SharePoint farm, you must install a feature on all of them manually. The same is true when you update features.

EXAM TIP

Although administrators can install SharePoint features by using Windows PowerShell cmdlets, this operation has become rare because solution files are easier to deal with. In your exam preparation, focus on feature scopes and activation, rather than installation, as these are more likely to come up.

Farm Solutions

SharePoint solutions were introduced to ease the deployment of custom components. They make use of the feature infrastructure. For example, each SharePoint solution can include multiple features of different scopes. SharePoint solutions are single files with a .wsp extension. All the custom components are present within this file together with a manifest that describes the components and defines where they should be installed in the SharePoint hierarchy.

NOTE EXAMINING THE CONTENTS OF SOLUTION FILES

To find out what is inside a solution file, a developer would normally use Visual Studio. However, the format of information within a .wsp file is the same as a cabinet file. You can use any cabinet file viewer to open .wsp files. For example, some compression utilities can open these files.

As you learned in Lesson 1, SharePoint solution files can be created by a developer in Visual Studio. Such a solution can include an entire site definition, a single custom component such as a Web Part, or any combination of custom components. Alternatively, a user can create a solution file by using the Save As Template tool in the web browser. Such a solution will always contain all the components of the saved site as a Site Template.

Regardless of the creation method, a farm solution is a SharePoint solution that has been deployed to the farm-level solution store. This is a task that can only be completed by farm administrators.

Farm solutions do not run in the sandbox. Therefore, a poorly written solution can potentially cause security problems and instability in the SharePoint system. For example, by writing a lot of information to the hard disk, a farm solution could crash the server and cause a denial of service. Therefore, before you deploy a farm solution, you must be sure that it is well tested and trustworthy, particularly if you have a Service Level Agreement (SLA) that guarantees high availability.

You should consider testing farm solutions thoroughly in a lab environment before you deploy them. Such a test environment should consist of SharePoint servers configured as closely to the production farm as possible. When you are satisfied that the solution is trustworthy, you must install it and activate it on the production farm.

User Solutions

A user solution is a SharePoint solution file that is deployed in the solution gallery. There is a solution gallery for every SharePoint site collection. Any user who has the manage Web site permission can upload a solution file to this gallery and deploy it in the site collection. Site owners, for example, have permission to complete this task.

This arrangement can mean that many users can upload and activate user solutions but administrators can be confident that user solutions will not hinder availability and security. This is because user solutions always run in the sandbox. The sandbox protects SharePoint from poorly written solutions by imposing the following limitations:

- **Resource Quotas** Solutions in the sandbox cannot overuse server resources such as memory, CPU, and database queries. When the solution exceeds certain criteria, it scores a point. Administrators can configure the maximum number of points each solution can score in 24 hours. When a solution exceeds this number it is shut down. Points scored depend on the resource that is used, for example, when the percentage processor time exceeds 85 percent a point is scored. Similarly, if the solution uses more than 100 MB of memory a point is scored.

- **No calls to web services** Many web services of the Internet are considered untrustworthy, so user solutions are prevented from accessing web services.

- **No access to data outside the local site collection** User solutions can only access SharePoint items and documents if they are within the same site collection where the solution is deployed.

- **No access to files on the hard disk** User solutions can neither read from nor write to the file system of the server directly.

- **Limited access to the SharePoint object model** The SharePoint object model is the set of classes that developers can call from managed code. User solutions have access to many powerful classes but some, with facilities that may compromise security or stability, are blocked. For example, the sandbox blocks access to the *SPFarm* object, which represents the SharePoint farm itself.

- **A separate host process** User solutions run within a protected worker process so that poor solutions cannot threaten the stability of other services, such as other web applications.

Administrators or users who wish to deploy a user solution must first upload the solution file to the site collection solution gallery, as shown in Figure 10-5, and then activate it.

EXAM TIP

Make sure you are clear about the difference between a farm solution and a user solution. Ultimately, the difference is where they are deployed: farm solutions are deployed in Central Administration; user solutions are deployed in the site collection solution gallery. User solutions in the solution gallery are restricted by the sandbox; farm solutions are not restricted. Also remember that only farm administrators can upload and activate farm solutions. User solutions are a key innovation in SharePoint 2010, so they are likely to come up often.

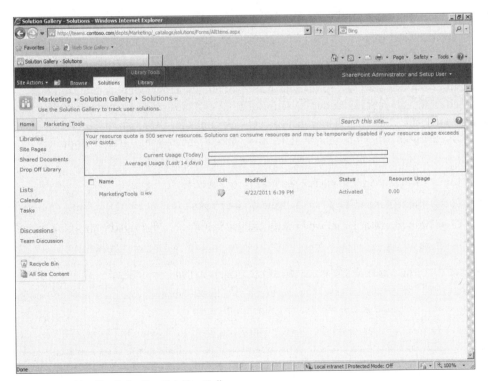

FIGURE 10-5 The Site Collection Solution Gallery

Feature Management

Administrators might need to install features provided by developers or third parties. You might also want to remove features that are no longer needed. Installed features must be activated and deactivated in different locations depending on their scope.

INSTALL A FEATURE IN WINDOWS POWERSHELL

To install a new feature in your SharePoint farm, follow these steps. If you have more than one web front-end server in your SharePoint farm, you must install the feature on all of them. The feature should be supplied in the form of a folder with both files and subfolders. The root of this folder should contain a file called Feature.XML.

1. Open Windows Explorer and browse to the following location: **C:\Program Files\ Common Files\Microsoft Shared\Web Server Extensions\14\TEMPLATE\FEATURES**.

2. Paste the feature as a subfolder of FEATURES.

3. Click Start, All Programs, Microsoft SharePoint 2010 Products, and then click SharePoint 2010 Management Shell.

4. Type the following Windows PowerShell cmdlet:

    ```
    Install-SPFeature -Path <FeatureName>
    ```

    where *<FeatureName>* is the name of the subfolder you just copied.

ACTIVATE OR DEACTIVATE A FARM FEATURE IN CENTRAL ADMINISTRATION

Many out-of-the-box features included in SharePoint are not activated by default. You may also need to activate features added by farm solutions and those features that you have installed manually. The location in which you activate or deactivate a feature depends on its scope. Use the following steps to activate or deactivate a feature with the farm scope:

1. In the Central Administration Quick Launch, click System Settings.

2. Under Farm Management, click Manage Farm Features.

3. Locate the feature you want to activate or deactivate.

4. Click the Activate or Deactivate button. Active features are displayed with a blue Active label.

ACTIVATE OR DEACTIVATE A SITE OR SITE COLLECTION FEATURE

If a feature has site or site collection scope, steps to activate or deactivate it are similar except that the feature is found in the site or site collection feature list:

1. In Internet Explorer, open the site for which you want to activate the feature. If the feature has the site collection scope, open the top-level site in the site collection.

2. Click Site Actions and then click Site Settings.

3. If the feature has the site scope, then under Site Actions, click Manage Site Features. If the feature has the site collection scope, then under Site Collection Administration, click Site Collection Features.

4. In the Features list, locate the feature you want to activate or deactivate.

5. Click the Activate or Deactivate button.

ACTIVATE OR DEACTIVATE A WEB APPLICATION FEATURE

If a feature has web application scope, use the following steps to activate or deactivate it:

1. In the Central Administration Quick Launch, click Application Management.

2. Under Web Applications, click Manage Web Applications.

3. Select the web application for which you want to enable the feature.

4. On the ribbon, click Manage Features.

5. In the Features list, locate the feature you want to activate or deactivate.

6. Click the Activate or Deactivate button.

ACTIVATE A FEATURE IN WINDOWS POWERSHELL

You can use the *Enable-SPFeature* Windows PowerShell cmdlet to activate any installed feature. For example:

```
Enable-SPFeature –identity <MyFeature> -URL <http://myserver.mydomain.local/mysite>
```

Where:

- *<MyFeature>* is the name of the feature you want to activate.
- *<http://myserver.mydomain.local/mysite>* is the URL of the site, site collection, or web application for which you want to activate the feature.

> **NOTE THE –*URL* PARAMETER AND FARM SCOPED FEATURES**
>
> The –*URL* attribute is required for all features except those with the farm scope. Because farm features are activated for the entire SharePoint system, the URL is superfluous and you will receive an error if you include it.

To disable Features, use the very similar Windows PowerShell *Disable-SPFeature* cmdlet.

REMOVE A FEATURE

You cannot remove a feature unless it is disabled in all sites, site collections, and web applications. All features that depend on it must also be disabled. You must use the *Uninstall-SPFeature* Windows PowerShell cmdlet to remove a feature:

```
Uninstall-SPFeature –path <MyFeature>
```

where *<MyFeature>* is the name of the Feature folder.

User Solution Management

Both administrators and users might need to upload solution files to a site collection solution gallery and then install it. Remember that solutions uploaded to the site collection solution galleries are user solutions and run within the sandbox.

UPLOAD AND INSTALL A USER SOLUTION IN THE BROWSER

Solution files have a .wsp extension. Use the following steps to upload a solution to the site collection solution gallery and install it in the farm.

> **NOTE** **SOLUTION FILES IN MULTI-SERVER FARMS**
>
> Unlike SharePoint features, SharePoint solution files don't need to be uploaded and installed on every web front-end server in a multi-server SharePoint farm. However, when you upload a solution file to a site collection solution gallery, you can only use it in that site collection. When you want to use a User Solution in many site collections, you must manually upload and install it in each one.

1. Browse to the top-level site in the site collection in which you want to use the user solution.

2. Click Site Actions and then click Site Settings.

3. Under Galleries, click Solutions. The list of current user solutions is displayed, along with a summary of resource usage.

4. On the ribbon, click the Solutions tab.

5. Click Upload Solution.

6. In the Name text box, type the path to the .wsp solution file you want to upload. Alternatively, use the Browse button to locate it.

7. Click OK.

8. When the upload is complete, click the new solution in the list.

9. In the ribbon, click Activate.

10. In the Details dialog box, click Activate.

UPLOAD AND INSTALL A USER SOLUTION IN WINDOWS POWERSHELL

Alternatively, you can use the *Add-SPUserSolution* and *Install-SPUserSolution* cmdlets to upload and activate user solutions. Use these commands in Windows PowerShell scripts when you want to automate the tasks. For example, if you want to use a user solution in many site collections, you could write a script that evaluates all the site collections in a farm and installs a user solution in all of them.

This example script uploads and installs a solution file to a single site collection:

```
Add-SPUserSolution -LiteralPath <PathToSolutionFile>
-Site <http://myserver.mydomain.local>

Install-SPUserSolution -Identity <SolutionFileName>
-Site <http://myserver.mydomain.local>
```

Where:

- *<PathToSolutionFile>* is the location where you have stored the .wsp file. This can be on a local hard drive or on a shared folder.

- *<http://myserver.mydomain.local>* is the URL of the site collection where you want to use the user solution.

- *<SolutionFileName>* is the name of the solution file you uploaded to the site collection solution gallery.

UNINSTALL AND REMOVE A USER SOLUTION IN THE BROWSER

If a user solution is no longer required or has proved unreliable, you might want to remove it from the solution gallery. To do this, you must first deactivate it by using the following steps:

1. In the browser, open the site collection in which the user solution is installed.
2. Click Site Actions and then click Site Settings.
3. Under Galleries, click Solutions.
4. Select the user solution you want to deactivate.
5. On the ribbon, click the Solution tab and then click Deactivate.
6. In the Deactivate Solution dialog box, click Deactivate.
7. Select the user solution you want to remove.
8. On the ribbon, click Delete and then click OK.

UNINSTALL AND REMOVE A USER SOLUTION IN WINDOWS POWERSHELL

You can also use Windows PowerShell to uninstall and remove a user solution:

```
Uninstall-SPUserSolution -Identity <SolutionFileName>
-Site <http://myserver.mydomain.local>

Remove-SPUserSolution -Identity <SolutionFileName>
-Site <http://myserver.mydomain.local>
```

where:

- *<SolutionFileName>* is the name of the solution file you uploaded to the site collection solution gallery.

- *<http://myserver.mydomain.local>* is the URL of the site collection where you want to use the user solution.

Farm Solution Management

Farm solutions are solution files that farm administrators upload and activate in the farm solution gallery. Farm solutions are not restricted by the sandbox. Therefore, you should be sure that a solution is well tested and trustworthy before you use it; otherwise, it could compromise security or stability and cause problems for your users.

UPLOAD A FARM SOLUTION

To upload a solution file to the farm solution list, you must use the *Add-SPSolution* Windows PowerShell cmdlet:

```
Add-SPSolution -LiteralPath <PathToSolutionFile>
```

where *<PathToSolutionFile>* is the location where you have stored the .wsp file. This can be on a local hard drive or on a shared folder.

INSTALL A FARM SOLUTION IN CENTRAL ADMINISTRATION

When the solution file is present in the farm solution list, use the following steps to install it:

1. In the Central Administration Quick Launch, click System Settings.
2. Under Farm Management, click Manage Farm Solutions.
3. Click the solution you want to install.
4. Review the configuration information and then click Deploy Solution.
5. Optionally, you can specify a date and time when the solution should deploy.
6. Click OK.

INSTALL A FARM SOLUTION IN WINDOWS POWERSHELL

You can also install an uploaded farm solution by using Windows PowerShell:

```
Install-SPSolution -Identity <SolutionFileName> -Time <DateTime> -GACDeployment
```

where:

- *<SolutionFileName>* is the name of the solution file you uploaded.
- *<DateTime>* is the date and time when you want the solution to be installed. If you omit the *–Time* parameter, the solution is installed immediately.

Some solutions created in Visual Studio by developers need components added to the Global Assembly Cache (GAC). When this is the case the developer should inform you and you must use the *–GACDeployment* parameter or the solution will not function fully. When no components need to be added to the Global Assembly Cache, you can omit this parameter.

UNINSTALL A FARM SOLUTION IN CENTRAL ADMINISTRATION

If a farm solution is no longer required, you can uninstall it from the farm by completing the following steps:

1. In the Central Administration Quick Launch, click System Settings.
2. Under Farm Management, click Manage Farm Solutions.
3. Click the solution you want to uninstall.
4. Click Retract Solution.
5. Optionally, you can specify a date and time when the solution will be uninstalled.
6. Click OK.

> **IMPORTANT REMOVING FARM SOLUTIONS**
>
> You can uninstall farm solutions in Central Administration but you cannot remove them from the farm. Farm solutions will remain in the farm solution list and any farm administrator can reinstall them. To remove a farm solution completely, you must use the Windows PowerShell *Remove-SPSolution* cmdlet as described in the next section.

UNINSTALL AND REMOVE A FARM SOLUTION IN WINDOWS POWERSHELL

In this example, Windows PowerShell cmdlets are used to uninstall a farm solution and then remove it completely:

```
Uninstall-SPSolution –Identity <SolutionFileName>
Remove-SPSolution –Identity <SolutionFileName>
```

where *<SolutionFileName>* is the name of the solution file you uploaded to the farm.

PRACTICE **Managing Features and Solutions**

Practices are designed to guide you through important procedures. The instructions in the Training Kit are high-level instructions that will challenge you to think carefully and to apply the procedures that are covered in this lesson and elsewhere in the Training Kit. If you need assistance, consult the detailed, step-by-step instructions in the Practice Answers on the companion media.

In this practice, you practice activating both features and solutions. You will also upload the user solution you created in the last practice and use a farm solution.

Prepare for the Practice

Before you perform this practice, ensure that your lab environment has been built according to the instructions found in the Introduction to this Training Kit. You must also have performed the practice in Lesson 1 of this chapter. You must be logged off of SP2010-WFE1 before beginning the exercises.

EXERCISE 1   Enable a Feature

In this exercise, you enable one of the built-in SharePoint features at the site collection level:

1. Use Internet Explorer to browse to ***http://teams.contoso.com/depts/marketing***.
2. Open the list of site collection scoped features.
3. Activate the Search Server Web Parts Feature.
4. Open the list of site scoped features.
5. Activate the Content Organizer feature.

EXERCISE 2   Upload and Activate a Site Template

In this exercise, you upload the site template you created in the first practice to the Marketing site collection. You also activate the solution:

1. In Internet Explorer, browse to the Marketing site collection solution gallery.
2. Upload the MarketingTools.wsp file from the Desktop to the solution gallery.
3. Activate the solution file.

EXERCISE 3   Create a Site from a Site Template

In this exercise, you create and test a new site in the Marketing site collection based on the Marketing Tools site template you created in Practice 1:

1. Create a new site in the Marketing site collection. Use the following settings and guidance:
   - Site Template: MarketingTools
   - Title: Marketing Tools
   - URL Name: marketingtools

2. Examine the site. Notice that master page you created is in use, and that the Leads and Follow Up Tasks lists are in place.

3. Add a new lead to the Leads list. The workflow creates a new task in the Follow Up Tasks list.

4. Close all windows and log off SP2010-WFE1.

EXERCISE 4   Upload and Activate a Farm Solution

In this exercise, you upload and activate a solution to the farm solution list. The solution file used is a simple tool that displays whether it is running inside or outside the sandbox:

1. Log on to SP2010-WFE1 as **CONTOSO\Administrator** with the password **Pa$$w0rd**.

2. View the list of farm solutions in Central Administration. It should be empty.

3. Use the Add-SPSolution cmdlet to add the DetectSandbox.wsp solution file to the farm solution list. This solution file is located at C:\70667TK\Practice Files\10_02\ DetectSandbox.wsp.

4. Refresh the list of farm solutions in Central Administration. The Detect Sandbox solution is displayed.

5. Close all windows and log off SP2010-WFE1.

6. Log on to SP2010-WFE1 as **CONTOSO\SP_Admin** with the password **Pa$$w0rd**.

7. Open the site collection at ***http://teams.contoso.com/depts/marketing***.

8. Go to the list of site collection features and activate the Detect Sandbox Web Part feature.

9. Go to the Marketing Tools site homepage.

10. Add the custom DetectorPart Web Part to the homepage.

11. Stop editing the page. The Sandbox Detector Web Part shows that it is operating outside the sandbox.

EXERCISE 5   Retract and Remove a Farm Solution

In this exercise, you retract and remove a farm solution:

1. In Central Administration, browse to the list of farm solutions.

2. Retract the detectsandbox.wsp solution.

3. Close all windows and log off SP2010-WFE1.

4. Log on to SP2010-WFE1 as **CONTOSO\Administrator** with the password **Pa$$w0rd**.

5. Open the SharePoint 2010 Management Shell and get the list of farm solutions.

6. Type a command to remove the detectsandbox.wsp solution.

7. Get the list of farm solutions again.

8. Close all programs and log off SP2010-WFE1.

Lesson Summary

- SharePoint Features are units of functionality that administrators can enable or disable.
- The feature scope defines where it is activated, who can activate it, and where its custom components can be installed.
- Each feature can have the site, site collection, web application, or farm scope.
- Administrators occasionally have to install features and often have to activate or deactivate them in different locations.
- Some features depend on other features to ensure that prerequisite functionality is in place.
- Solution files are single .wsp files that package many custom components for simple deployment in a SharePoint farm.
- Users can create a solution file by using the Save As Template tool.
- Developers can create a solution file by using Visual Studio.
- User solutions are deployed in a site collection solution gallery and are restricted by the sandbox.
- The sandbox ensures that a user solution cannot threaten stability or security.
- Farm solutions can only be deployed by farm administrators and are not restricted by the sandbox.
- You should ensure that farm solutions are trustworthy and thoroughly tested before you deploy them.

Lesson Review

You can use the following questions to test your knowledge of the information in Lesson 2, "Deploy and Manage Solutions and Features." The questions are also available on the companion media in a practice test if you prefer to review them in electronic form.

> **NOTE** **ANSWERS**
>
> Answers to these questions and explanations of why each answer choice is right or wrong are located in the "Answers" section at the end of the book.

1. You have a large SharePoint production environment. A developer has created and tested a Web Part and built it into a feature for deployment. You have installed and activated the feature on a web front-end server but not all users can see the Web Part in the Web Part gallery. What is the cause of this problem?

   A. The feature is created with the farm scope and you are not a farm administrator.

   B. The developer should have used the Save As Template tool in the browser to create the feature.

   C. The feature requires the *-GACDeployment* parameter to be used in Windows PowerShell.

   D. You must install the feature on all web front-end servers, not just one.

   E. The developer must create a solution file for deployment.

2. A developer is creating a custom solution that will be used in many sites throughout your global organization. She wants users to be able to install and activate the solution themselves without involving administrators. Which of the following capabilities can she include in her solution? (Choose all that apply.)

   A. A Web Part that displays information from the local site collection

   B. A Web Part that displays information from another site collection

   C. A Web Part that displays information obtained from a newsfeed web service on the Internet

   D. A Web Part that writes logging information to the hard disk

   E. A master page that imposes a look and feel on the solution site

Lesson 3: Support Custom Solutions

Administrators throughout your SharePoint organization may need to reconfigure objects to support the requirements of custom solutions. A good example is the Search service application: if you want users to be able to search the contents of a custom site column, you must reconfigure the crawler to index that column. Users expect words to be indexed regardless of which column they appear in. If they know a word is used in an item but it doesn't appear in search results because the custom column is not indexed, they may become disillusioned with the enterprise search tools and stop using them. In this lesson, you'll see what administrative tasks you must complete to integrate custom solutions fully with all aspects of the SharePoint farm. To optimize SharePoint for a new custom solution requires both a thorough understanding of SharePoint, such as that which you have acquired while studying for SharePoint exams, and a thorough understanding of the custom solution itself.

> **After this lesson, you will be able to:**
> - Optimize a SharePoint farm to support a custom solution.
> - Understand the User Code Host service.
> - Balance the load of running user solutions across multiple SharePoint servers.
> - Plan and implement resource usage quotas to constrain user solutions.
> - Authorize users to manage user solutions.
> - Authorize users to manage features and farm solutions.
> - Plan staging and testing for any customization.
> - Configure the Search service application to support custom solutions.
>
> **Estimated Lesson Time: 40 minutes**

Introducing Supporting Custom Solutions

In Lesson 2, you saw how administrators upload, enable, disable, and remove features, user solutions, and farm solutions. These are the most common tasks for administrators because they manage customizations, but this is not the end of the story.

As soon as you have installed SharePoint, the farm is ready to host custom features and solutions and it will usually perform well at this task. However, in unusual circumstances, you may find that the default configuration is not optimal and some tuning is required. This lesson describes how to tune your farm in a variety of ways to ensure trouble-free hosting of SharePoint Composites, custom features, and custom solutions.

An Example Scenario: A Rich Web Content Management Solution

To explore the need for optimization further, let's consider a hypothetical scenario. Suppose that Contoso Ltd. wants to host its public website on SharePoint but have a number of specialist requirements and want to include a lot of rich content. Their development team has created the following components:

- Custom content types that describe each of the 25 product ranges in the Contoso catalog. These include the custom ProductID and PartNumber site columns.

- Twenty-five Silverlight applications to engage users as they explore each of the product ranges.

- A master page that includes two of these Silverlight applications in the page header and the left-side navigation.

- A custom field control that editors can use to upload product photos and that displays a slide show to site visitors.

- A custom Web Part that displays product videos when users click links in some of the Silverlight applications.

The first thing to notice about this solution is that no part of it breaks the limitations placed on user solutions. For example, none of the custom components accesses data from a web service or writes directly to the file system. Where possible, both developers and administrators will prefer to create user solutions rather than farm solutions. Developers find it easier to deploy and update their solutions and Administrators have the extra reassurance of the sandbox to prevent instability. In this case, therefore, a user solution is possible and preferable.

However, many of the customizations included are resource-intensive. If website traffic is high, it's quite possible that the default resource quota for user solutions will be exhausted. If this happens, the user solution will be temporarily disabled and site visitors will find that all the most engaging functionality in the site does not work. Remember that the default resource quotas are designed for situations in which several user solutions run simultaneously on farms with many SharePoint sites and service applications. Contoso, however, has a dedicated SharePoint farm specifically to host the company website. Therefore, you should significantly increase the resource usage quotas to enable this intensive user solution.

You should also give some thought to permissions for user solution management. Although developers should be able to deploy their own solutions in the testing and staging farms, the production farm should be more carefully controlled. Your team might decide to authorize only administrators to deploy user solutions or perhaps only a subset of senior developers.

Finally, it is clearly important that site visitors can locate products by their Product ID or Part Number. You must reconfigure the crawler to index these custom fields. You might also want to display them in search results.

As you can see, the administrative tasks described in this section can make a huge difference to the behavior of a custom application built on SharePoint.

Supporting User Solutions

As we have seen in previous lessons, when a solution file is uploaded to a site collection solution gallery, it will run within the sandbox and is prevented from taking actions that could jeopardize security and stability. The sandbox is so named because it provides a safe environment in which immature, untested, and untrustworthy code cannot cause damage to the SharePoint farm. In this section, you will see how the sandbox is implemented, how to govern resource quotas, and how to influence the way quota points are calculated. You will also see how to isolate and load balance user solutions to make the best use of your server hardware.

The Architecture of the Sandbox

To manage the sandbox well, you must understand how it is built and implemented in the SharePoint architecture. Its components are shown in Figure 10-6.

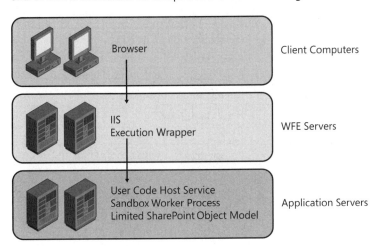

FIGURE 10-6 The architecture of the sandbox

As you can see, given enough servers it is possible to separate the majority of the sandbox architecture onto a separate, dedicated application server. If you do this, only a simple execution wrapper runs on the web front-end servers. This wrapper receives calls from the IIS worker process, looks up the location of the User Code Host Service, and forwards the request to the right application server. On that application server, the user code host service verifies that sandboxed solutions are permitted on this application server and forwards the request to the sandbox worker process. This worker process isolates the user solution and ensures that it can call only the limited subset of the SharePoint object model. This subset excludes all classes that have security implications or may affect stability when poorly used.

Planning Resource Usage Quotas

In Chapter 4, "Administering and Securing SharePoint Content," you learned how to set quotas on site collections. These quotas limit the total amount of data that can be stored in a site collection and are vitally important because they alert administrators to pending disk consumption issues. When you set the site collection quotas, you can also set the sandbox resource usage quotas that restrict user solutions and prevent them from overusing server resources and causing contention.

By default, each user solution can score up to 300 points in a day. If the solution exceeds this number it is disabled. Site collection administrators are alerted if any user solution exceeds 100 point in a day. This gives time for administrators to take action before functionality is disabled and users start to receive error messages.

To set quotas appropriately, you should first understand how these points are scored. Table 10-2 lists all the indicators that are involved and the value that scores a single point.

TABLE 10-2 Sandbox Point Scoring

INDICATOR	RESOURCES TO SCORE 1 POINT	DESCRIPTION
Abnormal Process Termination	1	If a single process terminates unexpectedly, a point is scored.
CPU Execution Time	3600	If the solution uses too much CPU time, a point is scored.
Critical Exception Count	3600	If the number of fatal errors exceeds 3600, a point is scored.
Invocation Count	100	If a solution is invoked more than 100 times, a point is scored.
Percent Processor Time	85	If the solution uses more than 85 percent of the processor time, a point is scored.
Process CPU Cycles	100 Billion	If the solution uses more than 100 billion CPU cycles, a point is scored.
Process Handle Count	10,000	If the solution process has more than 10,000 handles, a point is scored.
Process IO Bytes	10 Million	If the solution uses more than 10 MB I/O, a point is scored.

INDICATOR	RESOURCES TO SCORE 1 POINT	DESCRIPTION
Process Thread Count	10,000	If the solution uses more than 10,000 threads, a point is scored.
Process Virtual Bytes	100 Million	If the solution users more than 100 MB of memory, a point is scored.
SharePoint Database Query Count	20	If the solution queries the SharePoint content database more than 20 times, a point is scored.
SharePoint Database Query Time	120 ms	If a SharePoint content database query takes longer than 120 ms, a point is scored.
Unhandled Exception Count	50	If more than 50 unhandled exceptions occur, a point is scored.
Unresponsive Process Count	2	If a solution has more than two unresponsive processes, a point is scored.

These indicators and the default threshold are set to reflect a typical server running SharePoint. It is not possible for an administrator to adjust the indicators and thresholds, but developers can make adjustments through the SharePoint object model.

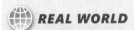 **REAL WORLD**

Alistair Matthews

In fact it's not quite true that administrators cannot adjust the metrics that are used to calculate resource usage points. Because the SharePoint object model has classes that can make these adjustments and you can call object model classes from Windows PowerShell scripts, you can write a Windows PowerShell script to adjust the metrics. However, it is strongly recommended that you do not make such adjustments unless you have an overriding need to do so. If you want to know more about this topic, and you don't mind reading some C# code, see "Developing, Deploying, and Monitoring Sandboxed Solutions in SharePoint 2010" in the MSDN magazine at *http://msdn.microsoft.com/en-us/magazine/ee335711.aspx*.

Implementing Resource Usage Quotas

To administer resource usage quotas you can use settings on the site collection in Central Administration. You must be a farm administrator to change these settings. It is not sufficient to have site collection administrative permissions.

SET THE RESOURCE USAGE QUOTA FOR A SITE COLLECTION

To set the resource usage quotas for user solutions within a site collection, follow these steps:

1. In the Central Administration Quick Launch, click Application Management.

2. Under Site Collections, click Configure Quotas And Locks.

3. In the Site Collection section, ensure that the site collection you want to administer appears in the Site Collection box.

4. Under Site Quota Information, in the Limit Maximum Usage text box, type the number of points you want to allow for each solution.

5. If you want administrators to be alerted when a certain number of points are reached, select the Send Warning Email check box and type the threshold in the text box.

6. You can also review the current number of points scored and the daily average for the last 14 days.

7. Click OK.

Isolating and Load Balancing Sandboxed Solution Code

Administrators can choose where to place and run the user solution worker process. All user solution code runs within this process; you can take two approaches to configuring its location:

- **Local Mode**   In this approach, the worker process runs on the web front-end server that received the request. If you have more than one web front-end server in your farm, the user solution code will be load balanced by whatever means you use to load balance front-end servers. This is the default mode. For more information about load balancing front-end servers, see Chapter 11, "Implementing Business Continuity."

- **Remote Mode**   In this approach, the worker process runs on a separate application server. Remote mode can be more efficient because when the first request is received, the user solution is loaded into memory. When subsequent requests arrive, the user solution is already running and can respond more quickly. The application server must be running the Sandboxed Code Service.

> **IMPORTANT   MODES CANNOT BE MIXED**
>
> Since the worker process location mode is a farm-wide setting, you cannot mix local mode and remote mode in a single SharePoint farm. Furthermore, you must be a SharePoint farm administrator to control this setting.

Local mode requires no administrative changes, as it is the default, and you should consider that even in this approach, the sandbox restricts user solutions to safe operations. There should be no possibility for a solution to compromise security or stability.

Remote mode, by contrast, requires administrative time to set up and—if you want to use dedicated servers—extra hardware to host the worker process. However, many administrators will consider that the extra isolation it affords for user solutions is worth the extra cost. Furthermore, by using several dedicated servers, you can create an extremely scalable environment for user solutions that can handle the most intensive customizations.

When a request for a user solution arrives at a web front-end server, the front-end server checks the list of application servers that run the Sandboxed Code Service. If this is the first request for that solution, the front-end server sends the request to the application server with the least current load. The user solution is started on this server and responds to the request. When subsequent requests arrive for the same user solution, they are automatically sent by front-end servers to the application server that is already running that user solution. This is known as *solution affinity*.

SET THE USER SOLUTION EXECUTION MODE FOR A SHAREPOINT FARM

A farm administrator can set the execution mode for an entire SharePoint farm by taking the following steps:

1. In the Central Administration Quick Launch, click System Settings.
2. Under Farm Management, click Manage User Solutions.
3. Under Load Balancing, if you want to use local mode, select All Sandboxed Code Runs On The Same Machine As A Request.
4. If you want to use remote mode, select Requests To Run Sandboxed Code Are Routed By Solution Affinity.
5. Click OK.

CONFIGURE A SERVER TO RUN THE SANDBOXED CODE SERVICE

For remote mode, you must ensure that the Sandboxed Code Service is running on at least one server in your farm. To enable the service, use the following procedure:

1. In the Central Administration Quick Launch, click System Settings.
2. Under Servers, click Manage Services On Server.
3. In the Server selection box, choose the server where you want the Sandboxed Code Service to run.
4. Scroll down the list of services to locate the Microsoft SharePoint Foundation Sandboxed Code Service.
5. In the Action column, click Start.

Security and Stability Considerations

Administrators and system architects are responsible for providing the stable platform on which custom solutions run. Security is always an important factor to consider when designing a stable system because, if permissions are too weak, malicious users or unintentional administration mistakes can result in system downtime.

Permissions for Managing Features and Solutions

Both SharePoint features and farm solutions run outside the sandbox and do not benefit from its protection. There are many ways in which features and farm solutions could interfere with business continuity and cause failures and system downtime. For example:

- Custom components can write information directly to the file system if they are outside the sandbox. If a poorly written component does this intensively, it could fill a hard disk and cause a server to halt.

- Custom components can run with elevated permissions. A poorly written or deliberately malicious custom component can reconfigure farm-level settings and interrupt service to users.

- Custom components can use any class in the SharePoint object model. Some SharePoint classes, such as *SPFarm*, are extremely powerful and enable callers to make drastic changes to the SharePoint configuration.

Therefore, it is extremely important to carefully control who can upload and activate features and solutions. If you do not take such precautions, untested, unproven, and untrustworthy code can end up running on your SharePoint farm. Table 10-3 lists who can manage features at different scopes and farm solutions.

TABLE 10-3 Groups for Feature and Farm Management

TASK	SCOPE	REQUIRED MEMBERSHIP
Upload a feature	Farm	Farm Administrators
Activate a feature	Farm	Farm Administrators
	Web Application	Farm Administrators
	Site Collection	Site Collection Administrator or Site Collection Owner
	Site	Site Owner or Site Administrator
Upload a farm solution	Farm	Farm Administrator
Activate a farm solution	Farm	Farm Administrator

RESTRICT ACCESS TO THE USER SOLUTION GALLERY

User solutions are stored in a specialized library at the site collection level. You can assign permissions to this gallery in the same way you would for any other document library in SharePoint.

By default the permissions for the solutions gallery are inherited from the top-level site permissions. If you want to modify these permissions, you must break this inheritance. To assign access to the solutions gallery, take the following steps:

1. Browse to the top-level site in the site collection you want to administer.
2. Click Site Actions and then click Site Settings.
3. Under Galleries, click Solutions.
4. On the ribbon, click the Library tab.
5. In the Settings section, click Library Settings.
6. Under Permissions And Management, click Permissions For This Gallery.
7. On the ribbon, click Stop Inheriting Permissions.
8. In the Message from Webpage, click OK.
9. Click Grant Permissions.
10. In the Users/Groups text box, type the name of the group you want to assign permissions to.
11. Click the Check Names button.
12. Choose your permission level. To upload solution files, users must have at least Contribute permission.
13. Click OK.

> **NOTE PERMISSIONS AND OTHER GALLERIES**
> You can use similar steps to assign permissions to the master page gallery and the Web Part gallery. In this way you can restrict who can make these other types of custom components.

Testing and Staging Customizations

Custom solutions in SharePoint are powerful and flexible but can cause problems. A poorly written solution can malfunction and deny users access to the custom functionality and other parts of the SharePoint system. To weed out poor code from sound and robust code, you must implement a thorough testing regime.

The sandbox helps to mitigate any problems caused by user solutions so you may consider publishing less thoroughly tested code. A sandboxed solution cannot crash SharePoint or Windows processes, compromise security, or overuse server resources and cause contentions. If a sandboxed solution fails it only affects itself. However, sandboxed solutions can become popular, widely used, and sometimes critical to productivity. Therefore, when failures can prevent or hinder productivity, testing is still important.

Development methodologies, such as the Microsoft Solution Framework and Agile, include detailed recommendations for testing and staging. Three separate environments are frequently required:

- **The development farm**   This is the SharePoint farm developers use to create code and solve problems. Sometimes developers install SharePoint on their own computers or use Hyper-V, VMware, or other virtualization technologies for these purposes. In other cases, there may be a dedicated development farm for the entire development team. Because this environment runs untested code, many failures are expected.

- **The testing farm**   As a solution reaches completion and functionality is completed, an alpha or beta testing period begins. Bugs are identified and eliminated. Stress testing determines the scalability of the solution. Tested should be completed in a dedicated SharePoint farm that resembles the production environment as closely as the budget will allow.

- **The staging farm**   Staging differs from testing in that the contents of the staging farm should closely resemble the production farm. In other words, you test your solution not only with SharePoint but also with the documents, items, and media stored in your production environment. The staging farm should closely match the production farm.

The number of staging and testing steps you actually run depends on the budget you have for development and the expected impacts of any failures. Larger companies with many users depending on SharePoint will invest in extensive tests before deployment. However, even small businesses with tiny budgets should test custom solutions before deployment on a production farm.

Configuring Search to Support Customizations

In Chapter 7, "Administering SharePoint Search," you learn about the very flexible and tunable search systems available in SharePoint. When you develop and deploy custom SharePoint Composites, solutions, and other unique components, you should always consider whether to reconfigure search to better index and query custom content. Think about the following refinements:

- **New managed properties**   If you deploy or create new site columns and content types, users often expect their values to be searchable. You should consider adding managed properties to the search configuration for each new site column.

- **New search scopes**   Consider whether users might need a dedicated search scope for your solution. For example, if it consists of a single customized SharePoint site, might users need to search for results only in this site? If so, create a search scope for the site.

- **New search pages**   A custom solution, especially a site definition or site template, might require its own search page, or the search box Web Part on its master page.

- **New keywords and best bets**   Custom solutions, with a dedicated purpose, often become the best place to find information on a topic. For example, if your solution manages HR information, you might need a best bet to direct users to it when they search for "Employee ID."

- **New refinement panel filters**   Like keywords and best bets, refinement panel filters can be used to direct users to the right information. For example, a refinement panel filter can enable users to drill down to results based on values in a custom site column.

- **FAST Search** The extra capabilities included in the FAST search engine may assist users of your new solution. For example, if the solution includes product photographs, visual best bets—which are only available with FAST—may help users.

For more details about these refinements and step-by-step implementation procedures, see Chapter 7.

PRACTICE Supporting Custom Solutions

Practices are designed to guide you through important procedures. The instructions in the Training Kit are high-level instructions that will challenge you to think carefully and to apply the procedures that are covered in this lesson and elsewhere in the Training Kit. If you need assistance, consult the detailed, step-by-step instructions in the Practice Answers on the companion media.

In this practice, you administer resource usage quotas and set up remote mode load balancing for the Sandbox Code Service.

Prepare for the Practice

Before you perform this practice, ensure that your lab environment has been built according to the instructions found in the Introduction to this Training Kit. You must also have performed the practice in Lesson 2 of this chapter. You must be logged off of SP2010-WFE1 before beginning the exercises.

EXERCISE 1 Set Resource Usage Quotas

In this exercise, you set a large resource usage quota for user solutions in the Marketing site collection:

1. Log on to SP2010-WFE1 as **CONTOSO\SP_Admin** with the password **Pa$$w0rd**.
2. Open Application Management in Central Administration.
3. Configure quotas and locks for the Marketing site collection in the Contoso Teams web application. Use the following settings and guidance:
   - Limit Maximum Usage to: 500 points
   - Send Warning Email When Usage Per Day Reaches: 200 points
4. In Internet Explorer, browse to the Marketing site collection.
5. Open the site collection solutions gallery. Notice that the new resource quota applies.

EXERCISE 2 Examine Resource Usage Quota Indicators

In this exercise, you use Windows PowerShell to examine the indicators that SharePoint uses to calculate resource quota points:

1. Type the following command in the SharePoint 2010 Management Shell:

   ```
   [Microsoft.SharePoint.Administration.SPUserCodeService]::Local.ResourceMeasures
   ```

2. Examine the results.

EXERCISE 3   Lock a User Solution

Farm administrators can block a user solution to ensure that it is never used in a SharePoint farm. In this exercise, you use this tool:

1. Use Central Administration to manage user solutions.

2. Block the user solution file you created in Practice 1 and saved to the Desktop.

EXERCISE 4   Enable Remote Mode Load Balancing

In this exercise, you enable remote mode load balancing for the SharePoint farm and enable the Sandboxed Code Service:

1. Use Central Administration to manage user solutions.

2. Select Requests to Run Sandboxed Code are Routed by Solution Affinity.

3. Configure the Microsoft SharePoint Foundation Sandboxed Code Service to run on the SP2010-WFE1 server.

4. Close all windows and log off SP2010-WFE1.

Lesson Summary

- Custom components, whether created in place or deployed by features and solutions, add unique functionality and frequently can only perform at their best when administrators reconfigure the farm.

- You must thoroughly understand both SharePoint and the customization to configure the farm optimally.

- Resource usage quotas are set on site collections and close down user solutions that overuse resources to prevent contentions.

- Each user solution scores points as it uses resources. If it exceeds the defined limit in 24 hours, SharePoint closes it.

- You must ensure that the resource usage quotas, which are intended to restrict poorly written user solutions, do not restrict solutions that are well written but resource-intensive by design.

- Consider dedicating one or more application servers to run the user solution worker process in remote mode for extra isolation and scalability.

- Carefully control who can manage farm solutions, users solutions, and features by assigning group memberships.

- Restrict who can upload and activate user solutions, master pages, and Web Parts by assigning group memberships or direct permissions on galleries.

- Customizations that run outside the sandbox must be thoroughly tested to ensure stability and security.

- User solutions, which are restricted by the sandbox, can fail and impact user productivity. You should test them where possible.

- When you create or deploy a custom component, reassess your search configuration to ensure that it serves the customized farm optimally.

Lesson Review

You can use the following questions to test your knowledge of the information in Lesson 3, "Support Custom Solutions." The questions are also available on the companion media in a practice test if you prefer to review them in electronic form.

> **NOTE ANSWERS**
>
> Answers to these questions and explanations of why each answer choice is right or wrong are located in the "Answers" section at the end of the book.

1. Your organization manufactures engine parts. Your development team has created a SharePoint user solution for the engineering department to manage the product development process. This solution includes new content types to store CAD drawings, workflows, product photography, and videos. You want to ensure that this intensive solution runs as fast as possible without contending for resources with the other sites in your SharePoint farm. Which of the following steps should you take? (Choose all that apply.)

   A. Decrease the server resource usage quota for user solutions in the appropriate site collection.

   B. Increase the server resource usage quota for user solutions in the appropriate site collection.

   C. Enable local mode for the user solution worker process.

   D. Enable remote mode for the user solution worker process.

   E. Start the Sandboxed Code Service on one or more dedicated application servers.

   F. Use Windows PowerShell to adjust the indicators used to score resource usage points in the sandbox.

2. A developer has created a solution file for deployment in your SharePoint farm. You would like to deploy the solution in the sandbox for the extra stability and reassurance it includes but you want to ensure that it does not exceed the resource usage quota. Which of the following events score a resource usage point? (Choose all that apply.)

   A. A query against the SharePoint content database.

   B. An abnormal process termination.

   C. Use of 90 percent of the processor time.

   D. A query against a web service hosted on the Internet.

   E. A process stops responding.

Chapter Review

To further practice and reinforce the skills you learned in this chapter, you can perform the following tasks:

- Review the chapter summary.
- Review the list of key terms introduced in this chapter.
- Complete the case scenarios. These scenarios set up real-world situations involving the topics of this chapter and ask you to create a solution.
- Complete the suggested practices.
- Take a practice test.

Chapter Summary

- You can customize SharePoint 2010 in many ways to adapt it to the needs of your company or team.
- Many customizations can be made by power users or administrators. In this way, you can adapt SharePoint without waiting for developer time.
- Some advanced customizations, such as custom workflow activities, can only be added by developers using Visual Studio.
- The sandbox restricts user solutions to prevent them from reducing the farm's stability and security.
- You can use the browser to create your own content types, Web Part pages, lists, libraries, and other custom objects.
- You can use SharePoint Designer to create workflows, master pages, BCS connections, and other custom objects.
- You can modify any default form by using InfoPath 2010.
- Administrators can upload new features and solutions by using Windows PowerShell and activate them in Central Administration.

Key Terms

The following terms were introduced in this chapter. Do you know what they mean?

- SharePoint Features
- SharePoint Farm Solutions
- SharePoint User Solutions
- SharePoint Composites
- Site Templates

- Site Definitions
- Sandbox
- Master Page
- Workflow
- Web Parts
- Web Part Pages
- Web Part Zones

Case Scenario: Deploying a Third-Party Custom Relationship Management Solution

In the following case scenario, you will apply what you've learned about subjects of this chapter. You can find answers to these questions in the "Answers" section at the end of this book.

Customer Relationship Management (CRM) systems come in many forms. Your company is evaluating a CRM system from a third-party developer. The system is design to run on SharePoint, which you have already implemented and are using very successfully. You want to ensure that the CRM system runs rapidly but does not threaten stability.

1. You want to know if the solution can be run in the sandbox. What should you ask the developers about their system?

2. How should you configure your SharePoint solution to maximize the scalability of the CRM system in the sandbox?

Suggested Practices

To help you successfully master the exam objectives presented in this chapter, complete the following tasks.

Practice 1: Create Your Own Custom User Solution

Within the limits of a single chapter, it's not possible to demonstrate fully the capabilities of SharePoint customizations. To explore custom solutions more fully, create one or more of your own custom solutions that addresses a specific need within your organization. Create such a solution in a dedicated development farm:

1. Interview stakeholders about their needs. Include potential users, IT staff who must administer the solution, and managers who need performance data and other analysis.

2. Begin by planning site columns and content types. Create lists and libraries to store your users' information.

3. Tune the user interface to be as responsive and streamlined as possible. In particular, you should spend more time on the master page than was possible in Lesson 1 and add company branding.

4. Create more complex workflows that model actual business processes. Explore the available actions and add steps that send emails, log to history lists, and wait for user input.

5. Create a site template that encapsulates your solution. Use this to create the solution in testing, staging, and eventually production farms.

Practice 2: Configure Sandboxed Code Load Balancing in a Multi-Server Farm

In Lesson 3, you enabled remote mode load balancing for sandboxed user solutions. However, in a single server environment, it is not possible to load balance sandboxed code across multiple SharePoint application servers:

1. Install and configure a SharePoint farm with one or more dedicated web front-end servers.

2. Add two or more application servers to host the Microsoft SharePoint Foundation Sandboxed Code Service.

3. Enable remote mode load balancing for the farm.

4. Start the Microsoft SharePoint Foundation Sandboxed Code Service on all the application servers.

Take a Practice Test

The practice tests on this book's companion media offer many options. For example, you can test yourself on only the lesson review content, or you can test yourself on all the 70-667 certification exam objectives. You can set up the test so that it closely simulates the experience of taking a certification exam, or you can set it up in study mode so that you can look at the correct answers and explanations after you answer each question.

> **MORE INFO** **PRACTICE TESTS**
>
> For details about all the practice test options available, see the "How to Use the Practice Tests" section in this book's Introduction.

CHAPTER 11

Implementing Business Continuity

The extensive and versatile content management facilities built into SharePoint Server 2010 make it a business-critical system for most organizations that implement it. If you use SharePoint as a document management system, for example, authors and editors may not be able to do their jobs when the system is unavailable. If you use SharePoint to run your website, users may not be able to get information, buy your products, or contact you when the system is down. Therefore, you should ensure that such times are minimized. By providing multiple failover systems you can build a SharePoint farm that resists all but the most catastrophic failures. By implementing a well-designed backup and restore plan, you can ensure that even in the worst circumstances, the service interruption is as short as possible. In this chapter you'll see how to plan, implement, and run such a farm.

Exam objectives in this chapter:

- Configure SharePoint farms.
- Back up and restore a SharePoint environment.

Lessons in this chapter:

Before You Begin

To complete the lessons in this chapter, you must build your lab environment according to the instructions found in the Introduction to this Training Kit and have done the following:

- Performed the practices in Chapter 1
- Performed the practices in Chapter 5

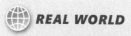

REAL WORLD

Alistair Matthews

Business continuity is the most thankless and yet perhaps the most important of the IT department's responsibilities. Like a soccer goalkeeper, when you do an excellent job few will notice, but everyone will be on your case when things go wrong. All you can do is prepare very thoroughly!

Creating a highly available network, for example, is expensive and requires extensive expertise. When it works well, nobody notices because SharePoint is always there when they need it. In fact they will take it for granted. For this reason, some budget holders argue against the extra expense. In discussions like that, you must stand your ground for the necessary funds or at least point out that downtime will be a direct consequence of cutting corners.

Backup and restore operations also consume the day-to-day budget. Tapes and other media cost money but, more important, administrators often spend a significant amount of time configuring and verifying backups and rehearsing disaster recovery. This money will be considered a good investment when you can restore the farm in two or three hours and people can get back to work quickly. If you are tempted to take shortcuts, consider the possible consequences if you cannot restore all the content!

Lesson 1: Configure High Availability

Any complex, server-based IT system relies on an extensive hardware and software infrastructure. Even if your software and hardware is of the highest quality, there are inevitably multiple points of failure and many things that can go wrong. In addition, malicious users and hackers will often attack and try to compromise your system. You can configure SharePoint to continue running when many types of failure occur by adding failover components and redundancy. You can also protect SharePoint from attack with edge-security and antivirus solutions. In this lesson you'll see how to take steps to create a highly available SharePoint farm.

After this lesson, you will be able to:

- Understand the failures that threaten stability and availability.
- Plan hardware architectures that resist failures.
- Plan and implement SharePoint components to support high availability.
- Plan SQL Server clusters and database mirroring.
- Monitor a SharePoint farm to preempt failures.

Estimated Lesson Time: 70 minutes

What Is High Availability?

Users and board members would like a system to be available all the time and they often assume that this is the case. This is called *continuous availability,* but it is difficult and very expensive to achieve because many threats can interrupt service, including:

- Server hardware failures

  Disk faults are among the most common hardware failures, perhaps because of the moving parts involved and the high continuous load to which disks must typically respond. Network cards also frequently cause problems, and memory and CPUs sometime fail, albeit less frequently.

- Network hardware failures

  Access to SharePoint also requires a functional network. This involves hardware such as routers, switches, and long cable runs. Wi-Fi networks rely on powered wireless hubs.

- Power interruptions

  Most hardware in your system requires mains power, also referred to as *alternating-current electric power.* Laptops can run for perhaps two or three hours on battery power. Uninterruptable Power Supplies (UPSs) can prevent service interruption for a short time but often only grant servers time to shut down cleanly and avoid data loss.

- WAN connection drop-outs

  If a user is at a remote location, such as a regional office, at home, or at a client site, a WAN technology is required to connect to the SharePoint server. Microwave links are sometimes susceptible to bad weather, ADSL connection equipment can fail, and telephone wires can be damaged.

- Software faults, such as memory leaks

  You should ensure that software is thoroughly tested before deployment. However, occasionally faults may slip through the net and cause interruptions by over consuming resources or crashing processes.

- Contention for resources, such as disk space

  A server that runs out of disk space will not be able to respond to user requests until you free some space or add capacity. If too much load is placed on processors or memory, the interruption in service is temporary but should still be considered critical.

- Scheduled maintenance tasks

  Windows Server 2008 requires far fewer reboots than earlier versions. However, sometimes an expected maintenance task, such as the installation of a software update, requires a reboot to complete.

- Configuration mistakes

  When you diagnose a system failure, you should ask yourself what has recently changed. Often an administrator has just made a mistaken setting. For example, a stricter firewall configuration may be considered essential but may result in SharePoint servers that cannot communicate with each other, with clients, or with database servers.

- Malicious attacks

  When you have a connection to the Internet, you are open to all kinds of malicious attacks and must ensure that edge security systems are tight. However, do not discount the possibility of an attack that originates within your local area network.

As you can see, problems have many potential sources, each of which can prevent users from doing their jobs. With a well-designed SharePoint farm, you may suffer no interruptions in service in a given year, but most experienced system administrators would not guarantee this as part of their Service Level Agreement (SLA).

When you host SharePoint or other services for tenant companies, the contract customers sign almost always includes an SLA that guarantees a certain percentage of availability. If you do not meet this percentage, you breach the contract and customers may withhold subscriptions. That has an immediate impact on your bottom line. Even within a single organization, IT often commits to an SLA and faces sanctions if it is not met.

Consider the percentages of availability, shown in Table 11-1, that are common in SLAs.

TABLE 11-1 Availability Levels

NAME	PERCENTAGE AVAILABILITY	PERMITTED DOWNTIME PER YEAR
Three Nines	99.9 percent	8.76 hours
Four Nines	99.99 percent	52.6 minutes
Five Nines	99.999 percent	5.26 minutes

A highly available system is usually defined as one that ensures a guaranteed agreed level of service over a contractual period. The period is usually a year and the level you guarantee depends on the budget you have for hardware and software. In this lesson, you will see how to design and implement a SharePoint farm that guarantees a high level of availability.

The Importance of High Availability in SharePoint

SharePoint can take many different roles in an organization. You must carefully consider what SharePoint does for your users and assess the consequences of downtime before you plan and budget for a given availability level. SharePoint often provides one or more of the following services:

- **Document Management** SharePoint stores documents as authors and editors write, review, and amend them. When SharePoint is unavailable, users cannot check out documents and edit them and therefore become unproductive. Authors and editors who have a document checked out and downloaded can continue to work on it. However, they will usually want to upload a version at least once a day.

- **Records Management** SharePoint stores complete versions of documents and other content for compliance with legislation. When SharePoint is down, new records and versions cannot be created. A record also cannot be discovered for use in a court case, for example. Although this is a business-critical system, short service interruptions may have less impact. However, long interruptions may cause legal problems for the organization.

- **Intranet Portal Management** SharePoint hosts portal websites on the intranet for internal users. These sites may include project management tools, scheduling tools, sales dashboards, business intelligence dashboards, and many other facilities. When SharePoint is down, therefore, the impact on productivity can be varied and extensive.

- **Extranet Portal Management** SharePoint hosts portal websites for both internal users and partner organizations. When SharePoint is down, in addition to the impact on internal user productivity, partners are also prevented from working.

- **Web Content Management** SharePoint hosts the customer-facing website and enables authors and editors to make managed changes. When SharePoint is down, a principal line of communication with customers is interrupted. If you sell through your website, the impact on revenue is immediate. Even if sales do not happen through the website, customers quickly locate and communicate with your competitors. Authors and editors cannot do their jobs.

- **Search** SharePoint indexes and queries content in SharePoint, file shares, databases, and other stores throughout your organization. When SharePoint is down, users cannot locate documents and records they need. Users can continue work with existing knowledge, but research, learning, and reference location is impossible.

Each of these services should be considered business-critical and, given that SharePoint often provides several of these services simultaneously, you can see that SharePoint is usually at the heart of a business's IT infrastructure. Even if you do not have an SLA to work to, the availability of the SharePoint farm should be among your highest priorities.

IMPORTANT **SCHEDULED AND UNSCHEDULED DOWNTIME**

Some SLAs distinguish between scheduled and unscheduled downtime. Scheduled downtime consists of service interruptions for maintenance tasks such as hotfix installation, service pack installation, and hardware upgrades. Scheduled downtime is predictable and expected. Service interruptions caused by power failures, process crashes, poorly tested custom code, memory leaks, and other accidents are considered unscheduled.

If you provide SharePoint services to users in one time zone, for example, you can regularly take the farm offline at low-demand times such as Sunday evening to perform maintenance and thus improve reliability at peak times. However, when you have a large, globally distributed user base, demand may simply never drop that low, and scheduled downtime may have the same impact as unscheduled downtime. The nature of your business and users will determine whether you can schedule regular maintenance. Your SLA should reflect this.

NOTE **AVAILABILITY AND OFFICE WORKSPACE 2010**

By configuring Office Workspace 2010 to synchronize with SharePoint sites, users can easily take all the content in a site with them when they disconnect. Workspace is designed to enable users to be productive on the train, at home, at client sites, and at other times when a connection to SharePoint is unavailable.

You should not consider Workspace to be an availability solution because a interruption in SharePoint service will count as downtime, even if users can continue to work in Workspace. It is not, therefore, a means to meet your SLA commitments. However, by installing Workspace on all client computers and educating users on synchronization, you can lessen the impact of both scheduled and unscheduled maintenance. Users can make changes to documents, media, and list items on their laptops and desktops, and upload them when SharePoint comes back online.

The Importance of Good Security

High security and high availability are generally considered as separate goals in system design. However, it is important to note that many successful malicious attacks result in downtime. Consider the following examples of attacks:

- **Denial of Service** Any type of malicious attack that aims to interrupt a system's service to users is known as a *Denial of Service (DoS) attack.* Any successful DoS attack will cause downtime and immediately threaten your SLA. A common and sophisticated attack, for example, involves infecting thousands of client computers on the Internet with a virus. After infection the code runs, but only awaits commands from a central computer. At such a command, all the infected computers may make requests of a target website. Such a group of infected computers is called a *botnet.* Large botnets, which often include tens of thousands of computers, deny service to legitimate users by flooding a site with traffic.

- **Virus Infection** Less sophisticated viruses, or those with different intentions, deny service by infecting computers directly. After infection, such viruses may hog CPU and memory resources, overwrite critical hard disk files, or crash critical processes. Direct infection usually requires malicious code to be executed on a computer, so you can protect your SharePoint server by protecting it with firewalls and a good virus scanner.

- **Website Hijack** Malicious users often like to penetrate a web server's defenses and replace its content with their own message. Although HTTP functionality remains in place, this is still considered a DoS attack, because users cannot reach the content intended for them.

It is largely true to say that an insecure system cannot be highly available.

EXAM TIP

The use of firewalls, application-layer security, and antivirus software to secure SharePoint is not mentioned in the list of skills measured in the 70-667 exam. However, this subject is so important that we have included it even though strictly speaking it is outside the scope of this book. This is not a complete treatment of the subject but intended to ensure that you are aware of critical issues. It should not be revised as part of your exam preparation.

Most malicious attacks originate outside your company on the Internet. One excellent way to ensure security is, therefore, to physically separate SharePoint from the Internet and prevent all connections. However, if you host Internet sites, extranet sites, or have remote users, this approach prevents functionality. Today, almost all SharePoint farms will be available to Internet connections.

The second most secure approach is to protect your SharePoint farm by using firewalls. A sensible configuration that includes a perimeter network (sometimes called DMZ) is shown in Figure 11-1.

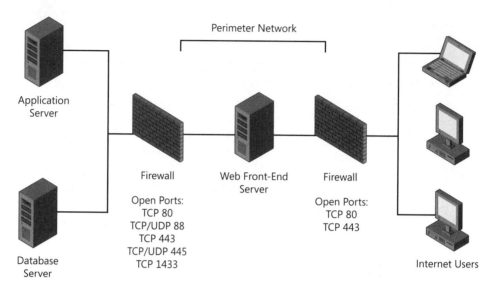

FIGURE 11-1 SharePoint protected by firewalls

Firewalls examine request packet properties and reject all but those that satisfy certain requirements. Clients access SharePoint front-end servers through TCP port 80 or TCP port 443 when HTTPS is used. All other ports on the external firewall can be closed. By filtering on the internal firewall so that only packets from the SharePoint front-end servers are passed, you ensure that no direct connection can be made to the application and database servers.

Recently more sophisticated attacks have exploited weaknesses in web services or dynamic websites. Because these attacks work through port 80, the configuration in Figure 11-1 may not intercept them. This is because conventional firewalls only filter the headers of each packet and do not examine the contents. Modern advanced firewalls, such as Microsoft Forefront Threat Management Gateway (Forefront TMG) and Microsoft Forefront Unified Access Gateway (Forefront UAG), can spot threats in the content of packets. This is called *application-layer security* and is considered essential for today's Internet connected networks. Recent versions of third-party firewalls, such as CheckPoint or Cisco PIX, also include application-layer security.

You must also plan to immunize your SharePoint farm against computer viruses. Windows runs on many computers, so it is a prime target for virus writers. Any file that includes executable code, such as Office macros or JavaScript files, could include a virus. Usually such viruses infect client computers because this is where viral code runs—SharePoint itself may remain infection-free but stores the virus from where it infects many user computers. Occasionally a weakness in Windows or SharePoint may potentially be exploited by viruses to infect SharePoint servers themselves.

To protect against viruses, install a SharePoint-aware antivirus product. Such antivirus software uses the SharePoint Antivirus API to scan and quarantine infected files. Microsoft Forefront Protection 2010 for SharePoint is an excellent example of a SharePoint-aware antivirus tool but you should also consider solutions from third parties.

It is also important to regularly apply updates, such as hotfixes and service packs, to all your software. Most viruses exploit weaknesses such as buffer overruns. Security hotfixes close such vulnerabilities as soon as Microsoft becomes aware of the problem. This is usually before a virus writer can create an exploit.

> **IMPORTANT   TESTING UPDATES**
>
> In the past, certain hotfixes and service packs have introduced extra vulnerabilities or conflicts with other software. Occasionally you may find that an update interrupts your SharePoint service. Today such events are rare but companies that need to guarantee a very high level of availability still mistrust software updates. Before they install an update on a production SharePoint farm, such companies install it on a test environment that matches the production farm as closely as possible. If tests are successfully passed, the update can be rolled out on the production farm.

High-Availability Hardware Architectures

Perhaps the most important threat to availability (in that it causes most service interruptions) is hardware reliability. Current disk technology, for example, has become remarkably reliable and you can expect many years of service from almost all your disks. However, disks include tiny moving parts and are placed under constant load. Wear and tear is inevitable and occasional manufacturing faults reduce disk lifetime. Solid-state components, such as CPUs, may overheat, although in a properly air-conditioned server room this is unusual even in high-load farms. Cooling technologies are also now very advanced. Memory units may also overheat on occasion. Interruptions in power are an unavoidable danger. Network components can also fail.

Server hardware has been continuously improved to increase its resilience to failures and ensure that they do not interrupt service. The solutions described in this section are built into hardware systems and underlie the SharePoint infrastructure. Hardware solutions like these tend to be more expensive than software configurations but often represent the best improvement in availability.

Fault-Tolerant Disk Arrays

You can build a system that is resilient to disk failures by using multiple disks and storing data on more than one of them. Such sets of disks usually implement the Redundant Array of Independent Disks (RAID) technology. Several RAID levels describe different methods of spreading data across disk arrays. In each level, when a disk failure occurs, one or more of the other disks in the array can be used to return data to users.

Some commonly used RAID levels include:

- **RAID 0**   In a RAID 0 array, data is written in stripes across multiple disks with no parity. Be clear that this is not a fault-tolerant design because a single disk failure will interrupt service from the entire array and all data on the disk will be lost. RAID 0 improves disk performance but does not provide resilience.

- **RAID 1**   A RAID 1 array has two disks; data is written to both. If a disk failure occurs, the other disk in the array is used to read and write, and service is not interrupted. RAID 1 is also called *disk mirroring*.

- **RAID 5**   A RAID 5 array has at least three disks. Data is written in stripes across all disks. For each stripe, one disk contains parity information. When a disk fails, the parity information is used to reconstruct the data that was on that disk so that read-and-write operations can continue, although performance decreases.

- **RAID 1+0**   A RAID 1 + 0 array (also known as a RAID 10 array) is an example of a nested RAID system. Each disk is mirrored to a second disk. Each disk is also striped across multiple disks. Mirroring the disks makes the array fault tolerant. Striping makes the array perform faster for read-and-write operations.

You can implement software-based RAID levels by installing standard single disks and configuring the array in the Windows Disk Management console. Alternatively, you can buy hardware RAID controllers that implement all RAID functions—these appear as simple disks to Windows. Hardware-based RAID levels provide the best performance. Table 11-2 compares software RAID and hardware RAID.

TABLE 11-2 Comparing Software and Hardware Fault Tolerance

RAID IMPLEMENTATION	ADVANTAGES	DISADVANTAGES
Windows	<ul><li>Built into Windows Server</li><li>Requires no specialist hardware</li></ul>	<ul><li>Several steps are required to recover from a disk failure.</li><li>Parity calculation and other processes place load on the CPU.</li><li>Supports only RAID 0, 1, and 5.</li><li>Places extra load on the server CPU.</li><li>Lower performance.</li></ul>
Hardware	<ul><li>Simple hotswapping</li><li>Parity calculation and other processes are handled by the hardware controller.</li><li>Some controllers include a RAM cache to improve performance.</li></ul>	<ul><li>Relatively expensive.</li></ul>

As you can see, although Windows has a flexible implementation of RAID, hardware RAID has significant advantages—as long as your budget permits it. Most SharePoint servers should use hardware RAID to ensure availability, particularly if you have guaranteed an availability level in your SLA.

> **IMPORTANT**   **RAID AND BACKUP**
>
> Although RAID levels use multiple copies of data, it is important to note that they are not replacements for a proper backup regime. Many disasters may occur that destroy all the disks in an array. If you do not have backups, significant data loss will occur despite your fault-tolerant design. For more information about backing up SharePoint, see Lesson 2 in this chapter.

Fault-Tolerant Power Hardware

No national power grid is 100 percent reliable. Power outages are caused by lightning strikes, high winds, floods, and many other events. Carefully consider the risks before you place servers in remote locations or countries where electricity delivery can be unreliable. Wherever you place your farm, you must assume that power will sometimes be unavailable.

Two hardware technologies are available to protect against power outages:

- **UPSs**   An Uninterruptable Power Supply (UPS) consists of a rechargeable battery connected between the power mains and the server's power socket. When power is available, the battery is charged. When a power outage occurs, the battery automatically takes over. Because the battery's capacity is limited, it cannot run the server indefinitely but may be able to sustain demand for up to an hour, by which time the power may be back on. Most modern UPSs include a USB connection to the host server. Through this the server can sense when a power outage occurs and determine how long the UPS can continue to provide power. You can configure the server to shut down a few minutes before the battery expires to ensure that all data is saved. Advanced UPSs can also alert administrators to power outages by sending emails or text messages. Enterprise class datacenters are usually equipped with large, sophisticated UPS systems that can sustain entire datacenters for several hours.

- **Emergency Generators**   For the highest level of protection against power outages, you can use emergency generators. These usually run on gasoline or natural gas and generate electricity with a dynamo. They are used in enterprise class datacenters to ensure continuity.

High-Availability SharePoint Architectures

You can build a SharePoint system on a single server to support many hundreds of users. However, except in very small business, single-server farms are unusual. SharePoint is more commonly deployed over several servers in a farm. This approach increases scalability because user load is spread over many servers and hardware can be dedicated to a single role. More relevantly to this chapter, multi-server farms also provide fault tolerance because, when a server fails, services can fail over onto other servers in the farm. The users receive no interruption in services. In this section, you will see how to design resilient SharePoint farms.

> **MORE INFO** **PLANNING FOR HIGH AVAILABILITY**
>
> High availability is a specialized topic and this section can only provide an overview within the scope of this training kit. Microsoft includes an excellent discussion of availability techniques in Microsoft TechNet, with links to many more resources, at *http://technet .microsoft.com/en-us/library/cc748824.aspx.*

Multiple Web Front-End Servers

Web front-end servers provide the contact point for all users with the SharePoint farm. If your farm has only one front-end server, and a failure occurs, there is an immediate and complete interruption in service. Therefore, unless you are supremely confident in your hardware, a highly available SharePoint farm requires at least two front-end servers and more are desirable in case more than one server fails.

Installing more than one web front-end server is a straightforward procedure. Install the SharePoint binaries as normal but, when asked whether you want to create a new farm, select an existing farm and provide the name of content database server. Then configure the new server to host one or more of the web applications you have created in SharePoint.

Care must be taken to ensure that user requests are distributed equally between all the running front-end servers in the farm and that the farm automatically compensates for any server failure. You can use one of the following methods to configure this:

- DNS Round Robin

  When multiple DNS A records point to the same fully qualified domain name, DNS responds to name requests by cycling through the associated IP addresses to distribute load. For example, suppose you created the following A records in DNS:

  ```
  sharepoint.contoso.com     A     10.0.0.1
  sharepoint.contoso.com     A     10.0.0.2
  sharepoint.contoso.com     A     10.0.0.3
  ```

  When the first name resolution request is received, the DNS server returns all three results in this order:

  ```
  sharepoint.contoso.com     A     10.0.0.1
  sharepoint.contoso.com     A     10.0.0.2
  sharepoint.contoso.com     A     10.0.0.3
  ```

  When the second name resolution request is received, the DNS server returns all three results in this order:

  ```
  sharepoint.contoso.com     A     10.0.0.2
  sharepoint.contoso.com     A     10.0.0.3
  sharepoint.contoso.com     A     10.0.0.1
  ```

DNS continues to cycle results for subsequent requests. Because client applications usually try the first record in the response, their requests are distributed among the servers.

DNS round robin is not a reliable fault-tolerance method because the actions of client applications are not standardized. If the 10.0.0.1 server fails, some client applications may send an error message to the user. Others may wait for a timeout period and then try the 10.0.0.2 server. This degree of uncertainty cannot be used to satisfy an SLA! You should consider DNS round robin as a basic load-balancing solution but not a fault-tolerant solution.

■ Windows Network Load Balancing (NLB)

Windows Server Enterprise edition has included the NLB service since Windows Server 2000. This is a sophisticated technology that both evenly distributes network load between servers and takes immediate action to mitigate server failures. You can use NLB to ensure fault tolerance for your SharePoint front-end servers.

To use NLB with SharePoint, you must first create an NLB cluster. This is a set of servers that share the load of user requests. Each server in the cluster has two network cards:

- A dedicated network card. This card has a unique IP address and is used for communications other than user requests.

- A cluster network card. This card has the same IP address as all the other cluster network cards on other servers in the cluster. A user request sent to the cluster IP address, therefore, is automatically received by all the servers in the cluster.

Only one server needs to respond to each user request. The servers use a load-balancing algorithm to determine which server should respond. All the other servers simply drop the request.

Servers in the NLB cluster exchange heartbeat messages at regular intervals through their dedicated IP addresses. If a server fails, other servers in the cluster notice its lack of heartbeat and initiate the convergence process. During convergence, servers determine the number of running servers in the cluster and adjust the load-balancing algorithm to redistribute responses onto servers that remain online. This process is automatic.

NLB is an efficient fault-tolerant technology that you can use to make your SharePoint web front-end servers resilient to failures.

■ Hardware Network Load Balancing

Several manufacturers make network load-balancing hardware. In general, it is more expensive to use a hardware solution, but higher-availability levels are possible. Consider, for example, a hardware solution if your SLA guarantees five nines availability. The architecture varies with the manufacturer but in general, hardware solutions consist of a router that distributes requests to the web server in a cluster. The router polls each server regularly to spot failures and estimate its speed of response. A new request is sent to the server that responds most quickly to ensure that load is spread according to server speed. Hardware solutions often have lower failover times and can alert administrators to server failures. Some hardware solutions have their own redundancy to remove any single point of failure from the system. Cisco and F5 make popular hardware solutions.

> **MORE INFO** **COMPARING NLB AND HARDWARE LOAD BALANCERS**
>
> Joel Olsen's blog contains a thorough comparison of NLB and hardware load-balancing solutions, based on extensive real world experience: *http://www.sharepointjoel.com/Lists/Posts/Post.aspx?List=0cd1a63d-183c-4fc2-8320-ba5369008acb&ID=209.*

Multiple Application Servers

Throughout this training kit, you've seen service applications such as the Managed Metadata service application, the Search service application, and the Excel Services service application. In small and medium SharePoint farms you may choose to run these service applications on web front-end servers. You would do this when user load is not high and servers can easily cope with both roles. You would also consider such an architecture when the budget for extra servers is restricted.

With large numbers of users and intensive operations, you should separate service applications onto dedicated application servers. Here are some possible approaches:

- Install a single application server for all service applications.

    In this case, Excel Services, Search, Managed Metadata, Business Connectivity Services, and other service applications all run on the same server. This approach separates the demands of service applications from web front-end servers, and results in better scalability suitable for medium-sized farms. However, service applications do contend with each other for the application server's resources and you must ensure that the server is powerful enough to effectively deliver services.

    If the application server fails, no service applications are available and users are likely to receive errors very quickly. Some SharePoint functionality, such as document check in/check out, remain operational. Although this limits the impact of failures, this should not be considered a thoroughly fault-tolerant architecture.

- Install one application server for each service application.

    For example, install separate single servers for Search, Excel, Managed Metadata, and other service applications. This enables you to specify hardware that closely matches the needs of the service. For example, if you have many Excel spreadsheets with complex calculations and connections to data sources, specify a server with fast CPUs and a large amount of RAM.

    From the point of view of fault tolerance, this approach further limits the impact of application server failures. If a server fails, users notice that only one service application is unavailable. So, for example, they may find they cannot choose terms in managed metadata fields while search is still fully functional. Again, this should not be considered a fully fault-tolerant solution because application server failures do have an impact, albeit a limited impact, on users.

■ Install multiple application servers for each service application.

In this approach you install two or more dedicated application servers for each service application. As with the previous approach, you can specify hardware according to the unique demands of each service application.

This approach results in a more fault-tolerant farm because when an application server fails, at least one other server is always running that shared service to maintain functionality. This architecture is the most expensive because at least two servers are required for each service application.

In your server farms it is likely that you will use a mixture of the preceding approaches. Suppose, for example, you rate the Search service application and Managed Metadata service application as business-critical. You might install three application servers for each of these service applications to ensure that they are always available. All other service application you might consider less important and run on a single application server.

You are not required to use NLB or a hardware load balancer with service applications because round-robin load balancing is built into the service application infrastructure. This functionality is actually provided by the Application Discovery and Load Balancer service application. This service application is not visible in Central Administration but is automatically installed and configured in all SharePoint 2010 farms. When a consuming component, such as a Web Part, requests access to a service application, the service application proxy, which runs on the web front-end server, calls the Application Discovery and Load Balancer service application to find out which servers host the requested service. The replies automatically spread load to all the appropriate application servers using a round-robin method.

When an application server fails, if there are other application servers that host the service, the consequences depend on the type of service application:

■ Service applications that store data outside SQL Server

Excel Services and Access Web Services store some data outside SQL Server and use timer jobs to complete tasks. If a server fails while a timer job is running, some data loss may occur. Otherwise, the service application fails over onto another application server smoothly.

■ Service applications that store data in SQL Server

Other service applications store data in SQL Server databases. For example, the Search service stores the crawl database, the property database, and the search administration database in SQL Server. In such cases, if you have configured clustering or mirroring in SQL, application services can fail over onto other application servers without any data loss or interruption in service. For more information about SQL Server clustering and mirroring, see the next section.

FAST Search Architectures

One of many good reasons to add FAST Search Server 2010 to your SharePoint farm is the possibility for building multi-server farms. Such farms are designed to scale FAST to extreme corpus sizes and user numbers. However, multi-server FAST farms also make FAST functionality highly resilient to failures.

In Chapter 7, "Administering SharePoint Search," you saw how FAST servers reside in a separate FAST Search farm between the SharePoint farm and the SQL Servers. Consider the following components when architecting a highly available FAST solution:

- **The Query Search Service Application** You must deploy only one Query Search Service Application (SSA) in your SharePoint farm, but this shared service can run on more than one application server. Configure this topology by adding extra query components—one on each application server in the SharePoint farm. If one query server fails, other query components exist to take on query tasks.

- **The Content Search Service Application** You must deploy only one Content SSA in your SharePoint farm. Just as with the Query SSA, you should create only one Content SSA in the SharePoint farm. You can install extra crawl components on other application servers to create a fault-tolerant system.

> **NOTE CONSEQUENCES OF CONTENT SSA FAILURES**
>
> Bear in mind that when you plan high availability for the FAST farm, the consequences of Content SSA failures are not likely to be severe for several hours afterward. When the Content SSA is not available, users can still make queries and FAST can index all content sources except the SharePoint farm. Eventually users may notice that new SharePoint documents are not returned by searches, but this is not an immediate problem.

- **The FAST Farm** The FAST Search technology includes industry-leading availability. This is because almost all the FAST farm components support redundancy. For example, the Item Processing component can be run in separate instances on two or more FAST servers. If a server failure occurs, a batch of items may not be processed but a flow control protocol ensures that it is resubmitted to another instance. For more information about using redundancy in all the FAST components, see *http://technet .microsoft.com/en-us/library/ff599525.aspx*.

- **SQL Databases** FAST requires several databases in the SQL Server farm, just like the native SharePoint Search service application. Specifically, these are the Property and Crawl databases for People Search and the administration databases for the FAST farm and the SSAs. Notice that no property and crawl databases are stored in SQL. If SQL became unavailable, FAST would still run for both crawls and queries. However, people searches would fail and administration changes could not occur. Problems would also arise if FAST servers or SSA servers were restarted. If you consider these faults to be mission-critical, use database clusters or mirroring to protect the databases, as described in the next section.

High-Availability Database Architectures

SharePoint relies on Microsoft SQL Server 2003 or 2008 to host databases. Of highest importance are the content databases, one for each web application. However, many other databases are required by different components. For example, many of the service applications must store their configurations and other information in SQL databases. Therefore, a highly available SharePoint farm cannot be created without a highly available SQL Server system.

SQL Server is an industry-leading server database system and as such it includes advanced redundancy systems that ensure that you can meet the strictest SLAs. Two techniques can be used to provide redundancy to SharePoint:

- Failover Clustering

  A SQL cluster has two or more servers—each called a *cluster node*—that share at least two disks, an IP address, and a network name. A failover cluster appears as a single server to SharePoint and other client applications. The databases and transaction logs are stored on the shared disks and all nodes in the cluster can access them.

  Under normal circumstances, only one node—called the *primary node*—accesses databases and responds to SQL queries. As in NLB, nodes use heartbeats to check availability. If the primary node fails, another node takes ownership of the shared disks, IP address, and network name and responds to SQL queries. In this way, the impact on users is minimized.

  A failover cluster also enables administrators to take a node offline for maintenance tasks such as upgrades or hardware changes without interrupting service to users.

- Database Mirroring

  Failover clustering is an excellent redundancy solution, but requires specialized hardware and resources. Database mirroring, by contrast, works entirely in software and can be implemented with two conventional servers.

  In database mirroring, you copy a database from a principal server to a mirror server. The two databases are linked so that any change in the principal database is applied to the mirror database as well. This is done by sharing transaction records. Each transaction is compressed, sent across the network to the mirror server, and applied to the mirror database.

  If the principal server fails, the mirror server brings its copy of the database online, with little or no data loss. You can configure this failover to occur automatically or perform it manually. In an upgrade, by applying the upgrade to one server at a time, you can ensure availability at all times.

  Database mirroring also protects against data corruptions: if a principal server cannot read a page in its database, it asks for the same page from the mirror database and restores consistency.

EXAM TIP

A full discussion of SQL and Windows clustering is beyond the scope of this SharePoint textbook. For the 70-667 exam, you should know only that SQL clustering provides redundancy and high availability for the database servers. For more information about SQL failover clustering, see *http://technet.microsoft.com/en-us/library/ms189134.aspx*.

Similarly, SharePoint administrators are not usually expected to be experts on SQL database mirroring. The steps required to configure database mirroring for a SharePoint content database are included in the practice for this lesson. For more information about mirroring, see *http://technet.microsoft.com/en-us/library/ms189852.aspx*.

Example Farms

In this section, you will see and investigate three example SharePoint farms, each with a different set of priorities and a different design. All of these examples are designed with redundancy to provide some level of high availability.

A Highly Available Small Farm

You have been asked to implement SharePoint for document management on a small company's intranet. The hardware budget is limited but availability is a high priority because business-critical processes will rely on SharePoint. You want to create a system with no single point of failure for the smallest possible cost. Figure 11-2 shows a suitable architecture.

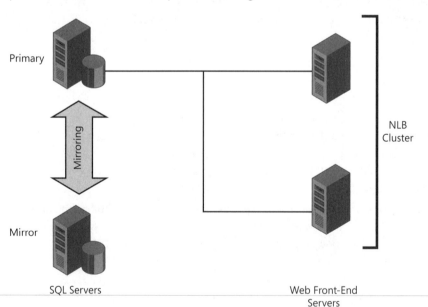

FIGURE 11-2 A highly available small SharePoint farm

Notice the following features:

- Two SharePoint front-end servers also host all service applications.
- NLB is used to provide fault tolerance and load balancing for the front end.
- There are two SQL Servers.
- All databases are mirrored across both SQL Servers.
- Databases are stored on RAID 5 arrays configured in Windows.
- Transaction logs are stored on RAID 1 mirror sets configured in Windows.

This architecture illustrates that a limited hardware budget need not be a barrier to high availability.

A Highly Available Medium-Sized Farm

You have been asked to design a server architecture for a larger company. The hardware budget is generous but not unlimited. Search and managed metadata are considered business-critical and must be available 99.99 percent of the time. Other service applications are lower priority. Figure 11-3 shows a suggested architecture.

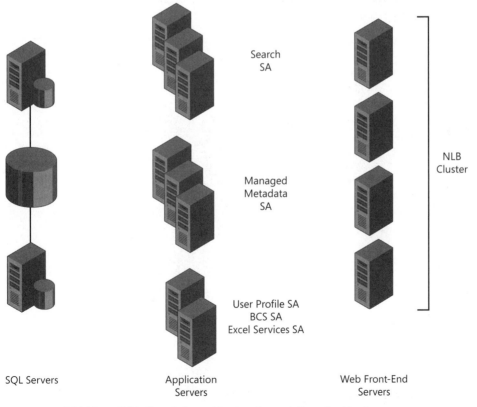

FIGURE 11-3 A highly available SharePoint architecture for a medium-sized business

Notice the following features:

- Four web front-end servers are load balanced with NLB.

- No service applications are hosted on web front-end servers.

- No service application is hosted on a single application server.

- Search and Managed Metadata service applications have three dedicated application servers each.

- Database servers are clustered.

- All disks include hardware RAID controllers.

This architecture illustrates a typical server configuration for a medium or large SharePoint installation on an intranet or extranet.

A Hosted SharePoint Farm

You have been asked to architect a SharePoint farm for an ISP that wants to host SharePoint services for multiple global clients. The SLA specifies four nines availability for all functionality. Search, Managed Metadata, and User Profiles are the only service applications that will be provided. The high reliability of the solution will be a unique selling point for marketing. Figure 11-4 shows a suitable architecture.

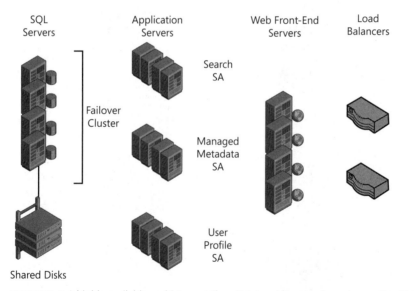

FIGURE 11-4 A highly available multi-tenant SharePoint architecture for a demanding SLA

Notice the following features:

- A hardware network load-balancing solution is included with redundancy.

- There are many web front-end servers, none of which hosts service applications.

- At least three application servers are dedicated to each service application.
- Database servers are clustered.
- All servers include hardware RAID controllers.

This architecture illustrates design decisions you can make when availability is a top priority and outweighs budgetary concerns.

> **IMPORTANT HIGH AVAILABILITY AND MONITORING**
>
> Many of the server failures that infuriate real-world IT departments have foreseeable causes that could have been spotted and fixed before they became critical. For example, everyone knows that you should maintain free space on hard disks. However, when you have 10 or 20 servers in a SharePoint farm, each with multiple drives, it can become harder to keep track. For this reason it is essential to demand a strict monitoring routine from your IT personnel to reach the availability level guaranteed in your SLA.
>
> Many monitoring tools are available in both Windows, SharePoint, and third-party vendors. For example, critical counters can be monitored and alerts set in the Windows Performance Monitor console. SharePoint's Health Analyzer tool is also excellent and informative. Many third-party solutions can be configured to alert on-call personnel of drive usage thresholds and service issues. For more information about monitoring SharePoint, see Chapter 12, "Monitoring and Optimizing SharePoint Performance."

PRACTICE Configure High Availability

Practices are designed to guide you through important procedures. The instructions in the Training Kit are high-level instructions that will challenge you to think carefully and to apply the procedures that are covered in this lesson and elsewhere in the Training Kit. If you need assistance, consult the detailed, step-by-step instructions in the Practice Answers on the companion media.

In this practice, you configure database mirroring for the Contoso intranet content database.

Prepare for the Practice

Before you perform this practice, ensure that your lab environment has been built according to the instructions found in the Introduction to this Training Kit.

> **IMPORTANT REASSIGNING MEMORY**
>
> In this practice, you install SQL Server on the CONTOSO-DC virtual machine. SQL Server requires at least 1 GB of RAM so you must reassign memory as described in the following steps.

1. Apply the snapshot CHAPTER 05 to CONTOSO-DC.

2. Apply the snapshot CHAPTER 05 to SP2010-WFE1.

3. If you are using Hyper-V, use the following steps to adjust memory usage:

    A. Right-click the CONTOSO-DC virtual machine and click Settings.

    B. In the Hardware list, click Memory.

    C. In the RAM text box, type **1500** and then click OK.

    D. Right-click the SP2010-WFE1 virtual machine and click Settings.

    E. In the Hardware list, click Memory.

    F. In the RAM text box, type **4500** and then click OK.

    If you are using VMWare Workstation, use the following steps to adjust memory usage:

    A. In VMware Workstation, select CONTOSO-DC, and then click Edit Virtual Machine Settings.

    B. In the Device list, click Memory.

    C. Increase the amount of memory to 1500 MB, and then click OK.

    D. In VMware Workstation, select SP2010-WFE1, and then click Edit Virtual Machine Settings.

    E. In the Device list, click Memory.

    F. Decrease the amount of memory to 4500 MB, and then click OK.

4. Start CONTOSO-DC.

    Wait for the virtual machine to complete startup, at which time the Press Ctrl+Alt+Delete prompt appears.

5. Start SP2010-WFE1.

6. Log on to SP2010-WFE1 as **CONTOSO\SP_Admin** with the password **Pa$$w0rd**.

EXERCISE 1   Install SQL Server 2008 R2 on the Domain Controller

In this exercise, you install SQL Server 2008 R2 on the CONTOSO-DC image so that in the next exercise you can mirror the intranet content database.

> **IMPORTANT**   **SQL SERVER AND DOMAIN CONTROLLERS**
>
> In a production environment, it is not recommended that you install SQL Server on any domain controller. This procedure is only appropriate in a lab or demonstration environment.

1. Connect to the CONTOSO-DC virtual machine.

2. Log on as **CONTOSO\Administrator** with the password **Pa$$w0rd**.

3. Use the Windows Firewall with Advanced Security administrative tool to turn off the Windows Firewall.

4. Install SQL Server 2008 R2. Use the following settings and guidance:
   - SQL Server Features: Database Engine Services, SQL Server Replication, Reporting Services, Management Tools – Basic, Management Tools – Complete
   - Instance: Default Instance
   - Instance ID: MSSQLSERVER
   - Service Accounts: Use CONTOSO\SQL_Service for all service accounts.
   - SQL Server Administrators: CONTOSO\Administrator and CONTOSO\SQL_Admin
   - Reporting Services Configuration: Install the SharePoint Integrated Mode Default Configuration.
   - Use default settings for all other values.

EXERCISE 2   **Back Up the Intranet Content Database**

To set up database mirroring, you must back up the database primary partner and restore it on the mirror server. In this exercise, you back up the Intranet content database to a file share on the CONTOSO-DC virtual server:

1. Create a new folder on the CONTOSO-DC virtual server C: drive called Backups.
2. Share the Backups folder. Ensure that CONTOSO\SQL_Admin has Read/Write permission.
3. Switch to the SP2010-WFE1 virtual server.
4. Log on as **CONTOSO\SQL_Admin** with the password **Pa$$w0rd**.
5. Create a new folder on the SP2010-WFE1 virtual server C: drive called Backups.
6. Use the Windows Firewall with Advanced Security administrative tool to turn off the Windows Firewall.
7. Use SQL Server Configuration Manager to manage the Network Configuration.
8. Enable TCP/IP connections.
9. Use SQL Server Management Studio to start the SQL Server Agent.
10. Use SQL Server Management Studio to back up the SharePoint_Content_Intranet database. Use the following settings and guidance:
    - Backup Type: Full
    - Destination: Remove the default destination
    - Destination: Add C:\Backups\IntranetDatabase.bak
11. Use SQL Server Management Studio to back up the SharePoint_Content_Intranet database again. Use the following settings and guidance:
    - Backup Type: Transaction Log
    - Destination: Remove the default destination
    - Destination: Add C:\Backups\IntranetTransactionLogs.bak
12. Copy both of the backup files you have created from C:\Backups to \\CONTOSO-DC\Backups.

EXERCISE 3   Restore the Intranet Content Database on the Mirror Partner

In this exercise, you restore the database on the CONTOSO-DC virtual server in preparation for configuring mirroring:

1. Switch to the CONTOSO-DC virtual server.

2. Use SQL Server Configuration Manager to manage the Network Configuration.

3. Enable TCP/IP connections.

4. Use SQL Server Management Studio to connect to the localhost SQL Server.

5. Start the SQL Server Agent.

6. Add the following Logins:
    - CONTOSO\SP_Farm
    - CONTOSO\SP_Admin

7. Create a new database called SharePoint_Content_Intranet.

8. Perform a Database restore operation on the SharePoint_Content_Intranet database. Use the following settings and guidance:
    - Source for Restore: Device
    - Source for Restore: C:\backups\IntranetDatabase.bak
    - Options: Overwrite the Existing Database.
    - Options/Recovery State: Leave the Database Non-Operational

9. Perform a Transaction Log restore operation on the SharePoint_Content_Intranet database. Use the following settings and guidance:
    - Restore Source: File or Tape
    - Restore Source: C:\Backups\IntranetTransactionLogs.bak
    - Options/Recovery State: Leave the Database Non-Operational

EXERCISE 4   Mirror the Intranet Content Database

In this exercise, you configure mirroring from the principal database on the SP2010-WFE1 server to the restored database on the CONTOSO-DC server:

1. Switch to the SP2010-WFE1 virtual server.

2. Right-click the SharePoint_Content_Intranet database and, under Tasks, click Mirror.

3. Run the Configure Security Wizard. Use the following settings and guidance:
    - Include Witness Server: No
    - Principal Server: SP2010-WFE1
    - Mirror Server: CONTOSO-DC
    - Service Accounts/Principal: CONTOSO\SQL_Service
    - Service Account/Mirror: CONTOSO\SQL_Service

4. Start mirroring.

EXERCISE 5 Configure the Intranet Web Application

In this exercise, you configure SharePoint to automatically fail over to the mirrored database partner:

1. Log off the SP2010-WFE1 server.
2. Log on as **CONTOSO\SP_Admin** with the password **Pa$$w0rd**.
3. In Central Administration, access the Manage Content Databases page.
4. Configure the SharePoint_Content_Intranet database. Use the following setting:
   - Failover Database Server: CONTOSO-DC

Lesson Summary

- High-availability architectures ensure that SharePoint is responsive to users almost all the time.
- The availability level you must work to is defined in your SLA.
- High availability can be achieved by designing a SharePoint farm with multiple redundancy at all levels.
- Redundancy requires extra hardware and is therefore more expensive.
- The key role played by SharePoint in many organizations requires high availability to ensure that users can always be productive.
- High security is essential to high availability because many malicious attacks cause denials of service to users.
- Many hardware solutions, including fault-tolerant disk arrays and network load balancers, are available and provide the highest levels of availability.
- Software solutions, such as NLB and Windows-based RAID, are effective and cheaper to implement.
- You can use multiple web front-end servers with NLB or a hardware load balancer.
- Service applications that run on more than one application server are load balanced automatically by the Application Discovery and Load Balancer Service Application.
- FAST Search farms can include multiple levels of redundancy.
- Databases should be protected by using a failover cluster or database mirroring.
- Regular monitoring is essential for high availability.
- High availability is not a substitute for a strict backup and restore regime.

Lesson Review

You can use the following questions to test your knowledge of the information in Lesson 1, "Configure High Availability." The questions are also available on the companion media in a practice test if you prefer to review them in electronic form.

1. You want to install a highly available SharePoint farm and are in the process of planning the server hardware to support it. Which of the following design features will improve availability for your users? (Choose all that apply.)

   A. A hardware-controlled RAID 0 stripe set on which you will store the Search service application index files.

   B. A hardware-controlled RAID 1 mirror set on which you will store transaction logs for the SharePoint content database.

   C. A hardware-controlled RAID 5 stripe set on which you will store the SharePoint content database.

   D. UPSs for all web front-end, application, and database servers.

   E. High-speed DAT tape backup hardware for database servers.

2. You set up three web front-end servers in your SharePoint farm and use Windows NLB to load balance between them. You install three application servers and configure all service applications to run on all three of them. Which of the following statements about the farm are true? (Choose all that apply.)

   A. Each web front-end server must have at least two network cards.

   B. Each web front-end server must respond to the farm IP address.

   C. Each web front-end server must be able to ping all the others.

   D. Each application server must have at least two network cards.

   E. Each application server must respond to the farm IP address.

   F. Web front-end servers automatically load balance the application servers.

Lesson 2: Back Up and Restore SharePoint

In Lesson 1, you saw how SharePoint supports highly available and scalable architectures with redundancy at all levels. If you have the budget to implement such a system you may feel reasonably secure and invulnerable to common problems. However, no amount of redundancy is a substitute for a strict backup and restore regime because disasters may occur at any time. Although such events are rare, the consequences may be very severe, especially in a modern knowledge-based company whose existence may be guaranteed only by the information it stores. For example, think of a software house: If the painstakingly developed source code for a flagship product is lost, it is difficult to see how the company can continue trading. Although this is often a thankless task, it is the IT administrator's responsibility to ensure that your system can recover from even worst-case scenarios.

After this lesson, you will be able to:

- Describe typical situations in which the administrator must restore data.
- Understand the SharePoint Recycle Bin and its role in data protection.
- Back up a SharePoint farm in Central Administration.
- Perform granular backups in Central Administration.
- Restore data in Central Administration.
- Use Windows PowerShell cmdlets to script backup and restore operations.
- Use SQL Server tools to back up and restore SharePoint databases.

Estimated Lesson Time: 60 minutes

The Importance of Backup and Restore

Most IT administrators understand the vital role played by backup and recovery methods. However, it is worth reviewing situations that frequently require data to be restored from whatever backup media you use. With a thorough understanding of these situations you can plan to accelerate recovery operations and reduce your workload and the impact of any disasters.

> **NOTE BACKUP MEDIA**
>
> Because this is a SharePoint textbook, this chapter does not go into detail about backup media. You should find your organization has already chosen a preferred medium but sometimes you may be involved in the choice. Common choices are DAT tapes, hard disks, and optical disks. Internet-based remote backup services are also becoming more popular. When you select a medium, consider the cost of storage per megabyte, the speed of backup and, critically, the speed of restore operations. Long restore times mean greater impact on user productivity after a disaster.
>
> You should read extensively on the subject of storage media before you commit to a system.

Recovering Accidentally Deleted Items

The backup is the ultimate recourse when users, or even administrators, delete information erroneously. Nobody is perfect and non-descriptive filenames and unclear folder hierarchies can often confuse people. Although a delete operation usually prompts an Are You Sure? dialog box, many users are so used to this question that they click Yes without a moment's thought. Administrators are also not immune from such errors and they can make mistakes during bulk operations that remove hundreds or thousands of items. Poorly tested custom code can also cause similar deletions.

Traditionally, the IT administrator regularly spent time locating files on backup tapes and restoring them to file servers. Now that Recycle Bins are so prevalent, this task is less frequent, but strict Group Policy can empty the local Recycle Bin every day—such as when users log off.

SharePoint has a highly functional Recycle Bin with flexible retention settings. If you configure this carefully, it can avoid the need to recover accidentally deleted items from backup media in almost all cases.

Disaster Recovery

A disaster, in the context of backup and restore, is any catastrophic failure that results in data loss from your production systems. The potential causes are many and varied:

- **Acts of God**   Fires and floods are perhaps the most common but earthquakes may be a threat in your location as might extreme weather events. Server centers housed in basements in cities on floodplains are especially vulnerable to flooding and surprisingly common.

- **Incompetence**   SharePoint does not allow users to cause major damage but ill-informed administrators could delete sites or lists. Training is a high priority for administrators. Badly written Windows PowerShell scripts or custom code can potentially cause extensive damage and must be well tested.

- **Sabotage**   Disgruntled employees with high-level permissions or physical access to your servers have occasionally caused data loss.

- **Malicious Attacks**   Hackers—most often on the Internet but occasionally within your network—can wreak havoc if your system is not properly protected by firewalls and antivirus software.

These disasters all threaten even the most highly available system. However, if your hardware budget did not permit for multiple redundancy, more mundane events, such as disk failures and power interruptions, can require recovery from backups. In single-server or small SharePoint farms your backup regime is of prime importance.

Migrating Content

Backups are also frequently used to migrate content from one store to another. Consider, for example, a custom development project: Developers require a testing environment that closely matches the real SharePoint farm that their code will eventually run on. It is important, particularly in the latter stages of development, that the test farm is a very accurate model of the production farm. A large and realistic set of test content is vital to ensure that the custom solution can handle data as it exists in your production environment.

You can migrate content to such a test environment in several ways. For example, the SharePoint Content Deployment service can automatically deploy content from one farm to another. However, best practice often requires a physical separation between production and testing systems, so a network copying tool such as the Content Deployment service cannot be used. However, by taking physical backup media to the test farm and restoring it there, you can create a test environment that matches the production system right down to the level of individual items.

Planning a Disaster Recovery Strategy

With content so important to many companies in modern economies, protection against data loss has become one of the IT department's most important functions. Disasters are mercifully rare, but when they do happen, the effectiveness of the recovery is an excellent measure of your planning—you must endeavor to think of everything that could go wrong. Of prime importance is to consider the durations of backup and restore operations:

- **Backups** Backups are often scheduled for off-peak hours, but you must ensure that they are complete before users arrive at work in the morning. With large content stores that can include lots of videos or other large files, this might not be the case. You must consider how many GB your hardware can back up per hour. In companies without off-peak hours, such as global companies or those with 24-hour shift patterns, backups must take place while users are working, so you should ensure that servers have enough resources to avoid contention.

- **Restores** When disaster strikes, users become unproductive and the company begins to lose money. If you have an SLA to work to, you immediately begin to consume your permitted downtime. Therefore, you should plan to minimize the duration of restore operations within the restrictions of your hardware budget.

It's also important to consider the cost per MB of data storage in your chosen medium.

Begin by planning to purchase the fastest backup hardware you can afford. The money saved when you can restore data quickly should justify this cost.

In SharePoint Central Administration, you can also choose from two backup types:

- **Full** A full backup always copies all the content and configuration data. This uses a lot of tape, or space on your chosen medium. However, this backup type is often used because you can restore all data in a single operation.

- **Differential** A differential backup copies only the content that has changed since the last full backup. In this way, you can use less tape and reduce storage costs. However, bear in mind that a complete restore will require two backup sets: the previous full backup and the most up-to-date differential backup. Therefore, a restore will take longer.

You should create a regular backup schedule to ensure that all data is protected. For example, when you want to minimize the duration of restores, you might run a full backup every night. When you want to conserve media costs, you could run differential backups every night except Sunday, when a full backup is run. Differential backups should not be used without occasional full backups.

Also give some thought to the location where you store your backups. When they are onsite they can be quickly accessed for disaster recovery. However, the worst disasters may destroy entire buildings, so you should store some copies at remote locations.

Finally, you should rehearse disaster recovery procedures in a lab environment. If you don't run such rehearsals you may miss a systematic error in your plan. Even small problems could result in data loss and the only way to be completely sure your plan works is to practice it.

Backup and Restore Tools and Techniques

This section describes the tools and techniques the SharePoint administrator can use to ensure data continuity. Make regular backups part of your daily administrative routine and never assume they are running smoothly without checking. SharePoint administrators can use SharePoint tools for backup and restore or, alternatively, they can back up databases directly in SQL Server. The following discussions compare all these techniques.

The Recycle Bin

SharePoint includes its own Recycle Bin that is used whenever items, documents, and other files are deleted. This is not an alternative to a proper backup regime but it does enable accidentally deleted items to be restored without resorting to the backup media. If you configure the Recycle Bin carefully, you should find that you rarely if ever have to spend time recovering from accidental deletions.

This is a two-stage Recycle Bin:

- **Site Recycle Bin**   When a user deletes an item, the item is placed in the site-level Recycle Bin folder and remains there for 30 days by default. When a user opens the site Recycle Bin, she sees the items she herself has deleted. She can restore a deleted item to its original location, or delete it permanently. The site-level Recycle Bin is shown in Figure 11-5.

- **Site Collection Recycle Bin**   When the 30-day retention period expires, or when a user permanently deletes an item, SharePoint moves the item to the site collection–level Recycle Bin. Only site collection administrators can access this Recycle Bin. Administrators can restore items or delete them permanently.

Farm administrators can configure the behavior of the Recycle Bin for each web application. It can be switched off and the stage-one retention period can be adjusted. Items in stage two remain until the Recycle Bin reaches a certain percentage of the live site quota. Then the oldest items are deleted. Farm administrators can set this percentage.

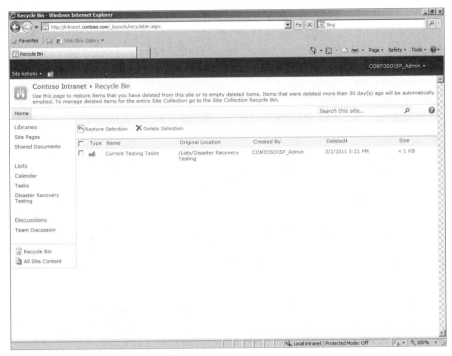

FIGURE 11-5 The site-level Recycle Bin

When you configure the Recycle Bin, you should consider that longer retention times reduce the likelihood that you will have to restore an item from the backup media. However, long retention times also increase the disk consumption for all sites in your farm and you should ensure that you have enough disk space to support them.

> **IMPORTANT   THE RECYCLE BIN AND SITE QUOTAS**
>
> Items in the site Recycle Bin count towards the site quota. Therefore, bear in mind that deleting an item does not immediately free space in the quota. Only when items are removed from the site Recycle Bin is space made available.
>
> By contrast, items in the site-collection Recycle Bin do not count towards the quota and you must take this into consideration when planning disk space. If, for example, you have two sites and a quota of 200 MB you may expect disk consumption to stop increasing at 400 MB. However, if you set the site collection Recycle Bin to retain items until its total size is 50 percent of the quota, you must ensure that you have disk space for an extra 200 MB.

CONFIGURE THE RECYCLE BIN

Farm administrators can use the following steps to configure the Recycle Bin:

1. In the Central Administration Quick Launch, click Application Management.

2. Under Web Applications, click Manage Web Applications.

3. Select the web application that you want to configure.

4. On the ribbon, click General Settings.

5. Scroll down to locate the Recycle Bin section.

6. Under Recycle Bin Status, you can choose to turn the Recycle Bin off. Note that when you use this setting, deleted items must be restored from backups.

7. When the Recycle Bin is on you can choose how long items are retained in the site Recycle Bin.

8. Under Second Stage Recycle Bin you can specify the size of the site-collection Recycle Bin as a percentage of the site quota. You can also turn off the second-stage Recycle Bin.

9. Click OK.

Farm Backup in Central Administration

Perhaps the most popular tool for SharePoint backup and restore is located in Central Administration. Farm administrators can use this tool to perform backups of the entire farm or more granular objects, such as site collections, sites, or single lists.

In the Farm Backup tool, you can select the following for a backup operation:

- **Complete Farm**   The entire farm, including all content and configuration data, is backed up.

- **Farm Configuration Only**   No content reaches the backup media. All configuration values, such as service application settings and web application settings, are backed up.

- **Farm Components**   You can also select certain SharePoint components for the backup. For example, you could choose to back up the configuration database, the State Service, or the SharePoint Diagnostics service.

BACK UP A SHAREPOINT FARM

To make a complete backup of the SharePoint farm, use the following steps. The procedure is similar when you want to back up the farm configuration or a farm component.

1. In Central Administration Quick Launch, click Backup And Restore.

2. To specify a backup location, under Farm Backup And Restore, click Configure Backup Settings.

3. Under Backup File Location, type the path to the folder where you want to save backups.

4. Click OK.

5. Under Farm Backup And Restore, click Perform A Backup.

6. In the list of components, select the check box to the left of the top Farm object. All the other check boxes are also selected.

7. Click Next.

8. Under Backup Type, select Full or Differential.

9. Under Back Up Only Configuration Settings, choose whether to back up content with configuration values.

10. Under Backup File Location, type a path to the backup media.

11. Click Start Backup. The Backup And Restore Job Status page displays the state of the backup as it progresses.

> **IMPORTANT** **BACKUP FILES**
>
> The Farm Backup and Granular Backup tools create many .bak files and a single backup manifest file in XML format. All these files must be available when you perform a restore.

Granular Backup in Central Administration

In SharePoint 2010, administrators can back up a site collection, site, or individual list. In earlier versions of SharePoint, this capability is only available in the Stsadm.exe command-line tool.

> **NOTE** **GRANULAR BACKUPS AND CPU DEMAND**
>
> When you run a granular backup, bear in mind that the process places extra load on the CPUs in your web front-end servers. In particular, granular backups are more processor-intensive than farm backups. You should ensure that granular backups do not cause contention for processor time.

BACK UP A SITE COLLECTION

To back up a single site collection, follow these steps:

1. In the Central Administration Quick Launch, click Backup And Restore.

2. Under Granular Backup, click Perform A Site Collection Backup.

3. Under Site Collection, choose the site collection you want to back up.

4. Under File Location, type a path where you want to save the backup package. This path must include the name of the .bak file to create.

5. Click Start Backup.

BACK UP A SITE

To back up a site, follow these steps. You can back up a list or library in a very similar way:

1. In the Central Administration Quick Launch, click Backup And Restore.

2. Under Granular Backup, click Export A Site Or List.

3. Under Site Collection, choose the site collection that contains the site you want to back up.

4. In the Site picker, choose the site you want to back up.

5. Under File Location, in the Filename text box, type a path where you would like to save the backup file. Include the name of the file.

6. Under Export Full Security, choose whether to include permissions and roles defined in the site.

7. Under Export Versions, choose whether major and minor versions of documents will be exported.

8. Click Start Export.

Restoring Data in Central Administration

It is vital that you ensure that the data you have backed up can be rapidly and reliably restored in the event of a disaster. When such an event occurs, speed is of the essence because users' ability to work within SharePoint will be affected until your restore operation is complete and SharePoint is back online. Therefore, it is a good idea to rehearse the procedures in a lab environment to ensure that mistakes are minimized.

RESTORE A FARM BACKUP

Complete the following steps to restore a farm backup:

1. In the Central Administration Quick Launch, click Backup And Restore.

2. Under Farm Backup And Restore, click Restore From A Backup.

3. In the Backup Directory Location text box, you may need to type the path to the backup files and then click Refresh.

4. A list of completed backup jobs is displayed. Select the backup job you want to restore and then click Next.

5. A list of all the components present in the backup files is displayed. Select the components you want to restore and then click Next.

6. Under Restore Only Configuration Settings, choose whether to restore the content or only the configuration in the backup files.

7. Under Restore Options, choose whether to restore to a farm with the same computer names, web application names, and database servers as the backup farm. This is the situation when restoring after a disaster to the farm that was backed up. The New Configuration option enables you to restore to a farm with different service account credentials, site and site collection names, web application names, and so on.

8. If the service account credentials have changed, type the details in the Credentials section.

9. Click Start Restore. The Backup And Restore Job Status page displays the progress of the restore operation.

Backup and Restore in Windows PowerShell

Windows PowerShell is an effective way to automate repetitive and complex procedures by writing scripts to perform them. If you find that your daily backup routine—which may involve many SharePoint farms, web applications, content databases, and service applications—has become complex and difficult, you can simplify matters by placing all backup operations into a single Windows PowerShell script. As well as reducing the workload, this approach standardizes and increases the reliability of a complex backup process because administrators may mistakenly miss steps in a complex backup procedure.

You can use the following SharePoint cmdlets in your backup scripts:

- **Backup-SPFarm**   You can use this cmdlet to back up the entire farm or an individual database or web application.
- **Backup-SPSite**   You can use this cmdlet to back up a site collection.
- **Backup-SPConfigurationDatabase**   You can use this cmdlet to back up the configuration information for the farm.

The following example command performs a full backup of a SharePoint farm and stores the backup files on a file server called \\backupserver:

```
Backup-SPFarm –BackupMethod full –Directory \\backupserver\backupshare\SharePointFarm
```

The following example command performs a backup of the Contoso intranet site collection to the same file server:

```
Backup-SPSite -Identity http://intranet.contoso.com
–Path \\backupserver\backupshare\IntranetSiteCollection.bak -UseSqlSnapshot
```

> **NOTE   THE -USESQLSNAPSHOT OPTION**
>
> When you use the *-UseSqlSnapshot* option, SharePoint creates a SQL database snapshot at the beginning of the process. All data is backed up from that snapshot, not the live database. At the end of the backup operation, the snapshot is removed.
>
> When you use this option, users can continue working in the live database while the backup takes place. If you do not specify it, SharePoint sets a read-only site lock on the site collection while the backup completes and users cannot make changes. Alternatively you can use the *-NoSiteLock* option to enables users to continue working, but in this case the site collection might not be in a consistent state when it is restored.
>
> *-UseSqlSnapshot* is therefore highly recommended. However, you can only use it when your edition of SQL Server supports snapshots. For example, Enterprise and Developer editions support database snapshots.

You can use the following cmdlets in your restore scripts:

- **Restore-SPFarm**   You can use this cmdlet to restore one or more items from a SharePoint farm backup.
- **Restore-SPSite**   You can use this cmdlet to restore a SharePoint site collection from a .bak file.

The following example command restores a backup from the \\backupserver file server and overwrites the original configuration and content:

```
Restore-SPFarm –Directory \\backupserver\backupshare\SharePointFarm
–RestoreMethod Overwrite –BackupId 12345678-90ab-cdef-1234-567890abcdef
```

The following example command restores the Contoso Intranet site collection from
a backup file to its original location, forcing an overwrite. It also specifies the database server
and content database to restore the content to:

```
Restore-SPSite –Identity http://intranet.contoso.com –Force –DatabaseServer SP2010-WFE1
–DatabaseName SharePoint_Content_Intranet
–Path \\backupserver\backupshare\IntranetSiteCollection.bak
```

Backing Up the IIS Configuration

It is important to note that the configuration of IIS is not backed up by any of the preceding
methods. If a catastrophic failure occurs and you must restore the entire farm, you will have
to configure IIS from scratch unless you perform the following procedure.

BACK UP THE IIS CONFIGURATION

You will need to use an account with local administrative permissions to complete
the following steps:

1. Click Start, right-click Command Prompt, and then click Run As Administrator.

2. In the User Account Control dialog box, click Yes.

3. Type the following command, and then press Enter:

   ```
   cd %windir%\system32\inetsrv
   ```

4. Type the following command, and then press Enter:

   ```
   appcmd add backup myiisbackup
   ```

5. Include the IIS backup file as part of your system file-level backup strategy.

You can restore the configuration backup by using the following command:

```
appcmd restore backup myiisbackup
```

SQL Server Backup Methods

SharePoint uses Microsoft SQL Server for almost all its data storage. In addition to the main SharePoint content databases, many databases are also used by service applications. For example, the Search service application has three separate databases. As you have seen in the practices for this book, 20 or more databases may be stored in SQL for SharePoint support. SQL Server includes its own backup and restore methods that administrators can use for disaster recovery and data migration. These have both advantages and disadvantages over the SharePoint backup and restore tools—in reality you may decide to use both in your backup routines.

You should consider using SQL backup tools for the following reasons:

- Important SQL Server system databases, such as Master, MSDB, and TempDB, can only be backed up by using SQL backup.

- SQL backup tools provide integration with tape media hardware. For example, you can choose to rewind and/or eject the tape on completion.

- SQL backup tools provide advanced verification options. For example, you can verify the entire backup after completion or choose to calculate the checksum before writing to the media.

However, you should also bear in mind that not all SharePoint information is stored in SQL. Notably, the Search index files are stored on the index and query server hard drives. If these were lost, a complete crawl operation would be required to rebuild them, which would take time and much processing and memory on the index application servers. The IIS configuration cannot be backed up by using the SQL tools.

When a change is made in a SQL Server database, it is first written to transaction logs, then to the main database files. The server can write to transaction logs fast and sequentially—writing a change to a database can require several separate operations on the hard disk. You should place transaction logs on a separate physical disk from the database files to accelerate performance and improve recoverability. The point to which you can recover data after a disaster depends on the recovery model that you set for each database. The following recovery models are available:

- **Simple** If you choose this model, you can recover a database up until the point when the last backup was taken.

- **Full** In certain circumstances that depend on the nature of the disaster, you can recover right up to the point just before the disaster occurred. This applies when the disaster destroyed the database files but not the transaction logs. When you restore, the transaction logs are replayed to recover changes after the backup was taken. If the disaster destroyed the transaction logs as well, you can only restore to the point of the backup. This is one excellent reason to place transaction logs and database files on separate disks—a disaster that affects only the database file disk does not destroy the transaction logs.

- **Bulked Logged** This recovery model is used to maximize performance while large quantities of data are written to the database. A transaction log is maintained but may not be as up to date as in the Full recovery model. SQL Database Administrators (DBAs) use this model temporarily when some high-input operation takes place.

SQL Server also supports more backup types than the SharePoint backup tools:

- **Full** Transaction logs are committed to the database. All data is backed up and the transaction logs are purged.
- **Differential** Only the transaction logs are backed up. Transaction logs are not purged. Differential backups effectively back up all the changes since the last Full backup.
- **Transaction Log Backup** Only the transaction logs are backed up. Transaction logs are purged. Transaction Log backups effectively back up all the changes since the last Full backup or the last Transaction Log backup.
- **File and File Group Backup** If the DBAs have subdivided the database file into several files and file groups, you can use this backup type to back up one or more files or file groups.
- **Partial Backup** In a partial backup, all data is backed up except data stored in read-only file groups.
- **Differential Partial Backup** This backup type is similar to a Partial backup except that only changed data is backed up.
- **Copy-Only** When you want to create a backup of the database without affecting the backup history or purging the transaction logs, use a Copy-Only backup.

> **NOTE SQL BACKUP COMPRESSION**
>
> If you use SQL Server 2008 Enterprise edition to store databases, you have the option to use compression in backup operations. Data is compressed before it is written to the media. Depending on the data in the database, the compressed data may be as little as 20 percent of the original database so this option can reduce storage costs.
>
> If you use this option, you should consider first that CPU load is increased during both backup and restore operations. Ensure that you have the resources to cope with this load on the SQL Servers. Second, because data must be uncompressed, the duration of a restore may be increased and users may be unproductive for longer.

SET A DATABASE RECOVERY MODEL

This procedure illustrates how to set the recovery model. It sets the Full recovery model on the Contoso Intranet content database, which is called SharePoint_Content_Intranet:

1. Click Start, All Programs, Microsoft SQL Server 2008 R2, and then click SQL Server Management Studio.
2. In the Connect To Server dialog box, select the SQL Server that stores the content database you want to configure, and then click Connect.

3. Expand Databases, right-click SharePoint_Content_Intranet, and then click Properties.

4. In the Select A Page pane, click Options.

5. In the Recovery Model drop-down list, select Full, and then click OK.

6. Close SQL Server Management Studio.

BACK UP A SHAREPOINT CONTENT DATABASE

This procedure illustrates how to use the SQL Server backup tools by using them on the SharePoint content database for the Contoso intranet site collection. In this example, a full backup is taken to a disk location:

1. Click Start, All Programs, Microsoft SQL Server 2008 R2, and then click SQL Server Management Studio.

2. In the Connect To Server dialog box, select the SQL Server that stores the content database you want to configure, and then click Connect.

3. Expand Databases, right-click SharePoint_Content_Intranet, click Tasks, and then click Back Up.

4. In the Backup Type drop-down list, ensure that Full is selected.

5. In the Backup Set section, in the Name box, type a descriptive name. You should consider including the data in this name to help administrators select a database to restore.

6. In the Description box, type whatever text you think might help administrators.

7. In the Destination section, select the Disk option.

8. Click Remove to delete the default destination for a disk backup.

9. Click Add.

10. In the Select Backup Destination dialog box, in the File Name text box, type the path to the folder where you want to create the backup. Include the filename with a .bak extension.

11. Click OK.

12. In the Back Up Database dialog box, click OK.

13. When the backup operation is complete, click OK.

SQL Server Restore Methods

In the discussion of SharePoint disaster recovery, you saw the importance of a thorough plan for disaster recovery and the need to rehearse your procedures to ensure that everything runs smoothly at the times of greatest need. These arguments apply just as much to the SQL Server backup and restore techniques. If you choose SQL backup and restore, you must plan recovery steps carefully before any disaster takes place and practice them. In this section you will see the procedure for SQL Server database restoration.

In SharePoint 2010, you can detach a content database. This removes the database from the SharePoint configuration and makes its content unavailable to users but the database is not destroyed and can still be accessed in SQL Server Management Studio. You can also attach a content database; this technique is useful in several scenarios:

- When you have restored the content to a new database with the SQL Server restore tools, you must reattach it to SharePoint to make it available to users.

- When you have protected a database with SQL database mirroring and the primary database has failed, you must attach the mirrored database to SharePoint.

- If you want to restore a single site collection, site, list, or library from a database backup, you can restore the entire database in SQL, then back up individual items from the restored unattached database in Central Administration. Finally, you can restore those backed up items to your live SharePoint farm.

- When you want to migrate content from a backed-up database into a new SharePoint farm.

RESTORE A DATABASE TO SQL SERVER

If you used the SQL backup tools to protect any database, you can restore it by following these steps. You can restore any database this way, including SharePoint content databases, service application databases, and SQL system databases. While the restore takes place, the database is taken offline, so there is an interruption in service to users. In this example, the Contoso intranet content database is restored.

> **IMPORTANT** **SQL SERVER ROLES**
>
> To complete the restore procedure, you must be logged on with a user account that has the sysadmin server role.

1. Click Start, All Programs, Microsoft SQL Server 2008 R2, and then click SQL Server Management Studio.

2. In the Connect To Server dialog box, select the SQL Server that stores the content database you want to configure, and then click Connect.

3. Expand Databases, right-click SharePoint_Content_Intranet, click Tasks, click Restore, and then click Database.

4. In the Source For Restore section, select From Device, and then click the Browse button.

5. In the Specify Backup dialog box, in the Backup Media drop-down list, select File, and then click Add.

6. Browse to and select the file you want to restore from, and then click OK.

7. In the Specify Backup dialog box, click OK.

8. In the list of Backup Sets, select the backup set you want to restore. You can see the date and time each set was backed up in this list.

9. In the Select A Page pane, click Options.

10. Select the Overwrite The Existing Database check box.

11. Click OK.

> **NOTE** **RESTORING AN UNATTACHED DATABASE**
>
> In this example, the restored database is automatically attached to SharePoint. To create an unattached database, create a new, empty database in SQL Management Studio and then restore the backup into it.

ATTACH A RESTORED DATABASE

If you have a content database in SQL that is not attached to SharePoint, you can attach it with the following steps. You might have an unattached database if you have restored a backup to a new SQL database or if you have a mirrored database. You can also use this technique to migrate an entire content database from one SharePoint farm to another.

> **IMPORTANT** **THE DBOWNER SQL PERMISSION**
>
> To complete the following procedure, you must ensure that the SharePoint farm service account has the dbowner role on the unattached content database.

1. In the Central Administration Quick Launch, click Application Management.

2. Under Databases, click Manage Content Databases.

3. Click Add A Content Database.

4. Under Web Application, select the web application to which you want to attach the content database.

5. In the Database Server text box, type the name of the SQL Server that hosts the unattached content database.

6. In the Database Name text box, type the name of the unattached content database.

7. Click OK.

RECOVER ITEMS FROM AN UNATTACHED DATABASE

If you want to recover only certain site collections, sites, lists, or libraries from an unattached content database, you must begin by backing up those items from the unattached content database. In the following example procedure, a site collection is backed up:

1. In the Central Administration Quick Launch, click Backup And Restore.

2. Under Granular Backup, click Recover Data From An Unattached Content Database.

3. Under Database Name And Authentication, in the Database Server text box, type the name of the SQL Server that hosts the unattached content database.

4. In the Database Name text box, type the name of the unattached content database.

5. Under Operation To Perform, select Browse Content, and then click Next.

6. Under Site Collection, select the site collection you want to back up.

7. Under Operation To Perform, select Backup Site Collection, and then click Next.

8. In the Filename text box, type the path and filename where you want to create the backup file and then click Start Backup.

9. When the backup is complete use a Granular Restore operation in Central Administration to create the site collection in your SharePoint farm.

PRACTICE   Configure User Profiles

Practices are designed to guide you through important procedures. The instructions in the Training Kit are high-level instructions that will challenge you to think carefully and to apply the procedures that are covered in this lesson and elsewhere in the Training Kit. If you need assistance, consult the detailed, step-by-step instructions in the Practice Answers on the companion media.

   In this practice, you use the Recycle Bin to recover accidentally deleted items and back up the SharePoint farm configuration. You will also back up the Teams content database, restore it to an unattached database, and then import items from the restored database into the intranet site collection.

Prepare for the Practice

Before you perform this practice, ensure that your lab environment has been built according to the instructions found in the Introduction to this Training Kit.

1. Apply the snapshot CHAPTER 05 to CONTOSO-DC.

2. Apply the snapshot CHAPTER 05 to SP2010-WFE1.

3. Start CONTOSO-DC.

   Wait for the virtual machine to complete startup, at which time the Press Ctrl+Alt+Delete prompt appears.

4. Start SP2010-WFE1.

5. Log on to SP2010-WFE1 as **CONTOSO\SP_Admin** with the password **Pa$$w0rd**.

EXERCISE 1   Create a List in the Teams Site

In this exercise, you create a list and some items in the Teams site collection for use in later exercises:

1. Open Internet Explorer and browse to the Teams site collection.

2. Create a new List. Use the following guidance and settings:

   - Template: Announcements
   - Name: Disaster Recovery Testing

3. Create a new announcement in the list with the title Current Testing Tasks.

4. The body of new announcement should describe that you will test the Recycle Bin, the backup of configuration values, and the unattached database.

EXERCISE 2   Configure the Recycle Bin

In this exercise, you configure the retention times for the Teams site collection Recycle Bins:

1. Open Central Administration.

2. In the General Settings for the Contoso Team Web Application, locate the Recycle Bin Settings.

3. Configure the first-stage Recycle Bin to delete items after 40 days.

4. Configure the second-stage Recycle Bin to add 60 percent of the live site quota.

EXERCISE 3   Delete and Recover Items from the Recycle Bin

In this exercise, you use the Recycle Bin to restore accidentally deleted items:

1. Browse to the Disaster Recovery Testing list in the Teams site collection.

2. Delete the Current Testing Tasks announcement.

3. Click the Recycle Bin link in the Quick Launch to display the stage 1 Recycle Bin.

4. Delete the Current Testing Tasks announcement from the stage 1 Recycle Bin.

5. Go to Site Settings and open the Site Collection Recycle Bin.

6. Examine the list of items deleted from the end user Recycle Bin.

7. Restore the Current Testing Tasks announcement.

8. Check the Disaster Recovery Testing list to ensure that the announcement has reappeared.

EXERCISE 4   Back Up the Farm Configuration

In this exercise, you use the SharePoint Central Administration backup tools to protect the farm configuration settings:

1. Create a new folder called **backups** in the root of the C: drive.

2. In Central Administration, use the Farm Backup and Restore tool to perform a backup.

3. Back up the entire Farm object. Use the following guidance and settings:

   - Backup Type: Full
   - Back up only configuration settings
   - Backup Location: C:\backups

4. When the backup is complete, examine the contents of the C:\backups folder.

EXERCISE 5 Back Up a Content Database

In this exercise, you use the SQL Server backup tool to protect the Teams content database:

1. Start SQL Server Management and connect to the localhost SQL Server.

2. Back up the SharePoint_Content_Teams database. Use the following guidance and settings:

   - Description: Testing the SQL Backup Tools for SharePoint Recovery
   - Destination: C:\backups\sqlbackuptest.bak

3. When the backup is complete, examine the contents of the C:\backups folder.

EXERCISE 6 Restore a Content Database to an Unattached Database

In this exercise, you restore the backup you just created to a new, unattached content database:

1. Use SQL Server Management Studio to create a new database called SharePoint_Content_Teams_Unattached.

2. On the new database use the Restore Database tool. Use the following guidance and settings:

   - Source for Restore: From Device.
   - Source for Restore: C:\backups\sqlbackuptest.bak.
   - Select the only backup set.

3. On the Options page, use the following guidance and settings:

   a. Overwrite the existing database

   b. Change the database file path to: C:\Program Files \Microsoft SQL Server\MSSQL10_50.MSSQLSERVER \MSSQL\DATA\SharePoint_Content_Teams_Unattached.mdf

   c. Change the log file path to: C:\Program Files \Microsoft SQL Server\MSSQL10_50.MSSQLSERVER \MSSQL\DATA\SharePoint_Content_Teams_Unattached_log.ldf

4. Execute the restore.

EXERCISE 7 Export a List from an Unattached Content Database

In this exercise, you export a list from the unattached content database SharePoint_Content_Teams_Unattached so that you can import it into the intranet site in the next exercise:

1. In Central Administration, browse to Backup And Restore.

2. Use the Recover Data From An Unattached Content Database tool. Use the following guidance and settings:

   - Database Name: SharePoint_Content_Teams_Unattached
   - Site: /
   - List: Disaster Recovery Testing

- Operation to Perform: Export Site or List
- File Location: C:\backups\DisasterRecoveryTestingList.cmp

EXERCISE 8   Import a List to the Intranet Site Collection

In this exercise, you import the Disaster Recovery Testing list into the intranet site collection. This task can only be completed by using the *Import-SPWeb* Windows PowerShell cmdlet:

1. In the SharePoint 2010 Management Shell, issue a command to import the Disaster Recovery Testing list from the export file you just created. Use the following settings and guidance:

   - Cmdlet: *Import-SPWeb*
   - Identity: http://intranet.contoso.com
   - Path: C:\backups\DisasterRecoveryTestingList.cmp

2. When the import is complete, browse the lists in the Contoso intranet site. The Disaster Recovery Testing list is present with its original content.

Lesson Summary

- A thorough backup and restore plan is the ultimate resort when disasters happen.
- The critical role played by SharePoint in many organizations makes disaster recovery the highest priority.
- Backup and restore techniques can also be used to recover accidentally deleted items and to migrate content from one SharePoint farm to another.
- Your backup strategy should be planned carefully to maximize the speed of recovery operations within the available budget.
- You should rehearse recovery operations to overcome difficulties before they delay recovery or prevent user productivity.
- The Recycle Bin in SharePoint ensures that you rarely have to restore accidentally deleted items from backup media.
- Central Administration includes Farm Backup and Granular Backup tools.
- You can automate complex backup and restore procedures by encapsulating them in Windows PowerShell scripts.
- The IIS configuration should be backed up by using appcmd.exe.
- SQL Server backup methods can be used on any SharePoint database.

Lesson Review

You can use the following questions to test your knowledge of the information in Lesson 2, "Back Up and Restore SharePoint." The questions are also available on the companion media in a practice test if you prefer to review them in electronic form.

1. You want to back up all the data and configuration information for your SharePoint farm. You begin by using the Central Administration tool to perform a full backup on the entire farm, both content and configuration data. Which of the following steps should you also take to complete your backup? (Choose all that apply.)

    A. None. The full farm backup protects all content and configuration values.

    B. Use SQL tools to back up SQL System databases.

    C. Use SQL tools to back up the content databases.

    D. Use the Appcmd.exe tool to back up the IIS configuration.

    E. Use the Granular Backup tool in Central Administration to back up all site collections.

2. You have been using SQL Management Studio to back up a SharePoint content database for the past six months. You are using the Full restore model and transaction logs and database files are stored on a single disk. No other backup tool has been used. This morning users complained of SharePoint errors and you have determined that the database disk has failed. You replace the disk and begin restoring the database. Which of the following can you restore?

    A. The Search service application configuration.

    B. The Search index files.

    C. All SharePoint content up to the point of failure.

    D. All SharePoint content up to the point of the last backup.

    E. The IIS configuration.

Chapter Review

To further practice and reinforce the skills you learned in this chapter, you can perform the following tasks:

- Review the chapter summary.
- Review the list of key terms introduced in this chapter.
- Complete the case scenarios. These scenarios set up real-world situations involving the topics of this chapter and ask you to create a solution.
- Complete the suggested practices.
- Take a practice test.

Chapter Summary

- High-availability architectures ensure that your SharePoint farm is resilient to hardware and software failures.
- High-availability architectures enable SharePoint to conform to the strictest SLA availability requirements.
- To ensure the availability of your farm, you should design it without any single points of failure and with multiple levels of redundancy.
- Fault-tolerant hardware, such as RAID arrays and hardware load balancers, are highly effective but expensive.
- Software solutions, such as NLB and Windows RAID arrays, are cheaper but cannot guarantee the highest levels of availability.
- Application servers are automatically load balanced by SharePoint.
- Databases can be made fault-tolerant by using Failover Clustering or Database Mirroring.
- A strict and well-rehearsed backup and restore plan ensures that the impact of disasters is minimized.
- The SharePoint Recycle Bin can be used to restore the majority of accidentally deleted items without restoring them from backup media.
- The Farm Backup tool in Central Administration can back up the entire farm or just its configuration values.
- The Granular Backup tool in Central Administration can back up a site collection, site, list, or library.
- You can use Windows PowerShell to script complex backup and restore routines.
- SQL Server includes backup tools that you can use to back up most SharePoint data.

Key Terms

- High availability
- Fault tolerance
- Service Level Agreement
- Scheduled downtime
- Unscheduled downtime
- Denial of service
- Botnet
- Application-layer security
- RAID array
- UPS
- DNS round robin
- NLB
- The Application Discovery and Load Balancer Service
- Failover Clustering
- Database Mirroring
- Full backups
- Differential backups
- Disaster recovery
- Farm backup
- Granular backup
- SQL Server recovery models
- Transaction log backup
- Unattached content database

Case Scenario: Improving Resilience and Recovery Times

In the following case scenario, you apply what you've learned about subjects of this chapter. You can find answers to these questions in the "Answers" section at the end of this book.

Your SharePoint farm consists of a single web front-end server, a single application server that runs all service applications, and a single database server. The rollout has been highly successful and business-critical documents and processes are now dependent on SharePoint. In the last month, three service failures caused downtime for different reasons. The board has asked you to improve the availability of SharePoint and make it resilient to the specific failures that occurred. You have a generous but not unlimited budget for hardware changes.

1. You traced the first failure to a hard disk on the Search service application servers. Users were unable to run searches without errors because the index files were unavailable. How can you ensure that such an event does not cause a service interruption in the future?

2. You traced the second failure to a network card failure on the web front-end server. Users were unable to connect to SharePoint at all. How can you ensure that such an event does not cause a service interruption in the future?

3. The third event was a localized fire that affected a portion of your datacenter. The board recognizes that IT cannot prevent such disasters but they would like you to improve the speed of recovery, which took many hours because you initially restored backups in the wrong order. How can you guarantee that future restore operations proceed more smoothly?

Suggested Practices

To help you successfully master the exam objectives presented in this chapter, complete the following tasks.

Practice 1: Set Up a Multi-Server SharePoint Farm in the Lab

The practices in this book are designed to run on virtualized hardware with limited memory. Therefore, it's not possible to simulate building a SharePoint farm with several web front-end and application servers or demonstrate SQL Server failover clustering. If you have a virtualization platform with a very large amount of RAM or a lab environment with many computers, you can practice setting up a highly available network:

1. Add several servers to the SharePoint farm and configure them as web front-end servers.

2. Experiment with DNS round robin and NLB to distribute the load between front-end servers. Examine what happens when one server fails—can users still connect and how long does any service interruption last?

3. Add application servers dedicated to one or more service applications to the farm. Investigate how load is distributed across these servers and test what happens when an application server fails.

4. If you have sufficient hardware, set up a SQL Server failover cluster. Test how long failover takes and whether uses receive errors if a cluster node fails.

Practice 2: Using Backups to Migrate Data

At the beginning of Lesson 2, you saw how backups can be used to migrate data, not just for disaster recovery. This is an excellent way, for example, to create a realistic lab environment in which administrators can practice procedures and developers can test code. If you have separate production and testing SharePoint farms:

1. Use a SQL Server backup on the production environment to create a backup file of the content databases and service application databases.

2. Use the SQL Restore tools to create these databases in the lab environment.

3. Attach the content databases in SharePoint Central Administration.

4. Test whether users can access the content.

Take a Practice Test

The practice tests on this book's companion media offer many options. For example, you can test yourself on only the lesson review content, or you can test yourself on all the 70-667 certification exam objectives. You can set up the test so that it closely simulates the experience of taking a certification exam, or you can set it up in study mode so that you can look at the correct answers and explanations after you answer each question.

> **MORE INFO**   **PRACTICE TESTS**
>
> For details about all the practice test options available, see the "How to Use the Practice Tests" section in this book's Introduction.

CHAPTER 12

Monitoring and Optimizing SharePoint Performance

The speed with which a SharePoint farm serves content to users is critical to the success of your system. Many users, especially on the Internet, are very unforgiving of slow responses and you can lose customers if pages take longer than five seconds to load. On intranets and extranets, users might be working with large documents, videos, and other content that quickly become unwieldy if SharePoint cannot retrieve them fast. Users also expect search results within a very short time frame. By purchasing more and faster hardware you can often solve these problems, but unless you fully understand a bottleneck, you may waste your budget. For example, a network contention issue will not be solved by extra server memory. SharePoint Server 2010 includes many rich tools for performance analysis. In this chapter, you will learn how to use them to dissect the performance of your SharePoint farm and how to spot bottlenecks before they become a barrier to productivity. You will also see many techniques for optimizing your SharePoint configuration so that it makes maximum use of hardware resources.

Exam objectives in this chapter:

- Manage operational settings.
- Monitor and analyze a SharePoint environment.
- Manage site collections.
- Optimize the performance of a SharePoint environment.

Lessons in this chapter:

Before You Begin

To complete the lessons in this chapter, you must build your lab environment according to the instructions found in the Introduction to this Training Kit and have done the following:

- Performed the practices in Chapter 1
- Performed the practices in Chapter 7

 **REAL WORLD**

Alistair Matthews

Although the SharePoint documentation and the SharePoint IT Pro community discuss performance frequently and in depth, many less efficient IT departments do not analyze the performance of their systems. I suppose the reasoning is "If it ain't broke don't try to fix it," but omission often causes trouble. It's a bit like driving a car in fog—you might be about to run into a brick wall. By keeping a careful eye on your performance and how it changes over time, you can disperse the fog and spot problems before they affect users.

If you are a consultant and arrive at a new client's office to deal with a farm you have not configured before, I recommend that you ask to see the benchmark performance test results. You'll be surprised by the number of times this request results in a blank look or an embarrassed silence. If you've been hired to improve performance, such data is essential.

Lesson 1: Monitor Performance

A SharePoint farm is a complex system. It may have multiple servers all taking different roles and running different services. Each role places specific demands on its server's hardware. If at any point in this system demand exceeds capacity, performance suffers and user productivity may fall. The biggest challenge in such a situation is often to identify the component that is at fault. Multiple servers are involved in delivering a page to a user—which server is causing the problem and what services or software components are overtaxing hardware resources? To answer such questions, you must analyze the performance of your farm in detail. In this way you can determine how to resolve the contention and maximize the speed of delivery. In this lesson, you learn how to examine and profile your SharePoint system's performance to ensure that users always get their content delivered quickly.

After this lesson, you will be able to:

- Use Performance Monitor to analyze a SharePoint farm.
- Ensure that a SharePoint farm architecture has enough resources to support your users.
- Create benchmark performance records and identify trends.
- Resolve bottlenecks and troubleshoot poor performance.
- Configure your SharePoint farm for monitoring and troubleshooting.
- Choose the right counters to examine a performance issue.
- Use the developer dashboard to obtain page rendering performance data.

Estimated Lesson Time: 90 minutes

Introduction to Monitoring SharePoint

Any experienced system architect monitors her systems regularly and for many different purposes, although the ultimate goal in every case is to ensure that the system responds rapidly to users. The process begins before SharePoint is deployed to users—monitoring simulated stress placed on a test farm can identify performance problems that arise from your unique requirements. Monitoring continues through the deployment phase and into day-to-day running of the system to spot potential problems before they affect users.

A key concept in performance analysis is that of the bottleneck. A bottleneck is a component of the system for which demand exceeds supply and it represents the point at which you should reconfigure or add resources to increase the performance of the system. For example, consider a SharePoint web front-end server that serves many videos to site visitors. At times of peak site traffic, videos take too long to stream and users are browsing to other sites. If the server processors cannot render video rapidly enough, they are the bottleneck. Adding memory will do nothing to accelerate rendering. Unless you can identify bottlenecks, you may waste budget on upgrades that do not address the root cause.

Always have a clear idea of the question you wish to answer by testing performance. For example, you may want to determine how a custom Web Part will add load to your farm, how long it will take to import user profiles, or how a Business Connectivity Services (BCS) connection might load an external database. Each of these questions requires a different testing approach and your choice of counters and test conditions will be distinctive.

In the following sections, you learn how to approach performance testing before and after deployment and for different purposes.

Pre-Deployment Performance Testing

In the design phase of a deployment project, you can use published recommendations and scalability results to specify your server hardware. You start with estimated numbers of users, documents, media files, search requirements, and other values and work toward numbers of servers, processors, memory sizes, and so on.

> **MORE INFO CAPACITY PLANNING GUIDELINES FOR SHAREPOINT 2010**
>
> TechNet includes an excellent article on this capacity planning process: *http://technet .microsoft.com/en-us/library/ff758645.aspx*.

You should be clear, however, that this capacity planning process can only create an architecture that is *likely* to satisfy performance requirements. This is because the recommendations are created by measurements in typical SharePoint farms. You must bear in mind that your farm may not be typical and that some unique condition, such as a custom component or an unusual methodology, may place extra load on the system and give rise to a bottleneck.

For example, a custom Web Part that is used extensively in many sites and for many users may be memory-intensive even if it is designed and coded well. Your server memory may exceed all the published recommendations and still not support the requirements of the Web Part.

To run realistic tests before you deploy SharePoint, you must create a test environment. You should do this after you have completed your capacity planning and have a good architecture for a farm that you think will respond well to demand. The test environment requires the following components:

- **A Test SharePoint Farm**   This must match the proposed production farm as closely as possible both in terms of server numbers and hardware specifications for each server. In fact, it is a good idea to purchase all the hardware for the production environment and use it for the test environment first. It is not appropriate, for example, to use virtualization in the test environment unless you plan on using virtualization in production as well. This would render all performance test results meaningless. Some organizations with larger budgets and stricter Service Level Agreements (SLAs) maintain matching test and production farms after deployment. The test farm can be used to ensure that content and custom code run securely and efficiently and that they do not compromise security and scalability.

- **Custom Components** Any custom components that you have developed in-house or purchased from third parties may significantly alter the performance of some part of your farm. It is critical to include these in your test environment to generate results that are close to your proposed production farm.

- **Realistic Sample Content** The closer the match between the content in the test and production farms, the more accurate and reliable your tests will be. Ideally, you may have content that you can import into the test farm. For example, if you are upgrading from SharePoint 2007, you can use the migration techniques described in Chapter 9, "Deploying and Upgrading to SharePoint 2010," to import your organization's actual content into the test environment. Bear in mind that if you do this, some data might be sensitive and your migration should not allow members of the test team to access data in the test farm that they are denied access to in the legacy system.

- **Load Simulation Tools** The test environment lacks actual users to place a load on the servers. Therefore, you must simulate load. A wide range of tools are available to help you with this. Microsoft publishes the SharePoint Load Test Kit as part of the SharePoint 2010 Administration Toolkit. This can be used with Visual Studio Ultimate to run complex and thorough load simulation tests. Later in this chapter, you will see how to configure these tools.

Once this infrastructure is in place, you can run tests to find out whether your proposed architecture supports the load you expect users to impose. Focus your tests on detailed and precise performance questions such as:

- How are server resources consumed by serving a single page?

- How are server resources consumed by serving a single document of average size?

- How are server resources consumed by serving a piece of rich media such as a video or Silverlight application?

- How are server resources consumed by more complex sequences of operation? For example, what happens when a user checks a document out, downloads it, uploads a new version, and checks it in?

- How long is a crawl likely to take?

- How does a crawl affect the system's response time to user requests?

- How long is a backup likely to take and how does it affect the system's response time to user requests?

Later in this chapter, you will learn how to configure tests that address such questions and build a full picture of the performance of your proposed farm.

Benchmarking and Regular Performance Monitoring

Monitoring should by no means cease during and after deployment. In fact, the deployment phase of a role-out project should be the time that your production environment is most intensively monitored. Both during and after deployment, you must identify trends in usage and demand to intercept bottlenecks before they become critical.

In most cases, you will move users onto the new system in phases. For example, you may choose to introduce users one department at a time or add new projects, with their users, on SharePoint as they begin. As each new group of users is added, you must profile performance both to ensure that their needs are met and to guarantee that the next groups can be accommodated. By monitoring each phase of the deployment in this way, you can gain confidence in the capacity of the system while minimizing the consequences of failures.

When the deployment is complete and everyone is using your production SharePoint farm, do not think that regular performance monitoring can be dispensed with. This is because patterns of use and demand rarely stay constant over long periods of time. For example, as users become confident with SharePoint, discover more features, and receive proper training, they are likely to make higher demands and encourage their coworkers to do the same. In many cases you will observe a gradual increase in demand over the first few months. New sites, service applications, and custom components are also all likely to alter demand.

The identification of such trends in demand is made complex by the cycles that every system experiences. For example:

- During each work day, you will observe peaks and troughs as users arrive at work, have lunch, complete their tasks, and leave for home. If your farm serves people in more than one time zone, two or more such cycles will be superimposed.

- Some companies, such as accountancies, are closed on weekends and you will see low demand. Other companies, such as retailers, may be busier on Saturdays. Other cultures have different work patterns that accommodate religious observances.

- During a year, you may notice high and low demand. For example, when schools are out, many users take vacations. By contrast, in the run up to Christmas, retailers are likely to be very busy.

In addition to these cyclical variations, one-off events can influence demand. For example, during a product launch demand may be unusually high. If many of your users attend the same conference, demand is likely to be low.

If you want to identify meaningful long-term trends in performance, you must filter out such daily, weekly, and annual cycles and compare like with like. Take the following precautions to ensure that you identify real trends that are not confused with one-off or cyclical variations:

- Begin by identifying typical cyclical variations for your own company. In your organization, these may be very different from those in the preceding list.

- Monitor over a significant time period. For example, monitor over a full 24 hours and compare average values or compare charts of demand variation.

- Avoid monitoring performance on unusual days. Try to monitor a typical work day for the users of your farm.

- Choose to monitor similar days in cyclical variations. For example, the second Monday in March should occupy a similar position in annual and weekly cycles for many companies. By monitoring on that day in two or more years, you can spot increasing or decreasing trends in demand.

By monitoring performance in these ways soon after deployment, you can create a detailed profile of the demands placed on your system and the way it responds. Such an initial profile is called a *benchmark*. It is intended as a reference against which to compare similar profiles taken at later dates. When you compare the benchmark with later performance data, you can diagnose changes in demand and respond before they cause bottlenecks.

Identifying Bottlenecks and Troubleshooting

By benchmarking and regular monitoring as described in the previous section, you can stay ahead of gradual changes in demand and upgrade or reconfigure your farm before bottlenecks arise and responsiveness degrades. However, unexpected events such as sudden changes in user behavior or working practices can result in sudden leaps in demand that your system cannot respond to. For this reason, it is not possible to make your system invulnerable to bottlenecks. If they develop, you must diagnose their precise nature as quickly as possible. This information will enable you to make an appropriate upgrade or reconfiguration so that the system returns to high performance.

> **IMPORTANT FOCUS ON PEAK DEMAND**
>
> In the previous section you saw how demand varies in cycles of different lengths and in response to one-off events. When benchmarking, you must try to avoid monitoring at unusual times so that you can compare times of similar demand and identify trends.
>
> Things are different when you are identifying bottlenecks. Usually, these are only restrictive at times of peak demand. Therefore you should try to run tests at peak times in the day and week, and you shouldn't be interested in average values. And in the event of a one-off event that you expect to cause extra demand, you should monitor so that you can observe the bottleneck in action.

When you understand the bottleneck clearly, you can choose an appropriate upgrade, such as extra memory, an upgraded processor, or even an additional server. However, because SharePoint has a flexible architecture, bear in mind that you may be able to resolve the issue without spending budget on new hardware. For example, if your monitoring has identified the bottleneck on a heavily utilized application server, you may be able to resolve it by moving a service application to another under-utilized server in the farm.

Sources of Information

In SharePoint 2010, you have many sources of performance data that can help you to test and optimize a farm, including:

- **Diagnostic Logs** SharePoint records activity in diagnostic logs. You can configure the classes of events that are saved here as well as the log's location. Diagnostic logs are most useful for troubleshooting but may also help profile the farm's performance. Diagnostic logs are also known as trace logs and Unified Logging Service (ULS) logs.

- **Performance Monitor**   This rich Windows administration tool can be used to examine performance live or make logs over long time periods for later analysis. Many counters are available for Windows, SharePoint, and SQL Server so that you can analyze the system in great detail.

- **Developer dashboard**   This tool displays components of a SharePoint web page together with their load times. Although the developer dashboard is designed to assist developers to author fast code, administrators can also use it to view the performance of user interface components.

- **Usage Reports and Web Analytics**   SharePoint includes native tools for recording usage and server health. You can view this data in a range of reports in Central Administration. Web Analytics reports are similar but targeted at website administrators. You will learn more about SharePoint's native reporting tools in Lesson 3.

- **Fiddler**   Fiddler is a tool for observing and debugging HTTP traffic between a browser and a web server. SharePoint delivers all its content via HTTP, so Fiddler can tell you a lot about how SharePoint responds to users. You can download Fiddler from *http://www.fiddler2.com/fiddler2/*.

Preparing for Monitoring

Before you monitor performance in a test or production farm, you should make some configuration changes so that more information is gathered than normal. In a test environment, you must also prepare the load simulation tools.

Configuring SharePoint for Monitoring

In the default configuration SharePoint collects some information for monitoring and troubleshooting. However, when you are profiling performance or diagnosing bottlenecks, extra information is helpful. You should therefore consider altering the settings in Table 12-1.

TABLE 12-1 Settings for Monitoring and Troubleshooting

SETTING	DEFAULT VALUE	VALUE FOR MONITORING	DESCRIPTION
Event Log Flooding Protection	Enabled	Disabled	This setting prevents SharePoint logging many events to the Event Logs. When you are troubleshooting, these events may help to identify the problem.
The Microsoft SharePoint Foundation Usage Data Import Timer Job	30 minutes	5 minutes	This timer job imports data from logs into the usage database. When you are troubleshooting, you may want to ensure that the database is as current as possible, so increase the frequency of the timer job is appropriate.
Enable all diagnostic providers	Disabled	Enabled	Only the "Search Health Monitoring – Trace Events" provider is enabled by default. Other diagnostic providers may help to diagnose problems or bottlenecks.
Job Diagnostics Performance Counter Providers	5 minutes	1 minute	These providers limit the frequency that counters can poll the performance of web front-end and SQL Servers. By lowering them, you can increase their resolution when you record them in Performance Monitor.
Usage Data Collection Counters	Disabled	Enabled	You can enable the following counters to get a better understanding of usage patterns in your farm: Content Import Usage Content Export Usage Page Requests Feature Use Search Query Use Site Inventory Usage Timer Jobs Rating Usage

CONFIGURE THE FREQUENCY OF THE MICROSOFT SHAREPOINT FOUNDATION USAGE DATA IMPORT TIMER JOB

To ensure that usage database is updated frequently, take the following steps:

1. In the Central Administration Quick Launch, click Monitoring.

2. Under Timer Jobs, click Review Job Definitions.

3. Scroll down and click the Microsoft SharePoint Foundation Usage Data Import timer job.

4. Under Recurring Schedule, select minutes and type **5** in the Every Minute(s) box.

5. Click OK.

CONFIGURE USAGE DATA COLLECTION

Use the following steps to enable usage data collection and configure the data that will be collected. You can specify a SQL Server database where usage information will be stored and a maximum log file size:

1. In the Central Administration Quick Launch, click Monitoring.

2. Under Reporting, click Configure Usage And Health Data Collection.

3. Under Usage Data Collection, select the Enable Usage Data Collection checkbox.

4. Under Event Selection, select the events that interest you. For example, if you are monitoring website usage, select Page Requests.

5. Under Logging Database Server, fill in the name of the server and database where you want to store usage and health data.

6. At the bottom of the page, click OK.

CONFIGURE DIAGNOSTIC LOGGING

Diagnostic logs are useful for both troubleshooting and performance tuning. Although the logs themselves are difficult to read and analyze in their raw form, the ULS Viewer tool mentioned earlier provides a simple way to mine them for information. When you configure diagnostic logging, you can specify where the location logs are stored, as well as the logging level for events of different types. These logging levels apply to both diagnostic logs and the event logs. This is also where you enable event log flood protection. To configure these logs, follow these steps:

1. In the Central Administration Quick Launch, click Monitoring.

2. Under Reporting, click Configure Diagnostic Logging.

3. To view the Event and Diagnostic logging level for an event category, expand the appropriate containers. For example, to view the levels for SharePoint Cache, expand All Categories and SharePoint Server. The logging levels are listed to the right of the SP Cache category.

4. To alter the logging levels for a category, select its check box, then under the list of categories, select the least critical event to report to the event logs and the diagnostic logs.

5. To disable event log flood protection, clear the Enable Event Log Flood Protection checkbox.

6. To configure the location of diagnostic logs, under Trace Log, type your preferred location in the Path textbox.

> **IMPORTANT** DIAGNOSTIC LOG LOCATION
>
> The path you use for diagnostic logs must exist on all SharePoint servers in the farm.

7. In this section, you can also configure a maximum time to retain diagnostic logs and a maximum for the logs. These settings prevent diagnostic logs from consuming disk space but may cause important events to be removed. When one of these maximum values is reached, the oldest entries in the log are removed.

8. At the bottom of the page, click OK.

> **IMPORTANT** RECONFIGURING FOR PERFORMANCE
>
> Be aware that the configuration changes described in Table 12-1 aid diagnosis but decrease system performance slightly. They also log more information to the hard disk. When you have finished diagnosis and troubleshooting operations, it is important to set them back to the default values so that your farm performance is at its best.

Stress Simulation Tools

In a production farm, load is generated by normal user operations. However, a test environment has few or no real users. Therefore you must simulate the load that users place on the system so that you can identify the performance limits of your proposed farm.

Microsoft provides the following tools that you can use to generate simulated loads for performance tests:

- **Visual Studio Ultimate 2010** This software package includes a range of tools for application life-cycle management and is designed to help teams of developers to collaborate on software packages. Its testing tools enable users to create and run elaborate and flexible load simulations on software.

- **The SharePoint 2010 Administration Toolkit** This toolkit includes a range of tools for advanced administration, such as a Security Configuration Wizard that reduces the vulnerability of a SharePoint farm to various malicious attacks. Part of this toolkit is the Load Testing Kit (LTK). The LTK includes two command-line utilities that prepare a SharePoint farm for load testing and a Visual Studio project file with preconfigured tests for a SharePoint farm.

Using Performance Monitor

In the Windows Server 2003 or 2008 Administrative Tools, you can find the Performance Monitor snap-in. This tool can measure and record a large range of performance data generated by Windows services and components, SharePoint, SQL, and other software packages you may be using. The versatility of the tool is due to the large number of counters that are available. Many of these are built into Windows. Others are added by software packages, such as SharePoint, Exchange, and SQL Server.

You should already be familiar with this tool from your Windows administration experience so this section will present a short reminder of Performance Monitor's main features and then concentrate on counters that are relevant to SharePoint tuning.

Performance Monitor, Data Collector Sets, and Reports

Within the Performance Monitor snap-in, you will find the following containers:

- **Monitoring Tools**   In this container, you can use the Performance Monitor tool to examine performance counters in real time as the system responds to users. You can also view logged data saved by data collector sets.

- **Data Collector Sets**   A data collector set is a collection of performance counters, trace logs, and configuration logs. Having defined a data set, you can use it to start recording data over short or long periods. For example, you could run a data collector for 24 hours to examine the system performance over an entire daily cycle.

- **Reports**   When you run a data collector set, the values of counters and logs are recorded periodically and stored on the hard disk. The Reports container shows detailed summary reports of this data.

> **MORE INFO**   **USING PERFORMANCE MONITOR**
>
> For more information on using the Windows Performance Monitor tool, see this step-by-step guide: *http://technet.microsoft.com/en-us/library/cc771692%28WS.10%29.aspx*.

Windows Performance Counters

Because Windows Server underlies SharePoint, many generic operating systems counters are relevant to SharePoint. SharePoint cannot function efficiently unless Windows is optimally configured and hardware is well specified. Table 12-2 shows counters you can use to diagnose problems with hardware.

TABLE 12-2 Hardware Counters

OBJECT	DESCRIPTION
Processor	Counters for the Processor object describe the behavior of CPUs in a server. If you have multiple CPUs or multiple cores in a single CPU, multiple instances of the Processer object appear and you can choose between them. You can also choose to monitor the Total instance—that is, all instances. The % Processor Time, for example, should be sustained above 80 percent, although it will frequently peak over this level.
Network Interface	Counters for the Network Interface object describe how fast data is sent and received. Ensure that network traffic remains below about 50 percent of network segment capacity.
Logical Disk and Cache	Logical Disk counters relate to a partition on a hard drive. Physical Disk counters relate to an entire hard drive. Note, however, that hardware RAID arrays appear as single physical disks to Windows. You should ensure that % Disk Time is less than 80 percent and that queues do not reach excessive lengths. Disk caches should not register frequent failures.
Memory and Paging File	Ensures that the working set is usually significantly less than physical memory. Page faults, which occur when an item is not in physical memory but must be retrieved from the page file, should be fewer than five per second.

Table 12-3 shows counters for Windows components and services that you should examine when tuning SharePoint.

TABLE 12-3 Software Counters

OBJECT	DESCRIPTION
Process	Note that many of the counters in the Processor object are also available in the Process object. So, for example, you can monitor the % Processor Time for an individual process, such as the sqlserver process.
ASP.NET	Microsoft SharePoint Foundation and SharePoint Server 2010 are built on the ASP.NET technology. Therefore the ASP.NET counters are relevant to SharePoint performance. The Requests Queued counter, for example, should remain small and static on web front-end servers and the Request Wait Time should be less than a second or so.

OBJECT	DESCRIPTION
.NET CLR Memory	.NET technology underlies ASP.NET, so this object is relevant to SharePoint. In particular, counters in this object describe how garbage collection is behaving. This is the removal of objects that are no longer in use from memory. Therefore, poor performance can indicate a memory problem. For example, the % Time in GC counter indicates the proportion of time that was spent in garbage collection. It should be less than 5 percent at all times in normal operation.

SharePoint Counters

When you install SharePoint on a Windows server, a large number of objects and counters are added to Performance Monitor so that you can analyze the behavior of SharePoint service applications, caches, and other components. Table 12-4 describes some of the most important SharePoint counters.

TABLE 12-4 SharePoint Performance Monitor Counters

OBJECT	DESCRIPTION
SharePoint Foundation	This object includes some general SharePoint counters. For example, the Responded Page Requests Rate is the number of pages served to users per second and you can use it to determine the speed of a proposed SharePoint farm in a test environment. If you are using page throttling, you can assess its impact by using the Throttled Page Requests counter. This object includes counters for the Object Cache.
Sandboxed Code Process Pool	Counters in this object describe the behavior of custom code run in the SharePoint sandbox. This includes user solutions. For example, you can use the Requests/Sec counter to measure the speed requests that are serviced by the sandbox process.
Excel Calculation Services	Counters in this object describe the Excel Calculation Services application within SharePoint. Because this service application can generate intensive load, use these counters to distinguish Excel load from other demands. Your results may argue, for example, for a separation of Excel Services onto a dedicated application server.
Shared Service Provider	Although Shared Service Providers have been replaced in SharePoint 2010 with service applications, the Shared Service Provider object is still found in Performance Monitor. With these counters, you can monitor the progress of user profile synchronization and My Sites throughput.

OBJECT	DESCRIPTION
SharePoint Foundation Search Gatherer	Counters in this object describe the behavior of the native SharePoint Search crawler. For example, the Active Queue Length is the number of items and documents in the crawler's indexing queue. The Server Objects counter is the number of servers, of all types, the crawler is currently connected to and indexing.
SharePoint Foundation Search FAST Content Provider	Counters in this object describe the behavior of the FAST Content service application as it crawls and indexes content. If you are using FAST instead of SharePoint Search, use these counters instead of the SharePoint Foundation Search Gatherer object.
SharePoint Disk-Based Cache	Several of the SharePoint objects in Performance Monitor enable you to monitor the caches SharePoint uses to optimize content delivery. Counters in this object describe the behavior of the BLOB Cache, which retains temporary copies of Binary Large Objects (BLOBs) for subsequent requests.
SharePoint Publishing Cache	Counters in this object describe the behavior of the SharePoint Output Cache. This cache stores copies of rendered page so that subsequent requests for the same page can be delivered rapidly.

> **MORE INFO**   **TUNING THE SHAREPOINT CACHES**
>
> Table 12-4 mentions counters for the BLOB cache, the object cache, and the output cache. Tuning the behavior of these caches is crucial to performance optimization. With these counters you can analyze cache performance. In Lesson 4, you will see how to adjust settings to optimize them.

SQL Server Counters

Like Windows services, SQL Server underlies SharePoint because it is used to store content and also data for service applications. If SQL performs poorly, SharePoint and user productivity are directly affected. SQL Server monitoring is therefore integral to SharePoint monitoring. Table 12-5 describes some of the more important SQL Server counters and objects.

TABLE 12-5 SQL Server Performance Monitor Counters

OBJECT	DESCRIPTION
SQL Server: General Statistics	The counters in this object describe server-wide quantities, such as the number of current connections to the server, the number of temporary tables, and the rate at which connections are reset.

OBJECT	DESCRIPTION
SQL Server: Databases	The counters in this object describe the behavior of the databases on the server. You can choose a single database or use the Total instance to study all of them. For example, you can use these counters to examine the performance of database transaction logs.
SQL Server: Transactions	By recording, in your baseline, the number of transactions per second for individual databases, you can diagnose trends in SQL Server usage.
SQL Server: Plan Cache	SQL Server uses the plan cache to retain stored procedures, Transact-SQL statements, and triggers. Counters in this object describe the behavior of this cache and are critical to SQL performance tuning.

MORE INFO **SQL SERVER MONITORING**

A full description of this very large topic is beyond the scope of this SharePoint book and we have listed only the most important SQL counters in this section. For more information on SQL Server monitoring tools and methods see *http://msdn.microsoft.com/en-us/library/ee377023%28v=bts.10%29.aspx.*

Using the Developer Dashboard

Page rendering time is a key value in SharePoint performance. If you use SharePoint to run an Internet-facing website, it is particularly critical because customers are particularly impatient with slow responses. Surveys show that, when pages typically take longer than five seconds to load, site visitors lose patience and browse elsewhere. On intranets and extranets, although users may persist for longer, slow page rendering has a direct impact on user productivity.

A SharePoint page often has multiple components, including the master page, content page, and multiple Web Parts. If a page is slow to load, it can be difficult to determine which component is causing the problem. This is the problem that the developer dashboard is designed to address. The developer dashboard is shown in Figure 12-1.

The dashboard shows the total execution time and other general information about the page, together with the time each phase of page rendering took to complete. Critically, the render times for all page components are displayed.

Although this dashboard is designed as a developer tool to encourage high-performance custom components, administrators will also frequently use it as a source of performance data and a troubleshooting tool.

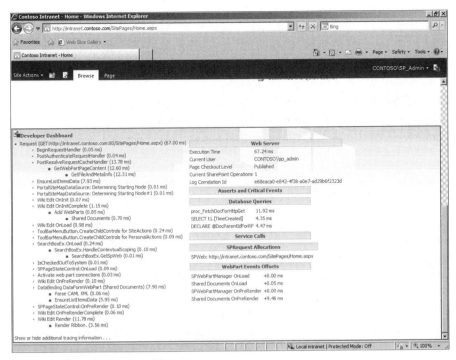

FIGURE 12-1 The developer dashboard

ENABLING THE DEVELOPER DASHBOARD

The developer dashboard has three modes:

- **Off** In this mode, the dashboard is never shown. This mode is appropriate for production and customer-facing sites when you are not troubleshooting page performance.

- **On** In this mode, the dashboard is always shown. This mode is appropriate when you are testing the performance of every page in a lab environment.

- **On Demand** In this mode, an icon appears in the top right of the page. Users can click this icon to view the dashboard. This mode is appropriate when you are troubleshooting individual pages.

To set the developer dashboard mode for a web application, you must run the following Windows PowerShell script:

```
$DevDashboardSettings =
[Microsoft.SharePoint.Administration.SPWebService]::
ContentService.DeveloperDashboardSettings;
$DevDashboardSettings.DisplayLevel = '<Mode>';
$DevDashboardSettings.RequiredPermissions = 'EmptyMask';
$DevDashboardSettings.TraceEnabled = $true;
$DevDashboardsettings.Update()
```

Where *<Mode>*is either "On", "Off", or "OnDemand".

PRACTICE   Monitor SharePoint Performance

Practices are designed to guide you through important procedures. The instructions in the Training Kit are high-level instructions that will challenge you to think carefully and to apply the procedures that are covered in this lesson and elsewhere in the Training Kit. If you need assistance, consult the detailed, step-by-step instructions in the Practice Answers on the companion media.

In this practice, you use a Performance Monitor data collector set to record some counters relevant to SharePoint performance. You simulate some user activity and examine the logged data. You enable and use the developer dashboard.

Prepare for the Practice

Before you perform this practice, ensure that your lab environment has been built according to the instructions found in the Introduction to this Training Kit.

1. Apply the snapshot CHAPTER 07 to CONTOSO-DC.
2. Apply the snapshot CHAPTER 07 to SP2010-WFE1.
3. Start CONTOSO-DC.

   Wait for the virtual machine to complete startup, at which time the Press Ctrl+Alt+Delete prompt appears.
4. Start SP2010-WFE1.
5. Log on to SP2010-WFE1 as **CONTOSO\SP_Admin** with the password **Pa$$w0rd**.

EXERCISE 1   Configure Diagnostic Logging and Usage Data Collection

In this exercise you configure locations for diagnostic logging and usage data. You also increase the amount of diagnostic information recorded.

1. Create a new folder in the root of the C:\ drive called **SPLogs**.
2. In the SPLogs folder, create a folder called **UsageData** and a folder called **TraceLogs**.

3. Open Central Administration and configure usage and health data collection. Use the following settings and guidance:

   ■ Enable usage data collection.

   ■ Do not log Content Import and Content Export events.

   ■ Usage data log file location: C:\SPLogs\UsageData.

   ■ Enable health data collection.

4. Configure diagnostic logging. Use the following settings and guidance:

   ■ Change the Event Log and Trace log reporting level to Verbose for SharePoint Server\Event Throttle and SharePoint Server\SP Cache objects.

   ■ Disable event log flood protection.

   ■ Trace log path: C:\SPLogs\TraceLogs.

5. Examine the contents of the C:\SPLogs\UsageData folder.

6. Examine the contents of the C:\SPLogs\TraceLogs folder.

EXERCISE 2   Configure a Data Collector Set in Performance Monitor

In this exercise, you create a data collector set in Performance Monitor and add several relevant counters to it:

1. Start Performance Monitor and create a new Data Collector Set. Use the following settings and guidance:

   ■ Name: SharePoint Analyzer

   ■ Create manually; do not use a template.

   ■ Sample Interval: 1 sec.

2. Add the following performance counters to the SharePoint Analyzer Data Collector Set:

   ■ Processor/%Processor Time (_Total instance)

   ■ Memory/Page Faults/Sec

   ■ SharePoint Foundation/Current Page Requests

   ■ SharePoint Search Gatherer Process/Crawls In Process.

3. Configure the Data Collector Set to store data in the C:\SPLogs\PerfMonLogs folder.

EXERCISE 3   Simulate User Activity

In this exercise, you start the data collector set you just created, and simulate user activity:

1. Start the SharePoint Analyzer data collector set you just created.

2. Open the Contoso intranet homepage and refresh the page several times.

3. Browse to other pages in the site and make frequent requests.

4. Switch back to Performance Monitor and stop the SharePoint Analyzer data collector set.

EXERCISE 4   Examine Performance Logs

In this exercise, you examine the performance data you just recorded:

1. Within the Monitoring Tools node, click the Performance Monitor object.

2. View Log Data. Open the log files you just recorded.

3. Add all the counters in the log files to the chart.

4. Examine the counters and note all the average values.

EXERCISE 5   Enable the Developer Dashboard

In this exercise, you put the developer dashboard into On Demand mode by issuing Windows PowerShell commands:

1. Use SharePoint 2010 Management Shell to issue the following commands in this order:

```
$DevDashboardSettings = [Microsoft.SharePoint.Administration.SPWebService]::
ContentService.DeveloperDashboardSettings;
$DevDashboardSettings.DisplayLevel = 'OnDemand';
$DevDashboardSettings.RequiredPermissions = 'EmptyMask';
$DevDashboardSettings.TraceEnabled = $true;
$DevDashboardSettings.Update();
```

2. Close the SharePoint 2010 Management Shell.

EXERCISE 6   Examine the Performance Data in the Developer Dashboard

In this exercise, you examine the data in the developer dashboard:

1. In Internet Explorer, browse to the Contoso intranet homepage.

2. Display the developer dashboard.

3. Identify the page component that took the longest to render.

4. Close all windows and log off of SP2010-WFE1.

Lesson Summary

- To make maximum use of your server hardware and ensure that the SharePoint farm responds rapidly to user requests, you must analyze its performance regularly.

- When a system approaches its capacity, bottlenecks develop. The bottleneck is the component of the system that limits performance. By identifying a bottleneck you make the right upgrade or reconfiguration to improve capacity.

- Before you deploy a SharePoint farm, test it in a lab environment with simulated user load to ensure that it can cope with the demand you expect.

- Test the farm during and after deployment to ensure that your load predictions were correct.

- By creating baselines and testing regularly, you can identify performance trends and prevent bottlenecks from arising.

- When you want more information for troubleshooting, configure SharePoint to record more information in logs and to collate diagnostic data more often.

- When you have finished troubleshooting and want to maximize SharePoint performance, reduce the data stored in logs.

- The Windows administration tool Performance Monitor can analyze a system in real time or record data for later analysis.

- Windows and SQL Server must be performing optimally for SharePoint to perform optimally.

- Windows, SharePoint, and SQL Server all have their own counters that you can examine in Performance Monitor.

- Use the SharePoint Load Testing Kit from the SharePoint Administration Toolkit, together with Visual Studio Ultimate 2010, to run realistic load simulations in the lab environment.

- You can use the developer dashboard to examine how long each SharePoint page takes to render and to identify slow Web Parts and other components.

Lesson Review

You can use the following questions to test your knowledge of the information in Lesson 1, "Monitor Performance." The questions are also available on the companion media in a practice test if you prefer to review them in electronic form.

> **NOTE ANSWERS**
>
> Answers to these questions and explanations of why each answer choice is right or wrong are located in the "Answers" section at the end of the book.

1. You suspect that a SQL Server that hosts your SharePoint content databases is not optimally configured and you want to upgrade it. You want to find out which component to upgrade to increase responsiveness. Which of the following counters should you examine in Performance Monitor? (Choose all that apply.)

   A. The Processor: % Processor Time counter.

   B. The Memory: Page Faults per Second counter.

   C. The Process: % Processor Time counter for the sqlserver process.

   D. The ASP.NET: Requests Queued counter.

   E. The SharePoint Foundation: Throttled Page Requests counter.

   F. The SQL Server: Plan Cache object and its counters.

2. You are preparing to roll out SharePoint for your entire organization of 5,000 users. You have designed a farm and built an accurate version of it in a lab environment. You want to test the farm to see whether it will have sufficient capacity for the

expected user load. Which of the following tools will you need to configure and run these tests? (Choose all that apply.)

A. Central Administration

B. The SharePoint Load Testing Kit

C. Visual Studio 2010 Professional

D. Visual Studio 2010 Ultimate

E. Performance Monitor

F. The developer dashboard

Lesson 2: SharePoint Health Analyzer

The Health Analyzer is a new feature in SharePoint 2010 that is designed to run regular, automatic checks on the configuration of the SharePoint farm. It can spot common configuration mistakes and explain their consequences in the reports it generates. In some cases it can also repair problems automatically and inform administrators of the actions it took. Because SharePoint is a complex system, even the most scrupulous of administrators can occasionally forget regular checks or make configuration mistakes. It's therefore reassuring to know that Health Analyzer is keeping an eye on things for you. In this lesson, you will see how to configure and use Health Analyzer to improve the reliability of your farm.

> **After this lesson, you will be able to:**
> - Understand how Health Analyzer gathers data.
> - Describe the architecture of the Health Analyzer.
> - Configure Health Analyzer job definitions.
> - Add new job definitions.
> - Configure Health Analyzer timer jobs.
>
> **Estimated Lesson Time: 30 minutes**

Introducing SharePoint Health Analyzer

The Health Analyzer is designed to be an extra pair of eyes for farm administrators. Even in small farms with only a few administrators, configuration mistakes can arise but not become obvious. Some may directly affect users and you will learn of them as users begin to complain or make support requests. In other cases you may not find out about mistakes until periodic actions such as backups or indexing operations. In the worst cases, the mistake affects a critical operation, such as a restore operation after a major disaster. The last thing you need at times like that is to find your restore invalid or out of date because a poor configuration was not spotted.

Health Analyzer applies a set of health rules to the farm on an hourly, daily, weekly, or monthly basis. A set of categorized rules ships with SharePoint. It is also possible to add extra rules of your own, although this task requires some .NET code.

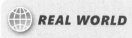
Alistair Matthews

SharePoint is complex and requires you to remember many details. Most experienced SharePoint administrators have lists of items to check regularly. I've found such lists extremely useful, especially because as a consultant, I frequently work with SharePoint farms that are new to me. At such times, I don't really know all the administrators and their levels of experience or knowledge. Even if the staff I've met are competent, there's no guarantee that some more junior administrator hasn't made some fundamental configuration mistake. I usually take an hour or so to run through a range of checks to give me confidence in the system and the people that run it. Very often this process identifies problems that may cause problems in the future. This is also a good way to impress clients, although you should try to be polite about it!

The SharePoint Health Analyzer is an extension of this checklist concept. Its extra advantage is that it runs automatically and on a schedule that you specify. This is reassuring because when things are busy, your own regular checks may get postponed but the Health Analyzer will keep watch on things for you.

Using Health Analyzer

Health Analyzer is found in Central Administration, as shown in Figure 12-2. To use it or configure rules you must be a farm administrator. You will find it on the Monitoring Page. To review rule results, click Review Problems And Solutions.

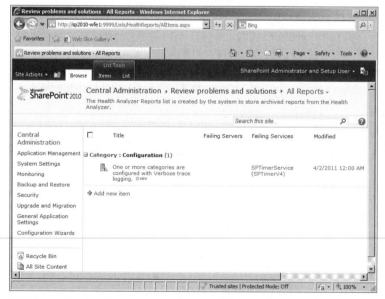

FIGURE 12-2 The Health Analyzer Problems and Solutions Page

Health rules are categorized and presented on this page within their categories, which you can expand or collapse. To see more details about a report, click its title, as shown in Figure 12-3.

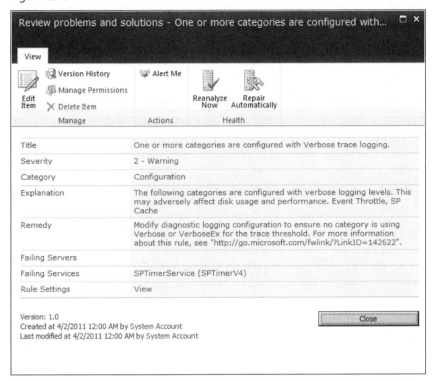

FIGURE 12-3 A Health Analyzer Report

Each report includes the following values:

- **Title**   The title for a report matches that of the corresponding rule. It is frequently one to two lines and quite descriptive.
- **Severity**   The severity can be:
  - 1 – Error. This is a problem that you must fix to maintain full SharePoint functionality.
  - 2 – Warning. This is also a problem but may not have an immediate or obvious effect. It may, for example, indicate that the configuration is not optimal.
  - 3 – Information. This severity indicates that the report is simply to help administrators and does not represent a problem.
  - 4 – Success. This severity indicates that a rule executed successfully with no problems.
  - 0 – Rule Execution Failure. This severity indicates that the rule did not execute properly. You should investigate such a problem and resolve it—otherwise, the rule cannot monitor the farm for you.

- **Category**   The four built-in categories are: configuration, security, performance, and availability. You can also configure new categories.

- **Explanation**   This field provides a detailed explanation of the problem and its possible effects.

- **Remedy**   This field describes how to fix the problem. It frequently includes a link to a Microsoft TechNet article or other location.

- **Failing Servers**   This field shows the server in the farm where the problem occurs.

- **Failing Services**   This field shows the SharePoint service where the problem occurs.

When errors occur, a red bar is displayed on the Central Administration homepage. This alerts all administrators to the problem.

Health Analyzer Architecture

The SharePoint Health analyzer consists of the following components:

- **Timer Jobs**   Eighteen timer jobs run health rules, prepare reports, and sometimes make repairs. Some of these run hourly, some daily, some weekly, and one is configure to run monthly. Among the weekly timer jobs, for example, one checks the user profile service, another checks web application configuration settings, and a third checks Central Administration settings.

- **A SharePoint List**   Health rules are stored in a dedicated list called Health Analyzer Rule Definitions.

- **Health Rules**   All health rules derive from either the *SPHealthAnalysisRule* class or the *SPRepairableHealthAnalysisRule* class. Developers can inherit these classes when they create custom health rules. Administrators can configure each rule. For example, you can choose whether the rule runs hourly, daily, weekly, or monthly.

Health Analyzer Configuration

The default Health Analyzer configuration is suitable for most organizations and, from day to day, you can usually just examine the reports periodically. However, in some circumstances, you may want to adjust the properties of job definitions or tune the execution of the 18 timer jobs.

CONFIGURE JOB DEFINITIONS

To set the properties one of the default health rules, follow these steps:

1. In the Central Administration Quick Launch, click Monitoring.

2. Under Health Analyzer, click Review Rule Definitions.

3. There are 4 categories and 45 health rules by default. Locate the rule you wish to configure. You may have to click the right arrow to view the second page.

4. Click the title of your chosen rule and examine the details.

5. On the ribbon, click Edit Item.
6. In the Edit dialog box, you can specify the title, schedule, and version number for the rule. You can also disable the rule and specify whether the rule should attempt an automatic repair. Only some rules can make such repairs. Finally, in the scope field, you can specify whether the rule should run on all servers that host the relevant service or on the first server that becomes available.

7. When you are satisfied with your settings, click Save.

CONFIGURE HEALTH ANALYZER TIMER JOBS

You should not delete the timer jobs associated with the Health Analyzer or rules may not execute properly. Also it is not recommended that you change the frequency of timer job execution. Instead, if you want a rule to run more or less frequently, edit the rule itself.

However, you may want daily, weekly, or monthly rules to execute at off-peak times or to coincide with your administrative schedule. To adjust timer job schedules, follow these steps:

1. In the Central Administration Quick Launch, click Monitoring.
2. Under Timer Jobs, click Review Job Definitions.
3. Scroll down to find the timer job you want to configure. All the Health Analyzer timer jobs have names that begin with "Health Analysis Job".
4. Click the title of the timer job you want to configure.
5. Under Recurring Schedule, select the time period when you want the timer job to run. The options displayed depend on whether the timer job runs hourly, daily, weekly, or monthly.
6. Click OK.

PRACTICE   **Use SharePoint Health Analyzer to Diagnose Issues**

Practices are designed to guide you through important procedures. The instructions in the Training Kit are high-level instructions that will challenge you to think carefully and to apply the procedures that are covered in this lesson and elsewhere in the Training Kit. If you need assistance, consult the detailed, step-by-step instructions in the Practice Answers on the companion media.

In this practice, you examine Health Analyzer reports and configure timer jobs. You also simulate a problem and observe how Health Analyzer diagnoses it.

Prepare for the Practice

Before you perform this practice, ensure that your lab environment has been built according to the instructions found in the Introduction to this Training Kit. You must also have performed the practice in Lesson 1 of this chapter. You must be logged off of SP2010-WFE1 before beginning the exercises.

EXERCISE 1   Examine Health Analyzer Alerts

In this exercise, you examine the Health Analyzer alerts in your farm:

1. Log on to SP2010-WFE1 as **CONTOSO\SP_Admin** with the password **Pa$$w0rd**.
2. Open the Health Analyzer Problems and Solutions page in Central Administration.

EXERCISE 2   Configure Health Analyzer Timer Jobs

In this exercise, you configure the schedule for a timer job that underpins Health Analyzer. You also manually start the timer job:

1. Use Central Administration to review timer job definitions.
2. Configure the following timer job: Health Analysis Job (Daily, Microsoft SharePoint Foundation Timer, All Servers).

3. Configure the timer job to run between 1:00 AM and 5:00 AM.

4. Run the timer job manually.

EXERCISE 3   Configure a Job Definition

In this exercise, you edit a Health Analyzer rule definition and configure it to run less frequently:

1. Open the Monitoring page in Central Administration.

2. Edit the following Health Analyzer rule definition: Trial Period For This Product Is About To Expire.

3. Configure the rule to run monthly.

EXERCISE 4   Diagnose Problems by Using Health Analyzer

In this exercise, you simulate a SharePoint problem by stopping a web service. You observe how Health Analyzer highlights the problem and resolves it:

1. In Central Administration, review the Health Analyzer Rule Definitions.

2. Run the following rule definition manually: The Security Token Service Is Not Available.

3. Review the Health Analyzer Rule Definitions again and note any problems.

4. Open Internet Information Services (IIS) Manager and browse to the Application Pools.

5. Stop the SecurityTokenServiceApplicationPool.

6. In Central Administration, open the Review Rule Definitions page.

7. Run the following rule manually: The Security Token Service Is Not Available.

8. Go to the Review Problems And Solutions page. You should see a warning about the Security Token Service.

9. Switch back to Internet Information Services (IIS) Manager and restart the SecurityTokenServiceApplicationPool.

10. Close Internet Information Services Manager and return to Central Administration.

11. On the Review Problems And Solutions page, open the warning about the Security Token Service and click Reanalyze Now.

12. Refresh the page. After a few seconds, the warning disappears.

13. Close all windows and log off of SP2010-WFE1.

Lesson Summary

- Health Analyzer is a new tool in SharePoint 2010 that automatically runs a broad range of tests, called health rules, on the SharePoint farm.

- If the system fails a health rule, a warning is displayed on the Central Administration homepage and you can view full details, including a suggested remedy.

- Health Analyzer consists of a set of 18 timer jobs that run the health rules, and a list of the health rules.

- Some rules can automatically attempt to repair the problem they diagnose.

- Administrators can configure rules by selecting a schedule, disabling automatic repair, or disabling the rule itself.

- Administrators can ensure that health rules run at appropriate times by configuring the 18 timer jobs.

- Developers can create custom health rules and encapsulate them in SharePoint solution files for administrators to install.

Lesson Review

You can use the following questions to test your knowledge of the information in Lesson 2, "SharePoint Health Analyzer." The questions are also available on the companion media in a practice test if you prefer to review them in electronic form.

> **NOTE ANSWERS**
>
> Answers to these questions and explanations of why each answer choice is right or wrong are located in the "Answers" section at the end of the book.

1. You are troubleshooting the SharePoint timer service and you want to configure SharePoint to check its status hourly. You notice the "Timer service failed to recycle" health rule, which runs weekly by default. You want to ensure that this rule runs hourly until you have solved the problem. Which of the following steps should you take?

    A. Edit the health rule in the Health Analyzer Rule Definitions list. In the Schedule drop-down list, choose Hourly.

    B. Edit the "Health Analysis Job (Weekly, Central Administration, All Servers)" timer job. Reconfigure this timer job to run hourly.

    C. Edit the "Health Analysis Job (Weekly, Central Administration, Any Server)" timer job. Reconfigure this timer job to run hourly.

    D. Write a Windows PowerShell script that runs the "Timer service failed to recycle" health rule. Use Windows Task Scheduler to execute the script hourly.

2. A developer gives you a custom health rule in the form of a SharePoint solution file. You install and activate the solution and configure the rule to run hourly on any server. You select the Repair Automatically check box. Sometime later the Central Administration homepage shows a warning stating that this rule has failed. Why did the rule not automatically repair the problem?

A. Because you should have configured the health rule to run with the "All Servers" scope, not "Any Server".

B. Because one of the hourly Health Analysis timer jobs is not running.

C. Because the developer did not use the *SPRepairableHealthAnalysisRule* class and include code to make the repair.

D. Because you have not enabled the developer dashboard.

E. Because you did not use the Run Now button to manually run the rule the first time.

Lesson 3: Usage Reports and Web Analytics

SharePoint 2010 includes a range of usage and Web Analytics reports that describe what users have been doing and how the farm has responded to their demands. These reports are designed to help all administrators, including site, site collection, and farm administrators. You will find them to be an excellent source of information both when troubleshooting capacity issues and also in day-to-day administration when you want an overview of performance. In this lesson, you will see how these reports are generated and how to configure the logs that underlie them. Web Analytics also extends usage reports and enables you to use Excel, Web Parts, and workflows for further analysis. Finally, SQL Server Reporting Services (SSRS) can be used to report on SharePoint usage and behavior. You will see how to configure this component and dissect the results it generates.

> **After this lesson, you will be able to:**
> - Use Central Administration reports to diagnose problems in a SharePoint farm.
> - Understand the logs required for SharePoint reports.
> - Describe how SQL Server Reporting Services (SSRS) can be used to analyze SharePoint usage patterns.
> - Describe how Web Analytics can be used to optimize the performance of SharePoint content.
> - Configure SharePoint diagnostic logs, trace logs, and web logs.
> - Configuring and use SSRS to analyze a SharePoint farm.
> - Configure the Web Analytics service application.
> - Use Web Analytics tools such as workflows and the Web Analytics Web Part.
>
> **Estimated Lesson Time: 60 minutes**

Introducing SharePoint Web Analytics Reports

SharePoint's usage and Web Analytics reports are another rich source of information on the behavior of your system and your users. SharePoint creates a default set of reports in sites, in site collections, and in Central Administration. Because these reports are created automatically, you can use them with no previous configuration. However, if you are interested in specific aspects of behavior, you can optimize the collection of data on which the reports are based. In this section, you will learn about the default set of reports throughout SharePoint and the purposes you can put them to. You will also see how SSRS extends the reporting capabilities available to you.

Reports in Central Administration

A range of reports is available in the Reporting section of the Central Administration site, as long as you have configured SharePoint to collect usage and health data. You can configure data collection either by running the SharePoint Farm Configuration Wizard or manually. The manual procedure is outlined later in this lesson.

The usage reports visible in Central Administration depend on the service applications running in your farm. For example, if you have not deployed the Search service application or FAST, the Search Administration Reports are not available. Figure 12-4 shows the list of Search reports. As you can see, the list includes reports to analyze the performance of both crawling and querying.

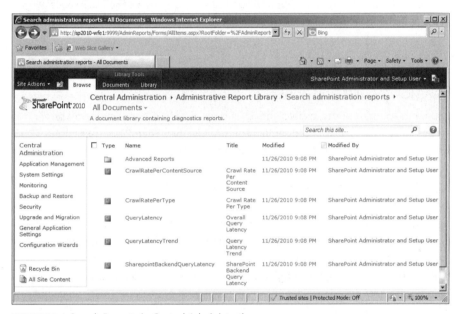

FIGURE 12-4 Search Reports in Central Administration

In the Monitoring section of Central Administration, you will also find the Health Reports, including two key reports:

- **Slowest Pages**   This report displays the pages that, on average, load most slowly. Before the report is constructed, you must specify the server, web application, and date range that interests you. You can also specify the number of items to show in the report and then click Go to view the results. Along with average load times, this report shows maximum and minimum load times and database query counts. After you identify slow pages with this report you can investigate them further by enabling the developer dashboard.

- **Top Active Users**   This report displays the users that most frequently access your server or farm. For each user returned, you can see the number of requests he made, the time he last made a request, and the percentage of his requests that were successful.

Usage and Health Reporting Process

The usage and health reports described in the preceding section are created from a database hosted on the SQL Server. The process is as follows:

1. Raw usage data is stored as users make requests and the system responds. These logs are saved in the following location by default, although you can specify your own location. This is also the default location for trace logs:

   C:\Program Files\Common Files\Microsoft Shared\Web Server Extensions\14\LOGS

2. Health data is collected from a range of sources such as web logs. Snapshots are taken on a schedule that you can specify.

3. The Microsoft SharePoint Foundation Usage Data Import and Usage Data Processing timer jobs collate usage and health data and add it to the reporting database.

4. When you execute a report in Central Administration, it is built with queries against the reporting database.

Web Analytics Reports and Tools

If you are running an Internet site, a clear understanding of both user behavior and server response is essential if you are going to remain competitive. Any SharePoint user might become annoyed with performance but on an intranet site, she often has no choice but to persist. Internet users, by contrast, are notoriously impatient with slow response times, mostly because they have plenty of other sites to visit instead of yours. Slow Internet servers, therefore, have a direct effect on your company's bottom line.

If you're using SharePoint 2010 to run your Internet site, you need to know all about what users browse, how they move through your site, what they search for, and other details. You will use this information to optimize the site's structure and navigation, move your site to the top of results pages in Internet search engines, and streamline your site's internal search tools. If you're using SharePoint on an intranet or extranet, this kind of analysis is less critical but remains extremely useful.

For these purposes, SharePoint 2010 has a new, rich set of reports and services for web traffic analysis called Web Analytics. In this section, you'll see the kind of data that you can obtain. Later in the lesson, you'll see how to configure the service and use the data generated.

Web Analytics reports are visible for single SharePoint sites or for Site Collections. Farm administrators can also run reports in Central Administration for individual sites, site collections, or for the entire farm. Default Web Analytics reports are grouped into three categories:

- **Traffic reports**   These reports describe the visitors and requests that your SharePoint site receives. Some example reports are:

  - Number of Page Views: This report shows how much traffic your site gets.
  - Top Visitors: This report describes who visits your site.
  - Top Referrers: This report shows how visitors located your site.

- **Search reports**   These reports describe how the search service is used so that you can optimize it with best bets, keywords, and so on. Some example reports are:
  - Number of Queries: This report shows how often users ran searches.
  - Top Queries: This report shows what terms users most frequently searched for.
  - Failed Queries: This report shows what queries have high failure rates.
- **Inventory reports**   These reports describe the content stored within your sites, including list items, documents, and rich media. Some example reports are:
  - Storage Usage: This report shows how much disk drive space the content database uses.
  - Number of Sites: This report shows how many sites exist in site collections.

In addition to viewing reports in the browser, Web Analytics includes a range of tools for more detailed analysis and broader publication:

- **Customize Report Tool**   When you view any Web Analytics report, you also see a "Customize Report" in the Quick Launch. This link opens the report in Excel. You can use Excel's advanced analysis tools to make calculations and charts based on the report data. When you refresh the Excel spreadsheet, the latest data from Web Analytics is automatically imported, so you know your analysis is up to date.
- **Web Analytics Workflows**   Web Analytics includes workflows that enable you to schedule reports on a periodic basis, such as once a week. You can also run reports when certain conditions are met, such as when the number of page views increases by 10 percent in a week.
- **Best Bet Suggestions**   As you saw in Chapter 7, "Administering SharePoint Search," a best bet enables search administrators to direct users to certain pages and documents when they search for specific terms. However, it can be difficult to know what terms they most frequently search for and what page they usually access for each common search term. Web Analytics can provide this information in the Best Bets Suggestions report.
- **Web Analytics Web Part**   This Web Part is designed to automatically supply site visitors with links to popular content or common search terms. You can add it to any web page in SharePoint and, in this way, provide a continuously updated set of popular links or searches.

Figure 12-5 shows the components of Web Analytics within the SharePoint farm.

Notice that the Usage Data logging components described in the previous section, including the Usage Data timer jobs, are required because Web Analytics uses the same staging and reporting databases. Also notice that Web Analytics has its own service application that runs on the application server of your choice. You must install and configure this service application, either manually or by running the Farm Configuration Wizard. The Web Analytics service application requires that the State service application be installed and running.

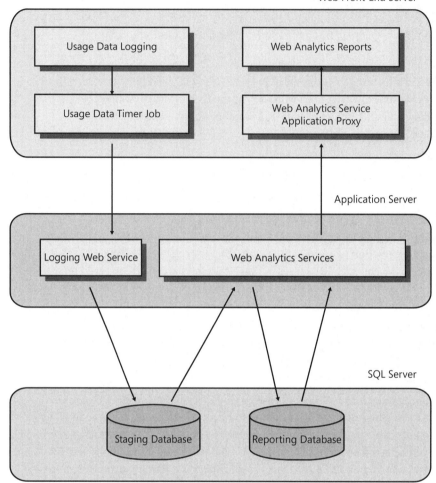

Web Front-End Server

Usage Data Logging

Web Analytics Reports

Usage Data Timer Job

Web Analytics Service
Application Proxy

Application Server

Logging Web Service

Web Analytics Services

SQL Server

Staging Database

Reporting Database

FIGURE 12-5 Web Analytics Architecture

SQL Server Reporting Services

So far in this chapter, you have seen the reporting tools and breadth of reports available out of the SharePoint box. These are extremely informative and useful, especially in terms of things like web traffic, user behavior, and search optimization. However, SharePoint requires SQL Server to store content and service application databases and SQL Server is an industry-leading database server. As such it includes a world-class set of reporting tools—SQL Server Reporting Services (SSRS), which you can use to analyze and visualize data held both in SharePoint and in other databases. By integrating SharePoint with SSRS, you can also use a SharePoint document library for report storage, which makes it easy to publish your reports to other company members, and add reports to SharePoint dashboards and other pages.

To integrate SSRS and SharePoint 2010, you must install the Reporting Services Add-In on SharePoint web front-end servers and make several configuration changes. The Reporting Services Add-In is a free download. The installation procedures are described later in this chapter. When you have completed them, SSRS integration runs in the configuration shown in Figure 12-6.

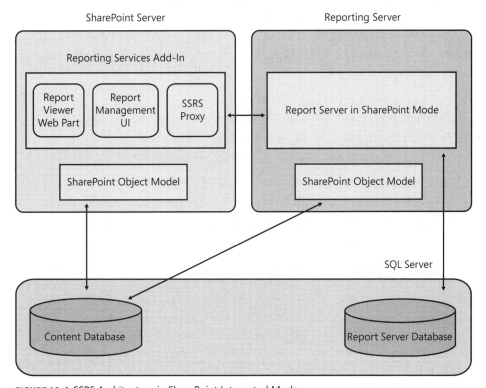

FIGURE 12-6 SSRS Architecture in SharePoint Integrated Mode

The Reporting Services Add-In on the SharePoint WFE servers consists of three components:

- **The SSRS Proxy**   This component communicates with SSRS on the reporting server. You must configure the name of the reporting server and the right authentication credentials in Central Administration.

- **The Report Management User Interface**   This component consists of application pages that enable administrators to view, store, and manage report server content on the SharePoint farm.

- **The Report Viewer Web Part**   This Web Part presents reports and can be used on any Web Part Page anywhere in the SharePoint farm. You can enhance business intelligence dashboards with SSRS reports by using this Web Part.

For integrating with SharePoint 2010, you must use SSRS 2008 R2 or later.

Configuring and Using Usage Reports and Logs

Usage and health reports are only available if you have configured SharePoint to collect the appropriate data. When you run the Farm Configuration Wizard, it always enables usage and health data collection but you may want to alter the default configuration. If you have not used the wizard in your farm, you must enable usage and health data collection manually, as described in this section. The procedures in this section also describe how to view usage and health reports.

CONFIGURE USAGE AND HEALTH DATA COLLECTION

SharePoint must collect a broad range of data before it can construct usage and health reports. To enable this data collection, take the following steps:

1. In the Central Administration Quick Launch, click Monitoring.

2. Under Reporting, click Configure Usage And Health Data Collection.

3. Under Usage Data Collection, select the Enable Usage Data Collection checkbox.

4. Under Event Selection, select the types of events that interest you. For example, for monitoring user activity, select the Page Requests checkbox.

> **NOTE PERFORMANCE AND USAGE DATA COLLECTION**
>
> When you are tuning to maximize performance, select as few event types as possible or disable usage data collection, which can place extra load on servers. During troubleshooting or if you are confident that SharePoint can handle both user load and data collection simultaneously, you can select all these checkboxes so that reports are as rich and functional as possible.

5. Under Usage Data Collection Settings, you can specify the location where usage logs are stored. The default is the LOGS folder in the 14 hive. You can also specify the maximum size for usage logs.

6. Under Health Data Collection, select the Enable Health Data Collection checkbox.

7. Under Logging Database Server, you can specify the SQL Server and database where usage and health data will be collated for reporting.

8. At the bottom of the page, click OK.

CONFIGURE THE LOG COLLECTION SCHEDULE

The following two timer jobs must execute to collate usage and health logs and store data in the reporting database:

- **Microsoft SharePoint Foundation Usage Data Import**   This is the job that imports data from the logs to the reporting database. Until this job executes, no reports can be viewed in Central Administration.

- **Microsoft SharePoint Foundation Usage Data Processing**   This job searches for expired usage data in the reporting database and deletes it. Expired data includes any records that are older than 30 days. If you are using the Web Analytics service application, this job does not delete data but instead moves it to the Web Analytics Reporting database.

You may want to adjust the schedule for these timer jobs to run at off-peak hours. When troubleshooting, you may want to run these timer jobs more frequently. To adjust the schedules, follow these steps:

1. In the Central Administration Quick Launch, click Monitoring.

2. Under Reporting, click Configure Usage And Health Data Collection.

3. Under Log Collection Schedule, click the Log Collection Schedule link.

4. Click the title of the timer job you want to manage.

5. Under Recurring Schedule, select the frequency with which you want the job to run, and the time period. For example, if you choose Hourly, you can specify the number of minutes past the hour when the job should start.

6. Click OK. Alternatively, to run the job immediately, click Run Now.

Configuring and Using Web Analytics

Before you can use Web Analytics reports, export data to Excel, and use the Web Analytics Web Part, you must create and configure the Web Analytics services application. Remember that this service application relies on the usage data processing components. Therefore, for example, the Microsoft SharePoint Foundation Usage Data Import timer job must be functional before you complete the following procedures.

CREATE A WEB ANALYTICS SERVICE APPLICATION

If you ran the Farm Configuration Wizard, and selected the Web Analytics Service Application checkbox after installing SharePoint, you don't need to complete the following steps because the service application will already have been provisioned. To set up the service application manually, follow these steps:

1. In the Central Administration Quick Launch, click Application Management.

2. Under Service Applications, click Manage Service Applications.

3. Click New, and then click Web Analytics Service Application.

4. In the Service Application Name textbox, type an appropriate name for the service application.

5. Under Application Pool, select an existing application pool or create a new one to match your deployment plan.

6. Under Database Server, type the name of the SQL Server where you want to create the two databases that the Web Analytics service application requires.

7. Under Staging Database Name, type an appropriate name for the Web Analytics staging database.

8. Under Reporting Database Name, type an appropriate name for the Web Analytics reporting database.

9. In the Data Retention drop-down list, choose the number of months you want data to remain in the reporting database.

10. Click OK. SharePoint creates the service application.

11. When the installation is complete, click OK.

12. In the Central Administration Quick Launch, click System Settings.

13. Under Servers, click Manage Services on Server.

14. In the Server box, select the SharePoint server where you want the Web Analytics services to run.

15. To the right of the Web Analytics Web Service, click Start.

16. To the right of the Web Analytics Data Processing Service, click Start.

VIEW A REPORT AND EXPORT IT TO EXCEL

After you provision and start the Web Analytics service application, data begins to appear in the Web Analytics reports. However, because user activity and usage data collection is required before data reaches the reporting database, you should expect to wait 24 hours or so before reports become available. After this time, you can examine reports by following these steps. This example uses Central Administration, but you can also view Web Analytics reports at the site and site collection levels.

1. In the Central Administration Quick Launch, click Monitoring.

2. Under Reporting, click View Web Analytics Reports.

3. The Summary page displays pages views, unique visitors, and search queries for each site collection. Click the name of the site collection that interests you.

4. The Summary report is displayed for the site you selected. This includes data such as Average Number Of Page Views Per Day and Total Number Of Referrers. The more detailed reports are listed in the Quick Launch in three categories: Traffic, Search, and Inventory.

5. In the Quick Launch, click the report that interests you. The analysis is displayed.

6. To export the report to Excel, in the ribbon, click the Analyze tab.

7. In the Export section, click Export To Spreadsheet.

USE WEB ANALYTICS WORKFLOWS

The Web Analytics workflows can be configured to run reports and send out the results to administrators on a fixed schedule or when certain conditions are met. Web Analytics workflows can only be configured on reports at the site or site collection level. To configure a workflow, follow these steps:

1. In the site you want to analyze, click Site Actions and then click Site Settings.

2. Under Site Actions, if you want to schedule a site-level report, click Site Web Analytics Reports. If you want to schedule a site collection–level report, click Site Collection Web Analytics Reports. The Summary report is shown.

3. In the Quick Launch, click the report that you want to schedule.

4. In the ribbon, click the Analyze tab.

5. In the Workflow section, click Schedule Alerts Or Reports.

6. Under Workflow, select whether to schedule an alert or a report. An alert is a simple message sent to administrators when conditions are met. A report is an analysis with more details.

7. Under Name, type a unique name for the workflow.

8. Each workflow must have a task list, where tasks for workflow participants will be created, and a history list, where the progress of the workflow will be recorded. Select these lists in the two drop-down lists.

9. Click Next.

10. Use the Recipients people picker control to select a user or distribution group to send reports to.

11. In the Message textbox, type an explanatory message for recipients of the report.

12. Under Frequency, specify how often this workflow will run. This option is specific to the reports option.

13. Use the Start Date and End Date to specify the period over which the report will run. This option is specific to the reports option.

14. Under Web Analytics Reports, select the reports to send and then click Finish.

USE THE WEB ANALYTICS WEB PART

You can display a Web Analytics report on any SharePoint web page by using the Web Analytics Web Part. This is extremely helpful when you want to create a dashboard for administrators. To add the Web Part to a page, follow these steps:

1. In Internet Explorer, open the SharePoint page where you want to display reports.

2. On the ribbon, click the Page tab, and then click Edit Page.

3. Place the cursor where you want the reports to appear.

4. On the ribbon, click the Insert tab, and then click Web Part.

5. In the Categories list, click Content Rollup.

6. In the Web Parts list, click Web Analytics Web Part, and then click Add.

7. In the title bar of the Web Analytics Web Part, click the down arrow, and then click Edit Web Part.

8. Scroll to the top right of the page to find the Web Part Properties sheet.

9. In the Information To Display drop-down list, specify whether to display information about content, search queries, or search center queries.

10. In the Site Scope drop-down list, specify whether the report should cover the entire site collection, this site and sub-sites, or only this site.

11. In the Period drop-down list, specify the duration for the reports.

12. At the bottom of the properties sheet, click OK.

13. On the ribbon, click the Page tab, and then click Save & Close.

Configuring SSRS

The steps that you take to install and configure SSRS SharePoint integration differ depending on whether you have already set up your organization's SharePoint farm. The procedures listed in this section assume that the SharePoint farm is already up and running. If you do not already have a SharePoint farm and are about to install it, the recommended stages are as follows:

1. Use the SharePoint PrerequisiteInstaller.exe tool on all servers in your farm. Among other prerequisites, this tool will install the Reporting Services Add-In for SharePoint.

2. Install and configure your SharePoint farm.

3. If your reporting server is separate from the SharePoint WFE servers, you must install SharePoint on it as well and join it to the SharePoint farm.

4. Install SQL Server Reporting Services on the reporting server and configure a database in SharePoint Integrated Mode.

5. Configure the SSRS Proxy component by setting properties in Central Administration.

6. Create a SharePoint document library to store and publish reports.

> **NOTE** **PRESENCE OF THE REPORTING SERVICES ADD-IN**
>
> Whether you are starting from scratch or installing SSRS on a preexisting farm, it is important to have the Reporting Service Add-In and other main components installed before you configure the SSRS Proxy in Central Administration.

INSTALL THE REPORTING SERVICES ADD-IN

You must install the Reporting Services Add-In on each SharePoint server in the farm. You can obtain the Add-In from this location: *http://www.microsoft.com/download/en/details .aspx?id=622*.

Alternatively you can use the SharePoint Prerequisite Installer to install this add-in. You can find this executable in the root of your SharePoint installation media. To install the add-in, follow these steps:

1. After downloading the rsSharePoint.msi file, double-click it.
2. In the Security Warning dialog box, click Run.
3. On the Welcome page of the installation wizard, click Next.

> **NOTE** **PROGRAM MAINTENANCE PAGE**
>
> If the wizard displays the program maintenance page, with Repair and Remove options, at this stage, you already have the add-in installed—probably because you used the prerequisite installer when you installed the SharePoint server. You can click Cancel and exit this installation.

4. Enter your name and company and click Next.
5. Click Install. The add-in is installed and configured.
6. Click Finish.

ACTIVATE THE REPORT SERVER FEATURE

SSRS integration requires a site-collection level SharePoint feature called Report Server Integration Feature. Activate this feature in the following way:

1. In Internet Explorer, open the top-level site in the site collection where you want to publish SSRS reports.
2. Click Site Actions and then click Site Settings.
3. Under Site Collection Administration, click Site Collection Features.
4. Scroll down to locate the Report Server Integration Feature. To the right of this feature, click Activate.

CONFIGURE THE REPORT DATABASE IN SHAREPOINT INTEGRATED MODE

These steps assume that you already have SQL Server Reporting Services installed on your reporting server. If not, you must rerun the SQL Server Installation wizard and add the Reporting Services feature to your existing instance.

1. Click Start, All Programs, SQL Server 2008 R2, Configuration Tools, and then click Reporting Services Configuration Manager.

2. Click the Database container in the Connect pane and then click Change Database.

3. Ensure that the Create A New Report Server Database option is selected, and then click Next.

4. Enter the Server Name and Authentication details for the server where you want to store the Reporting Database. This is often the local server.

5. Click Next.

6. In the Database Name textbox, type a descriptive name for the reporting database.

7. Select the SharePoint Integrated Mode option, and then click Next.

8. Under Credentials, specify the username and password of an existing user account that report services will use to connect to the reporting database. Click Next.

9. Review your specifications and then click Next.

10. When the configuration is complete, click Finish.

> **NOTE** **INSTALLING SHAREPOINT ON THE REPORTING SERVER**
>
> If your reporting server is not already a SharePoint server, you must install SharePoint on it at this point. This is because Report Services needs SharePoint classes and binary files to access SharePoint databases. See Chapter 1, "Creating a SharePoint 2010 Intranet," for more information about installation. You must add the reporting server to the SharePoint farm but you do not need to host any SharePoint sites on it.

> **IMPORTANT** **REPORTING SERVICES AND DOMAIN ACCOUNTS**
>
> When the reporting server also hosts the SharePoint content databases in SQL Server, you must configure the Report Server service to run with under a domain account, not a local account.

CONFIGURE REPORT SERVICES INTEGRATION IN SHAREPOINT CENTRAL ADMINISTRATION

Now that both SharePoint and SQL Reporting Services have the right components installed, you must configure the SSRS Proxy component to connect successfully to the reporting server. Complete the following steps:

1. In the Central Administration Quick Launch, click General Application Settings.

2. Under Reporting Services, click Reporting Services Integration.

3. Under Report Server Web Service URL, type the URL of the reporting server.

4. Use the Authentication Mode and Credentials sections to configure the user account that SharePoint will use to connect to the reporting server. This account must be a member of the Administrators group on the reporting server.

5. Optionally, you can choose to activate the Reporting Services feature in all site collections or in specific site collections.

6. Click OK.

7. When the feature activation is complete, click Close.

PRACTICE **Analyze SharePoint Usage**

Practices are designed to guide you through important procedures. The instructions in the Training Kit are high-level instructions that will challenge you to think carefully and to apply the procedures that are covered in this lesson and elsewhere in the Training Kit. If you need assistance, consult the detailed, step-by-step instructions in the Practice Answers on the companion media.

In this practice, you execute the Usage Data Import timer job to collate usage data. You also configure the Web Analytics service application and view reports.

Prepare for the Practice

Before you perform this practice, ensure that your lab environment has been built according to the instructions found in the Introduction to this Training Kit. You must also have performed the practice in Lesson 2 of this chapter. You must be logged off of SP2010-WFE1 before beginning the exercises.

EXERCISE 1 Configure and Execute the Usage Data Import Timer Job

In this exercise, you adjust the schedule for the timer job that collates usage data:

1. Log on to SP2010-WFE1 as **CONTOSO\SP_Admin** with the password **Pa$$w0rd**.

2. Use Central Administration to access the Configure Usage and Health Data Collection page and click the Log Collection Schedule link.

3. Edit the Microsoft Foundation Usage Data Import timer job and configure it to run every 10 minutes.

4. Run the timer job manually.

EXERCISE 2 Create a State Service Application

Before the Web Analytics service application can run fully, you must have a functional State service application. In this exercise, you create such a service application in the Contoso farm:

1. Start the SharePoint 2010 Management Shell.

2. Issue the following commands in this order to create the State service application:

```
$serviceapp = New-SPStateServiceApplication –Name "State Service Application
-Enterprise"

New-SPStateServiceDatabase –Name "SharePoint_Service_State" –ServiceApplication
$serviceapp

New-SPStateServiceApplicationProxy –Name "State Service Application Proxy"
-ServiceApplication $serviceapp
```

3. Close SharePoint Management Shell.

EXERCISE 3 Create a Web Analytics Service Application

In this exercise, you install and configure the Web Analytics service application:

1. In Central Administration, view the list of service applications.

2. Create a new Web Analytics Service Application. Use the following guidance and settings:

   - Name: Web Analytics Service Application – Enterprise
   - Application Pool: SharePoint Service Applications
   - Database Server: SP2020-WFE1
   - Staging Database Name: SharePoint_Service_WebAnalytics_Staging
   - Reporting Database Name: SharePoint_Service_WebAnalytics_Reporting

3. Start the following services on the SP2010-WFE1 server:

   - Web Analytics Data Processing Service
   - Web Analytics Web Service

EXERCISE 4 Configure a Web Analytics Workflow

In this exercise, you configure a Web Analytics Workflow to run a report on a chosen schedule:

1. Open the Contoso intranet homepage in Internet Explorer.

2. In Site Settings, click Workflow Settings.

3. Add a new workflow. Use the following settings and guidance:

   - Workflow Template: Schedule Web Analytics Reports
   - Name: Top Pages Report
   - Recipient: CONTOSO\SP_Admin
   - Message: There is a new top pages report
   - Web Analytics Reports: Top Pages

EXERCISE 5 View Web Analytics Reports

In this exercise, you view a Web Analytics report for the Contoso intranet.

> **IMPORTANT WAIT BEFORE PROCEEDING**
>
> You must give the Web Analytics service application time to collate data and compile reports before performing this procedure. This may take up to 24 hours.

1. Browse the Contoso intranet site in Internet Explorer.

2. In Site Settings, click Site Web Analytics Reports.

3. Examine the data in Top Pages and other reports of your choice.

4. Close all windows and log off of SP2010-WFE1.

Lesson Summary

- Native SharePoint usage and Web Analytics reports are another rich source of information on the behavior of your servers and users.

- Usage log information is collated by the Microsoft SharePoint Foundation Usage Data Import time job and placed in a reporting database.

- Health reports in Central Administration are built on this reporting database.

- Web Analytics reports are available at the site, site collection, and farm levels and analyze site visitor activity, web traffic, search tool use, and content statistics.

- Web Analytics extends the SharePoint health and usage reports and includes a dedicated service application.

- You can import Web Analytics reports into Excel for deeper analysis and merges with other data.

- You can use Web Analytics workflows to run reports or alert administrators to changing behavior.

- Use the Web Analytics Best Bets Suggestions report to help tune your search solution to terms that are frequently queried.

- The Web Analytics Web Part can place popular content or search terms on your web page. These links are continuously updated with the latest activity on your site.

- SSRS can be integrated with SharePoint so that you can publish reports in your SharePoint intranet or extranet.

Lesson Review

You can use the following questions to test your knowledge of the information in Lesson 3, "Usage Reports and Web Analytics." The questions are also available on the companion media in a practice test if you prefer to review them in electronic form.

1. You have been running SharePoint for several months successfully but now require more details about user activity in your sites. You are about to install and configure Web Analytics. Which of the following must you complete before Web Analytics can work? (Choose all that apply.)

   A. Configure and start the Managed Metadata service application.

   B. Configure and start the State service application.

   C. Configure and start the User Profile service application.

    D. Ensure that the Microsoft SharePoint Foundation Usage Data Import timer job runs regularly.

    E. Install the Reporting Services Add-In on at least one SharePoint Server in the farm.

2. You want to ensure that the Top Pages report is run on Monday morning and emailed to all farm administrators so that they can assess SharePoint performance. Which of the following tools can you use to do this?

    A. Usage Reports

    B. The Web Analytics Web Part

    C. Web Analytics Workflows

    D. The Report Viewer Web Part

    E. The SSRS Proxy

Lesson 4: Optimize Content Storage and Access

So far in this chapter, you have seen techniques for monitoring and reporting on the health and performance of your SharePoint farm. If you want a fast system that responds quickly to user requests, these techniques are essential. The next stage is to take the information you have gained and use it to accelerate your servers. You can take two approaches to this task: first, you can upgrade the farm by adding servers, or by adding processors, memory, faster disks, and other resources to servers. In other words, you can upgrade by adding extra hardware. The performance data you now have enables you to choose the right hardware to resolve your bottlenecks. The second approach is to reconfigure SharePoint to optimize its use of the hardware it already has. You can do this by ensuring optimal use of hard disks, caches, and databases in your farm. The advantage to this approach is that it frequently can be completed without buying any extra hardware. It also ensures that you get the maximum value for money from the hardware you already have.

> **After this lesson, you will be able to:**
> - Understand how resource throttling, BLOB storage, compression, and disposable objects can affect performance.
> - Describe the three types of caching that you can use to optimize performance.
> - Describe optimal disk configurations and storage locations for SharePoint components.
> - Optimize the SQL Servers that support your SharePoint farm.
>
> **Estimated Lesson Time: 60 minutes**

Introducing Optimization

SharePoint 2010 is designed and configured to perform well straight out of the box. Many companies use none of the techniques described in this lesson and still get very quick response from their farm, even at times of high traffic. However, its configuration is designed to work well in a typical SharePoint farm. The default configuration assumes several things:

- **Typical users**   If users, for example, stream an unusually large number of videos from SharePoint media libraries every day, this assumption might not be valid.

- **Typical content**   Most companies' content consists predominantly of Office documents, with some videos and other rich media. If you deal exclusively in video content, for example, or have a lot of custom document formats, this assumption might not be valid.

- **The farm hosts an intranet or extranet**   If you use SharePoint to host a customer-facing Internet site, the right configuration to serve pages rapidly may differ from the out-of-the-box settings.

In fact, a "typical" SharePoint installation is a fictitious concept because every installation has some unusual requirements. This is why SharePoint's default configuration cannot be optimal for every farm. Every administrator should make time to evaluate the changes described in this lesson. If you have very unusual requirements or if performance is critical, you should make this evaluation a high priority because some configurations may yield significant improvements. Occasionally, for example, you may find that one of these optimizations may save you from spending extra budget on upgraded hardware.

However, you must also beware of optimization changes and make them carefully and with proper tests. You should take the following approach:

- Whenever possible, test your proposed optimization in a lab environment with simulated user load, before you implement it on your production farm. This is both to ensure that your change does not mistakenly interrupt service and to observe that the change increases performance.

- Before you implement an optimization, both in the lab and in production, establish a thorough benchmark by using Performance Monitor. The counters in this benchmark should target aspects of performance you expect to change.

- Implement an optimization during off-peak hours when the smallest number of users is likely affected by problems.

- After you implement an optimization, test again and compare your performance results to the benchmark.

It is vital to measure accurately how much a configuration change alters performance. For example, if your change improves page rendering by 10 percent, that is a good result and very worthwhile—but users may not notice a change. Unless you measure performance changes properly, you may even harm responsiveness without being aware of it.

Furthermore, you must justify the time you spend testing and implementing changes to your superiors, and they want to see hard data. Unless you can back up your assertions of increased performance with statistics, they may not be convinced that you are not wasting your time.

High-Performance SharePoint Configuration

In this section, you will see some general techniques that may help to optimize your farm performance. In each case the potential benefits are described and steps to implement each technique are listed.

Resource Throttling

Resource throttling is a new feature in SharePoint 2010. When you configure it, SharePoint monitors server resources every five seconds. If these checks are unsuccessful three times in a row, server resources are throttled according to the rules you specify. When the next successful check occurs, throttling ceases and things return to normal.

Resource throttling prevents servers from becoming critically overloaded and is particularly helpful when your system includes very large lists. However, use the throttle sparingly because when it is engaged, users may see error pages in their browser and timer jobs will not run.

CONFIGURE RESOURCE THROTTLING

You configure resource throttling for each web application. Set up resource throttling by following these steps:

1. In the Central Administration Quick Launch, click Application Management.

2. Under Web Applications, click Manage Web Applications.

3. Click the web application you want to configure.

4. On the ribbon, click General Settings, and then click Resource Throttling.

5. Under List View Threshold, in the textbox, type the maximum number of items that a user can view in a list. Large numbers of items in a single operation can significantly impact performance.

6. Under Object Model Override, select Yes if you want an authorized user to be able to circumvent the List View Threshold when using custom code.

7. In the List View Threshold For Auditors And Administrators textbox, you can specify a larger threshold for members of these specific groups.

8. Under List View Lookup Threshold, specify the maximum number of lookup fields that a database query can include. These fields place extra load on database servers.

9. Under Daily Time Window For Large Queries you can specify a time period when queries that exceed the previous thresholds can be run by anyone. This should be an off-peak time when the extra load is manageable.

10. Under Backward-Compatible Event Handlers, choose whether event handlers should be compatible with code written for previous versions of SharePoint. Because these event handlers are inefficient, you should turn them off unless a developer specifically needs them and cannot re-code.

11. Under HTTP Request Monitoring and Throttling, choose whether to enable or disable throttling for web requests on WFE servers.

12. Under Change Log, specify a maximum number of days long entries are kept in the change log. Lowering this value helps to conserve disk space.

13. Click OK.

Remote BLOB Storage

When discussing databases, a BLOB is a Binary Large Object. This is any file that you want to store in the database, including Office files, pictures, videos, and rich content of various other types. SharePoint is designed for document management, so it almost always stores a lot of BLOBs in the content database. This is not necessarily a bad thing, but in certain circumstances you may find an improvement in performance when BLOBs are stored on the hard disk outside the database files. Such external storage is called *Remote BLOB Storage* (RBS). Be sure that you test this thoroughly because RBS is as likely to decrease performance as increase it. The effect depends on your system and its hardware.

One good reason to use RBS is to reduce the size of unwieldy databases. If your content database is 4 GB or larger, consider using RBS to reduce it.

To configure RBS you must:

1. Install and configure the RBS add-on feature pack for SQL Server 2008.
2. Set up the FILESTREAM provider on the SQL Server.
3. Install the RBS provider on each SharePoint server.
4. Enable RBS for each content database.

> **MORE INFO** **CONFIGURING RBS**
>
> Configuring RBS is a complex SQL Server task. The details of this operation are outside the scope of this SharePoint book. If you want to make this optimization, you can get more details and complete step lists at the following location: *http://technet.microsoft.com/ en-us/library/ee748638.aspx*.

BLOB Cache

SharePoint uses three different caches on web front-end servers to temporarily store content as it is served to a user. If another user requests the same resource while it remains in the cache, the WFE server can serve it the second time without calling SQL Server, calling Application servers, or executing ASP.NET code to render a page. In this way, caches accelerate SharePoint's response to users.

Caches must be carefully configured and used. If you increase the cache time, for example, items are cached for longer. This means that the cache is used more often because items are more likely to be in it, so the performance of the server goes up. However, if the item in the content database changes, the copy in the cache will not change until it expires. This means that out-of-date items can be returned to users. Ideally, you would use caching with items that rarely change. In practice, the cache settings are compromises between performance and content freshness.

The first of these caches is called the *BLOB Cache*. This stores BLOB files such as documents, images, and videos. This cache reduces the load on SQL Servers and serves documents more quickly if they have been used recently.

CONFIGURE THE BLOB CACHE

To configure the BLOB Cache, you must edit the Web.config file for the relevant web application. Use the following steps:

1. Click Start, Administrative Tools, and then click Internet Information Services (IIS) Manager.

2. In the Connections pane, expand the server that hosts the web application.

3. Expand the Site container.

4. Right-click the web application you want to configure, and then click Explore.

5. Right-click the Web.config file and then click Open.

6. Locate the line that begins with "<BlobCache".

7. In the *Location* attribute, specify a folder on a disk that has enough space for the cache. This location should not be on the same disk as the operating system swap file or the SharePoint diagnostic logs for performance reasons.

8. In the *maxSize* attribute, type the maximum size of the BLOB Cache in GB.

9. Set the *Enabled* attribute to **"true"**.

10. Save the Web.config file and close it. IIS automatically restarts the web application and users may notice a brief interruption in service.

Output Cache

This cache, sometimes known as the Page Output Cache, stores rendered versions of web pages to accelerate their distribution to users and to reduce load on content database servers. Different versions of each page are stored depending on the permissions of the user who made the request so that security is maintained.

> **IMPORTANT   THE OUTPUT CACHE AND THE PUBLISHING FEATURE**
> You can only use the Output Cache if you have activated the Publishing feature in all the relevant sites.

To enable the Output Cache, you must edit Web.config as you did for the BLOB Cache:

1. Click Start, Administrative Tools, and then click Internet Information Services (IIS) Manager.

2. In the Connections pane, expand the server that hosts the web application.

3. Expand the Site container.

4. Right-click the web application you want to configure, and then click Explore.

5. Right-click the Web.config file and then click Open.

6. Locate the line that begins with "<OutputCacheProfiles".

7. Set the *useCacheProfileOverrides* attribute to **"true"**.

8. Save the Web.config file and close it. IIS automatically restarts the web application and users may notice a brief interruption in service.

Object Cache

The Object Cache reduces traffic between the WFE servers and the SQL Server by storing SharePoint objects such as lists, libraries, site settings collections, page layouts, content types, and so on. This cache stores objects in memory, so you must have enough RAM to support your object cache without recourse to the paging file. As for the Output Cache, you can only use the Object Cache if you enable the Publishing feature on all the relevant sites.

To configure the Object Cache, edit Web.config by following these steps:

1. Click Start, Administrative Tools, and then click Internet Information Services (IIS) Manager.

2. In the Connections pane, expand the server that hosts the web application.

3. Expand the Site container.

4. Right-click the web application you want to configure, and then click Explore.

5. Right-click the Web.config file and then click Open.

6. Locate the line that begins with "<ObjectCache".

7. In the *maxSize* attribute, set the size you want the Object Cache to be in memory in MB.

8. Save the Web.config file and close it. IIS automatically restarts the web application and users may notice a brief interruption in service.

> **EXAM TIP** **KNOW WHICH CACHE IS WHICH**
>
> Although all caches use the same principle to accelerate performance, they will result in different improvements. For example, if you have a problem with large objects, such as large lists, enabling the BLOB Cache will not help. For the exam, make sure you can differentiate the benefits of each of the three caches so you can choose the right one for a given scenario.

Optimizing Storage

SharePoint relies on SQL Server to store its content, and SQL is a high-performance database server capable of supporting the largest and busiest databases. The most optimal SQL databases, however, must be designed carefully to realize the best performance. In particular, you must place the database files carefully on different hard disks in your servers. You must also consider other SharePoint files not stored in SQL Server, such as index files and diagnostic logs. In this section, you will learn how to locate databases, transaction logs, and other files to accelerate the delivery of content.

The optimal disk configurations described in this section require that certain files are separated onto dedicated disks or disk arrays. In small companies with limited hardware budgets, such separation is not always possible and you may have to find a compromise.

Content Databases

As the ultimate location for content storage, the content databases in any SharePoint farm are critical to performance. In Chapter 4, "Administering and Securing SharePoint Content," you saw how to design content databases, taking into account the time required for backup and restore, the structure of your sites and site collections, and other factors. In this section you will learn where database files should be located on your server's hard disk.

Every database in SQL Server consists of the following files. This includes SharePoint content databases, service application databases, and non-SharePoint databases:

- **Database files** This is the file storage location for data and files (unless you are using RBS). It is structured in tables, and a single change, such as a new item in a SharePoint list, usually requires SQL to make changes in multiple tables. Writing to this file, therefore, is complex and relatively slow. These files have .mdf or .ndf extensions.

- **Transaction logs** This is the first location changes are written to. The database engine moves through these logs, writing each transaction to the database files. A write operation to a transaction log is relatively fast because all data is added to the end of the file.

The most important consideration when placing your database files is to keep database files on a separate disk from transaction logs. This increases performance because the disk write head does not have to process both files. The write head for transaction logs, in particular, can remain in one place, sequentially writing transactions to the end of the logs and not needing to jump to other locations to write to database files and so on. As you saw in Chapter 11, "Implementing Business Continuity," this also increases recoverability. You should also separate database files and transaction logs from operating system files where possible.

You can also maximize performance by using RAID arrays. Ideally, database files should be placed on a RAID 5 array. Transaction logs should be placed on a RAID 10 array.

If you have chosen to implement RBS, as described in the previous section, you can optimize its performance by separating BLOB files from both the database and the transaction logs.

In compromise situations, when you do not have enough disks to separate all the preceding files onto separate drives, your priority should be to separate the transaction logs for both performance and recoverability reasons.

Service Applications and Other Databases

So far, we have considered only content databases because serving content is SharePoint's principal purpose. However, there may be many other SQL Server databases in a SharePoint farm. There is always the Configuration Database to store and service applications that require other databases of their own. Table 12-6 lists all the databases you might need to store. You must consider locations for all these databases when you plan service application deployment.

TABLE 12-6 SharePoint Database Types

SERVICE APPLICATION	DATABASE	DESCRIPTION
None	Configuration Database	Most configuration data for the SharePoint farm is stored here and many operations require a query against this database. For example, when a WFE server receives a request for a page, it checks the Configuration Database to determine which site and content database holds the page. Optimizing this database is a high priority.
Usage and Health Data Collection Service	Logging Database	Health and usage data are collated into this database for supporting health reports.

SERVICE APPLICATION	DATABASE	DESCRIPTION
Search Service Application	Search Administration Database	Stores the search service application configuration, including the definitions of managed properties, best bets, content sources and so on.
	Property Database	Stores crawled properties and document metadata.
	Crawl Database	Stores crawled data and access control lists. Optimizing all three search databases is a high priority to ensure that your enterprise search system can deal with the load of queries and crawls.
Web Analytics Service Application	Staging Database	Stores un-aggregated fact data, metadata, and other information from which reports will be generated.
	Reporting Database	Stores aggregated report tables and classified data.
User Profile Service	Profile Database	Stores personal data such as colleagues and team members, projects, expertise, and so on. Optimize this database whenever social networking is widely used in your farm.
	Synchronization Database	Stores data temporarily as it is imported from Active Directory or another external source. User profile synchronization is a high-demand service so optimize this database whenever you expect large amounts of data to be exchanged.
	Social Tagging Database	Stores comments and "like" tags.
Managed Metadata Service Application	Term Store Database	Stores keywords and term sets. Users can tag content throughout the farm with these words to categorize information.
State Service Application	State Database	This service application maintains state information for InfoPath forms.

SERVICE APPLICATION	DATABASE	DESCRIPTION
Business Connectivity Services	BCS Database	Stores the configuration of connections, external content types, and external lists.
Secure Store Service Application	Secure Store Database	Stores credentials and mappings that enable SharePoint users to access external resources without manually logging in.

As you can see, there may be a very large number of databases that support a SharePoint farm with many service applications deployed. It is unlikely that a single server will have enough drives to separate all the database files from each other and to separate all transaction logs. However, because you can specify different locations for each database when you install the service application, you can dedicate a database server to individual service applications.

> **MORE INFO BEST PRACTICES FOR OPERATIONAL EXCELLENCE**
>
> You can find further recommendations and best practices for optimizing a SharePoint farm at the following location: *http://technet.microsoft.com/en-us/library/cc850692.aspx*.
>
> You can read a detailed case study that describes how optimization techniques were used to speed up the sharepoint.microsoft.com site here: *http://sharepoint.microsoft.com/blog/ Lists/Comments/ViewComment.aspx?ID=1202*.

PRACTICE **Optimize Content Access**

Practices are designed to guide you through important procedures. The instructions in the Training Kit are high-level instructions that will challenge you to think carefully and to apply the procedures that are covered in this lesson and elsewhere in the Training Kit. If you need assistance, consult the detailed, step-by-step instructions in the Practice Answers on the companion media.

In this practice, you optimize the performance of SharePoint by configuring resource throttling and the SharePoint caches.

Prepare for the Practice

Before you perform this practice, ensure that your lab environment has been built according to the instructions found in the Introduction to this Training Kit. You must also have performed the practice in Lesson 3 of this chapter. You must be logged off of SP2010-WFE1 before beginning the exercises.

EXERCISE 1   Configure Resource Throttling

In this exercise, you configure resource throttling parameters for the Contoso Intranet Web application:

1. Log on to SP2010-WFE1 as **CONTOSO\SP_Admin** with the password **Pa$$w0rd**.
2. In Central Administration, open the list of web applications.
3. For the Contoso Intranet Web application, configure resource throttling. Use the following settings and guidance:
   - List View Threshold: 2000
   - List View Threshold for Auditors and Administrators: 5000
   - List View Lookup Threshold: 6

EXERCISE 2   Enable the Publishing Feature

The output and object caches require the site-level Publishing feature. In this exercise, you enable this feature:

1. Browse to the Contoso intranet homepage.
2. Go to Site Settings and access the Site Collection Features list.
3. Enable the SharePoint Server Publishing Infrastructure feature.
4. Go to the Site Features list.
5. Enable the SharePoint Server Publishing feature.

EXERCISE 3   Configure SharePoint Caches

In this exercise, you edit the Web.config file for the Contoso Intranet Web application to enable the BLOB Cache, the Object Cache, and the Output Cache:

1. Open Internet Information Services Manager and access the list of sites.
2. Explore the Contoso intranet site.
3. Edit the Web.config file using Notepad.
4. Find and edit the <BlobCache> tag. Set the following attributes:
   - *maxSize*: 5
   - *enable*: true
5. Find and edit the <ObjectCache> tag. Set the *maxSize* attribute to 200.
6. Find and edit the <OutputCacheProfiles> tag. Set the *useCacheProfileOverrides* attribute to true.
7. Save the file and close Notepad.

Lesson Summary

- If you have unusual or unique SharePoint requirements, the default SharePoint configuration may not be optimal.
- Configure resource throttling on a web application to restrict resource-intensive tasks such as rendering large lists.
- RBS enables you to store images, document, and other binary files outside the content database. This reduces the size of the content database and sometimes increases performance.
- Configure the BLOB Cache to accelerate the delivery of images, documents, and other binary files by caching them on WFE servers.
- Configure the Output Cache to enable SharePoint WFE servers to store rendered web pages. Subsequent requests for cached pages can be delivered rapidly from this cache.
- The Object Cache stores SharePoint objects such as lists, libraries, content types, and so on. You can accelerate page delivery by configuring this cache.
- To optimize database performance, separate transaction logs from database files and operating system files.
- Consider all the databases in the SharePoint farm when you locate database files and transaction logs.

Lesson Review

You can use the following questions to test your knowledge of the information in Lesson 4, "Optimize Content Storage and Access." The questions are also available on the companion media in a practice test if you prefer to review them in electronic form.

> **NOTE ANSWERS**
>
> Answers to these questions and explanations of why each answer choice is right or wrong are located in the "Answers" section at the end of the book.

1. You have several large lists in a SharePoint site that stores information about your product catalog. Users are complaining about poor performance and you have traced the problem to a Web Part that displays all the items in the largest of these lists. You want to prevent the Web Part from displaying more than 1,000 items. How can you achieve this?

   A. Use resource throttling to set a list view threshold.

   B. Use resource throttling to set a list view lookup threshold.

   C. Use resource throttling to enable backward-compatible event handlers.

   D. Enable RBS in the SQL Server database.

   E. Configure the maximum size of the BLOB Cache.

2. You have installed a new database server in your SharePoint farm specifically to host the Search service application databases. It has four RAID 10 arrays and one RAID 5 array. How should you place the operating system, database files, and transaction logs to maximize performance?

   A. Place all database files and transaction logs on the RAID 5 array. Place the operating system on the first RAID 10 array. Use the remaining RAID 10 arrays for backups.

   B. Place the operating system on the RAID 5 array. Separate the database files for the Search Administration, Property, and Crawl databases onto three of the RAID 10 arrays. Place all transaction logs on the final RAID 10 array.

   C. Place the operating system on the RAID 5 array. Place all the database files on the first RAID 10 array. Separate transaction logs for the Search Administration, Property, and Crawl databases onto the remaining three RAID 10 arrays.

   D. Place the operating system on a RAID 10 array. Separate the database files for the Search Administration, Property, and Crawl databases onto the remaining three RAID 10 arrays. Place all transaction logs on the RAID 5 array.

   E. Place the operating system on a RAID 10 array. Place all the database files on the RAID 5 array. Separate the transaction logs for the Search Administration, Property, and Crawl databases on the remaining RAID 10 arrays.

Chapter Review

To further practice and reinforce the skills you learned in this chapter, you can perform the following tasks:

- Review the chapter summary.
- Review the list of key terms introduced in this chapter.
- Complete the case scenarios. These scenarios set up real-world situations involving the topics of this chapter and ask you to create a solution.
- Complete the suggested practices.
- Take a practice test.

Chapter Summary

- SharePoint administrators use Performance Monitor to study and understand how the farm responds to user requests.
- By studying the performance of the farm in the lab and in production, administrators can ensure that SharePoint responds well to users, even during expected or unexpected peaks in demand.
- Before you deploy SharePoint, you should simulate load in the lab and record how SharePoint responds.
- During a phased deployment, monitor performance again to ensure that users behave as you predicted.
- After deployment, create a benchmark performance profile. You can use this benchmark later to spot trends in SharePoint usage.
- If performance is poor, you must monitor to identify the bottleneck. Otherwise you may make ineffective upgrades that do not increase performance.
- In Performance Monitor, take care to choose counters that target the question you are trying to answer.
- For troubleshooting, you can increase the amount of information SharePoint logs and records. Reduce this amount when you have finished and want to tune for performance.
- The developer dashboard can be a valuable source of performance data for components of the user interface.
- Health Analyzer regularly checks a range of configuration values to ensure that SharePoint functions well.
- When problems are found, a banner alerts you in Central Administration and you can access suggested remedies. Some rules can resolve problems automatically.

- SharePoint includes several built-in reporting tools and can integrate will SQL Server Reporting Services.

- Web Analytics provides a wide range of reports targeted to website administrators who want to optimize site structure, navigation, and search.

- You can prevent resource intensive actions, such as querying large lists, by setting Resource Throttling limits.

- By using Remote BLOB Storage in SQL Server, you can sometimes increase database performance.

- SharePoint can use the BLOB Cache, the Output Cache, and the Object Cache to increase performance. Increasing cache times can increase performance but you must be careful to ensure that out-of-date pages are not returned to users.

- The location of database files and transaction logs, for all databases in the SharePoint farm, is critical to optimal performance.

Key Terms

The following terms were introduced in this chapter. Do you know what they mean?

- Performance Monitor counters
- Data collector sets
- Performance bottleneck
- Developer dashboard
- Load simulation
- Performance benchmark
- Diagnostic logs (also known as trace logs and ULS logs)
- Usage Data Collection
- Usage reports
- Web Analytics
- Web Analytics workflow
- Best bet suggestion
- SharePoint 2010 Load Testing Kit
- Health Analyzer
- Health rule
- SQL Server Reporting Services
- The Reporting Services Add-In
- SSRS Proxy
- Resource throttling

- BLOB Cache
- Output Cache
- Object Cache

Case Scenario: Monitoring Web Part Deployment

In the following case scenario, you will apply what you've learned about subjects of this chapter. You can find answers to these questions in the "Answers" section at the end of this book.

You have an existing SharePoint farm with around 3,000 users authoring and editing a broad range of documents. Sites are created for each document authoring project. The farm performs well and responds quickly to user requests. A developer in your team has created a new Web Part that will be used on every page in the project sites. You expect the Web Part to increase demand on the SharePoint farm but you are not sure which servers or components will be affected.

1. You want to start by ensuring that the Web Part, which will run outside the sandbox, will not affect stability. You also want to make an estimate of the load that a single user will add when the new Web Part is included on a page. How should you approach this task?

2. Next, you want to deploy the Web Part into the farm and start using it. You want to measure exactly how much extra load this places on the farm. How should you approach this task?

Suggested Practices

To help you successfully master the exam objectives presented in this chapter, complete the following tasks.

Practice 1: Deploy SSRS

In the practice in Lesson 3, you configured Web Analytics and used it to generate web traffic reports. To understand the advantages of integrating SharePoint and SSRS, you should practice deploying SSRS in the lab:

1. Install the Reporting Services Add-In for SharePoint to all SharePoint servers in the farm using the rsSharePoint.msi file.

2. Activate the Report Server Integration Feature at the site collection level.

3. Configure a new Reporting Database in SQL Server Reporting Services. Ensure that you use the SharePoint Integrated mode.

4. If your reporting server is not already a SharePoint server, install SharePoint. Add the new SharePoint server to the SharePoint farm. You do not need to host any sites or service applications on the new SharePoint server.

5. Configure Report Services Integration in Central Administration.

Practice 2: Test How Caching and Resource Throttling Affect Performance

In the practice in Lesson 4, you configured resource throttling and three types of caching. In a real environment, you must prove that these changes have increased performance and measure how much. This requires performance tests before and after you change the configuration:

1. Begin by making a thorough benchmark of the performance of your test farm with Performance Monitor. Use Visual Studio Ultimate to generate simulated user demand.

2. Make your proposed optimizations.

3. Rerun the same tests and compare the results with the benchmark results.

4. Tune settings. For example, you may find a larger or smaller BLOB Cache size increases performance. Rerun the tests.

Take a Practice Test

The practice tests on this book's companion media offer many options. For example, you can test yourself on only the lesson review content, or you can test yourself on all the 70-667 certification exam objectives. You can set up the test so that it closely simulates the experience of taking a certification exam, or you can set it up in study mode so that you can look at the correct answers and explanations after you answer each question.

> **MORE INFO** **PRACTICE TESTS**
>
> For details about all the practice test options available, see the "How to Use the Practice Tests" section in this book's Introduction.

Answers

Chapter 1

Lesson 1

1. **Correct Answer: D**

   A. Incorrect: SQL Server 2005 (64-bit) does not support SharePoint 2010. Service Pack 3 is required.

   B. Correct: SQL Server 2005 SP3 (64-bit) is the minimum version of SQL Server that supports SharePoint Server 2010.

   C. Incorrect: SQL Server 2008 (64-bit) does not support SharePoint. SP1 is required. However, SQL Server 2008 SP1 (64-bit) is not the minimum version required by SharePoint—earlier versions are supported.

   D. Incorrect: SQL Server 2008 R2 supports SharePoint, but is not the minimum version required—earlier versions are supported.

2. **Correct Answers: C and D**

   A. Incorrect: The sysadmin role is not necessary for the setup user.

   B. Incorrect: The serveradmin role is not necessary for the setup user.

   C. Correct: The dbcreator server role is required for the setup user. The setup user credentials are used during configuration of the farm to create the SharePoint configuration database.

   D. Correct: The securityadmin server role is required for the setup user. The setup user credentials are used during configuration of the farm to assign database roles to the SharePoint farm account.

3. **Correct Answers: C and D**

   A. Incorrect: Setup.exe is used to install SharePoint. The setup wizard will report that prerequisites are missing, but it cannot install missing prerequisites.

   B. Incorrect: The SharePoint 2010 Products Preparation Tool cannot download missing prerequisites without Internet connectivity unless it is supplied with parameters that direct the prerequisite installer to prerequisite installation files.

   C. Correct: A PrerequisiteInstaller. Arguments.txt file can direct the Preparation Tool to an offline source of prerequisite installation files.

   D. Correct: PrerequisiteInstaller.exe accepts command-line parameters that point to an offline source of prerequisite installation files.

Lesson 2

1. **Correct Answer: B**

   A. **Incorrect:** PrerequisiteInstaller. Arguments.txt is used to automate the installation of SharePoint prerequisites, but not of SharePoint binaries.

   B. **Correct:** Config.xml can be used by Setup.exe to automate installation of SharePoint binaries.

   C. **Incorrect:** Unattend.xml is used to automate the installation of Windows, but not of SharePoint.

   D. **Incorrect:** Windows PowerShell can be used to launch the installation of SharePoint binaries (Setup.exe), but by itself cannot automate the configuration of the installation.

2. **Correct Answers: A and C**

   A. **Correct:** SharePoint Products Configuration Wizard steps you through the configuration of a SharePoint server.

   B. **Incorrect:** Setup.exe is used to install the SharePoint binaries, but is not used to configure the server.

   C. **Correct:** Windows PowerShell can be used to configure the server.

   D. **Incorrect:** Central Administration is used to configure and manage the farm after a server has joined the farm, but cannot be used to manage a server until after the server has been configured.

3. **Correct Answers: B and C**

   A. **Incorrect:** The Farm Administrators group is not configured by the Farm Configuration Wizard.

   B. **Correct:** A managed account is created, if it does not already exist, and is given permissions required by the service applications that are configured by the wizard.

   C. **Correct:** The selected service applications are deployed and configured by the wizard.

   D. **Incorrect:** Connections to back-end data sources are not configured by the Farm Configuration Wizard.

   E. **Incorrect:** The outgoing email server is not configured by the Farm Configuration Wizard.

4. **Correct Answers: A, D, and E**

   A. **Correct:** The Administrators group of the SharePoint server is a default member of the Farm Administrators group.

   B. **Incorrect:** The Domain Admins group is not a default member of the Farm Administrators group. However, if Domain Admins is a member of the local Administrators group on the SharePoint server, then users in Domain Admins will be farm administrators.

   C. **Incorrect:** The *dbowner* role on the SQL server is not a default member of the Farm Administrators group.

   D. **Correct:** The farm account is a default member of the Farm Administrators group.

   E. **Correct:** The setup user account is a default member of the Farm Administrators group.

Lesson 3

1. **Correct Answer: B**

   A. **Incorrect:** A unique authentication provider is not required simply because a server hosts multiple web applications on the same IP address and port.

   B. **Correct:** If a server hosts multiple web applications on the same IP address and port, each web application must be configured with a unique host header.

   C. **Incorrect:** A unique application pool is not required simply because a server hosts multiple web applications on the same IP address and port.

   D. **Incorrect:** A unique application pool identity is not required simply because a server hosts multiple web applications on the same IP address and port.

2. **Correct Answers: A and C**

   A. **Correct:** When you create a SharePoint web application, an IIS Web site is also created.

   B. **Incorrect:** A DNS record is not created when you create a SharePoint web application. You must add a DNS record as a separate step.

   C. **Correct:** A content database can be associated with only one web application. When you create a web application by using Central Administration, a content database is created.

   D. **Incorrect:** No content is created in a web application until you create a site collection.

3. **Correct Answers: A, D, and E**

   A. **Correct:** When you create a site collection, a top-level website is also created.

   B. **Incorrect:** An IIS Web site is created when you create a web application, not when you create a site collection.

   C. **Incorrect:** A content database is not created when you create a site collection.

   D. **Correct:** A home page is created in the site collection, based on the selected site definition for the top-level site.

   E. **Correct:** Lists and libraries are created in the site collection, based on the selected site definition for the top-level site.

Case Scenario: Deploying SharePoint Servers and Farms

1. A stand-alone installation of SharePoint Server 2010 installs SQL Server Express on the server. This ensures that the changes made on one server will not impact any other training or production server.

2. SharePoint 2010 can be installed on Windows Vista SP1 and Windows 7 clients with only 4 GB of RAM.

3. You can script the installation and configuration of SharePoint servers and then run the scripts in both the test and production environments. This will ensure that the installation and configuration parameters are identical.

Chapter 2

Lesson 1

1. **Correct Answer: B**

   A. **Incorrect:** Central Administration allows you to assign only two site collection administrators.

   B. **Correct:** Site collection administrators can enable and disable features and perform other configuration for the site collection.

   C. **Incorrect:** The Owners group of a site has full control of content but cannot configure site collection settings.

   D. **Incorrect:** The Designers group of a site cannot configure site collection settings.

2. **Correct Answers: B, C, E, and G**

   A. **Incorrect:** The Site Collection Administrators group, as defined by using the top-level site's Site Settings page, does not receive email notifications. Only the primary site collection administrator and the secondary site collection administrator receive email notifications. Because Lola would be the third member of Site Collection Administrators, she would not be made a site collection owner.

   B. **Correct:** The Primary Site Collection Administrator, as defined by using Central Administration, receives email notifications related to quotas if quotas are enabled.

   C. **Correct:** A storage limit must be configured for a quota and its notification settings to have any effect.

   D. **Incorrect:** The requirement is for Lola to receive a notification when her site reaches its storage limit, not before it reaches its limit.

   E. **Correct:** The quota template must be applied to the site collection for its settings to take effect.

   F. **Incorrect:** When you select Individual Quota, you must configure the storage limit directly on the site collection. No step is listed in which the storage limit is configured on the site collection.

   G. **Correct:** Outgoing email settings must be configured for a quota notification to be sent successfully.

   H. **Incorrect:** Incoming email settings are not required for notifications to be sent successfully.

3. **Correct Answer: B**

   A. **Incorrect:** You can configure the primary owner of a site collection by using Stsadm. The Stsadm command executed correctly—it produced an Access Denied error—so the problem is not due to the lack of functionality.

B. **Correct:** An access denied error suggests that you did not run Stsadm with administrative credentials.

C. **Incorrect:** The Stsadm command executed correctly—it produced an Access Denied error—so the problem is not due to the lack of a path to stsadm.exe.

D. **Incorrect:** You cannot remove the primary site collection administrator.

Lesson 2

1. **Correct Answers: B and C**

   A. **Incorrect:** The *Get-SPWebApplication* cmdlet works with *SPWebApplication* objects— web applications—not *SPWeb* (website) applications.

   B. **Correct:** If provided an identity of a specific web application, such as a URL, the *Get-SPWebApplication* cmdlet returns an object representing that web application.

   C. **Correct:** If no identity is provided, the *Get-SPWebApplication* cmdlet returns a collection of all web applications in the farm, except Central Administration. If the *–IncludeCentralAdministration* parameter is supplied, Central Administration is also included in the collection.

   D. **Incorrect:** The *Get-SPWebApplication* cmdlet does not work with service application objects.

2. **Correct Answer: D**

   A. **Incorrect:** *Delete-SPSite* is not a Windows PowerShell cmdlet. In fact, *Delete* is not a valid Windows PowerShell verb.

   B. **Incorrect:** *Remove-SPWebApplication* removes an entire web application, not a single site collection.

   C. **Incorrect:** *Remove-SPWeb* removes a website, not a site collection.

   D. **Correct:** *Remove-SPSite* can be used to delete a site collection.

3. **Correct Answers: A, B, C, and D**

   A. **Correct:** The *Get-SPWebApplication* cmdlet is necessary. Without using *Get-SPWebApplication* with the *-IncludeCentralAdminsitration* parameter, you cannot retrieve the site collection for Central Administration with the *Get-SPSite* cmdlet. The resulting command is: Get-SPWebApplication -IncludeCentralAdministration | Get-SPSite -Limit ALL.

   B. **Correct:** The *-IncludeCentralAdminsitration* parameter is necessary. Without using *Get-SPWebApplication* with the *-IncludeCentralAdminsitration* parameter, you cannot retrieve the site collection for Central Administration with the *Get-SPSite* cmdlet. The resulting command is: Get-SPWebApplication -IncludeCentralAdministration | Get-SPSite -Limit ALL.

C. **Correct:** The *Get-SPSite* cmdlet retrieves a collection of objects representing all site collections in the farm. The resulting command is: Get-SPWebApplication -IncludeCentralAdministration | Get-SPSite -Limit ALL.

D. **Correct:** Without the *-Limit ALL* parameter, the *Get-SPSite* cmdlet returns only 20 site collections per web application. The resulting command is: Get-SPWebApplication -IncludeCentralAdministration | Get-SPSite -Limit ALL.

Case Scenario: Reporting Properties of the SharePoint Farm

1. The *Get-SPWebApplication*, *Get-SPSite*, and *Get-SPWeb* cmdlets can return .NET objects representing all websites in the farm. The *Select-Object* cmdlet can retrieve specific properties of the websites.

2. The *Export-CSV* cmdlet exports pipeline objects to a .csv file, which can be opened by Microsoft Excel.

3. You can create a Scheduled Task to run the reports automatically.

4. The credentials used by the scheduled task must be given permissions to all content databases in the farm by using the *Add-SPShellAdmin* cmdlet. The scheduled task credentials and the user account of the compliance officer must also have permissions to a shared location to which the reports will be saved.

Chapter 3

Lesson 1

1. **Correct Answers: A, B, and D**

   A. **Correct:** The third step is to add an HTTPS binding to the IIS Web site that uses the certificate.

   B. **Correct:** The first step is to create a SharePoint Web application. While creating the web application, click Yes for the Use Secure Sockets Layer (SSL) setting.

   C. **Incorrect:** SharePoint does not store certificates. Certificates and the handling of SSL are managed by IIS.

   D. **Correct:** The second step is to create or add a certificate to the server.

2. **Correct Answer: D**

   A. **Incorrect:** The outgoing email server setting is not scoped to the site or site collection, it is scoped to the web application or farm.

   B. **Incorrect:** The Configure Outgoing E-Mail Server on the General Settings page of Central Administration configures the outgoing email server for all web applications in the farm. You can specify only one SMTP server.

C. **Incorrect:** If a message has already been sent to an SMTP server, it is too late to distribute that message to one of several SMTP servers.

D. **Correct:** You can configure an SMTP server for each web application and, if you do so, outgoing email including alerts are sent to the specified SMTP server rather than to the farm's default SMTP server.

3. **Correct Answer: A**

A. **Correct:** You can configure the Recycle Bins to retain items for a specified length of time.

B. **Incorrect:** The requirement does not state that users should not be able to delete items.

C. **Incorrect:** Information management policies are features that can be used within a list or library. They do not affect the behavior of items that have been deleted.

D. **Incorrect:** User policy is a set of permissions that applies to all content in a web application, and overrides permissions configured on content in the web application.

Lesson 2

1. **Correct Answer: A**

A. **Correct:** SetSPN is used to add the service principal name of a web application in the application pool account.

B. **Incorrect:** An SSL binding is not required for Kerberos to function.

C. **Incorrect:** A trusted identity provider is registered for SAML token-based authentication, not for Kerberos authentication.

D. **Incorrect:** The Web.config file must be modified for forms-based authentication, not for Kerberos authentication.

2. **Correct Answers: C and E**

A. **Incorrect:** The Negotiate method does not force Kerberos—a browser can request NTLM. Kerberos is the preferred protocol, so if a browser and the connection can support Kerberos, it will be used, but it is not guaranteed.

B. **Incorrect:** The client security log will not reflect the authentication protocol used in the connection to the web application.

C. **Correct:** The Security event log on the server will show a logon event. The general information of the event will show the Security ID of the user, and the protocol that was used.

D. **Incorrect:** The KList command on the server will not show that a ticket has been used to successfully connect with the server.

E. **Correct:** The KList command can be used to examine and purge Kerberos tickets that have been issued to a client.

F. **Incorrect:** SetSPN is used to add the service principal name of a web application in the application pool account. It cannot be used to verify that the Kerberos protocol was actually used for a connection.

3. **Correct Answers: B and C**

   A. **Incorrect:** The site collection administrators will manage the access permissions granted to anonymous users. Your goal is only to ensure that, even if a site collection administrator grants permissions greater than read-only to anonymous users, that the access is limited to read-only.

   B. **Correct:** A Deny Write anonymous user policy will override any permissions granted by site collection administrators, thus ensuring that the maximum available access is read-only.

   C. **Correct:** You must enable anonymous authentication on the web application: otherwise, anonymous users cannot connect to the web application.

   D. **Incorrect:** The site collection administrators will manage the access permissions granted to anonymous users. Your goal is only to ensure that, even if a site collection administrator grants permissions greater than read-only to anonymous users, that the access is limited to read-only.

4. **Correct Answers: C, D, and E**

   A. **Incorrect:** Port 389 is not required for this scenario.

   B. **Incorrect:** SQL logins are permissions for the partner users to access the SQL database. This is not required. However, you must create SQL logins for the application pool identity used by the web application.

   C. **Correct:** You must modify Web.config files to specify the membership provider and role manager provider.

   D. **Correct:** Forms Based Authentication is supported only by Claims Based Authentication.

   E. **Correct:** You must configure the authentication provider of the web application itself to use Forms Based Authentication, which requires defining the membership provider and the role provider.

5. **Correct Answers: A, C, D, and E**

   A. **Correct:** You must specify the membership provider, the role manager provider, and any required connections in the Web.config file of Central Administration. Additionally, you should configure the wildcards used by the People Picker control to search the user directory.

   B. **Incorrect:** The Secure Store Service is not involved with inbound authentication of users to a web application. As you'll learn in Chapter 8, the Secure Store Service is used to authenticate to back-end data sources.

   C. **Correct:** You must specify the membership provider, the role manager provider, and any required connections in the Web.config file of the Security Token Service Application. Additionally, you should configure the wildcards used by the People Picker control to search the user directory.

D. **Correct:** You must specify the membership provider, the role manager provider, and any required connections in the Web.config file of the web application. Additionally, you should configure the wildcards used by the People Picker control to search the user directory.

E. **Correct:** Application pool identities—including those used by the web application, Central Administration, and the STS—must be given permission to access the user directory specified by the membership provider and the role manager provider.

Lesson 3

1. **Correct Answers: A and D**

   A. **Correct:** You must add a host header binding to the IIS site for *http://timecards*. There should already be a host header binding for *http://timecards.contoso.com*.

   B. **Incorrect:** The Web.config file does not have to be modified to support this scenario.

   C. **Incorrect:** Managed paths are used to define the URL namespaces within which site collections can be created. Managed paths are not needed to support this scenario.

   D. **Correct:** You must add an internal URL to the default zone, *http://timecards*.

   E. **Incorrect:** The scenario does not require SharePoint to render outgoing URLs as *http://timecards*—the scenario only requires that users can browse to the site with that URL. It is recommended to create additional zones only when it is absolutely necessary.

2. **Correct Answers: A, B, C, and D**

   A. **Correct:** You must create a new zone to allow users to access the web application with two different protocols and URLs.

   B. **Correct:** When you extend the web application, you must enable SSL, and configure the public URL as *https://server1.contoso.com*.

   C. **Correct:** You must use IIS Manager to add the SSL binding to the IIS Web site of the new zone.

   D. **Correct:** You must install the SSL certificate on the IIS Web server.

3. **Correct Answer: C**

   A. **Incorrect:** In this scenario, the URL that IIS will receive is *http://partners.contoso.com*.

   B. **Incorrect:** In this scenario, the URL that IIS will receive is *http://partners.contoso.com*. SSL is processed on the intermediary device.

   C. **Correct:** You must modify the alternate access mappings of the default zone so that the public URL is *https://partners.contoso.com* and the internal URL remains *http://partners.contoso.com*.

   D. **Incorrect:** User access will be through the single URL, *https://partners.contoso.com*. There is no requirement for an additional zone.

4. **Correct Answers: A and B**

   A. **Correct:** You must extend the web application to a new zone so that you can apply a unique security policy to the new zone.

   B. **Correct:** You can apply a user policy, such as Deny Write, to restrict content access through the new zone.

   C. **Incorrect:** If you set the content database to read-only by using SQL Server Management Studio, the content will be read only for the entire web application, through all zones.

   D. **Incorrect:** Permissions applied to the site collection affects access through all zones. Users will not be able to change content on the internal URL.

   E. **Incorrect:** There is no requirement for anonymous access, so users are authenticated. Anonymous access restrictions apply only to anonymous connections.

5. **Correct Answers: B, D, and F**

   A. **Incorrect:** The default zone is *http://server1*. The requirement is for anonymous access through *https://server1.contoso.com*.

   B. **Correct:** You must bind the certificate to the IIS Web site supporting the extended zone.

   C. **Incorrect:** When you extend the web application, a new zone is created with the correct public and internal URL, *https://server1.contoso.com*.

   D. **Correct:** You must extend the web application to create a new zone and IIS site, to which you will bind the incoming SSL requests.

   E. **Incorrect:** Anonymous access restrictions are used to limit the access of anonymous users to content in zones that they can already access. Anonymous access restrictions do not enable anonymous access in the first place.

   F. **Correct:** You must modify the authentication provider of the new zone to enable anonymous access.

Case Scenario: Troubleshooting Web Application Configuration

1. Sign In is displayed by the Welcome control in the upper-right corner of the page when a user is not authenticated—that is, it is displayed to anonymous users. The site is allowing users to connect as anonymous users.

2. The only way that anonymous authentication could be disabled on *http://intranet* and enabled on *http://intranet.contoso.com* would be for the two URLs to be two different zones. The previous administrator extended the intranet to an additional zone.

3. First, you must unextend the web application, deleting the zone and the IIS site. Then, add the URL of the zone you just deleted as an internal URL for the default zone, and add a host header binding to the IIS Web site. Finally, check the authentication provider settings of the web application to ensure that anonymous authentication is disabled.

Chapter 4

Lesson 1

1. **Correct Answer: D**

   A. **Incorrect:** Lola and April are currently receiving email notifications, which suggests that the outgoing SMTP server setting is already correct.

   B. **Incorrect:** The Specify Quota Settings page allows you to configure storage limits and warning levels, but does not allow you to specify the recipients of email notifications.

   C. **Incorrect:** Changing the order of users by using the Site Settings page does not change the site collection owners as defined in Central Administration.

   D. **Correct:** The two site collection owners—as defined in Central Administration—receive email notifications about site collection storage.

2. **Correct Answer: A**

   A. **Correct:** The Manage Web Applications page allows you to disable self-service site creation.

   B. **Incorrect:** The Site Settings page will not prevent the creation of new site collections.

   C. **Incorrect:** The scsignup.aspx page is used to create a new site collection when self-service site creation is enabled.

   D. **Incorrect:** A site lock can prevent the creation of new content in a site collection, but cannot prevent the creation of new site collections.

3. **Correct Answer: A**

   A. **Correct:** The *Move-SPSite* cmdlet can move a site collection to another content database.

   B. **Incorrect:** Stsadm does not have a *splitdatabase* operation.

   C. **Incorrect:** The Manage Content Database page of Central Administration allows you to create and delete content databases, but does not allow you to move content between content databases.

   D. **Incorrect:** Content deployment is used to copy content from a source site collection to a destination site collection. It is used to support scenarios such as a staging and production environment for a public-facing website. It does not move content between content databases.

Lesson 2

1. **Correct Answer: B**

   A. **Incorrect:** User policy applies to the web application. This policy would prevent all users from deleting all content in all site collections.

   B. **Correct:** Create a custom permission level that includes all of the permissions of the Contribute permission level. Replace the default permission level of the Project A Members group—Contribute—with the new permission level.

     C. **Incorrect:** SharePoint does not provide Deny permissions for site content.

     D. **Incorrect:** Configuring the content database as read-only would prevent all changes, not just deletions, for all site collections in the content database.

2. **Correct Answers: A, C, and D**

     A. **Correct:** A custom permission level that includes the Override Check Out permission will allow managers to check in documents that were checked out by another user.

     B. **Incorrect:** The Contribute permission level does not include the Override Check Out permission.

     C. **Correct:** The Full Control permission level includes the Override Check Out permission.

     D. **Correct:** The Design permission level includes the Override Check Out permission.

3. **Correct Answer: D**

     A. **Incorrect:** User policy applies to the web application. This policy would prevent all users from changing all content in all site collections.

     B. **Incorrect:** Moving users into the site's Visitors group would give the users only Read permission to content, and would thereby prevent users from changing other pages in the library.

     C. **Incorrect:** Removing the site's Members group from the permissions to the library would prevent users from changing other pages in the library.

     D. **Correct:** Blocking inheritance for the page and removing the site's Members group will prevent users from changing the page. Remaining pages in the library would continue to inherit the permissions assigned to the library.

Case Scenario: Configure Site Collections and Content Databases

1. The web application is implemented as a single site collection in a single content database. The user information list is scoped to a site collection. The fact that partner administrators can see each other's users is an indication that there is only one site collection.

2. You should create a total of 10 site collections, so that the partner company's users are partitioned from each other.

3. Only one content database is necessary, because the backup requirements are the same for all partners, and a content database that will grow to a maximum size of 50 GB can be backed up overnight.

4. You can apply a Full Control user policy to the Compliance group for the partners.contoso.com web application. The permissions in a user policy take precedence over any permissions in a site collection.

Chapter 5

Lesson 1

1. **Correct Answers: B and C**

   A. **Incorrect:** Excel Services is part of SharePoint Server 2010. You do not need to install Microsoft Office on the server.

   B. **Correct:** You must start a service instance of Excel Calculation Services on at least one server in the farm.

   C. **Correct:** You must deploy an Excel Services Application.

   D. **Incorrect:** There is no requirement for a web application with a specific name to support Excel Services.

2. **Correct Answers: A, E, and F**

   A. **Correct:** You must publish the service in the farm hosting the service.

   B. **Incorrect:** The service must be started on servers in the farm hosting the service, but not in the farm connecting to the service.

   C. **Incorrect:** The service is published in the farm hosting the service, not in the farm subscribing to the service.

   D. **Incorrect:** The connection is made in the farm connecting to the service, not in the farm hosting the service.

   E. **Correct:** You must connect to the service from the farm subscribing to the service.

   F. **Correct:** The service must be started on servers in the farm hosting the service.

Lesson 2

1. **Correct Answers: C and D**

   A. **Incorrect:** You do not require an additional Managed Metadata Service application to address this scenario. You can assign sales managers the correct role within an existing Managed Metadata Service application.

   B. **Incorrect:** You do not require an additional term store to address this scenario. A new term store would require a new Managed Metadata Service application. You can assign sales managers the correct role within an existing Managed Metadata Service application.

   C. **Correct:** You can create a term group, and then assign the Contributors role to the sales managers. The term group Contributors can modify term sets and terms within the term group.

   D. **Correct:** You can create a term set for Customers. The term set can then be used in a managed metadata column in a list, library, or content type.

   E. **Incorrect:** The Keywords set is an open term set that is designed to support folksonomy.

2. **Correct Answers: C and E**

   A. Incorrect: Content types are scoped to a site and cannot be shared between site collections unless you have configured the Managed Metadata Service correctly.

   B. Incorrect: The human resources site collection is subscribing to the content types of the legal site collection. The legal site collection is the content type hub.

   C. Correct: You must configure the properties of the Managed Metadata Service application so that the legal site collection is the content type hub.

   D. Incorrect: Content deployment is not used to share content types.

   E. Correct: The application connection of a Managed Metadata Service must specify that web applications consume content types from the content type hub.

Case Scenario: Configure Service Applications and the Managed Metadata Service

1. A Managed Metadata Service application should be created in the new farm. The terms for the joint venture should be created in that Managed Metadata Service application. The service application can be published, and the Contoso farm can connect to the service application, and then web applications in the Contoso farm can use terms from the joint venture term set. Likewise, the Litware farm can connect to the service application and thereby consume terms in the term store.

2. You must add the users as Term Store Contributors. Additionally, you must add them to the Delegated Administrators group in Central Administration so that they can access Central Administration.

3. For Contoso and Litware to provide content types for the joint venture farm, each must create a Managed Metadata Service application, configure content type syndication, and publish the service application. The joint venture farm must connect to each of the published service applications. In the properties of the connection, you must specify that web applications consume content types from the content type hub.

Chapter 6

Lesson 1

1. **Correct Answers: D and E**

   A. Incorrect: There must already be a BCS connection because some fields synchronize correctly. You do not need an external content type.

   B. Incorrect: There must already be a user profile synchronization connection because some fields synchronize correctly.

C. **Incorrect:** By adding a filter to the user profile synchronization connection you would prevent some users from synchronizing—you would not synchronize the Office field.

D. **Correct:** The problem likely results from a naming difference between the SharePoint Office field and its equivalent in the HR database.

E. **Correct:** It is a good precaution to run a full synchronization to ensure that the mapping takes effect for all users.

2. **Correct Answers: B and D**

A. **Incorrect:** Because the *New-SPProfileServiceApplication* command ran, the SharePoint snap-in must be loaded.

B. **Correct:** When you create a User Profile service application in Central Administration, a proxy is automatically created. When you create a User Profile service application in Windows PowerShell, you must use the *New-SPProfileServiceApplicationProxy* command to create a proxy to go with it.

C. **Incorrect:** The SharePoint farm does need local administrator rights, but if it did not have them, the User Profile Synchronization Service would not have started.

D. **Correct:** An IISReset is required after you start the User Profile services.

E. **Incorrect:** Self-service site creation is required for My Sites but not for user profiles.

Lesson 2

1. **Correct Answers: D and E**

A. **Incorrect:** There must already be a BCS connection because some fields synchronize correctly. You do not need an external content type.

B. **Incorrect:** There must already be a user profile synchronization connection because some fields synchronize correctly.

C. **Incorrect:** By adding a filter to the user profile synchronization connection you would prevent some users from synchronizing—you would not synchronize the Office field.

D. **Correct:** The problem likely results from a naming difference between the SharePoint Office field and its equivalent in the HR database.

E. **Correct:** It is a good precaution to run a full synchronization to ensure that the mapping takes effect for all users.

2. **Correct Answers: B and D**

A. **Incorrect:** Because the *New-SPProfileServiceApplication* command ran, the SharePoint snap-in must be loaded.

B. **Correct:** When you create a User Profile service application in Central Administration, a proxy is automatically created. When you create a User Profile service application in Windows PowerShell, you must use the *New-SPProfileServiceApplicationProxy* command to create a proxy to go with it.

C. **Incorrect:** The SharePoint farm does need local administrator rights, but if it did not have them, the User Profile Synchronization Service would not have started.

D. **Correct:** An IISReset is required after you start the User Profile services.

E. **Incorrect:** Self-service site creation is required for My Sites but not for user profiles.

Case Scenario: Configuring User Profiles and Social Networking

1. You must separate user profiles and My Sites into two SQL Server databases. This requires two User Profile service applications, two web applications, and two site collections. For the permanent consultants:

   - Create a web application and configure the content database to be stored on a SQL Server cluster with RAID disks.
   - Create a site collection in the new web application based on the My Site Host template.
   - Enable self-service site creation and create a managed path for personal sites on the web application.
   - Set up user profile synchronization. Select AD DS organizational units or add filters to ensure that only permanent consultants are synchronized.
   - Create an audience that contains permanent staff only. Use this audience to target My Sites in this User Profile service application.
   - Back up the content database regularly and fully.

   For the freelance consultants:

   - Create a web application and configure the content database to be stored on a single SQL Server with cheaper hardware.
   - Create a site collection in the new web application based on the My Site Host template.
   - Enable self-service site creation and create a managed path for personal sites on the web application.
   - Set up user profile synchronization. Select AD DS organizational units or add filters to ensure that only freelance consultants are synchronized.
   - Create an audience that contains freelance consultants only. Use this audience to target My Sites in this User Profile service application.
   - Back up the content database less often. You may also decide to use incrememental backups.

   When this configuration is complete, add each My Site host site collection as a trusted My Site host in the other User Profile service application. This ensures that permanent staff can browse freelancers' My Sites and vice versa.

2. For both User Profile service applications edit the user permissions. Remove the Use Social Features permission from All Authenticated Users. Grant it to a security group that contains permanent staff but not freelancers.

Chapter 7

Lesson 1

1. **Correct Answers: A, B, D, F, and G**

   A. **Correct:** The Search service runs under the context of a managed account.

   B. **Correct:** The Search service account must be a member of WSS_WPG.

   C. **Incorrect:** The Search service account need not be a member of WSS_Admin_WPG.

   D. **Correct:** You want to create a single search solution for your entire enterprise, so a single Search service application is appropriate.

   E. **Incorrect:** By installing a separate service application for each content source you will partition search and not create a single enterprise solution.

   F. **Correct:** Although you could add start addresses for all the content to a single content source, creating four separate content sources permits you to create separate index schedules for each and is more flexible.

   G. **Correct:** A Search site of some kind is required. A site based on the Enterprise Search Center template is the most functional.

2. **Correct Answers: A, B, and F**

   A. **Correct:** The file share may not be among the start addresses for any of the content sources. You can remedy this by creating a dedicated content source with the file share as its only start address.

   B. **Correct:** A dedicated content source is not required. You can also solve the problem by adding a new start address for the file share to an existing content source.

   C. **Incorrect:** A Protocol Handler for file shares is included by default.

   D. **Incorrect:** PDF is not a storage technology, such as file shares or HTTP. Therefore, there is no Protocol Handler for PDF files.

   E. **Incorrect:** File shares are not a file type. Therefore, there is no IFilter for file shares.

   F. **Correct:** PDF files are a file type so an IFilter must be present for SharePoint to index them. A PDF IFilter is not present by default in SharePoint. You must install a third-party IFilter.

Lesson 2

1. **Correct Answer: B**

   A: **Incorrect:** An increment crawl is sufficient if there is a new item with the new column populated.

   B: **Correct:** The crawler must have processed an item with the new column populated before the column appears in the Crawled Properties list.

C. **Incorrect:** It is not necessary to re-create the lists and their contents from scratch.

D. **Incorrect:** The dbowner role is not required by the site administrator because she does not make any changes to that database.

E. **Incorrect:** The dbowner role is not required for your account because you do not make any changes to that database.

2. **Correct Answer: E**

A. **Incorrect:** Managed properties do not enable thumbnails for results.

B. **Incorrect:** Keywords boost relevance for certain words. They do not enable thumbnail display.

C. **Incorrect:** Best bets display a link whenever certain keywords are searched for. They do not enable thumbnail display.

D. **Incorrect:** The Refinements Panel Web Part cannot display thumbnails.

E. **Correct:** FAST is required to display thumbnails for all results.

Lesson 3

1. **Correct Answers: A, C, and E**

A. **Correct:** Only one Query SSA is possible for each FAST Farm.

B. **Incorrect:** Many index columns can be created across multiple servers in each FAST Farm.

C. **Correct:** Multiple servers within a single Content SSA will help to scale to large corpus sizes.

D. **Incorrect:** Although multiple servers within a single Query SSA are possible, they do not increase the supported corpus size. Instead, they support more frequent queries and larger numbers of users.

E. **Correct:** Multiple index columns within a single Search Cluster can be used to scale to large corpus sizes.

2. **Correct Answer: D**

A. **Incorrect:** Separating crawlers and query servers increases scalability but does not create separate indexes for each tenant.

B. **Incorrect:** Separating crawl servers and query servers increases scalability but does not create separate indexes for each tenant.

C. **Incorrect:** Five search sites are required, but if they all use the same Search service application, there is only one index and each tenant can see results from other tenants.

D. **Correct:** By creating a Search service application for each tenant you create a separate index for each tenant and ensure that they cannot see each other's results.

E. **Incorrect:** FAST Search Server is not required to create separate indexes and index columns partition a single index.

Case Scenario: Optimizing an Enterprise Search Solution

1. Add a keyword for the phrase "Electronic." Add "Electrical" as a synonym of the keyword. Add a best bet to the keyword that links to the Internet-facing site. Ensure that the Best Bets Web Part is included at the top of the results page, above the Search Core Results Web Part.

2. Add a keyword for "circuit board etching." Results that satisfy this phrase will receive a relevancy boost and so should appear closer to the top of results lists.

3. Add a managed property called Component Type to your search configuration. Map this to the appropriate crawled property. SharePoint will not index the Component Type column.

Chapter 8

Lesson 1

1. **Correct Answers: B and E**

    A. Incorrect: The BDC Server Runtime runs on the WFE servers.

    B. Correct: The BDC Service runs on the application servers you specify in Central Administration.

    C. Incorrect: The BCS Web Parts are user interface components that run on the WFE servers.

    D. Incorrect: The BCS Package Store holds configuration details in memory on the WFE servers.

    E. Correct: The Secure Store Service runs on application servers and is required by BCS to manage authentication details.

    F. Incorrect: The BDC Service database must be hosted on a SQL Server database computer.

2. **Correct Answers: C, D, and F**

    A. Incorrect: The user interface technology used in the sales application is irrelevant to BCS.

    B. Incorrect: The user interface technology used in the sales application is irrelevant to BCS.

    C. Correct: BCS can connect to any Web Service that publishes data for reading or writing operations.

    D. Correct: BCS can connect to any WCF Service that publishes data for reading or writing operations.

    E. Incorrect: BCS cannot connect to an Access database without custom coding.

    F. Correct: BCS can connect to a SQL Server database to read or write data.

Lesson 2

1. **Correct: C**

    A. Incorrect: Because this is a simple data-collection form, it can be run in the sandbox and does not need administrator approval.

B. **Incorrect:** The user does not need to use SharePoint Designer to edit forms.

C. **Correct:** Simple forms can be uploaded by users and run in the sandbox.

D. **Incorrect:** This simple functionality—like all of the more advanced options in InfoPath forms—does not require custom code.

2. **Correct Answers: A and B**

   A. **Correct:** The State service application is required for SharePoint to render InfoPath forms to the browser without errors.

   B. **Correct:** Farm administrators can and sometimes do disallow browser-enabled forms in Central Administration.

   C. **Incorrect:** Farm administrators can disable cross-domain access for user form templates, but this is unlikely to cause an error when you have only added static links to the form. Also, if this was the problem, InfoPath users would also receive errors.

   D. **Incorrect:** SharePoint can render InfoPath forms that display without errors in many modern web browsers.

   E. **Incorrect:** If the details in the data connection file were incorrect, InfoPath users would also receive errors.

Lesson 3

1. **Correct Answer: E**

   A. **Incorrect:** An Excel Services service application must already be in use if intranet users can publish spreadsheets successfully. A second service application cannot be expected to solve the problem.

   B. **Incorrect:** The Excel Shared Service must be started on at least one application server if intranet users can publish spreadsheets successfully.

   C. **Incorrect:** Excel spreadsheets should render in the browser no matter which load balancing method you choose.

   D. **Incorrect:** If the View In Browser tool does not work, the Excel Web Access Web Part will not successfully display the spreadsheet either.

   E. **Correct:** Because the Intranet and Finance portals are in separate site collections they use separate content databases. The Excel Services user account requires the dbowner role on all content databases that contain spreadsheets for rendering in the browser.

2. **Correct Answers: D and E**

   A. **Incorrect:** You can import Excel spreadsheets into a SharePoint list without Excel Services.

   B. **Incorrect:** Because you do not need Excel Services to import a spreadsheet, there is no Excel Services user account.

   C. **Incorrect:** Because you do not need Excel Service to import a spreadsheet, there is no Excel Shared Service.

- **D. Correct:** The Import Spreadsheet list template can be used to import a spreadsheet, even when there is no Excel Services service application.
- **E. Correct:** Because the Employees spreadsheet contains salaries and probably other confidential information, you must use permissions to preserve security.

Lesson 4

1. **Correct Answer: C**

   - **A. Incorrect:** Because most of the marketing web database works, there is no reason to think that a template would solve the problem, and it would take significant effort to adapt a template to the marketing requirements.
   - **B. Incorrect:** Microsoft SQL Server 2008 R2 is not required to support Access Web Services.
   - **C. Correct:** The Microsoft SQL Server 2008 R2 Reporting Services Add-in for SharePoint Technologies 2010 is required for reports in web databases to work.
   - **D. Incorrect:** Because the web database works partially, the Access Web Services service application must be in place in the farm already.
   - **E. Incorrect:** Because the web database works partially, the Access Database Service must already be running in the SharePoint farm.

2. **Correct Answers: A, B, D, and E**

   - **A. Correct:** Access 2010 is required to create web database templates.
   - **B. Correct:** The .accdb format must be used to create web database templates.
   - **C. Incorrect:** If other web databases work, the Access Web Services service application must be present in the farm.
   - **D. Correct:** The Maximum Template Size prevents very large databases from being used as templates.
   - **E. Correct:** A web database is a SharePoint site, so a user must have create sites permission to create one from an Access template.

Lesson 5

1. **Correct Answers: A, B, and D**

   - **A. Correct:** Only drawings created in Visio 2010 are supported by Visio Web Services.
   - **B. Correct:** The user must save the drawing in the .vdw web drawing format.
   - **C. Incorrect:** Because the error does not appear when the user opens the drawing in Visio, she must have appropriate permissions in the SharePoint list.
   - **D. Correct:** Visio Services can only connect to SharePoint lists in the same farm as the library that stores the drawing.
   - **E. Incorrect:** Because other users can view drawings in their browsers, the Visio Graphics service must be running already.

Lesson 6

1. **Correct Answer: D**

   A. **Incorrect:** Because intranet site users can open Word documents, the Word Viewing service application must be present in the farm.

   B. **Incorrect:** Because intranet site users can open Word documents, the Word Viewing shared service started on at least one application server in the farm.

   C. **Incorrect:** Users do not require the Office suite to be installed on their local computers to use Office Web Applications.

   D. **Correct:** The Office Web Apps SharePoint Feature must be enabled at the site collection level for all web applications.

   E. **Incorrect:** Silverlight is not required to access Office Web Applications, although users with Silverlight receive the richest functionality.

Case Scenario: Configuring User Profiles and Social Networking

1. Create and configure a Business Data Connection service application. Use SharePoint Designer to make a BCS connection to the LOB system. Create an external content type to describe the products. Create an external list to hold products in SharePoint.

2. Use SharePoint permissions and AD DS security groups to deny write permission to Internet site users. In addition, when you create Operations for your external content type, create Read Operations only.

Chapter 9

Lesson 1

1. **Correct Answer: D**

   A. **Incorrect:** SQL Server 2005 can support a SharePoint 2010 farm. Although you should upgrade to SQL Server 2008 R2, this is not the best answer. In addition, SQL Server 2008 R2 cannot be installed on a server running Windows Server 2003.

   B. **Incorrect:** Windows Server 2003 Service Pack 3 is not required by SQL Server 2005 to support a SharePoint 2010 farm. This is not the best answer.

   C. **Incorrect:** Windows Server 2008 R2 is not required by SQL Server 2005. This is not the best answer.

   D. **Correct:** Windows Server 2008 R2 is required to install SharePoint on the SharePoint servers.

2. **Correct Answer: A**

   A. **Correct:** Service Pack 2 includes the Pre-Upgrade Check.

B. Incorrect: Windows PowerShell 2.0 is a requirement for SharePoint Server 2010, but it is not a prerequisite for running the Pre-Upgrade Check.

C. Incorrect: The Pre-Upgrade Check does not require read-only databases.

D. Incorrect: Although Windows Server 2008 SP1 or Windows Server 2008 R2 is required for SharePoint Server 2010, the Pre-Upgrade Check can run in the existing environment.

3. **Correct Answer: B**

A. Incorrect: The *Test-SPContentDatabase* cmdlet can be used on a SharePoint Server 2010 farm before mounting the content database.

B. Correct: The *preupgradecheck* operation helps you to evaluate the health and upgrade readiness of a SharePoint farm.

C. Incorrect: PSConfig is not used to evaluate upgrade readiness.

D. Incorrect: The SharePoint Administration Toolkit is not used to evaluate upgrade readiness.

Lesson 2

1. **Correct Answers: C and E**

A. Incorrect: Although a container for service connection points will help you monitor installations of SharePoint, a container is not required to install SharePoint.

B. Incorrect: Although you needed to know the farm password in MOSS 2007, you do not need to know the account's password in SharePoint Server 2010.

C. Correct: You must know the farm passphrase to add a server to a farm.

D. Incorrect: The account used to add the server to the farm does not require the sysadmin fixed server role.

E. Correct: You must specify the name of the SQL server hosting the farm configuration database, and then you must specify the name of the database.

2. **Correct Answer: A**

A. Correct: The *DisableInstall* value blocks the installation of SharePoint Server 2010.

B. Incorrect: This container is used to host *serviceConnectionPoint* objects, which represent existing SharePoint deployments. It is not used to restrict installation.

C. Incorrect: This parameter is used when upgrading SharePoint, not when installing an instance of SharePoint on a new server.

D. Incorrect: The *Set-SPFarm* cmdlet changes properties of an existing farm. It is not used to block or allow installation of new servers in the farm.

3. **Correct Answer: B**

A. Incorrect: The Password Management Settings page of Central Administration allows you to configure several settings related to managed accounts and password changes, but it does not allow you to configure automatic password changes.

B. **Correct:** The Managed Accounts page of Central Administration allows you to configure automatic password change for a managed account. After you configure automatic password change for a managed account, the administrative effort required to maintain that managed account is significantly reduced.

C. **Incorrect:** The Delegated Administrators group represents users that have limited access to Central Administration.

D. **Incorrect:** The *New-SPManagedAccount* cmdlet registers a managed account. The *Set-SPManagedAccount* cmdlet allows you to configure automatic password changes for a managed account.

Case Scenario 1: Determining an Upgrade Strategy

1. You must do the following before upgrading to SharePoint 2010:

   - Upgrade the server operating system on each server to Windows Server 2008 or Windows Server 2008 R2.

   - Upgrade the SQL server to SQL Server 2008 R2, which is required to support mirroring.

   - Add at least 4 GB of RAM to each of the SharePoint servers.

   - Install Service Pack 2 and the October 2009 Cumulative Update or later to each of the SharePoint servers.

2. You should recommend a database attach upgrade approach. With a database attach upgrade, you reduce the level of effort required to upgrade hardware and software. Additionally, you can provide availability to the SharePoint 2007 farm by setting databases to read-only while they are attached to the new farm. In the SharePoint 2010 farm, you can attach multiple databases to perform a parallel upgrade, which reduces overall upgrade time. In the event of a failed upgrade, you can simply continue to provide access to sites on the SharePoint 2007 farm.

Case Scenario 2: Managing SharePoint Farms in the Enterprise

1. Configure the *DisableInstall* registry value on all computers in the domain and set the value to 1. This can be done by using Group Policy to deploy the change to all domain computers. For example, you can configure the setting in the Default Domain Policy Group Policy Object (GPO), or in a custom GPO linked to the domain. Then, on developer VMs only, set the value to 0. This can be done by using Group Policy to deploy the change only to developer VMs. For example, the computer accounts for developer VMs can be placed in a single OU and a Group Policy linked to the OU can set the value to 0. By default, a policy setting in a GPO linked to an OU will override a policy setting in a GPO linked to the domain.

   Your answer may vary. What is important is that you identify that the *DisableInstall* registry value is used to block or allow SharePoint installation, and that you must somehow specify *DisableInstall*=1 for all computers in the domain except for those on which SharePoint installation is allowed.

2. SharePoint farms can be tracked by reporting the *serviceConnectionPoint* objects for each farm. To enable tracking, you must create a container in the domain. Follow the procedure described in Lesson 2 to create the container. Each new SharePoint farm will automatically generate a *serviceConnectionPoint* object for the farm. For existing farms, you can use Windows PowerShell to generate the markers. A Windows PowerShell script can query and report all *serviceConnectionPoint* objects in the domain.

Chapter 10

Lesson 1

1. **Correct: C**

   A. **Incorrect:** The sandbox is specifically designed to run user solutions developed both in the local farm and also other farms.

   B. **Incorrect:** Developer involvement is not required. A user solution can be created by using the Save As Template tool in the SharePoint site.

   C. **Correct:** Site templates, created by users, are based on out-of-the-box templates, such as Blank Site or Team Site. There are language-specific versions of these templates. If the French version of the base template is not available in the North American SharePoint farm, the solution may not be functional after deployment.

   D. **Incorrect:** If all the required Web Parts were not available in the North American farm, the user solution would deploy successfully, although some functionality in Web Part pages may be missing.

   E. **Incorrect:** SharePoint can render InfoPath forms in the browser. It is not necessary for InfoPath forms to be installed on all clients.

2. **Correct: A**

   A. **Correct:** The master page can impose a consistent look and feel on every page in the site. This can include corporate branding.

   B. **Incorrect:** A workflow models a business process. It does not influence the look and feel of the site or impose branding.

   C. **Incorrect:** Although you could add the corporate branding to every Web Part page, this repetitive task can be avoided if you edit the master page instead.

   D. **Incorrect:** Although developers could add corporate branding to every Web Part, administrators and users cannot edit Web Parts. You may also wish to use these Web Parts elsewhere without the corporate branding.

   E. **Incorrect:** Site definitions are used by developers to package their solutions for deployment to other sites and farms. This solution was not created from a site definition.

Lesson 2

1. **Correct Answer: D**

   A. Incorrect: If the feature had farm scope and you were not a farm administrator, you could not have installed or activated the Feature at all.

   B. Incorrect: The Save As Template tool creates a solution file, not a feature.

   C. Incorrect: The –*GACDeployment* parameter is only available when you install farm solutions, not features.

   D. Correct: In a multi-server farm, a feature must be manually installed on all web front-end servers before it is available to all users all the time.

   E. Incorrect: Although solution files make deployment and installation easier, they are not required for deploying features.

2. **Correct Answers: A and E**

   A. Correct: User solutions can access data stored anywhere in the same site collection.

   B. Incorrect: User solutions cannot access data stored in any site collection other than the one where they are deployed.

   C. Incorrect: User solutions cannot access web services.

   D. Incorrect: User solutions cannot read or write data directly to the file system.

   E. Correct: User solutions can include master pages.

Lesson 3

1. **Correct Answers: B, D, and E**

   A. Incorrect: This intensive user solution is likely to need more resource usage points per day, not fewer.

   B. Correct: You should increase the quota for this intensive user solution or it may be temporarily disabled.

   C. Incorrect: To support an intensive user solution, you should use remote mode and run the user solution worker process on dedicated application servers.

   D. Correct: Remote mote enables you to dedicate application servers to run user solutions.

   E. Correct: Dedicated applications servers can respond to intensive user solutions without consuming resources on web front-end servers or other application servers.

   F. Incorrect: It is not recommended to adjust the resource usage points indicators.

2. **Correct Answers: B and C**

   A. Incorrect: Twenty SharePoint database queries are required to score a single point.

   B. Correct: A single abnormal process termination scores a point.

   C. Correct: Using more than 85 percent of the processor time scores a point.

   D. Incorrect: Solutions in the sandbox cannot query a web service.

   E. Incorrect: Two unresponsive processes are required to score a point.

Case Scenario: Deploying a Third-Party Custom Relationship Management Solution

1. Your questions should reflect the limitations placed on a user solution by the sandbox. For example, does the solution write directly to the file system or call web services? Does the solution need to access data from other site collections in SharePoint? What objects in the SharePoint object model are used? Most developers will know whether their solution is compatible with the sandbox.

2. Configure two or more dedicated application servers to run the Sandboxed Code Service and enable remote mode load balancing.

Chapter 11

Lesson 1

1. **Correct Answers: B, C, and D**

   A. **Incorrect:** RAID 0 does not provide improved availability because there is no parity or mirroring to reconstruct data in the event of a disk failure.

   B. **Correct:** A RAID 1 mirror set improves availability because in the event of a disk failure, data can be read from the mirror disk.

   C. **Correct:** A RAID 5 stripe set improves availability because in the event of a disk failure, data can be reconstructed from the parity data.

   D. **Correct:** A UPS improves availability because for a limited time it can power a server in the event of a mains supply interruption.

   E. **Incorrect:** Although a high-speed backup system is an excellent idea, it does not improve availability but protects against catastrophic data loss.

2. **Correct Answers: A, B, C, and F**

   A. **Correct:** Servers in an NLB cluster must have a network card to respond to user requests and a second network card for other communications, such as the heartbeat.

   B. **Correct:** Servers in an NLB cluster share a farm IP address. User requests are sent to this address.

   C. **Correct:** Servers in an NLB cluster ping each other to ensure that all servers are online. This is called the heartbeat. When communication is lost with a server in the cluster, convergence takes place to distribute the user requests to online servers.

   D. **Incorrect:** Application servers do not use NLB and do not need two network cards.

   E. **Incorrect:** Application servers do not respond directly to user requests and therefore should not respond to the farm IP address.

   F. **Correct:** The Application Discovery and Load Balancer service automatically load balances the application servers.

Lesson 2

1. **Correct Answers: B and D**

    A. Incorrect: A full farm backup in SharePoint Central Administration backs up all SharePoint content and SharePoint configuration values. However, certain SQL and IIS configuration values are not backed up.

    B. Correct: SQL System databases are not protected by a SharePoint full farm backup.

    C. Incorrect: The SharePoint full farm backup protects all SharePoint content.

    D. Correct: The IIS configuration is not protected by a SharePoint full farm backup.

    E. Incorrect: The SharePoint full farm backup protects all SharePoint site collections.

2. **Correct Answer: D**

    A. Incorrect: The Search service application is stored in a separate database, not the content database you have backed up.

    B. Incorrect: The Search index files are not stored in a SQL database but on the Search application servers' hard disks.

    C. Incorrect: Because you placed database files and transaction logs on the same disk, the disk failure has destroyed both. If the transaction logs had been stored on a separate disk that did not fail, you could have restored up to the point of failure.

    D. Correct: All SharePoint content up to the point of the last backup is present in the backups you created.

    E. Incorrect: The IIS configuration is not stored in any SharePoint content database.

Case Scenario: Improving Resilience and Recovery Times

1. You have a good hardware budget, so consider purchasing a hardware-based RAID array. You should install this array in the application server and move the search index onto it.

2. Install a second web front-end server into your existing SharePoint farm and use a load-balancing solution to distribute load among them. Although your budget is good, it is unlikely to permit a hardware-based load balancer for a farm of this size. Instead, consider configuring NLB to distribute user requests.

3. Because you have a good hardware budget, you can certainly consider purchasing faster backup and restore hardware. However, it is clear that the long delay was caused by an administrative mistake. Ensure that all IT personnel involved in disaster recovery have rehearsed their procedures in a lab environment.

Chapter 12

Lesson 1

1. **Correct Answers: A, B, C, and F**

   A. **Correct:** The %Processor Time counter will help to identify any CPU bottlenecks.

   B. **Correct:** The Page Fault per Second counter will be over five per second if there is insufficient memory in your SQL Server.

   C. **Correct:** The % Processor Time counter for the sqlserver process measures the amount of CPU load caused by SQL Server.

   D. **Incorrect:** ASP.NET is not involved on the SQL Server. In fact, these counters will not be present because IIS is not installed on SQL Server.

   E. **Incorrect:** SharePoint is not installed on the SQL Server and therefore this counter will not be available.

   F. **Correct:** The Plan Cache and its behavior are critical to the performance of SQL Server.

2. **Correct Answers: A, B, D, and E**

   A. **Correct:** Before you run tests, you should increase the amount of information SharePoint logs by making changes in Central Administration.

   B. **Correct:** The SharePoint Load Testing Kit includes tools for generating simulated loads in lab environments.

   C. **Incorrect:** Visual Studio 2010 Professional does not include the testing components required by the LTK.

   D. **Correct:** Visual Studio 2010 Ultimate does include the testing components required by the LTK.

   E. **Correct:** As you run tests with the LTK, you will use Performance Monitor to measure, record, and analyze performance.

   F. **Incorrect:** The developer dashboard is used to analyze performance in individual web pages, not the SharePoint farm as a whole.

Lesson 2

1. **Correct Answer: A**

   A. **Correct:** By choosing a schedule in the health rule definition, you select the timer job that will run this rule and ensure that it executes hourly.

   B. **Incorrect:** You should not reconfigure the frequency of the Health Analysis timer jobs because, by doing this, you would affect more than one of the health rules, not just the "Timer service failed to recycle" rule.

    C. **Incorrect:** This answer is incorrect for the same reason that answer B is incorrect.

    D. **Incorrect:** Although this approach would work, it is too complex when a simple Central Administration setting has the intended effect.

2. **Correct Answer: C**

    A. **Incorrect:** The scope property does not influence whether a repair is attempted by a health rule.

    B. **Incorrect:** If the appropriate timer job was not running, the health rule would not run at all, so the warning would not appear in Central Administration.

    C. **Correct:** The developer must use the *SPRepairableHealthAnalysisRule* class and include code so that the rule can fix the problem. If this is not the case, selecting the Repair Automatically check box has no effect.

    D. **Incorrect:** The developer dashboard is not involved in the Health Analyzer.

    E. **Incorrect:** It is not necessary to run a health rule manually.

Lesson 3

1. **Correct Answers: B and D**

    A. **Incorrect:** The Web Analytics service application does not require the Managed Metadata service application.

    B. **Correct:** The Web Analytics service application requires the State service application.

    C. **Incorrect:** The Web Analytics service application does not require the User Profile service application.

    D. **Correct:** The Microsoft SharePoint Foundation Usage Data Import collects data and places it in the Web Analytics staging database. If this timer job does not run, no Web Analytics reports will be visible.

    E. **Incorrect:** The Reporting Services Add-In is required by SSRS, not by Web Analytics.

2. **Correct Answer: C**

    A. **Incorrect:** Usage reports show visitor behavior but you cannot configure SharePoint to email them to administrators.

    B. **Incorrect:** The Web Analytics Web Part can be used to display popular content or searches on a SharePoint page, not email reports to administrators.

    C. **Correct:** You can configure a workflow on any Web Analytics report to run the report and email the results to administrators on a schedule of your choice.

    D. **Incorrect:** The Report Viewer Web Part can display SSRS reports in SharePoint web pages but not email them to administrators.

    E. **Incorrect:** The SSRS Proxy communicates between the SharePoint WFE servers and the SSRS Reporting server. It does not email reports to users.

Lesson 4

1. **Correct Answer: A**

   A. Correct: The list view threshold limits the number of items that SharePoint will return for any list in the web application.

   B. Incorrect: List view lookups are lookup fields within a single query. This threshold may help but it is not the cause of the problem as it is described in the question.

   C. Incorrect: Backward-compatible event handlers do not affect the performance of large lists.

   D. Incorrect: RBS concerns the storage on binary files in the content database. It does not help with large lists.

   E. Incorrect: The BLOB Cache increases general performance when used carefully but it is not directly related to rendering large lists.

2. **Correct Answer: E**

   A. Incorrect: For best performance, do not store transaction logs on the same disk as the database files.

   B. Incorrect: You should place the database files on the RAID 5 array. Also, you should separate transaction logs for different databases onto separate drives.

   C. Incorrect: You should place the database files on the RAID 5 array. You were correct to separate transaction logs from the database files and from each other.

   D. Incorrect: Separating database files from each other does not improve performance. Instead you should separate transaction logs.

   E. Correct: RAID 5 gives best performance for database files. RAID 10 gives best performance for transaction logs. The database files should be separated from the operating system and from all transaction logs. Transaction logs should be separated from each other where possible.

Case Scenario: Monitoring Web Part Deployment

1. Start by deploying the Web Part in a lab environment. Use a SharePoint farm that is as close to the production environment as possible. Add the Web Part to a page and use Visual Studio Ultimate to generate multiple requests to that page. Attempt to simulate a typical number of page requests for a single user per minute. Use Performance Monitor to profile the behavior of Processor, Memory, and PhysicalDisk objects during these tests. Repeat the test but double the rate of requests so that you can assess the load of two users. These tests should enable you to prove the Web Part stable and how much load a single user requesting the Web Part adds.

2. You must ensure that you have thoroughly benchmarked the performance of the SharePoint farm before you deploy the Web Part. This is so you can later diagnose the *difference* that the Web Part makes to performance. Then deploy the Web Part and have users place it on pages. You might want to phase in the Web Part by getting a small number of users to use it initially. Rerun your performance tests and compare the results to the benchmark. This should illustrate how the Web Part increases load.

Index

Symbols and Numbers

$error, 90
$false, 90
$true, 90
.accdb files, 493, 495
.asmx files, service application endpoints, 289
.bak files, 657
.dll files, 96
.iqy (query) files, 483
.mdb files, 493, 495
.NET CLR Memory, 688
.NET Framework 3.5
    ADO.NET DATA Service Update, 15
    SharePoint prerequisites, 12
.ps1. *See* PowerShell
.svc files, service application endpoints, 289
.udcx files, upgrades, 536–37
.vdw files, 506–07
.wsp files
    customizing, 584–85
    farm solutions, 597–98
    user solutions, 601–02
.xsn files, 536–37
_Layouts pages, master page settings, 124–25
~$_, 85
~% (ForEach-Object alias), 90–91
~($) dollar sign, 89–90
~32-bit environments, upgrades, 525–26
~64-bit environments, upgrades, 525–26

A

abbreviations, terms, 322
Abnormal Process Termination, 612
About Me, 253

absolute URLs, 199
Access. *See* Access Web Services
access control. *See also* authentication
    Access Web Services, 493
    application pool identities, 112–13
    service applications, 297–301
    site access requests, 259
    user policies, configuring, 133
    user solutions, 598–99, 616–17
Access Control List (ACL), configuring
        search, 397
access mappings
    configuring, overview, 185–89
    defined, 109
    internal and public URLs, 194–95
    load-balancing with request
        overwrites, 193–94
    off-box SSL termination, 192–93
    practice configuring, 204–07
    single-label host names, 190–92
Access Services, requirements, 5
access to content, optimizing
    BLOB storage and cache, 725–27
    Object Cache, 728
    Output Cache, 727–28
    overview, 723–24
    practice, optimizing content access, 732–33
    resource throttling, 724–25
    storage, optimizing, 728–32
Access Web Services
    enhancements, 494–96
    implementing and configuring, 496–97
    overview, 493–95
    practice configuring, 498–500
    using, 498
AccessServiceName, 496
acounts, managed, 556–61

D

G

H

hardware
   fault-tolerant power hardware, 635
   network load balancing, 637–39
   performance counters, 686–87
   requirements, 5–6
   upgrade requirements, 524–27, 540
header, host
   page requests, 41
   web applications, creating, 42
Health Analyzer
   configuration, 700–02
   overview, 697–700
   Rule Definition list, 700
Health Reports, Web Analytics, 707
heartbeat messages, 637
help desk, customizing, 578–79
Help File Collections, 551
Hierarchy Managers group, 253
high-availability
   architectures for, 633–35
   backup and restore
      accidentally deleted items, 652
      Central Administration
         restore, 658
      disaster recovery, 652
      disaster recovery, planning, 653–54
      Farm Backup tool, 656–57
      granular backup, 657–58
      IIS configuration backup, 660
      migrating content, 652–53
      overview, 651
      PowerShell scripts, 658–60
      practice, user profile, 666–69
      Recycle Bin, 654–56
      SQL Server, backup, 661–63
      SQL Server, restore, 663–66
   case scenario, 672–73
   configuring, 627–33
   database architectures, 641–42
   farm examples, 642–45
   FAST search architectures, 640
   overview, 625–26
   practice, configuring, 645–49
   SharePoint architectures, 635–40
hijacking, Websites, 631–33
Holme, Dan, 522

host header
   IIS Web site binding, 110–11
   IIS Web site settings, 115–16
   page requests, 41
   web applications, creating, 42
host names, service principal names, 151
hosted service
   high-availability, 644–45
   requirements, 6
HostHeader, 164
HostHeader, New-SPWebApplication, 146
host-named site collection, best practices, 203
Hotfix for Microsoft Windows, 12
HTTP
   Fiddler, HTTP traffic, 682
   multiple zones, 202
   Office Web Applications, 512
   service class, service principal names, 151
HTTP Data Connections, 475
HTTPS
   IIS Web site requests, 110–11
   multiple zones, 202
   service principal names, 151
human resources integration, 579–80

I

identities, application pool design, 112–13
identities, SQL Server services, 9–10
identity claim, 173
Identity parameter, 78–81
identity provider STS (IP-STS), 161, 173–75
IFilters, 401, 405–07
IIS. *See* Internet Information Services (IIS)
illustrations. *See* Visio Services
import
   administrator-deployed form templates, 536–37
   practice, Intranet site collection lists, 669
Import Spreadsheet List Template, 483
Import Term Set, 325
ImportTrustCertificate, 174–75
Incremental Crawl, search process, 406–08, 411
Incremental synchronization, 365
Index Partitions, search logical topology, 435
indexing
   best practices, 203
   case scenario, adminstering search, 449–50

L

Q

service accounts
    configuring, 30–31
    in-place upgrades, 534–36
    managed account, 560–61
    passwords, changing, 30–31
    passwords, managed accounts, 556
    service principal names, configuring, 152–53
Service Application Associations, 293
Service Application Framework (SAF). *See also* service
      applications
    access, restricting, 297–301
    administrators, assigning, 297
    application associations, 295–96
    case scenario, configuring, 338
    connection groups (proxy groups), 292–95
    design, 307
    endpoint, 289–90
    Managed Metadata Service (MMS)
      content type syndication, 329–31
      content type syndication, design, 331–32
      information architecture, overview, 311–14
      items and documents, applying terms, 317–19
      keywords, 320–21
      local term sets, 326
      overview, 311
      practice implementing, 332–35
      term sets, managing, 323–25
      term store design, 327–29
      term store, managing, 325–26
      terms, creating, 314–18
      terms, managing, 321–23
      terms, using, 313
    overview, 283–84, 288
    practice administering, 307–09
    publish service application, 304–05
    remote connections, 305–06
    service application, creating, 290–91
    service scalability and redundancy, 290
    sharing across farms
      overview, 301
      trusts, configuring, 302–04
Service Application Name; 292
Service Application URL, 306
service applications. *See also* Service Application
      Framework (SAF)
    Access Web Services
      enhancements, 494–96
      implementing and configuring, 496–97

      overview, 493–95
      practice configuring, 498–500
      using, 498
    administrators, 57, 65
    Business Connectivity Services (BCS)
      architecture, 457–60
      BCS Web Parts, 463–64
      external data, connecting to, 460–63
      overview, 455–57
      practice configuring, 464–67
    case scenarios, user profiles and social
      networking, 519
    configuring, 29–30
    connections
      configuring, 111, 119
      overview, 292
    content storage, 730–32
    databases, adding, 552–53
    Excel Services
      architecture, 485–86
      business intelligence and dashboards, 484–85
      collaboration, 483–84
      configuring, 486–87
      Excel Access Web Part, 488–89
      overview, 482–85
      practice configuring, 489–91
      publishing spreadsheets, 488
    FAST Search, 439–40
    feature administrators, role of, 57
    InfoPath forms service
      adding, 470–71
      administering, 473–76
      architecture for, 472–73
      overview, 469
      practice configuring, 478–80
      sandboxed forms, creating, 476–78
      scenario for, 471–72
    Office Web Applications
      architecture, 512–13
      deploying, 513–14
      overview, 510–12
      practice configuring, 515–16
      testing, 514–15
    overview, 283–84, 453–54
    pool accounts, installation, 10–11
    service instance
      overview, 285
    service instances

X

Z

About the Authors

DAN HOLME As Chief SharePoint Evangelist at AvePoint, Dan Holme utilizes both his expertise in Microsoft technologies and proven experience solving customers' IT business challenges to educate the global SharePoint community, as well as develop solutions that will set the standard for the next generation of collaboration platforms.

A graduate of Yale University and Thunderbird School of Global Management, Dan spent 17 years as a consultant and trainer, delivering solutions to tens of thousands of IT professionals from the most prestigious organizations and corporations around the world.

In addition to earning the prestigious title of Microsoft MVP (Windows Server Directory Services, 2007, and SharePoint Server, 2008-2011), Dan has been recognized as one of the Top 50 Influencers by The SharePoint50 Project and one of the top 10 Microsoft Partner MVPs. Dan is a contributing editor for *Windows IT Pro* and *SharePoint Pro* magazines as well as the community lead of SharePointProMag.com, and has authored several books and courses, including training kits and Microsoft Official Curriculum courses for Active Directory and SharePoint.

Prior to joining AvePoint, Dan founded Aptillon, a SharePoint consulting and development firm, with seven of the world's top SharePoint MVPs. He also played an instrumental role as Microsoft Technologies Consultant for NBC Olympics during the Winter Olympics in Vancouver (2010), Beijing (2008), and Torino (2006)—a role he plans to play again for the broadcast of the 2012 Summer Olympics from London.

ALISTAIR MATTHEWS A consultant with extensive and cutting-edge experience in Microsoft technologies, Alistair has spent the last 10 years developing with, consulting on, and communicating about both the developer and IT professional sides of SharePoint, Visual Studio, Active Directory, Exchange, and Windows. He is currently most interested in SharePoint Web Content Management and likes to impress clients with elegant publishing workflows and custom UI elements. He's also more excited about Office 365 than he cares to admit.

Alistair has a particular passion for writing about technology and has contributed to many Microsoft Learning courses, MSDN and TechNet articles, and white papers. He is the principal consultant at Web Dojo Ltd and lives the telecommuting dream in Cornwall, UK.

Windows Server 2008— Resources for Administrators

Windows Server® 2008 Administrator's Companion

Charlie Russel and Sharon Crawford

ISBN 9780735625051

Your comprehensive, one-volume guide to deployment, administration, and support. Delve into core system capabilities and administration topics, including Active Directory®, security issues, disaster planning/recovery, interoperability, IIS 7.0, virtualization, clustering, and performance tuning.

Windows Server 2008 Administrator's Pocket Consultant, Second Edition

William R. Stanek

ISBN 9780735627116

Portable and precise—with the focused information you need for administering server roles, Active Directory, user/group accounts, rights and permissions, file-system management, TCP/IP, DHCP, DNS, printers, network performance, backup, and restoration.

Windows Server 2008 Resource Kit

Microsoft MVPs with Microsoft Windows Server Team

ISBN 9780735623613

Six volumes! Your definitive resource for deployment and operations—from the experts who know the technology best. Get in-depth technical information on Active Directory, Windows PowerShell® scripting, advanced administration, networking and network access protection, security administration, IIS, and more—plus an essential toolkit of resources on CD.

Internet Information Services (IIS) 7.0 Administrator's Pocket Consultant

William R. Stanek

ISBN 9780735623644

This pocket-sized guide delivers immediate answers for administering IIS 7.0. Topics include customizing installation; configuration and XML schema; application management; user access and security; Web sites, directories, and content; and performance, backup, and recovery.

Windows PowerShell 2.0 Administrator's Pocket Consultant

William R. Stanek

ISBN 9780735625952

The practical, portable guide to using *cmdlets* and scripts to automate everyday system administration—including configuring server roles, services, features, and security settings; managing TCP/IP networking; monitoring and tuning performance; and other essential tasks.

ALSO SEE

Windows PowerShell 2.0 Best Practices

ISBN 9780735626461

Windows® Administration Resource Kit: Productivity Solutions for IT Professionals

ISBN 9780735624313

Windows Server 2008 Hyper-V™ Resource Kit

ISBN 9780735625174

Windows Server 2008 Security Resource Kit

ISBN 9780735625044

Microsoft® Press

microsoft.com/mspress

Get Certified—Windows® 7

Desktop support technicians and administrators—demonstrate your expertise with Windows 7 by earning a Microsoft® Certification focusing on core technical (MCTS) or professional (MCITP) skills. With our 2-in-1 *Self-Paced Training Kits*, you get a comprehensive, cost-effective way to prepare for the certification exams. Combining official exam-prep guides + practice tests, these kits are designed to maximize the impact of your study time.

EXAM 70-680

MCTS Self-Paced Training Kit: Configuring Windows 7

Ian McLean and Orin Thomas

ISBN 9780735627086

EXAM 70-685

MCITP Self-Paced Training Kit: Windows 7 Enterprise Desktop Support Technician

Tony Northrup and J.C. Mackin

ISBN 9780735627093

EXAM 70-686

MCITP Self-Paced Training Kit: Windows 7 Enterprise Desktop Administrator

Craig Zacker and Orin Thomas

ISBN 9780735627178

Great for on the job

**Windows 7
Resource Kit**

Mitch Tulloch, Tony Northrup, Jerry Honeycutt, Ed Wilson, and the Windows 7 Team at Microsoft

ISBN 9780735627000

**Windows 7
Inside Out,
Deluxe Edition**

Ed Bott, Carl Siechert, Craig Stinson

ISBN 9780735656925

**Windows 7
Administrator's
Pocket Consultant**

William R. Stanek

ISBN 9780735626997

microsoft.com/mspress

Windows Server 2008 Resource Kit— Your Definitive Resource!

Windows Server® 2008 Resource Kit

Microsoft® MVPs with the Microsoft Windows Server Team

ISBN 9780735623613

Your definitive reference for deployment and operations—from the experts who know the technology best. Get in-depth technical information on Active Directory®, Windows PowerShell® scripting, advanced administration, networking and network access protection, security administration, IIS, and other critical topics—plus an essential toolkit of resources on CD.

ALSO AVAILABLE AS SINGLE VOLUMES

Windows Server 2008 Security Resource Kit

Jesper M. Johansson et al. with Microsoft Security Team

ISBN 9780735625044

Windows Server 2008 Active Directory Resource Kit

Stan Reimer et al. with Microsoft Active Directory Team

ISBN 9780735625150

Windows Powershell Scripting Guide

Ed Wilson

ISBN 9780735622791

Windows Server 2008 Networking and Network Access Protection (NAP)

Joseph Davies, Tony Northrup, Microsoft Networking Team

ISBN 9780735624221

Windows® Administration Resource Kit: Productivity Solutions for IT Professionals

Dan Holme

ISBN 9780735624313

Internet Information Services (IIS) 7.0 Resource Kit

Mike Volodarsky et al. with Microsoft IIS Team

ISBN 9780735624412

microsoft.com/mspress

What do you think of this book?

We want to hear from you!
To participate in a brief online survey, please visit:

microsoft.com/learning/booksurvey

Tell us how well this book meets your needs—what works effectively, and what we can do better. Your feedback will help us continually improve our books and learning resources for you.

Thank you in advance for your input!